Wireshark® Network Analysis

The Official Wireshark Certified Network Analyst™ Study Guide

1st Edition (Version 1.0)

Laura Chappell

Founder, Chappell University™
Founder, Wireshark University™

Wireshark® Network Analysis

The Official Wireshark Certified Network Analyst™ Study Guide
1st Edition (Version 1.0)

To arrange bulk purchase discounts for sales promotions, events, training courses, or other purposes, please contact Chappell University at the address listed on the next page.

Book URL: *www.wiresharkbook.com*
13-digit ISBN: 978-1-893939-99-8
10-digit ISBN: 1-893939-99-8

Distributed worldwide for Chappell University through Protocol Analysis Institute, LLC.

For general information on Chappell University or Protocol Analysis Institute, LLC, including information on corporate licenses, updates, future titles or courses, contact the Protocol Analysis Institute, LLC at 408/378-7841 or send email to *info@chappellU.com*.

For authorization to photocopy items for corporate, personal or educational use, contact Protocol Analysis Institute, LLC at email to *info@chappellU.com*.

Trademarks. All brand names and product names used in this book or mentioned in this course are trade names, service marks, trademarks, or registered trademarks of their respective owners. Protocol Analysis Institute, LLC is the exclusive developer for Chappell University.

Limit of Liability/Disclaimer of Warranty. The author and publisher have used their best efforts in preparing this book and the related materials used in this book. Protocol Analysis Institute, LLC, Chappell University and the author(s) make no representations or warranties or merchantability or fitness for a particular purpose. Protocol Analysis Institute, LLC and Chappell University assume no liability for any damages caused by

This book and the book website, *www.wiresharkbook.com*, references Chanalyzer software created by Metageek (*www.metageek.net*).

This book and the book website, *www.wiresharkbook.com*, references GeoLite data created by MaxMind, available from *www.maxmind.com*.

PhoneFactor™ SSL/TLS vulnerabilities documents and trace files referenced on the book website, *www.wiresharkbook.com*, were created by Steve Dispensa and Ray Marsh (*www.phonefactor.com*).

This book and the book website, *www.wiresharkbook.com*, references trace files from MuDynamics (*www.pcapr.net*).

Protocol Analysis Institute, LLC
5339 Prospect Road, # 343
San Jose, CA 95129 USA
www.wiresharkbook.com

Chappell University
5339 Prospect Road, # 343
San Jose, CA 95129 USA
info@chappellU.com
www.chappellU.com

Cover design by Gary Lewis, Kinetic-Creations (*www.kinetic-creations.com*)

Dedication

This book is dedicated to Gerald Combs, creator of Wireshark. I feel tremendously fortunate to consider Gerald a friend.

About 10 years ago, I sent Gerald a note—just out of the blue—"may I include Ethereal on my CD? I want to give it away at conferences." Expecting some pushback—after all, he didn't know who the heck I was—I was amazed and thrilled to receive his response stating "sure, go ahead—that would be great!"

Gerald is more than the creator of Wireshark. Gerald is one of us. He struggled with a problem. He formulated a solution. Then he did something extraordinary— he shared his solution with the world. In his typical unselfish mode, Gerald opened up his project for others to contribute to and participate in.

Ethereal morphed into Wireshark… and Wireshark continued to mature. Wireshark has surpassed every other network analyzer product in the industry to become the de facto standard for network traffic analysis. Gerald has remained one of the most honest, humble, dedicated professionals in our field.

Thank you Gerald.

p.s. Very, very special thanks to Gerald's wife, Karen, and their absolutely cute-beyond-belief, I-have-my-Daddy-wrapped-around-my-little-finger, smarty-pants-who-melts-your-heart daughter! Gerald beams when he talks about you two very special ladies and it is a treat spending time with you <girl power!>. I am grateful for the love, support and inspiration you have provided Gerald. Your tremendous humor and joie de vivre inspires me!

ACKs

There are many people who were directly and indirectly involved in creating this book.

First and foremost, I would like to thank my children, **Scott and Ginny**, for your patience, support and humor during the many hours I was huddled over my computer to complete this book. Your words of encouragement really helped me balance work and life during some long days and nights of deadlines. (Oh, and thanks also to **Pyra** who patiently sat up late nights with me as my schedule became insane.)

Mom, Dad, Steve and Joe—ahh... yes, the "fam." You guys have given me so much material for my presentations! Mom, thanks for instilling in me a twisted sense of humor (hopefully I'll make it up to the casino sometime soon!). Dad, thanks for keeping me laughing while you try to find out which cable is the power cord on your laptop (scary). Steve and Joe—I wish we could hang out more as you two rejuvenate me (and give me even more great material after a glass of wine or two!).

Special thanks to **Brenda Cardinal and Jill Poulsen** who have worked with me for over 10 years each—you masochists! I appreciate you both keeping everyone else at bay (sorry everyone else) as I focused on the brain dumping process to get this book out of my head and the gut-wrenching editing process. Thanks for politely smiling and pretending to listen to my geek rants when I found something new and cool to add to the book! I am fortunate to have both of you around to brighten my days and put life in perspective. I can hardly wait to meet our new little protocol analyst, Colton. Brenda, this might be a good book to read in the evenings to help him sleep! Jill—I'll catch you soon for another "remote cocktail" chat!

Joy DeManty—wow—bet you're sick of reading this book over and over and over again! I appreciate your reviewing skills and how quickly you jumped on board with this project and waded through thousands of pages and notes to guide this title to completion. Besides being a great friend (and party pal) over the years I've now been fortunate to work with you twice!!! Are you ready for more (after we have a cocktail or two to decompress from this project, of course)?

Lanell Allen—you really pulled through for us on this project! I was thrilled when you offered to edit this book. Your tireless hours and hours of work put into finding my typos, half-sentences and dangling prepositions (he he) had a huge impact on this book. Your Wireshark experience and ability to spot technical errors was a blessing! Thank you for taking on this project and projecting such a positive attitude—there were many nights I really needed to read your upbeat emails!

Gerald Combs—what can I say? You have selflessly shared with us a tremendous tool and I am so very grateful for your devotion to Wireshark. This book is dedicated to you.

The Wireshark developers—what a group! It has been a pleasure meeting so many of you in person at the Sharkfest conferences over the past two years as well as via email. Your continued efforts to improve and enhance Wireshark have helped so many IT professionals find the root of network issues. Thank you for the many hours you have dedicated to making Wireshark the world's most popular network analyzer solution! You can find the developer list at **Help | About Wireshark | Authors**. I hope this book accurately explains the features you have spent so many hours implementing. If I missed anything you'd like included in future editions of this book, please let me know.

Gordon "Fyodor" Lyon—the creation of this book was triggered when you released "Nmap Network Scanning"—an excellent book that every networking person should own. I appreciate your time and effort looking over the network scanning section and participating at the Summit 09 conference. I look forward to working with you on some future projects—there are so many possibilities!

Ryan Woodings and **Mark Jensen** of **Metageek**—it has been a pleasure collaborating with you folks on ideas and microwave popping methods (g)! It has been a blast showing Wi-Spy/Chanalyzer at conferences and sharing these hot products with the IT community. I look forward to more brainstorming sessions. Special thanks to **Trent Cutler** for reviewing the WLAN chapter and sneaking in under the wire with some great feedback.

Steve Dispensa and **Marsh Ray** of **PhoneFactor** (*www.phonefactor.com*)—thank you both for kindly allowing me to include your *Renegotiating TLS* document and trace files at *www.wiresharkbook.com.* You two did a great job documenting this security issue and your work benefits us all.

Stig Bjørlykke, Wireshark Core Developer—you came up with so many great additions to this book! Your understanding of the inner workings of Wireshark as well as the areas that often perplex people helped make this book much more valuable to the readers. Thanks so much for offering to take the time to review multiple chapters. We all appreciate your development efforts to make Wireshark such a valuable tool!

Sean Walberg—Thanks for being such a great resource on the VoIP chapter. You really have such a wonderful talent explaining the inner workings of VoIP communications. I loved your presentation at Sharkfest '09—funny and geeky at the same time! I appreciate your efforts to clarify the VoIP chapter in this book.

Martin Mathieson, Wireshark Core Developer—I am so grateful for the fixes and tips you provided for the VoIP chapter and the time you took to explain the duplicate IP address detection feature you added to Wireshark. I appreciate you providing the RFC references to be included and understanding that the readers may be new to VoIP analysis. The time and energy you have put into enhancing Wireshark are a benefit to us all!

Betty DuBois—Thanks for all your review time and talent—not only on this book project, but also on the Wireshark University Instructor-Led courses. It's always great to talk/work with a fellow packet-geekess!

Keith Parsons—Thanks for clarifying the concepts in the WLAN chapter and adding the awesome "To DS/From DS" graphic and table! You always have great ideas and teaching methods—and you're truly the "geek toy king" as well!

Anders Broman, Wireshark Core Developer—Thanks for taking the time to look through the VoIP chapter and ensure the information was accurate and presented clearly. Thank you so much for all your efforts as a Wireshark core developer.

The pcapr Team—I appreciate you allowing me to provide readers with several trace files from your online repository at *www.pcapr.net*. Thank you to **Mu Dynamics** (*www.mudynamics.com*) for supporting the *pcapr.net* project.

My Students—Sincere thanks to the **hundreds of thousands of students** who have taken my online training courses, instructor-led courses and self-paced courses over nearly 20 years of teaching. I've gotten to know so many of you as friends. Your honest and direct feedback has always helped me hone my training materials (and my jokes).

Gary Lewis—you wacky guy, you! Your emails definitely crack me up. If anyone out there needs design services, Gary is the "go to" guy with a great (and somewhat twisted) sense of humor. Thanks for a great cover design—can you believe that ugly first piece of *#&$(*&# I sent to you?

Case Study Submitters—Case studies were submitted from all around the world. Thanks to all of you who overloaded my email with your Wireshark success stories. The following individuals provided case studies that were included in this book to offer a glimpse into how folks use Wireshark to save time and money.

"Anonymous"
Roy B.
Martin B.
Bill Bach
Coleen D.
Todd DeBoard and Team
Mitch Dickey
Thanassis Diogos
Steve Dispensa
Todd Dokey
Vik Evans
Russ F.
Allen Gittelson
Richard Hicks

Rob Hulsebos
Jennifer Keels
Christian Kreide
LabNuke99
Todd Lerdal
Robert M.
Jim McMahon
P.C.
Karl R.
Mark R.
Guy Talbot
Delfino L. Tiongco
Sean Walberg
Christy Z.

And of course—Finally, I'd like to thank those folks who create lousy applications, cruddy TCP/IP stacks, scummy operating systems, pathetic interconnecting devices and sad default configurations and the users who bring their muck onto the network— you make life so interesting!

If I've missed anyone in this ACK section, I apologize and plead brain-drain at this point!

Contents at a Glance

This page intentionally left blank.

Perhaps a good spot for you to jot down your notes or draw something—
maybe a list of network issues you'd like to solve… or what about drawing a picture
depicting your most dreaded network user?

Table of Contents

Foreword by Gerald Combs, Creator of Wireshark

 When you first lifted this book, feeling your back strain under its enormous weight, your first thoughts probably were "How am I going to get through this?

Is there really that much to Wireshark? Where's the pain reliever? How many of these protocols are there? Is protocol analysis that important?"

To answer your questions in order...

You'll get through this because Laura is the best instructor I've ever met. Each time I've had the opportunity to see her teach I've been impressed with her ability to convey the most arcane technical details in an easy-going, down to earth way. She has a unique talent for making protocol analysis accessible (and even fun). This book continues that style.

Wireshark is the result of a lot of hard work by a lot of very talented developers. By one estimate, over 500 person-years of effort have gone into the current release. Professionals in every branch of networking have contributed code to Wireshark to make it work better in their environment. As a result you can capture traffic anywhere in the world (and even off world![1]) and be able to tell what's going on.

Try the medicine cabinet. If it's empty, look in your luggage to see if any fell out the last time you traveled.

Computer networking touches nearly every aspect of our lives. This is reflected in the huge number of protocols and networks in use.

As our society relies more and more on network connectivity, it's important for people like you to be well-versed in protocol analysis. This book, which is no doubt causing your desk to strain and creak with its massive, tree-killing weight, will help you acquire the skills necessary to do your job better.

---

[1] Yes, really. Wireshark can dissect the protocols used in the Interplanetary Internet.

Consider the following questions before you venture forth:

1. Where is the best location to run Wireshark to identify the cause of network problems?

2. What should the traffic look like (when everything is running properly)?

3. Where is the anomaly?

4. Do I need to move Wireshark to another location for a closer look?

5. Have I filtered on the traffic of interest to see the problem more clearly?

6. Can Wireshark's charts and graphs aid in interpretation?

Preface

Wireshark is a FIRST RESPONDER tool that should be employed immediately when the cries of "the network is slow" or "I think my computer is infected" echo through the company halls.

In the first case, you are using Wireshark to quickly identify the cause of performance issues. In the second case you are using network forensics to look for evidence of a security breach. In both cases you are looking for signatures in the traffic or packets—the ultimate purpose being isolation of unusual or unacceptable patterns.

I've used the phrase "the packets never lie" for years now. It is true.

> **Network analysis is a key skill that every IT professional should possess and Wireshark is the world's most popular network analyzer tool.**

Twenty years ago I presented a session on ARCnet communications to a group of peer instructors. I delved into the idea of packet structure and the mythical belief at that time that everyone cared. Somehow though, I related the ARCnet networking rules and limitations to Sister Gerald, the militant no-nonsense head of discipline at my Catholic boarding school… and I got a few laughs. Imagine that… networking can be funny!

Now—before you think I'm going to mention any of the nuns, my techno-challenged father, my WoW-addicted son (go Alliance!), my iPhone toting daughter (who I hope will grow up and make iTunes a less pathetic application) and my Pavlovian response to a trace file filled with hideous communications issues and delicious security flaws—this book is not a breezy stroll through the world of packets.

This book is packed with basic through advanced techniques, tips and tricks to analyze a variety of network types. It is designed to get you from point A to point Z (or perhaps I should say point 0x00 to point 0xFF) as fast as possible with a solid understanding of the processes, protocols, and putrid things that occur under our noses (or under our feet or over our heads).

If you don't have Wireshark loaded on every computer within reach, stop now! Wireshark is the best girlfriend/boyfriend, wife/husband, mother/father, sister/brother, dog/cat or lover your network will ever have.

Who is always there to listen to you with a patient and understanding silence when you are crying in your latte because the users keep complaining about network performance?

Wireshark!

Who never threatens to fire you if you don't get those file transfers to occur at 'acceptable speeds' before lunch today?

Wireshark!

Who smiles and sits around all day long just waiting for the moment you say "I need help"?

Wireshark!

That's right!

So… it's time to elevate your copy of Wireshark from "network wallflower" to network powerhouse. It's time to roll up your sleeves, get rid of the training wheels, put on your helmet and reflective gear, tell everyone to get the hell out of your way, get on that bike—and ride!

By the way—you have no idea how difficult it was to refrain from adding humor (or at least what I call humor) to this book. It crept in at various points—some I left in, most I simply moved aside for a later book that might focus on the humorous side of packet analysis. We will have to wait and see…

Laura Chappell
Founder, Chappell University
Founder, Wireshark University

About This Book

Wireshark Network Analysis: the Official Wireshark Certified Network Analyst™ Study Guide offers you a solid foundation in the key skills of network analysis, troubleshooting, optimization and security. By purchasing this book, you have indicated your desire to learn packet-level communications and develop skills necessary to analyze, troubleshoot and secure networks more efficiently and achieve the Wireshark Certified Network Analyst certification.

Download the Supplements from *www.wiresharkbook.com*

Each chapter concludes with a "Practice What You've Learned" section that references traffic files (trace files), configuration files and other files related to the current chapter. These files are available for download at *www.wiresharkbook.com*. Before delving into this book, it is recommended that you install Wireshark from *www.wireshark.org*[2] and download at least the trace files from *www.wiresharkbook.com*. Create a *traces* directory on your local system and copy these trace files into that directory.

Who is this Book For?

This book offers an ideal reference for information technologists responsible for key network tasks including:

- identify poor network performance due to high path latency
- locate internetwork devices that drop packets
- validate optimal configuration of network hosts
- analyze application functionality and dependencies
- optimize application behavior for best performance
- learn how TCP/IP networks function
- analyze network capacity before application launch
- verify application security during launch, log in and data transfer
- identify unusual network traffic indicating potentially compromised hosts
- studying for the Wireshark Certified Network Analyst Exam

---

[2] If you are interested in working with the latest Development Release of Wireshark, visit *www.wireshark.org/download/automated*.

How is this Book Organized?

Chapter 1: The World of Network Analysis explains the key uses of network analysis and provides lists of tasks used for troubleshooting, securing and optimizing network traffic. This chapter also provides insight into the "needle in the haystack issue" that overwhelms many new network analysts.

Chapter 2: Introduction to Wireshark details Wireshark internals, the elements of the Wireshark graphical interface and functions of the Main Menu, Main Toolbar, Filter Toolbar, Wireless Toolbar, and Status Bar. In addition, this chapter offers a list of resources recommended for network analysts.

The next eleven chapters (Chapters 3 through 13) focus on Wireshark functionality with numerous examples of use and references to trace files available at *www.wiresharkbook.com*. If you are new to Wireshark, focus on these sections to obtain foundational skills used in later chapters.

Chapters 14 through 25 concentrate on the key protocols and applications of the TCP/IP suite including ARP, DNS, IP, TCP, UDP, and ICMP. Identifying or absolving TCP/IP as part of the troubleshooting process helps isolate the cause of performance issues and locate security holes. In addition, these are the chapters you should focus on if you are troubleshooting DHCP-based configurations or HTTP/HTTPS sessions.

Chapter 26: Introduction to 802.11 (WLAN) Analysis explains how to capture wireless traffic, identify basic WLAN problems caused by RF (radio frequency) interference, WLAN retries and access point availability. This chapter also provides tips on filtering on specific WLAN traffic. This is an introductory chapter and does not delve deeply into WLAN analysis techniques as such detail would likely require an additional 500 pages.

Chapter 27: Introduction to Voice over IP (VoIP) Analysis offers an overview of call setup and voice traffic. In addition, this chapter explains the use of Wireshark's key VoIP analysis features including RTP stream analysis and call playback. This is also an introductory chapter and does not offer an exhaustive resource on VoIP analysis—that also would require an additional 500 pages.

Chapter 28: Baseline Normal Traffic Patterns and *Chapter 29: Find the Top Causes of Performance Problems* offers details on baselines that should be created before network problems arise and examples of traffic patterns indicating delays along a path, faulty internetworking devices, misconfigured hosts and other issues affecting performance.

Chapters 30 through 32 focus on the security application of Wireshark including an overview of network forensics and analysis of network discovery processes that often preclude a security breach. In *Chapter 31: Detect Scanning and Discovery Processes*, we used Nmap[3] to generate a variety of scans against a target as we analyzed the signatures of this type of traffic. *Chapter 32: Analyze Suspect Traffic* examines evidence of compromised hosts and unsecure application traffic.

Chapter 33: Effective Use of Command-Line Tools details the use of the command-line tools used to split trace files, alter trace file timestamps, automatically start the GUI version of Wireshark with specific parameters, capture traffic with minimal overhead and merge trace files.

---

[3] In this section, you will see recommendations for the *Nmap Network Scanning* book—get the book ordered and put that on your reading list right now! For more information on Nmap Network Scanning, visit *nmap.org.book*.

Appendix A: Resources on the Book Website includes a list of all the files available at *www.wiresharkbook.com* at the time of publication (content may be added over time). This includes a comprehensive list of the trace files that you will use in the "Practice What You've Learned" section at the end of each chapter.

What Do Those Icons Mean?

Icons used to denote special information included throughout this book.

 Tip, Trick or Technique—examples of using a Wireshark feature for faster problem resolution, isolation of security flaw or other communication feature—stop and try these tips out!

 Case Study—example of how Wireshark was used in the real world (many case studies were submitted by Wireshark users and developers)—do the problems sound familiar? How would you have attacked the problem? Can you implement some of the steps described?

 Nmap Syntax—tips on launching the Nmap scans analyzed in *Chapter 31: Detect Scanning and Discovery Processes*—the best way to know how an application really functions is to analyze it as it runs. We analyzed Nmap scans and also Aptimize Website Accelerator™ in this book.

 Book Website Resources—the book website, *www.wiresharkbook.com* contains additional resources (*Appendix A* provides more details on these resources. You can also provide feedback, suggestions, reviews and critiques of the book on this site. Read the next section.

What's Online at *www.wiresharkbook.com?*

There are numerous references and resources referred to in this book at *www.wiresharkbook.com*. These files include:

- **Loads of trace files** (.pcap files) referenced in images throughout the book—the entire set of trace files is listed with descriptions in *Appendix A*.

- **Chanalyzer recordings (.wsr files)** to evaluate RF interference from numerous sources including a portable phone and various microwave ovens—the list of the Chanalyzer recordings is included in Appendix A. For more information on using Chanalyzer to identify RF interference, refer to *Chapter 26: Introduction to 802.11 (WLAN) Analysis*.

- **MaxMind® GeoIP® database files** (.dat files) as well as an installation and use video (mp4 format). For more information on GeoIP, refer to *Chapter 17: Analyze Internet Protocol (IPv4) Traffic*.

- **PhoneFactor™ SSL/TLS vulnerabilities documents and trace files** created by Steve Dispensa and Ray Marsh from Phone Factor (see the case study written by Steve Dispensa in *Chapter 30: Network Forensics Overview*).

- **Wireshark configurations** for customized profiles created for use on WLAN, VoIP, malicious traffic, etc. For more information on using Wireshark profiles, refer to *Chapter 11: Customize Wireshark Profiles*.

You can download individual sets of files or grab the entire set in ZIP or ISO image format. Please review the usage restrictions on the materials before you use them. Thanks.

Which Version of Wireshark Did You Use to Write This Book?

Wireshark is a moving target—constantly changing and evolving with new features, bug fixes and more dissectors. This book was written using the Wireshark Windows development release series 1.3 which preceded the stable release 1.4. You can live on the bleeding edge and access the development versions at *www.wireshark.org/download/automated* or grab the most recent stable release at *www.wireshark.org/download.html*.

Where noted, we have indicated features added in the newest versions of Wireshark.

Wireshark was created using Graphical Toolkit (GTK). GTK offers a toolset for creating graphical interfaces that are cross platform compatible. In most cases the steps shown throughout this book can be used if you are working on *nix or MAC OS X platforms. There are few differences between the Windows version and other Wireshark versions. Most of these differences are due to the GTK capabilities on those underlying operating systems.

How Can I Submit Comments/Change Requests for this Book?

Wireshark is updated quite often. In 2009, Wireshark went through eight stable release versions. Periodically you may find information about major functionality changes at *www.wiresharkbook.com*. In addition, you can provide your comments or change requests for future book editions by sending email to *updates@wiresharkbook.com*.

Wireshark Certified Network Analyst™ Program Overview

The revised Wireshark Certified Network Analyst ("Wireshark CNA") Exam is a globally-available, proctored exam to meet the secure and widely available delivery requirements desired by candidates.[4]

Visit *www.wiresharkU.com* for additional information on the Wireshark CNA Certification Program. Questions regarding your Wireshark CNA Certification status may be directed to *wcna@wiresharkU.com*.

Why Should I Pursue the Wireshark CNA Certification?

Successful completion of the Wireshark CNA Certification Exam indicates you have the knowledge required to capture network traffic, analyze the results and identify various anomalies related to performance or security issues.

How Do I Earn the Wireshark CNA Certified Status?

To earn the Wireshark CNA status, you must pass a single exam—the WCNA-100x exam. For details on booking your exam, visit *www.wiresharkU.com*.

Upon completion of the Wireshark CNA Certification Exam, an individual will receive a pass/fail score. Candidates who successfully pass the Wireshark CNA Certification Exam will receive their Wireshark CNA Certification Exam Confirmation within ten (10) working days. The Wireshark CNA Certification Exam Confirmation contains the candidate's certificate, additional information regarding analysis resources and details on maintaining Wireshark CNA status. For more information on the Wireshark CNA program, visit *www.wiresharkU.com*.

Questions regarding Wireshark CNA Certification status may be directed to *wcna@wiresharkU.com*.

Wireshark CNA Exam Objectives

Each chapter title page in this book provides a list of exam objectives for the Wireshark CNA program. For additional information regarding exam preparation, visit *www.wiresharkU.com*.

---

[4] The earlier version of the test and Wireshark CNA Certification Program was put on hold in late 2009 to accommodate the transition to a proctored format. Individuals who obtained their Wireshark CNA Certification under the prior program were automatically imported into the new program.

Wireshark University™ and Wireshark University™ Training Partners

After numerous talks with Gerald Combs and the CACE Technologies team, Wireshark University was launched in March 2007.

The goal of Wireshark University is to provide education on how to analyze, troubleshoot, secure and optimize network communications using Wireshark.

Wireshark University is responsible for creating and maintaining the Wireshark Certified Network Analyst Exam and Wireshark Certified Network Analyst Members Program, Wireshark University Certified Training Partner Program, Wireshark University Certified Instructor Program, and the Wireshark University Certified Training Materials.

Currently, Wireshark University courses are offered in instructor-led format throughout the world and in self-paced format through Chappell University (*www.chappellU.com*).

For more information on Wireshark University, visit *www.wiresharkU.com* or send email to *info@wiresharkU.com*.

Schedule Customized Onsite/Web-Based Training

If you are interested in training a team in a fast, effective, hands-on course environment, contact us directly. Customized courses can be developed and delivered by Laura Chappell. Customized courses are based on your network traffic. Course lengths can run from 2 days to 10 days and even include a web-based delivery option to meet the training needs of geographically dispersed students.

Contact us at *info@chappellU.com* for more information on scheduling customized training for your organization or visit *www.chappellU.com*. Online recorded courses are available from Chappell Seminars (*www.chappellseminars.com).*

Chapter 1:
The World of
Network Analysis

Wireshark Certified Network Analyst Exam Objectives covered:

- Defining Network Analysis
- Troubleshooting Tasks for the Network Analyst
- Security Tasks for the Network Analyst
- Optimization Tasks for the Network Analyst
- Application Analysis Tasks for the Network Analyst
- Understand Security Issues Related to Network Analysis
- Be Aware of Legal Issues of Listening to Network Traffic
- Overcome the "Needle in the Haystack Issue"
- Review a Checklist of Analysis Tasks

- ❖ Case Study: Pruning the "Puke"
- ❖ Case Study: The "Securely Invisible" Network
- ❖ Summary
- ❖ Practice What You've Learned
- ❖ Review Questions and Answers

Defining Network Analysis

Network analysis is the process of listening to and analyzing network traffic. Network analysis offers an insight into network communications to identify performance problems, locate security breaches, analyze application behavior, and perform capacity planning. Network analysis (aka "protocol analysis") is a process used by IT professionals who are responsible for network performance and security.

Whether you are completely new to network analysis or just returning after a hiatus of setting up servers, architecting your company's security plan, deploying Voice over IP, or jumping through hoops to get WLAN issues fixed... *Welcome and welcome back!*

Network analysis is not brain surgery. Anyone can analyze network communications. You do, however, need to acquire three basic skills to be a top notch network analyst who can spot the cause of performance problems, evidence of breached hosts, misbehaving applications or the impending overload of the network.

1. A solid understanding of TCP/IP communications
2. Comfort using Wireshark
3. Familiarity with packet structures and typical packet flows

Many of you have probably installed and configured TCP/IP networks—in fact, I imagine many of you have set up hundreds if not thousands of TCP/IP clients and servers. Excellent! You already understand TCP/IP addressing and realize the role that DNS and DHCP servers play on your network.

From a network analyst's perspective, you need to understand the purpose of those devices and protocols and how they interact. For example, how exactly does a DHCP server offer an IP address and configuration information to a DHCP client? What if there is a relay agent in use? What happens when the user's address lease time expires? How does the user learn the right IP address to use when the user wants to reach *www.wireshark.org*? What happens if the local name server does not have the answer? What happens if the local name server is down?

Seeing these processes in action at packet level is a fast way to learn the inner workings of your network. You build your baseline of understanding—the baseline is your foundational knowledge of how the processes are supposed to work.

Network analyzer tools are often referred to as "sniffers" and may be sold or distributed as a hardware-plus-software solution or as a software-only solution. Wireshark is distributed as an open source software-only solution, but there are add-on adapters that can enhance Wireshark's capabilities. The AirPcap adapter from CACE Technologies is an example of a hardware add-on. The AirPcap adapter is used on Windows hosts running Wireshark to listen in to wireless traffic in Monitor Mode.[5]

---

[5] Monitor Mode (also referred to as *rfmon* mode and wireless network analysis is covered in *Chapter 26: Introduction to 802.11 (WLAN) Analysis.*

Follow an Analysis Example

The typical network analysis session includes several tasks:

- Capture packets at the appropriate location
- Apply filters to focus on traffic of interest
- Review and identify anomalies in the traffic

For example, watch your own traffic as you browse to *www.wireshark.org/download.html* to grab the latest copy of Wireshark. This is what you might see in the traffic...

Your system requests the MAC (hardware) address of a local DNS server before asking for the IP address for *www.wireshark.org*. Hopefully, the DNS server responds with the information you need and then you're off!

Your client makes a TCP connection to *www.wireshark.org* and then sends an HTTP GET request asking for the download page as shown in Figure 1.

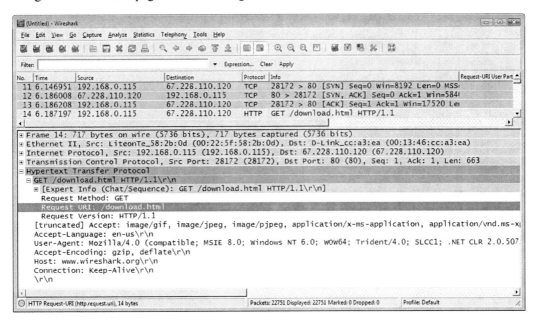

Figure 1. The client requests the Wireshark download.html page

If all goes well up to this point, you will see the HTTP server respond with an HTTP/1.1 200 OK response and then the page download begins. You will see various GET requests sent from your system—you are requesting the style sheets for the page and graphics to build the page.

When you select to download Wireshark, you see your system make a new TCP connection to another IP address and send a GET request for the Wireshark software as shown in Figure 2.

So far everything makes sense. You located the Wireshark site. You asked for the download.html page. Now you are downloading the file you want.

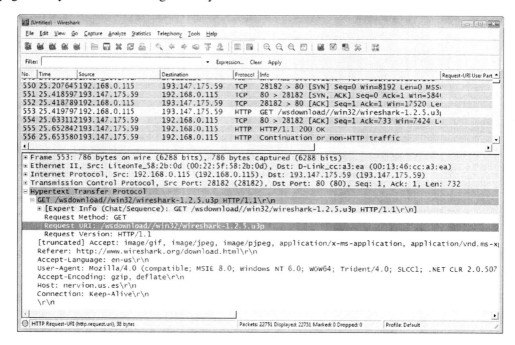

Figure 2. You request the Wireshark executable

You can watch the process as the file is transferred to your local system. It all makes perfect sense. It is all quite logical.

Until it all goes "to hell in a hand basket" as my mother would say.

You sit patiently waiting for the download to finish—tapping your fingers ever so irritatingly on your desk. Your eyes wander… looking for some distraction that will make the time pass more quickly. Waiting… waiting… waiting… until finally you just can't stand it anymore.

You type a new URL and decide to come back to the *www.wireshark.org* site later to get the latest copy of Wireshark. The other site loads quickly (oh… yeah… speed is good). You find another open source software package that is on your 'must have' list. You begin the download process and are filled with excitement at the thrill of taking charge and grabbing software at blazing speed (after all, your company did pay big money to upgrade that Internet connection)… until…

Your heart sinks…

This is taking waaaaay too long. At this rate you will miss lunch, dinner and potentially your summer vacation!

Maybe it's not *www.wireshark.org* that's having the problem. Maybe it's the Internet or (gasp!) your WAN link or (heaven's forbid!) your network or (shivers!) your DNS server or (unthinkable!) your desktop system.

Well? Which is it?

If you'd been running Wireshark in the background, you'd have known the answer long before I typed in that comment about your summer vacation. The packets never lie. They always point to where the problem is.

Network analysis adds an indispensible tool to the network—just as an x-ray is an indispensible tool to the hospital emergency room.[6]

Network analysis allows us the opportunity to look inside the network communication system. We can pull back the curtains and watch the packets travel back and forth. We can **SEE** the DNS query being sent out and catch the timely DNS response providing an answer. We can watch our local system send a TCP connection request packet to *www.wireshark.org*. We can measure how long it takes *www.wireshark.org* to answer and get a general feel for the round trip time to get to that site. We proudly beam as our system sends the HTTP GET request for the file—just as a good system should. We can gleefully…uh… what's that? The data transfer just stopped? How rude! Why did the transfer stop?

Well… you'll just have to look at the packets to know the answer. Then you can point the finger! In the world of finger pointing, *it's only the network analyst's finger that counts*.

The scenario above is quite common. The page loads nicely—all those little pieces and parts zipping on down to your system, gently placed in your TCP receive buffer awaiting pick-up by the browser you used to download the file. Waiting… waiting… waiting… You are not the only one who is wondering what the *#$)(#! is taking so long. Your packets could wither and die in that buffer waiting to be picked up by the browser.

Wait… more data is coming in… and more… and… *SCREECH!* The TCP buffer is full and it kindly tells the *www.wireshark.org* server that it can't possibly handle another byte so please "shut up!" The file transfer stops. The buffer waits for the application to pick up data. The user waits to see the file download is complete. Everyone waits…

Where is that <insert "*bleep*" here> browser? Doesn't it have any sense of time? There's data down here to be delivered to the user. Someone's gonna get mad! Oh yeah—someone is mad.

In this case the problem is caused by a browser that is not picking up data out of the TCP receive buffer in a timely manner. The TCP receive buffer fills. The TCP stack at the client sends a TCP packet to the server to let it know that there is no more room to buffer data. The server stops sending the file until the client indicates there is more buffer space.

---

[6] Imagine if you took a bad fall ice skating (computer geeks should not ice skate—that's another story). You think you broke your arm. At the emergency room the doctors huddle around you perplexed. "It's probably just a sprain—a pain killer and no movement for a week and you'll be fine." chimes in one doctor. "No. I think it's broken—let's re-break it and set it" Eeek… this scenario gets even uglier when you consider appendicitis.

The problem is not at *www.wireshark.org*. The problem is not at the download server. The problem is not at the WLAN link. The problem is not the internal network. The problem IS at the client—specifically the browser. You know where to begin troubleshooting. In this book we cover several reasons why file transfers slow to a crawl.

Troubleshooting Tasks for the Network Analyst

Troubleshooting is the most common use of Wireshark and is performed to locate the source of unacceptable performance of the network, an application, a host or other element of network communications. Troubleshooting tasks that can be performed with Wireshark include, but are not limited to:

- Locate faulty network devices
- Identify device or software misconfigurations
- Measure high delays along a path
- Locate the point of packet loss
- Identify network errors and service refusals
- Graph queuing delays

Security Tasks for the Network Analyst

Security tasks can be both proactive and reactive and are performed to identify security scanning processes, holes or breaches on the network. Security tasks that can be performed with Wireshark include, but are not limited to:

- Perform intrusion detection
- Identify and define malicious traffic signatures
- Passively discover hosts, operating systems and services
- Log traffic for forensics examination
- Capture traffic as evidence
- Test firewall blocking
- Validate secure login and data traversal

Optimization Tasks for the Network Analyst

Optimization is the process of contrasting current performance with performance capabilities and making adjustments in an effort to reach optimal performance levels. Optimization tasks that can be performed with Wireshark include, but are not limited to:

- Analyzing current bandwidth usage
- Evaluating efficient use of packet sizes in data transfer applications
- Evaluating response times across a network

Application Analysis Tasks for the Network Analyst

Application analysis is the process of capturing and analyzing the traffic generated by a network application. Application analysis tasks that can be performed with Wireshark include, but are not limited to:

- Analyzing application bandwidth requirements
- Identifying application protocols and ports in use
- Validating secure application data traversal

Understand Security Issues Related to Network Analysis

Network analysis can be used to improve network performance and security—but it can also be used for malicious tasks. For example, an intruder who can access the network medium (wired or wireless) can listen in on traffic. Unencrypted communications (such as clear text user names and passwords) may be captured and thus enable a malicious user to compromise accounts. An intruder can also learn network configuration information by listening to the traffic—this information can then be used to exploit network vulnerabilities. Malicious programs may include network analysis capabilities to sniff the traffic.

Define Policies Regarding Network Analysis

Companies should define specific policies regarding the use of a network analyzer. Your company policies should state who can use a network analyzer on the network and how, when and where the network analyzer may be used. Ensure these policies are well known throughout the company.

If you are a consultant performing network analysis services for a customer, consider adding a "Network Analysis" clause to your non-disclosure agreement. Define network analysis tasks and be completely forthcoming about the types of traffic that network analyzers can capture and view.

Files Containing Network Traffic Should be Secured

Ensure you have a secure storage solution for the traffic that you capture because confidential information may exist in the traffic files (referred to as *trace files*).

Protect Your Network against Unwanted "Sniffers"

As you will learn in *Chapter 3: Capture Traffic*, switches make network analysis a bit more challenging. Those challenges can be overcome using taps or redirection methods. Switches are not security devices. Unused network ports and network ports in common areas (such as building lobbies) should be deactivated to discourage visitors from plugging in and listening to network traffic.

The best protection mechanism against network sniffing is to encrypt network traffic using a robust encryption method. Encryption solutions will not protect the general network traffic that is broadcast onto the network for device and/or service discovery however. For example, DHCP clients broadcast DHCP Discover and Request packets on the network. These packets contain information about the client (including the host name, requested IP address and other revealing information). These DHCP broadcasts will be forwarded out by all ports of a switch. A network analyzer connected to that switch is able to capture the traffic and learn information about the DHCP client.

Be Aware of Legal Issues of Listening to Network Traffic

We aren't lawyers, so consult your legal counsel on this issue.

In general, Wireshark provides the ability to eavesdrop on network communications—have you heard the terms "wiretapping" or "electronic surveillance"? Unauthorized use of Wireshark may be illegal. Certain exceptions are in place to cover government use of wiretapping methods in advance of a crime being perpetrated.

In the U.S., Title I of the ECPA (Electronic Communications and Privacy Act), often referred to as the Wiretap Act, prohibits the intentional, actual or attempted interception, use, disclosure, or "procure[ment] [of] any other person to intercept or endeavor to intercept any wire, oral, or electronic communication."

Title I offers exceptions for operators and service providers for uses "in the normal course of his employment while engaged in any activity which is a necessary incident to the rendition of his service" and for "persons authorized by law to intercept wire, oral, or electronic communications or to conduct electronic surveillance, as defined in section 101 of the Foreign Intelligence Surveillance Act (FISA) of 1978." Cornell University Law School provides details of Title I at *www.law.cornell.edu/uscode/18/usc_sup_01_18_10_I_20_119.html*.

In the European Union, the Data Protection Directive, Directive 95/46/EC of the European Parliament and of the Council of 24 October 1995, defines the protection of individuals with regard to the processing of personal data and on the free movement of such data requires Member States to ensure the rights and freedoms of natural persons with regard to the processing of personal data, and in particular their right to privacy, in order to ensure the free flow of personal data in the Community. For details on the EU Data Protection Directive, visit *ec.europa.eu/justice_home/fsj/privacy/*.

Avoid Prison

Company policies may also forbid unauthorized tapping into network communications. Disregard for these policies may result in disciplinary actions or termination. Tom Quilty, CEO of BD Consulting and Investigations (www.bdcon.net), offered this note:

"If they are capturing traffic with Personally Identifiable Information (PII), HIPAA (health records), or other protected information, the trace files should not leave the facility. If lost, it may require that the client report a data breach, which could be very costly for the person capturing the traffic. They should also ensure that they have an appropriate General Liability and Errors & Omissions rider. I would recommend that they understand what information is going across the wire (or air) and review the client's Data Breach Policies and Response Plan (assuming they have one—most don't). They may also have to testify about how they protected any information captured (hopefully, they have developed procedures for this before this comes up)."

Many countries have similar laws in place regarding protection of information—make sure you understand your local laws and look into professional insurance… just in case.

Overcome the "Needle in the Haystack Issue"

Many times new analysts capture thousands (or millions) of packets and are faced with the "needle in a haystack issue"—the feeling that they are drowning in packets. Several non-pharmaceutical analysis procedures can be used to avoid or deal with this situation:

- Place the analyzer appropriately (covered in *Chapter 3: Capture Traffic*)
- Apply capture filters to reduce the number of packets captured (covered in *Chapter 4: Create and Apply Capture Filters*)
- Apply display filters to focus on specific conversations, connections, protocols or applications (covered in *Chapter 9: Create and Apply Display Filters*)
- Colorize the conversations in more complex multi-connection communications (covered in *Chapter 6: Colorize Traffic*)
- Reassemble streams for a clear view of data exchanged (covered in *Chapter 10: Follow Streams and Reassemble Data*)
- Save subsets of the captured traffic into separate files (covered in *Chapter 12: Save, Export and Print Packets*)
- Build graphs depicting overall traffic patterns or apply filters to graphs to focus on particular traffic types as shown in Figure 3 (covered in *Chapter 8: Interpret Basic Trace File Statistics* and *Chapter 21: Graph IO Rates and TCP Trends*).

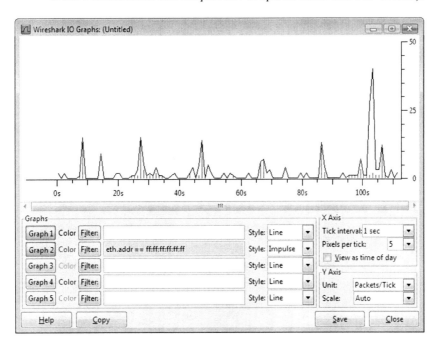

Figure 3. Use filters in graphs to identify traffic patterns

Throughout this book we will show and work with trace files obtained and manipulated using these techniques.

Review a Checklist of Analysis Tasks

Analysis tasks can be considered preventive or reactive. Preventive methods include baselining network communications to learn the current status of the network and application performance. Preventive analysis can also be used to spot network problems before they are felt by the network users. For example, identifying the cause of packet loss before it becomes excessive and affects network communications helps avoid problems before they are even noticed.

Reactive analysis techniques are employed after a complaint about network performance has been reported or when network issues are suspected. Sadly, reactive analysis is more common.

The following lists some of the analysis tasks that can be performed using Wireshark:

- Find the top talkers on the network
- Identify the protocols and applications in use
- Determine the average packets per second rate and bytes per second rate of an application or all network traffic on a link
- List all hosts communicating
- Learn the packet lengths used by a data transfer application
- Recognize the most common connection problems
- Spot delays between client requests due to slow processing
- Locate misconfigured hosts
- Detect network or host congestion that is slowing down file transfers
- Identify asynchronous traffic prioritization
- Graph HTTP flows to examine website referrals rates
- Identify unusual scanning traffic on the network
- Quickly identify HTTP error responses indicating client and server problems
- Quickly identify VoIP error responses indicating client, server or global errors
- Build graphs to compare traffic behavior
- Graph application throughput and compare to overall link traffic seen
- Identify applications that do not encrypt traffic
- Play back VoIP conversations to hear the effects of various network problems on network traffic
- Perform passive operating system and application use detection
- Spot unusual protocols and unrecognized port number usage on the network
- Examine the start up process of hosts and applications on the network
- Identify average and unacceptable service response times (SRT)
- Graph intervals of periodic packet generation applications or protocols

Networks vary greatly in the traffic seen. The number and type of network analysis tasks you can perform depends on your network traffic characteristics.

Understand Network Traffic Flows

Let's start at the packet level by following a packet as it makes its way from one host to another. We'll start by looking at where we can capture the traffic (more in-depth information on capturing can be found in *Chapter 3: Capture Traffic*). We will examine how a packet is encapsulated, then stripped nearly naked by some high-priced router only to be re-encapsulated and sent on its way again just before hypothermia sets in. Let's chat about packets whizzing past switches so quickly there really isn't even time for a proper introduction. Then we peak at the effect that Quality of Service (QoS) has on our traffic and where devices and technology puff up their chests, whip out their badges and throw up roadblocks that make us fear for our little packet lives.

Switching Overview

Switches are considered Layer 2 devices—a reference to Layer 2 of the Open Systems Interconnection (OSI) model—the data link layer which includes the Media Access Control (MAC) portion of the packet, such as the Ethernet header.

Switches forward packets based on the destination MAC address (aka the destination hardware address) contained in the MAC header. As shown in Figure 4, switches do not change the MAC or IP addresses in packets.[7]

When a packet arrives at a switch, the switch checks the packet to ensure it has the correct checksum. If the packet's checksum is incorrect, the packet is considered "bad" and the packet is discarded. Switches should maintain error counters to indicate how many packets they have discarded because of bad checksums.

If the checksum is good, the switch examines the destination MAC address of the packet and consults its MAC address table to determine if it knows which switch port leads to the host using that MAC address. If the switch does not have the target MAC address in its tables, it will forward the packet out all ports in hopes of discovering the target when it answers.

If the switch does have the target MAC address in its tables it forwards the packet out the appropriate port. Broadcasts are forwarded out all ports on a switch. Unless configured otherwise, multicasts are also forwarded out all ports on a switch.

To learn about the challenges of and solutions for capturing traffic on a switched network, refer to *Capture Traffic on Switched Networks* on page 82.

---

[7] In Figure 4 we use a symbolic letter to represent the MAC addresses of the client and server.

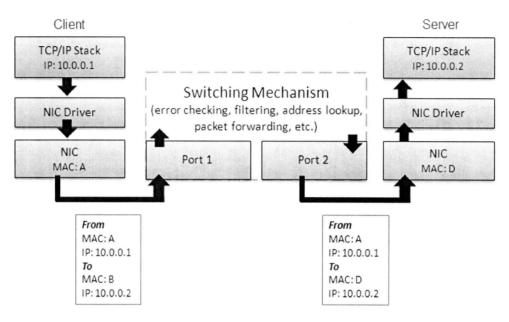

Figure 4. Switches do not alter the MAC or IP address in a packet

Routing Overview

Routers forward packets based on the destination IP address in the IP header. When a packet is sent to the MAC address of the router, that router examines the checksum to ensure the packet is valid. If the checksum is invalid, the packet is dropped. If the checksum is valid, the router strips off the MAC header (such as the Ethernet header) and examines the IP header to identify the "age" (in Time to Live) and destination of the packet. If the packet is too "old" (Time to Live value of 1), the router discards the packet.

The router consults its routing tables to determine if the destination IP network is known. If the router is directly connected to the target network, it can send the packet on to the target. The router decrements the IP header Time to Live value and then creates and applies a new MAC header on the packet before forwarding it, as shown in Figure 5.

If the target is not on a locally connected network, the router forwards the packet to the next-hop router that it learned about when consulting its routing tables.

Routers may contain rules that block or permit packets based on the addressing information. Many routers provide firewall capabilities and can block/permit traffic based on other characteristics.

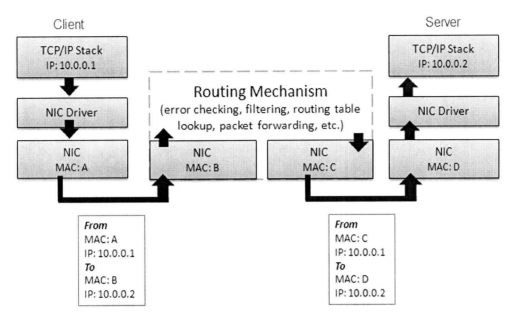

Figure 5. Routers change the destination MAC address to the target (if the target is local) or next router (if the target is remote)

Proxy, Firewall and NAT/PAT Overview

Firewalls are created to examine the traffic and allow/disallow communications based on a set of rules. For example, you may want to block all TCP connection attempts from hosts outside the firewall that are destined to port 21 on internal servers.

Basic firewalls operate at Layer 3 of the OSI model—the network layer. In this capacity, the firewall acts like a router when handling network traffic. The firewall will forward traffic that is not blocked by the firewall rules. The firewall prepends a new MAC header on the packet before forwarding it. Additional packet alteration will take place if the firewall supports added features, such as Network Address Translation (NAT) or proxy capabilities.

NAT systems alter the IP addresses in the packet as shown in Figure 6. This is often used to hide the client's private IP address. A basic NAT system simply alters the source and destination IP address of the packet and tracks the connection relationships in a table to forward traffic properly when a reply is received. Port Address Translation (PAT) systems also alter the port information and use this as a method for demultiplexing multiple internal connections when using a single outbound address. The IP addresses you see on one side of a NAT/PAT device will not match the IP addresses you see on the other side of the NAT/PAT device. To correlate the communications on both sides of a NAT device, you will need to look past the IP header to identify matching packets.

Proxy servers also affect traffic. Unlike the communications seen when you use a standard firewall, the client connects to the proxy server and the proxy server makes a separate connection to the target. There are two totally separate connections to examine when troubleshooting these communications.

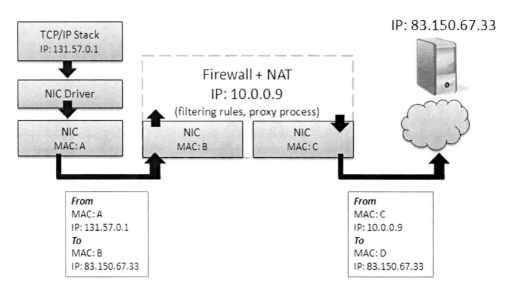

Figure 6. The firewall uses NAT to hide the true source IP address

Other Technologies that Affect Packets

There are numerous other technologies that affect network traffic patterns and packet contents.

Virtual LAN (VLAN) tagging (defined as 802.1Q) adds an identification (tag) to the packets. This tag is used to create virtual networks in a switched environment. Figure 7 shows a VLAN tag in an Ethernet frame. In this case, the sender belongs to VLAN 32.

Multiprotocol Label Switching (MPLS) is a method of creating virtual links between remote hosts. MPLS packets are prefaced with a special header by MPLS edge devices. For example, a packet sent from a client reaches an MPLS router where the MPLS label is placed on the packet. The packet is now forwarded based on the MPLS label, not routing table lookups. The MPLS label is stripped off when the packet exits the MPLS network.

```
⊞ Frame 26: 414 bytes on wire (3312 bits), 414 bytes captured (3312 bits)
⊞ Ethernet II, Src: AniCommu_40:ef:24 (00:40:05:40:ef:24), Dst: 3com_9f:b1:
⊟ 802.1Q Virtual LAN, PRI: 0, CFI: 0, ID: 32
    000. .... .... ....  = Priority: 0
    ...0 .... .... ....  = CFI: 0
    .... 0000 0010 0000  = ID: 32
    Type: IP (0x0800)
⊞ Internet Protocol, Src: 131.151.32.129 (131.151.32.129), Dst: 131.151.32.2
⊞ Transmission Control Protocol, Src Port: 1162 (1162), Dst Port: 6000 (600
⊞ X11, Request, opcode: 2 (ChangeWindowAttributes)
⊞ X11, Request, opcode: 61 (ClearArea)
⊞ X11, Request, opcode: 59 (SetClipRectangles)
```

Figure 7. VLAN tags separate virtual networks using the ID field

Warnings About "Smarter" Infrastructure Devices

You paid a bunch of money for those brilliant infrastructure devices and you didn't expect them to be the cause of your network problems, did you? Numerous "security devices" do more than route packets based on simple rules—they get in there and mess up the packets. For example, Cisco's Adaptive Security Appliance (ASA) performs "TCP normalization." Billed as stateful firewalls and VPN concentrators, these lovely boxes had a little problem that caused them to strip off some TCP functionality during the connection process. In essence, an ASA device forced TCP hosts on both sides of it to go back to pre-2006 capabilities.

Wide Area Network (WAN) optimization techniques can also alter the packet and data stream process by compressing traffic, offering locally-cached versions of data, optimizing TCP or prioritizing traffic based on defined characteristics (traffic "shaping").

The best way to know how these technologies affect your traffic is to capture the packets before and after they pass through a traffic-altering device.

Launch an Analysis Session

You can start capturing and analyzing traffic right now. Follow these steps to get a feel for analyzing traffic on a wired network first.

Step 1:   Get Wireshark installed (refer to the System Requirement information at *www.wireshark.org/docs/wsug_html_chunked/ChIntroPlatforms.html*). Visit *www.wireshark.org/docs/wsug_html_chunked/ChapterBuildInstall.html* for details on installing Wireshark on numerous platforms.

Step 2:   Launch Wireshark and click on your wired network adapter listed in the Interface List on the Start Page. If your adapter is not listed, you cannot capture traffic. Visit *wiki.wireshark.org/CaptureSetup/NetworkInterfaces* for assistance. If your adapter was listed, Wireshark should be capturing traffic now.

Step 3:   If you have browsed to *www.chappellU.com* recently, clear your browser cache before this step. Refer to your browser Help for details on how to clear your browser cache. In addition, consider clearing your DNS cache.[8] While Wireshark is capturing traffic, launch your browser and visit *www.chappellU.com*.

Step 4:   Select **Capture | Stop** or click the **Stop Capture** button.

---

[8] To clear your DNS cache on a Windows host, go to a command prompt and type `ipconfig /flushdns`. On a Linux host, restart the `nscd` (name service cache) daemon. For MAC OS X 10.5.x or 10.6.x, type `dscacheutil -flushcache` at the terminal prompt.

Step 5: Look through the captured traffic. You should see a DNS query (unless you did not clear your DNS cache in Step 3). After you make a connection to *www.chappellU.com*, your browser sent a GET request to the server and should have received an HTTP/1.0 302 Moved Temporarily response as shown in Figure 8. You are redirected to *www.chappellseminars.com/chappellu.html*.

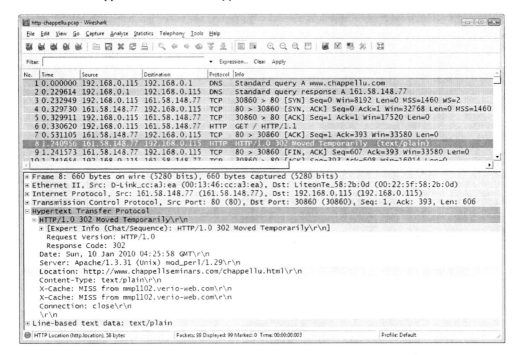

Figure 8. The HTTP server indicates that a page has been moved

You may see traffic from other processes in the trace file. For example, if your browser performs a website blacklist check to identify known malicious sites, you will see this traffic preceding connection to *www.chappellU.com*. Display filters can be used to remove unrelated traffic from view so you can focus better on the traffic of interest. For more information on display filtering, refer to *Chapter 9: Create and Apply Display Filters*.

Step 6: Select **File | Save** and create a *\mytraces* directory. Save your file using the name *chappellu.pcap* (Wireshark automatically appends the .pcap extension if you forget to include it).

You did it! Well done. You are well on your way to learning network analysis—one of the most valuable and fundamental skills of network management and security.

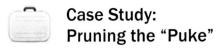

Case Study:
Pruning the "Puke"

Submitted by: **Mitch Dickey**
                 Frederick County Public Schools, VA

Our school district is comprised of 24 buildings and roughly 50 VLANS. Generally speaking, each campus has one VLAN for data and one for voice. For the most part each campus is its own VLAN, with some smaller sites sharing a single VLAN. We operate in a NetWare environment with at least one NetWare server at each campus. Each campus links back to an aggregate location before it is sent on to the router; what some like to call "Router on a Stick."

I use Wireshark on a regular basis to monitor traffic patterns and remove unnecessary traffic from the VLANs that I manage. Two types of traffic that I have eliminated are NetBIOS and SMB. Since we are in a NetWare environment we use NDPS for our printing services and do not require Windows File and Printer Sharing. Because of this I turn off NetBIOS and SMB on the machines that I manage. I recently sampled four other VLANs (out of my control) by taking a five minute PCAP. After the capture, I sifted through the traffic using filters to determine what percentage of traffic was NetBIOS and SMB. Although the results are lower than what I expected, trimming what I did find could be beneficial to switch/router processing, and most of all security.

- A capture containing 50,898 packets returned a combined total of 1,321 packets or 2.5% NetBIOS/SMB traffic.
- A capture containing 175,824 packets returned a combined total of 16,480 packets or 9% NetBIOS/SMB traffic.
- A capture containing 295,911 packets returned a combined total of 14,102 packets or 5% NetBIOS/SMB traffic.
- A capture containing 115,814 packets returned a combined total of 333 packets or less than 1% NetBIOS/SMB traffic.

I have used Wireshark to track down and remove other unnecessary protocols like SNMP and SSDP as well. We only use SNMP on Cisco equipment so eliminating it from network printers has cleaned up the network.

Case Study:
The "Securely Invisible" Network

One customer's network consisted of 22 buildings in a campus-style setting. Management complained that the network is slow at times and had asked a consultant to come onsite to determine the cause of poor network performance.

Upon arrival, I was asked to sign a legal document stating that I would not listen to the network traffic to isolate the problem (you, as I must question why they called me).

The management at this company was concerned that confidential data may traverse their network in an unencrypted form.

The management was ignoring the fact that there are many ways for someone to tap into their network. If their data is visible to a network analyst, it would be best to verify that and fix the problem, not just assume that no one is listening.

It took several meetings with various individuals to convince management that they were a bit "off" on their thinking.

Once I began listening to their network traffic it became evident that they had good reason to be concerned. Their Lotus Notes implementation was misconfigured—all emails traveled through the network in clear text.

Over the next few hours of listening to the network traffic we found several applications that sent sensitive data across the network. By the time I left they had a list of security enhancements to implement on the network.

Summary

Network analysis offers an insight into network communications. When performance problems plague the network, guesswork can often be time consuming and lead to inaccurate conclusions costing you and your company time and money. A full understanding the network traffic flows is necessary to (a) place the analyzer properly on the network and (b) identify possible causes of network problems.

At this point it is recommended that you follow the procedures listed in *Launch an Analysis Session* on page 15 and review the section entitled *Follow an Analysis Example* on page 3.

Practice What You've Learned

 Download the trace files available in the Download section of the book website, *www.wiresharkbook.com*. There are many trace files and other book supplement files available on the book website. Consider copying them all to your drive now.

In Wireshark, open *gen-googlemaps.pcap*. This trace file contains the traffic from a web browsing session to *maps.google.com*.

Our client is 192.168.0.106. Our default gateway, 192.168.0.1, offers DNS services as well.

Answer the following questions about this trace file.

- What is the hardware address of the client that is browsing to *maps.google.com*?
- What is the IP address of the DNS server (which is also the router)?
- What is the hardware address of the DNS server/router?
- What is IP addresses are associated with *maps.google.com*?

No.	Source	Destination	Protocol	Info
1	AsustekC_b0:30:23	Broadcast	ARP	who has 192.168.0.1? Tell 192.168.0.106
2	D-Link_cc:a3:ea	AsustekC_b0:30:23	ARP	192.168.0.1 is at 00:13:46:cc:a3:ea
3	192.168.0.106	192.168.0.1	DNS	Standard query A maps.google.com
4	192.168.0.1	192.168.0.106	DNS	Standard query response CNAME maps.1.google.com A 74.125.19.147
5	192.168.0.106	74.125.19.147	TCP	twsdss > http [SYN] Seq=0 win=65535 Len=0 MSS=1460
6	74.125.19.147	192.168.0.106	TCP	http > twsdss [SYN, ACK] Seq=0 Ack=1 win=5720 Len=0 MSS=1430
7	192.168.0.106	74.125.19.147	TCP	twsdss > http [ACK] Seq=1 Ack=1 win=65535 Len=0
8	192.168.0.106	74.125.19.147	HTTP	GET / HTTP/1.1
9	74.125.19.147	192.168.0.106	TCP	http > twsdss [ACK] Seq=1 Ack=888 win=7096 Len=0
10	74.125.19.147	192.168.0.106	TCP	[TCP segment of a reassembled PDU]

```
⊞ Frame 1: 42 bytes on wire (336 bits), 42 bytes captured (336 bits)
⊞ Ethernet II, Src: AsustekC_b0:30:23 (00:17:31:b0:30:23), Dst: Broadcast (ff:ff:ff:ff:ff:ff)
⊟ Address Resolution Protocol (request)
    Hardware type: Ethernet (0x0001)
    Protocol type: IP (0x0800)
    Hardware size: 6
    Protocol size: 4
    Opcode: request (0x0001)
    [Is gratuitous: False]
    Sender MAC address: AsustekC_b0:30:23 (00:17:31:b0:30:23)
    Sender IP address: 192.168.0.106 (192.168.0.106)
    Target MAC address: 00:00:00_00:00:00 (00:00:00:00:00:00)
    Target IP address: 192.168.0.1 (192.168.0.1)
```

❶ The first two packets—ARP packets—obtain the hardware address of the DNS server. What can we learn just from these two packets? Well—the client is 192.168.0.106. The DNS server is at 192.168.0.1. The hardware addresses of the client and the DNS server are listed in the Source and Destination columns (the first three bytes of the hardware address—the OUI value—and "broadcast" has been resolved to a more readable format by Wireshark). The hardware address of the client is listed as AsustekC_b0:30:23 in the Packet Info pane and 00:17:31:b0:30:23 in the Ethernet II summary line and inside the ARP packet.

❷ Packets 3 and 4 are the DNS query/response packets. The client is trying to get the IP address of *maps.google.com*. The DNS query packet is addressed to the hardware address and IP address of the DNS server (this DNS server is local to the client). The DNS server provides 7 IP addresses and indicates that *maps.google.com*'s real name (CNAME) is *maps.l.google.com*. The first address provided is 74.125.19.147.

❸ The client makes a TCP connection to *maps.google.com* in packets 5, 6 and 7. Now the client sends the packet to the hardware address of the router (which is also the DNS server) and the IP address of *maps.google.com* (*maps.l.google.com*).

❹ In packet 8 the client asks for the main page (GET / HTTP/1.1). In packet 9, the server acknowledges receipt of that request. In packet 10 the server begins sending the main page to the client.

The following table lists the trace file you worked with and a couple other trace files at *www.wiresharkbook.com* that you might want to review.

gen-googlemaps.pcap	This trace file depicts a simple web browsing session to *www.google.com*. The client performed an ARP query to get the hardware address of the DNS server and then sent a query to that DNS server to resolve the IP address for *www.google.com*. After receiving a successful response, the client makes a TCP connection to the server on port 80 and requests to GET the main page. The page is downloaded successfully.
telnet.pcap	Someone makes a telnet connection to a Cisco router to run the `show version` command which is echoed back, as is the `exit` command. The password, however, is not echoed back. Follow the DO, DON'T, WILL and WON'T command as the client and server negotiate the connection behavior.
icmp-ping-basic.pcap	This trace shows a basic ICMP ping test preceded by the DNS query/response to obtain the IP address of *www.chappellU.com*.

Review Questions

Q1.1   **What is the purpose of network analysis?**

Q1.2   **Name at least three troubleshooting tasks that can be performed using network analysis.**

    1.

    2.

    3.

Q1.3   **Why is network analysis considered a security risk by some companies?**

Answers to Review Questions

Q1.1   **What is the purpose of network analysis?**

A1.1   Network analysis offers an insight into network communications to identify performance problems, locate security breaches, analyze application behavior, and perform capacity planning.

Q1.2   **Name at least three troubleshooting tasks that can be performed using network analysis.**

A1.2   1.   Locate faulty network devices

2.   Measure high delays along a path

3.   Locate the point of packet loss

Q1.3   **Why is network analysis considered a security risk by some companies?**

A1.3   Some companies consider network analysis to be a security risk because it involves tapping into network traffic and eavesdropping on communications. These companies fear that unencrypted information (data, email, etc.) may be seen by the network analyst. In reality, however, the network analyst can identify unsecure network communications to prevent unauthorized eavesdroppers from gaining insight into confidential communications.

Chapter 2: Introduction to Wireshark

Wireshark Certified Network Analyst Exam Objectives covered:

- What is Wireshark?
- Obtaining the Latest Version of Wireshark
- Compare Wireshark Release and Development Versions
- Report a Wireshark Bug or Submit an Enhancement
- Capturing Packets on Wired or Wireless Networks
- Opening Various Trace File Types
- Understanding How Wireshark Processes Packets
- Using the Start Page
- Identifying the Nine GUI Elements
- Navigating Wireshark's Main Menu
- Using the Main Toolbar for Efficiency
- Focusing Faster with the Filter Toolbar
- Making the Wireless Toolbar Visible
- Accessing Options through Right-Click Functionality
- Functions of the Menus and Toolbars

  - ❖ Case Study: Detecting Database Death
  - ❖ Summary
  - ❖ Practice What You've Learned
  - ❖ Review Questions and Answers

What is Wireshark?

Wireshark is the world's most popular network analyzer. Available for free to all as an open source tool, Wireshark runs on a variety of platforms and offers the ideal 'first responder' tool for IT professionals.

In 1997, the analysis world was dominated by commercial network analyzers that ranged in price from $5,000 to $20,000. The cost was prohibitive to most business and information technologists. Gerald Combs was one of these technologists who felt the budget constraints of the expensive commercial tools. Prior to creating Ethereal, Gerald Combs was lugging around a Sniffer™ portable at the University of Missouri in Kansas City. The limited budget at his next job at a small Internet service provider limited his tools to tcpdump and snoop.

He decided to create his own network analyzer program.

Gerald Combs originally released his network analyzer program under the name Ethereal™ (version 0.2.0) on July 14, 1998 although Gerald's original development notes are dated several months earlier (late 1997).[9] When Gerald began working with CACE Technologies In June 2006, trademark ownership issues of the name Ethereal forced the development efforts to move to the new name, Wireshark[10].

Wireshark is maintained by an active community of developers from all over the world. For more information on the Wireshark developers, see *Thanks to the Wireshark Developers!* on page 26.

Obtaining the Latest Version of Wireshark

Wireshark is available for numerous operating systems including Windows, Apple Mac OS X, Debian GNU/Linux, FreeBSD, Gentoo Linux, HP-UX, Mandriva Linux, NetBSD, OpenPKG, Red Hat Fedora/Enterprise Linux, rPath Linux, Sun Solaris/i386, Sun Solaris/Sparc and Ubuntu.

Visit *www.wireshark.org/download.html* to locate the appropriate Wireshark version for your operating system.

Wireshark is released under the GNU (pronounced guh-*new*) General Public License (referred to as the GNU GPL). For information on the GNU GPL, visit *www.gnu.org/licenses/gpl-faq.html*. To view the Wireshark License, choose **Help | About Wireshark | License** as shown in Figure 9. For details on the estimated cost to develop Wireshark, see *Calculating the Value of the Wireshark Code* on page 26.

---

[9] If you'd like to get a glimpse of the Wireshark development process, watch the video at *www.vimeo.com/9329501*. Loris Degioanni (creator of WinPcap) used **code_swarm**, an organic visualization tool and the Wireshark code commits to graphically represent the entire life of Wireshark in a short 3-minute video.

[10] Gerald Combs states that the Wireshark "shark" is carcharodon photoshopia. It is most definitely based on carcharodon carcharias also known as the Great White shark. When the name change was imminent, one of the potential future names considered, and dismissed thankfully, was "EtherWeasel". Sounds a bit like a porn project, eh?

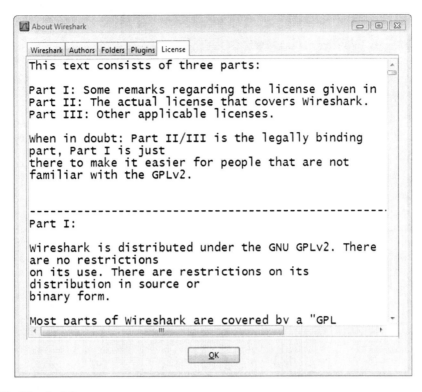

Figure 9. The Wireshark license

Compare Wireshark Release and Development Versions

The most recent stable version of Wireshark is available at *www.wireshark.org/download.html* while the most recent development release version can be found at *www.wireshark.org/download/automated/*.

The version number used for stable releases contain an even number after the decimal point (such as 1.2 and 1.4) while development release version numbers contain an odd number after the decimal point (such as 1.1 and 1.3). In addition, development releases contain "SVN" in the title indicating the development release version is managed using the Subversion open source version control system.

Get Notified of New Wireshark Releases
Sign up for the Wireshark-announce mailing list at www.wireshark.org/lists *to receive notification of releases.*

Thanks to the Wireshark Developers!

Currently there are approximately 700 developers credited with building and enhancing Wireshark. There are between 10 and 20 active developers at any given time. Wireshark's capabilities and resulting popularity is a direct result of the tireless efforts of the development team.[11]

The list of "Core Developers" is maintained at *wiki.wireshark.org/Developers*. The complete list of contributors is available at **Help | About Wireshark | Authors**. At the time this book was written, the core developers are listed as:

Olivier Abad	Mike Hall	Luis Ontanon
Olivier Biot	Guy Harris	Tim Potter
Stig Bjørlykke	Jaap Keuter	Kovarththanan Rajaratnam
Graham Bloice	Tomas Kukosa	Gilbert Ramirez
Sake Blok	Ulf Lamping	Balint Reczey
Hannes Boehm	Graeme Lunt	Lars Roland
Anders Broman	Martin Mathieson	Ronnie Sahlberg
Gerald Combs[12]	Joerg Mayer	Richard Sharpe
Laurent Deniel	John McDermott	Sebastien Tandel
Gerasimos Dimitriadis	Bill Meier	Michael Tuexen
Mike Duigou	Stefan Metzmacher	Richard Van Der Hoff
Stephen Fisher	Greg Morris	Alejandro Vaquero
Jeff Foster	Jeff Morriss	Jelmer Vernooij
Uwe Girlich	Ashok Narayanan	Ed Warnicke
Jun-ichiro itojun Hagino	Nathan Neulinger	Jim Young

Calculating the Value of the Wireshark Code

SLOCCount (*sourceforge.net/projects/sloccount/*) is a tool used to count source lines of code and estimate development cost and time. According to SLOCCount, Wireshark contains 1.8 million lines of code (LoC) and has taken 545 person-years to develop at an estimated development cost of $73 million. Wireshark's automated build system generates a report after each check in at *www.wireshark.org/download/automated/sloccount.txt*.

Report a Wireshark Bug or Submit an Enhancement

Wireshark uses the Bugzilla bug tracking system at *bugs.wireshark.org/bugzilla* as shown in Figure 10. Sometimes things just don't seem right in Wireshark. Maybe a field doesn't seem to be decoded properly or a button is only partially visible—you can view the entire list of open bugs to see if someone else feels your pain or if the bug is being worked on.

---

[11] All of us who solve network problems, optimize communications, spot security flaws faster and more accurately because of Wireshark owe a big THANKS to all the developers! Please report bugs and offer enhancement ideas to help the developers.

[12] Gerald Combs is listed as the original author (and fearless leader).

Bugs can be reported on the Wireshark GUI, Tshark, dumpcap, Editcap, Mergecap, Capinfos, Text2pcap and other related utilities. The bug tracking system also supports the Wireshark web sites, including *www.wireshark.org*, *wiki.wireshark.org*, and *anonsvn.wireshark.org*. Problems with other network services such as Subversion, mail, FTP, and rsync should be reported here as well.

You can search for a bug based on a key word, submit a new bug or request product enhancements here as well.

Figure 10. You can view all open bugs in Wireshark's Bugzilla bug database

You will need to create an account and login before you can file a bug. You do not need to create an account or login to search for a bug or show open bugs. To learn more about using Bugzilla, visit *bugs.wireshark.org/bugzilla/docs/html/using.html*.

Following Export Regulations
Wireshark has the ability to decrypt DCERPC, IPsec, ISAKMP, Kerberos, SNMPv3, SSL/TLS, WEP, WPA/WPA2 and a number of other protocols. Wireshark's primary distribution point is in the United States through the *www.wireshark.org* site, and subsequently falls under U.S. encryption export regulations.

Export regulation issues are covered in the Wireshark FAQ:

> *"To the best of our knowledge, Wireshark falls under ECCN 5D002 and qualifies*
> *for license exemption TSU under Section 734.3(b)(3) of the EAR. Downloading*
> *Wireshark in Cuba, Iran, North Korea, Libya, Sudan, and Syria is prohibited."*

The FAQ references a document written by Frank Hecker that details Mozilla's Export Control Classification Number used for U.S. encryption export control regulations. The document is located at *hecker.org/mozilla/eccn*.

Identifying Products that Leverage Wireshark's Capabilities

Numerous products either embed Wireshark within their product offerings or provide complementary services based on Wireshark.

- AirPcap adapters by CACE Technologies enable simultaneous 802.11 a/b/g/n capture and dissection by Wireshark (*www.cacetech.com*)

- CACE Pilot® by CACE Technologies offers long-term trending of network traffic and export of selected sections of traffic directly into Wireshark (*www.cacetech.com*)

- Cisco's Nexus 7000 Series switches includes Wireshark as a built-in protocol analyzer (*www.cisco.com/en/US/products/ps9402*)

Capturing Packets on Wired or Wireless Networks

When Wireshark is connected to a wired or wireless network, traffic is processed by either the WinPcap, AirPcap or libpcap link-layer interface, as illustrated in Figure 11.

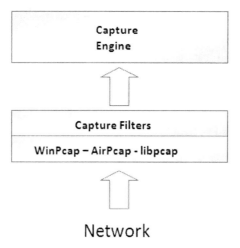

Figure 11. Traffic capture process

Libpcap

The libpcap library is the industry standard link-layer interface for capturing traffic on *NIX hosts. Information regarding patches related to libpcap can be found at *www.tcpdump.org*.

WinPcap

WinPcap is the Windows port of the libpcap link-layer interface. WinPcap consists of a driver that provides the low-level network access and the Windows version of the libpcap API (application programming interface). Visit *www.winpcap.org* for more information on WinPcap and WinPcap-capable utilities.

AirPcap

AirPcap is a link-layer interface and network adapter to capture 802.11 traffic on Windows operating systems. AirPcap adapters operate in passive mode to capture WLAN data, management and control frames. Visit *www.cacetech.com* for more information on AirPcap adapters.

Opening Various Trace File Types

WinPcap, AirPcap and libpcap interfaces are not used when opening trace files. Opened trace files are processed through the Wireshark wiretap library as illustrated in Figure 12.

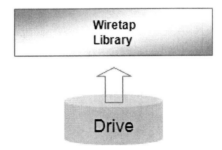

Figure 12. The Wiretap Library is used when you open trace files

The Wireshark wiretap library enables Wireshark to read a variety of trace file formats including the following:

Wireshark/tcpdump-libcap	Microsoft NetMon	Endace ERF capture
AIX tcpdump-libcap	Network General Sniffer	TamoSoft CommView
RedHat 6.1 tcpdump-libpcap	NI Observer	Shomiti/Finisar Surveyor
SuSE 6.3 tcpdump-libpcap	Sun snoop	WildPackets *Peek

To view the entire list of trace file formats in the Wireshark wiretap library, launch Wireshark and select **File | Open**. Open the **Files of Type** drop down list.

Understanding How Wireshark Processes Packets

Trace files that are processed by libpcap, WinPcap or AirPcap or are opened up with the wiretap library are processed in the core engine as shown in Figure 13.

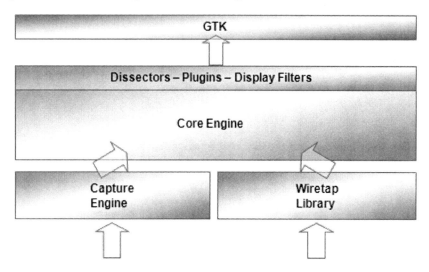

Figure 13. Packet processing elements

Core Engine

The core engine is described as the 'glue code that holds the other blocks together.'

Dissectors, Plugins and Display Filters

Dissectors (also referred to as decodes), plugins (special routines for dissection) and display filters (used to define which packets should be displayed) are applied to the incoming traffic at this time. Dissectors decode packets to display field contents and interpreted values (if available).[13]

Graphical Toolkit (GTK)

GTK is the graphical toolkit used to create the graphical user interface for Wireshark and offers cross-platform compatibility.

---

[13] This is where the real power of Wireshark shines! Can you imagine decoding an HTTP GET request one byte at a time from a hex dump?! That is the kind of *fun* that screams "you have no life!"

Using the Start Page

A Start Page was added to Wireshark when it reached version 1.2.0.

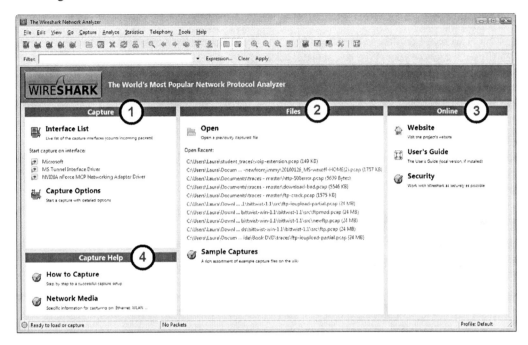

Figure 14. The Wireshark Start page

There are four sections on the Start Page.

- Capture Area ❶
- Files Area ❷
- Online Area❸
- Capture Help Area ❹

The Capture Area

The Capture Area consists of three sections: Interface List link, the active interface list and Capture Options. The Interface List shows the interfaces recognized by Wireshark. Click on the **Interface Link** to open a list of the interfaces recognized by Wireshark. To begin capturing immediately on one of the interfaces listed, click **Start**.

No Interface? No Capture!

Wireshark cannot begin capturing traffic on an interface that is not listed. If you are certain an interface is available on your system, but Wireshark does not display it on the active interface list, consider restarting Wireshark. If the interface still does not appear in the list, try rebooting your system.

The Capture Options portion of this area is used to define a capture filter, specify capture stop conditions, activate/deactivate name resolution methods and more. Capture methods and options are covered in *Chapter 3: Capture Traffic*.

The Files Area

The Files Area consists of three sections: Open, the Open Recent list and a link to Sample Captures. Click **Open** to browse your drive and select a trace file to open. Click on one of the files listed in the Open Recent list to open that file immediately. Click on the **Sample Captures** link to launch a browser and view *wiki.wireshark.org/SampleCaptures*, the Wiki page that contains sample trace files.[14]

The Online Area

The Online Area contains links to the main Wireshark website, the User's Guide and the Wireshark security page at *wiki.wireshark.org/Security*. The link to the User's Guide will open up the local copy of the User's Guide if it is available.[15]

The Capture Help Area

The Capture Area contains links to two locations—the How to Capture page at *wiki.wireshark.org/CaptureSetup* and the Network Media page at *wiki.wireshark.org/CaptureSetup/NetworkMedia*.[16]

Frames vs. Packets

The terms "frame" and "packet" are both used in Wireshark. In Figure 15, the Packet Details Pane uses the term "Frame" as the heading at the top of each packet. The term "packet" is used throughout most of the other areas of Wireshark. In this book we use the term "packet" and only use the term "frame" when referring to the Frame summary line or data link frame structure.

---

[14] Another great resource for trace files is *www.pcapr.net*. This site is managed by Mu Dynamics and contains thousands of trace files. Members can edit and download trace files.

[15] Ulf Lamping, Richard Sharpe and Ed Warnicke created the Wireshark User's Guide which is remarkably comprehensive and includes examples of Wireshark usage and tips throughout.

[16] The Network Media Specific Capturing page contains a matrix listing the various operating systems that Wireshark can run on and the physical interface types that libpcap/WinPcap can capture on. For example, the matrix indicates you cannot capture Bluetooth traffic when running Wireshark on a Windows host, but you can capture Bluetooth traffic when running Wireshark on a Linux host.

Identifying the Nine GUI Elements

When you open an existing trace file or begin a capture session, you are now working in the main Wireshark window. There are nine distinct sections in the main Wireshark window:

Title ❶

Menu (text) ❷

Main Toolbar (icons) ❸

Filter Toolbar ❹

Wireless Toolbar ❺

Packet List Pane ❻

Packet Details Pane ❼

Packet Bytes Pane ❽

Status Bar ❾

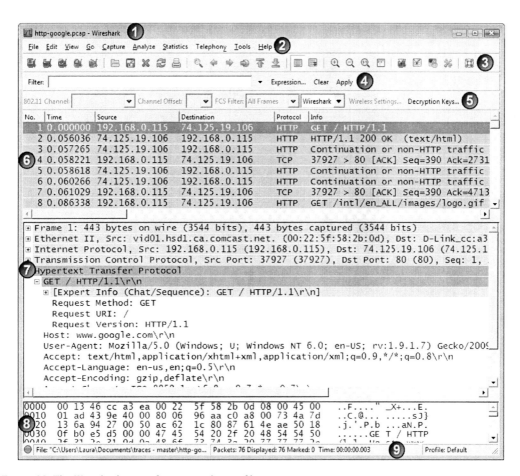

Figure 15. The Wireshark view of an unsaved trace file

Customizing the Title Bar

The title bar can be customized by selecting **Edit | Preferences | Layout** and filling in the Custom window title field. Your new title will precede the existing title such as the trace file name or "(Untitled)" on an unsaved capture session. If you have installed multiple versions of Wireshark, you can differentiate each version by adding the version information to the title bar.

Displaying the Wireless Toolbar

Wireshark includes a Wireless Toolbar that is used when you use an AirPcap adapter with Wireshark. To view the Wireless Toolbar, select **View | Wireless Toolbar**. For more information on wireless analysis, see *Chapter 26: Introduction to Analyzing 802.11 (WLAN) Analysis*.

Opening and Closing Panes

There may be times when you want to alter which panes are open. On the menu, select **View** and check or uncheck the pane that you want to display/hide. The most common pane to open/close is the Packet Bytes pane to allow more space for the Packet List and Packet Details panes.[17]

Figure 16. Hide and show the Packet List, Details and Bytes panes

---

[17] If you really want to impress someone, close the Packet List and Packet Details pane. Use the Accelerator Keys Ctrl+Down Arrow (next) and Ctrl+Up Arrow (back) to scroll through the packets as you mumble "hmmm... I see....".

Interpreting the Status Bar

The Status Bar at the bottom of the Wireshark window consists of four sections: the Expert Info Composite button, the file information column, the packets information column and the profile column.

Expert Info Composite Button

Wireshark includes an Expert system that can help you identify the cause of performance problems. Like all other "expert systems" included with analysis tools, you should verify the information provided by examining the actual traffic—don't just rely on the Expert system alone. The Expert Info Composite button is color coded as follows:

- Red   The highest level is Errors
- Yellow   The highest level is Warnings
- Cyan (light blue) The highest level is Notes
- Blue   The highest level is Chats
- Grey   There are no Expert Info Composite items

File Information Column

As you capture packets, Wireshark saves the packets to a temporary file—these are unsaved trace files. The File Information Column indicates the directory and file name of the unsaved trace file or opened trace file.

The file information column indicates the file size and time duration of the unsaved or opened trace file.

Figure 17. The Expert Info Composite and File Information portion of the Status Bar

Packet Information Column

The packet information column includes the total count of packets in the saved or unsaved trace, the count of displayed packets if a display filter is set, the count of marked packets (if any) and the note of dropped packets (relevant for packets captured through the capture engine only).[18] If you have used the "ignore" feature, the number of ignored packets will be displayed here as shown in Figure 18. The "ignore" feature was added to Wireshark in development release 1.3. A trace file load time indicator was also added to Wireshark v1.3 (development release) and Wireshark 1.4 (stable release).

```
Packets: 2436 Displayed: 110 Marked: 0 Ignored: 2
```

Figure 18. The packet information column indicates if packets are filtered, marked or ignored

---

[18] Some combinations of libpcap and WinPcap with certain OS versions may not be able to detect and report dropped packets. If you experience packet drops while running Wireshark on a Windows host, consider increasing the Buffer size in the Capture Options window. This buffer stores the packets until they are written to disk. The default value is 1 megabyte.

Profile Column

You can create profiles to customize Wireshark for a specific situation. For example, if you are analyzing WLAN traffic, you may create a "WLAN Profile" that includes a "retries" column in the Packet List pane, contains display filters for specific WLAN control frames and colorizes all disassociations with a black background and a red foreground.

The active profile is displayed in the right column of the Status Bar as shown in Figure 19. Click on the **Profile** column to change to select another profile from the list.

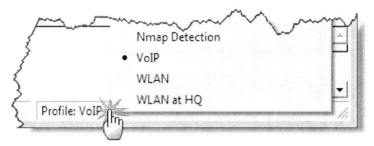

Figure 19. The current profile is listed at the right of the Status Bar

Use **Edit | Configuration Profiles** to create a new profile, edit an existing profile name, or delete a profile. By default, Wireshark stores profiles in a *profile* folder in your Wireshark Personal Configuration directory. As you work with that profile to and add capture, display or color filters, additional files are placed in the profile's directory.[19]

Navigating Wireshark's Main Menu

The main menu consists of ten sections. Unlike the Main Toolbar, Filter Toolbar, Wireless Toolbar and Status Bar, you cannot hide the menu.

File Menu Items

The items in the File menu are covered at *www.wireshark.org/docs/wsug_html_chunked/ChUseFileMenuSection.html*. In this Study Guide, we provide a bit more depth on several items and focus on the uses of these items.

Open Recent

Select **Edit | Preferences** and enter a number in the "Open Recent" max list entries section to configure the number of items listed in the Open Recent menu option by. The default value is 10.[20]

---

[19] Rather than share the entire profile directory with another user, consider sharing the individual files contained in the profile's directory. Be careful with the *preferences* file—some settings, such as gui.fileopen.dir (the directory to start in when opening a trace file) may not match the target host.

[20] When working through network issues, I constantly switch back and forth between different trace files. I set my Open Recent max. files setting to 30 so I can avoid wading through a directory of hundreds of trace files. You will learn some tricks on Wireshark customization in *Chapter 5: Define Global and Personal Preferences*.

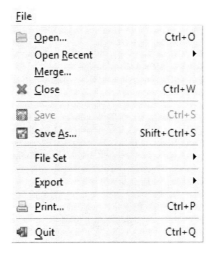

Figure 20. The File menu items

Merge

There may be times when you want to merge multiple trace files together. In addition, you can merge trace files at the command line using Mergecap (see *Chapter 33: Effective Use of Command Line Tools* on page 693).

Why would you want to merge trace files? Perhaps you have captured trace files at two points on the network—one trace file at the client and another at the server. You want to compare the traffic at each end of the communication. Another example would be if you tapped into a full-duplex network using a non-aggregating tap (a tap that does not combine the data streams from each direction into a single data stream). You could have captured traffic on two separate hosts running Wireshark, or from two separate interfaces on the same Wireshark host (running two instances of Wireshark). For more information on dual captures, refer to *Dual Capture* on page 92.

File Set

Wireshark may have processing problems after you capture a large amount of traffic or open a large trace file. Using Wireshark's Capture Options, you can save to a file set—a series of files linked together by Wireshark.

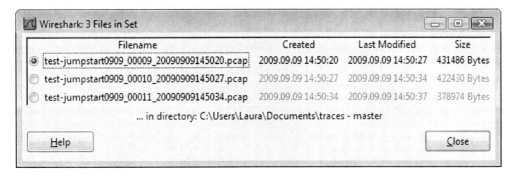

Figure 21. The File Set View window

Export

The export feature offers the ability to export the entire trace file into another format and define the packets to be included in the export. Using this feature you can easily create a subset of the trace file that you are viewing. If you have selected a field in a packet, the Selected Packet Bytes option is available. The export feature allows you to export HTTP objects. Select **File | Export | Objects | HTTP**.

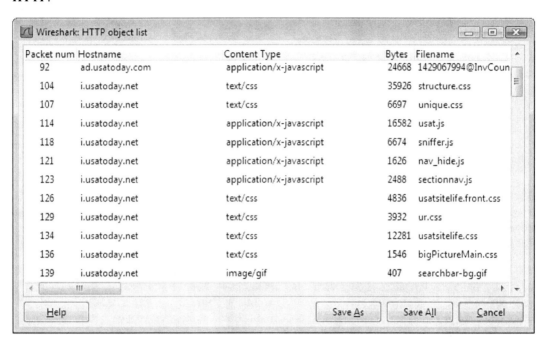

Packet num	Hostname	Content Type	Bytes	Filename
92	ad.usatoday.com	application/x-javascript	24668	1429067994@InvCoun
104	i.usatoday.net	text/css	35926	structure.css
107	i.usatoday.net	text/css	6697	unique.css
114	i.usatoday.net	application/x-javascript	16582	usat.js
118	i.usatoday.net	application/x-javascript	6674	sniffer.js
121	i.usatoday.net	application/x-javascript	1626	nav_hide.js
123	i.usatoday.net	application/x-javascript	2488	sectionnav.js
126	i.usatoday.net	text/css	4836	usatsitelife.front.css
129	i.usatoday.net	text/css	3932	ur.css
134	i.usatoday.net	text/css	12281	usatsitelife.css
136	i.usatoday.net	text/css	1546	bigPictureMain.css
139	i.usatoday.net	image/gif	407	searchbar-bg.gif

Figure 22. The exported HTTP object list

> **Overloading HTTP Object Export**
> *When you capture a trace file of HTTP communications that contain a large number of HTTP options, be careful using the Save All feature of HTTP object export. There are times when this has crashed Wireshark.*

Edit Menu Items

The items in the Edit menu are covered at *www.wireshark.org/docs/wsug_html_chunked/ChUseEditMenuSection.html*. In this Study Guide we provide a bit more depth on several items and focus on the uses of these items.

You can also use the Main Toolbar to Find a packet and open the Preferences window. (You can also right click on a protocol or application in the Packet Details pane to set preferences quickly.)

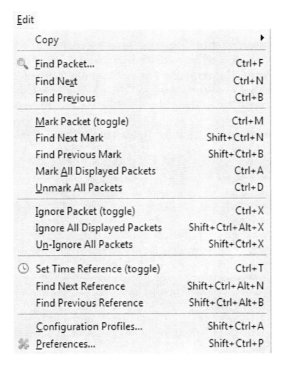

Figure 23. The Edit menu items

Mark Packets

Marked packets are listed with a black background and white foreground. Packet marking is a temporary setting—when you reopen the trace file, the packet marking is gone.

To mark a packet, select **Edit | Mark Packet**. Marks are toggled on and off. To unmark a packet, repeat the steps. In addition, you can right click on a packet in the Packet List pane and select **Mark Packet**. To mark an entire set of packets, apply a filter on the packets first and then select **Mark All Displayed Packets**.

Ctrl+M is a Wireshark Accelerator Key. Wireshark Accelerator Keys enable you to use Wireshark more effectively.

Use Packet Marking to Identify Interesting Packets

Packet marking is a feature that allows you to highlight and quickly navigate among interesting packets. When you are examining a trace file, consider marking packets of interest to review later. Remember, however, packet marking is only temporary. When you close the trace file, packet marking is removed.

Ignore Packets

This feature was added in version 1.4 of Wireshark. Ignoring packets offers a quick way to remove packets from view. When you are working with a large, complex trace file, remove distracting packets to focus in on the interesting traffic. In Figure 24 we are focusing in on unusual traffic generated by an iPhone that has just been turned on.[21] We ignored packets so we could just view the packets of interest[22]. The Status Bar indicates that we have ignored 38 packets.

To quickly restore the ignored packets, click the **Reload** button on the Main Toolbar.

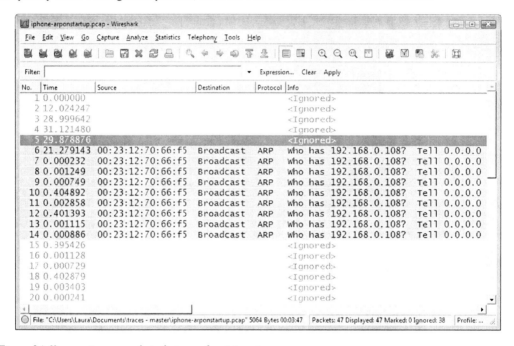

Figure 24. You can ignore packets that are of no interest

Time Reference

The Time Reference setting is also toggled on and off and is only temporary. When you reopen the file the current time column setting will be in effect and no time references will be set.

Time Reference is used to measure the time from one packet to another in a trace file. For example, if a trace file contains 1,000 packets and packets 23 through 340 contain a login sequence that you want to measure from start to end, select **packet 23** and press **Ctrl+T**. Wireshark enters the value *REF* in the Time column and sets the time as 0.000000. The time column value after the *REF* indicates when packets arrived compared to the arrival time of the Time Reference packet. When you jump to packet 340, the time column displays the time difference between packet 23 and packet 340.

---

[21] We can only hope an "ignore user" setting will be added someday.

[22] These are unique ARP packets because the source IP address is shown as 0.0.0.0. For more information on analyzing ARP communications, refer to Chapter 16: Address Resolution Process (ARP) Analysis.

If you are interested in measuring the time from the end of one packet to the end of another packet, consider adding a delta time column or changing the current Time column value to display Seconds Since Previous Displayed Packet. Refer to *Identify Delays with Time Values* on page 173 for more information on working with time in trace files.[23]

Configuration Profiles

You can customize Wireshark to work more effectively by creating a series of profiles for the various network environments you work in. For example, you could create a WLAN Analysis profile that contains columns of interest for WLAN sessions such as frequency/channel, WLAN retries and signal strength columns.

When you create a new profile, a folder using the same name as the profile is created in the Personal Configuration directory.[24] By default, a file called "recent" is placed in your new profile directory. This file contains the general Wireshark window settings, such as visible toolbars, timestamp display, zoom level and column widths.

If you create capture filters, display filters and color filters while working in a custom profile, additional files will be created and stored in your custom profile's directory (*cfilters*, *dfilters* and *colorfilters*, respectively). For more information on creating custom profiles, refer to *Chapter 11: Customize Wireshark Profiles*.

Preferences

The Preferences item opens the Global Configuration settings for Wireshark. These settings include:

- User Interface—General Wireshark interface settings, such as the "Always Start in" directory which Wireshark accesses when you select **File | Open**, the number of files to retain for the "recent files" list, the number of display filters to retain for the display filter drop-down list and whether to wrap to the beginning of a trace file. In addition, this is the area for configuring the layout of the panes (Packet List, Packet Details and Packet Bytes), columns displayed in the Packet List pane, font style and type and colors for marked packets and followed streams

- Capture—Default capture interface, whether to update the list of packets in real time, whether to use automatic scrolling during packet capture

- Printing—The output format and target when you select to print packets or a trace file

- Name Resolution—Enable or disable MAC name resolution, transport (port name) name resolution, network (host) name resolution, SMI (Structure of Management

---

[23] You absolutely MUST consider time whenever you are troubleshooting network communications. Networking is a messy, dirty job. You may find that a process requests something 400 times unsuccessfully—but the entire process is over with in less than one-half of a second. It is doubtful that any user (no matter how "retentive" they are) recognizes your efforts if you cut that 400 packets to 200 and save them one-quarter of a second. Heck—they never say thank you when you save them thirty minutes!

[24] You can locate the Personal Configuration directory by selecting **Help | About Wireshark | Folders**.

Information) resolution for Simple Network Management Protocol (SNMP) traffic and the GeoIP database location[25]

- Statistics—Define the number of channels that should display in the RTP (Real-time Transport Protocol) player

- Protocols—This key configuration area contains individual configurations for many of the Wireshark protocol dissectors. For an example of altering a protocol configuration, refer to *The Purpose of TCP* on page 374.

View Menu Items

The items in the View menu are covered at
www.wireshark.org/docs/wsug_html_chunked/ChUseViewMenuSection.html. In this Study Guide, we provide a bit more depth on several items and focus on the uses of these items.

You can also click on the **Main Toolbar** icons to enable coloring, enable autoscroll, zoom in/out/1:1/resize and access the coloring rules. The View menu allows you to hide/show the various toolbars[26], the Status bar, the Packet List, Packet Details and Packet Bytes panes.

The zooming and resizing options enable you to improve viewing ease.

Time Display Format

By default, Wireshark sets the Time column to "Seconds since Beginning of Capture" where each packet timestamp is based on the arrival time since the first packet in the trace file.

The Time Display Format setting is maintained in the "Recent" file in the Wireshark Personal Configuration folder or the current Profile directory. The entry for the Time Display Format is shown below.

```
# Timestamp display format.

# One of: RELATIVE, ABSOLUTE, ABSOLUTE_WITH_DATE, DELTA,
DELTA_DIS, EPOCH

gui.time_format: RELATIVE
```

For more details on using timestamps when analyzing traffic, refer to *Use Time to Identify Network Problems* on page 166.

---

[25] Not all versions of Wireshark support GeoIP location services which maps IP addresses to an OpenStreetMap location.

[26] In earlier versions of Wireshark, the option of showing the Wiresless Toolbar was only available when you are using an AirPcap adapter and AirPcap driver. This is another reason to stay current with the latest Wireshark releases.

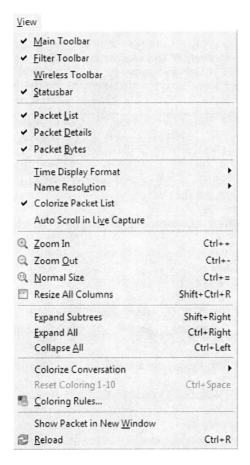

Figure 25. The View menu items

Use the Perfect Timestamp for Troubleshooting

This is one of the most important settings to understand and use when troubleshooting performance. Capturing a user's traffic as they perform tasks and setting the timestamp to "Seconds Since Previous Displayed Packet" enables you to sort the Time column and identify large gaps in time.

Name Resolution

The basic name resolution processes offered by Wireshark are MAC layer, network layer (host name) and transport layer (port name) resolution. The setting in use is defined by the Global Preferences for the profile in use.

To temporarily override the Global Preferences setting when viewing a saved or unsaved trace file, select **View | Name Resolution** and choose to resolve the name for an IP host (Resolve Name) or toggle on or off the MAC, network or transport layer name resolution processes.

Don't Let Wireshark Flood a DNS Server

Be careful of enabling network name resolution as this causes Wireshark to send a DNS PTR (pointer) query for every IP address identified in the trace file (unless the name is located in a hosts file). A DNS PTR query generated by Wireshark is shown in Figure 26.

```
⊞ Frame 415 (88 bytes on wire, 88 bytes captured)
⊞ Ethernet II, Src: 00:21:97:40:74:d2 (00:21:97:40:74:d2
⊞ Internet Protocol, Src: 192.168.0.113 (192.168.0.113)
⊞ User Datagram Protocol, Src Port: 61508 (61508), Dst
⊟ Domain Name System (query)
    [Response In: 416]
    Transaction ID: 0x2290
  ⊞ Flags: 0x0100 (Standard query)
    Questions: 1
    Answer RRs: 0
    Authority RRs: 0
    Additional RRs: 0
  ⊟ Queries
    ⊞ 217.136.121.128.in-addr.arpa: type PTR, class IN
```

Figure 26. Wireshark sends DNS PTR queries when network name resolution is enabled

Transport name resolution uses Wireshark's *services* file[27] and converts a port number, such as 80, to a name—in this case HTTP. The *services* file is based on IANA's Well Known Port Number list at *www.iana.org/assignments/port-numbers*. Many people find the transport name resolution process confusing as it will resolve ephemeral (temporary) port numbers often used as source port numbers to a registered IANA port number, even though the communications are not related to the registered service. You can edit Wireshark's *services* file if desired.

Editing Wireshark's *Services* File is OK, but...

It is possible to edit Wireshark's services file to remove some of the entries, but we suggest you make a copy of the original file in case you totally mess it up and want to restore it someday. Alternately, you can copy the services file from another Wireshark host.

In some instances, you will need to click the **Reload** button to see the resolved names. These settings are maintained until you restart Wireshark.

Colorize Conversations

To make specific conversations (based on characteristics such as Ethernet address, IP address or transport port number) more visible in a trace file, consider colorizing a conversation. These are temporary colorizations only, but will be applied each time you open that trace file—until you restart Wireshark. If you want consistent colorization every time you start Wireshark, build a coloring rule.

---

[27] This is a different *services* file than the native OS services file. This file is only used by Wireshark when correlating port numbers with service names when transport name resolution is enabled.

When you are working with complex communications using numerous connections (such as your login process or perhaps a web browsing session to *www.espn.com*), consider colorizing the conversations to separate them visually. This will save you a LOT of time and confusion when wading through your trace files.

To remove conversation colorizing, select **View | Reset Coloring 1-10**.

Coloring Rules

Coloring Rules are persistent settings maintained in the *colorfilters* file. You can have a unique set of coloring rules in each Profile. Wireshark consists of several default coloring rules as shown in Figure 27.[28]

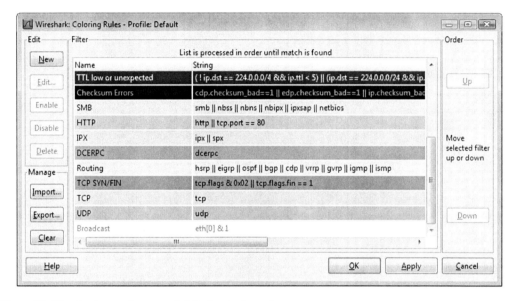

Figure 27. Wireshark contains several default coloring rules

Toggle coloring rules on and off using the Colorize Packet List button on the Main Toolbar or **View | Colorize Packet List**.

For more details on using packet colorization to analyze traffic more efficiently, refer to *Chapter 6: Colorize Traffic*.[29]

---

[28] Coloring rules are the "ring tones" of the analysis world. They alert you to possible problem traffic ("your ex-wife/ex-husband is calling") or just packets of particular interest ("your attorney is calling"). Spend some time in *Chapter 6: Colorize Traffic* to set up your Wireshark system to be more visually effective.

[29] One fun trick with coloring rules (I use it with ugly NetBIOS traffic that I don't want to 'see') is to set the foreground and background of these packets to white... now you can filter on these ugly packets and select **Edit | Ignore all displayed packets** to avoid those gag reflexes from kicking in on ugly packets.

Show Packet in a New Window

Showing individual packets in new windows is one technique used to compare the contents of two or more packets in a trace file. You can also simply double-click on a packet in the Packet List pane to open a packet in a new window.

> **Compare Packets with Side-by-Side Views**
>
> *If you want to compare two packets to identify differences, simply double-click on each packet to open new packet windows.*

Reload

The most common reason to reload a trace file is when you alter the name resolution setting when viewing a trace file. There are some other settings that may require you to reload a trace file. There is reload button on the Main Toolbar as well.

Go Menu Items

The items in the Go menu are covered at *www.wireshark.org/docs/wsug_html_chunked/ChUseGoMenuSection.html*. In this Study Guide, we provide a bit more depth on several items and focus on the uses of these items.

You can also use the Main Toolbar to quickly navigate forwards/backwards through packets, jump to specific packets or go to the top/bottom of the trace file.

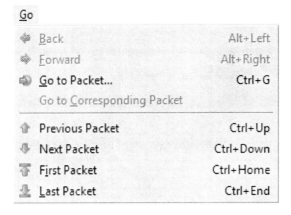

Figure 28. The Go menu items

Go to Corresponding Packet

Most items in the Go menu are self explanatory and available on the Main Toolbar, but the Go to Corresponding Packet requires some explanation.

Wireshark attempts to link related packets, such as ACKs to data packets and duplicate ACKs. This item is grayed out unless you have selected a packet that contains a link to another packet. In Figure 29, Wireshark contains a link to another packet –packet 415. In this example, we are examining the trace file called *download-bad.pcap*.

Practice Jumping Between Corresponding Packets

This trace file (download-bad.pcap) is available at www.wiresharkbook.com. When you open this trace file, go to packet 417 and expand the TCP SEQ/ACK Analysis section to see the corresponding packet information shown in Figure 29. Double-click on the **"Duplicate to the ACK in frame: 415"** *line to jump directly to packet 415.*

Although you can use the **View | Go to Corresponding Packet** method, the link embedded in the packets allows you to double-click inside the packet to jump to the linked packet.

```
⊞ Frame 417: 66 bytes on wire (528 bits), 66 bytes captured (528
⊞ Ethernet II, Src: Sony_f4:3a:09 (08:00:46:f4:3a:09), Dst: 3Com
⊞ Internet Protocol, Src: 10.0.52.164 (10.0.52.164), Dst: 61.8.
⊟ Transmission Control Protocol, Src Port: ads (2550), Dst Port:
      Source port: ads (2550)
      Destination port: http (80)
      [Stream index: 0]
      Sequence number: 446    (relative sequence number)
      Acknowledgement number: 318610    (relative ack number)
      Header length: 32 bytes
   ⊞ Flags: 0x10 (ACK)
      window size: 256960 (scaled)
   ⊞ Checksum: 0x18fc [correct]               Double-click to jump
   ⊞ Options: (12 bytes)                         to packet 415
   ⊟ [SEQ/ACK analysis]
      ⊟ [TCP Analysis Flags]
           [This is a TCP duplicate ack]
           [Duplicate ACK #: 1]
      ⊟ [Duplicate to the ACK in frame: 415]
           ⊟ [Expert Info (Note/Sequence): Duplicate ACK (#1)]
                [Message: Duplicate ACK (#1)]
                [Severity level: Note]
                [Group: Sequence]
```

Figure 29. Use Go To Corresponding Packet when a link is available

Capture Menu Items

The items in the Capture menu are covered at *www.wireshark.org/docs/wsug_html_chunked/ChUseCaptureMenuSection.html*. In this Study Guide, we provide a bit more depth on several items and focus on the uses of these items.

Use the Main Toolbar to quickly list interfaces, show interfaces, start a new capture, stop a running capture, restart a running capture or view the capture filters.

The Capture Menu items are mostly self-explanatory. Capture Interfaces, Options and Capture Filters are covered in detail in *Chapter 4: Create and Apply Capture Filters.*

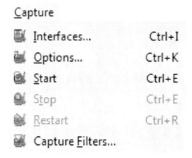

Capture	
Interfaces...	Ctrl+I
Options...	Ctrl+K
Start	Ctrl+E
Stop	Ctrl+E
Restart	Ctrl+R
Capture Filters...	

Figure 30. The Capture menu items

Capture Interfaces

Select **Capture Interfaces** to view the interfaces that Wireshark recognizes. If no interfaces are shown, Wireshark cannot capture traffic from a wired or wireless network. In the Capture Interfaces window you can start capture immediately, set capture options or view interface details (if shown).[30]

For more information on the Capture Interfaces window, read *Select the Right Capture Interface* on page 92.

See Packet Counts Without Capturing Anything

The Capture Interfaces window depicts a running packet count indicating which interfaces "see" packets. During the count process, however, packets are not being captured or buffered. This is a valuable method for identifying interfaces on the most active network segments. For example, if you have two wired interfaces listed, you can identify which one is seeing the most traffic before beginning your capture.

Capture Options

The Capture Options window enables you to set the capture interface, multiple file capture options, ring buffer options, stop capture options, display options, name resolution and wireless settings (if using AirPcap adapters) and remote capture settings (if connecting to a host running *rpcapd*, the remote packet capture daemon). You can also define a capture filter in this window. For more details on the Capture Options window and capabilities as well as remote capture methods, refer to *Chapter 3: Capture Traffic.*

Start, Stop and Restart Capturing

These three menu options are not the fastest way to start capturing—examine *Capture Toolbar Icons* on page 62 to use the icons on the menu toolbar to start, stop and restart faster.

Capture Filters

This menu option opens the Capture Filters window allowing you to create or edit capture filters. For more details on these filters, read *Chapter 4: Create and Apply Capture Filters.*

---

[30] The Details option is not available on all operating systems.

Analyze Menu Items

The items in the Analyze menu are covered at
www.wireshark.org/docs/wsug_html_chunked/ChUseAnalyzeMenuSection.html. In this Study Guide,
we provide a bit more depth on several items and focus on the uses of these items.

Only one item is duplicated on the Main Toolbar—Display Filters. You can also open the Display
Filters window by clicking the **Display** button to the left of the Display Filter window.

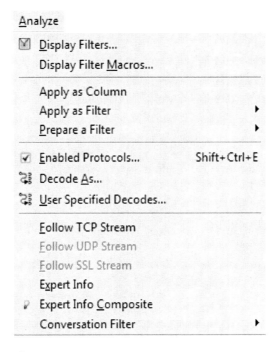

Figure 31. The Analyze menu items

Display Filters

Display filters are applied to focus on a specific conversation, protocol other feature of traffic.
Effective use of display filters decreases the time required to identify the cause of poor network
performance, unusual network traffic patterns or other traffic of interest.

There are over 96,000 possible display filters available. Of course, these filters are not all listed on
the Display filters window, but they are accessible through the auto-complete display filter feature
and the Expressions feature.

Display filters can be applied during a live capture or to a saved trace file.

With a few exceptions, display filters do not use the same syntax as capture filters. Display filters *do* use the same syntax as coloring rules. For more details on how to use display filters effectively, refer to *Chapter 9: Create and Apply Display Filters*.

Display Filter Macros

This item allows you to create macros for more complex display filters. The macros contain the syntax and structure of the display filter and the argument placement. For more details on how to create and use display filter macros, refer to *Use Display Filter Macros* on page 223.

Apply as Column

This feature is only available after you select a field in the Packet Details pane.[31] You can also simply right click on a field in the Packet Details pane and select Apply as Column. A new column is added to the Packet List pane. You can click and drag to move the new column or right click on the new column heading to change alignment, rename or delete the column.

Apply as Filter and Prepare a Filter

These two options are applied by right clicking on a packet in the Packet List pane or a heading or field in the Packet Details pane. You cannot use this feature by right clicking in the Packet Bytes pane.

When you chose Apply as Filter, the filter is immediately listed in the display filter field and applied to the traffic. When you select Prepare a Filter, the filter is immediately listed in the display filter field, but it is not applied to the traffic. This allows you to alter the syntax of the display filter before applying it.

Enabled Protocols

Using this item, you can enable or disable certain protocol dissectors. Your setting is retained even after you restart Wireshark.

 Disabling a Protocol May Blind You

Be careful with this setting. If you disable a protocol, higher protocols and applications will not be decoded. For example, if you disable UDP, then applications that use UDP (such as DHCP and DNS) will not be decoded either as shown in Figure 32.

---

[31] This feature was added in the development version 1.3 and stable version 1.4.

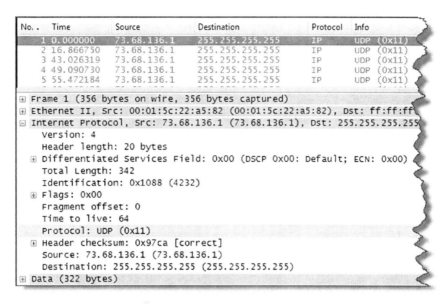

Figure 32. Disabling UDP also disables the DHCP dissector

Decode As

This item is used to force Wireshark to use a specific dissector on the traffic based on the highest layer recognized. In Figure 33, we have selected a DHCP packet and opened the Decode As window.

This is a temporary setting—it will be applied each time the criteria are seen in any saved or unsaved trace file, but it will be reset when you restart Wireshark.

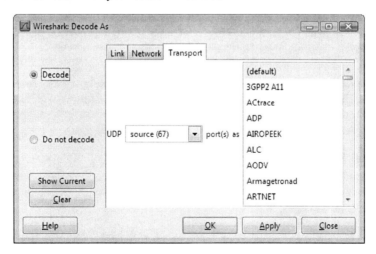

Figure 33. Decode As forces a dissector to be applied

User Specified Decodes

This feature is used in conjunction with the Decode As item. If we applied the ADP dissector to traffic from port 67 and to port 68 (commonly used for DHCP traffic), this setting is now shown in the User Specified Decodes window as shown in Figure 34.

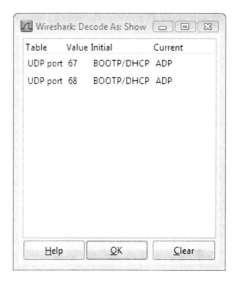

Figure 34. User Specified Decodes correspond to the Decode As setting

Follow UDP, TCP or SSL Streams

This feature is very useful when you are interested in seeing the commands and data that are exchanged between hosts.

Reassemble Streams for Faster Interpretations

If you find yourself constantly focused on the ASCII interpretations shown in the Packet Bytes pane, consider following the stream for faster interpretations.

When you choose to follow a UDP stream, Wireshark creates a filter based on source/destination IP addresses and source/destination port numbers. When you choose to follow a TCP stream or SSL stream, Wireshark creates a filter based on the stream number. For more information on following streams, refer to *Chapter 10: Follow Streams and Reassemble Data.*

Expert Info and Expert Info Composite

Wireshark can identify unusual or interesting traffic in a trace and apply a categorization and colorization to this traffic. In addition, Wireshark tracks the interesting traffic in the Expert Info and Expert Info Composite windows.

The button on the left of the Status Bar links to the Expert Info Composite window. For more information on Wireshark's Expert Info capabilities and uses, refer to *Chapter 13: Use Wireshark's Expert System.*

Conversation Filter

The Conversation Filter item can only be used to identify PROFINET/IO (PN-IO) traffic. PROFINET/IO is an open industrial standard for an advanced version of Ethernet. For more information on PROFINET, visit *www.profibus.com*.

Statistics Menu Items

The items in the Statistics menu are covered at *www.wireshark.org/docs/wsug_html_chunked/ChUseStatisticsMenuSection.html*. In this Study Guide, we provide a bit more depth on several items and focus on the uses of these items.

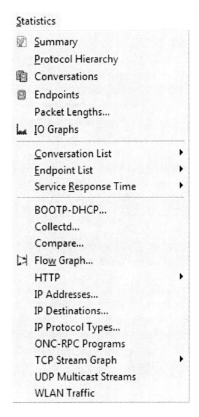

Figure 35. The Statistics menu items

The Statistics Menu consists of many of the powerful interpretation features of Wireshark. Many of the items fall into the category of basic traffic statistics and are relatively self-explanatory. The majority of these statistics items are covered in more detail in other chapters, as referenced in the sections that follow.

For more information on using and interpreting Wireshark Statistics, refer to *Chapter 8: Interpret Basic Trace File Statistics*.

Summary

The Summary window provides an overview of the packet and byte counts, time elapsed and capture filter (if applied). This summary provides basic information on all packets captured, displayed packets and marked packets. For more information on using and interpreting summary statistics, refer to *Chapter 7: Define Time Values and Interpret Summaries*.

Protocol Hierarchy

This item is particularly useful in detecting protocol anomalies in a trace file (refer to *Chapter 32: Analyze Suspect Traffic*). Wireshark indicates the packet count, byte count and percentage of all traffic in the trace file or, if a display filter has been applied, the packet count, byte count and percentage details on the filtered traffic.

Conversations and Endpoints

A conversation is a pair of devices communicating with each other. An endpoint is one side of a communication. For example, if 10.1.1.1 is browsing to 10.2.2.2, their communication is seen as a conversation whereas 10.1.1.1 and 10.2.2.2 are seen as separate endpoints. When you are working with a large trace file that contains many hosts communicating, the conversations and endpoints traffic can be sorted to identify the most active hosts or conversations.

Packet Lengths

Packet lengths are an important characteristic to watch in any data transfer process. Transferring a file using small packet sizes is much less efficient than using full packet sizes. For more details on using this feature, see *Evaluate Packet Lengths* on page 192.

IO Graphs

IO (or Input/Output) graphs offer a view of the total amount of bytes in a saved or unsaved trace file. This graph can be run while capturing traffic to see a dynamic view of the bytes captured by Wireshark.

IO graphs are very powerful in telling a story about the traffic by applying display filters, altering the styles and X and Y axis values. Using advanced IO graphs, you can also use functions such as MIN, MAX and AVG. Figure 36 shows an IO Graph that compares all traffic in a trace file with TCP duplicate ACK packets. For more information on basic and advanced IO Graphing, refer to *Chapter 21: Graph IO Rates and TCP Trends*.

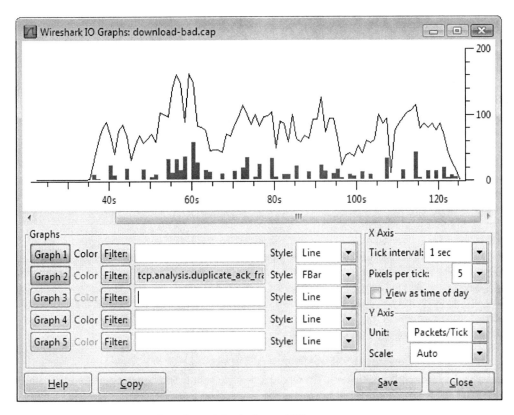

Figure 36. An IO Graph depicts all traffic and the duplicate ACKs

Conversation and Endpoint Lists

This is a quick way to view specific conversations or endpoints—it is faster than loading **Statistics | Conversations** or **Statistics | Endpoints** and then choosing IP, TCP, UDP or another criteria.

Service Response Time

This option provides graphs of minimum, maximum and average service response times (SRT) for many processes including SMB, SMB2, LDAP and NCP.[32]

BOOTP-DHCP

This statistic simply lists the type of BOOTP-DHCP packets captured. This is a useful statistic to examine when you are looking for the cause of DHCP problems in a large trace file that includes the DHCP startup sequences of hundreds of hosts.

Collectd

Collectd is an open source project that includes a daemon that collects system performance information using a series of over 90 plugins to track information such as CPU usage, DNS traffic

---

[32] This is a great feature for analyzing Microsoft's SMB traffic—if you are a Microsoft shop, capture your login sequence and a file transfer sequence. Open the **Statistics | Service Response Time** window to identify average service response times in the trace file.

types, connection information, disk data, email statistics, cache usage and more. Collectd was created by Florian Forster and can be downloaded at *collectd.org*. The Collectd statistics feature was added after Wireshark v1.2.6 to display information about statistics traffic captured and sent across the network from the Collectd daemon.

Compare

At the time this book was written, the Compare feature did not perform in a logical manner. Updated information on this feature will available at *www.wiresharkbook.com* when it becomes available.

Flow Graphs

Flow graphs create a packet-by-packet interpretation of the traffic, separating source and target hosts by columns. This is particularly useful when interpreting HTTP traffic. Flow graphs are covered in more detail in *Chapter 8: Interpret Basic Trace File Statistics*.

HTTP

The HTTP statistics include load distribution information, packet counter and requests. Load distribution lists HTTP requests by server host and server address. The packet counter information breaks down the HTTP request types (such as GET and POST) with the HTTP response codes (such as 200, 403 or 404). Finally, the HTTP requests lists out every target HTTP server and every file requested from each server. HTTP statistics are covered in more detail in *Chapter 23: Analyze Hypertext Transfer Protocol (HTTP) Traffic*.

IP Addresses, IP Destinations, IP Protocol Types

These are somewhat self-explanatory. These items provide counts and percentages for each subject. The IP Protocol Types item lists packet count and percentages for UDP and TCP traffic.

ONC-RPC Programs

This statistic displays the minimum, average and maximum service response time for the Open Network Computing (ONC) variation of Remote Procedure Call (RPC).

TCP Stream Graphs

This is one of the most impressive (and unfortunately one of the least understood) features of Wireshark. You must select a TCP-based packet in the Packet List pane in order to select TCP Stream Graphs. These four TCP graphs are covered in *Chapter 21: Graph IO Rates and TCP Trends*.

- Round Trip Time Graphs
- Throughput Graphs plot
- Time-Sequence Graph (Stevens)
- Time-Sequence Graph (tcptrace)

Each of these graphs is unidirectional graphs requiring that you select your TCP packet carefully before building TCP graphs.

UDP Multicast Streams

As multicasting (sending packets to a group of hosts based on a target multicast address) has become more popular for uses such as video streaming, the UDP multicast streams item becomes more valuable. For more information on multicast analysis, refer to *Chapter 8: Interpret Basic Trace File Statistics.*

WLAN Traffic

This item discovers WLAN traffic in a saved or unsaved trace file and provides basic information about that WLAN traffic. This information includes the SSID, channel, packet count, packet type and protection method detected as shown in Figure 37. If you are interested in getting your feet wet analyzing 802.11 networks, refer to *Chapter 26: Introduction to 802.11 (WLAN) Analysis.*

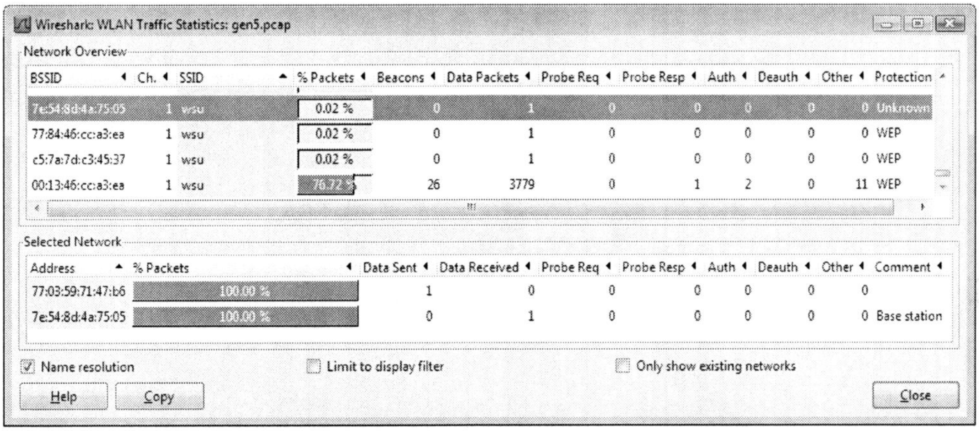

Figure 37. WLAN traffic information includes the SSID and encryption method detected

Telephony Menu Items

The 15 Telephony Menu items are shown in Figure 38. This is a good indication of the popular use of Wireshark as a VoIP analysis tool. For more information on VoIP analysis, refer to *Chapter 27: Introduction to Voice over IP (VoIP) Analysis.*

Some of the telephony items in the telephony menu are covered under the Statistics section of the Wireshark online documentation since that was where many of the items were listed prior to Wireshark v1.2. This item in the Tools menu is covered at *www.wireshark.org/docs/wsug_html_chunked/ChUseTelephonyMenuSection.html.*

Three key areas in this list are RTP, SIP and VoIP Calls.

Figure 38. The Telephony menu items

RTP

The RTP (Real-time Transport Protocol) item displays and analyzes RTP streams and indicates if there are possible problems in a unidirectional RTP stream (as denoted by the somewhat unusual "Pb?" column). The RTP window defines packet loss and jitter rate information.

When Wireshark Doesn't Recognize RTP Traffic

*If you have captured an RTP stream and not the Session Initiation Protocol (SIP) call setup traffic or Wireshark did not understand the signaling traffic, Wireshark may not recognize your traffic as RTP traffic. In this case, select **Edit | Preferences | Protocols | RTP** and enable **"Try to Decode RTP Outside of Conversations"**.*

SIP

SIP, or Session Initiation Protocol, is used to set up and manage the call such as INVITE and ACCEPT methods and the numerical response codes indicating success, redirection, client errors, server errors and global failures.

VoIP Calls

This is an area that thrills many VoIP analysts[33] as it enables the playback of some unencrypted VoIP calls. First Wireshark automatically detects VoIP calls (remember, if Wireshark does not detect call setup traffic it may not detect the call either), then it builds a table with the start/stop time of the call, the initial speaker, information on the source and destination of the call as well as the protocol used for the call setup.

---

[33] Yes—VoIP analysts can be a strange and misunderstood bunch. It really messes with your mind when you are in charge of the application that is at the top of the QoS food chain!

Wireshark can graph out the VoIP traffic in a trace file as shown in Figure 39. In this case, a caller has requested to be transferred to extension 204.

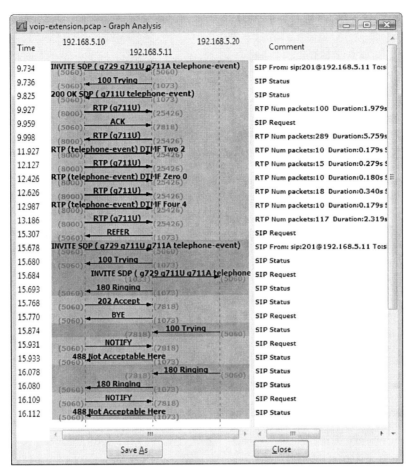

Figure 39. Wireshark graphs out VoIP traffic

For more information on analyzing VoIP traffic, refer to *Chapter 27: Introduction to Voice over IP (VoIP) Analysis.*

Tools Menu Items

There is only one item on the Tools menu, the Firewall ACL (Access Control List) Rules item.[34]

Figure 40. The Tools menu items

This item in the Tools menu is covered at
www.wireshark.org/docs/wsug_html_chunked/ChUseToolsMenuSection.html.

Firewall ACL Rules

After clicking on a packet or field and selecting Tools | Firewall ACL Rules, Wireshark builds a
Cisco IOS (Standard) firewall rule based on the source IP address in the packet as shown in Figure
41.

Figure 41. Wireshark can automatically create ACL rules

Wireshark can create ACL rules for the following firewall formats:

- Cisco IOS (standard and extended)
- IP Filter (ipfilter)
- IPFirewall (ipfw)
- Netfilter (iptables)
- Packet Filter (pf)
- Windows Firewall (netsh)

Once you create the desired filter, simply click the **Copy** button and paste the filter into your firewall
configuration.

---

[34] Honestly, this is one of the weakest features of Wireshark. If you are the infrastructure administrator, I doubt
you need Wireshark to build these relatively simple rules for you. It seems a bit pathetic to have one entire menu
item ("Tools") holding a place for this feature—perhaps it will fade away like William Hung someday.

Help Menu Items

You can quickly launch Wireshark's Help from the Main Toolbar.

The items in the Help menu are covered at
www.wireshark.org/docs/wsug_html_chunked/ChUseHelpMenuSection.html.

Figure 42. The Help menu items

Most items in the Help menu are self explanatory. One of the key items in the Help menu is the About Wireshark section. This section includes the folder information that defines where Wireshark elements are located as shown in Figure 43. The Folders area includes a short list of the typical files contained in each folder and links to each the folders.

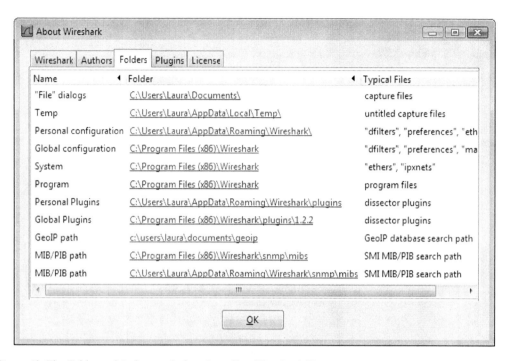

Figure 43. The Folders tab indicates the location of key Wireshark files

Using the Main Toolbar for Efficiency

The Main Toolbar contains the icon-based navigation for Wireshark which provides a faster method to perform many common tasks. The Main Toolbar is separated into seven sections as shown and defined below.

Toolbar Icon Definitions

Capture Toolbar Icons

From left to right, List Interfaces, Capture Options, Start Capture, Stop Capture and Restart Capture

Trace File and Print Toolbar Icons

Open File, Save File, Close File, Reload File, Print

Navigation Toolbar Icons

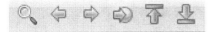

Find, Go Back, Go Forward, Jump To, Go to First Packet, Go to Last Packet

- Find locates a packet based on a display filter, hex value or string
- Back returns to last packet located by Find, Go To, First or Last
- Next is only active after Back has been used
- Go To takes you to a specific packet number
- First jumps to the first packet in the trace file (based on the packet number, regardless of sorting)
- Last jumps to the last packet in the trace file (based on the true packet number, regardless of sorting)

The Packet Number Never Changes

The packet number value never changes for a packet, regardless of how columns are sorted.

Finding a Packet

Use the **Find** button on the Main Toolbar or **Ctrl+F** to open the Find Packet window as shown in Figure 44. You can locate packets based on a display filter value, hex value contained in the packet or an ASCII string.

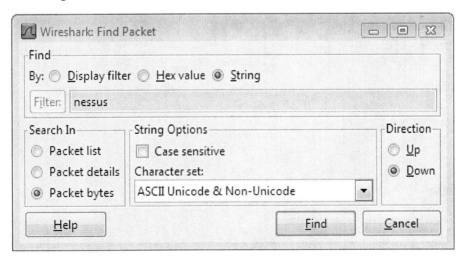

Figure 44. You can find packets based on display filter, hex value or string

Searching can be limited to summary information in the Packet List pane, the decoded values in the Packet Details pane or the entire packet contents in the packet bytes pane. You can also choose the direction your search should use—up or down from the currently-selected packet.

"Wrap to end/beginning of the file during a Find" is set in the **Edit | Preferences | User Interface** area.

The String option is used to perform a case sensitive search and define the character set as ASCII Unicode & Non-Unicode (default), ASCII Unicode or ASCII non-Unicode. The string options section is only applicable when performing a string search.

Color and Scroll Toolbar Icons

Packet Coloring (toggle on/off), Auto Scroll (toggle on/off)

Auto scroll is most useful when you have applied a capture filter to limit the number of packets that scroll across the screen. If Wireshark is dropping packets, consider turning off auto scroll and packet coloring. If that doesn't help enough, disable "Update list of packets in real time" in **Edit | Preferences | Capture**.

Viewer Toolbar Icons

Zoom In, Zoom Out, Zoom 100%, Resize All Columns

As you add more columns and adjust the contents of those columns, click the **Resize Columns, Zoom in, Zoom out** or **1:1 (100%)** buttons to set the column sizes for best visibility.[35]

Filter, Color and Configuration Toolbar Icons

Capture Filter Editor, Display Filter Editor, Coloring Rules Editor, Global Preferences

Help Toolbar Icon

Help Window

---

[35] The older I get, the more valuable this feature becomes.

Focusing Faster with the Filter Toolbar

The Filter Toolbar consists of a Display Filter button (marked just "Filter"), the display filter area, the display filter drop-down, Expression, Clear and Apply buttons as shown in Figure 45.

Display filtering is covered in detail in *Chapter 9: Create and Apply Display Filters*.

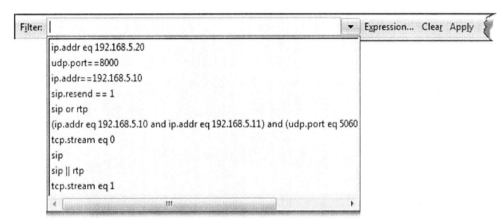

Figure 45. The Display Filter toolbar contains six elements

Set the number of recently used display filters that Wireshark remembers in the **Edit | Preferences | User Interface | Filter display list max. entries** setting. The display filter auto-complete feature and use of Expressions is covered in detail in *Chapter 9: Create and Apply Display Filters*.

Making the Wireless Toolbar Visible

The Wireless Toolbar can be used to select the WLAN channel, define decryption keys to use on wireless traffic and indicate whether a pseudoheader should be applied to incoming wireless packets. Many of the Wireless Toolbar options are only available if Wireshark detects that an AirPcap adapter is connected to the local system.

The Wireless Toolbar is hidden by default. To view the Wireless Toolbar, select **View | Wireless Toolbar**. The Wireless Toolbar consists of six sections, as shown in Figure 46. The 802.11 Channel, Channel Offset, FCS Filter and Wireless Settings fields are only available if you have an AirPcap adapter connected to your Wireshark system.

Figure 46. The Wireless Toolbar consists of six sections

The details of the Wireless Toolbar sections are covered in *Chapter 26: Introduction to 802.11 (WLAN) Analysis*.

Accessing Options through Right-Click Functionality

Many Wireshark tasks can be completed quickly using right-click functionality. Different right-click options are available for the Packet List pane, Packet Details pane and Packet Bytes pane. Different right-click windows appear depending on where you clicked in each pane as well.

Figure 47 shows the right-click functions available when you right click on a packet in the Packet List pane. Figure 48 shows functions available when you right click on a packet in the Packet Details pane. Hex view and bits view are the only two right-click options available in the Packet Bytes pane.

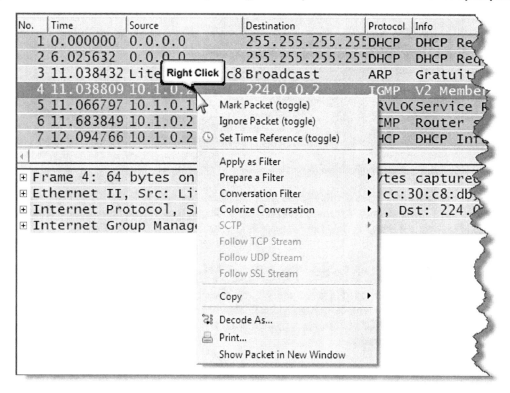

Figure 47. Right-click *functionality offers a faster way to perform some operations*

Two of the newer right-click functions are Copy and Apply as Column.[36] Copy is available when you right click on the Packet List and Packet Details panes. Apply as Column is only available in the Packet Details pane as shown in Figure 48.

---

[36] **Apply As Column** is available with Wireshark v1.3 (development version) and Wireshark v1.4 (stable version) and later. To obtain the development versions of Wireshark, visit *www.wireshark.org/download/automated/*.

Don't Kill Wireshark Performance

To display custom columns, Wireshark must look inside packets to locate the desired field and extract the contents of that field to display in the Packet List pane. All this work adds overhead to Wireshark and may slow down the process of displaying trace file contents or update the list of packets in real-time while capturing.

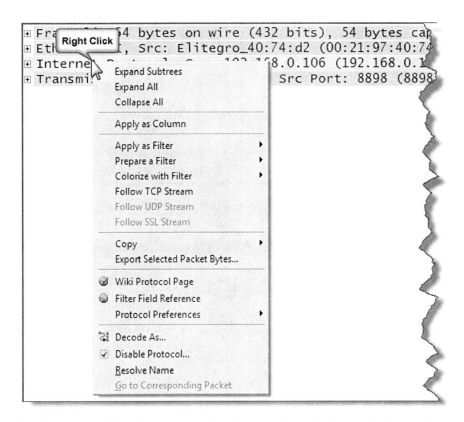

Figure 48. Different right-click *options are available when you select a field in the Display Details pane*

Right Click | Copy

One time saving option available on the right-click window is the Copy option. Figure 49 shows the additional window that appears when you select the Copy option.[37]

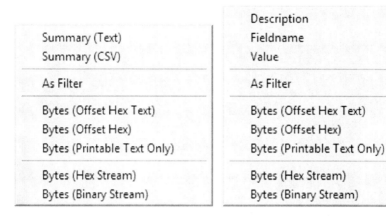

Figure 49. The Copy options available when you click on a field in the Packet List pane (left) and Packet Details pane (right)

The following section shows the values buffered when you use various Copy options on a UDP packet in the Packet List pane.

An example of the Summary (text) value is shown below.

```
2    16.866750    73.68.136.1    255.255.255.255
     DHCP    DHCP ACK - Transaction ID 0x426b999
```

An example of the Summary (CSV) is shown below.

```
"2","16.866750","73.68.136.1","255.255.255.255","DHCP","DHCP ACK
- Transaction ID 0x426b999"
```

An example of the As Filter value is shown below (note that Wireshark can detect which column you right click on to buffer the information contained on that row for that column).

```
frame.time_relative == 43.026319
```

The following section shows the values buffered when you use various Copy options on a UDP header in the Packet Details pane.

Description: `Length: 310`
Fieldname: `udp.length`
Value: `310`
As Filter: `udp.length == 310`

---

[37] This is a GREAT timesaving feature—especially if you are a horrible typist!

Right Click | Apply As Column

This option is available (after Wireshark version 1.2.6) when you right click on a field in the Packet Details pane. It offers a fast way to add a column to the Packet List pane. Figure 50 shows the Packet List pane with two new columns—one showing the TCP window size value and another showing the TCP sequence number value. A value does not appear in rows that do not have packets containing those two fields.[38]

To add the columns shown in Figure 50, simply open a trace file that contains a TCP conversation. Right click on the **Window size** field in the TCP header and select **Apply As Column**. Do the same for the **TCP Sequence Number** field. If you don't have a good TCP trace to use for this, use *http-espn2010.pcap* that is available in the Download section at *www.wiresharkbook.com*.

You can right click on any column heading to align left, center or right, rename the column or remove the column.

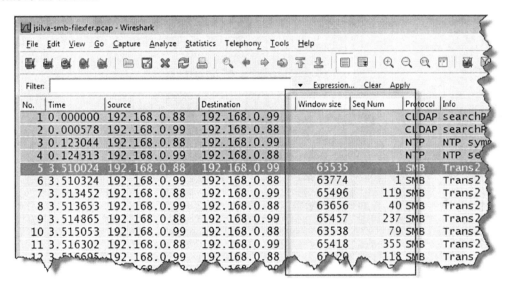

*Figure 50. Add columns to the Packet List pane using **right click | Apply As Column***

Right Click | Wiki Protocol Page (Packet Details Pane)

Wireshark has links to the related Wiki pages from the protocol summary line and protocol fields in the Packet Details pane. For example, click on the **Hardware Size** field in an expanded ARP packet. Select **Wiki Protocol Page** and click **OK** on the information pop-up. Your default browser will display the related protocol page (if one exists).

---

[38] This feature calls for a margarita party! Finally! After years of getting cramps in my hands from going through the long and convoluted method of adding columns using **Edit | Preferences | Columns | New**, we can now two clicks and the new column is added!

Right Click | Filter Field Reference (Packet Details Pane)

Right click on any field in any packet and select **Filter Field Reference** to open the latest Wireshark filter list in your default browser. For example, click on the **Protocol Type** field in an ARP packet and select **Filter Field Reference**—Wireshark opens the list of available ARP display filter fields as shown in Figure 51.

Display Filter Reference: Address Resolution Protocol
Protocol field name: arp
Versions:
Back to Display Filter Reference

Field name	Type	Description	Versions
arp.dst.atm_num_e164	String	Target ATM number (E.164)	1.0.0 to 1.2.6
arp.dst.atm_num_nsap	Byte array	Target ATM number (NSAP)	1.0.0 to 1.2.6
arp.dst.atm_subaddr	Byte array	Target ATM subaddress	1.0.0 to 1.2.6
arp.dst.hlen	Unsigned 8-bit integer	Target ATM number length	1.0.0 to 1.2.6
arp.dst.htype	Boolean	Target ATM number type	1.0.0 to 1.2.6
arp.dst.hw	Byte array	Target hardware address	1.0.0 to 1.2.6
arp.dst.hw_mac	6-byte Hardware (MAC) Address	Target MAC address	1.0.0 to 1.2.6
arp.dst.pln	Unsigned 8-bit integer	Target protocol size	1.0.0 to 1.2.6
arp.dst.proto	Byte array	Target protocol address	1.0.0 to 1.2.6
arp.dst.proto_ipv4	IPv4 address	Target IP address	1.0.0 to 1.2.6
		Target ATM address	1.0.0 to

Figure 51. You can quickly load the display filter reference by right clicking in the Packet Details pane

Right Click | Protocol Preferences

Many of the protocols and applications dissected by Wireshark have preference settings that can be altered using Edit | Preferences | Protocols. You can also right click on a summary line as shown in Figure 52. The protocol preference settings defined using the right click method are saved and in effect the next time you start Wireshark.

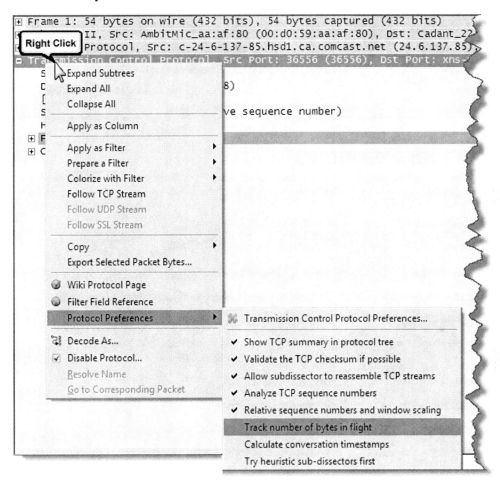

Figure 52. You can quickly set protocol preferences by right clicking on a protocol line in the Packet Details window

Sign Up for the Wireshark Mailing Lists

You should become familiar with the various sections on the Wireshark website and consider registering for one of the five Wireshark mailing lists defined below.

Mailing List	Description
Wireshark-announce	Announcements about releases (low volume)
Wireshark-users	Community-driven support for Wireshark (high volume)[39]
Wireshark-dev	Developer discussion for Wireshark (high volume)
Wireshark-commits	SVN (subversion) repository commit messages (high volume)
Wireshark-bugs	Bug tracker comments (high volume)

Know Your Resources

There are numerous sites that provide assistance with Wireshark functionality or resources for network analysis.

www.wireshark.org	Main Wireshark home page
www.wireshark.org/docs	Wireshark documentation links
wiki.wireshark.org	Wiki page for Wireshark support
www.wireshark.org/download	Download page (current and development versions)
blog.wireshark.org/	The Wireshark blog
www.wiresharkU.com	Wireshark University home page and Wireshark CNA certification exam information
www.winpcap.org	WinPcap home
www.tcpdump.org	libpcap/tcpdump home
www.iana.org	Internet Assigned Numbers Authority (IANA)
www.ietf.org	Internet Engineering Task Force (IETF)

---

[39] What Gerald considers 'high volume' is nothing compared to the numerous Viagra mailing lists that I must be on!

Case Study:
Detecting Database Death

Submitted by: **Bill Bach**
                   Goldstar Software, Inc.

I was troubleshooting an application problem for a client, which started as a simple
"Database Version 6 or Higher Required" message for a given file. More interesting
were the facts: A) the database files was already in version 6 format, and B) the error
only spewed spontaneously, about 1/10 of the time, and sometimes it would report on a
different database file.

After working on this issue for a while and quadruple-checking all the usual suspects,
we were stumped and decided to enable the database vendor's trace feature. This feature
is very handy because it reports to a simple text file every database request and every
corresponding reply -- a great troubleshooting aid for unusual problems like this. Of
course, that text file grows VERY rapidly in a production environment and really takes a
toll on performance, so we had to use it sparingly.

After several attempts of testing at random, we finally managed to capture a series of
events with the "Database Version..." message getting returned. Whew.

Upon digging through an 80MB trace file, we were able to locate the database request
where the version number was requested. Interestingly, the application had provided a 0
value for one of the parameters, instead of a -1 (which indicates that the file version
should be returned). With the 0 in there, no file version was returned, which explains
why a 0 got returned for the file version, and subsequently the program complained
about the version number.

So, we complained to the application vendor, who dug through the code and could find
NO instances of ever passing a 0 -- they ALWAYS passed a-1 to get the database
version. Strange.

Back to the database trace file again, we watched a "normal" application launch and
indeed confirmed that 19 times out of 20, the database file version was being requested,
but only periodically was the parameter a 0. More strange!

On a lark, we decided to capture traffic from the same application startup process,
capturing both a trace with the version request working and one with it not working. As
expected, when the version request worked, we saw the -1 value getting passed from the
application to the server. However, when the version request failed, we saw -- a -1
value! Most strange!

We took another trace on the server side.

Again, we duplicated the problem. This time, though, we had EVERYTHING running
at the same time. We watched as the application sent a -1 for the version request, the -1
was seen in the workstation-side trace file, the -1 was seen on the server-side trace file,
and a 0 was seen by the database vendor trace file.

Aha! Finally, indisputable proof!

When we provided this information to the database vendor, they did a detailed review of their own networking code and indeed found a case where some functions (and the version request was one of them) could have parameters overwritten with a 0. Since it was occurring in the communications module, the database feature only saw the 0 value and responded accordingly. Of course, the database trace feature was implemented in the engine, so it also reported the 0 value. For most applications, this would be completely transparent as they typically don't care which database version they are running on, but because this application DID rely on the return value, and it failed because of it. The next week, we had a new communications module from the developer and things were working once again.

What did we learn?

A) You need to involve the application developer, the back-end developer, AND a networking professional to troubleshoot some issues.

B) You may need multiple network traces (at the client and at the server) to watch packets going through the network.

C) Just because a vendor provides a trace log, doesn't mean that you can rely on it!

Summary

From its humble beginnings as Ethereal, Wireshark has matured to a feature rich tool for analyzing wired and wireless network traffic. As long as you stay within the laws and corporate policies that regulate use of Wireshark, you can troubleshoot and secure your network more efficiently with an inside look at network communications.

All versions of Wireshark use packet capture drivers to capture traffic on wired and wireless networks and the wiretap library to open various types of trace files. Wireshark supports a common interface across multiple platforms with menu-based, icon-based or right-click functionality for trace file manipulation and interpretation.

Practice What You've Learned

Download the practice trace files available from the Download section on the book website, *www.wiresharkbook.com*. Use these trace files to practice what you've learned in this chapter.

1. In Wireshark's Start Page, select **File | Open** and select *ftp-dir.enc*. This trace file was captured and saved by a host running an old DOS version of Network General's Sniffer product. That version saved files with the *.enc* format. Wireshark used Wiretap Library to open that trace file.

2. Scroll through the trace file to see the traffic generated from a File Transfer Protocol (FTP) session. In this FTP session the user logged in to an FTP server with the user name "Fred" and the password "Krueger." In packet 22, the user typed in "dir" at the command line and their FTP software generated the LIST command to the FTP server.

3. Examine the Status Bar at the bottom of the window. On the left side you can see the path and name of the trace file you loaded. You can also see the file is 4,297 bytes in size and the total packet time is 37 seconds.

File: "C:\Users\Laura\Documents\traces\ftp-dir.enc" 4297 Bytes 00:00:37

4. To jump quickly to packet 39 in the trace file, click the **Go To Packet** button on the Main Toolbar. Enter **39** and click **Jump To**. Packet 39 is highlighted in the Packet List pane (top pane) and dissected in the Packet Details pane (middle pane).

5. Right click on the **Frame** line in the Packet Details pane and select **Expand All**. Wireshark is now showing you all the dissected fields of the FTP packet.

6. Scroll down and right click on **Frame Length: 73 bytes (584 bits)** and Select **Apply as Column**.[40] In the Packet list pane you should now have a new column entitled "Frame length on the wire." If you want to remove a column, right click the **column heading** and select **Remove Column**.

---

[40] Available in Wireshark versions as of 1.3.

7. On the Packet List pane (top pane), right click on **packet 39** and select **Follow TCP Stream**. You should clearly be able to read client FTP commands in red and server responses in blue.

Find the following information using the information contained in this chapter:

- What is the highest level of Expert Information contained in this trace file?
- What profile are you working with?
- What is the time display format you are working with?
- Are you resolving IP addresses to names?
- How many capture interfaces are currently available on your system (do not return to the Start Page to learn this information)?

Each of these items can be determined through the Wireshark Status Bar or main menu system.

Practice navigating Wireshark's interface with the following trace files:

icmp-standardping.pcap	This trace shows a standard ICMP-based ping process. By default, the ping.exe file sends a separate ICMP Echo Request packet out at approximately 1 second intervals.
http-microsoft.pcap	This is a sample web browsing session to *www.microsoft.com*. Ensure your packet colorization is enabled to distinguish between DNS and HTTP.
smb-filexfer.pcap	This trace shows the file transfer process between a Microsoft client and server using SMBv1. The file transferred is OOo_2.4.1_SolarisSparc_install_en-US.tar.gz. You can see the periodic SMB Read ANDX Request and Read ANDX Response interruptions during the file download process.
sec-nmapscan.pcap	This trace depicts an Nmap scan. Open the **Statistics	Conversation** window and examine the TCP conversations. Do you see any common port number used by Nmap to perform this scan? Did Nmap hit any ports more than once? Refer to *Chapter 31: Detect Network Scanning and Discovery Processes* for more information on Nmap detection.

Review Questions

Q2.1   **What is the purpose of WinPcap?**

Q2.2   **What is the purpose of Wireshark's dissectors?**

Q2.3   **What is the purpose of the Wiretap library?**

Answers to Review Questions

Q2.1   **What is the purpose of WinPcap?**

A2.1   WinPcap is the Windows port of the libpcap link-layer interface. WinPcap provides the low-level network access for packet capture on a Windows host.

Q2.2   **What is the purpose of Wireshark's dissectors?**

A2.2   Wireshark dissectors decode packets to display field contents and interpreted values (if available). An HTTP packet will use several dissectors—Ethernet, IP, TCP and HTTP.

Q2.3   **What is the purpose of the Wiretap library?**

A2.3   The Wireshark wiretap library enables Wireshark to read a variety of trace file formats such as the formats used by Network General Sniffer and WildPackets OmniPeek products.

Chapter 3:
Capture Traffic

Wireshark Certified Network Analyst Exam Objectives covered:

- Know Where to Tap Into the Network
- Run Wireshark Locally
- Capture Traffic on Switched Networks
- Use a Test Access Port (TAP) on Full-Duplex Networks
- Set up Port Spanning/Port Mirroring on a Switch
- Analyze Routed Networks
- Analyze Wireless Networks
- Capture at Two Locations Simultaneously (Dual Captures)
- Select the Right Capture Interface
- Capture Traffic Remotely
- Automatically Save Packets to One or More Files
- Optimize Wireshark to Avoid Dropping Packets
- Conserve Memory with Command-line Capture

- ❖ Case Study: Dual Capture Points the Finger
- ❖ Case Study: Capturing Traffic at Home
- ❖ Summary
- ❖ Practice What You've Learned
- ❖ Review Questions and Answers

Know Where to Tap Into the Network

The most common reason people avoid analyzing network traffic is total and utter confusion at the hundreds of thousands of packets whizzing by. This is a sure sign that the analyst is embroiled in the "Needle in the Haystack" issue.

Given a large enterprise network where numerous users are complaining about network performance, placing the analyzer in the right spot is just as important as applying the right filters to focus on traffic of interest and interpreting traffic correctly.

Consider the network diagram shown in Figure 53. Client A is complaining.

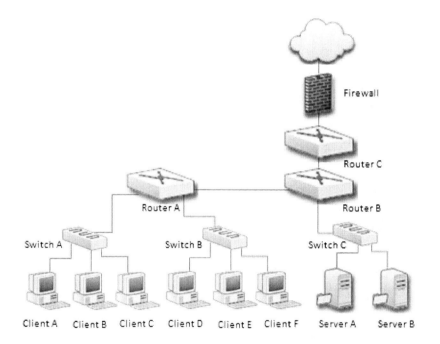

Figure 53. Basic network diagram—consider the user complaints when determining where to place the analyzer.

Begin by placing your analyzer as close to Client A as possible to identify traffic issues from Client A's perspective.[41] By capturing at this location you can measure round trip time and identify packet loss at the point where Client A connects into the network.

---

[41] This can be one of the more unpleasant aspects of network analysis—sitting close to the complaining user. Consider dazzling them with a dissertation on how the TCP sliding window and congestion avoidance mechanisms help improve throughput rates of packets as long as the MTU size is supported end-to-end. This is another great time to close the Packet List and Packet Details panes and just peruse the Packet Bytes panes while randomly shouting hex values. They'll leave you alone right away.

If everyone connecting to Server A is complaining, you may still want to capture traffic from the clients' perspectives. If you find the problem is packet loss, you can move Wireshark closer to Server A until you find the location where packets are being dropped.[42]

Run Wireshark Locally

One option for capturing traffic is simply to run Wireshark or Tshark on the system that you want to capture traffic to or from. Since Wireshark runs on most operating systems, this is a simple solution. This solution is not employed very often because of the common need to bypass security measures in order to get Wireshark or Tshark installed on the user machine and the hesitation to load another application on that machine, especially if it is a server.[43]

Portable Wireshark

Portable Wireshark can be installed onto a PortableApps-enabled device—this lets you to run Wireshark on a host without installing Wireshark on that host. Wireshark runs on the PortableApps-enabled device.

Figure 54 shows the PortableApps menu—note that Portable Wireshark has been added to the menu. You do not need to install Wireshark inside the PortableApps menu system; Portable Wireshark can be run as a separate portable application by simply copying it into a directory on the Portable Apps device.

To download Portable Wireshark, visit *www.wireshark.org/download.html*. Currently, Portable Wireshark is only supported on 32-bit operating systems. For more information on Portable Wireshark, visit *wiki.wireshark.org/WiresharkPortable*.

Install the PortableApps Suite on a USB stick. Next visit *www.wireshark.org/download.html* and select **Windows PortableApps (32-bit)**. Save the executable to the local drive. When you launch Portable Apps, select or create a WiresharkPortable directory on your USB stick for the target. To install Wireshark inside the PortableApps package, choose the **Options | Install New App** option from the main PortableApps menu and select the file ***wireshark-<version>.paf.exe***. A Wizard installs the package on your USB flash device and a new menu item for Wireshark will be added to the main PortableApps menu.

---

[42] Network analysis is not a "sit down and do it" type of process. Get a hot laptop loaded with power and memory and a comfortable pair of shoes. Don't hesitate to move your analyzer to another location when tracking down problems on the network.

[43] The down side of installing Wireshark on Client A's computer is that they will want to keep it on their systems. The term "ignorance is bliss" means that when the users are ignorant about Wireshark and packet analysis in general, we feel blissful.

Figure 54. Wireshark can be run as a portable application

Wireshark U3

U3 devices can auto-launch applications—they are specially formatted USB flash drives that adhere to the U3 specification. U3 smart drives use the U3 Launchpad that works with recent Windows systems only.

Capture Traffic on Switched Networks

You bought a switch to help control and isolate network traffic, thereby allowing more efficient use of the bandwidth. This is a great technique for reducing unnecessary traffic on connected ports, but it creates anguish for the protocol analyst.

When you connect Wireshark into a switch port, you will only see up to four types of traffic by default:

- Broadcast traffic
- Multicast traffic (if forwarded by the switch)
- Traffic to and from your own hardware address
- Traffic to an unknown hardware address

Traffic from one device connected to a switch flows directly to the destination device on another port. In Figure 53, Client A's traffic flows up through Switch A, Router A, Router B and Switch C on the way to Server A. Client A's traffic is not sent down any other ports on Switch A.

If you plug Wireshark into Switch A, you won't be able to listen to Client A's communications because Switch A is doing what it should be doing—it is isolating local conversations based on hardware addresses.[44]

There are several ways to capture network traffic on a wired network.

- Hub into half-duplex traffic
- Tap into half or full-duplex traffic
- Span a switch port
- Install Wireshark on a system

Use a Simple Hub on Half-Duplex Networks

Standard hubs can be used to monitor half-duplex network traffic by connecting the hub in-line between half-duplex devices. Hubs are dumb devices that simply forward bits that arrive on one port out all other ports.

If you plan to use a hub to monitor half-duplex networks, ensure you test the hub. Numerous manufacturers have sold devices described as hubs that are, in fact, switches. To test an alleged hub, connect two half-duplex test stations and Wireshark to the hub as shown in Figure 55. Ping one test station from the other test station. If Wireshark can see the ping traffic, the hub really is a hub and it is forwarding traffic down all ports. If Wireshark does not see the ping traffic, the hub is likely a switch and should not be used for traffic monitoring.[45] You must either connect the switch to the hub's crossover port or use a crossover cable to connect the two.

---

[44] It's a good idea to test this. Capture traffic on your host that is connected to a switch. If you see traffic between other devices, then your switch has a problem. It's acting like a hub—probably a very expensive hub.

[45] Be careful with devices sold as "hubs"—some "hubs" are actually switches. In addition, dual-speed hubs (hubs that can connect to 10Mbps or 100Mbps hosts) can become switches between the different media speeds.

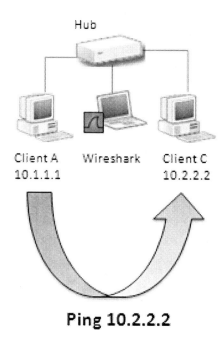

Ping 10.2.2.2

Figure 55. Test your hubs before using them to monitor half-duplex traffic

Use a Test Access Port (TAP) on Full-Duplex Networks

Network taps can be used on half and full-duplex networks to listen in on the traffic between a client or server and a switch or router. Taps are passive devices that are placed in-line (in the path) between devices. Unlike spanned ports, taps can forward packets that contain physical layer errors (such as CRC errors) to the monitor port(s).

Taps do not introduce delays or alter the contents of traffic flowing through them. In addition, taps should "fail open" so they will not disrupt traffic if power to the tap is lost.

Figure 56. A Net Optics 10/100/1000BaseT Non-aggregating tap

Tap Installation

Tap installation procedures vary depending on the tap features. Figure 57 shows the configuration of a non-aggregating tap and two systems running Wireshark.

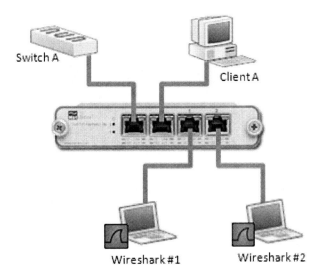

Figure 57. Setting up a non-aggregating tap and two Wireshark systems

Non-Aggregating Taps

Non-aggregating taps pass full-duplex communications out two separate ports. A device running Wireshark requires two network interface cards to receive traffic from the two monitor ports. Two instances of Wireshark would be run—each instance capturing traffic from a different interface. Alternately, two separate devices running Wireshark can be connected to the two ports.

Use **File | Merge** or Mergecap to combine the separate trace files captured on non-aggregating taps.

Watch Timestamp Issues on Multiple NIC Captures

When configuring a single computer with two network interface cards to listen to traffic from both the monitor ports on a non-aggregating tap, be aware of the timestamp differences between the two network interface cards. If one of the network interface cards is USB-based, delays may be significant enough to cause problems when merging the two trace files together to get a complete picture of the communications.

Aggregating Taps

Aggregating taps combine the bi-directional traffic into a single outbound port. Devices with only one network interface card can be connected to the aggregating tap to listen into full-duplex communications.

Figure 58. Net Optics 10/100 Dual Port Aggregator Tap

Regenerating Taps

Regenerating taps are used when you have more than one monitoring tool to use for listing in on traffic. For example, perhaps you want to analyze the traffic with Wireshark and perform intrusion detection with another tool, such as Snort (*www.snort.org*). Regenerating taps have more than one outbound port, allowing connection of two (or more) monitoring devices.

Figure 59 shows a regenerating tap with fiber ports. The first 8 ports on the left are regeneration ports. The two ports on the right are the inline ports. If you were using this tap to monitor traffic between a server and switch, one inline port on the right side would connect to the server and the second would connect to the switch.

Figure 59. Net Optics 10 Gigabit Regeneration Tap

Link Aggregation Taps

Link aggregation taps are used when you have more than one link to monitor. For example, if you want to monitor the traffic to and from two separate servers. Instead of using multiple taps, a single link aggregation tap can be connected to both servers. The link aggregating tap combines the traffic from these links and sends the stream out one or more monitoring port.

Intelligent Taps

Intelligent taps can make decisions on inbound traffic, provide timestamps for each packet received, filter packets and more. The features available depend on the intelligent tap solution.

NetOptics is a global manufacturer of passive access with network taps, aggregator taps, regeneration taps, converter taps and bypass switches. For more information, visit *www.netoptics.com*.

Using Analyzer Agents for Remote Capture

Analyzer agents are used by distributed analyzers. These agents are typically software programs that are loaded on switches to enable them to capture traffic from all ports and send the data to a management console. Analyzer agents may enable you to manage switched traffic from a central location. Unfortunately, however, you might get caught up in a proprietary solution or find that this type of feature makes the switch too expensive. For more information on remote capture methods, see *Capture Traffic Remotely* on page 94.

Set up Port Spanning/Port Mirroring on a Switch

Some vendors call this technique port spanning (SPAN stands for switched port analysis), others call it port mirroring. In this book we use the term port spanning. Cisco also uses the term port snooping when referring to this feature on Catalyst 8500 switches.

In a switched environment port spanning is used to configure a switch to send a copy of any port's traffic down a monitor port—the port that a Wireshark system would be connected to. This method of analyzing switched networks can only be used if the switch supports this functionality.

SPAN Terminology

The following table lists common SPAN terminology.

Term	Definition
Source SPAN Port	The source SPAN port is a port that is monitored by the SPAN feature. In Figure 60, port 4 is the source SPAN port.
Source SPAN VLAN	The source SPAN VLAN is a VLAN whose traffic is monitored by the span feature.
Destination Span Port or Monitor Port	The Destination SPAN port or Monitor port is the port that monitors source ports—in Figure 60, port 1 where Wireshark is connected is the destination span port or monitor port.
Ingress Traffic	Ingress traffic is traffic that is flowing into the switch. Some switches require that you define if you are interested in monitoring ingress and egress traffic or just ingress traffic to a port.
Egress Traffic	Egress traffic is traffic that is flowing out of the switch. Some switches require that you define if you are interested in monitoring ingress and egress traffic or just egress traffic from a port.

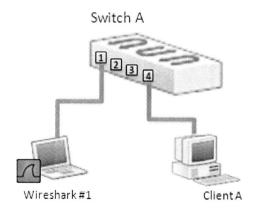

Figure 60. Port 4 is spanned to port 1

As shown in Figure 60, the traffic from port 4 is copied down to port 1 where Wireshark is located.

Example of Span Commands

The following example includes sample span commands used for a Cisco switch which uses the syntax **set span** *source_port destination_port.*

```
switch (enable) set span 1/4 1/1
```

If you want to span multiple ports to Wireshark, the syntax would be **set span** *source_port, source_port, destination_port.* The following example would span ports 3 and 4 to port 1.

```
switch (enable) set span 1/3,1/4 1/1
```

For more details on configuring spanning on a switch, refer to your manufacturer documentation.

Spanning VLANs

You can use a tap or span a port to listen to VLAN traffic. We will address the process of spanning a VLAN device.

In order to span the traffic to or from devices in a VLAN, span the port of a device in the VLAN. Define the destination port as the one that Wireshark is connected to on the switch. In order to see VLAN tags, do not configure Wireshark's interface connected to the switch as a member of a VLAN.

There is still no guarantee you will be able to see VLAN tags, however, because different operating systems and drivers handle VLAN tags in different manners.

If the VLAN tag is handled by the network interface card or driver on the system that Wireshark is loaded on, the tag will not be handed up to Wireshark and you won't be able to see the tag when you analyze the traffic. If the card or driver passes the VLAN tag to the upper layer on the Wireshark system, you will be able to see and analyze the VLAN tag field, as shown in Figure 61.

For more details on spanning VLAN ports, refer to the manufacturer's documentation.

```
⊞ Frame 1 (64 bytes on wire, 64 bytes captured)
⊞ Ethernet II, Src: Cisco_ea:b8:c1 (00:19:06:ea:b8:c1), Dst: Broadcast (ff:ff:ff:ff:ff:ff)
⊟ 802.1Q Virtual LAN, PRI: 0, CFI: 0, ID: 123
     000. .... .... .... = Priority: 0
     ...0 .... .... .... = CFI: 0
     .... 0000 0111 1011 = ID: 123
     Type: ARP (0x0806)
     Trailer: 000000000000000000000000000000000000
⊞ Address Resolution Protocol (reply/gratuitous ARP)
```

Figure 61. Wireshark decodes VLAN fields if the card and driver pass them up

Analyze Routed Networks

Routers isolate traffic based on the network address, such as an IP address. If you place Wireshark on one side of a router, you will only see traffic that is destined to or coming from that network.

Figure 62 consists of two networks (10.1.0.0 and 10.2.0.0, subnetted 255.255.0.0). Traffic between the clients and servers on network 10.1.0.0 will not be visible to Wireshark #2 on network 10.2.0.0.

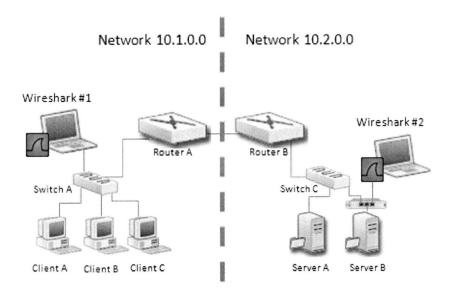

Figure 62. Placing Wireshark on each side of a router

Wireshark #1 is configured through port spanning to listen to the port connecting to Router A. This enables Wireshark #1 to listen in on traffic to and from Clients A, B and C.

Wireshark #2 is connected to an aggregating tap that connects Server B to Switch C.

Analyze Wireless Networks

Start from the bottom and move up through the protocol stack when analyzing WLAN environments. "From the bottom" in the WLAN environment means to analyze the strength of radio frequency (RF) signals and look for interference.

Wireshark cannot identify unmodulated RF energy or interference. Use a spectrum analyzer to identify these problems. Metageek makes an excellent affordable set of WLAN spectrum analyzer adapters and software. For more information, visit *www.metageek.net.*

Wireshark's location on a wireless network is similar to the location in a wired network—start as close as possible to the complaining user. You want to learn the signal strength, packet loss rate and round trip latency time at the location of the user who is complaining.

Figure 63 shows a portion of a network where a user, Client C, is complaining of performance problems. We have placed Wireshark close to that user.

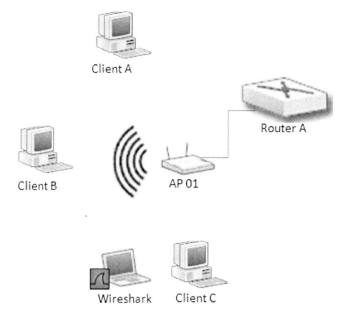

Figure 63. Place Wireshark close to the client to analyze traffic from the client's perspective

Once you have determined that interference is not an issue, move up to the packet level to examine the WLAN traffic such as the connection process and authentication. Examine the WLAN control and management processes to make sure everything is functioning properly before inspecting the data packets.

If everything is fine up to this point, you are now following the same steps as you would follow with traditional wired network analysis. To effectively analyze WLAN traffic, your Wireshark system should have a WLAN card and driver that can be put into both promiscuous mode and monitor mode.

Monitor Mode

Monitor mode and promiscuous mode are not the same.

Promiscuous mode enables a network card and driver to capture traffic that is addressed to other devices on the network, not just to the local hardware address.

In promiscuous mode only (without monitor mode), an 802.11 adapter only captures packets of the SSID the adapter has joined. Although it can receive, at the radio level, packets on other SSID's, those packets are not forwarded to the host.

In order to capture all traffic that the adapter can receive, the adapter must be put into "monitor mode", sometimes called "rfmon mode". In this mode, the driver doesn't make the adapter a member of any service set.

Monitor Mode Blocks Other Connectivity

In monitor mode, the adapter won't support general network communications (web browsing, email, etc.). It only supplies received packets to a packet capture mechanism, not to the network stack.

In monitor mode, an adapter and driver pass *all* packets of *all* SSID's from the currently selected channel up to Wireshark.

Monitor mode is not supported by WinPcap (so it doesn't work with Wireshark or TShark on Windows). Monitor mode is supported, for at least some network interface cards, on some versions of Linux, FreeBSD, NetBSD, OpenBSD, and Mac OS X. You will have to test your network interface cards/drivers on these platforms to see if they will work in monitor mode.

Due to this limitation (particularly in the Windows environment), CACE Technologies developed AirPcap adapters. These adapters can capture data, management and control frames and multi-channel monitoring. In addition, CACE developed an AirPcap aggregating adapter that allows you to capture on multiple AirPcap adapters (and therefore multiple channels) simultaneously.

Figure 64. CACE Technologies created the AirPcap adapter for WLAN capture

View *www.cacetech.com* for more information on the AirPcap adapters. Refer to *Chapter 26: Introduction to 802.11 (WLAN) Analysis* for details on configuring capture channels, WLAN decryption and interpretation.

Native Adapter Capture Issues

You can capture on your native WLAN adapter as long as Wireshark displays that adapter in the interfaces list.

You may find, however, that your trace files only contain data packets (and no WLAN control or management packets) and have an Ethernet header on each packet. These are fake Ethernet headers applied to the packet in place of the 802.11 header.

These fake headers are put on the packets by the native 802.11 network interface card or driver after stripping off the original 802.11 header. These adapters won't pass up the management or control frames. Your ability to analyze WLAN issues is quite limited.

For more information on capturing WLAN traffic, visit *wiki.wireshark.org/CaptureSetup/WLAN*. For details on analyzing WLAN traffic, refer to *Chapter 26: Introduction to 802.11 WLAN Analysis*.

Launch Wireshark and determine (a) if your native WLAN adapter is recognized by Wireshark in the interface list, (b) what happens when you attempt to capture on this interface and (c) what you can capture, if anything.

Capture at Two Locations Simultaneously (Dual Captures)

There are times when two or more Wireshark systems may be required to capture traffic on the network. For example, if you want to measure one-way time to a target you can set up Wireshark at both ends of the connection and measure how long it takes packets to travel through the network. Another example is if you are using a non-aggregating tap and you've connected two separate Wireshark systems to the two monitor ports of the tap.

It is important to consider the following issues when performing dual captures:

- Traffic can be captured using Tshark, dumpcap or the Wireshark GUI interface
- Both analyzer systems should be time synchronized using Network Time Protocol (NTP)—visit *www.ntp.org* for information on Network Time Protocol
- Capture filters may be used to define specific traffic of interest
- Editcap may be used to alter timestamps if trace files are not synchronized
- Mergecap can be used to combine trace files

Refer to the Case Study at the end of this chapter for an example of using two Wireshark systems to analyze network problems.

Select the Right Capture Interface

Open the Capture Interfaces window to verify packets are being seen on the desired interface. Select **Capture | Interfaces** or click the **Capture Interfaces** button to view the interfaces that Wireshark recognizes as shown in Figure 65.

If no interfaces are shown, there is likely a problem with libpcap (on *nix platforms), the AirPcap or WinPcap driver. It is recommended that you first restart Wireshark and, if your interfaces are still not appearing on the interfaces list, consider restarting your system.

Easily Remove Duplicate Packets in Your Capture

At one customer site all the traffic they captured had duplicates—just packets sent from their local Wireshark hosts were duplicated. In essence, they would see SYN-SYN-SYN/ACK-ACK-ACK for the three-way TCP handshake initiated from their systems. It turned out that a VPN client program (Global VPN Client) caused the problem. See wiki.wireshark.org/CaptureSetup/InterferingSoftware for details of other interfering programs. If you have this problem, use Editcap with the –d parameter to remove duplicates that occur within 5 packet proximity.

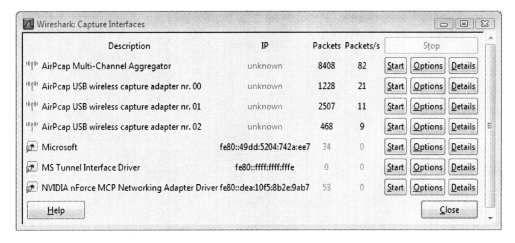

Figure 65. The Interfaces List shows traffic activity without capturing traffic

Understand Why There are Checksum Errors on YOUR Traffic Only

What if your Wireshark system captures traffic perfectly well—except that each packet from your host appears to contain checksum errors? If you receive responses to your TCP connection attempts, web browsing requests and other requests, your packets are getting through in acceptable shape. Likely, your network interface card/driver uses checksum offloading (task offloading) which calculates the IP and TCP checksums on the card, after Wireshark has obtained a copy of the outbound packet. Consider disabling the Checksum Error coloring rule if it bothers you.

Interface Details

The Interfaces Detail window (shown in Figure 66) lists interface and link type characteristics and statistics and task offload capabilities. This information is provided by the network interface card driver and is subject to the driver's accuracy.

Figure 66. The Interface Details window

Capture Traffic Remotely

There may be times when you want to capture traffic at a remote location, but analyze that traffic locally.

Some switches offer a remote spanning capability—referred to as *rspan*. Consult your switch manufacturer documentation to learn more about these capabilities.

One simple option for remote capture is to run Wireshark and remote control software on the target. UltraVNC (free), Logmein and Anyplace Control are three examples of remote control software programs.

You can also use the remote capture abilities included with WinPcap. WinPcap includes *rpcapd*, a remote capture daemon that can be run on a remote host to capture and send packets to a local Wireshark host. The *rpcapd* file is copied to the \winpcap directory during WinPcap installation.

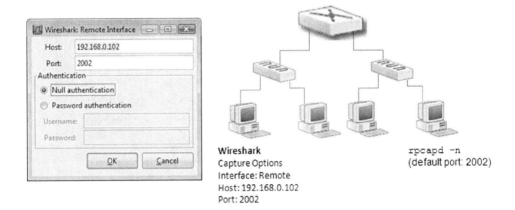

Wireshark
Capture Options
Interface: Remote
Host: 192.168.0.102
Port: 2002

rpcapd -n
(default port: 2002)

Figure 67. Performing remote capture using rpcapd

In Figure 67, we are running `rpcapd -n` on a remote Windows host. The −n parameter indicates that we are not using authentication between the Wireshark and remote capture host. The default port used to transfer the captured packets from the remote host to Wireshark is 2002.

Figure 68 shows Wireshark's Capture Options window. We selected "Remote" on the Interface drop down list to open the Remote Interface Settings window. We entered the remote host IP address and indicated that we will be using port 2002 for the rpcap replay traffic. We also indicated that we will not use authentication.

Use the−n parameter for null authentication—consider using the −l parameter with rpcapd to define which hosts can connect to the rpcap daemon.

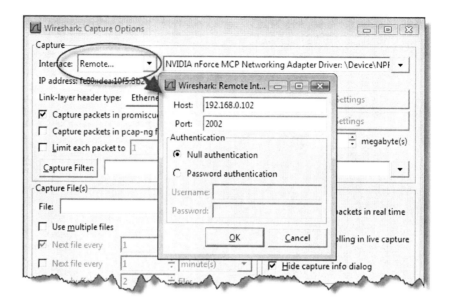

Figure 68. Once you have set up a remote session you can adjust parameters using the Interface dropdown

Configuration Parameters for rpcapd

The following section lists the rpcapd parameters that can be used to configure the remote host for packet capture.

Usage: rpcapd [-b <address>] [-p <port>] [-6]
                           [-l <host_list>] [-a <host,port>]
                           [-n] [-v] [-d] [-s <file>] [-f <file>]

Parameter	Description
-b <address>	The address to bind to (either numeric or literal). Default: it binds to all local IPv4 addresses
-p <port>	The port to bind to. Default: it binds to port 2002
-4	Use only IPv4 (default both IPv4 and IPv6 waiting sockets are used)
-l <host_list>	A file that keeps the list of the hosts which are allowed to connect to this server (if more than one, list them one per line). It is suggested to use literal names (instead of numeric ones) in order to avoid problems with different address families
-n	Permit NULL authentication (usually used with -l)
-a <host,port>	Run in active mode when connecting to host on port. If port is omitted, the default port (2003) is used

Parameter	Description
-v	Run in active mode only (default: if -a is specified, it accepts passive connections as well
-d	Run in daemon mode (UNIX only) or as a service (Win32 only). Warning (Win32): this switch is provided automatically when the service is started from the control panel
-s <file>	Save the current configuration to file as shown in Figure 70.
-f <file>	Load the current configuration from file; all the switches specified from the command line are ignored
-h	View the rpcapd help screen

The −1 parameter enables you to list 'allowed' Wireshark hosts. If your *hosts* file does not contain the information from a host attempting to connect for remote capture, it will receive an error response. Figure 69 shows the error popup window.

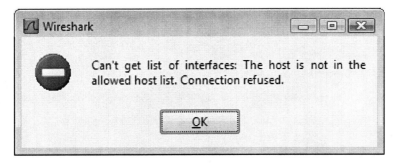

Figure 69. The Wireshark host is not listed in the hosts file on the system running rpcapd

Remote Capture: Active and Passive Mode Configurations
Configure the remote capture device to run in Active Mode to enable the remote host to initiate the connection to the Wireshark host for packet transfer.

If you specify the −a parameter, include at least the host information for the system running Wireshark. If you do not include port information, port number 2003 will be assumed.

Experiment with Remote Capture Traffic
Remote capture is one of the features that you should experiment with before you need it. Note that you will be adding a significant amount of traffic to the network as rpcapd sends the remotely captured traffic to Wireshark.

Save and Use Remote Capture Configurations

You can create a file called `rpcapd.ini` that includes the configuration commands and launch this configuration file using the `-f` parameter.

You can automatically create a configuration file using the `-s <file>` parameter. The daemon parses all the parameters used and saves them into the specified configuration file. Figure 70 shows the contents of a configuration file that was automatically generated using the command `rpcapd -a 192.168.0.105,2003 -n -s amode.txt`.

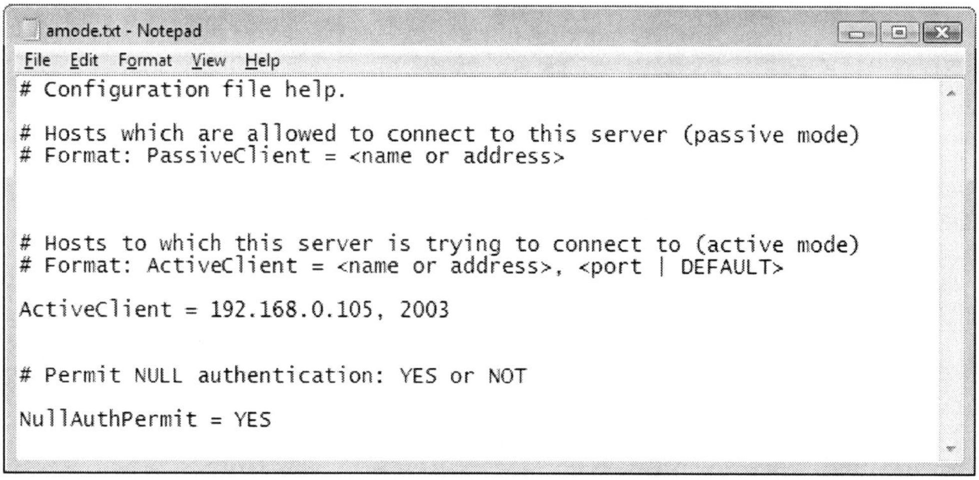


```
# Configuration file help.

# Hosts which are allowed to connect to this server (passive mode)
# Format: PassiveClient = <name or address>


# Hosts to which this server is trying to connect to (active mode)
# Format: ActiveClient = <name or address>, <port | DEFAULT>

ActiveClient = 192.168.0.105, 2003

# Permit NULL authentication: YES or NOT

NullAuthPermit = YES
```

Figure 70. Use the `-s <filename>` parameter to automatically save configurations to a file

Automatically Save Packets to One or More Files

When you need to capture a large amount of traffic, consider capturing to a file set and possibly using a ring buffer. File sets are opened and manipulated with **File | File Set**.

Create File Sets for Faster Access

File sets are contiguous files that are saved to disk and can be accessed using File | File Set. File sets can be opened and examined faster than individual files.

If you create a file set using the file name *corp01.pcap*, the files will be named using the *corp01* stem, a five-digit sequential number, the year, hour (24-hour time value), minute, seconds and the .pcap extension.

File sets taken at a five minute interval would have names similar to the following:

corp01_00001_20090119191348.pcap
corp01_00002_20090119191848.pcap
corp01_00003_20090119192348.pcap
and so on…

To create file sets, select **Use multiple files** in the capture options window as shown in Figure 71. If you use select multiple files, you must define criteria for the creation of the next file.

Next file criteria can be based on file size (kilobytes, megabytes, gigabytes) or time (seconds, minutes, hours, days).

Select Multiple Criteria for Capture Stop

If you select both file size and time criteria, the first criteria matched will trigger a new file to be created. For example, if you defined that the next file should be created when a file reached 10 megabytes and 20 seconds and the network traffic consists of minimum size packets, you will likely hit the 20 second criteria before the 10 megabytes criteria. The new file would be created after 20 seconds and the previous file would not contain 10 megabytes of packets.

Figure 71. Capture Options for file sets and stop criteria

Use a Ring Buffer to Limit the Number of Files Saved

A ring buffer limits the number of files saved. For example, a ring buffer of two, as set in Figure 71, would only save the last two files in the set, maintaining the sequential numbering scheme.

The files saved would begin with corp01 and be followed with the file number and the timestamp. If the entire capture process created 90 files, only the last two would be saved.

Define an Automatic Stop Criteria

Stop criteria can be defined on the number of files created, the number of packets captured, the captured file size or time.

In Figure 71, Wireshark will stop capturing after 40 minutes. There will only be two files since we have configured a ring buffer setting of two files.

Optimize Wireshark to Avoid Dropping Packets

If you are capturing on a very busy network, you might consider optimizing Wireshark to avoid dropping packets. Packet loss may be noted on the Wireshark Status Bar.

Any configuration that consumes extra processing power should be examined to determine if it can be disabled or another capture method can be used.

Capture Options for Optimization

The following capture options can affect Wireshark's efficiency.

- Update List of Packets in Real Time (disable)
- Name Resolution (disable network name resolution)
- Buffer Size (increase; pertains to Windows only)
- Protocol Tasks (examine individually to remove unneeded features)
- Command-Line Capture (consider using Tshark)

Display Options for Optimization

The following display options can affect Wireshark's efficiency.

- Number of Columns (reduce the number of columns)
- Split the trace file (use Editcap to split the trace file into smaller sizes)

Conserve Memory with Command-line Capture

Consider one of the command-line capture methods to capture packets at the command line if you consistently experience packet loss when using the Wireshark GUI. Three command-line capture tools are included with Wireshark:

- Tshark
- Dumpcap
- Rawshark

Tshark is covered in *Chapter 33: Effective Use of Command-Line Tools*.

Another popular tool, tcpdump, is not included with Wireshark but offers command-line capture. For more information on tcpdump, visit *www.tcpdump.org/tcpdump_man.html.*

Most likely you will look at either Tshark or Dumpcap for capturing traffic at command-line. Tshark offers greater flexibility through more parameters, but it also uses more resources. In fact, Tshark relies on Dumpcap so you will see both Dumpcap and Tshark launched when you've just loaded Tshark.

Dumpcap uses much less memory as you can see from the table below. If memory usage and performance is an issue, Dumpcap is the right choice. If functionality and capability is most important to you, then Tshark is the right choice.

Tool	Memory (Private Working Set)
Dumpcap	2,824 Kb
Tshark	2,608 Kb (dumpcap) + 83,208

For details on Dumpcap and Tshark parameters, refer to *Chapter 33: Effective Use of Command-Line Tools.*

Case Study:
Dual Capture Points the Finger

Submitted by: ***Karl R.***
                   Systems Integrator

Our client was complaining about performance when downloading files from Server B. When analyzing the traffic close to Client A, we noticed that there is a significant delay before each file is received at the client.

We decided to capture traffic at both the client and the server to compare traffic flows at both locations.

Figure 72 shows the basic network with two Wireshark systems. Wireshark #1 is connected to a spanned port listening to the traffic to/from Client A. Wireshark #2 is connected to an aggregating tap and is listening to the traffic to and from Server B.

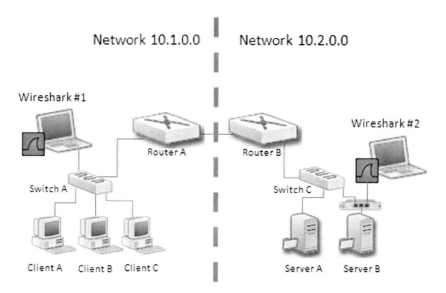

Figure 72. To compare a traffic flow at separate locations, we set up two Wireshark systems

In this case, the analyst merged the trace files together. Upon doing so, the trace consisted of duplicate packets throughout. Comparing the timestamps in the duplicate packets revealed that packets containing file requests were delayed, whereas ACK packets were not.

Wireshark Says "Where," but Not Always "Why"

Although Wireshark could identify the location where this problem occurred, it could not identify the cause of the problem. This is often the case in network analysis. Cooperation with IT members responsible for the devices along the path is imperative to identify the actual reason the problem occurred.

The next step was to move the Wireshark #1 system along the path towards the server to identify the point at which delays were incurred. The culprit was Router B—statistics at that router showed that it had a large number of packets in the queue. Working with the vendor we identified several configuration errors that had given high priority queuing to all traffic destined to Server A and low priority to all traffic to server B. We reconfigured the router and things were back to normal.

Case Study: Capturing Traffic at Home

Submitted by: Rob Hulsebos

Several years ago my first broadband internet modem gave me trouble—every 15 minutes my connection was closed, causing all sorts of errors on my PC.

According to the internet provider's remote diagnostics there was nothing wrong with the modem.

But even after re-installing Windows, using different PC's, removing the wireless router used and making a wired connection, the problem remained. I then used an Ethernet tap to check the network traffic between the modem and my provider, with my wife's PC running Wireshark to intercept the traffic from my PC.

It then turned out that the modem closed the connection regularly, apparently because it thought it was using a dial-up line which it disconnected automatically if there was no network traffic for 1 minute—this to save on telephone costs. But the modem was not configured to do that—I had a fixed fee line, no need to disconnect. Apparently I ran into a firmware bug where it ignored the fixed line setting.

So I re-installed the modem's firmware, and from that moment on it all worked fine.

If it wasn't for Wireshark I would have believed the modem's webpage showing me that it was configured for a fixed line, while actually it ignored that configuration setting.

Summary

Before you can analyze network traffic, you need to capture it. Tapping into the network at the most appropriate location can help capture the traffic that will help you the most in your analysis processes.

When working on switched networks—the most common network configuration—you have the option of running Wireshark locally, spanning a switch port or using a full-duplex tap. You have several options for remote capture as well—you can use open source or commercial remote control software, remote spanning (if your switch supports this function), or *rpcapd* which is included with the WinPcap download.

When you are capturing WLAN traffic, you should use an adapter/driver that can function in monitor mode to listen into traffic on all SSIDs within range. If you are using a native adapter to capture WLAN traffic, it may substitute the 802.11 header with an Ethernet II header and not capture and display management or control traffic or traffic from other WLAN devices.

If you need to capture a large amount of traffic, consider saving to file sets to make the trace files more manageable. If the Wireshark GUI cannot keep up with the traffic, optimize Wireshark or consider using a command-line capture tool such as Tshark or Dumpcap.

Practice What You've Learned

Download the trace files available in the Download section of the book website, *www.wiresharkbook.com*. Use these trace files to practice the tasks and tricks contained in this book.

Here is a list of tasks that you should practice at this point:

- Try capturing web browsing traffic on your local system—learn what you can capture without port spanning or using a full-duplex tap.
- Select **Capture | Interfaces** and wait a few moments to see which interface(s) are seeing traffic. Click the **Start** button to begin capturing on one of these interfaces.
- Launch your web browser and browse to *www.chappellU.com*.
- After the page has loaded, select **Capture | Stop** or click the **Stop Capture** button on the Main Toolbar. Select **File | Save** and call your trace file *chappellU1.pcap*.
- If you have a wireless adapter on your system, start a capture using that WLAN interface. If you receive an error message indicating that the "capture session could not be initiated (failed to set hardware filter to promiscuous mode)", close the alert window and select **Capture | Options** and choose your WLAN adapter in the Interface section. Disable (uncheck) **Capture packets in promiscuous mode** and click **Start**. Browse to *www.chappellU.com* and then stop your capture session. Examine the traffic to see what data link header was placed on your traffic. For more information on WLAN capture options using promiscuous and monitor mode, refer to *Chapter 26: Introduction to 802.11 (WLAN) Analysis*.
- If you have a switch, practice spanning a port that connects to a system configured as a testing host. To ensure your spanning works properly, use that testing system

to browse to *www.chappellU.com*. If your spanning process worked correctly you should be able to see all traffic to or from your testing host.

- If you have a tap, connect the tap between a switch and your testing host. Connect your Wireshark host to the tap as well. Browse to *www.chappellU.com* from that host and verify that you captured all traffic to and from the testing host.

- Perform a remote capture test by installing WinPcap on another network host and running `rpcapd -n` on that host. On your local Wireshark system, open **Capture | Options** and select **Remote** in the Interfaces option. Define the IP address of the host running rpcap. Select the remote interface to capture from and begin capturing. Analyze the traffic you have captured from the remote host to verify the process worked.

- Practice capturing your own traffic to file sets. Name your capture files *testset1.pcap* and use multiple files—create the next file every 30 seconds. Use a ring buffer to save the last 5 files and stop capturing after 10 files. Start your capture and begin browsing a number of web sites for the next 7 minutes or so. Check to determine if Wireshark automatically stopped capturing and identify your five files of the file set. Their names should begin with *testset1_00006*, *testset1_00007*, *testset1_00008*, *testset1_00009*, and *testset1_00010*.

Review Questions

Q3.1   If you connect a Wireshark host directly into a switch, what traffic can you expect to see by default?

Q3.2   What is the difference between monitor mode and promiscuous mode?

Q3.3   What is the purpose of file sets?

Answers to Review Questions

Q3.1 **If you connect a Wireshark host directly into a switch, what traffic can you expect to see by default?**

A3.1 By default, switches forward all broadcast packets, multicast packets (unless configured to block multicast forwarding), packets destined to the Wireshark host's hardware address and packets destined to unknown hardware addresses.

Q3.2 **What is the difference between monitor mode and promiscuous mode?**

A3.2 In monitor mode, the driver doesn't make the adapter a member of any service set. In this mode, an adapter and driver pass *all* packets of *all* SSIDs from the currently selected channel up to Wireshark.

Promiscuous mode enables a network card and driver to capture traffic that is addressed to other devices on the network, not just to the local hardware address.

Q3.3 **What is the purpose of file sets?**

A3.3 File sets are used to create a contiguous set of trace files during a capture process. Instead of opening and navigating through one large trace file (which may be a slow process), you can create file sets and move faster among the smaller trace files.

Chapter 4: Create and Apply Capture Filters

Wireshark Certified Network Analyst Exam Objectives covered:

- The Purpose of Capture Filters
- Build Your Own Set of Capture Filters
- Filter by a Protocol
- Create MAC/IP Address or Host Name Capture Filters
- Capture One Application's Traffic Only
- Use Operators to Combine Capture Filters
- Create Capture Filters to Look for Byte Values
- Manually Edit the Capture Filters File
- Share Capture Filters with Others

The Purpose of Capture Filters

Capture filters limit the packets saved in either the \temp location while capturing or to another directory when you save a trace file. Capture filters cannot be applied to existing trace files—they are applied during live capture processes only. Capture filters are very useful in limiting the packets you capture when you are on a busy network or you are focusing in on a specific type of traffic. Packets that pass the capture filter criteria are passed up to the Wireshark capture engine as shown in Figure 73.

Capture filters use the same filter syntax as tcpdump.

Capture filters are not as flexible and granular as display filters. In addition, at this time, Wireshark does not have an auto-complete feature or error checking colorization feature (although Wireshark will generate an error window if your capture filter syntax is incorrect).

To view saved capture filters, select **Capture | Capture Filters** or click the **Capture Filters** icon on the Main Toolbar.

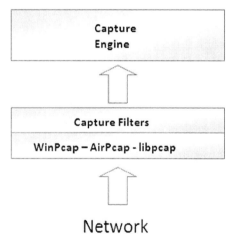

Figure 73. Capture Filters are only applied to packets arriving from the network

 Use Capture Filters Sparingly and Display Filters Generously

When you filter out traffic with capture filters, you cannot get the discarded packets back. They were dropped before being handed up to the capture engine. If you capture generously, you can apply and remove display filters to focus on certain traffic. You can easily save subsets of the traffic based on display filters. You can't get traffic back after it has been dropped due to a capture filter.

Wireshark's default capture filters include the following:

Capture Filter Name	Capture Filter Syntax
Ethernet address 00:08:15:00:08:15	`ether host 00:08:15:00:08:15`
Ethernet type 0x0806 (ARP)	`ether proto 0x0806`
No Broadcast and no Multicast	`not broadcast and not multicast`
No ARP	`not arp`
IP only	`ip`
IP address 192.168.0.1	`host 192.168.0.1`
IPX only	`ipx`
TCP only	`tcp`
UDP only	`udp`
TCP or UDP port 80 (HTTP)	`port 80`
HTTP TCP port (80)	`tcp port http`
No ARP and no DNS	`not arp and port not 53`
Non-HTTP and non-SMTP to/from *www.wireshark.org*	`not port 80 and not port 25 and host www.wireshark.org`

Wireshark includes a set of default capture filters that are kept in the Wireshark program file directory. The capture filter file name is *cfilters*. You may have multiple *cfilters* files on your system. When you create a profile (covered in *Chapter 11: Customize Wireshark Profiles*) and create a new capture filter while using that profile, a *cfilters* file is created in the profile directory.

For example, if you create a WLAN profile, you might consider creating a series of WLAN-specific capture filters, such as a filter for 802.11 traffic to and from the MAC address of an access point or a capture filter for beacon frames only (see *Chapter 26: Introduction to 802.11 (WLAN) Analysis* for more filter options).

Build Your Own Set of Capture Filters

You can easily create your own capture filters and change the default capture filters. If you try to capture traffic using incorrect capture filter syntax, an error message (such as the error message in Figure 74) appears. To learn more about the tcpdump filter format, see *www.tcpdump.org/tcpdump_man.html*. Capture filters consist of identifiers and qualifiers.

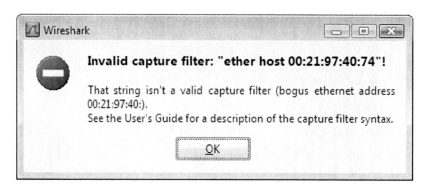

Figure 74. Capture filter syntax error message

Identifier

The identifier is the element for which you are filtering. In a capture filter for traffic to or from port 53, "53" is the identifier. The identifier can be a number or a name.

Qualifiers

There are three qualifiers used in capture filters:

- Type
- Dir
- Proto

Type Qualifier

The type of qualifier indicates what type of name or number to which the identifier refers. For example, in a capture filter for traffic to or from port 53, "port" is the type qualifier. *Host*, *net* and *port* are three type qualifiers.

Dir (Direction) Qualifier

The direction qualifier is used to indicate the flow of traffic in which you are interested. Two commonly used direction qualifiers are *dst* and *src*. If a direction qualifier is not provided, it is assumed that *dst or src* is desired.

Proto (Protocol) Qualifier

The protocol qualifier is used to limit the captured traffic to a particular protocol such as *tcp* or *udp*. An example of using a protocol qualifier would be *udp net 10.2* where *udp* is the protocol qualifier, *net* is the type qualifier and *10.2* is the identifier. If you removed the protocol qualifier and created a capture filter of *net 10.2* then all protocols to or from IP addresses beginning with 10.2 would be captured.

Primitives

Primitive keywords can also be used. The following list defines primitives available for use in capture filters:

- dst host *host*
- src host *host*
- host *host*
- ether dst *ehost*
- ether src *ehost*
- ether host *ehost*
- gateway *host*
- dst net *net*
- src net *net*
- net *net*
- net *net* mask *netmask*
- dst port *port*
- src port *port*
- less *length*
- greater *length*
- ip proto *protocol*
- ip6 proto *protocol*
- ip6 protochain *protocol*
- ip protochain *protocol*
- ip broadcast
- ether multicast
- ip multicast
- ip6 multicast
- ether proto *protocol*
- decnet src *host*
- decnet dst *host*
- decnet host *host*
- ip, ip6, arp, rarp, atalk, aarp, decnet, iso, stp, ipx, netbeui
- lat, moprc, mopdl
- vlan vlan_id
- tcp, udp, icmp
- clnp, esis, isis
- iso proto *protocol*
- *proto[expr:size]*

For more detail on the primitives shown above, refer to the tcpdump man page at *www.tcpdump.org/tcpdump_man.html*. For information on *proto[expr:size]*, refer to *Capture Filter Operator Examples* on page 118.

Filter by a Protocol

Filtering by protocol uses primitives. For example, to filter on all ICMP traffic, the syntax is simply `icmp`. Wireshark interprets this filter as "look at the Protocol field in the IP header for the value 0x01" (the protocol number used to indicate that ICMP is next in the packet). [46]

If a protocol does not have a primitive, you will need to build the filter based on a distinct field value used by that protocol or use a filter based on offsets and byte values.

Common protocol filters are *tcp, udp, ip, arp, icmp* and *ip6*.[47]

Create MAC/IP Address or Host Name Capture Filters

When you want to capture traffic to and/or from a specific network device, base your capture filter on either a hardware address, IP address or host name as shown in the table below.

Capture Filter Syntax	Capture Filter Example	Capture Filter Description
dst host *host*	`dst host www.wireshark.org`	Traffic to the IP address associated with *www.wireshark.org*
dst host *host*	`dst host 67.228.110.120`	Traffic to 67.228.110.120
src host *host*	`src host www.google.cn`	Capture traffic from the IP address associated with *www.google.cn*.
host *host*	`host www.espn.com`	Capture traffic to or from the IP address associated with *www.espn.com*.
ether dst *ehost*	`ether dst 08:3f:3d:03:32:03`	Capture traffic **to** the Ethernet address 08:3f:3d:03:32:03.
ether src *ehost*	`ether src 08:3f:3d:03:32:03`	Capture traffic **from** the Ethernet address 08:3f:3d:03:32:03.
ether host *ehost*	`ether host 08:3f:3d:03:32:03`	Capture traffic **to or from** the Ethernet address 08:3f:3d:03:32:03.

---

[46] ICMP is one of the rare filters that use the same syntax for capture filters and display filters by chance.

[47] This is not a mistake, the capture filter for IPv6 traffic is simply `ip6`.

Capture Filter Syntax	Capture Filter Example	Capture Filter Description
gateway *host*	`gateway rtrmain01`	[Requires that a host name is used and can be found by the local system's name lookup process.] Capture traffic **to or from** the hardware address of `rtrmain01`, but not to the IP address of `rtrmain01`. This filter captures traffic going through the specified router. Another option for creating this using MAC and IP addresses is listed next.
ether host *ehost* **and not** *host*	`ether host 00:13:46:cc:a3:ea and not host 192.168.0.1`	Capture traffic flowing **to or from** the hardware address defined but not **to or from** the IP address defined—this is an alternate to using the `gateway` primitive and more suitable if name resolution is not available—the `ether host <address>` would be the hardware address of the router and the `host <address>` would be the IP address of the router.
dst net *net*	`dst net 192.168`	Capture traffic **to** IP addresses starting with 192.168. This filter will also capture ARP packets that have 192.168.*.* in the Target IP Address field.
src net *net*	`src net 10.2.2`	Capture traffic **from** any IP address starting with 10.2.2. This filter will also capture ARP packets that have 10.2.2.* in the Source IP Address field.
net *net*	`net 130.57`	Capture traffic **to or from** IP addresses starting with 130.57.
net *net* **mask** *netmask*	`net 172.16 mask 255.240.0.0`	Capture traffic **to or from** IP addresses starting with 172.16 through 172.31.
net net/len	`net 172.16/12`	Capture traffic **to or from** IP addresses starting with 172.16 through 172.31.
wlan host *ehost*	`wlan host 00:22:5f:58:2b:0d`	Capture traffic **from** the WLAN source address 00:22:5f:58:2b:0d.

When creating capture filters for addresses, `host` can be defined as a number or a name. For example, `host 67.228.110.120` and `host www.wireshark.org` would capture the same traffic as long as *www.wireshark.org* is resolved to that IP address.

Avoid host Capture Filters When Analyzing Web Browsing Sessions

In Chapter 23: Analyze Hypertext Transfer Protocol (HTTP) Traffic you learn about web site redirection. If you use a capture filter such as host www.espn.com, *Wireshark captures traffic to the IP address associated with that location. If you are redirected to another site, the traffic to the next site won't be captured. It is more effective to use a capture filter for* port 80.

Use a "My MAC" Capture Filter for Application Analysis

When you are analyzing an application, be careful of making assumptions regarding the protocols and ports used by that application. When you run an application on your own system and want to analyze just the traffic to and from your system to identify the traffic generated by that application, use a filter based on your MAC address, not your IP address. This ensures you get all traffic to or from your hardware address including packets that do not have an IP header (such as ARP traffic).

When you are analyzing an application running on another host, consider filtering on the traffic to and from the hardware address of the test system.

An example of a capture filter for your own traffic is ether host 00:21:97:40:74:D2 (if that is your MAC address).

Filter Your Traffic *Out* of a Trace File (Exclusion Filter)

When you are capturing traffic to and from another host on a network, you may want to filter your own traffic out of the trace file so you can browse the internet, send and receive email and continue working in the background while not having your own traffic show up in the trace files. This is called an "exclusion filter" because you are excluding packets from being captured.

In this case you might create a "Not my MAC" filter that captures all traffic except the traffic to or from your hardware address. The syntax for an exclusion filter for a hardware address is not ether host <*ehost*> or ether host 00:21:97:40:74:D2 referencing the example above and shown in Figure 75.

When to Use MAC Capture Filters Instead of IP Address Filters

We recommend creating this filter based on MAC address instead of IP address as IP addresses may change as you move from one network to another. Remember that these MAC address filters only work if you are on the same network as defined in the MAC address filter. MAC address information is stripped off and reapplied by routers.

In Figure 75, we have connected Wireshark to an aggregating tap to analyze traffic to and from Client A. We have created and applied a "Not My MAC" filter to ensure traffic to and from our Wireshark system is not in the trace files. This allows us to browse the Internet while capturing Client A's traffic, but keep our traffic out of the trace file. The filter syntax is not ether host 00:21:97:40:74:D2.

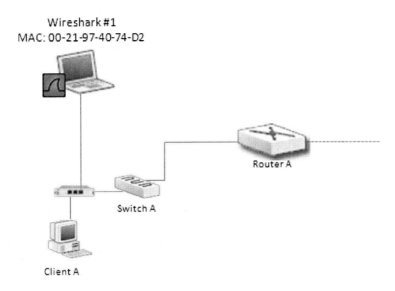

Figure 75. Consider filtering out traffic to or from your MAC address

Capture One Application's Traffic Only

Application filtering is performed using primitives for the port number the application uses. Once you know the port number that your application uses, you can build your capture filter to look for your application traffic over UDP or TCP, focus on one transport type or capture traffic flowing in a single direction.

For example, DNS queries and responses typically run over UDP on port 53. DNS zone transfers, however, run over TCP on port 53.

- To filter on all DNS traffic (UDP and TCP) that use port 53, use the capture filter `port 53`. Since you have not specified a transport, both UDP and TCP traffic will be captured.
- If you are only interested in capturing DNS zone transfers over TCP that use port 53, use the capture filter `tcp port 53`.
- If you are only interested in capturing UDP-based DNS queries and responses that use port 53 (not zone transfers), use the capture filter `udp port 53`.
- If you are interested in capturing DNS responses only, use the capture filter `src port 53` since DNS responses come from port 53.

DNS filtering provides a perfect comparison between the process to create a capture filter and the process to create a display filter. Wireshark understands the common acronym of numerous applications, such as DNS. While you must specify a port number for DNS capture filters, you can simply use `dns` for a display filter.

You can use `portrange` as a quick method to filter on a range of ports. The capture filter `tcp portrange 6881-6999` will capture TCP traffic to or from ports between 6881 and 6999. These are the commonly used ports for BitTorrent Tracker communications.

Use Operators to Combine Capture Filters

There are three primary operators available for capture filters:

- Negation (`!` or `not`)
- Concatenation (`and`)
- Alternation (`or`)

These operators enable you to make more specific capture filters.

If you wanted to expand your DNS filter created earlier to also include an address filter, use an operator.

The capture filter `host 192.168.1.103 and tcp dst 53` will capture all DNS queries (sent to port 53) from 192.168.1.103. When using the "and" operator, packets must match <u>both</u> sides of the operator to pass through the filter.

If you used the "or" operator, the interpretation would be entirely different. When using the "or" operator, each packet must match only one side of the operator to pass through the filter. `host 192.168.1.103 or tcp dst 53` will capture all traffic to or from 192.168.1.103 regardless of the destination ports as well as any traffic sent to port 53 regardless of the IP addresses in use.

Capture Filter Operator Examples

The capture filter `not src net 10.2.0.0/16` only captures traffic to or from IP addresses that do not begin with 10.2. The capture filter `host www.wireshark.org and not port 80 and not port 25` only captures traffic to or from *www.wireshark.org*, but not any traffic to or from ports 80 and 25.

Create Capture Filters to Look for Byte Values

In some cases you may need to create a capture filter that looks for a specific value at a specific offset in the packet. The syntax for byte offset capture filters is `proto [ expr:size ]` where proto is one of `ether, fddi, tr, ip, arp, rarp, tcp, udp, icmp` or `ip6`. "Expr" identifies the offset of the field and "`size`" (optional) defines the length (in bytes) that you are interested in. This is followed by the operator and the value.

For example, perhaps you want to create a capture filter for all TCP packets that contain a TCP window size value of 65,535.

We can see in Figure 76 that the TCP header starts with the value 0x0050. The window size field is 15 bytes from the start of the TCP header. When we count the offsets, we start counting at zero so the offset of the window size field is 14.

To create the filter, we will start with the highest protocol, TCP. Next, we define the offset and the length of the field (optional) followed by the operator and value. The capture filter is `tcp[14:2]` `= 0xffff`. We started at the TCP header and started counting from 0 until we reached the window size field.

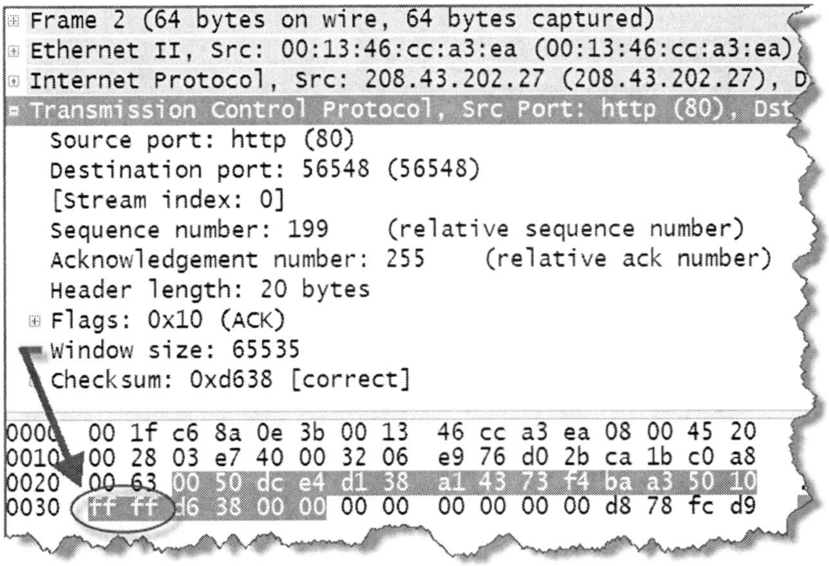

```
⊞ Frame 2 (64 bytes on wire, 64 bytes captured)
⊞ Ethernet II, Src: 00:13:46:cc:a3:ea (00:13:46:cc:a3:ea)
⊞ Internet Protocol, Src: 208.43.202.27 (208.43.202.27), D
⊟ Transmission Control Protocol, Src Port: http (80), Dst
    Source port: http (80)
    Destination port: 56548 (56548)
    [Stream index: 0]
    Sequence number: 199     (relative sequence number)
    Acknowledgement number: 255     (relative ack number)
    Header length: 20 bytes
  ⊞ Flags: 0x10 (ACK)
    Window size: 65535
    Checksum: 0xd638 [correct]

0000  00 1f c6 8a 0e 3b 00 13  46 cc a3 ea 08 00 45 20
0010  00 28 03 e7 40 00 32 06  e9 76 d0 2b ca 1b c0 a8
0020  00 63 00 50 dc e4 d1 38  a1 43 73 f4 ba a3 50 10
0030  ff ff 16 38 00 00 00 00  00 00 00 00 d8 78 fc d9
```

Figure 76. The TCP header decode

The capture filter (`tcp[2:2] > 100 and tcp[2:2] < 150`) captures only the traffic to ports between 100 and 150. The destination port field is located at offset 2 from the start of the TCP header and the field is two bytes long - `tcp[2:2]`. Fortunately, we can simply use `portrange 100-150` for this purpose.

Another example, `wlan[0] = 0x50` captures WLAN probe response packets. This filter is based on the 802.11 Type and Subtype field values that are located at offset 0 in the WLAN header. The length field is optional and not used in this example. Refer to *Analyze Frame Control Types and Subtypes* on page 527.

Manually Edit the Capture Filters File

The capture filters window has some limitations. You cannot sort the capture filters or categorize capture filters. These capabilities are possible by manually editing the *cfilters* file. Figure 77 shows an edited *cfilters* file in the capture filter window.

To manually edit the *cfilters* file, open the file in a text editor. The capture filter syntax is "name" `filter`. Ensure you add a line feed after the last capture filter listed or Wireshark will not display the last filter in the list.

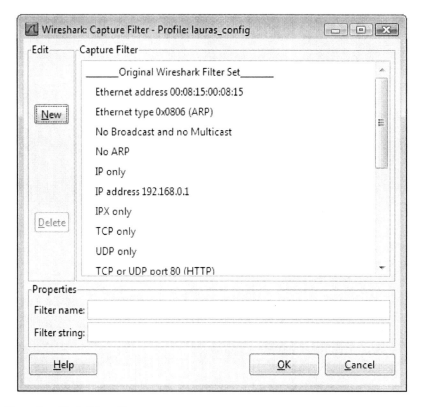

Figure 77. Manually edited cfilters file

The book website (*www.wiresharkbook.com*) contains the following *cfilters* file in the Download section. Consider creating a "Wireshark Book" profile and copying this *cfilters* file into that profile directory. For more information on creating custom Wireshark profiles, refer to *Chapter 11: Customize Wireshark Profiles*.

Sample *cfilters* File

```
"_____Original Wireshark Filter Set_____" Installed with Wireshark
"    Ethernet address 00:08:15:00:08:15" ether host 00:08:15:00:08:15
"    Ethernet type 0x0806 (ARP)" ether proto 0x0806
"    No Broadcast and no Multicast" not broadcast and not multicast
"    No ARP" not arp
"    IP only" ip
"    IP address 192.168.0.1" host 192.168.0.1
"    IPX only" ipx
"    TCP only" tcp
"    UDP only" udp
"    TCP or UDP port 80 (HTTP)" port 80
"    HTTP TCP port (80)" tcp port http
"    No ARP and no DNS" not arp and port not 53
"    Non-HTTP and non-SMTP to/from www.wireshark.org" not port 80 and not
port 25 and host www.wireshark.org
"_____Laura's Wireshark Filter Set_____" Just My Stuff
```

```
"     My MAC (replace w/your MAC Address)" ether host 00:08:15:00:08:15
"     Not My MAC (replace w/your MAC Address)" not ether host
00:08:15:00:08:15
"     ARP or DHCP (Passive Discovery)" arp or port 67 or port 68
"     Broadcasts/Multicasts Only" broadcast or multicast
"     ICMP Only" icmp
"     IPv6 Only" ip6
```

Share Capture Filters with Others

Although the capture filter feature does not include an export or import feature at this time, you can share your capture filters by simply copying the *cfilters* file from one Wireshark system to another.

In order to avoid overwriting the default capture filters, make a backup copy of the *cfilters* file that is in the Global Configuration directory or create a new profile and put the shared capture filters file in that profile directory.

Case Study:
Kerberos UDP to TCP Issue

Submitted by: Thanassis Diogos

Arriving onsite I was given a brief description of a pretty strange problem. The customer was in the middle of Domain migration from Windows NT 4 to Windows 2003 Active Directory. They were using the well known tool for this job called ADMT (Active Directory Migration Tool). This tool was being used to migrate user and other objects from the source NT Domain to the destination. These users were required to use Terminal Services on a Terminal Server located in a perimeter firewall zone and joined to the same Active Directory.

A small number of the users migrated were not able to login and use the Terminal Server and the error message received during logon was "The RPC Server is unavailable". Oh great! As a workaround they found that deleting faulty accounts and recreating them allowed users to login normally. Of course this was not acceptable and I had to find out what was the initial cause of the issue.

Through event viewer and other logs I was not able to find out the real cause, Wireshark was installed locally on Terminal Server and started to monitor traffic.

I used the default capture filter to exclude port 3389/RDP (not port 3389) since I was not interested in Remote Desktop Protocol (RDP) but I was interested in logon traffic. The image below shows what we captured.

Source	Destination	Protocol	Info
10.74.24.29	10.72.100.224	CLDAP	searchRequest(364) "<ROOT>" baseObject
10.72.100.224	10.74.24.29	CLDAP	searchResEntry(364) "<ROOT>" searchResDone
10.74.24.29	10.72.100.224	KRB5	AS-REQ
10.72.100.224	10.74.24.29	KRB5	KRB Error: KRB5KRB_ERR_RESPONSE_TOO_BIG
10.74.24.29	10.72.100.224	TCP	xdtp > kerberos [SYN] Seq=0 Win=64512 Len=
10.74.24.29	10.72.100.224	TCP	xdtp > kerberos [SYN] Seq=0 Win=64512 Len=
Cisco_e6:25:c3	CDP/VTP/DTP/P	CDP	Device ID: Blade_D_U> Port ID: GigabitEth
10.74.24.29	10.72.100.224	TCP	xdtp > kerberos [SYN] Seq=0 Win=64512 Len=
Cisco_e6:25:c3	CDP/VTP/DTP/P	DTP	Dynamic Trunking Protocol
10.74.24.29	10.74.27.20	TDS	Remote Procedure Call Packet
10.74.27.20	10.74.24.29	TDS	Response Packet
10.74.24.29	10.74.27.20	TDS	Remote Procedure Call Packet
10.74.27.20	10.74.24.29	TDS	Response Packet
10.74.24.29	10.74.27.20	TDS	Remote Procedure Call Packet

So in frame No 3 we monitor the AS-REQ normal Kerberos traffic asking for initial authentication, but in frame 4 server responds that "KRB Error: KRB5KRB_ERR_RESPONSE_TOO_BIG" which means that answer cannot fit inside UDP packet which has the limitation of 512 bytes maximum payload for Kerberos traffic.

Using this response, the server is asking our client to switch over to TCP communication. This is exactly what the client does by initiating a TCP 3-way handshake. In frame 5 clients sends a TCP packet with SYN flag enabled but as we can see it resends that packet two more times which is typical TCP behavior.

The answer was quick and easy—the firewall between the host and server was configured to allow only UDP port 88 traffic, but not allow TCP port 88 traffic. The issue appeared only for a number of users because the Kerberos answers containing group memberships were directly affecting the UDP payload size. If the group membership information could not fit inside 512 bytes of space allowed by Kerberos over UDP, it simply switched over to TCP.

I do not think this problem could be solved without any kind of network tracing because events were very general and no other information was available. It's also an example that the solution is not always just "delete, recreate or reboot."

Summary

Capture filters are used to reduce the number of packets captured and therefore allow you to focus in more specifically on traffic of interest. Capture filters use the tcpdump syntax and are not interchangeable with display filters. You cannot apply capture filters to existing trace files and you cannot recover packets that did not match your capture filter already applied.

Capture filters are saved in the *cfilters* file. The default *cfilters* file is located in the Global Configuration directory—if you have added or altered the default capture filters another *cfilters* file will be located in the Personal Configurations folder.

Capture filters can be created based on a protocol, address or specific port number(s). Capture filters consist of Type, Direction and Protocol qualifiers or primitives. You can also define capture filters based on an offset and byte value if desired. Operators such as and, or and not allow you to combine capture filters to be more selective regarding the traffic you capture.

Practice What You've Learned

Download the *cfilters* file from the Download section of the book website, *www.wiresharkbook.com*. Copy this file to your Personal Configurations folder when instructed in the practice exercise below.

Create and Apply a Capture Filter for Your Own Traffic

- Create and save a "My MAC" capture filter based on your own hardware address.
- Start capturing your traffic using this capture filter. Do not touch your keyboard for at least 5 minutes. Did you capture any traffic? The packets would be generated by automated processes running in the background on your computer.
- Try another test—using the My MAC filter, open your browser and access *www.wireshark.org*. Do not navigate through the site—just browse to the main page.
- Stop capturing and examine the traffic you captured. If your browser performs site safety checks or the Wireshark site drops cookies on your drive, it will be visible in your trace file.

Replace your Capture Filter File

- Identify your Personal Configurations folder (**Help | About Wireshark | Folders**).
- Rename the existing *cfilters* file in that folder (if one exists) to *old-cfilters*.
- Copy the sample *cfilters* file from the Download section of the book website, *www.wiresharkbook.com*, to your Personal Configurations folder.
- Restart Wireshark and then select **Capture | Capture Filters**. You should see a customized capture filter set appear.

Review Questions

Q4.1   **What is the difference between capture filters and display filters?**

Q4.2   **What format is used by Wireshark's capture filtering?**

Q4.3   **What is the purpose of the following capture filters?**

```
ether dst 08:3f:3d:03:32:03

gateway rtrmain01

host www.espn.com
```

Answers to Review Questions

Q4.1   **What is the difference between capture filters and display filters?**

A4.1   Capture filters are applied to traffic during the capture process only. Capture filters cannot be applied to existing trace files. Display filters can be used while capturing, but do not limit the packet you capture—display filters only limit what is visible. Display filters can be applied to existing trace files. Each filter type uses a different filter syntax.

Q4.2   **What format is used by Wireshark's capture filters?**

A4.2   Capture filters use the tcpdump filter syntax.

Q4.3   **What is the purpose of the following capture filters?**

A4.3   **`ether dst 08:3f:3d:03:32:03`**

`ether dst 08:3f:3d:03:32:03` captures **all** traffic sent to the Ethernet address 08:3f:3d:03:32:03.

`gateway rtrmain01`

`gateway rtrmain01` captures traffic to or from the hardware address of `rtrmain01`, but not to the IP address of `rtrmain01`. This capture filter requires that a host name is used and can be found by the local system's name lookup process.

`host www.espn.com`

`host www.espn.com` captures traffic to or from the IP address associated with *www.espn.com.*

Chapter 5:
Define Global and Personal Preferences

Wireshark Certified Network Analyst Exam Objectives covered:

- Find Your Configuration Folders
- Set Global and Personal Configurations
- Customize Your User Interface Settings
- Define Your Capture Preferences
- Automatically Resolve IP and MAC Names
- Configure Statistics Settings
- Define ARP, TCP, HTTP/HTTPS and Other Protocol Settings
- Configure Protocol Settings with Right-Click

  ❖ Case Study: The Non-Standard Web Server Setup
  ❖ Summary
  ❖ Practice What You've Learned
  ❖ Review Questions and Answers

Find Your Configuration Folders

Wireshark consists of two types of configuration settings: Global Configurations and Personal Configurations.

Refer to **Help | About Wireshark | Folders**—as shown in Figure 78—to identify the location of Global and Personal Configuration folders. Double-click on any folder title to open the corresponding folder.

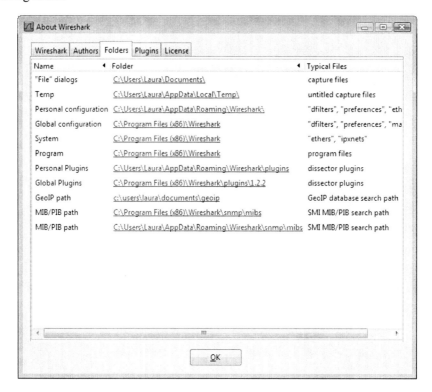

Figure 78. Wireshark folder information

Set Global and Personal Configurations

Wireshark global settings include the following text files:

- cfilters—default capture filters
- *dfilters*—default display filters
- *colorfilters*—default color filters
- *manuf*—default Organizationally Unique Identifier (OUI) list (global)
- *services*—default port list (global)
- *smi-modules*—default MIB modules to load

You can manually edit these global settings. For example, if you want to alter the transport name resolution of traffic on port 4308 because your custom-developed application uses that port, you can edit the *services* file for that entry from `compx-lockview 4308/tcp CompX-LockView` to `ourapp 4308/tcp Our-App`.

If you want to change an OUI value from one manufacturer name to another, simply edit the *manuf* file.

Some of these files, such as *cfilters*, *dfilters* and *colorfilters* can be edited to become personal settings. When you edit one of these files, Wireshark copies the original file from the Global Configuration folder and saves the new version (with your edits) into your Personal Configuration folder. When you make changes to your global preferences (such as Packet List pane columns, protocol settings and name resolution settings), a new *preferences* file is saved in your Personal Configuration folder as well.

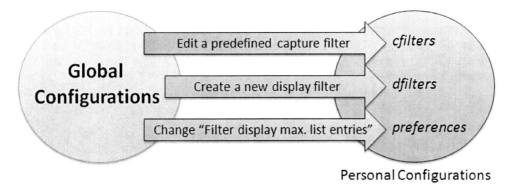

Figure 79. Personal Configuration files are based on Global Configuration files and settings

You can share these files with others by simply sending them the file. The new settings will be available after the receiver places the file(s) in their Personal Configuration folder and restarts Wireshark. Be careful of sharing Personal Configuration files, such as the *preferences* file that contain directory structure information. The directory information may not match the system to which you are copying this configuration information.

In addition, you can create a profile that uses its own configuration files. For example, if you work on WLANs part of the time, you might create a WLAN profile that includes filters, coloring and columns that assist you in analyzing WLAN traffic. For more information on creating and using Profiles, refer to *Chapter 11: Customize Wireshark Profiles*.

When you change global preferences while working in a profile, a new *preferences* file is saved in your profile folder. When you return to the default profile, you are using preferences contained in your Personal Configuration folder, not a profile subdirectory.

For details on each of the global preferences settings, refer to *www.wireshark.org/docs/wsug_html/#ChCustGUIPrefPage*. In this Study Guide we focus on key preference settings only.

Some of the most common global preferences to change include:

- "Open Recent" max list entries
- Pane layout
- Columns in Packet List pane
- Capture—Update list of packets in real time
- Capture—Automatic scrolling in live capture
- Name resolution settings
- Various protocol settings

When you update Wireshark, you are prompted to uninstall the previous version. During the uninstall process you can choose the components that you want to save as shown in Figure 80 (uninstall process on a Windows host).

By default, Wireshark maintains your personal settings during the update process, but overrides the global settings, such as the default *cfilters*, *dfilters*, *colorfilters*, *manuf* and *services* files. After installing Wireshark, consider making a copy of the original *preferences* file in case you need to restore it at some time in the future without going through a reinstallation.

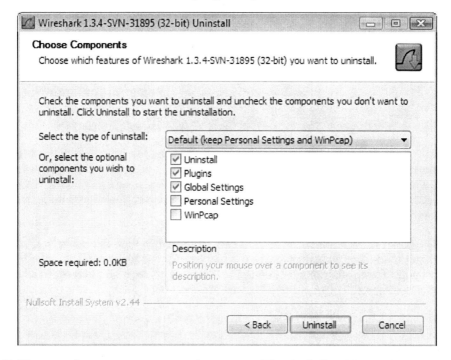

Figure 80. The uninstall options to remove an earlier version of Wireshark (the v1.3.4 development release)

It is important to stay up-to-date with the latest version of Wireshark as dissectors are fixed, features are added and security issues are addressed.

Customize Your User Interface Settings

The User Interface Settings area contains five sections, the main User Interface section, Layout, Columns, Fonts and Colors as shown in Figure 81. Many of these features are covered in the Wireshark online help files. In this section we focus on some of the key settings.

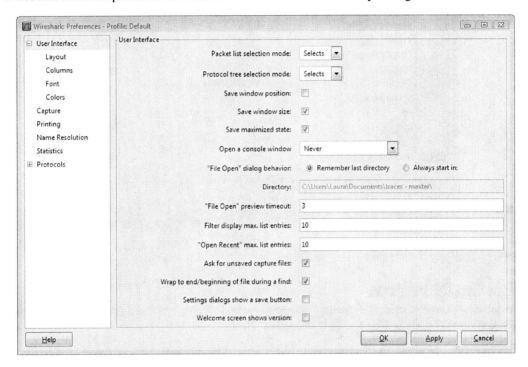

Figure 81. User interface preferences

"File Open" Dialog Behavior

When you select File > Open, Wireshark looks in the directory specified by this setting or in the last directory from which a trace file was opened. Consider creating a *mytraces* directory for all your trace files so you can set Wireshark to always look in this same directory.

Maximum List Entries

There are two "maximum list entries" settings available. The first, "Filter display" controls the number of recently-created display filters that should appear when you click the drop-down arrow next to the display filter field. The second, "Open Recent" controls the number of recently opened trace files that Wireshark displays when you select **File | Open Recent**.

Make Wireshark More Efficient

We move quickly between many, many trace files and constantly apply and clear display filters on our systems. We increase both the filter display list and open recent list values to 30 so Wireshark displays more options when we select File | Open Recent and click the drop-down arrow next to the display filter window. This saves a LOT of time.

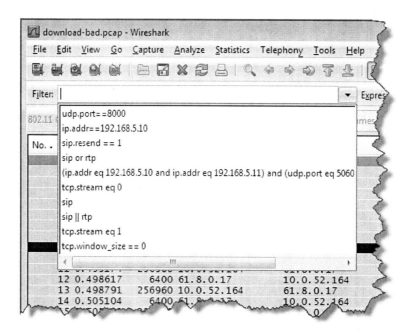

Figure 82. The Display filters max. list entries is set at 10

Pane Configurations

The default Wireshark pane configuration shows three stacked panes including the Packet List pane, the Packet Details pane and the Packet Bytes pane.

Use **View | <pane>** to toggle on or off the various panes. Alter the pane layouts by selecting **Edit | Preferences | User Interface | Layout**.

Columns

The default columns in the Wireshark Packet List pane are:

- No.   Packet number (this value never changes for each packet)
- Time   Setting based on View | Time Display Format setting
- Source   Highest layer source address identified (hardware/network)
- Destination Highest layer destination address identified (hardware/network)
- Protocol   Highest layer protocol identified
- Info   Protocol-specific details for each packet

Wireshark contains numerous pre-defined columns that can be added easily to the Packet List pane. Select **Edit | Preferences | Columns** and select **Add** to choose one of the pre-defined columns to add to the Packet List pane.

In addition, you can right click on a field in the Packet Details pane and select **Apply As Column**.[48] The new column will be added to the right side of the existing columns in the Packet List pane. Right click on a column heading in the Packet List pane to remove, rename, or align columns.

Columns can be reordered by dragging the columns up or down in the Preferences window or by dragging the columns into their new positions directly in the Packet List pane.

Several of the pre-defined columns are listed below:

- 802.1Q VLAN id
- Cisco Dst PortIdx
- Delta time (conversation)
- Destination port
- Fibre Channel OXID
- Frequency/Channel
- IEEE 802.11 TX rate
- Net Dest addr (resolved)

- Absolute data and time
- Cumulative Bytes
- Dest addr (unresolved)
- Expert Info Security
- Frame Relay DLCI
- IEEE 802.11 RSSI
- IP DSCP Value
- Packet length (bytes)

There may be times when you do not have a packet that has the desired column's field so you can't use Apply As Column. In addition, Wireshark may not have a predefined column you can simply select in the Preferences window. In this case, you can still create a custom column.

For example, if you want to create a column that displays the TCP window size field value, select **Edit | Preferences | User Interface | Columns | Add** and choose "**Custom**" in the field type. Enter the name of the field that you want to add a column for.

In Figure 83, we have set up a new column for the `tcp.window_size` field value and moved it to appear after the Time column. Packet 374 has a very low Window Size value—low enough to force the sender to stop sending data until a Window Update has been received. The time column indicates this caused a 2.75+ second delay. For more information on issues related to small window sizes, refer to *Chapter 20: Analyze Transmission Control Protocol (TCP) Traffic*.

Add a TCP Window Size Field Column to Spot Problems

Why is this column useful to add? The TCP window size field indicates the receive window buffer space available. When a host advertises a small or zero window size, network performance can be severely impacted.

In the worst case, this field can be used to perform a Denial of Service attack on a target. In September 2009, Microsoft's Security Bulletin MS09-048 addressed a vulnerability dealing with TCP window size field values. At a customer location, creating a column depicting the Window Size field value enabled us to easily see when Window sizes were unacceptably low.

A Window Size field column can help you spot these types of problems.

---

[48] Apply As Column and the ability to reorder columns directly in the Packet List pane was added in Wireshark v1.3 (development version) and Wireshark v1.4 (stable release).

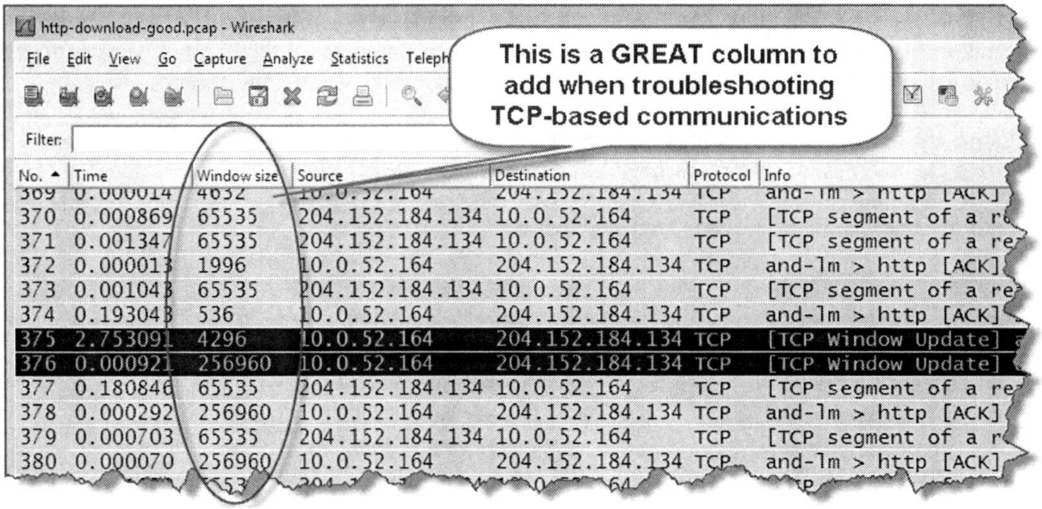

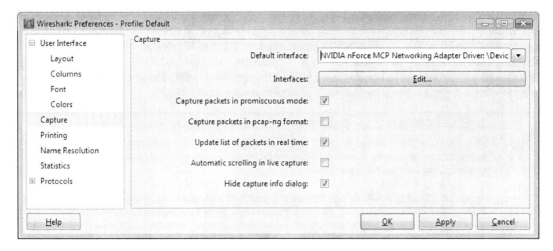

Figure 83. The new column provides fast information about the contents of a field

Define Your Capture Preferences

The capture preferences are used to select a default interface for capture and apply some configuration settings to that interface. Figure 84 shows the capture preferences window with promiscuous mode and real-time packet updates enabled and the capture info dialog hidden.

Figure 84. The Capture preferences window

Select a Default Interface for Faster Capture Launch

Selecting the default interface speeds up the time required to begin packet capture. If this is set for the interface you want to use, just click the **Start Capture** button on the Main Toolbar.

If an interface will never be used for packet capture, select **Edit | Preferences | Capture** and choose **Edit**, as shown in Figure 85. In this example, we have disabled the MS Tunnel Interface Driver which is used for IPv6 compatibility on a Vista 64 host.

Be Careful when Hiding Interfaces

This feature can cause problems if you hide an interface and then, months later, notice the interface missing in Wireshark's interface list (forgetting that you have hidden the interface). If an interface is not listed in the interface list, check the capture preferences.

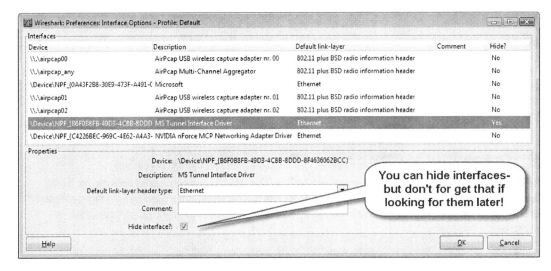

Figure 85. Altering interface settings

Enable Promiscuous Mode to Analyze Other Hosts' Traffic

Promiscuous mode enables an interface to capture packets that are not addressed to the interface's MAC address. In essence, this is the mode that allows analysts to listen in on traffic destined to other hosts on the wired network (refer to Chapter 26 for information about capturing WLAN traffic). Disabling promiscuous mode will limit the capture to packets to or from the local interface only.

The Future Trace File Format: Pcap-ng

Pcap-ng (the "ng" stands for next generation) format is considered an experimental trace file format at this time. Pcap-ng addresses three goals for capture file formats:

- Extensibility
- Portability
- Merge/append data

With these three goals in mind and future development on pcap-ng, meta data may be included with trace files to enhance interpretation and improve efficiency of network analysis processes. For more information about pcap-ng format, visit *www.winpcap.org/ntar/draft/PCAP-DumpFileFormat.html*. To view sample trace files in pcap-ng format, visit *wiki.wireshark.org/Development/PcapNg*.

See the Traffic in Real Time

Enable **Update list of packets in real time** to view the packets as they are captured. This feature allows you to start analyzing right away—while you are capturing. This feature can negatively affect Wireshark performance on a busy network. Consider disabling this feature if the Status Bar indicates Wireshark has dropped packets or you suspect packets have been dropped. For more recommendations for dealing with dropped packets, refer to *Optimize Wireshark* on page 100.

Automatically Scroll During Capture

On a very busy network, you will probably not be able to keep up with the packets as they scroll by quickly on the screen. This feature can be useful if you have applied a capture filter that limits the number of packets captured. It is also useful if you have applied a display filter that limits the number of packets that are displayed. This feature can also negatively affect Wireshark performance on a busy network. Consider disabling automatic scrolling if the Status Bar indicates Wireshark has dropped packets or you suspect packets have been dropped. For more recommendations for dealing with dropped packets, refer to *Optimize Wireshark* on page 100.

Automatically Resolve IP and MAC Names

Wireshark offers many options for name resolution. The most commonly used options are MAC name resolution, transport resolution and network name resolution. The name resolution preferences can severely impact performance in certain situations. Figure 86 shows the name resolution preferences window.

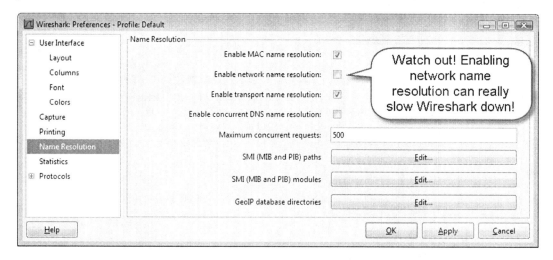

Figure 86. Wireshark name resolution preferences

Resolve Hardware Addresses (MAC Name Resolution)

MAC name resolution resolves the first 3 bytes of the MAC address to the OUI value contained in the *manuf* file in the Wireshark Global Configuration directory.

Wireshark's *manuf* file began as a subset of Michael Patton's "Ethernet Codes Master Page" and includes entries from IEEE's OUI list.

The *manuf* file consists of the three byte OUI value followed by the manufacturer short name and manufacturer long name (commented out) if available, as shown below.

```
00:E0:96      Shimadzu       # SHIMADZU CORPORATION
00:E0:97      CarrierAcc     # CARRIER ACCESS CORPORATION
00:E0:98      Trend
00:E0:99      Samson         # SAMSON AG
00:E0:9A      Positron       # Positron Inc.
00:E0:9B      EngageNetw     # ENGAGE NETWORKS, INC.
```

You can edit the *manuf* file—be certain to use a generic text editor that won't put in extraneous characters in the file.

You can also create an *ethers* file to enable Wireshark to resolve MAC addresses to names. The *ethers* file format is the same as the *hosts* file format. Place this file in your Wireshark Global Configuration or in your Personal Configuration directory. As long as Enable MAC name resolution is set, Wireshark will look for the *ethers* file to resolve MAC addresses.

In Figure 87, Wireshark has resolved two MAC addresses based on the information contained in the *ethers* file (also shown in the figure). ARP packets list the Ethernet address in the Packet List pane Source and Destination columns. TCP and UDP packets show the resolved addresses inside the Packet Details pane.

Using an *ethers* file does not have the same negative impact on performance that you may experience when enabling network name resolution (covered next) because it is a simple file lookup process.

Remember that MAC headers are stripped off and applied as packets cross routers on a network. If you focus on the MAC header addresses, you are only seeing addresses of local devices.

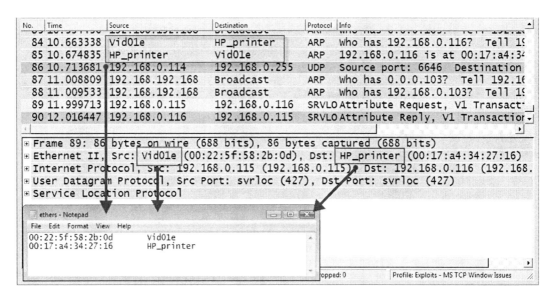

Figure 87. Use an ethers file to resolve MAC addresses

Resolve IP Addresses (Network Name Resolution)

Network name resolution uses a *host* file lookup process or inverse DNS queries (also referred to as Pointer or PTR queries) to resolve IP address to host names.

If network name resolution is enabled you can also enable concurrent DNS resolution and define the maximum concurrent requests for faster name resolution processing as shown in Figure 86.

Network Name Resolution Can Slow Wireshark to a Crawl

Enabling network name resolution when the name server is unavailable or name resolution latency times are high will severely impact Wireshark's performance. If you must use network name resolution, consider creating a hosts file as defined next.

You can create a Wireshark *hosts* file and place it in your Personal Configurations directory to speed up Wireshark's network name resolution process. When you enable network name resolution, Wireshark looks for this *hosts* file before generating DNS PTR queries to a DNS server. The Wireshark *hosts* file syntax is `ipaddress hostname` as shown below.

```
10.1.0.1    rtr01
10.1.0.99   server04
10.1.0.4    Fred
10.1.0.6    Michaela
```

You will need to restart Wireshark before it will recognize the new *hosts* file.

Warnings about Using a Special Wireshark *hosts* File

*Turning on network name resolution often causes undesirable effects (such as flooding the DNS server with DNS PTR queries). You can enable network name resolution and use a Wireshark hosts file as mentioned above, but any IP addresses seen in the trace file that do **not** have a hosts file entry will trigger the DNS PTR query process. Analyze your own traffic after you enable network name resolution and use a hosts file to see if your system still generates DNS PTR queries.*

Resolve Port Numbers (Transport Name Resolution)

The *services* file resides in the Global Configurations directory and contains a list of the port numbers and application/protocol names. The *services* file is a copy of the IANA port number file. You can edit this file using a text editor (as long as the editor does not put extraneous characters in the file). The original IANA file can be found at *www.iana.org/assignments/port-numbers*.

In Figure 87 Wireshark has resolved port 427 to "srvloc" (Service Location Protocol).

Resolve SNMP Information

Your copy of Wireshark must support libSMI to use MIBs and enable the SNMP dissector to resolve the object IDs (OIDs). For more information on Wireshark's handling of SNMP MIBs, refer to *wiki.wireshark.org/SNMP*.

The SNMP SMI (Structure of Management Information) paths setting indicates the path to MIB (Management Information Base) files used to resolve variable numbers to object names in SNMP communications.

The SNMP SMI modules are MIB (Management Information Base) files used to resolve ASN1 (Abstract Syntax Notation 1) numbers to object names in SNMP communications. The *smi-modules* file lists the default MIB modules to load when Wireshark is launched.

The default set of MIBs that load when you launch Wireshark is listed below:

IP-MIB
IF-MIB
TCP-MIB
UDP-MIB
SNMPv2-MIB
RFC1213-MIB
IPV6-ICMP-MIB
IPV6-MIB
SNMP-COMMUNITY-MIB
SNMP-FRAMEWORK-MIB
SNMP-MPD-MIB
SNMP-NOTIFICATION-MIB
SNMP-PROXY-MIB

SNMP-TARGET-MIB

SNMP-USER-BASED-SM-MIB

SNMP-USM-DH-OBJECTS-MIB

SNMP-VIEW-BASED-ACM-MIB

This list only includes the active MIBs. There are over 300 MIBs in Wireshark's \snmp\mibs folder as of Wireshark v1.4. Additional SNMP MIBs can be found at *www.mibdepot.com* or *www.oidview.com/mibs/detail.html*. If Wireshark can't resolve an SNMP MIB object, or OID (Object Identifier), it shows a partially resolved name such as `enterprises.9.9.41.2.0.1`.

In order to enable Wireshark to decode additional MIB information, (1) a MIB file must be created in the proper format and (2) the MIB must be placed in the \snmp\mibs folder (or in the SMI (MIB and PIB) Modules directory that you specify in the name resolution area of Wireshark's preferences). For details on formatting, naming and adding MIBs, refer to *wiki.wireshark.org/SNMP*.

If you are using secure SNMP communications available with SNMPv3, set the username, authentication model, password, privacy protocol, and privacy password in **Edit | Preferences | SNMP**.

Plot IP Addresses on a World Map

IP address mapping capability (GeoIP) was added in Wireshark v1.2[49]. Using the MaxMind databases, you can see IP addresses plotted on a world map. This setting indicates the path to files used to enable MaxMind's GeoIP mapping feature.

In order to use GeoIP, you must download the database files from *geolite.maxmind.com/download/geoip/database/* and point to the location of the files in the GeoIP settings[50].

GeoIP mapping is available from the IP tab in the conversations and endpoints windows. For details on using GeoIP mapping, refer to *List Endpoints and Map* on page 190.

Configure Statistics Settings

There are only two statistics settings—one that defines the tap update interval and another that defines the number of visible channels in the RTP player.

---

[49] You can only use this feature if "with GeoIP" is shown in the *Compiled with* section in **Help | About Wireshark**.

[50] The GeoLite data created by MaxMind is contained in the Download area of the book website, *www.wiresharkbook.com*. Updated versions of these database files are available from *www.maxmind.com*.

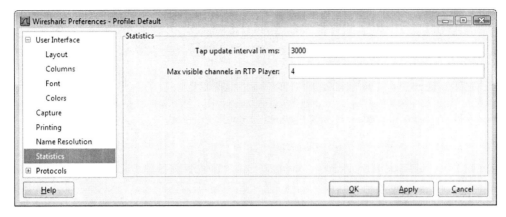

Figure 88. Wireshark statistics preferences

Define ARP, TCP, HTTP/HTTPS and Other Protocol Settings

Many of the protocols and applications interpreted by Wireshark have dissection options that can be changed. Those options could be as simple as changing the default port that an application uses or as complex as defining how dissectors should handle specific types of traffic.

Detect Duplicate IP Addresses and ARP Storms

Figure 89 shows the protocol preferences for the ARP/RARP dissector. Notice that you have the ability to enable detection of ARP storms and detect duplicate IP addresses.

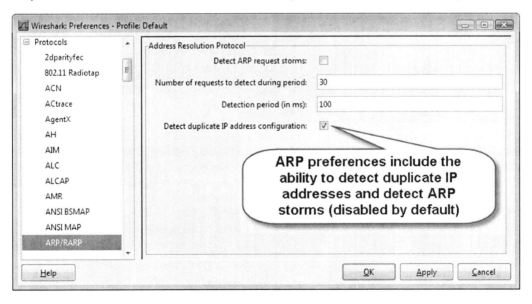

Figure 89. Wireshark protocol preferences

Duplicate IP address detection is on by default. To enable ARP storm detection you must define the number of ARP packets to detect during a specific detection period. When this is enabled as set in Figure 89, Wireshark looks for 30 ARP packets occurring within 100ms before triggering an event.

Define How Wireshark Handles TCP Traffic

One of the most commonly altered protocol preferences is the TCP dissector configuration, as shown in Figure 90. You can alter many key TCP dissector behaviors, such as:

- turn off TCP checksum validation
- analyze TCP sequence numbers (very helpful when troubleshooting)
- use relative sequence numbers and window scaling (also very helpful when troubleshooting)

Refer to *Chapter 20: Analyze Transmission Control Protocol (TCP) Traffic* for more details on TCP relative sequence numbers and window scaling.

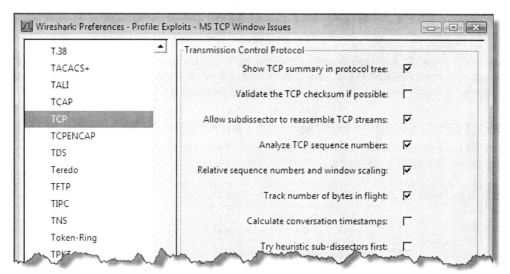

Figure 90. The TCP preference settings

One setting that you may find yourself turning on and off at times is the **Allow subdissector to reassemble TCP streams** setting. For example, for the clearest view of HTTP traffic in the Packet List pane, disable Allow subdissector to reassemble TCP streams to see the HTTP GET requests and the HTTP response codes in the Packet List pane. When you are working with HTTPS traffic, however, enable this setting to see and filter on all four SSL/TLS handshake packets. For more information on using this setting, refer to *Allow Subdissector to Reassemble TCP Streams* on page 391.

Set Additional Ports for HTTP and HTTPS Dissection

In the HTTP protocol preferences, you can add other ports that you might use for HTTP or HTTPS (SSL/TLS) traffic. For example, if you are running your HTTP server on port 3880, simply add this port number to the TCP ports list in the HTTP preferences area. For more details on working with HTTP/HTTPS traffic and settings, refer to *Chapter 23: Analyze Hypertext Transfer Protocol (HTTP) Traffic.*

Enhance VoIP Analysis with RTP Settings

In the RTP protocol preferences, you can configure the Wireshark RTP (Realtime Transport Protocol) dissector to try to decode RTP outside of conversations. This means that if you did not capture the call setup process (such as Session Initiation Protocol, SIP), Wireshark still examines the traffic to identify and decode RTP streams. This is an excellent setting to enable if Wireshark often cannot decode your RTP traffic. For more details on working with VoIP traffic, refer to *Chapter 27: Introduction to Voice over IP (VoIP) Analysis.*

Configure Wireshark to Decrypt SSL Traffic

In the SSL protocol preferences, you can define how SSL reassembly should work and enter one or more RSA keys to decrypt the SSL traffic detected by Wireshark. Wireshark can only decrypt SSL traffic if it is configured properly to reference an RSA key. Wireshark cannot be used to obtain the key. For more information on decrypting SSL traffic, refer to *Analyze HTTPS* on page 461.

Configure Protocol Settings with Right-Click

If you want to quickly change protocol settings while examining a packet, right click on a protocol section in the Packet Details pane (e.g., Ethernet, IP, TCP and HTTP). Select **Protocol Preferences** and set the value or toggle the setting on or off.

In Figure 91 we right clicked on the TCP summary line and selected Protocol Preferences. Preferences set this way are permanent and will be available again when you reload another trace file or restart Wireshark.

This is the fastest way to change protocol preferences for Wireshark.

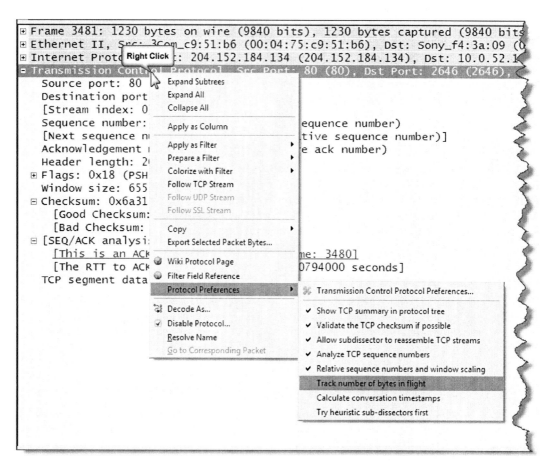

Figure 91. You can set protocol preferences by right clicking on the protocol in the Packet Details pane and selecting Protocol Preferences

Case Study:
The Non-Standard Web Server Setup

At one customer location they had configured a number of internal web servers to offer corporate information to all the employees, act as test servers, provide a site for uploading and downloading support files between departments, etc. The IT team had configured these servers with HTTP daemons running on unusual port numbers—from port number 159 to port 266.

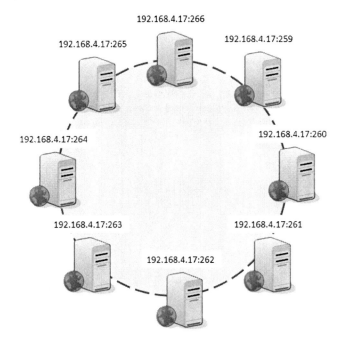

When the IT team is called in to troubleshoot communications to any one of these servers, Wireshark won't dissect the traffic as HTTP traffic.

To fix this problem, the team created a personal preference setting for HTTP traffic that included the additional port numbers they used for their HTTP traffic as shown in the next figure. Once Wireshark was configured with these additional ports, the IT team could easily dissect all the traffic to these servers as HTTP traffic.

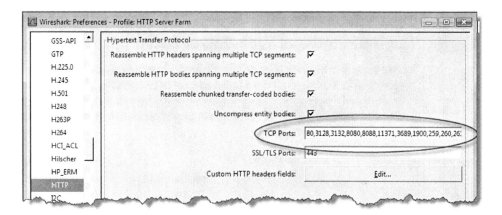

Because this IT team moved to many different branch offices and even partner companies, they decided to save this configuration in a profile so they could easily revert back to the default settings in case other traffic used those ports.

Summary

Wireshark can and should be customized for more efficient troubleshooting and security analysis.

You can customize the Wireshark interface, capture preferences, capture/display filters, packet colorization, name resolution processes, dissector behavior and more.

Various default settings are maintained in the Global Configurations directory while personal settings are maintained in the Personal Configurations folder. Additional confirmation information is saved in profile directories as well.

Locate your Global and Personal Configurations folders through **Help | Wireshark | Folders**.

Practice What You've Learned

 Download the trace files available in the Download section of the book website, *www.wiresharkbook.com*. You will use some of these trace files as you practice what you've learned in this chapter.

Customize Your User Interface

- Select **Edit | Preferences** and set your "Open Recent" max list entries value to 30.
- In the same area, set your **Filter display max. list entries** to 30.
- Select **Columns** and click the **Add** button. Name your column "*DSCP*". In the Field type list, select **IP DSCP Value**. Click and drag your new column to the row below the Time column.
- In the Layout section, add your name to the **Custom window title (prepend to existing titles)** field. Click **OK**. (This configuration will require a Wireshark restart to take effect.)
- Check your customization—you should see a new column for DSCP. Open *voip-extension.pcap* to see a communication that uses varying values in this field.

Add, Edit and Remove Custom Columns in the Packet List Pane

The column you created above is not a custom column—it was a built-in column available in the column field type list. You can create custom columns based on the fields in a packet.

- Open *tcp-winscaling-good.pcap*.
- Select any of the packets and expand the TCP header in the Packet Details pane.
- Right click on the **Window Size** field in the TCP header and choose **Apply as Column**.[51] Click on the new column's heading in the Packet List pane and drag the column to the right of the DSCP column.

---

[51] The **Apply as Column** feature was not available prior to Wireshark v1.3 (Development Release) and Wireshark v1.4 (Stable Release). Stay up-to-date with Wireshark releases at www.wireshark.org/download.

The following lists the trace files we worked with in this section. Both trace files are available on the book website, *www.wiresharkbook.com.*

voip-extension.pcap

This VoIP communication begins with a SIP call setup process. The call is directed to the VoIP server (operator). Later in the trace file the user enters extension 204. This was just a test call. If Wireshark does not recognize the RTP traffic, set the RTP preferences to decode RTP outside of conversations.

tcp-winscaling-good.pcap

Now this is the life! The client advertises a TCP window scale of 2 (multiply the window value by 4) and the server supports window scaling as well (although with a window scale of 0 which does it no good on the receive side of things). Check out Wireshark's ability to calculate the correct window size (packet 3) for the client. This is a feature you can turn on/off in the **Preferences | TCP** area.

Review Questions

Q5.1 How does Wireshark's network name resolution use DNS to associate an IP address with a host name?

Q5.2 Why would you want to alter Wireshark's preference settings?

Q5.3 What is the difference between a global preference and a personal preference setting?

Answers to Review Questions

Q5.1   **How does Wireshark's network name resolution use DNS to associate an IP address with a host name?**

A5.1   If network name resolution is enabled, Wireshark looks for a Wireshark *hosts* file first. If no Wireshark *hosts* file exists or the file does exist but does not have the desired information in it, Wireshark sends an inverse query to the DNS server to resolve the IP address. If this process is unsuccessful, Wireshark cannot resolve the IP address for a host name.

Q5.2   **Why would you want to alter Wireshark's preference settings?**

A5.2   You may want to alter Wireshark's preference settings to customize Wireshark for your network environment. These settings include the panes displayed in the main Wireshark window, capture settings, the name resolution processes, individual dissector behavior, etc.

Q5.3   **What is the difference between a global preference and a personal preference setting?**

A5.3   Global preferences are system-wide preferences. Personal preferences define customized Wireshark behavior and override the global preferences.

Chapter 6: Colorize Traffic

Wireshark Certified Network Analyst Exam Objectives covered:

- Use Colors to Separate Traffic
- Share and Manage Coloring Rules
- Identify Why a Packet is a Certain Color
- Color Conversations to Distinguish Them
- Temporarily Mark Packets of Interest
- Alter Stream Reassembly Coloring

  ❖ Case Study: Colorizing SharePoint Connections During Login
  ❖ Summary
  ❖ Practice What You've Learned
  ❖ Review Questions and Answers

Use Colors to Separate Traffic

Colorization can be a very effective tool to locate and highlight packets of interest. You can choose to colorize packets that indicate error conditions, contain evidence of a network scan or breached host, etc.

Wireshark contains several predefined coloring rules in the default coloring rules file (*colorfilters*) that resides in the Global Configurations directory. When you edit the coloring rules file, the new *colorfilters* file is saved in your Personal Configurations directory. If you create and work in a new profile, another *colorfilters* file is saved in that profile's directory.

The following table lists some of the predefined coloring rule string values.

Coloring Rule String	Description
`tcp.analysis.flags`	**Bad TCP (TCP retransmissions, out-of-order packets, duplicate ACKs, etc.)**
`hsrp.state !=8 && hsrp.state != 16`	**HSRP State Change (Hot Standby Router Protocol state changes)**
`stp.type == 0x80`	**Spanning Tree Topology Change**
`ospf.msg !=1`	**OSPF State Change (routing state changes)**
`icmp.type eq 3 || icmp.type eq 4 || icmp.type eq 11 || icmp.type eq 5`	**ICMP errors (ICMP destination unreachable, Source Quench, Redirect and Time Exceeded messages)**
`arp`	**ARP (all ARP traffic)**
`icmp`	**ICMP (all ICMP traffic; the ICMP errors colorization takes precedence because it is higher in the color rules list)**
`tcp.flags.reset eq 1`	**TCP RST (TCP connection refusal or termination packets)**
`ip.ttl < 5`	**Low TTL (packets that contain an IP header Time-to-Live value less than 5)**

Coloring rules require a name, a string (based on the display filter format), a foreground color and a background color.

Turn on and off colorization using the **Colorize Packet List** button on the Main Toolbar or select **View | Colorize Packet List**. Define coloring rules using the **Coloring Rules** button or select **View | Coloring Rules**. There is also an icon on the Main Toolbar to enable/disable colorization.

Coloring Rules are Processed in Order Top to Bottom

Coloring rules are processed in order from top to bottom. For example, using the default coloring rules, an HTTP packet that contains a TCP retransmission will be processed by the Bad TCP coloring rule, not the HTTP rule because the Bad TCP coloring rule is listed above the HTTP coloring rule.

Share and Manage Coloring Rules

You can easily share coloring rules using the Import or Export buttons in the Coloring Rules window. When you export a coloring rule, Wireshark prompts you for a file name. Wireshark uses the name *colorfilters* as the default name. If you want to share these rules with other users, consider using this name. In addition, you can delete or simply disable coloring rules.

One coloring rule you may consider disabling is Checksum Errors as shown in Figure 92. Disabling this coloring rule when you are analyzing traces taken on a system that uses checksum offloading (defined in *Chapter 3: Capture Traffic*).

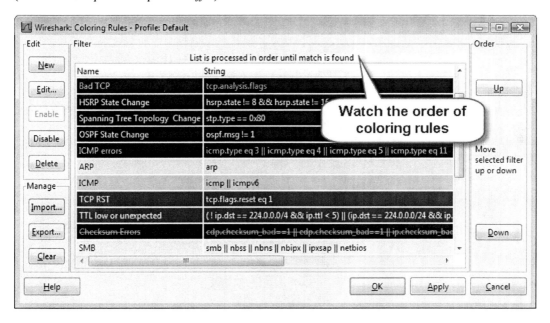

Figure 92. Coloring rules can be disabled

Identify Why a Packet is a Certain Color

To determine why a packet is colored a certain way, examine its frame section in the top of the Packet Details pane.

In Figure 93 we have expanded the frame section of the packet. This packet is colored based on a coloring rule named TCP SYN/FIN that uses the string `tcp.flags & 0x02 || tcp.flags.fin == 1` (only the SYN bit is set to 1 or the FIN bit is set to 1).

Although coloring rules are not actual fields in a packet, you can still filter on them. Right click on either the coloring rule name or the coloring rule string to create a display filter based on these two elements.

```
Frame 11 (74 bytes on wire, 74 bytes captured)
    Arrival Time: Apr  4, 2006 09:31:22.572592000
    [Time delta from previous captured frame: 0.062928000 seconds]
    [Time delta from previous displayed frame: 0.062928000 seconds]
    [Time since reference or first frame: 0.192846000 seconds]
    Frame Number: 11
    Frame Length: 74 bytes
    Capture Length: 74 bytes
    [Frame is marked: False]
    [Protocols in frame: eth:ip:tcp]
    [Coloring Rule Name: TCP SYN/FIN]
    [Coloring Rule String: tcp.flags & 0x02 || tcp.flags.fin == 1]
 Ethernet II, Src: Dell_be:9d:fd (00:14:22:be:9d:fd), Dst: Sony_f4:3a:
     Internet Protocol, Src: 10.1.0.1 (10.1.0.1)
```

Figure 93. Frame details include coloring rule information

Color Conversations to Distinguish Them

There are 10 temporary coloring options for conversations. Right click on a packet in the Packet List pane and select **Colorize Conversation**. Choose the conversation protocol to temporarily color a specific conversation as shown in Figure 94. The coloring rule remains in effect the next time you open the trace file, but it will not be in effect when you restart Wireshark.

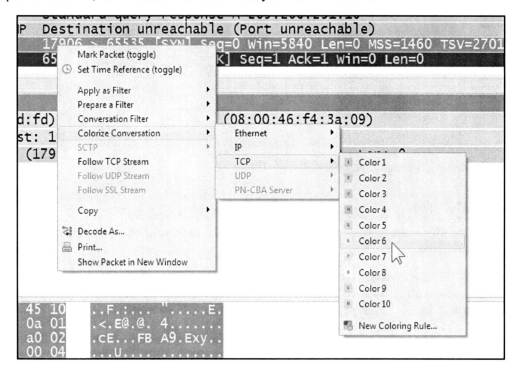

Figure 94. Right click on a packet to select it for colorization

To remove the conversation colorization, select **View | Reset Coloring 1-10**.

Temporarily Mark Packets of Interest

You can mark packets by right clicking on the packet and selecting **Mark Packet (toggle)**. Unmark the packet using the same step. Packet marking is useful to temporarily identify packets of interest.

You can also use several accelerator keys (keyboard shortcuts) to mark packets and move between marked packets.

Ctrl+M	Mark Packet (toggle)
Shift+Ctrl+N	Find Next Marked Packet
Shift+Ctrl+B	Find Previous Marked Packet

By default, Wireshark colors marked packets with a black background and white foreground. You can change the default coloring in **Edit | Preferences | Colors** as shown in Figure 96.

Use Packet Marking to Save Non-Contiguous Packets

Marking packets also allows you to save specific non-contiguous packets or ranges of packets between marked packets. For example, if you want to save packets 1, 3, 7 and 9 of a trace file, simply mark those packets. When saving the trace file, select to save only the marked packets.

The option for saving marked packets is shown in Figure 95. In this figure, Wireshark indicates that we have marked four packets. We have selected to save just those marked packets.

To clear marking, select **Edit | Unmark All Packets** or click the **Reload** button on the Main Toolbar.

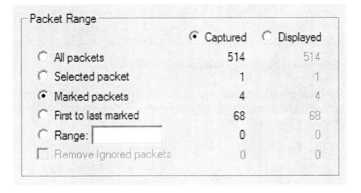

Figure 95. Use marked packets in the save process

Alter Stream Reassembly Coloring

When you right click on a packet and select Follow UDP stream, TCP or SSL streams, the streams are colorized to identify packets sent from a client (the device initiating the connection or conversation) and packets sent a server. For more information on following UDP, TCP or SSL streams, refer to *Chapter 10: Follow Streams and Reassemble Data.*

You can change the stream coloring using Edit | Preferences | User Interface | Colors as shown in Figure 96. Although only the stream coloring lists "Sample TCP stream client text" and "Sample TCP stream server text," these colors are also used for UDP stream reassembly and SSL stream reassembly—the setting can be interpreted simply as "stream client text" (the host that sent the first packet in the stream) and "stream server text" (the host that received the first packet in the stream).

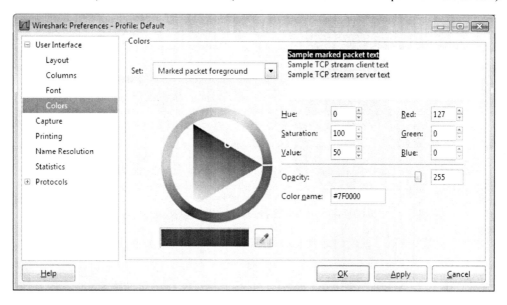

Figure 96. Stream coloring is defined through preferences

By default, a light red background and red font identify traffic sent by the client and light blue background and blue font identify traffic sent by the server. [52]The separate parts of a reassembled TCP stream are marked in Figure 97.

---

[52] You cannot tell the coloring difference because this book is printed in grey scale—why not open up Preferences | Colors and look for yourself?

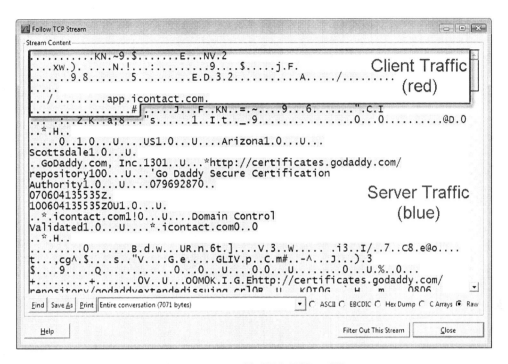

Figure 97. Stream coloring is seen when you reassemble UDP, TCP or SSL streams

Case Study:
Colorizing SharePoint Connections During Login

Colorization can help in the analysis of very complex communications. For example, SharePoint networks use numerous connections and numerous port numbers. Wading through the communications from a SharePoint client can be overwhelming and rekindle that "needle in the haystack" feeling.

During a recent onsite analysis and training session we analyzed a login sequence from a host that was a SharePoint client. In order to distinguish between the various connections made from the client, we systematically colorized the various conversations to tell them apart.

This colorization helped us quickly see which connections were established first and which connections had problems. We could slowly filter out conversations that didn't have problems—we were left with the conversations that we needed to focus on. Do a bit of "googling" to see how many ports are used in a typical SharePoint environment.

Summary

Colorization can be used to distinguish separate conversations, specific packet types and unusual traffic. A set of predefined coloring rules is included with Wireshark. Create custom coloring rules to improve your ability to identify unusual traffic in your analysis environment.

The predefined coloring rules are maintained in the *colorfilters* file in the Wireshark Global Preferences directory. New or customized coloring filter settings are maintained in the *colorfilters* file in your Personal Configuration folder. You can import, export and clear (return to default) your coloring rules.

Coloring rules are automatically applied to each packet as it is displayed (if packet coloring is enabled). Other colorization, such as conversation colorization and marked packets are applied on a temporary basis only. To identify the coloring rule applied to any packet, expand the Frame information in the Packet Details pane and examine the **[Coloring Rule Name]** and **[Coloring Rule String]** sections.

You can mark packets of interest and save just the subset of marked packets, if desired. You do not have the option to save packets based on any other colorization.

Reassembled UDP, TCP and SSL streams are colorized based on the Preferences settings. By default, data sent from clients is red and data from servers is blue. If desired, this can be changed.

Practice What You've Learned

Download the trace files available in the Download section of the book website, *www.wiresharkbook.com*. Use these trace files to complete the practice exercises that follow.

Deal with Checksum Offloading

- Open *ip-checksum-invalid.pcap*. Ensure packet coloring is enabled. Packets from 10.2.110.167 appear with a black background and a red foreground. Open the Frame section to examine the Coloring Rule Name and Coloring Rule String that these packets match.

- This trace was captured at 10.2.110.167. Since this communication appears to have worked properly, we can assume that the checksums were not incorrect when they went out on the network. This host uses checksum offloading (also referred to as task offloading).

- Open **View | Coloring Rules** and select the **Checksum Errors** coloring rule. Click **Disable** and then **OK**.

- What coloring rule does the traffic match now?

Separate Conversations using Colorization

Open *http-aol.pcap*. This trace file contains 18 separate TCP connections. We will use this trace file to practice colorizing traffic to help identify separate conversations in a single trace file.

- The first packet is a TCP handshake packet (SYN). Right click on **packet 1** in the Packet List pane and select **Colorize Conversation | TCP | Color 1**.

- Follow the same coloring process for the next TCP conversation that starts at packet 10—assign Color 2 to that conversation.

- Continue coloring the conversations each time you see a SYN packet.

- After you have colorized five separate conversations, scroll through the trace file. You should be able to see the separation between the conversations much easier now that they are colorized.

- Select **File | Close** to close the trace file.

- Open *http-1.pcap*—do you see your colorization in this trace file?

- Open *http-aol.pcap* again. Is your coloring still there? Your coloring will be lost if you restart Wireshark or select **View | Reset Coloring 1-10**.

Mark and Save Packets of Interest

In this exercise we want to create a new trace file that only contains packets that have the HTTP GET command in them. In addition, you want to include the first two packets of just two TCP connections to use as a snapshot of round trip latency time to the *www.aol.com* server.

- Using the same trace file, *http-aol.pcap*, apply the following display filter:

- `http.request.method == "GET"`

- How many packets matched your filter? You should see 57 packets.

- Select **Edit | Mark All Displayed Packets**. All the packets that contain the HTTP GET command should now be marked with a black background and white foreground. Click **Clear** to remove the display filter. Scroll through the trace file to see your marked packets.

- Right click on **packet 1** and choose **Mark Packet**. Perform the same steps for packet 2, packet 10 and packet 11.

- Select **File | Save As**. Your Packet Range area should look like the image below. Select **Marked Packets** and name your new file *get-syns.pcap*. Click **Save**. You now have created a new trace file containing the 57 packets plus the 4 additional packets you marked for a total of 61 packets.

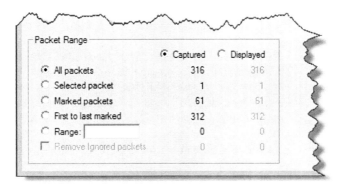

Clear your filter before opening the next trace file.

Add a Custom Coloring Rule for Packets Containing FTP Passwords

- Open *ftp-putfile.pcap*.
- Select **View | Coloring Rules** and click **New**.
- Enter the name **FTP PASS**. Enter `ftp.request.command == "PASS"` as the string (be sure to include the quotes around PASS in the string area).
- Define a red background and a white foreground. Click **OK**.
- Click the **Up** button multiple times to move your filter up to the top of the color filter list. Click **OK**. If your coloring rule worked correctly, packet 13 should be colorized with a red background and white foreground.

The following table provides more information about the two trace files we worked with in this section and lists additional trace files for practice.

ip-checksum-invalid.pcap	This is a classic case of checksum offloading (aka task offloading). We are capturing traffic on 10.2.110.167 and all traffic from that source appears to have invalid checksums. Open the Packet Details pane and look at which headers have invalid checksums. How do we know the checksums must be valid on the wire? Easy—the HTTP web browsing session was successful. Consider disabling the Checksum Errors coloring filter.
http-aol.pcap	It takes 18 different TCP connections to load the *www.aol.com* website. Have you analyzed the connection to your corporate website lately?
ftp-putfile.pcap	The client uses the STOR command during an active FTP connection. Note the Wireshark decode of the PORT command packets (packet 16) (packet 37) (packet 55) (packet 71). What data is being transferred across the secondary connections established by the server? Refer to *Chapter 24: Analyze File Transfer Protocol (FTP)*.

ip-127guy.pcap

This trace depicts an actual host that sends traffic to 127.0.0.1—something is terribly wrong with this host. Can you tell what application is triggering this traffic? Perhaps the application should be examined. Consider building a "butt-ugly" coloring rule for all traffic sent to 127.x.x.x.

tcp-window-frozen.pcap

A window frozen condition can kill file transfer speed. Set the Time Display Format to Seconds Since Beginning of Capture and right click on the first **ZeroWindow** packet (packet 30) to Set Time Reference. How much time did this condition waste? Consider building a coloring rule for all TCP packets that have a window size lower than 1460.

Review Questions

Q6.1   What is the difference between marking packets and applying a coloring rule?

Q6.2   How do you share coloring rules with other Wireshark users?

Q6.3   You have created a coloring rule for ICMP Type 3 traffic as shown in the figure below. How can you ensure that ICMP Type 3 packets are colored with this new rule?

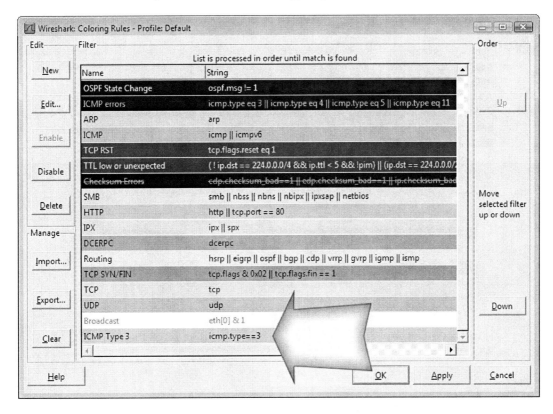

Answers to Review Questions

Q6.1   **What is the difference between marking packets and applying a coloring rule?**

A6.1   Packet marking is a temporary designation that is cleared when you reload the trace file, open the trace file again or toggle the packet marking off. Coloring rules are automatically applied to the traffic each time you open the trace file (if coloring is enabled).

Q6.2   **How do you share coloring rules with other Wireshark users?**

A6.2   By default, coloring rules are contained in the *colorfilters* file. This file can be copied to another Wireshark system. In addition, you can use the export and import feature in the coloring rules window to save the coloring rules file by another name and load it on another Wireshark system.

Q6.3   **You have created a coloring rule for ICMP Type 3 traffic as shown in the figure on the previous page. How can you ensure that ICMP Type 3 packets are colored with this new rule?**

A6.3   Coloring rules are processed in order from top to bottom. In order to have ICMP Type 3 packets colored as defined by the ICMP Type 3 color filter you created, move that color filter above the ICMP errors color filter as shown in the image below.

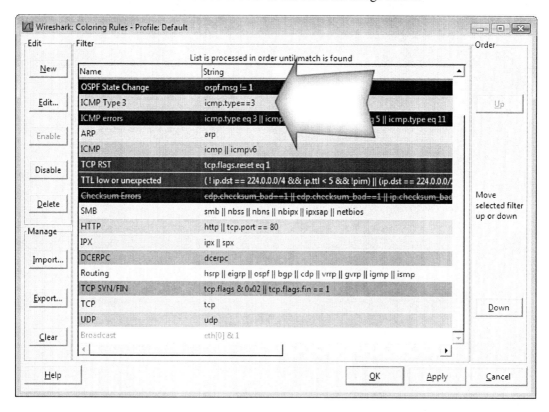

Chapter 7:
Define Time Values and Interpret Summaries

Wireshark Certified Network Analyst Exam Objectives covered:

- Use Time to Identify Network Problems
- Understand How Wireshark Measures Packet Time
- Choose the Ideal Time Display Format
- Deal with Time Accuracy and Resolution Issues
- Identify Delays with Time Values
- Create Additional Time Columns
- Measure Packet Arrival Times with a Time Reference
- Identify Client, Server and Path Delays
- View a Summary of Traffic Rates, Packet Sizes and Overall Bytes Transferred

Use Time to Identify Network Problems

When troubleshooting slow network communications, it is important to focus on the time column. Slow network performance can be due to high latency, access errors, excessive number of packets required to obtain data or a number of other causes.

When poor performance is due to delays in the communications, look for large gaps in time between a request and acknowledgement, an acknowledgement and a response, etc.

Understand How Wireshark Measures Packet Time

During the capture process, Wireshark gets the timestamps from the libpcap/WinPcap library. This library gets the timestamp from the operating system kernel. When you save a trace file, the packet timestamps are saved with that file so packet arrival time can be displayed when the file is opened.

The pcap file format consists of a record header for each packet. These record headers contain a 4-byte value that defines the timestamp of that packet in seconds since January 1, 1970 00:00:00 Coordinated Universal Time (UTC). This field is followed by another 4-byte value defining the microseconds since that point in time. The time zone and current time setting of the capturing host is used in defining the packet timestamp.

Note that packets captured using the pcap file formats cannot define nanosecond timestamp values. This feature is included in pcap-ng which is documented at *wiki.wireshark.org/Development/PcapNg*.

For more details on the pcap file format, refer to *wiki.wireshark.org/Development/LibpcapFileFormat*.

Choose the Ideal Time Display Format

Wireshark offers six time settings. Each time setting offers a different view of the timestamp value associated with each packet captured. Figure 98 shows the options available for the Time column setting.

Select **View | Time Display Format** to define the time column setting. If you prefer to see more than one time column at a time, you can add a column to the Packet List pane, as explained in *Create Additional Time Columns* on page 172.

It is recommended that you synchronize your system time using Network Time Protocol (NTP) to ensure timestamp accuracy.

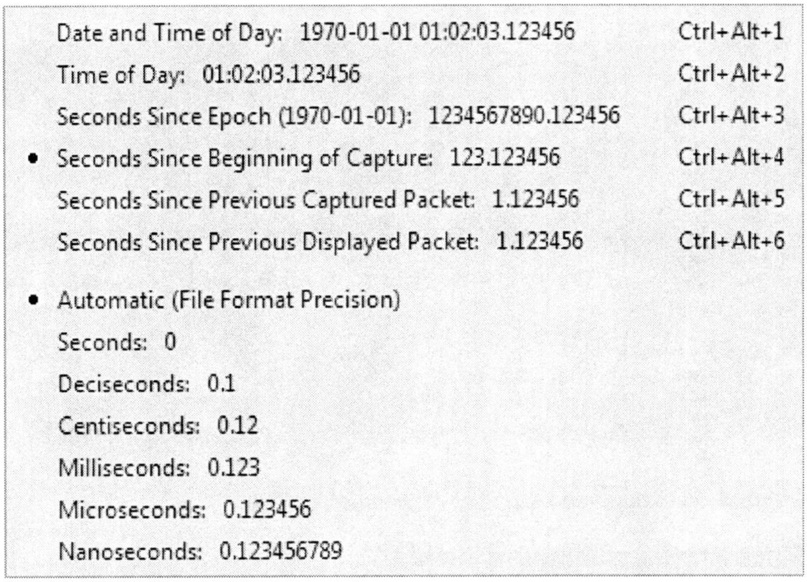

Date and Time of Day: 1970-01-01 01:02:03.123456	Ctrl+Alt+1
Time of Day: 01:02:03.123456	Ctrl+Alt+2
Seconds Since Epoch (1970-01-01): 1234567890.123456	Ctrl+Alt+3
• Seconds Since Beginning of Capture: 123.123456	Ctrl+Alt+4
Seconds Since Previous Captured Packet: 1.123456	Ctrl+Alt+5
Seconds Since Previous Displayed Packet: 1.123456	Ctrl+Alt+6
• Automatic (File Format Precision)	
Seconds: 0	
Deciseconds: 0.1	
Centiseconds: 0.12	
Milliseconds: 0.123	
Microseconds: 0.123456	
Nanoseconds: 0.123456789	

Figure 98. Time Display Format options

Date and Time of Day/Time of Day Setting

The Date and Time of Day and Time of Day options display the local time. If your local host time is off when you capture packets, the incorrect information will be saved with your trace file.

Seconds Since Epoch

Epoch time may rarely be used, but it is interesting. An epoch is a selected instance in time. Wireshark's Seconds since Epoch time is measured since January 1, 1970, which is also referred to as UNIX time.

Seconds Since Beginning of Capture

Seconds since Beginning of Capture is the default time setting for Wireshark. The first packet in the time column is set to a time value of 0. All other packet timestamps are measured in comparison to that first packet. In Figure 99, using this time setting we can see that packet 9 (the Window Update packet) occurs .335007 seconds after the connection setup began in packet 1.

This is an appropriate setting if your trace includes a single transaction, such as the process of loading a website.

No. ▲	Time	Source	Destination	Protocol	Info
1	0.000000	10.0.52.164	61.8.0.17	TCP	ads > http [SYN] Seq
2	0.167521	61.8.0.17	10.0.52.164	TCP	http > ads [SYN, ACK
3	0.167556	10.0.52.164	61.8.0.17	TCP	ads > http [ACK] Seq
4	0.169750	10.0.52.164	61.8.0.17	HTTP	GET /openoffice/stab
5	0.325404	61.8.0.17	10.0.52.164	TCP	http > ads [ACK] Seq
6	0.327342	61.8.0.17	10.0.52.164	TCP	[TCP segment of a re
7	0.335186	61.8.0.17	10.0.52.164	TCP	[TCP segment of a rea
8	0.335492	10.0.52.164	61.8.0.17	TCP	ads > http [ACK] Seq
9	0.335607	10.0.52.164	61.8.0.17	TCP	[TCP Window Update]
10	0.492885	61.8.0.17	10.0.52.164	TCP	[TCP segment of a r
11	0.493174	10.0.52.164	61.8.0.17	TCP	ads > http [ACK] Seq
12	0.498617	61.8.0.17	10.0.52.164	TCP	[TCP segment of a re
13	0.498791	10.0.52.164	61.8.0.17	TCP	ads > http [ACK] Se
14	0.505104	61.8.0.17	10.0.52.164	TCP	[TCP segment of a r
15	0.505252	10.0.52.164	61.8.0.17	TCP	ads > http [ACK] Seq
16	0.676139	61.8.0.17	10.0.52.164	TCP	[TCP segment of a re
17	0.676419	10.0.52.164	61.8.0.17	TCP	ads > http [ACK]

Figure 99. The default time setting is Seconds since Beginning of Capture

Seconds Since Previous Captured Packet

This setting is often called the delta time setting and measures the time from the end of one packet to the end of the next packet for all captured packets. If a display filter is set and a packet is not displayed, its timestamp is still calculated and shown on packets that are displayed.

Seconds Since Previous Displayed Packet

Seconds since Previous Displayed Packet only counts the delta time value from the end of one displayed packet to the next displayed packet.

If you are filtering on a conversation in the trace file, apply this time column setting to examine the delta time between packets in the conversation only.

Figure 100 compares the time column values for Seconds since Previous Captured Packet and Seconds since Previous Displayed Packet. Packets 3, 5 and 6 have been filtered out. For simplicity sake, we only used millisecond-level timestamping.

Seconds Since Previous...

	Captured Packet	Displayed Packet
1	0.000000	0.000000
2	0.001000	0.001000
3	0.013000	
4	0.002000	0.015000
5	0.034000	
6	0.006000	
7	0.018000	0.058000
8	0.005000	0.005000

Figure 100. Comparing Previous Packet and Displayed Packet timestamps

Deal with Time Accuracy and Resolution Issues

As discussed earlier, Wireshark does not create the packet timestamps. Timestamp accuracy may vary from one Wireshark system to another. The Wireshark documentation makes special reference to USB adapters and "bad timestamp accuracy" they offer. Those timestamps are passed to the operating system kernel which in turn is passed to the libpcap/WinPcap library.

Wireshark's libpcap/WinPcap capture libraries support microsecond resolution which is typically adequate. If you open a trace file captured with another network analyzer tool, you may find that the resolution is set to milliseconds and contains values after the decimal such as .342000, .542000, and .893000. There is nothing you can do to enhance the timestamp on these existing trace files.

Figure 101 shows the interpretation of Wireshark's timestamp value down to the nanosecond.

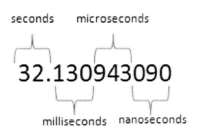

Figure 101. Timestamp resolution

Send Trace Files Across Time Zones

If you regularly travel, enable Network Time Protocol (NTP) to ensure your system is properly set on local time.

The "Date and Time of Day" and "Time of Day" values may not be an issue if you are only focused on the time between packets (Seconds since Previous Displayed Packet) or the comparative time between non-contiguous packets in a trace file. For example, if you are analyzing the response time to HTTP GET requests, you can simply use the Seconds Since Previous Displayed Packet setting.

If, however, you are interested in the exact date/time that a packet was captured and you send this trace file off to someone in another time zone, the trace file will have a different date/time value for the recipient. Remember—the pcap file format contains a record header for each packet that defines the difference between the local time and January 1, 1970 00:00:00 UTC. This value will be based on the time setting of the system that captured the trace file.

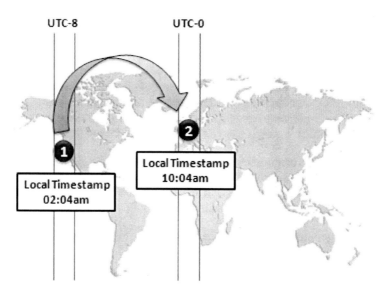

Figure 102. When trace files are sent across time zones

A trace file captured on a host in London, England will contain the GMT/UTC differential value of the capturing Wireshark system—GMT/UTC-0. When that user in London opens the trace file, the timestamp is set at 10:04am.

When the same trace file is emailed to someone on the west coast of the United States (Pacific Standard Time), the file still contains the GMT/UTC-0 value even though the user in the US is on GMT/UTC-8. When that user opens the trace file, the timestamp is seen as 2:04am as that system's GMT/UTC offset is quite different.

If you need to know the actual time that a packet was captured, you need to allow for the different time zone values.

Identify Delays with Time Values

To isolate slow performance caused by high latency, set the time column value to Seconds since Previous Displayed Packet using **View | Time Display Format | Seconds Since Previous Displayed Packet**. Wireshark retains this time setting in the *preferences* file.

You can sort the time column to identify packets that have a large delay between them.

In Figure 103, the time column is set to Seconds since Beginning of Capture. We have added another column for the delta time setting. We have clicked twice on the Delta Time column heading to sort from highest to lowest in delta times. (We turned off packet colorization for clarity's sake.)

In Figure 103, the trace file contains a single file download process. In the midst of the file download process, delta times jumped to over 16 seconds, 8 seconds, 4 seconds, 2 seconds and 1 second. It appears the performance issue occurs around the packet range 367-375. Note that colorization has been disabled for print clarity. When the colorization is disabled, you can clearly see the shading applied to the column on which you are sorting.[53]

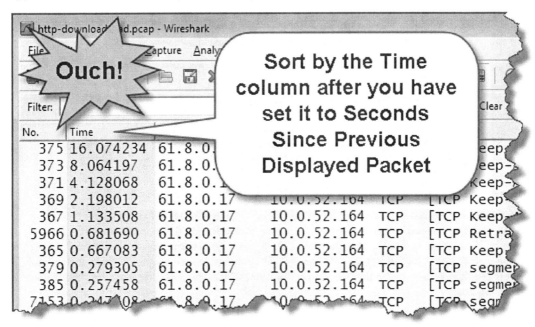

Figure 103. Sorting the Delta time column

Resorting the trace file by the number column enables us to look sequentially at traffic around the large gaps in time to see what lead up to the problem.

---

[53] This shading feature was implemented starting in Wireshark v1.3 (development release) and Wireshark v1.4 (stable release).

Create Additional Time Columns

If you want to view two or more time columns in your Packet List pane, use **Edit | Preferences** to add a predefined time column value or expand the **Frame** header, right click on a time field and select **Apply As Column**. .

Predefined time column options include:

- Absolute date and time—based on the date and time of the capturing host (this is the same as the Date and Time of Day setting)

- Absolute time—based on the time of the capturing host (this is the same as the Time of Day setting)

- Delta time (conversation)—time from the end of one packet to the end of the next packet in a conversation

- Delta time displayed—time from the end of one packet to the end of the next packet of displayed packets only (this is the same as Seconds Since Previous Displayed Packet)

- Relative time—time from the first packet in the trace file (this is the same as the Seconds Since Beginning of Capture setting)

- Relative time (conversation)—time from the first packet in the trace file for the conversation only

- Time (format as specified)—this setting displays the value set using View | Time Display Format

Using two time columns you can easily compare the arrival packet time (Time since Beginning of Capture) to the delta time (Time since Previous Displayed Packet).

Measure Packet Arrival Times with a Time Reference

Set a time reference and use Seconds since Beginning of Capture when you need to determine the time from the end of one packet to the end of another packet further down in the trace file. For example, if you want to find the time between a DNS query for *www.aol.com* and the final packet sent when the page is loaded, set the DNS query with a time reference and scroll down to the final packet. The time shown on the final packet sent indicates the entire load time including the DNS lookup process.

To set the time reference, right click on a packet and choose **Set Time Reference (toggle)**. The time reference packet is temporarily given a timestamp of 00:00:00 in the trace file (denoted by *REF* in the time column. The arrival time of all future packets is based on the arrival of the previous time reference packet. You can set more than one time reference packet in a trace file.

In Figure 104 we have set the time reference on packet 363. This is the last packet containing data before a zero window condition occurred. Scrolling down to packet 379, when data transfer resumes, we can see the entire delay time was 32.661522 seconds. For more information on Zero Window conditions, refer to *Chapter 20: Analyze Transmission Control Protocol (TCP) Traffic.*

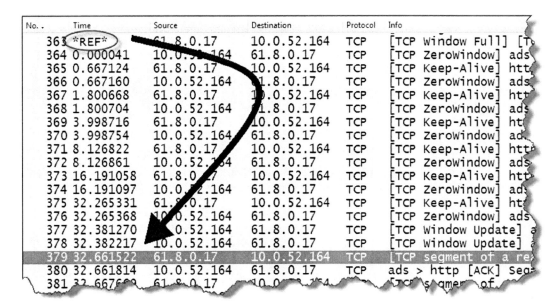

No. .	Time	Source	Destination	Protocol	Info
363	*REF*	61.8.0.17	10.0.52.164	TCP	[TCP Window Full] [T
364	0.000041	10.0.52.164	61.8.0.17	TCP	[TCP ZeroWindow] ads
365	0.667124	61.8.0.17	10.0.52.164	TCP	[TCP Keep-Alive] htt
366	0.667160	10.0.52.164	61.8.0.17	TCP	[TCP ZeroWindow] ads
367	1.800668	61.8.0.17	10.0.52.164	TCP	[TCP Keep-Alive] htt
368	1.800704	10.0.52.164	61.8.0.17	TCP	[TCP ZeroWindow] ads
369	3.998716	61.8.0.17	10.0.52.164	TCP	[TCP Keep-Alive] ht
370	3.998754	10.0.52.164	61.8.0.17	TCP	[TCP ZeroWindow] ad
371	8.126822	61.8.0.17	10.0.52.164	TCP	[TCP Keep-Alive] htt
372	8.126861	10.0.52.164	61.8.0.17	TCP	[TCP ZeroWindow] ads
373	16.191058	61.8.0.17	10.0.52.164	TCP	[TCP Keep-Alive] htt
374	16.191097	10.0.52.164	61.8.0.17	TCP	[TCP ZeroWindow] ad
375	32.265331	61.8.0.17	10.0.52.164	TCP	[TCP Keep-Alive] ht
376	32.265368	10.0.52.164	61.8.0.17	TCP	[TCP ZeroWindow] ads
377	32.381270	10.0.52.164	61.8.0.17	TCP	[TCP Window Update] a
378	32.382217	10.0.52.164	61.8.0.17	TCP	[TCP Window Update] a
379	32.661522	61.8.0.17	10.0.52.164	TCP	[TCP segment of a re
380	32.661814	10.0.52.164	61.8.0.17	TCP	ads > http [ACK] Seq
381	32.66766?	61.8.0.17	10.0.52.164		[TCP segment of

Figure 104. Using a Time Reference to sum total delay

Identify Client, Server and Path Delays

Figure 105 shows a TCP connection set up (three-way handshake in packets 1-3), an HTTP GET request (packet 4), a TCP ACK (packet 5) and a server responding with HTTP data (packet 6). You can use the packets in an HTTP connection setup to identify wire latency and processor latency. In this example, we use *http-download-bad.pcap* available from the Download section at *www.wiresharkbook.com*.

Handshakes Provide a Nice Snapshot of Latency

You can look at the SYN and SYN/ACK of a TCP connection establishment process to determine round trip latency time at that moment. Keep in mind that this measurement only provides a snapshot of round trip latency between the hosts. Just a few seconds later the round trip latency may be entirely different. Refer to the Tip in the section entitled Graph Round Trip Time on page 412 to learn how to build a graph of the average latency time in a trace file.

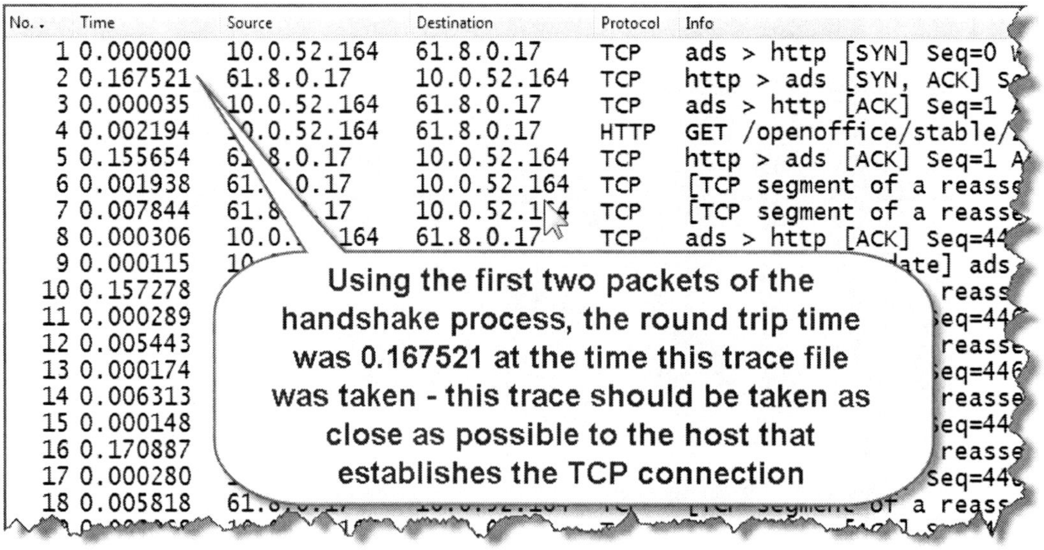

No. .	Time	Source	Destination	Protocol	Info
1	0.000000	10.0.52.164	61.8.0.17	TCP	ads > http [SYN] Seq=0
2	0.167521	61.8.0.17	10.0.52.164	TCP	http > ads [SYN, ACK] S
3	0.000035	10.0.52.164	61.8.0.17	TCP	ads > http [ACK] Seq=1
4	0.002194	10.0.52.164	61.8.0.17	HTTP	GET /openoffice/stable/
5	0.155654	61.8.0.17	10.0.52.164	TCP	http > ads [ACK] Seq=1 A
6	0.001938	61.8.0.17	10.0.52.164	TCP	[TCP segment of a reasse
7	0.007844	61.8.0.17	10.0.52.164	TCP	[TCP segment of a reasse
8	0.000306	10.0.0.164	61.8.0.17	TCP	ads > http [ACK] Seq=44
9	0.000115	10			ate] ads
10	0.157278				reass
11	0.000289				eq=44
12	0.005443				reasse
13	0.000174				eq=446
14	0.006313				reasse
15	0.000148				eq=44
16	0.170887				reasse
17	0.000280				Seq=44
18	0.005818	61.8			of a reas

Using the first two packets of the handshake process, the round trip time was 0.167521 at the time this trace file was taken - this trace should be taken as close as possible to the host that establishes the TCP connection

Figure 105. Evaluating latency with the time column

We can use this short section of the communications to identify three types of latency between the client and server: end-to-end path delays, slow server responses and overloaded clients.

Calculate End-to-End Path Delays

In Figure 105, Wireshark has been placed close to the client. The time between the initial TCP SYN (packet 1) and SYN/ACK (packet 2) packets indicate the round trip path latency time from the capture point. High latency times along a path should be evident by looking at the first two packets of the TCP handshake.

In this example, the time column has been set at Seconds since Previous Displayed Packet. The latency time between the SYN and SYN/ACK packet is over 167 milliseconds (.167521 seconds). We next examine the time between the GET request (4) and the ACK in response (packet 5). The round trip latency time is over 155 milliseconds (.155654 seconds). This also gives us a round trip latency time.

High latency along a path can be caused by interconnecting devices that make forwarding decisions on the packets, slow links along a path, the distance between end devices or other factors.

Locate Slow Server Responses

Examine the time between the server's ACK (packet 5) and the actual data packet (6) to identify potential server processor latency problems.

Servers may be slow responding when they are overwhelmed with other requests or processes or are underpowered (in processor capabilities or memory). Again, remember that this is simply a snapshot. Additional communications should be examined to verify that high server processor latency times are the problem.

Spot Overloaded Clients

Client latency issues are evident when a large delay occurs before a client makes a request for a service. For example, if there was a large delay between the ACK (packet 3) and GET Request (packet 4), the client is injecting latency into the communications.

Clients may be slow making the next request in a communication if the client is overloaded. This problem may be due to problems such as insufficient processing power, not enough memory available, or slow disk read/write operations, etc.

View a Summary of Traffic Rates, Packet Sizes and Overall Bytes Transferred

View **Statistics | Summary** for basic information about the saved or unsaved trace file. Summary statistics include: file format information, file length, time elapsed, number of packets, average packets per second, average packet size, total bytes, average bytes per second and average megabits per second. The summary information is particularly valuable when comparing proper network performance with problematic network performance.

Compare Up to Three Traffic Types in a Single Summary Window

You can compare three traffic types in one Summary window:

- All traffic in the trace file
- All marked packets in the trace file
- All displayed packets in the trace file

To compare three traffic types, as shown in Figure 106, follow these simple steps:

1. Apply a display filter for the first traffic type (such as DNS traffic) and select **Edit | Mark All Displayed Packets** then clear your filter.

2. Apply a new display filter for the second traffic type you are interested in (such as a specific conversation). Do not clear this display filter.

3. Select **Statistics | Summary** to view all traffic Captured compared to your marked packets and your filtered packets.

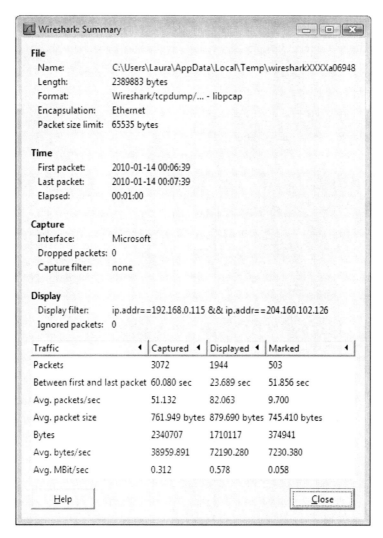

Figure 106. The Summary window can be used to compare three sets of data

Compare Summary Information for Two or More Trace Files

If you have created a baseline of network communications when performance was acceptable, you can use the summary window to compare basic statistics of your baseline traffic against the statistics of a current capture taken when performance was not acceptable. For more information on the baselines you should create, refer to *Chapter 28: Baseline "Normal" Traffic Patterns*.

Figure 107 shows two summaries side-by-side. In this case we launched two instances of Wireshark, loaded a separate trace file in each instance, and opened the summary window for each of the trace files.

Comparing the two summaries side-by-side, the trace file showing the slower download process has a much lower packet per second rate and average megabits per second rate than the trace file showing the faster download process.

To enhance these summary views further, we could filter each trace on a number of possible traits. In Figure 108 we have filtered both trace files on `frame.time_delta_displayed > 1` to locate the number of times the delta times were over 1 second.

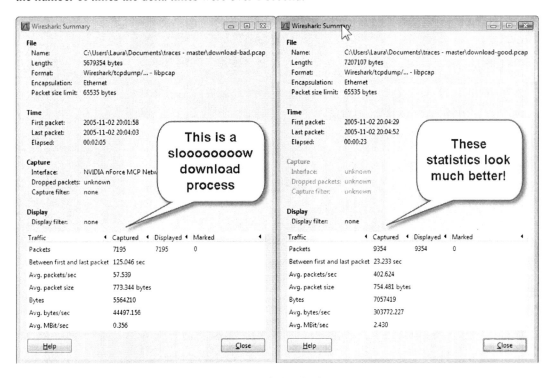

Figure 107. Comparing summaries in two instances of Wireshark

It is also possible to apply a filter for `tcp.analysis.flags` and then **Mark All Displayed Packets**. The marked column in the summary window would show the number of TCP analysis events in each trace file. For more information on display filtering, refer to *Chapter 9: Create and Apply Display Filters.*

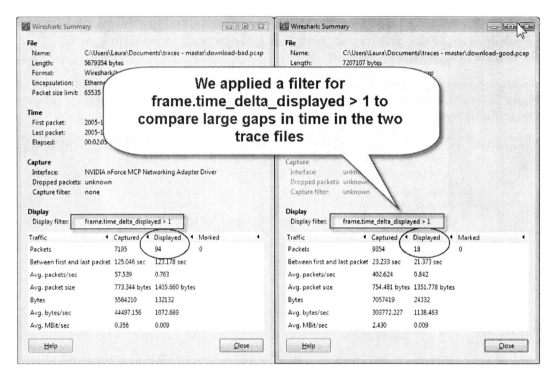

Figure 108. Compare traces with a filter on delta time over 1 second

Case Study:
Time Column Spots Delayed ACKs

Submitted by: Allen Gittelson

The customer complained that sending print jobs via 100 Mbps Ethernet to the print server was extremely slow.

I obtained network traces of the communication between their Windows Line Printer (LPR) client and our Line Printer Daemon (LPD) server and had my own baseline traces for comparison. It's usually very helpful to be able to compare a baseline trace to the "bad" or "abnormal" trace. I've found many times that we can identify at least where the differences between them start to occur and we can find the problem from analyzing the differences.

The first thing I did was look through the trace to see if there were any problems that were immediately obvious, and didn't see anything wrong in the LPR protocol (RFC 1179) communications. I normally have Wireshark's time column configured to show the interpacket timing (Time Since Previously Displayed Packet)—this is an example of a case when this was extremely helpful.

When I looked through the trace and paid attention to the interpacket timing, I noticed there were frequent and repeated ~200 ms (millisecond) gaps between packets in the LPR communication. Furthermore, there was a fairly clear pattern. The frequency and volume of these delays were making the data transfers extremely slow, because there were hundreds or thousands of these delays in a typical data transfer. The data transfer speed was slower than a telephone dialup connection at the time (approximately 56 Kbps).

One very easy way to identify this specific problem in the future was to use the display filter of Wireshark to view only the LPR traffic and then sort the trace by interpacket times with the largest times on top.

There were extremely frequent incidents of the ~200 ms delay times listed. Also, the Wireshark feature that is helpful to identify this type of problem is the IO Graphs feature. You can set the X Axis tick interval to 0.1 seconds and the Y Axis units to bytes/tick. In this situation, the IO Graph would show lots of bursts of traffic with delays between each burst set. I sometimes refer to this problem as the "hurry up and wait syndrome," because the data is transferred quickly with lots of time spent waiting for acknowledgements.

The customer believed that this problem was due to our specific device because they did not experience the problem with their other devices.

The root cause of the problem was in the implementation of the LPR client by Microsoft and how it interacted with the print server. I am unable to go into the details of how we worked around the problem for the products we manufactured, but you can see what the

Microsoft Knowledgebase has to say and recommend regarding this type of problem at *support.microsoft.com/kb/950326* and *support.microsoft.com/kb/823764*.

A work-around for this specific problem is to use other network printing protocols that are available such as SMB, Port 9100/raw, etc.

Summary

Performance problems can be caused by delays along a path, delays at the server or even delays at the client. You can change Wireshark's default time column setting or add more time column settings to help you measure the time between packets or from specific points (time references) in the trace file. Setting the time column to Seconds Since Previously Displayed Packet helps identify gaps between consecutive packets in a trace file.

Each trace file contains per-packet headers that include a main timestamp value based on the seconds since January 1, 1970 00:00:00. Wireshark references these headers when displaying packet timestamps in the Frame section of the Packet Details pane. When you open a trace file on hosts configured for different time zones, the trace file timestamp values displayed will be different.

You can set a time reference in a trace file by right clicking on a packet in the Packet List pane and selecting Set Time Reference (toggle). The time column will then provide the time from the current packet to the time reference packet.

You can use the TCP handshake to provide a snapshot of the round trip latency time between hosts. This is only a snapshot, however, and round trip time can vary over time.

You can use the trace file summaries to compare basic information for trace files and even use a time filter to identify how often large gaps in time are seen in a trace file.

Practice What You've Learned

 Download the trace files available in the Download section of the book website, *www.wiresharkbook.com*. You will use some of these trace files as you practice what you've learned in this chapter.

Measuring Slow DNS Response Time

- Open *dns-slow.pcap*. Select **View | Time Display Format | Seconds Since Previous Displayed Packet**.

- How much time elapsed between the first and second DNS query for *www.ncmec.org*? You should see 1.000620 seconds.

- How much time elapsed between the first and second DNS response for *www.ncmec.org*? Right click on the first DNS response and set a time reference to measure this value. (By the time the second DNS response arrived, the client had closed the listening port for the DNS response –that's why the client sent an ICMP Destination Unreachable/Port Unreachable response. For more information on analyzing ICMP traffic, refer to *Chapter 18: Analyze Internet Control Message Protocol (ICMP) Traffic*.) You should see 1.84489 seconds between the first and second DNS response packet.

- How much time did it take for the server to answer the DNS query in packet 98? You should see .207250 seconds elapsed between the DNS query in packet 98 and the DNS response in packet 107.

Measure a High Latency Path

- Open *http-download-good.pcap*. Reset the Time column to Seconds Since Previous Displayed Packet.[54] What is the latency time between the first and second packets of the TCP handshake (packets 1 and 2)? You should see 0.179989 seconds.

- Ensure the time column is set to Time Since Previous Displayed Packet. Sort the time column. What is the largest time delay in the trace file? You should see 2.753091 seconds is the largest time delay in the trace file.

- Resort by the Number column. What happened around the largest time delay in the trace file? You should see a TCP window update process occurred at this time. Refer to *Chapter 13: Use Wireshark's Expert System* for more information on Window Update packets.

When you experience slow performance when web browsing, accessing a file server, sending or receiving email, etc., capture your traffic and examine the time column.

The following table provides a summary of the two trace files we worked with in this section.

dns-slow.pcap	Compare how quickly the first and second DNS response packets come to the delay before the first DNS response is sent. Is the DNS response time better later in the trace (packet 98)?
http-download-good.pcap	The users are relatively happy with the download time required to obtain the OpenOffice binary depicted in this trace file. How long did the file transfer take? What is the average bytes/second rate? Set the time column to Seconds Since Previous Displayed Packet and then sort this column to find the large gaps in time.

---

[54] Even though Wireshark shows this as the active setting, when you set Time Reference packets it alters the actual setting to Seconds Since Beginning of Capture. You always need to reset it to Seconds Since Previous Displayed Packet.

Review Questions

Q7.1   **How can the time setting be used to identify the cause of network performance problems?**

Q7.2   **You have opened a trace file sent to you from another company. The timestamp only shows millisecond resolution. Why? Can you improve the timestamp resolution of the trace file?**

Q7.3   **You have opened a trace file that contains 5 separate conversations. How can Time Reference be used to measure the time elapsed in one of the conversations?**

Answers to Review Questions

Q7.1   **How can the time setting be used to identify the cause of network performance problems?**

A7.1   One way to identify network problems is to set the time column to Seconds since Previously Displayed Packet and look for large gaps in time in a conversation during what should be an automated streaming process. For example, during a file transfer process the file should be transferred without large gaps in time.

Q7.2   **You have opened a trace file sent to you from another company. The timestamp only shows millisecond resolution. Why? Can you improve the timestamp resolution of the trace file?**

A7.2   Most likely the analyzer used to capture the trace file could not provide more precise timestamps. You cannot alter the timestamp resolution of captured trace files.

Q7.3   **You have opened a trace file that contains 5 separate conversations. How can Time Reference be used to measure the time elapsed in one of the conversations?**

A7.3   You could set a Time Reference on the first packet of the conversation you are interested in and scroll to the end of the conversation. The time column will indicate the time elapsed from the Time Reference packet and the last packet of the conversation.

Alternately you could filter on the conversation of interest and then set the Time Reference on the first packet. The last packet displayed indicates the time elapsed for the conversation.

Chapter 8:
Interpret Basic
Trace File Statistics

Wireshark Certified Network Analyst Exam Objectives covered:

- Launch Wireshark Statistics
- Identify Network Protocols and Applications
- Identify the Most Active Conversations
- List Endpoints and Map Them on the Earth
- List Conversations or Endpoints for Specific Traffic Types
- Evaluate Packet Lengths
- List All IP Addresses in the Traffic
- List All Destinations in the Traffic
- List All UDP and TCP Ports Used
- Analyze UDP Multicast Streams
- Graph the Flow of Traffic
- Gather Your HTTP Statistics
- Examine All WLAN Statistics

  - ❖ Case Study: Application Analysis—Aptimize Website Accelerator™
  - ❖ Case Study: Finding VoIP Quality Issues
  - ❖ Summary
  - ❖ Practice What You've Learned
  - ❖ Review Questions and Answers

Launch Wireshark Statistics Windows

Wireshark can display statistics for a number of network packet types and overall behavior. To view Wireshark statistics, select **Statistics** on the menu. These statistics include:

- Protocol hierarchies
- Conversations and Endpoints
- Address and Port Information
- Packet Lengths
- Multicast Stream
- BOOTP-DHCP
- Flow Graphs
- WLAN Traffic

Identify Network Protocols and Applications

When examining a trace file that contains a variety of traffic types, consider selecting Statistics | Protocol Hierarchy to identify the protocols and applications in the trace file.

Figure 109 shows the protocol hierarchy information for *http-espn2007.pcap* which depicts a web browsing session to *www.espn.com*. The protocols and application are categorized according to their protocol layer.

The protocol hierarchy statistics window displays the packet count, bytes count, megabits per second and three end packets columns. The end packets column indicates the absolute number of packets, bytes and megabits of a protocol or application where that protocol or application was the highest decoded protocol or application.

In Figure 109, thirty-six of the packets were UDP-based (DNS requests and responses) and 261 packets were defined as HTTP packets that contain HTTP commands or response codes. The remainder of the traffic is listed as TCP which includes ACKs and the packets used to download the web page and its elements.

A display filter - !(nbdgm) && !(dcerpc) - was applied to the trace file before opening the protocol hierarchy window. The display filter removed NetBIOS datagram packets and DCE remote procedure call (DCERPC) packets from the trace file display.

You can right click on a row to apply or prepare a filter, find a packet or colorize a protocol.

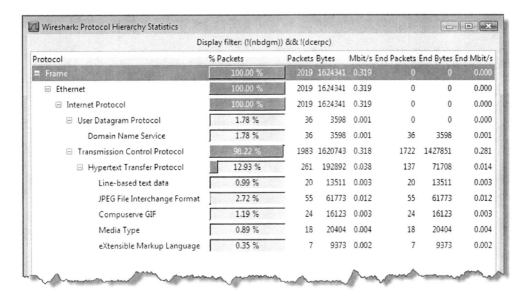

Figure 109. Protocol hierarchy information on a web browsing session

Characterize All Protocols and Applications Used by a Host

Apply an IP address display filter before opening the Protocol Hierarchy Statistics window to view traffic statistics for that host only. This is a great way to characterize all the protocols and applications that a host uses. For example, if you want to know what protocols and applications are active while a host is idle (without a user working on the system), filter on that host's IP address and open the Protocol Hierarchy Statistics window.

Examining the protocol hierarchy is a particularly important step when characterizing traffic to and from a host that you suspect may be compromised. Look for unusual protocols or applications, such as Internet Relay Chat (IRC), Trivial File Transfer Protocol (TFTP), Remote Procedure Call (RPC) or unrecognized applications.

In Figure 110 shows the Protocol Hierarchy information for a breached host. This network does not typically support Internet Relay Chat (IRC) or Trivial File Transfer Protocol (TFTP). At this point, you can right click on one of the unusual protocols or applications listed to create a filter on that traffic to examine it further.

For more examples of analyzing compromised hosts, refer to *Chapter 32: Analyze Suspect Traffic*.

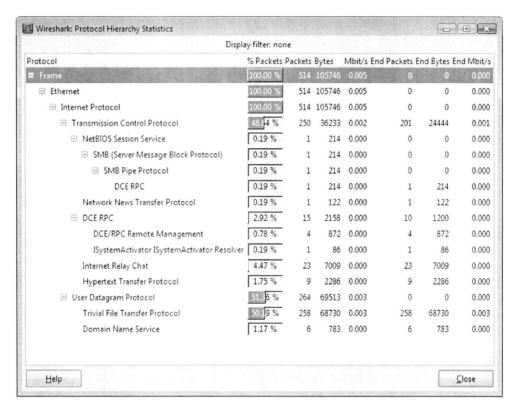

Figure 110. The protocol hierarchy displays some questionable traffic

Identify the Most Active Conversations

A conversation is a pair of devices communicating. Conversations can include just MAC layer addresses (ARP conversations for example), network layer addresses (ICMP ping conversations for example), port numbers (FTP conversations for example), etc.

Select **Statistics | Conversations** to view the Conversations window.

When working with a large trace file, sorting on the bytes transferred between hosts enables you to detect the most active connections based on packets, bytes, bits per second or total duration of conversation. Figure 111 shows a conversation list for TCP connections. Notice that there is only one Ethernet conversation, but numerous IP, TCP and UDP conversations that travel over that one Ethernet conversation.

In this example we have sorted on the bytes column to identify the most active conversation based on bytes transferred between TCP hosts.

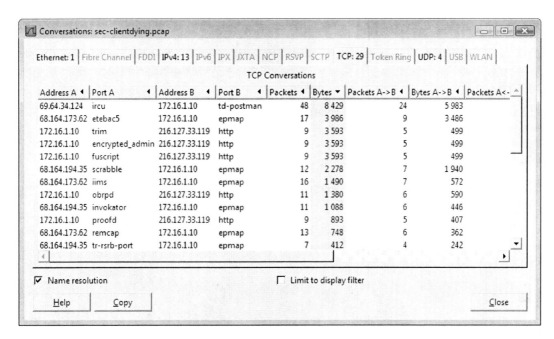

Figure 111. Conversations define pairs of hosts that communicate with each other

Conversations are pairs of hosts communicating while an endpoint is a single side of a conversation. Note that communications from a host to the broadcast address are listed as a conversation. Broadcast and multicast addresses are listed as endpoints in the endpoint window, even though there is no such host as a "broadcast" host or a "multicast" host.

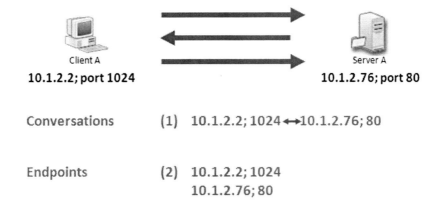

Figure 112. Comparing conversations with endpoints

List Endpoints and Map Them on the Earth

An endpoint is one side of a conversation—for example, an IP address and a port number used at that IP address would be defined as an endpoint. Select **Statistics | Endpoints** to view the endpoints window.

In Figure 113 we opened a trace file containing packets from a web browsing session to *www.aol.com* and opened the endpoint window. Note that the endpoint window displays details regarding packets, bytes, transmitted packets and bytes, received packets and bytes (as a destination address—there is no guarantee that the target ever received the packets).

If you have loaded the GeoIP database and configured GeoIP services in **Edit | Preferences | Name Resolution**, you may map some or all of the hosts listed under the IP tab in the endpoints window.[55]

If we had scrolled to the right in Figure 113 we would have seen the additional GeoIP columns that include location information such as Country, AS (Autonomous System) number, city, longitude and latitude.

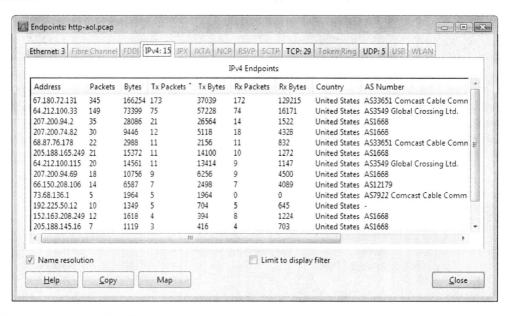

Figure 113. Examining IP address endpoints

The GeoIP mapping feature can only be used to map the location of IP addresses—you must select the **IP** tab in the Endpoints window to be able to use the Map button.

In Figure 114 we have mapped the IP addresses seen in our web browsing session to *www.aol.com*. The GeoIP feature launches an OpenStreetMap view of the world, plotting our IP addresses with red flags based on the GeoIP information detected for each address.

---

[55] Your version of Wireshark must support GeoIP. Check the "Compiled with" section under **Help | About Wireshark**—look for "with GeoIP".

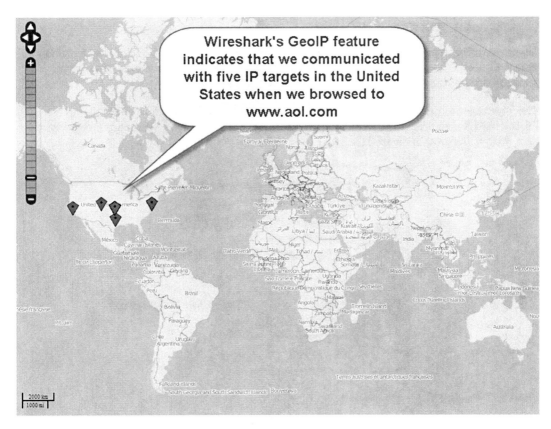

Figure 114. GeoIP can be run from the IP tab of the endpoints window

List Conversations or Endpoints for Specific Traffic Types

In addition to using Statistics | Conversations and Statistics | Endpoints, you can also click **Statistics | Conversation List** or **Statistics | Endpoints List** to view fourteen pre-defined conversation and endpoint criteria including Ethernet, FDDI, Fibre Channel, IPX, IPv4, JXTA, NCP, RSVP, SCTP, TCP (IPv4 and IPv6), Token Ring, UDP (IPv4 and IPv6), USB and WLAN.

The Endpoints List displays the GeoIP location information but does not have a Map button to link it to OpenStreetMap. To flag the location of IP addresses on a global map, select **Statistics | Endpoints | IP**.

Evaluate Packet Lengths

Select **Statistics | Packet Lengths** when baselining or analyzing a network application. Smaller packet sizes offer less-efficient file transfers and higher protocol overhead costs. For example, consider an application used to transfer a 500,000 byte file over TCP.

The most common network file transfer methods use TCP/IP communications over Ethernet. Ethernet 802.3 networks support 1518-byte packet sizes and a 1500-byte Maximum Transmission Unit (MTU) as shown in Figure 115.

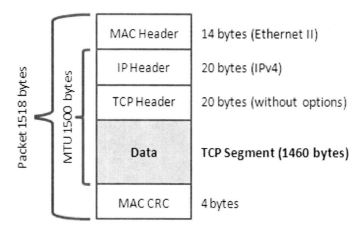

Figure 115. Standard TCP packet structure

The MAC, IP and TCP header overhead shown in Figure 115 does not factor in the unseen overhead elements such as the preamble and interpacket gap (if required).

When using a standard Ethernet II packet structure that can be 1,518 bytes and removing the overhead of the Ethernet header, IP header, TCP header and MAC Cyclical Redundancy Check (CRC) shown in Figure 115, you are left with 1,460 bytes available to handle TCP segment data. The Maximum Segment Size (MSS) that TCP can place in this packet is 1,460.

Some basic math can illustrate the problem of using small packet sizes to transfer large amounts of data across the network.

- If your application transfers the data using the full 1,460 byte available MSS size in all packets, it would take 343 packets to transfer 500,000 bytes of data. This would require 19,894 bytes (58 bytes overhead times 343 packets) for header overhead.

- If your application transfers the data sending only 320 bytes in a packet, it would take 1,563 packets to transfer 500,000 bytes of data. This would require 90,654 bytes (58 bytes overhead times 1,563 packets) for header overhead. This is certainly not as efficient for data transfer.

Database Communications are Weird

Database communications often use small packet sizes as they are transferring records and field values, not entire files. It is not the most efficient use of bandwidth, but it is not uncommon. Be sure to baseline your database traffic when users are not complaining. This provides a blueprint of how your database looks on a good day.

File transfer applications should be examined with particular attention focused on their packet lengths. If the application is transferring packets that are smaller than the maximum MTU allowed on the link, the reason may be:

- The application is transferring files that are smaller than the MTU—examine the file requests and file transfers to see if the application is indeed transferring small file sizes. For example, when you pick up or send email you may see lots of small packets as most emails are small and each email is typically treated as an individual file.

- A device along the path is limiting the MTU size. Transmit various sizes of ping packets or other packets along the path to determine if all traffic is throttled to a smaller MTU size. Consider that the MTU reduction may pertain to one particular port value or source/destination pair. Look for ICMP Type 3, Code 4 (Destination Unreachable, Fragmentation Needed but the Don't Fragment Bit is Set) packets. For more information on ICMP, refer to *Chapter 18: Analyze Internet Control Message Protocol (ICMP) Traffic.*

- The application was not developed to take advantage of maximum MTU sizes as shown in the Packet Lengths window in Figure 116. Compare other applications transferring files to and from the target. For example, try FTP or HTTP to test file transfers.

Figure 116 shows the Packet Lengths window of a trace file that contains small packets during a file transfer process. This application does not perform well as a file transfer method.

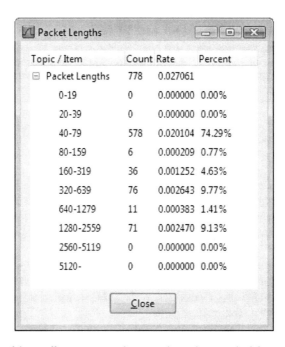

Figure 116. The majority of this traffic uses minimal size packets; this not ideal for transferring large files across the network

List All IP Addresses in the Traffic

Select **Statistics | IP Addresses** to list all the IP addresses seen in the trace file as shown in Figure 117. Wireshark prompts you for a display filter in case you want to focus on a specific address, subnet, protocol, application or other criteria. If you already have a display filter applied to the trace file, Wireshark includes the display filter when prompting you to create the statistics.

ARP Packets Do Not Match IP Address Filters

If you apply an `arp` *display filter when opening the IP Addresses statistic, no packets will appear. Although ARP packets have an IP address in the packet, they do not have an IP header. Therefore, IP address filters do not work on ARP packets.*

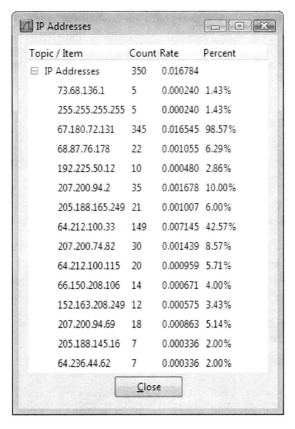

Figure 117. The IP address window does not list IP addresses seen in ARP packets

List All Destinations in the Traffic

Select **Statistics | IP Destinations** to examine each destination IP address as well as the destination transport (UDP or TCP) and destination port number.

Wireshark prompts you for a display filter in case you want to focus on a specific address, subnet, protocol, application or other criteria. If you already have a display filter applied to the trace file, Wireshark includes the display filter when prompting you to create the statistics.

For example, if you want to see all the hosts who have received a SYN+ACK (indicating a previous TCP connection attempt was successful), enter the display filter `tcp.flags == 0x12` before clicking **Create Stat**. (This looks for all packets with both SYN and ACK bits set.)

For more information on creating display filters for various TCP flags, refer to *Chapter 9: Create and Apply Display Filters*.

List All UDP and TCP Ports Used

Select **Statistics | IP Protocol Types** to summarize the traffic based on TCP or UDP port numbers. Only packets that contain UDP or TCP headers are counted in this statistic. Again Wireshark prompts you for a display filter in case you want to focus on a specific address, subnet, protocol, application or other criteria. If you already have a display filter applied to the trace file, Wireshark includes the display filter when prompting you to create the statistics.

Analyze UDP Multicast Streams

Wireshark automatically detects multicast streams—based on a target MAC address starting with 01:00:5E, the IANA-defined Ethernet multicast address identifier—and provides basic packet rate statistics and bandwidth usage details.

One example of multicast traffic is generated by Open Shortest Path First (OSPF) routers. OSPF is a link state routing protocol used to support large, heterogeneous IP networks. OSPF routers send multicast advertisements.

Another example is Internet Group Management Protocol (IGMP) multicast traffic. IGMP is used by hosts to dynamically join or leave multicast groups. Routers that are configured to support IGMP only forward packets down links that support a multicast member, as learned through IGMP.

Applications can also use multicast to transmit data to multiple hosts through a single datastream. In Figure 118 we examine the information for a multicast video stream.

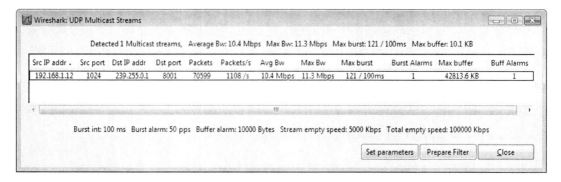

Figure 118. UDP Multicast Streams statistics include burst information

Select **Statistics | UDP Multicast Streams** to identify multicast source, destination and port information as well as the packet rate and burst statistics (based on settable parameters as shown in Figure 119).

The burst measurement interval measures the number of multicast packets within the given time (defined in milliseconds). Thresholds can be set to identify multicast traffic that falls outside a range of either a specific number of packets or bytes within the burst measurement interval.

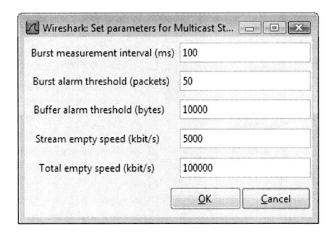

Figure 119. Multicast burst statistics are based on settable parameters

Graph the Flow of Traffic

Select **Statistics | Flow Graphs** to view the traffic with source and destination addresses distributed across columns as shown in Figure 120.

Flow graphs can be created based on all traffic, filtered traffic or just TCP flows. In Figure 120 we have graphed a web browsing session to *www.espn.com*. The start of the Flow Graph shows the DNS query for *www.espn.com* followed by the TCP handshake process.

As the client receives a redirection— indicating that the main page of *www.espn.com* is at another location—the client performs another DNS query (at timestamp 0.090) before the client launches another TCP handshake process to another server (timestamp 0.113).

Use Flow Graphs to Spot Web Browsing Issues

Creating Flow Graphs of web browsing sessions displays the number of sites you are redirected to for content when accessing a site. For example, to load www.espn.com*'s main web page, the Flow Graph indicates that a client must connect to six different web servers. If one of these other web servers responds slowly or with 404 errors, the client may complain about slow web browsing or state that part of the site does not load.*

You can save your Flow Graphs in ASCII text format. This format is not ideal, but it allows you to reformat and print out a full document depicting the flow of network communications.

Creating a Flow Graph of just TCP communications illustrates the TCP flags, sequence and acknowledgment number information for the traffic.

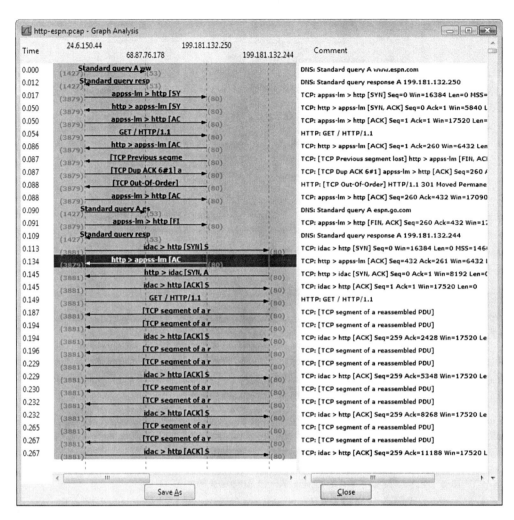

Figure 120. Flow graphs list sources and targets in columns

Gather Your HTTP Statistics

Select **Statistics | HTTP** to view load distribution information, packet counter and requests. Wireshark prompts you for a display filter in case you want to focus on a specific address, subnet, protocol, application or other criteria. If you already have a display filter applied to the trace file, Wireshark includes the display filter when prompting you to create the statistics.

Load distribution lists HTTP requests by server host and server address. The packet counter information breaks down the HTTP request types (such as GET and POST) with the HTTP response codes (such as 200, 403 or 404). Finally, the HTTP requests lists out every target HTTP server and every file requested from each server.

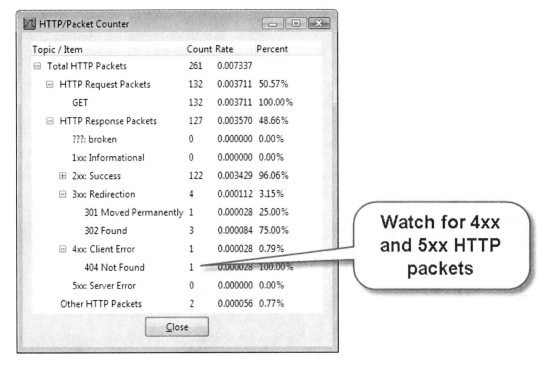

Figure 121. The HTTP Packet Counter shows a 404 error

Wireshark organizes the response packets according to the five numerical HTTP response code sets:

- 1xx Informational
- 2xx Success
- 3xx Redirection
- 4xx Client Error
- 5xx Server Error

HTTP statistics are covered in more detail in *Chapter 23: Analyze Hypertext Transfer Protocol (HTTP) Traffic*.

Examine All WLAN Statistics

Select **Statistics | WLAN** to list the BSSID, channels, SSID, packet percentages, management and control packet types and protection mechanisms of the WLAN traffic as shown in Figure 122. We can see in this figure that our lab network, *wsu* is only configured to use WEP at this time and the traffic flows on channel 1. Over 76% of WLAN traffic discovered is flowing to or from a DLink device.

Chapter 26: Introduction to 802.11 (WLAN) Analysis covers the process of analyzing wireless network traffic.

Figure 122. The WLAN statistics window includes management and control frame information

Apply a display filter before opening the WLAN Statistics window (such as `radiotap.channel.freq == 2437` for traffic arriving on Channel 6) to focus in on specific traffic.

In addition, you can choose to only show existing networks. When you enable this option, Wireshark will not send Probe Requests to locate additional WLAN networks.

Case Study:
Application Analysis: Aptimize Website Accelerator™

Wireshark offers an excellent open source solution for application testing. When vendors make grand claims of performance improvements offered by their products, I, like many in this industry, am skeptical. I must witness the improvements on my own turf at packet level. Wireshark provides insight into application behavior in a visible format. If there are performance changes, I can see them clearly and make a definitive judgment for or against an application's deployment on a customer's network.

Aptimize Website Accelerator (*www.aptimize.com*) claims to improve website performance without code changes or extra hardware—a perfect application analysis subject for Wireshark.

Step 1: Set up the Test
My good friend, Mike Iem, brought this case study to me—he informed me that Microsoft's SharePoint site had the Aptimize Website Accelerator product loaded on it. Mike provided me with the URL parameters that allowed me to access the site with and without Aptimize Website Accelerator enabled.

In order to capture only the traffic to and from the SharePoint site, I turned off all other applications that generated traffic on my local testing machine. This included my virus detection, safe website surfing tool, printer polling and background broadcasts. In addition, I created an exclusion filter to remove any extraneous communications from view.

Refer to *Chapter 9: Create and Apply Display Filters* for details on creating exclusion filters for application analysis.

Step 2: Running the Comparative Test
As Wireshark ran in the background, I entered the URL to access the SharePoint site **without** Aptimize Website Accelerator enabled:

```
http://sharepoint.microsoft.com/?wax=off
```

From my perspective the page loaded as sluggishly as most pages I browse (including my own company website). I stopped the capture after the page had completely loaded and Wireshark's packet counter stopped incrementing. I saved the displayed packets in a trace file called *aptimize-off.pcap*. (This file is named *app-aptimize-off.pcap* on the book website, *www.wiresharkbook.com*.)

Next, I cleared my browser cache, restarted my browser and used `ipconfig /flushdns` to clear my DNS resolver cache. Clearing the browser cache is imperative—if the browser cache is not cleared the browser sends "If-Modified-Since" HTTP requests and may load pages from cache instead of loading the pages across the network. Clearing DNS resolver cache is also a very important step in application analysis because DNS performance problems can have a severe impact on website loading times.

Again I started capturing traffic with my exclusion display filter set. This time I entered the URL to access the SharePoint site with Aptimize Website Accelerator enabled:

```
http://sharepoint.microsoft.com/?wax=on
```

I saved this new trace as *aptimize-on.pcap*. (This file is named *app-aptimize-on.pcap* and can be found in the Download section on the book website, *www.wiresharkbook.com*.) Wireshark would show me exactly how Aptimize Website Accelerator altered the traffic flow.

Step 3: Analyze the Results
My first step when analyzing "before and after" traffic is to run two instances of Wireshark and open the **Statistics | Summary** windows side by side.

Regardless of *how* Aptimize Website Accelerator altered the behavior, the improvement was visible from my user perspective and verified in the Summary window comparison, as shown in Figure 123.

I repeated the test numerous times for good measure. Each time, the Aptimize optimized download process showed an improvement in performance. The Summary window validated that Aptimize Website Accelerator improved the site load time by over 24% and reduced the packet overhead by over 22%.

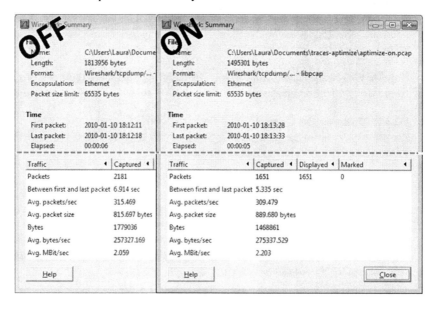

Figure 123. Performance before and after Aptimize Website Accelerator was enabled

What a dream! As I delved into the packets I could see exactly how Aptimize Website Accelerator dramatically improved website loading times and significantly reduced overhead on the network.

Looking through the trace files, I noticed a remarkable difference in the number of HTTP GET requests when the optimization was enabled—over 60% fewer GET requests on average requests. This has a great impact on the load time. Rather than asking for and receiving small pieces of the page bit-by-bit, the browser asks for a piece of the site (style sheets, graphics, etc.) and receives them in a stream.

The table below illustrates the numerous differences between the traffic before and after Aptimize Website Accelerator was enabled.

Statistic	Aptimize		Difference
	Off	On	
Time to Load Page Plus Links (secs)	6.91	5.33	24.30% faster launch
Packets to Load Page Plus Links	2,180	1,651	22.90% fewer packets
Bytes to Load Page Plus Links	1,779,036	1,468,861	17.44% fewer bytes
HTTP GET Requests	90	34	62.22% fewer GETs

The two-minute video on Aptimize's website (*www.aptimize.com*) offers an ideal analogy that explains why so many sites load slowly. In addition, they have a clear list of the features offered by Aptimize Website Accelerator. Using Wireshark I could witness the results of their optimization techniques including:

Reduce HTTP Requests: This was verified in the trace file—from 90 HTTP GET requests down to 34 HTTP GET.

Compress page resources: This is evident when we examine the smaller total bytes required to load the site—reduced from 2,180 packets to 1,651 packets.

When analyzing a web browsing session it is important to realize that loading a web page may require multiple connections. Each connection should be analyzed—not just the connection required to load the default page.

Using Wireshark, I created an IP address filter to display traffic to and from the SharePoint site only (`ip.addr==207.46.105.139`). Next, I opened the Statistics | Conversations window and clicked on the box Limit to display filter. I dragged the Duration column over to place it next to the Bytes column for better readability.

As shown in Figure 124, the web browsing session required six separate HTTP connections to the SharePoint site. Every connection required fewer packets, transferred fewer bytes and took less time when the Aptimize Website Accelerator was enabled.

The average improvement in connection speed was 37% for the six connections. Note that the site loading process made these connections concurrently. If they didn't, we would have seen a 24-second load without Aptimize Website Accelerator enabled and a 15-second load time with it enabled. Thank goodness for concurrent TCP connections.

Statistic	Aptimize		Difference
	Off	On	
Connection 1	4.8290	3.7866	22% improvement
Connection 2	4.4863	3.2607	27% improvement
Connection 3	4.0549	1.9541	52% improvement
Connection 4	3.5741	2.183	39% improvement
Connection 5	3.5518	1.9237	46% improvement
Connection 6	3.5604	1.9742	45% improvement

Now before you go running off to get Aptimize Website Accelerator loaded on your web server, you need to know this important fact:

If your site references third-party sites that are not optimized, your site visitor's performance may be negatively impacted.

For example, many sites link to partner sites. When elements load from these partner sites, your visitor must make separate TCP connections to those sites. I've used numerous sports reporting web sites as the perfect example of "letting your friends drag you down". As part of your improvement plan, analyze all connections your visitors establish when they visit your site. You can use the same steps shown in this case study and pay particular attention to **Statistics | Conversations**.

Since performing this application analysis, I learned that Aptimize added extensibility so that Aptimize Website Accelerator can cache these external scripts/images, etc. locally. This is a bonus for folks who link to third-party websites to load their pages. I expect this should really help improve website loading time and I plan on setting up a new application analysis lab test to check it out.

This Wireshark application analysis session proved definitively that the Aptimize Website Accelerator does improve web browsing speed, decrease the packet overhead and reduce the overall traffic required to view a website.

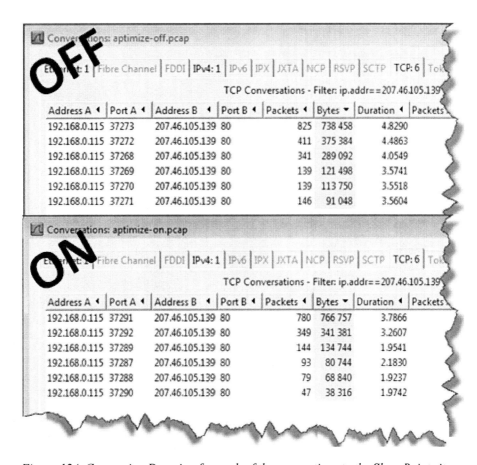

Figure 124. Comparing Duration for each of the connections to the SharePoint site

As a site becomes more complex and requires more connections and more data transfer capabilities, the advantages of using Aptimize Website Accelerator should also increase.

This was a dream project as it shows how easily you can use Wireshark to analyze a product to determine if it offers benefits to your company.

Case Study:
Finding VoIP Quality Issues

Submitted by: Roy B.

I use Wireshark to identify voice quality issues of VoIP calls over wired or wireless phones (like dual mode phones).

Wireshark is set to capture packets from the subnet of the VoIP phones or from the port of voice gateway.

I created an I/O graph using 2 filters:

- One filter for the outgoing traffic from the phone (using the phone MAC address or IP address)
- One filter for the incoming traffic to the phone (using the phone MAC address or IP address)

These VoIP phones are using the G.711 codec which sends traffic consistently at 50 packets per second in each direction. If all goes well, this traffic should appear as a straight line on the I/O graph showing at 50 packets per second on the Y axis.

If the line is not flat this means that there were voice quality issues.

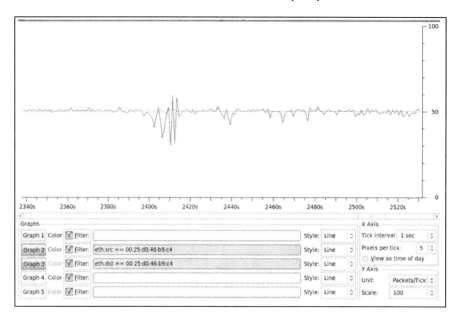

In the IO Graph shown you can see a trace from my Nokia dual mode phone communicating over the WLAN. Wireshark is capturing from the LAN subnet of the wireless phones.

The darker line represents the traffic coming *from* the phone, the lighter line represents the traffic going *to* the phone.

At around 2400 seconds (X axis), the darker line fluctuates—meaning that there are voice quality issues with traffic *from* the phone.

I use this technique with trace files to try and correlate the problems with WLAN interference. I monitor WLAN interference using a spectrum analyzer or through WLAN analysis.

This method is good for troubleshooting any constant traffic like voice, even if it is encrypted.

Summary

Wireshark's statistics provide details on the protocols and applications seen in saved or unsaved traces including the most active hosts or conversations, packet lengths, ports used and WLAN traffic.

In addition, you can graph the flow of traffic to analyze separate interwoven communications or spot dependencies on other hosts.

You should take time to baseline network communications to ensure you can spot unusual traffic statistics. Refer to *Chapter 28: Baseline "Normal" Traffic Patterns* for more information on the types of traffic that should be baselined.

Practice What You've Learned

Download the trace files available in the Download section of the book website, *www.wiresharkbook.com*. Open the following trace files and answer the statistics questions below. You should be able to find the answers to each of these questions by following the steps defined in this chapter. Refer to *www.wiresharkbook.com* for additional information.

app-aptimize-off.pcap	Which conversation is the most active (bytes)?
	How many UDP conversations are in the trace file?
	How many HTTP redirections occurred?
	How many TCP targets did 192.168.0.115 connect to?
	What was the average Mbits/second?
app-aptimize-on.pcap and *app-aptimize-on-fromcache.pcap*	Compare the following statistics from these two trace files to analyze the performance difference when you load a website from cache:

- HTTP Redirections
- Bytes
- Time from first to last packet

arp-sweep.pcap	This trace shows a class ARP sweep as mentioned in *Chapter 32: Analyze Suspect Traffic*. This ARP sweep isn't just one big nonstop sweep.
	What is the packet per second rate in this ARP sweep?
	Does the ARP sweep run consistently at this rate or does the packet per second rate vary?
	Using a Flow Graph, can you identify ARPs that are not part of the ARP sweep?

Review Questions

Q8.1   **How can you use the Protocol Hierarchy window to identify a breached host?**

Q8.2   **Your trace file contains over 100 TCP connections. How can you identify the most active (bytes/second) TCP connections?**

Q8.3   **What is the purpose of GeoIP?**

Answers to Review Questions

Q8.1   **How can you use the Protocol Hierarchy window to identify a breached host?**

A8.1   After capturing traffic to and from the host, open the Protocol Hierarchy window to look for unusual applications such as TFTP, IRC, etc. You can apply a display filter for the conversation from inside the Protocol Hierarchy window and then follow the TCP or UDP stream to reassemble the communications and identify commands or information exchanged.

Q8.2   **Your trace file contains over 100 TCP connections. How can you identify the most active TCP connection based on bytes per second?**

A8.2   Open the **Statistics | Conversations** window and select the **TCP** tab. Sort the information by the Bytes column. You can now right click and apply a filter based on the most active conversation for further analysis.

Q8.3   **What is the purpose of GeoIP?**

A8.3   GeoIP maps IP addresses in the Endpoints window to an OpenStreetMap view of the world. This feature is available if (a) Wireshark supports GeoIP, (b) the MaxMind GeoIP database files are loaded on the Wireshark system and (c) Wireshark's name resolution settings for GeoIP are configured properly.

Chapter 9: Create and Apply Display Filters

Wireshark Certified Network Analyst Exam Objectives covered:

- Understanding the Purpose of Display Filters
- Create Display Filters Using Auto-Complete
- Apply Saved Display Filters
- Use Expressions for Filter Assistance
- Make Display Filters Quickly Using Right-Click Filtering
- Understand Display Filter Syntax
- Combine Display Filters with Comparison Operators
- Alter Display Filter Meaning with Parentheses
- Filter on Specific Bytes in a Packet
- Use Display Filter Macros for Complex Filtering
- Avoid Common Display Filter Mistakes
- Manually Edit the *dfilters* File

  - ❖ Case Study: Using Filters and Graphs to Solve Database Issues
  - ❖ Case Study: The Chatty Browser
  - ❖ Case Study: Catching Viruses and Worms
  - ❖ Summary
  - ❖ Practice What You've Learned
  - ❖ Review Questions and Answers

Understanding the Purpose of Display Filters

Display filters enable you focus on specific packets based on a criteria you define. You can filter on traffic that you want to see (inclusion filtering) or filter undesired traffic out of your view (exclusion filtering).

Display filters can be created using several techniques:

- Type in the display filter (possibly using auto-complete)
- Apply saved display filters
- Use expressions
- Right-click filter
- Apply conversation or endpoint filters

When you apply a display filter, the Status Bar indicates the total number of packets and the packets displayed, as shown in Figure 125. In this example, the trace file contains 10,161 packets, but only 4,142 are displayed because they match our filter.

Figure 125. The Status Bar shows the displayed packet count

Wireshark's display filters use a specialized Wireshark filter format while capture filters use the Berkeley Packet Filtering (BPF) format—they are not interchangeable. The BPF filter format is also used by tcpdump. In rare instances, there just happen to be some capture and display filters that look the same because both filter mechanisms support identical filter syntax. For example, the capture and display filter syntax for TCP traffic is the same: `tcp`.

Wireshark includes a default set of display filters that are saved in a file called *dfilters* in the Global Configurations directory. When you edit the default display filters, a new *dfilters* file is saved in the Personal Configurations directory or in the active profile directory.

Display filters can be relatively simple. The filter field or protocol must be defined in lower case in most situations[56]. You can use uppercase characters for the value portion of the filter as we will cover later in this chapter.

---

[56] All field field or protocol text was in lowercase until VoIP filters were added. Some VoIP-related filters use uppercase and lowercase definitions. Use the auto complete feature to help with VoIP filters.

The following are examples of very basic display filters.

```
tcp
ip
udp
icmp
bootp⁵⁷
arp
dns
nbns
```

Display filters can be created based on a packet characteristic (not an actual field) if desired. For example, the following filters display packets that contain one of the TCP analysis flags packets and packets that have an invalid IP header checksum. These are not actual fields in a TCP packet.

```
tcp.analysis.flags
ip.checksum_bad
```

Using operators (see *Combine Display Filters with Comparison Operators* on Page 220) you can create display filters based on the contents of a field. The following list provides examples of filters based on field values.

```
http.request.method == "GET"
tcp.flags == 0x20
tcp.window_size < 1460
tcp.stream eq 1
icmp.type == 8
dns.qry.name == "www.wireshark.org"
```

Display filters can be quite complex and include numerous criteria that must be matched. The following are some examples of display filters using multiple criteria:

- The following filter displays ARP requests except ARP requests from the MAC address 00:01:5c:22:a5:82.
  ```
  (arp.opcode == 0x0001) &&
  !(arp.src.hw_mac == 00:01:5c:22:a5:82)
  ```

- The following display filter shows any BOOTP/DHCP packets to or from 74.31.51.150 that lists 73.68.136.1 as the relay agent.
  ```
  (bootp.ip.relay == 73.68.136.1) &&
  (bootp.ip.your == 74.31.51.150)
  ```

---

[57] Note that Wireshark does not recognize `dhcp` as a display filter. DHCP is based on BOOTP and Wireshark recognizes `bootp` as the filter to display all DHCP traffic.

- The following filter displays packets that have the TCP ACK bit set but not packets that have the TCP SYN bit set.
  ```
  (tcp.flags.ack == 1) &&
  !(tcp.flags.syn == 1)
  ```
- The following filter displays ICMP Destination Unreachable packets that indicate the host is unreachable or the protocol is unreachable.
  ```
  (icmp.type == 3) && ((icmp.code == 0x01)
  || (icmp.code == 0x02))
  ```

There is another form of display filter—one that uses the offset and a value calculated from a specific point in a packet. These types of display filter use the same format as offset capture filters *proto[expr:size]*. These filters may not be used often, but knowing how to create one when you need it can save you loads of time.

```
eth.src[4:2] == 22:1b
ip[14:2] == 96:2c
```

These offset filters are discussed in *Filter on Specific Bytes in a Packet* on page 222.

Use Your Display Filters in Command Line Capture

If you know how to build display filters efficiently, those filters can be used with the -R parameter with Tshark for command-line capture. You can even use Tshark to read an existing trace file, apply a display filter and output to a new trace file using the -r, -R and -w parameters together. Using display filters with Tshark during a live capture does not limit the packets you are capturing; it only limits the packets you see. Using these display filters with Tshark on previously saved captures can allow you to create a subset of the original trace file however. For examples of using display filters with Tshark, refer to *Tshark Examples* on page 686.

Create Display Filters Using Auto-Complete

If you know the display filter syntax you want to use, you can type it directly into the display filter area. Wireshark has an auto-complete feature that helps you create your filters. For example, if you type in tcp. (be sure to include the period after tcp) as shown in Figure 126, Wireshark's auto-complete feature lists possible display filter values that could be created beginning with tcp.

Note that tcp without the period is a valid display filter (as noted by the green background), but tcp followed by a period is not a valid display filter—you must either complete the filter by removing the period or add remaining text to the display filter as shown in the drop down list. For more information on Wireshark's validity checks, refer to *Let Wireshark Catch Display Filter Mistakes* on page 223.

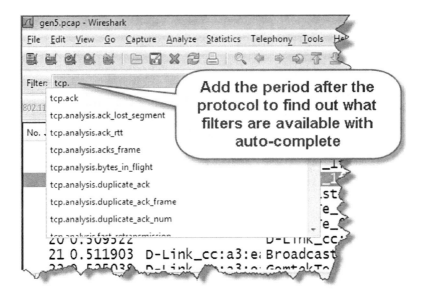

Figure 126. Wireshark's auto-complete feature helps you create valid filters

Apply Saved Display Filters

Click on the **Filter** button to the left of the display filter area to open the display filter window, shown in Figure 127. When you create filters that you want to use again, save them using the display filters window.

To create and save a new display filter, click **New** then enter the filter name and filter string. Wireshark supports error checking and auto-complete in the display filter box.

How to Ensure Your Display Filter is Saved

*If you do not see your filter listed in the display filters list, your filter cannot be saved. You must click **New** to create a new the filter. This is a common mistake people make when creating new display filters.*

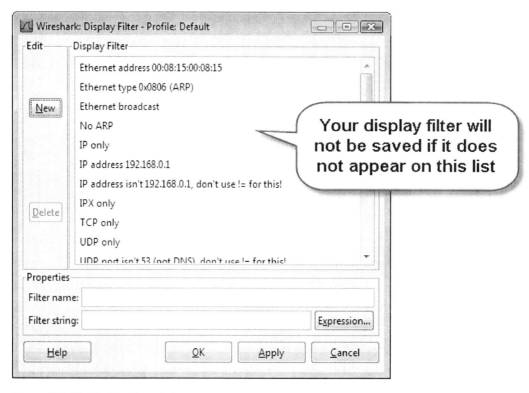

Figure 127. The display filter window

Use Expressions for Filter Assistance

In some cases you may want to make more complex filters, but you might not know the syntax. In addition, you might not be aware of the fields available for a specific type of communication. The Expression button is located to the right of the Display Filter field.

Expressions "walk you through" the filter creation process.

Some of the protocols and applications listed in the Filter Expression window include predefined values for individual fields. The FTP expression detail for `ftp.response.code` provides an example of a fully-defined expression as shown in Figure 128.

Expressions consist of field names, relations, values, pre-defined values (if available) and range. Selecting the "is present" relation simply builds a filter for the existence of the protocol, application or field. For example, selecting Mobile IP as the field name and "is present" in the relation area creates a `mip` filter that just looks for all Mobile IP traffic.

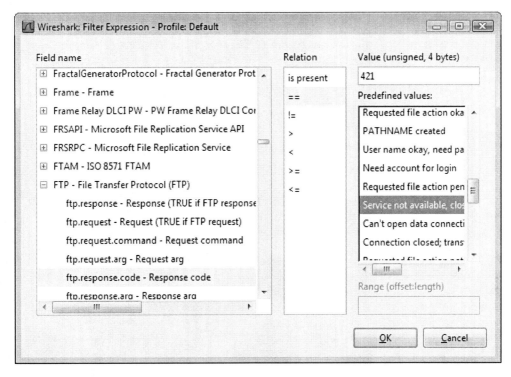

Figure 128. Some expression fields have pre-defined values

The following table provides examples of display filters created with Expressions:

Display Filter	Expression Path
`expert.severity == 1536`	Expert | Expert Severity | == | Warn
`expert.message`	Expert | Expert Message | is present
`bootp.type == 1`	BOOTP or DHCP | bootp.type | == | Boot Request
`dns.flags.opcode == 1`	DNS | dns.flags.opcode | == | Inverse Query

Make Display Filters Quickly Using Right-Click Filtering

You can use right-click filtering in the Packet List pane and the Packet Details pane. You cannot use this technique in the Packet Bytes pane.

You can right click on the Packet List pane and prepare or apply a filter based on the column and row that you right clicked on. You can also right click on a field or summary line in the Packet Details pane. Rather than type out a field value, right click on the field of interest and select either **Apply as Filter | Selected** or **Prepare a Filter | Selected**.

Apply as Filter

Use Apply as Filter to apply the filter immediately. You can edit the filter after it has been applied or expand the filter by using this technique and specifying one of the other filter options such as:

- Not Selected   (create an exclusion filter based on the selection)
- ... and Selected   (must match existing filter AND the selection)
- ... or Selected   (must match either existing filter OR the selection)
- ... and Not Selected   (must match existing filter AND NOT selection)
- ... or Not Selected   (must match either existing filter OR NOT selection)

Be careful—if you choose Apply as | Selected again or choose Apply as | Not Selected you will replace your original filter with the current field name and value. These two options replace anything already shown in your display filter window.

If you choose another option, an operator (&& or || or != or !) is placed after the existing filter portion and the field and value selected will be appended to the existing filter. For more information on display filter operators, refer to *Combine Display Filters with Comparison Operators* on Page 220.

For example, if you already have arp in your display filter window when you click on a source MAC address and select ...and Not Selected, your filter would display all ARP packets except those with the MAC address selected.

Prepare a Filter

Right click on a field and select **Prepare a Filter** to create a filter, but not apply it immediately. This process is useful for creating longer, more complex filters with numerous operators. For example, if you wanted to build a filter on ICMP Destination Unreachable/Port Unreachable packets, you could select the ICMP type value of 3 first and then select the ICMP code value of 3 using the **...and Selected** operation. You can edit your filter before applying it if necessary.

Copy | As Filter

One of the newer additions to Wireshark's display filter creation process is the right click ability to Copy | As Filter. Using this method, you can right click a field in either the Packet List pane or a field in the Packet Details pane and buffer a display filter based on that field using this copy feature. This technique is very useful for creating coloring rules or building more complex display filters.

Filter on Conversations and Endpoints

You can create a filter based on the conversations or endpoints window contents. Right click on a conversation of interest and select either **Prepare a Filter** or **Apply as Filter**. As shown in Figure 129, when creating filters based on a conversation, you are prompted for the direction of travel in addition to the basic filter type. The directions are based on the Address A and Address B column titles in the conversation window.

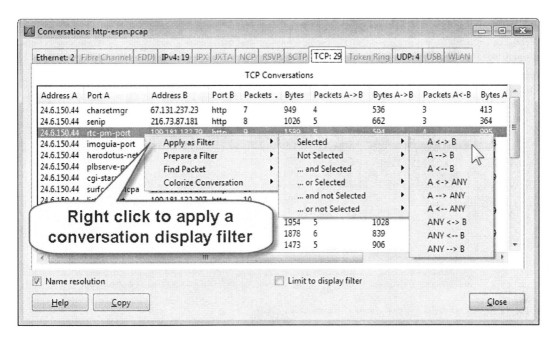

Figure 129. Create a bidirectional display filter based on a conversation

You can use the same steps to create display filters based on the endpoints window with one exception—the endpoints window does not offer an option to define the direction of the traffic.

Understand Display Filter Syntax

Display filters syntax is used to create display filters and coloring rules.

Every field shown in the Packet Details pane (whether that field actually exists in a packet or is simply a packet characteristic, such as a retransmission) can be used to create these filters. Highlight a field in the Packet Details pane and the related display filter value is shown in the status area. In Figure 130 we selected the TCP window size field. The field name is `tcp.window_size`. Now that we know the field name, we can create a `tcp.window_size == 65535` filter.

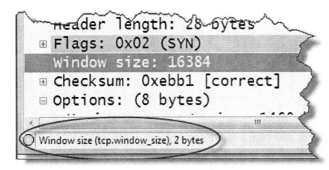

Figure 130. The field name selected in a packet is shown in the Status bar

As mentioned earlier, you can create display filters on packet characteristics as opposed to actual fields. In Figure 131 we selected the TCP analysis line stating "*[This is a tcp window update]*". The display syntax for all TCP window update packets is `tcp.analysis.window_update`. You can right click and apply a filter for TCP window update packets even though this field does not exist.

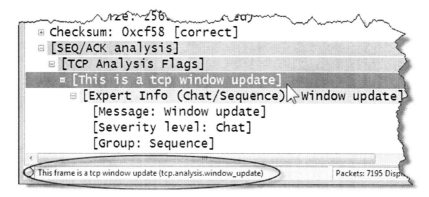

Figure 131. Not all fields displayed actually exist in a packet

Combine Display Filters with Comparison Operators

Comparison and logical operators enable you to combine multiple filters to further define the traffic of interest and offer a negative operand to filter out undesired traffic (exclusion filtering).

Description	Symbol	Text
equal to	==	eq
or	‖	or
and	&&	and
greater than	>	gt
less than	<	lt
greater than or equal to	>=	ge
less than or equal to	<=	le
not	!	not
not equal to	!=	ne
contains		contains
matches		matches

Understand Wireshark Warnings on Using `!=`

*Wireshark colorizes the display filter area in yellow whenever you use the != operator. It doesn't mean your filter won't work—it's just a warning that it **may not** work. See Let Wireshark Catch Display Filter Mistakes on page 223 for more details.*

You can create display filters with operators using the right-click method, expressions or just by typing in the filter. The following provides examples of various display filters using operators:

Display Filter	Description
`ip.addr == 10.2.3.4 && http`	Only display HTTP traffic to or from 10.2.3.4
`!arp && !icmp`	Display all traffic *except* ARP and ICMP traffic
`bootp || dns`	Only display BOOTP/DHCP or DNS traffic
`tcp contains "PASS"`	Only display packets that have the ASCII string "PASS" in the TCP segment
`dns.count.answers > 2`	Only display DNS responses that contain more than two answers
`tcp matches "zip"`	The TCP stream includes the text value "zip." This is a great filter if you are looking for HTTP downloads of compressed files. Consider using "exe" as the target content (note that "zip" may be included in the Accept-Encoding HTTP modifier)

You can use operators to make more complex inclusion display filters (indicating traffic you want to show) or exclusion display filters (traffic you want to hide).

The majority of the comparison operators are relatively intuitive—the **matches** operator is not, however. The *matches* operator is used with Perl regular expressions to search for a string within a field.

Check **Help | About Wireshark.** If the About box says "NOTE: this build doesn't support the "matches" operator for Wireshark filter syntax" then "matches" isn't supported.

The following is an example out of the wiki page (*wiki.wireshark.org/DisplayFilters*):

```
http.request.uri matches "gl=se$"
```

This filter examines the end (as denoted by the "$") of the URI Request line in an HTTP packet for the string "gl=se".

In the Practice What You've Learned section at the end of this chapter you will have a chance to test using "matches" on a trace file.

Alter Display Filter Meaning with Parentheses

Use parentheses to have the conditions evaluated in a specific order. For example, the two filters shown in the next table have different interpretations based on the parentheses set:

Filter with Parentheses	Interpretation
`(ip.src==192.168.0.105 and udp.port==53) or tcp.port==80`	DNS/port 53 traffic from 192.168.0.105 **plus** all HTTP/port 80 traffic on the network
`ip.src==192.168.0.105 and (udp.port==53 or tcp.port==80)`	DNS/port 53 **or** HTTP/port 80 traffic from 192.168.0.105

Filter on Specific Bytes in a Packet

Offset filters are also referred to as Subset Operators. These filters define a frame element, an offset, length (optional), operator and value. You can use these filters when no simpler filter method is available. For example, if you want to filter on Ethernet source addresses that end with a specific two-byte value, use an offset filter.

An example of an offset display filter is shown below.

```
eth.src[4:2] == 22:1b
```

The display filter shown above begins looking at the Ethernet Source Address field in a frame then counts over 5 bytes (we begin counting with zero) and looks for the two-byte value 0x221b. This means we are looking at the last two bytes in the Ethernet source field for the value 0x221b.

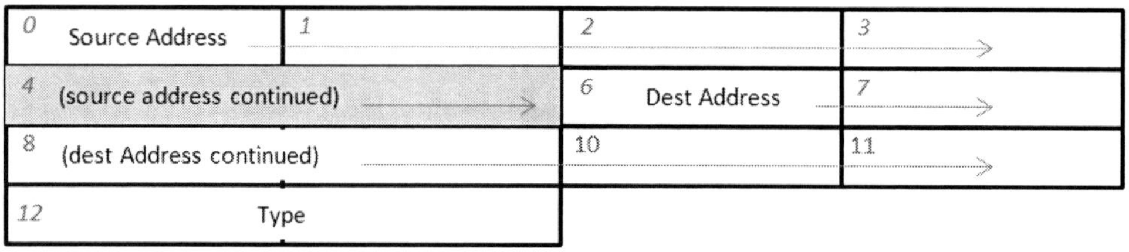

Figure 132. The filter `eth.src[4:2]` looks at the last two bytes of the Ethernet Source Address field

Another example of an offset filter is shown below.

```
ip[14:2] == 96:2c
```

This filter looks at the 15th and 16th bytes of the IP header (the last two bytes of the source IP address) for the value 0x962c (this would equate to a source IP address ending in 150.44). Figure 133 shows the breakdown of an IP header. Remember that the value [14:2] means we count over 15 bytes (start counting at 0) and look for a two-byte value.

0	Ver/Hdr Len	1	DiffServ	2	Total Length	
4	Identification			6	Flags/Fragment Offset	
8	TTL	9	Protocol	10	Hdr Checksum	
12	Source Address	13		14		15
15	Dest Address	16		17		18
19		20	Options (if any)			22

Figure 133. The filter `ip[14:2]` *looks at the 15th and 16th bytes(start counting at 0) in IP header source address field*

The need to create offset filters has been reduced because of the number of filters built into Wireshark. There are still times, however, when you need to use these offset filters to look inside fields for a partial value match.

Let Wireshark Catch Display Filter Mistakes

Wireshark contains error checking to help you avoid syntax problems and even practical display filter mistakes such as `ip.addr != 10.2.4.1`. This mistake is defined in *Avoid Common Display Filter Mistakes* on page 224.

- A green background indicates the filter syntax is correct and logical.
- A yellow background indicates the syntax is correct, but it may not be logically correct. For an example of a filter that would be colored yellow, see *Avoid Common Display Filter Mistakes* on page 225.
- A red background indicates a syntax error. Filters marked with a red background will not process correctly.

Not all display filter mistakes are caught by Wireshark's error checking mechanism. For example, consider the filter `http && arp`. How can a packet be both an HTTP packet *and* an ARP packet? It can't.

Use Display Filter Macros for Complex Filtering

Display filters macros are used to create shortcuts for more complex display filters. Select **Analyze | Display Filter macros | New** to create a new macro.

Display filter macros are saved in *dfilters_macros* in your Personal Configuration folder. If you create display filter macros under a profile other than the default profile, the *dfilters_macros* file is saved in the associated profile's directory. The syntax of this file is `"name","filter_string"`.

To create a display filter macro, first you must name the macro. You must use this name to call the macro in the display filter window. Figure 134 shows a display filter macro used to view traffic destined to five ports. Without using a display filter macro, this display filter syntax would be `tcp.dstport == 5600 || tcp.dstport == 5603 || tcp.dstport == 6400 || tcp.dstport == 6500 || tcp.dstport == 6700`.

The macro shown in Figure 134 is named "5ports". Dollar signs precede the variable numbers. The syntax to use this macro would be `${5ports:5600;5603;6400;6500;6700}`.

When we run this display filter macro, the five port variables will be substituted as follows:

$1   tcp.dstport == 5600
$2   tcp.dstport == 5603
$3   tcp.dstport == 6400
$4   tcp.dstport == 6500
$5   tcp.dstport == 6700

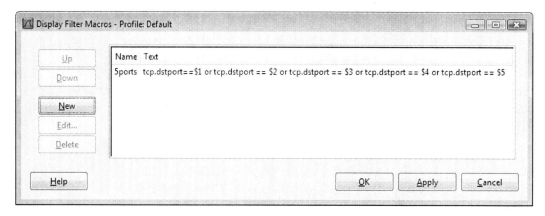

Figure 134. Display filter macros provide shortcuts for more complex filters

Another example of a time saving display filter macro would be one that focuses on a specific conversation—we'll call this macro "conv1". The display filter macro syntax would be:

```
(ip.src == $1 and ip.dst == $2 and tcp.srcport == $3 and
tcp.dstport == $4) or (ip.src == $2 and ip.dst == $1 and
tcp.srcport == $4 and tcp.dstport == $3)
```

In the example provided above, the display filter macro focuses on a specific conversation based on IP addresses and TCP port numbers. To run the macro, we would use the following command in the display filter window:

```
${tcp_conv:192.168.1.1;192.168.1.99;1201;2401}
```

You can share display filter macros by simply copying the *dfilters_macros* file from your Personal Configuration folder or profile folder to another Wireshark system.

Avoid Common Display Filter Mistakes

One of the most common filter mistakes involves the use of the ! or `not` operand. This problem is mostly seen when filtering out traffic to or from an IP address or port number.

Many people are familiar with the `ip.addr==10.2.4.1` syntax for displaying packets that contain the IP address 10.2.4.1 in either the source or destination IP address field. Naturally, they enter `ip.addr != 10.2.4.1` to try to view all packets *except* ones that contain the address 10.2.4.1. This filter structure does not work, however.

The filter `ip.addr != 10.2.4.1` actually means you are looking for a packet that has an `ip.addr` field that contains a value other than 10.2.4.1. There are two IP address fields in the packet, however and this filter will allow a packet to be displayed if it has 10.2.4.1 in *either* of those two fields. First Wireshark looks at the source IP address field to see if the filter matches. Next it looks at the destination IP address field.

The table below shows how packets are examined. Using the filter `ip.addr != 10.2.4.1`, if one of the IP addresses matches the filter then the packet will be displayed.

Source IP Address	Destination IP Address	Show Packet?
10.2.4.1 (no match)	255.255.255.255 (match)	Yes
10.99.99.99 (match)	10.2.4.1 (no match)	Yes
10.2.4.1 (no match)	10.99.99.99 (match)	Yes
10.2.2.2 (match)	10.1.1.1 (match)	No

The correct filter syntax is `!ip.addr==10.2.4.1`. Place the ! or `not` before `ip.addr`.

Manually Edit the *dfilters* File

You can add filters through the Wireshark GUI interface or edit the *dfilters* file directly. The default *dfilters* file is located in the Global Configurations directory. New filters are added to the *dfilters* file and a copy is placed in the Personal Configurations folder or in the current profile directory.

The syntax of the *dfilters* file is:

```
"filter name" filter string
```

The *dfilters* file does not have an extension and you must include a new line after the last display filter entry or it will not show up in the Wireshark display filter list.

The advantage of manually editing the *dfilters* file is the ability to reorder the display filters and add indenting and titles to your display filters list as shown in Figure 135.

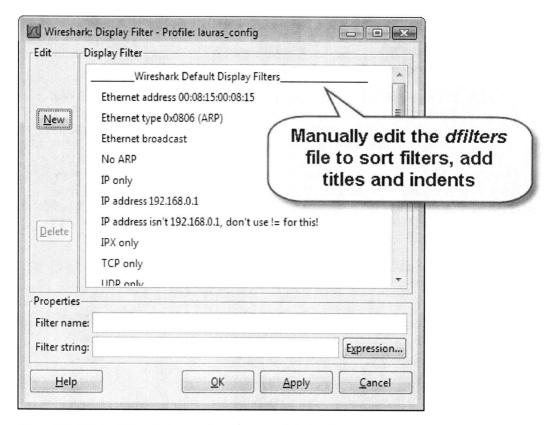

Figure 135. Edit the dfilters file to organize your personal display filters

To add the title and indents to your display filters list, manually edit the *dfilters* file and put underscores and spaces inside the quotes used around the name of the display filter, as shown in Figure 136.

The Download section of the book website, *www.wiresharkbook.com*, contains the *dfilters* file shown in Figure 136.

```
"_____Laura's Display Filters_____" Register for
Wireshark Certification Test Today
"    Default IRC TCP Ports 6666-6669 (IRC Traffic - Bot Issue?)"
tcp.port == 6666 || tcp.port == 6667 || tcp.port == 6668 || tcp.port ==
6669
"    DHCP NACK (DHCP Server Does Not Like Target)" (bootp.option.type
== 53) && (bootp.option.value == 06)
"    DNS Answers > 5 (Bot IRC List in this Packet?)" dns.count.answers
> 5
"    ICMP Protocol Unreachable (IP Scan Underway?)" icmp.type==3 &&
icmp.code==2
"    ICMP Response to TCP Packet (Sender Firewalled?)" (icmp) && (tcp)
```

Figure 136. An edited dfilters file

Using display filters helps avoid the "needle in the haystack issue" and speeds up the process of finding the cause of network problems and identifying unusual traffic patterns. For more information on the "needle in the haystack issue," see *Overcome the "Needle in the Haystack Issue"* on page 9.

The case studies at the end of this chapter provide examples of using display filters to solve network concerns and perform application analysis.

Case Study:
Using Filters and Graphs to Solve Database Issues

Submitted by: Coleen D.
Network Analyst

There appeared to be way too many connections to our documentation server at specific times during the day. The server administrators thought someone was attacking the server and they wanted to know how many active connections had been established to the server throughout the day and by whom.

I ended up using a display filter for the third packet of the TCP handshake to catch all successful connections and plotting this on an IO Graph. My filter is shown below.

```
(tcp.flags == 0x10) && (tcp.seq == 1) &&
(tcp.ack == 1)
```

The first part of my filter looked for packets that had just the ACK bit set in the TCP header. The second part looked for the TCP Sequence Number field set to 1 and the third part looked for the TCP Acknowledgment Number field set to 1.

We always have "relative sequence numbering" enabled in Wireshark's TCP preferences (otherwise this wouldn't work) and these field values are always seen in the third packet of the TCP handshakes.

To see these connections, I put this display filter in the red graph line in the IO Graph and used the Fbar format so it really showed up.

Sure enough, we did find that the connections spiked around 2pm each day.

Interestingly, it was one of the documentation server administrator machines that made over 1,000 connections to their own server around that time. It turned out someone in their group was testing out a new document management package that flooded the documentation server with connections every time they ran it.

We could easily show the source of the connections and recommend against the lousy program they were about to buy!

We saved the company a ton of money and headache using Wireshark!

Case Study:
The Chatty Browser

To analyze Twitter traffic, I created a filter for all traffic to/from my IP address (ip.addr==192.168.0.106) and then filtered out any of my unrelated traffic—the idle traffic and the background traffic sent when my browser connected to Web of Trust or other sites that had nothing to do with the Twitter communications.

I was working backwards and separating out my Firefox traffic and any other noise that my host generates without my interaction. I created a number exclusions to my display filter as I identified my background traffic to my printer, my router's management port, DHCP noise, ARP noise, traffic from my iPhone (which was being bridged onto the wired network), Google Analytics and Google Malware updates from Firefox, World News and BBC background feeds from Firefox and anything else not related to my Twitter communications.

When my convoluted display filter was completed, I could see no background traffic from superfluous processes.

My final display filter was extremely long:

```
ip.addr==192.168.0.106  && !srvloc && !dns &&
!ip.addr==74.6.114.56 && !ip.addr==239.255.255.250 &&
!ip.addr==96.17.0.0/16 && !ip.addr==192.168.0.102 && !smb
&& !nbns && !ip.addr== 192.168.0.103 &&
!ip.addr==64.74.80.187 && ! ip.addr==83.150.67.33 &&
!ip.addr==67.217.0.0/16 && !ip.addr==66.102.7.101 &&
!ip.addr==216.115.0.0/16 && !ip.addr==216.219.0.0/16 &&
!ip.addr==69.90.30.72
```

Although I started out analyzing Twitter traffic, I ended up finding out that all the plugins we added to Firefox made our browsers way too chatty—they were talking all the time.

We temporarily turned on network name resolution in Wireshark to make it easier to find out who the plugins were talking to. It made Wireshark really slow when we opened the Conversation and Endpoint statistics, but we could easily spot the plugin traffic by the targets.

We ended up uninstalling some of the plugins that were talking all day long in the background. We didn't need them and they just added too much garbage to the network.

Case Study: Catching Viruses and Worms

Submitted by: Todd Lerdal

Computer viruses and worms were a great learning time for me with packet analysis. I was very new at packet analysis and would just fire off traces on a VLAN to get a "feel" of what was running on my network. "Unofficial base-lining" is probably a better description—never documented anything other than getting an idea in my head of what was normal.

I knew the sorts of applications that I should expect to see, NCP, Web, Telnet, Citrix, etc. If there was something out there I didn't recognize, I'd filter down to it just to get a better understanding of "should this be running?"

Then, the worms hit.

I spent many hours/days with a monitor session on our server VLAN just watching how worms would spread to help identify, isolate, and inoculate infected workstations.

It doesn't take long once you start watching to see the unusual traffic on your LAN. What I would see is what appeared to be ping sweeps or port scans coming from multiple hosts.

Once I'd captured enough packets I was able to then build better display filters to identify just these sweeps so that I could then isolate the infected workstations and help the desktop and server teams to go clean these devices before allowing them back on the network.

With practice, it didn't take me long to generate lists of IP addresses or device names to provide the desktop folks so they could start cleaning.

Summary

Display filters are used to focus on specific packets, protocols, conversations or endpoints of interest. Display filters use the special Wireshark syntax—they are not interchangeable with capture filters which use the BPF filter syntax (also used by tcpdump).

Wireshark provides automatic error checking of your display filter syntax (green = correct syntax, red = incorrect syntax, yellow = may yield unexpected results). You can also use Wireshark's Expressions to create filters using predefined fields and field values.

One of the fastest ways to create a display filter is to right click on a field and select either Apply as Filter or Prepare a Filter. You can use comparison operators to combine multiple display filters, but be careful of the parentheses in your filters. The location of parentheses can alter a display filter's meaning.

Display filters are saved in the *dfilters* file and can be edited through the GUI or directly in the text file. You can share your display filters by simply sending someone a copy of your *dfilters* file.

 There are numerous Wireshark display filters contained in the Downloads section of the book website, *www.wiresharkbook.com*. One of the *dfilters* files available online is shown in Figure 136. This *dfilters* file includes the default set of display filters released with Wireshark and 15 additional display filters. To use this *dfilters* file, simply copy the file into your Personal Configuration folder or create a new profile and copy this file into the profile's folder. For more information on creating a new profile, refer to *Chapter 11: Customize Wireshark Profiles*.

Practice What You've Learned

The following table lists several trace files to use when practicing what you've learned in this chapter.

http-aol.pcap	It takes 18 different TCP connections to load the *www.aol.com* site. Have you analyzed the connection to your corporate website lately? Use `http.request.uri matches "laptop$"` as the display filter. Another example of using the matches operator is `http.request.uri matches "&+"`. This filter examines the URI field for the value "&" and display the packet if the value is found 1 or more times as denoted by the +.
app-norton-update2.pcap	This Symantec update process doesn't seem to work very well. Consider building a filter for `http.response.code == 404` and note the number of "File Not Found" responses. Now compare these two display filters and examine the difference in your results: (a) `!http.response.code == 404` (b) `http.response.code !=404`

ftp-crack.pcap

Apply the following display filter to the traffic:

```
ftp.request.command == "USER" ||
ftp.request.command == "PASS"
```

This reveals that the password cracking attempt is only focused on the admin account and the passwords are coming from a dictionary that includes names. Looks like they are cycling through the password list—we caught them on the letter M, but they start at the beginning later (packet 4739).

Review Questions

Q9.1   **What syntax type is used by Wireshark display filters?**

Q9.2   **Why is the display filter `arp && bootp` incorrect?**

Q9.3   **What is the difference between *Prepare a Filter* and *Apply as Filter*?**

Q9.4   **What is the difference between the following filters?**

```
(ip.src==192.168.0.1 and udp.port==53) or tcp.port==80
ip.src==192.168.0.1 and (udp.port==53 or tcp.port==80)
```

Answers to Review Questions

Q9.1 **What syntax type is used by Wireshark display filters?**

A9.1 Display filters use Wireshark's specialized display filter format. Capture filters use the Berkeley Packet Filtering (BPF) format (which is also used by tcpdump). Filters created with Wireshark's specialized display filter format and filters created with the BPF filter format are not interchangeable.

Q9.2 **Why is the display filter `arp && bootp` incorrect?**

A9.2 This filter displays packets that are both ARP and BOOTP/DHCP packets which is impossible. The correct filter would be `arp || bootp`.

Q9.3 **What is the difference between *Prepare a Filter* and *Apply as Filter*?**

A9.3 Prepare a Filter simply creates the filter and displays it in the display filter window—the filter is not applied yet. This allows you to add to the filter or edit the filter before applying it. Apply as Filter applies the filter to the traffic immediately.

Q9.4 **What is the difference between the following filters?**

```
(ip.src==192.168.0.105 and udp.port==53) or tcp.port==80

ip.src==192.168.0.105 and (udp.port==53 or tcp.port==80)
```

A9.4 The first filter displays DNS/port 53 traffic from 192.168.0.105 **plus** all HTTP/port 80 traffic on the network. The second filter displays DNS/port 53 or HTTP/port 80 traffic from 192.168.0.105.

Chapter 10: Follow Streams and Reassemble Data

Wireshark Certified Network Analyst Exam Objectives covered:

- Follow and Reassemble UDP Conversations
- Follow and Reassemble TCP Conversations
- Identify Common File Types
- Follow and Reassemble SSL Conversations

  - ❖ Case Study: Unknown Hosts Identified
  - ❖ Summary
  - ❖ Practice What You've Learned
  - ❖ Review Questions and Answers

Reassemble Traffic

Wireshark offers the ability to follow communications streams. The Follow Streams process reassembles the communications (minus the MAC header, network header and transport headers).

Figure 137 shows the result of following the TCP stream of an FTP command session. By default, Wireshark color codes the conversation in the streams window—red for traffic from the client (the host initiating the conversation) and blue for traffic from the server. You can change the color coding using **Edit | Preferences | Colors**.

Right click on a packet in the Packet List pane or Packet Bytes pane to select **Follow UDP Stream, Follow TCP Stream or Follow SSL Stream**. The traffic type that you have selected defines which option is available in the list.

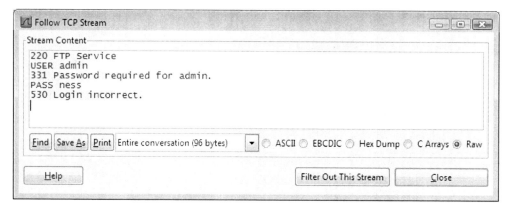

Figure 137. Following streams provides a clear view of commands and data transferred

Follow and Reassemble UDP Conversations

As long as the traffic has a UDP header, the option to Follow UDP Stream is available. Right click on a UDP packet and select **Follow UDP Stream**.

One example of using UDP stream reassembly is the process of reassembling a multicast video stream. As long as the video data is not encrypted, you can reassemble the data, use Save As to save the video stream in a video file format and open and replay it with a video player.

Consider VLC Player to Play Back Exported Video Files

We recommend VLC Player, an open source media player able to read numerous audio and video formats (MPEG-2, MPEG-4, H.264, DivX, MPEG-1, mp3, ogg, aac and more) as well as various streaming protocols. For more information on VLC, visit www.videolan.org.

Figure 138 shows a UDP stream in the background. Upon reassembling the UDP stream, a display filter was created for the UDP conversation - (ip.addr eq 192.168.1.12 and ip.addr eq 239.255.0.1) and (udp.port eq 1024 and udp.port eq 8001). In the

Stream Content window the data is displayed in raw format by default. Clicking Save As, we saved the data in a file called *videostream1*. We don't know the actual video format—VLC Player automatically detected the video type and, since it supports that video type, it could open and play the video.[58]

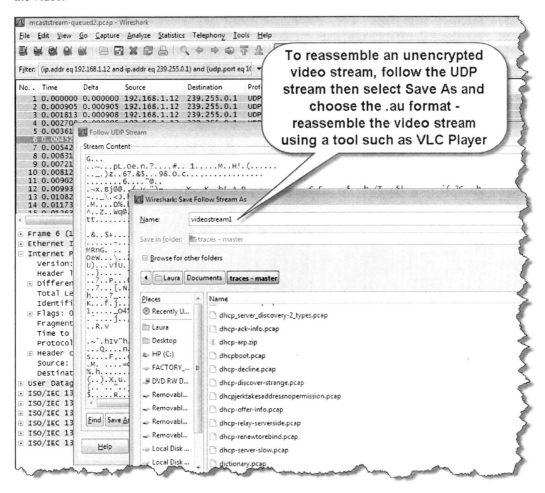

Figure 138. You can recreate a video stream using Follow UDP Stream

If the UDP stream you are examining is a VoIP RTP stream, use **Telephony | VoIP Calls | <select call> | Player | Decode** to reassemble an unencrypted VoIP call.

---

[58] Be aware of the file size you are working with when capturing video streams for reassembly. For example, a 5-minute YouTube video generates a 44 MB trace file. Wireshark v1.4 includes major improvements for dealing with larger trace files, but you still need to be aware that a larger trace file takes longer to load, longer to apply display filters, longer to reassemble data streams, etc. It is possible to fill an entire hard drive if you leave a Wireshark system capturing unattended.

Follow and Reassemble TCP Conversations

You can reassemble web browsing sessions, FTP command channel sessions, FTP data transfer channel sessions or any other TCP-based communications. Right click on a TCP packet and select **Follow TCP Stream**.

In some cases, you will see commands and application headers prefacing the data being transferred. For example, when reassembling an HTTP web browsing session, you will see the GET requests from the clients and the HTTP response codes from the server as well as the data that is being transferred.

When you follow TCP streams, a display filter based on the stream index number is created. The format of the filter is tcp.stream eq x. This filter syntax is also used when you follow SSL streams. The tcp.stream index value is listed in the TCP header as shown in Figure 139. Use this field to filter on a conversation from the Packet Details pane.

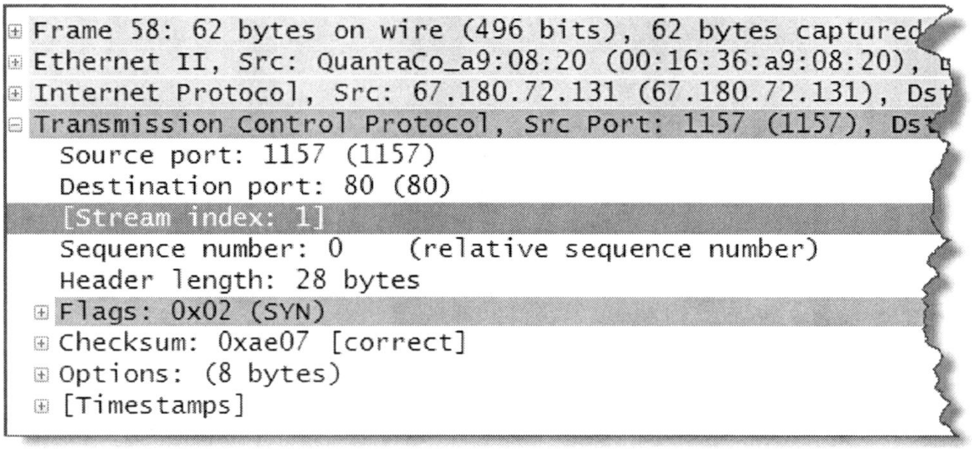

```
⊞ Frame 58: 62 bytes on wire (496 bits), 62 bytes captured
⊞ Ethernet II, Src: QuantaCo_a9:08:20 (00:16:36:a9:08:20),
⊞ Internet Protocol, Src: 67.180.72.131 (67.180.72.131), Dst
⊟ Transmission Control Protocol, Src Port: 1157 (1157), Dst
    Source port: 1157 (1157)
    Destination port: 80 (80)
    [Stream index: 1]
    Sequence number: 0     (relative sequence number)
    Header length: 28 bytes
⊞ Flags: 0x02 (SYN)
⊞ Checksum: 0xae07 [correct]
⊞ Options: (8 bytes)
⊞ [Timestamps]
```

Figure 139. The Stream Index value is in the TCP header

Figure 140 shows a reassembled FTP password cracking attempt. In this case the password cracking application uses the same TCP connection for each crack attempt. If we are interested in finding a particular password that was attempted, we can use the Find command in the Stream content window.

When analyzing or troubleshooting HTTP communications, **Follow TCP Stream** can be very useful to examine the commands and responses. In Figure 141 we reassembled an HTTP POST process where we can clearly see the data being sent from the client to the HTTP server. In this case, a user is filling out an online form on a web server.

Figure 140. Reassembling a password crack attempts that take place over a single TCP connection

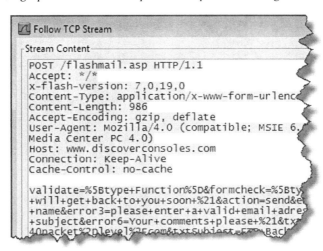

Figure 141. Reassembling an HTTP post session

What if we want to reassemble data in an HTTP communication? One option is to choose Export | Objects | HTTP to extract the objects downloaded during the entire HTTP session.

In some cases, however, you need to look through the data stream to find an embedded file. You can use a file extension or a file identifier to determine the type of file transferred. The file identifier is contained in the leading bytes of a file and is used to define whether a file is a Word document, a trace file, an Excel spreadsheet, an Open Office document, etc.

For more information on file types and file extensions, visit *mark0.net/soft-trid-deflist.html*.

In Figure 142, a TCP stream contains a file called *me.docx*. In this case we are aware that the file we are going to extract is a Word .docx file. These files start with the file identifier (50 4B 03 04 (in hex) which translates to the letters "PK" (also used for PKzip files). We can see these letters clearly in the TCP stream.

In Wireshark, we can save the entire TCP stream as a .docx file—Word 2007 generates an error when we try to open the file because there are leading bytes that are not part of the document. Word asks if we want to it to try to recover the file and, if we agree, it will look for the file identifier and rebuild the Word file from that point.

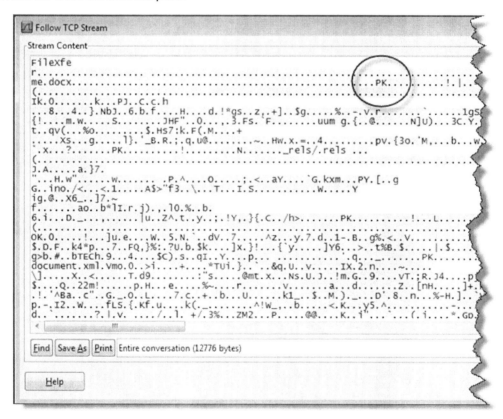

Figure 142. Sometimes you need to extract a file from inside a stream

Identify Common File Types

Files begin with file identifiers that indicate the application used to create or open the file. The following list provides some basic file identifier values. View streams in hex dump format so you can use the Find feature to locate these hex values in a stream.

Application	Extension	Value
Excel	xls	D0 CF 11 E0 A1 B1 1A E1 00
JPEG Bitmap	jpg	FF D8 FF
Open Office Document	odp	50 4B 03 04
Portable Network Graphics	png	89 50 4E 47 0D 0A 1A 0A 00 00 00 0D 49 48 44 52
Powerpoint Slide Deck	ppt	D0 CF 11 E0 A1 B1 1A E1 00
Powerpoint XML	pptx	50 4B 03 04
Wireshark .pcap Trace File	pcap	D4 C3 B2 A1
Wireshark XML File	docx	50 $B 03 04
Word	doc	D0 CF 11 E0 A1 B1 1A E1
Word 2007	docx	50 4B 03 04
PK Zip File	zip	50 4B 03 04

Reassemble an FTP File Transfer

It is an easy process to reassemble files transferred using FTP. The first step is to locate the FTP data channel. (Refer to *Chapter 24: Analyze File Transfer Protocol (FTP) Traffic* for details on FTP command and data channels.)

FTP data can run over any port number. Filter for `ftp.response.code == 227 || ftp.request.command == "PORT"` to view the FTP command channel traffic that will indicate the port used for data transfer. The response code 227 indicates that passive FTP data channel is being established. The FTP command PORT is used for an active command. Packets that match these two filters contain the IP address and port number of the data channel.

Figure 143 shows an FTP communication using a dynamic port number for the data transfer. In this example, the client has requested that the server enter passive mode (PASV). In packet 8 the server indicates that it is entering passive mode and defines the port number it will use for the FTP communications—port 30189. Immediately following the response, the client completes the TCP handshake to port 30189. The client sends two more commands on the FTP command channel: SIZE and RETR. The RETR command is the request to transfer the file *OS Fingerprinting with ICMP.zip* (the name is truncated in the screenshot).

Once you know what port the FTP data transfer takes place on, right click on a packet in that data stream and select **Follow TCP Stream**.

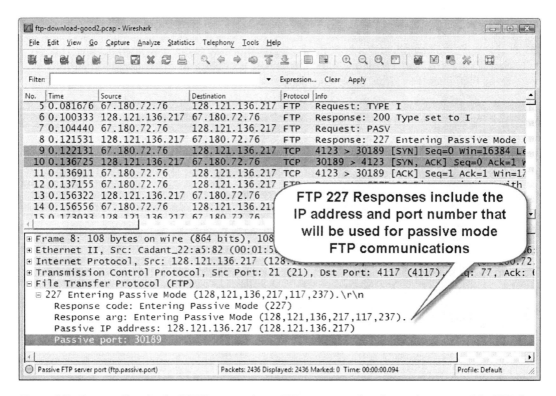

Figure 143. Create a filter for the PORT command or a 227 response code to locate the port used for FTP data

We can now right click on packet 9, the first packet of the data channel TCP handshake and select Reassemble TCP Stream. We know this is a .zip file based on the file name. Selecting Save As and naming the file allows us to unzip and open the PDF file contained therein.

When you follow a stream, Wireshark applies a display filter for the conversation based on the TCP stream index. You must clear this filter to see the entire contents of the saved or unsaved trace.

Follow and Reassemble SSL Conversations

Wireshark can decrypt SSL communications if you define RSA keys in **Edit | Preferences | Protocols | SSL**. For more information on SSL decryption and a sample SSL encrypted file, visit *Decrypt HTTPS Traffic* on page 466 and *wiki.wireshark.org/SSL*. In this example, we downloaded the *rsasnakeoil2.pcap* file and the RSA decryption key[59]. Right click on a decrypted SSL packet and select **Follow SSL Streams**.

Figure 144 shows the *rsasnakeoil2.pcap* trace file. We have not configured the SSL protocol with a link to the RSA key so no data is available when we follow the SSL stream.

---

[59] Wireshark is not a password cracking tool—you need to provide the key in order to decrypt WLAN or SSL communications.

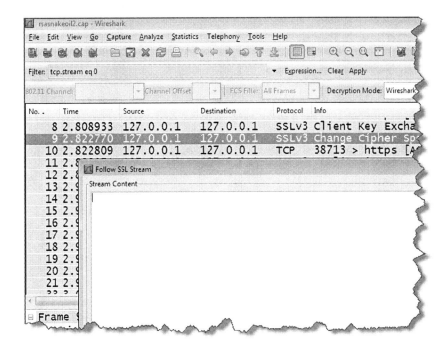

Figure 144. The rsasnakeoil2.pcap trace contains SSL traffic—until we apply the RSA key, the SSL stream is blank

In Figure 145 we have entered the RSA key information in the SSL protocol section under preferences. Our setting is `127.0.0.1,443,http,c:\keys\rsasnakeoil2.key`.

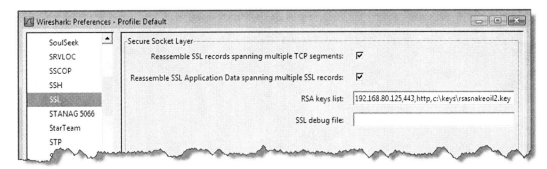

Figure 145. Adding the RSA key setting in the SSL preferences

In Figure 146, we have applied the RSA key to the Wireshark SSL protocol configuration. When we follow the SSL stream in the *rsasnakeoil2.pcap* trace, we can see the HTTP session contents and see the HTTP requests and responses clearly.

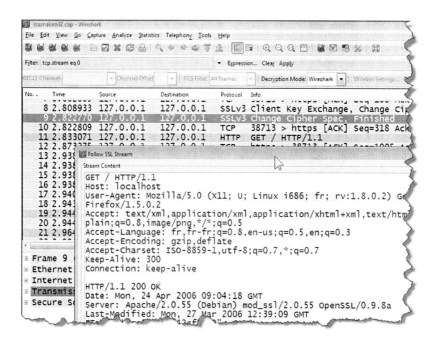

Figure 146. Follow the SSL stream after applying the RSA key to see the traffic in clearly

For another example of decrypting and analyzing SSL streams, refer to *Analyze HTTPS* on page 461.

Case Study:
Unknown Hosts Identified

The hospital IT staff stated they had 458 hosts and 7 servers at the location where we were working. The job was focused on training this staff to use Wireshark to quickly spot network problems and fix them fast.

During the analysis process, we captured all network traffic off a switch—we didn't span the port—we were just examining the broadcast and multicast traffic on the network. As we talked about broadcast traffic rates it became evident that this network had more than 458 hosts and 7 servers. We saw ARP broadcasts from over 600 devices throughout the day.

The IT team said this just could not be possible. In addition, they did not believe they had such a flat network—they had routers in place and no single subnet should have more than about 210 devices on it.

It was time to start spanning various switch ports to capture more than just ARP broadcasts from these devices. We decided to capture traffic to file sets to deal with the high amount of traffic we were capturing.

It didn't take long to see some undecoded traffic crossing the network from a host that the IT team did not recognize. We focused in on this traffic.

Since Wireshark didn't have a dissector for this traffic, we couldn't tell right away what the mysterious device was saying.

By reassembling the UDP streams we could see some interesting text strings that helped us identify these devices. They were various pieces of medical equipment that had embedded Windows XP running on them.

This raised serious concerns about the security of the network—were these systems patched and updated to protect them against known security issues? Who was responsible to keep these "closed devices" up-to-date?

This onsite analysis project lead to the customer coordinating a vendor/customer initiative to examine the security of devices with embedded operating systems. In some cases they pulled the devices from the network completely.

Summary

Following streams is a useful process to view the commands and data transferred in a conversation. Wireshark strips off the data link header, IP header and TCP or UDP header and color codes the traffic to differentiate between client and server traffic.

You can reassemble UDP, TCP and SSL streams. SSL streams only show reassembled data after they are decrypted.

On some communications, such as FTP data transfers, you can rebuild the original file transferred by saving the reassembled data. You can use the file identifier to determine what type of file was transferred.

Practice What You've Learned

 Download the trace files available in the Download section of the book website, *www.wiresharkbook.com*. Open the trace files listed below to practice reassembling streams.

app-nodissector.pcap   Even though Wireshark doesn't have a dissector for this application, following the TCP stream reveals the application in use. If Wireshark doesn't have a dissector for your traffic, examine the payload to look for some evidence to help identify the application or look up the port number used on *www.iana.org*.

ftp-clientside.pcap   You'll want to disable the Checksum Errors coloring rule when viewing this trace file. This is an FTP file transfer—note that you can follow the TCP stream of the data transfer and see the type of camera used to take the picture. This trace is the client side of the *ftp-serverside.pcap* trace file. Use **Save As** to make a new file from the data exchanged during this conversation.

http-proxy-problem.pcap   The client can't get communicate to other networks because of errors getting through the proxy server. Find and read the proxy response in clear text by following the TCP stream. Also note the slow handshake response time. Not a good day for this user.

Review Questions

Q10.1   You have selected a packet in the Packet List pane, but Follow TCP Stream, Follow UDP Stream and Follow SSL Stream are not available. Why not?

Q10.2   What is the syntax of the display filter created when you choose Follow TCP Stream?

Q10.3   How can you determine the type of file transferred over an FTP connection when you use Follow TCP Stream?

Q10.4   Why would the Stream window be empty when you select Follow SSL Streams?

Answers to Review Questions

Q10.1   **You have selected a packet in the Packet List pane, but Follow TCP Stream, Follow UDP Stream and Follow SSL Stream are not available. Why not?**

A10.1   You must have selected a packet that does not have a TCP header, UDP header or is not an SSL communication. For example, you cannot follow streams if you select an ARP packet in the Packet List pane.

Q10.2   **What is the syntax of the display filter created when you choose Follow TCP Stream?**

A10.2   `tcp.stream eq x` where x is the TCP stream number. This same syntax is used when you Follow SSL Streams. When you follow a UDP stream the syntax defines the IP addresses and port numbers—for example, `(ip.addr eq 24.6.150.44 and ip.addr eq 68.87.76.178) and (udp.port eq 1427 and udp.port eq 53)`.

Q10.3   **How can you determine the type of file transferred over an FTP connection when you use Follow TCP Stream?**

A10.3   You can look at the file name in the command channel or look for a file identifier inside the file itself.

Q10.4   **Why would the Stream window be empty when you select Follow SSL Streams?**

A10.4   The Stream window will be empty until you successfully apply decryption keys to the SSL stream.

Chapter 11: Customize Wireshark Profiles

Wireshark Certified Network Analyst Exam Objectives covered:

- Customize Wireshark with Profiles
- Sharing Profiles
- Create a Corporate Profile
- Create a WLAN Profile
- Create a VoIP Profile
- Create a Security Profile

  ❖ Case Study: Customizing Wireshark for the Customer
  ❖ Summary
  ❖ Practice What You've Learned
  ❖ Review Questions and Answers

Customize Wireshark with Profiles

Profiles can be used to work more efficiently with display filters, capture filters, color filters, columns and layouts specifically configured for the environment in which you are working.

For example, if you work on a network segment at a branch office that consists of routing traffic, web browsing traffic, VoIP call setup and VoIP call traffic and DNS traffic, you might want to create a profile called "Branch 01". This profile might contain coloring rules to make the various types of traffic more visible. You might also include a column to show the window size field values for TCP communications and an IP DSCP column to note asynchronous routing of your VoIP traffic.

Figure 147 shows the Wireshark Status bar. The current profile in use is listed in the right column. In this case we are working with the default profile, but we can quickly choose another profile in the list.

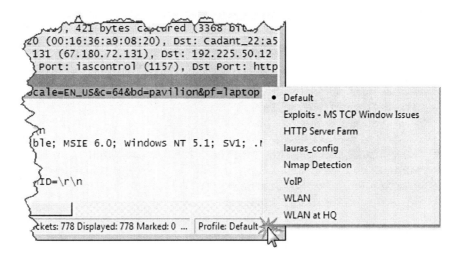

Figure 147. Click on the Profile column on the Status Bar to quickly change your profile selection

The number of files contained in the profile's directory depends on what you have added to your profile. The Default profile uses the configuration files located directly inside the Personal Configuration directory.

When you shut down Wireshark, the profile in use is saved and automatically loaded again when you restart Wireshark.

Create a New Profile

Select **Edit | Configuration Profiles | New** to create a new profile. Wireshark will create a new directory using the profile name you specify. This new directory is placed in a *profiles* directory under your Personal Configurations directory. You can also rename, copy or delete profiles in this area.

Figure 148 shows the contents of a Personal Configuration directory. When we defined our first profile, Wireshark created *profiles* in our Personal Configurations directory. Inside the *profiles* directory, we have five individual profile directories for our MS exploits, lauras_config, VoIP, WLAN and WLAN at HQ profiles.[60]

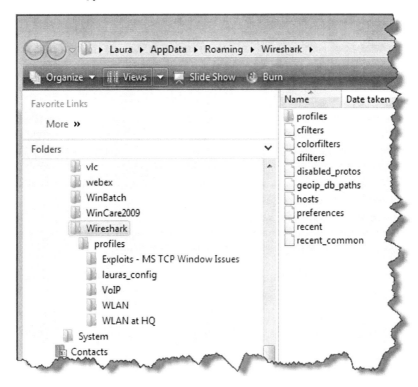

Figure 148. Our Personal Configurations directory contains a profiles folder

---

[60] Several profiles are available in the **Download** section at *www.wiresharkbook.com*.

There are several files that may be inside the profiles directory—which files exist depend on the settings established when working within a profile. The files may include:

> *cfilters*
>
> *dfilters*
>
> *colorfilters*
>
> *preferences*
>
> *disabled_protos*
>
> *recent*

When Wireshark creates a new profile, it uses the default settings from the Global Configurations directory. As you alter those settings, new profile configuration files are placed in the profile's directory.

Sharing Profiles

Profiles consist of a number of configuration files in a directory named after the profile itself. For example, if you make a profile called "Corporate HQ," Wireshark creates a "Corporate HQ" directory under the Wireshark *profiles* directory. To share the profile, copy the entire "Corporate HQ" directory to another Wireshark system's profile directory.

Be Careful Sharing Profiles

Be careful when copying the preferences file from one computer to another. Some settings may not be compatible with the new computer's directory structure or configuration. Two poential conflicts from the preferences file are shown below:

```
# Directory to start in when opening File Open dialog.
gui.fileopen.dir: C:\Users\Laura\Documents\traces - master

# Default capture device
capture.device: AirPcap USB wireless capture adapter nr. 00:
\\.\airpcap00
```

Create a Corporate Profile

A sample corporate profile might contain the following customized configurations:

cfilters	The *cfilters* file contains the capture filters for a key host based on its MAC address or its IP address (if statically assigned), key protocols and ports used and key web server host names.
dfilters	The *dfilters* file contains filters for a key host based on its MAC address or its IP address (if statically assigned), key protocols and ports used and key web server host names. All display filters should be defined as color filters as well so the traffic is easy to find in the trace files.
colorfilters	The *colorfilters* file contains colorization for unusual traffic on the network, such as low TCP window size values, traffic flowing between clients (this is built by excluding traffic that contains the IP address of a server in the source or destination IP address field) and application error responses.
preferences	The *preferences* file contains the column settings that include a Time Since Previous Displayed Packet, a column for the TCP window size setting and a column for the WLAN frequency/channel (consider adding other columns defined in the WLAN profile section below).

Create a WLAN Profile

A sample WLAN profile might contain the following customized configurations:

cfilters	The *cfilters* file contains the capture filters for key WLAN hosts based on either their MAC address (such as `wlan host 08:02:14:cb:2b:03`) or its IP address (if statically assigned), key protocols and ports used and key web server host names. In addition, create capture filters for beacon frames (`wlan[0] != 0x80`) and WLAN retries (`wlan.fc.retry == 1`).
dfilters	The *dfilters* file contains filters for all WLAN traffic (`wlan`), key hosts based on either its MAC address (such as `wlan.addr == 08:02:14:cb:2b:03`) or its IP address (if statically assigned), key protocols and ports used and key web server host names. In addition, the *dfilters* file contains filters for key WLAN traffic types, such as beacons (`wlan.fc.type_subtype == 0x08`) and management frames for a specific SSID (`wlan_mgt.ssid == "Corp WLAN1"`). All display filters should be defined as color filters as well so the traffic is easy to find in the trace files.
colorfilters	The *colorfilters* file contains colorization for unusual traffic on the network, such as low TCP window size values, traffic flowing between clients (this is built by excluding traffic that contains the IP address of a server in the source or destination IP address field) and application error

responses. The *colorfilters* file also contains colorization for certain WLAN traffic, such as disassociation frames (`wlan.fc.type_subtype == 0x0a`), retries (`wlan.fc.retry == 1`) and weak signal strength in Radiotap headers (`radiotap.dbm_antsignal < -80`). Use the auto-complete feature with `wlan.` (add the trailing period) to identify possible other display filter values. You might also want to add coloring rules based on the WLAN channel as explained in *Chapter 26: Introduction to Analyzing 802.11 (WLAN) Traffic*.

preferences   The *preferences* file contains the column settings that include a Time Since Previous Displayed Packet, a column for the TCP window size setting and a column for the WLAN Channel (`frequency/channel`), Radiotap Signal Strength value (custom: `radiotap.dbm_antsignal`) or PPI Signal Strength value (custom: `ppi.80211-common.dbm.antsignal`), 802.11 RSSI (`IEEE 802.11 RSSI`) and transmission rate (`IEEE 802.11 TX rate`). Use the auto-complete feature with `wlan.` (add the trailing period) to identify possible other column values. For more information on analyzing WLAN traffic, refer to *Chapter 26: Introduction to 802.11 (WLAN) Analysis*.

Create a VoIP Profile

A sample VoIP profile might contain the following customized configurations:

cfilters   The *cfilters* file contains the capture filters for a key host based on its MAC address or its IP address (if statically assigned), key protocols and ports used and key web server host names. Since SIP and RTP traffic is typically based on UDP, you may use the UDP capture filter (`udp`) more often than usual.

dfilters   The *dfilters* file contains filters for a key host based on its MAC address or its IP address (if statically assigned), key protocols and ports used and key web server host names. The *dfilters* file also contains filters for SIP (`sip`) and RTP (`rtp`) traffic as well as filters for various SIP error responses (such as `sip.Status-Code == 401`). All display filters should be defined as color filters as well so the traffic is easy to find in the trace files.

colorfilters   The *colorfilters* file contains colorization for unusual traffic on the network, such as low TCP window size values, traffic flowing between clients (this is built by excluding traffic that contains the IP address of a server in the source or destination IP address field) and application error responses. In this VoIP profile, the *colorfilters* file also contains colorization for SIP error responses (such as `sip.Status-Code == 401`) and retransmissions (`sip.resend == 1`).

preferences The *preferences* file contains the column settings that include a Time since Previous Displayed Packet, a column for the TCP window size values and a column for the DSCP (Differentiated Services Code Point) value (`ip.dsfield.dscp`). In addition, the RTP protocol preference setting "Try to Decode RTP outside of conversations" should be enabled. For more information on analyzing VoIP traffic, refer to *Chapter 27: Introduction to Voice over IP (VoIP) Analysis.*

Create a Security Profile

A sample security profile might contain the following customized configurations:

cfilters The *cfilters* file contains the capture filters for a key host based on its MAC address or its IP address (if statically assigned), key protocols and ports used and key web server host names.

dfilters The *dfilters* file contains filters for a key host based on its MAC address or its IP address (if statically assigned), key protocols and ports used and key web server host names. Display filters should be configured based on unusual traffic patterns—it is imperative that these display filters are also defined as color filters. Examples include a display filter for IRC traffic (`tcp.port == 6666 || tcp.port == 6667 || tcp.port == 6668 || tcp.port == 6669`), unusual ICMP traffic (`tcp && icmp.type==3 && (icmp.code==1 || icmp.code==2 || icmp.code==3 || icmp.code==9 || icmp.code==10 || icmp.code==13`) and ICMP OS fingerprinting (`icmp.type == 13 || icmp.type == 15 || icmp.type == 17`). All display filters should be defined as color filters as well so the traffic is easy to find in the trace files.

For more examples of security filters and colorization, refer to *Chapter 30: Network Forensics Overview, Chapter 31: Detect Scanning and Discovery Processes and Chapter 32: Analyze Suspect Traffic.* These chapters focus on detecting discovery processes and evidence of compromised hosts.

colorfilters The *colorfilters* file contains colorization for unusual traffic on the network, such as low TCP window size values (which can be signs of performance problems or TCP vulnerabilities being exploited), traffic flowing between clients, application error responses and unusual ICMP traffic. This filter is built by excluding traffic that contains the IP address of a server in the source or destination IP address field.

preferences The *preferences* file contains the column settings that include a Time since Previous Displayed Packet, a column for the TCP window size value.

Case Study:
Customizing Wireshark for the Customer

One of my customers had thousands of hosts and literally hundreds of applications. Capturing traffic from a client on the network inevitably ended up with too much traffic to sort through—we wanted to make the trace files easier to manage and analyze.

By creating a new profile for each of the three offices that we visited, we could analyze the traffic faster. The client was primarily interested in slow performance between the clients and one database server in particular—"DB912."

Here are the Wireshark areas we customized for this client:

- We created a coloring rule for large delays in the traffic from the DB912 server (`ip.src==10.6.2.2 && frame.time_delta_displayed > 0.200`). These packets were displayed with a red background and white foreground. Red backgrounds would be a symbol of problem traffic.

- We created a coloring rule for small Window Size field values because this client had Windows XP hosts that had not been configured to use Window Scaling—we could imagine there may be problems with the TCP buffer space. For more information, see *Chapter 20: Analyze Transmission Control Protocol (TCP) Traffic*. This coloring rule used a red background and a white background to alert us to a problem.

- We added two more ports to the HTTP preferences because they used more than the standard set of ports for web browsing to their internal servers.

- We created a special coloring rule for the first packet of the TCP handshake processes (`tcp.flags == 0x02`). These packets were colored with a dark green background and white foreground—we didn't use red because these were not problem packets.

- We created an *ethers* file that contained the hardware address of the network routers at each office. This made it easy to identify which router the clients' traffic went through to get off the network (this customer had more than one router on each network so watching the paths taken was important).

- We added `tcp.window_size` and `ip.dsfield.dscp` columns to the Packet List pane.

- We configured GeoIP and enabled GeoIP lookup in the IP preferences. This allowed us to look at the global target information right after the last IP header field. For more information on GeoIP mapping, refer to *List Endpoints and Map* on page 190.

Using all these customized settings, we could understand and troubleshoot the network problems much faster and more accurately.

Summary

Wireshark's profiles enable you to customize sets of Personal Configuration settings to work more efficiently in specific analysis environments. For example, a WLAN profile may have special coloring rules to identify traffic on separate channels and an extra column to indicate signal strength.

You can create an unlimited number of profiles and copy them to other Wireshark systems. Any configuration settings dealing with directory paths on the main Wireshark system may not work properly on other Wireshark systems if the directory structures do not match.

Consider creating profiles for your home environment, your office network, the branch offices or wireless networks. You could also build profiles for specific traffic types, such as wireless, database, VoIP or web browsing traffic.

Practice What You've Learned

There are 5 custom profiles in the Download section on the book website, *www.wiresharkbook.com*. Copy the profiles to your local Wireshark *profiles* directory. If a profiles directory does not exist you can create one and copy the profiles to that directory.

What elements might you include when creating your own set of profiles for the following network environments?

- Your corporate office
- Your home network
- A wireless network
- TCP-based applications

Open the trace files listed below to practice using the specified profiles.

wlan-airplane-laptopson.pcap	Use the *WLAN profile* on this traffic. This profile contains separate coloring rules for traffic on channels 1, 6 and 11 and WLAN retransmit frames, disassociation frames and probe request/reply frames. This traffic was broadcast on a flight that did not have a wireless network on board. So much for the old "please disable wireless on your laptops" speech, eh?
http-download-bad.pcap	Use the *lauras_config* profile on this traffic. In this trace, the client and the server can do window scaling, but there are still problems with the data flow. This profile contains two coloring rules for traffic with a low window size setting.
sec-strangescan.pcap	Use the *Nmap Detection* profile for this traffic. What on Earth is the scanner doing? Look at the TCP Flag settings in the scan packets.

icmp-dest-unreachable.pcap

Did any of the profiles affect this traffic? The client is trying to ping 10.4.88.88, but it appears that the local router can't locate the device on the next network. The local router sends an ICMP Destination Unreachable/Host Unreachable message indicating that it tried to ARP for the target, but didn't receive an answer. You MUST learn ICMP in depth to secure, optimize and troubleshoot your network effectively! Refer to *Chapter 18: Analyze Internet Control Message Protocol (ICMP) Traffic.*

Review Questions

Q11.1   **What elements can you customize using Wireshark profiles?**

Q11.2   **How can you move a custom profile to another Wireshark system?**

Q11.3   **Which file should you be cautious of sharing when copying a custom profile to another Wireshark system?**

Answers to Review Questions

Q11.1 **What elements can you customize using Wireshark profiles?**

A11.1 You can customize your preferences (such as name resolution, columns, stream coloring and protocol dissection settings), capture filters, display filters, coloring rules, etc.

Q11.2 **How can you move a custom profile to another Wireshark system?**

A11.2 You can copy the entire profile directory to the other Wireshark system.

Q11.3 **Which file should you be cautious of sharing when copying a custom profile to another Wireshark system**

A11.3 The preferences file may contain settings that are specific to the original Wireshark system. This file contains configurations such as the default directory setting for opening new trace files and the default capture device setting.

Chapter 12:
Save, Export and
Print Packets

Wireshark Certified Network Analyst Exam Objectives covered:

- Save Filtered, Marked and Ranges of Packets
- Export Packet Content for Use in Other Programs
- Save Conversations, Endpoints, IO Graphs and Flow Graph Information
- Export Packet Bytes

- ❖ Case Study: Saving Subsets of Traffic to Isolate Problems
- ❖ Summary
- ❖ Practice What You've Learned
- ❖ Review Questions and Answers

Save Filtered, Marked and Ranges of Packets

You can save a subset of packets based on the filters and marked packets. In addition, you can choose to save a range of packets regardless of the filter.

Avoid the "Needle in the Haystack Issue" by Saving Subsets

Consider saving subsets when you are baselining network communications. If you capture a trace of a workstation starting up, user logging in, user opening an application and user shutting down, save each function in a separate trace file for separate review.

Figure 149 shows the Save As window. We can choose whether to save the displayed packets only, the selected packet, marked packets, first to last marked packets or a range of packets. In our trace file, we have marked 3 packets and there are 104 packets that match the display filter.

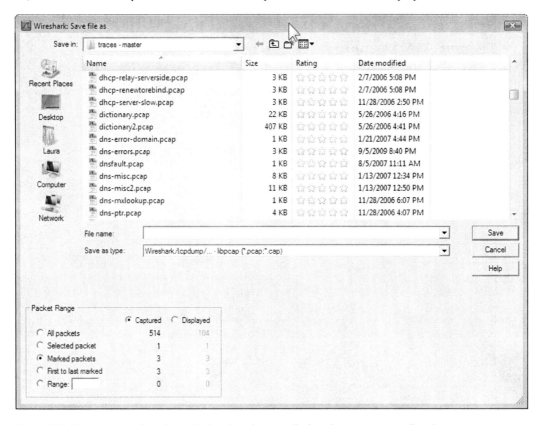

Figure 149. You can save all packets, displayed packets, marked packets or a range of packets

You can save trace files in numerous formats as well. Click on the **drop down arrow** to the right of the Save as type field to select a format other than tcpdump (.pcap or .cap) format. Alternately you can choose to print packets to a file (either a text file or a PostScript file). Select **File | Print** to open the Print window as shown in Figure 150.

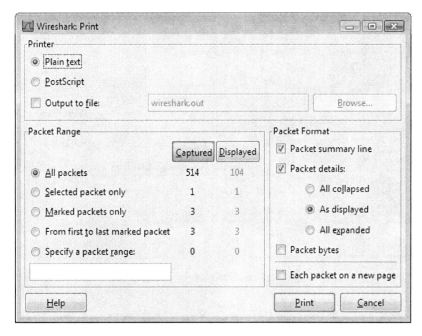

Figure 150. You can print to a text or PostScript file

When printing, you can choose to print just the Packet List pane summary line, the Packet Details (collapsed, as displayed, expanded) or the packet bytes. You can print each packet on a separate line (consider the number of packets you are printing, however). You have the same options to print displayed packets, selected packets, marked packets or a range of packets as you have when saving.

Print Packet Summaries in Landscape Mode

When printing the packet summary line, print in landscape format to see as much information as possible. You will still likely lose part of the information due to page size constraints. Consider printing to a file (print.txt for example) to reformat the data for best printing results.

```
Frame 14 (62 bytes on wire, 62 bytes captured)
    Arrival Time: Dec 22, 2004 18:29:00.896316000
    [Time delta from previous captured frame: 0.603304000 seconds]
    [Time delta from previous displayed frame: 0.603304000 seconds]
    [Time since reference or first frame: 6.581174000 seconds]
    Frame Number: 14
    Frame Length: 62 bytes
    Capture Length: 62 bytes
    [Frame is marked: True]
    [Protocols in frame: eth:ip:tcp]
    [Coloring Rule Name: TCP Handshake Packets (Connection Process/Attempt)]
    [Coloring Rule String: tcp.flags.syn == 1]
Ethernet II, Src: KinpoEle_01:20:e8 (00:01:e1:01:20:e8), Dst: AmbitMic_aa:af:80 (00:d0:59:aa:af:80)
    Destination: AmbitMic_aa:af:80 (00:d0:59:aa:af:80)
        Address: AmbitMic_aa:af:80 (00:d0:59:aa:af:80)
        .... ...0 .... .... .... .... = IG bit: Individual address (unicast)
        .... ..0. .... .... .... .... = LG bit: Globally unique address (factory default)
    Source: KinpoEle_01:20:e8 (00:01:e1:01:20:e8)
        Address: KinpoEle_01:20:e8 (00:01:e1:01:20:e8)
        .... ...0 .... .... .... .... = IG bit: Individual address (unicast)
        .... ..0. .... .... .... .... = LG bit: Globally unique address (factory default)
    Type: IP (0x0800)
Internet Protocol, Src: 68.45.134.187 (68.45.134.187), Dst: 172.16.1.10 (172.16.1.10)
    Version: 4
    Header length: 20 bytes
    Differentiated Services Field: 0x00 (DSCP 0x00: Default; ECN: 0x00)
        0000 00.. = Differentiated Services Codepoint: Default (0x00)
        .... ..0. = ECN-Capable Transport (ECT): 0
        .... ...0 = ECN-CE: 0
    Total Length: 48
```

Figure 151. Printed packets retain formats for readability

Export Packet Content for Use in Other Programs

Use **File** | **Export** to create additional graphs, search for specific contents, or perform other advanced procedures on data captured.

Packets can be exported in several formats:

- Plain text (*.txt)
- PostScript (*ps)
- Comma Separated Values—Packet Summary (*csv)
- PSML—XML Packet Summary (*psml)
- PDML—XML Packet Details (*pdml)
- C Arrays—Packet Bytes (*.c)

In the following example, we exported the contents of a filtered trace file to plot the beacons rate of WLAN packets—this same graph can be created using a filter with an IO Graph, but we exported to CSV format so we could graph and manipulate the information in a different format.

We worked with a profile that contained a column for the delta time value. We graphed the delta time value column only to view the frequency of beacons in the trace file.

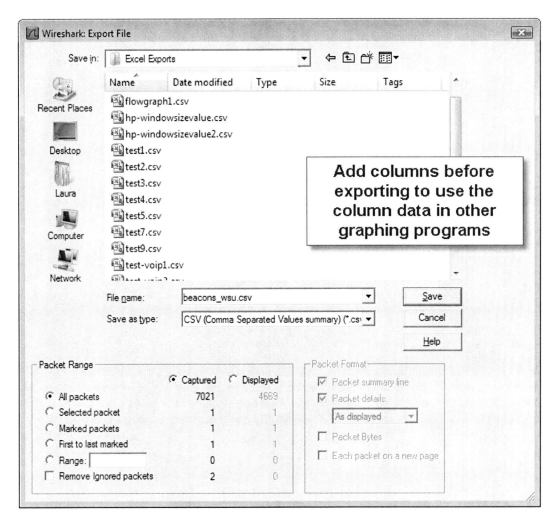

Figure 152. We have chosen to export displayed packets to CSV format

As shown in Figure 152, we named our exported file *beacons_wsu.csv*. Figure 153shows the file opened in Excel. The Delta time column is circled—that is the column we want graph.

	A	B	C	D	E	F	G	H	I	J	K
1	No.	Time	Delta	Source	Destinatic	Protocol	Info	TCPLen	WinSize	Freq/Char	RTapSig
2	1	0	0	D-Link_cc:	Broadcast	IEEE 802.1	Beacon frame, SN=2076, FN=0,			2412 [BG 1	-92
3	4	0.102554	0.102554	D-Link_cc:	Broadcast	IEEE 802.1	Beacon frame, SN=2077, FN=0,			2412 [BG 1	-92
4	5	0.204882	0.102328	D-Link_cc:	Broadcast	IEEE 802.1	Beacon frame, SN=2078, FN=0,			2412 [BG 1	-92
5	6	0.307253	0.102371	D-Link_cc:	Broadcast	IEEE 802.1	Beacon frame, SN=2079, FN=0,			2412 [BG 1	-92
6	7	0.409609	0.102356	D-Link_cc:	Broadcast	IEEE 802.1	Beacon frame, SN=2080, FN=0,			2412 [BG 1	-84
7	8	0.512044	0.102435	D-Link_cc:	Broadcast	IEEE 802.1	Beacon frame, SN=2081, FN=0,			2412 [BG 1	-84
8	9	0.615123	0.103079	D-Link_cc:	Broadcast	IEEE 802.1	Beacon frame, SN=2082, FN=0,			2412 [BG 1	-85
9	10	0.716834	0.101711	D-Link_cc:	Broadcast	IEEE 802.1	Beacon frame, SN=2083, FN=0,			2412 [BG 1	-85
10	11	0.819313	0.102479	D-Link_cc:	Broadcast	IEEE 802.1	Beacon frame, SN=2084, FN=0,			2412 [BG 1	-92
11	13	0.921637	0.102324	D-Link_cc:	Broadcast	IEEE 802.1	Beacon frame, SN=2085, FN=0,			2412 [BG 1	-91
12	14	1.023984	0.102347	D-Link_cc:	Broadcast	IEEE 802.1	Beacon frame, SN=2086, FN=0,			2412 [BG 1	-5
13	15	1.127111	0.103127	D-Link_cc:	Broadcast	IEEE 802.1	Beacon frame, SN=2087, FN=0,			2412 [BG 1	-92
14	16	1.228864	0.101753	D-Link_cc:	Broadcast	IEEE 802.1	Beacon frame, SN=2088, FN=0,			2412 [BG 1	-86
15	34	1.33123	0.102366	D-Link_cc:	Broadcast	IEEE 802.1	Beacon frame, SN=2094, FN=0,			2412 [BG 1	-85
16	42	1.433618	0.102388	D-Link_cc:	Broadcast	IEEE 802.1	Beacon frame, SN=2096, FN=0,			2412 [BG 1	-85
17	48	1.535925	0.102307	D-Link_cc:	Broadcast	IEEE 802.1	Beacon frame, SN=2097, FN=0,			2412 [BG 1	-8
18	50	1.6391	0.103185	D-Link_cc:	Broadcast	IEEE 802.1	Beacon frame, SN=2098, FN=0,			2412 [BG 1	-92
19	52	1.740707	0.101597	D-Link_cc:	Broadcast	IEEE 802.1	Beacon frame, SN=2099, FN=0,			2412 [BG 1	-92
20	54	1.843345	0.125	D-L		broadcast	on fra		2100	2 [B	

Figure 153. We will graph the contents of the Delta column

In Excel we selected the Delta column and Insert | Line to create the graph shown in Figure 154. Now that the data is graphed in Excel we can add labels, compare graphs in a single spreadsheet and more. Other graphs you may consider creating with exported CSV files include `tcp.analysis.bytes_in_flight`[61] and `wlan.analysis.retransmission`.

---

[61] You must have Track Number of Bytes in Flight enabled in **Preferences | Protocols | TCP** in order to use this column value.

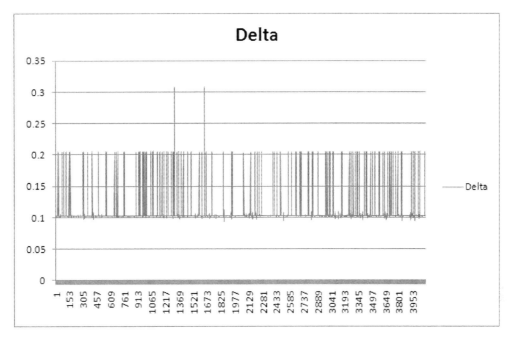

Figure 154. Plotting the delta time between beacons

Save Conversations, Endpoints, IO Graphs and Flow Graph Information

Conversations, endpoints, IO Graph information and other information may be saved as CSV format files, or in some cases, as graphic files (in the case of IO Graphs).

Flow graphs are saved in ASCII text format only. Click the **Save As** button to save the Flow Graph information.

In Conversations, Endpoints or IO Graph windows, click the **Copy** button to save the data in CSV format as shown in Figure 155. In the case of IO Graphs, only the plot point number and value are saved.

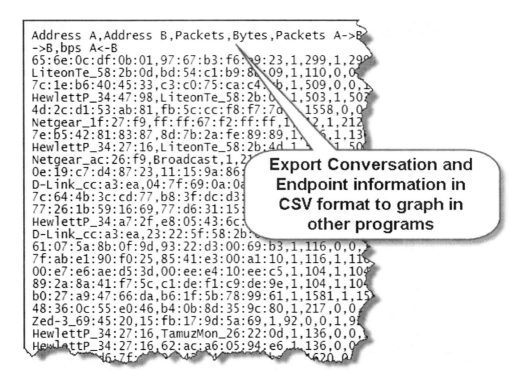

```
Address A,Address B,Packets,Bytes,Packets A->B
->B,bps A<-B
65:6e:0c:df:0b:01,97:67:b3:f6:?9:23,1,299,1,299
LiteonTe_58:2b:0d,bd:54:c1:b9:8?09,1,110,0,0
7c:1e:b6:40:45:33,c3:c0:75:ca:c4?b,1,509,0,0,1
HewlettP_34:47:98,LiteonTe_58:2b:0?1,503,1,50?
4d:2c:d1:53:ab:81,fb:5c:cc:f8:f7:7d?1558,0,0
Netgear_1f:27:f9,ff:ff:67:f2:ff:ff,1?2,1,212
7e:b5:42:81:83:87,8d:7b:2a:fe:89:89,1?5,1,13?
HewlettP_34:27:16,LiteonTe_58:2b:4d,1?1,50?
Netgear_ac:26:f9,Broadcast,1,2?
0e:19:c7:d4:87:23,11:15:9a:86?
D-Link_cc:a3:ea,04:7f:69:0a:0?
7c:64:4b:3c:cd:77,b8:3f:dc:d3?
77:26:1b:59:16:69,77:d6:31:15?
HewlettP_34:a7:2f,e8:05:43:6c?
D-Link_cc:a3:ea,23:22:5f:58:2b?
61:07:5a:8b:0f:9d,93:22:d3:00:69:b3,1,116,0,0,?
7f:ab:e1:90:f0:25,85:41:e3:00:a1:10,1,116,1,11?
00:e7:e6:ae:d5:3d,00:ee:e4:10:ee:c5,1,104,1,104
89:2a:8a:41:f7:5c,c1:de:f1:c9:de:9e,1,104,1,10?
b0:27:a9:47:66:da,b6:1f:5b:78:99:61,1,1581,1,15?
48:36:0c:55:e0:46,b4:0b:8d:35:9c:80,1,217,0,0
Zed-3_69:45:20,15:fb:17:9d:5a:69,1,92,0,0,1,9?
HewlettP_34:27:16,TamuzMon_26:22:0d,1,136,0,0,?
HewlettP_34:27:16,62:ac:a6:05:94:e6,1,136,0,0,?
```

Export Conversation and Endpoint information in CSV format to graph in other programs

*Figure 155. Click the **Copy** button to save the data from Conversation or Endpoint windows in CSV format*

Check out CACE Pilot™ for Graphing

For extensive graphing capabilities, consider CACE Pilot, the visualization and reporting tool that integrates with Wireshark. CACE Pilot is available from CACE Technologies (www.cacetech.com).

IO Graphs also have a Save button that allows you to save a graphic file in BMP, ICO, JPEG, PNG or TIFF format. The saved graphic is very limited, however as shown in Figure 156. You will not see the X- or Y-axis information.

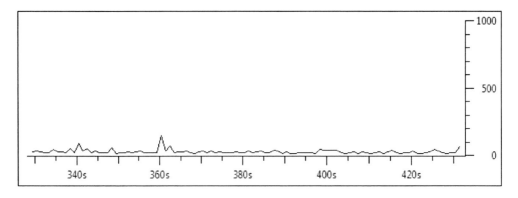

Figure 156. Saving an IO Graph does not provide much x-axis or y-axis information

Export Packet Bytes

To export packet bytes, you must select a field or byte(s) in the Packet Details pane or Packet Bytes pane. Right click and select **Export Selected Packet Bytes** or press **Ctrl+H**.

Using this function, packets can only be exported in raw data format. This format is a hex format of the field(s) selected with no formatting data. For example, select the IP header in a file, right click and choose **Export Selected Packet Bytes** to export the IP header of a packet into raw format. In Figure 157 we have opened the raw format file we exported using Neo, a free hex editing program for Windows (*www.hhdsoftware.com*).

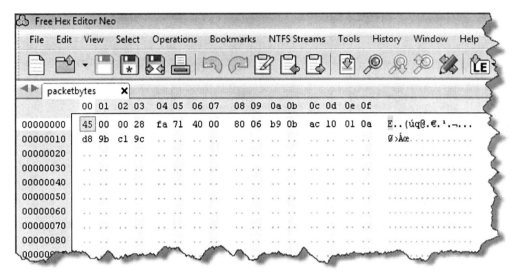

Figure 157. Opening a raw format file in the free hex editor Neo

Use Your Own Screen Capture Utility

Since many of the Wireshark screens do not support printing or export, consider using a third-party screen capture and print utility such as SnagIt by TechSmith Corporation (www.techsmith.com).

Case Study:
Saving Subsets of Traffic to Isolate Problems

The customer was having problems with connections to one of their database servers used by their personnel department. Sometimes the connections seemed to work fine—other times users couldn't get a connection. It was the dreaded "intermittent problem".

Because we didn't know when the problem would surface, we set up Wireshark off of a tap between one of the staff members and the switch. We configured Wireshark to capture traffic to a file set with each file set at a maximum of 30 MB. To reduce the traffic captured, we also used a capture filter set for all traffic to the database server (host 10.3.3.4).

Just to make sure we captured the problem while I was onsite, we repeated the same process for three other personnel department members. We didn't use port spanning on the switch because we were going to monitor three ports and I didn't want to rule out any physical layer issues that the port spanning would hide from us.

We asked the users to work on their database as they usually did—we let them know we were watching their traffic because (a) we wanted them to see that the IT team was working on the problem and (b) we were aware that they browsed some sites that weren't work related and we wanted to be able to subtly discourage them from doing so. <Grin.>

To help us spot the problems in the trace files we employed a little trick on the users' workstations. We gave the users a nice little icon named "Ouch" on their desktop to launch a ping to the database server. We told the users to double-click on the icon when they experienced a serious problem in the communications to the database server.

This helped us spot the problem points in the trace files.

After being informed that the problems were occurring again and that the four personnel department users had clicked "Ouch" at least three times each, we were ready to start looking at the traces.

We simply filtered on ICMP ping packets (icmp.type==8) and marked these packets. It didn't matter that the database server never responded—these were just markers in the file to help us find problem spots. Marking the packets made it easier to skip from one problem point to the next using Ctrl+Shift+N.

In each instance we saw the users were trying to access the same file and the server simply did not respond. The server sent the TCP ACK indicating that it received the request for the file, but it did not send the requested file. Repeated requests for that particular file went unanswered. The time column (set to Seconds since Previous Displayed Packet) indicated a delay averaging 23 seconds!

The request was ACKed by the server so we knew it arrived at the server. We didn't feel that this was a network problem.

We looked on the server to see if the file existed. It did. We used Find to look for the file name as an ASCII string and we were able to see times when users could get the file without problems.

It was time to do some research and ultimately contact the vendor. In this case we couldn't find much online to help us. We called the vendor and discussed the problem with them.

The vendor denied that the problem could ever occur. They implied that there must be packet loss on the network or the server was 'unstable.'

Rolling up our sleeves, we began to carve out the sections in the trace file that demonstrated the problem. We noted the numbers of the packets that included the file request and unmarked our ping packets (we did this quickly by filtering on `icmp.type==8` and choosing Ctrl+D to unmark the displayed packets).

Packet Range	Captured	Displayed
All packets	16549	16549
Selected packet	1	1
Marked packets	0	0
First to last marked	0	0
Range: 2304-25	201	201

We selected File | Save As and choose to save each range as separate trace files. We didn't need to give the vendor the entire trace file—we wanted to solve this one issue that was obviously causing problems. It's important to note that we did examine the trace file to ensure no confidential information was contained in it before sending it to the vendor.

After about three days the vendor responded to my customer stating that they were aware of an "anomaly" in their program that limited the number of times the file in question could be accessed by the program. If more than a certain number of users tried to access the file in a short period of time, the program would just discard the request.

Wireshark showed exactly where the problem was. It didn't tell us *why* the problem was occurring, but it saved the IT staff days of troubleshooting time through guesswork, indicated that the network was not at fault, validated the user's claims of performance problems and helped management avoid spending money on equipment that would not have solved the problem.

Summary

Wireshark offers numerous methods for saving packets, conversations, graphs and even bytes from a single packet.

To separate a trace file into smaller parts, you can save just the filtered packets, just the marked packets or even a range of packets. For example, if you find a single conversation that you want to share with a vendor, you can apply a filter on that conversation and save the conversation traffic in a separate trace file.

You can also export packet or file contents for manipulation in other programs. For example, you can add a column for the TCP Window Size field, export the file information to CSV format and build charts and graphs in another application.

Many of the statistics windows also offer the Save feature. For example, you can save the conversation or endpoint information as well as IO Graph plot points.

Practice What You've Learned

 Download the trace files available in the Download section of the book website, *www.wiresharkbook.com*. Test your skills at saving subsets of traffic and conversation information using the trace files listed below.

sec-evilprogram.pcap A truly classic trace file of a system infected with the Stopguard browser hijack spyware/malware/scumware program. Create a DNS filter to see the client look up Virtumonde's website. That's when the troubles begin. Save the DNS packets in a separate trace file called *vmonddns.pcap*.

icmp-redirect.pcap This trace contains ICMP redirection traffic. As you examine this trace, pay close attention to the MAC address in the packets and the contents of the ICMP Redirect packet (packet 2). That packet contains the IP address of the recommended router to get to 10.3.71.7. The client must already have the MAC address of that router (or perhaps the analyst filtered out ARP traffic). Filter out the ICMP packet and save it in a separate file called *icmpredir.pcap*.

sec-nessus.pcap Nessus (*www.nessus.org*), the penetration testing tool, doesn't try to be sneaky. Use the Find feature to search for the string 'nessus' in this trace file. You'll find the 'nessus' signature all over in this trace file. In addition, you'll see the unusual ping packet (packet 3) used by Xprobe2 when the Nessus scan runs. Open the Conversations window and select **Copy**. Open a text editor and paste the data into the file.

Review Questions

Q12.1   What save options are available when you only want to save a subset of packets contained in a trace file?

Q12.2   What export format could you use if you are going to import information from the Packet List pane into a spreadsheet program?

Q12.3   Which Wireshark feature should you use if you want to save a TCP header as a text file?

Answers to Review Questions

Q12.1   **What save options are available when you only want to save a subset of packets contained in a trace file?**

A12.1   When you select Save As, you can choose to save displayed packets, selected packets, marked packets, first to last marked packet or a packet range.

Q12.2   **What export format could you use if you are going to import information from the Packet List pane into a spreadsheet program?**

A12.2   Comma separated value (CSV) format imports easily into spreadsheet programs.

Q12.3   **Which Wireshark feature should you use if you want to save a TCP header as a text file?**

A12.3   Select the **TCP header** in a packet and choose **File | Export** and **Packet Bytes** in the Packet Format section.

Chapter 13:
Use Wireshark's
Expert System

Wireshark Certified Network Analyst Exam Objectives covered:

- Launch Expert Info Quickly
- Colorize Expert Info Elements
- Filter on TCP Expert Information Elements
- Understanding TCP Expert Information

  ❖ Case Study: Expert Info Catches Remote Access Headaches
  ❖ Summary
  ❖ Practice What You've Learned
  ❖ Review Questions and Answers

Let Wireshark's Expert Information Guide You

Wireshark's Expert Information is defined in the dissectors. For example, the TCP Expert Information is maintained in the *packet-tcp.c* file. You can access this file on *www.wireshark.org* when you select **Develop | Browse the Code**.

Expert Information is classified into one of four categories:

Errors	Packet or dissector errors
Warnings	Unusual responses from the application/transport
Notes	Unusual responses from the application/transport (may be a recovery process from a Warning)
Chats	Information about the workflow

Check Expert Notes AND Warnings

*Notice that both Warnings and Notes contain related information. For example, TCP Fast Retransmissions fall under Warnings while Retransmissions and Duplicate ACKs fall under Notes. Be certain to check **both** Warnings and Notes for potential issues.*

Launch Expert Info Quickly

As of Wireshark version 1.2, an Expert Info Composite button is available on the Status Bar, as shown in Figure 158.

Open the Expert Info Composite window by clicking on the **Expert Info** button on the left of the Status Bar or choose **Analyze | Expert Info Composite** from the menu. The Expert Info button is color coded according to the classification of Expert Information listed.

Errors	Red
Warnings	Yellow
Note	Cyan (Light Blue)
Chats	Blue
None	Grey

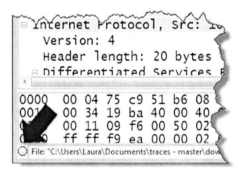

Figure 158. The button on the lower left corner of the Status Bar opens the Expert Info Composite window

Although future versions of Wireshark may expand on the number of Expert elements, currently, the majority of the elements are based on TCP communication issues.

Figure 159 shows the Expert Info Composite information for a trace file that depicts a network plagued with packet loss. In this case, a user was trying to download a large file from a website. The process seemed to be taking too long.

In the Warnings area we see 261 indications of Previous Segment Lost and 166 Fast Retransmissions. In the Notes area we see 759 Retransmissions. We can correlate the slow download with packet loss.

Always Double-Check Expert Findings

Although the Expert Info Composite window points to a likely cause of a problem, always verify the situation by examining the trace file. For example, in one situation we noticed that Wireshark defined a packet as "Out of Order" when it was actually a retransmission. The original packet had occurred almost 800ms earlier in the trace file and Wireshark did not relate the retransmission to the earlier original packet—instead, Wireshark saw the TCP Sequence Number field value was suddenly lower than the previous packet and indicated it was an Out of Order packet. Always double-check Expert findings.

Expand a selection in the Expert Info Composite window to click on a specific packet listed. Wireshark will highlight that packet in the trace file. For example, in Figure 159, we have expanded the Retransmissions information in the Notes section. We can click on the line listing packet 127 and Wireshark will highlight that packet in the Packet List pane.

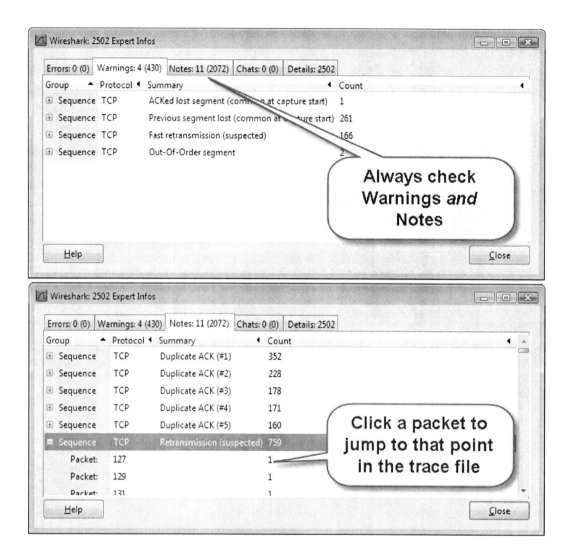

Figure 159. The Expert Info Composite window indicates packet loss problems

Colorize Expert Info Elements

By default, Wireshark colors packets that match the `tcp.analysis.flags` coloring rule with a black background and red foreground. These packets are listed in either the Expert Info Composite Warnings or Notes tabs. Expanding the frame information of a packet shows the coloring rule that a packet matches.

For example, in Figure 160, the packet matches the Bad TCP coloring rule that uses the string `tcp.analysis.flags`. You can change the colorization of these packets by editing the coloring rules.

```
⊟ Frame 1932 (74 bytes on wire, 74 bytes captured)
    Arrival Time: Jan 10, 2006 10:59:22.419867000
    [Time delta from previous captured frame: 0.006490000 seconds]
    [Time delta from previous displayed frame: 0.006490000 seconds]
    [Time since reference or first frame: 3768.478362000 seconds]
    Frame Number: 1932
    Frame Length: 74 bytes
    Capture Length: 74 bytes
    [Frame is marked: False]
    [Protocols in frame: eth:ip:tcp]
    [Coloring Rule Name: Bad TCP]
    [Coloring Rule String: tcp.analysis.flags]
⊞ Ethernet II, Src: Dell_cb:6b:15 (00:14:22:cb:6b:15), Dst: Dell_be:9d:fd
⊟ Internet Protocol, Src: 192.168.1.141 (192.168.1.141), Dst: 192.168.1.123
    Version: 4
    Header length: 20 bytes
```

Figure 160. Expand the frame section to identify the coloring rule applied

Filter on TCP Expert Information Elements

Apply a display filter for **tcp.analysis.flags** to show packets that match the Expert Info Composite Notes and Warnings triggers.

Figure 161 shows the result of applying a tcp.analysis.flags display filter to an entire trace file. This is a fast method to detect TCP-based problems in a trace file.

Use the tcp.analysis.flags Filter

Consider creating and saving this display filter. Although the Expert Info Composite window organizes Notes and Warnings in a tabbed format, this filter displays all "Bad TCP" packets in one window.

You can create a display filter to examine packets that meet a specific Expert Info severity level. The following provides examples of the four severity level filters ("Details" is not considered a severity level):

```
expert.severity==error
expert.severity==warn
expert.severity==note
expert.severity==chat
```

Another display filter available for packets that are part of a specific Expert Info group. The syntax is expert.group==<group>. Some of the Wireshark Expert Info groups are:

- Checksum—a checksum was invalid
- Sequence—sequence number was not correct or indicated a retransmission
- Malformed—malformed packet or dissector bug
- Protocol—invalid field value (possible violation of specification)

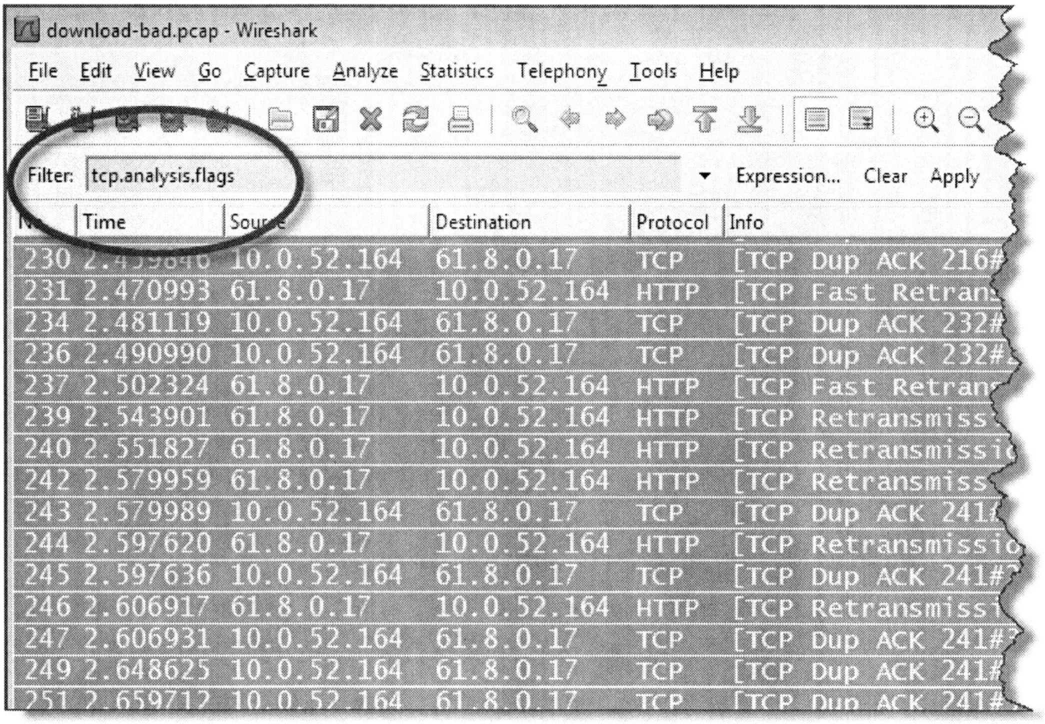

Figure 161. A tcp.analysis.flags display filter shows TCP problems

Understanding TCP Expert Information

The TCP dissector file, *packet-tcp.c*, lists the TCP Expert Information at the beginning of the file and the details of each Expert Information notification later in the file. The following lists the Expert Information contained in the *packet-tcp.c* file. Enable **Analyze TCP Sequence Numbers** (TCP preference) to use these TCP Expert notifications.

```
TCP_A_RETRANSMISSION            0x0001
TCP_A_LOST_PACKET               0x0002
TCP_A_ACK_LOST_PACKET           0x0004
TCP_A_KEEP_ALIVE                0x0008
TCP_A_DUPLICATE_ACK             0x0010
TCP_A_ZERO_WINDOW               0x0020
TCP_A_ZERO_WINDOW_PROBE         0x0040
TCP_A_ZERO_WINDOW_PROBE_ACK     0x0080
TCP_A_KEEP_ALIVE_ACK            0x0100
TCP_A_OUT_OF_ORDER              0x0200
TCP_A_FAST_RETRANSMISSION       0x0400
TCP_A_WINDOW_UPDATE             0x0800
TCP_A_WINDOW_FULL               0x1000
TCP_A_REUSED_PORTS              0x2000
```

The Expert system can speed up the process of locating potential problems in a trace file. The following section provides a definition of the fourteen TCP Expert notifications defined in the *packet-tcp.c* file. For more details on normal and unusual TCP communications, refer to *Chapter 14: TCP/IP Analysis Overview* and *Chapter 20: Analyze Transmission Control Protocol (TCP) Traffic*.

What Makes an Item a Warning vs. a Note?

Some Expert Info items are categorized as Warnings while others are defined as Notes. A warning indicates a problem in the communications (such as a lost packet detected) while a note indicates what could be considered "normal" traffic (such as a retransmission). True, a retransmission is not considered "good," but they are part of the proper TCP recovery process when packets are lost on a network. They are not considered an error.

What Triggers "TCP Retransmissions"

Retransmissions are listed under the Notes tab in the Expert Info Composite window. Retransmissions are the result of packet loss and triggered when the sender's TCP retransmission timeout (RTO) timer expires or a receiver sends Duplicate Acknowledgments to request a missing segment (see *What Triggers "Duplicate ACK"* on page 282).

If a TCP segment contains data and it uses the same sequence number as the previous packet, it must be a TCP retransmission or a fast retransmission (see *What Triggers "Fast Retransmission"* on page 283).

What Triggers "Previous Segment Lost"

Previous Segment Lost situations are listed under the Warnings tab in the Expert Info Composite window. Wireshark tracks the TCP sequence numbers of each packet as well as the number of data bytes in the packets. Wireshark, therefore, knows the next expected sequence number in a TCP stream. When an expected sequence number is skipped, Wireshark indicates a previous segment has been lost on the packet immediately following the missing packet in the stream.

What Triggers "ACKed Lost Packet"

ACKed Lost Packets are listed under the Warnings tab in the Expert Info Composite window. When Wireshark detects an acknowledgment, but it has not seen the packet that is being acknowledged, an ACKed Lost Packet warning is triggered.

What Triggers "Keep Alive"

TCP Keep Alive packets are listed under the Warnings tab in the Expert Info Composite window. Each side of a TCP connection maintains a keep alive timer. When the keep alive timer expires, a TCP host sends a keep alive probe to the remote host. If the remote host responds with a keep alive ACK (or any TCP packet, for that case), it is assumed the connection is still valid. If no response is received, it is assumed the connection is broken[62].

---

[62] Note that in some situations Zero Window Probe packets are interpreted as Keep Alive packets because they do not contain a single byte of data.

What Triggers "Duplicate ACK"

Duplicate ACKs are listed under the Notes tab in the Expert Info Composite window. A receiver tracks the incoming TCP sequence numbers. If a packet is detected as missing (the expected sequence number is skipped), the receiver generates an ACK indicating the next expected sequence number in the Acknowledgment Number field.

The receiver continues to generate duplicate ACKs—requesting the missing segment. When the host sending the TCP segments receives three identical ACKs (the original ACK and two duplicate ACKs), it assumes there is packet loss and it resends the missing packet—regardless of whether the RTO expired or not. A high number of duplicate ACKs may be an indication of high latency between TCP hosts as well as packet loss. A receiver continues to generate duplicate ACKs until the situation is resolved.

What Triggers "Zero Window"

Zero Window packets are listed under the Warnings tab in the Expert Info Composite window. When a receiver has no receive buffer space available, it sends Zero Window packets indicating the TCP window size is zero. This, in effect, shuts down data transfer to the receiver. The data transfer will not resume until that receiver sends a packet with a window size sufficient to accept the amount of queued data from the sender.

What Triggers "Zero Window Probe"

Zero Window Probes are listed under the Notes tab in the Expert Info Composite window. A zero window probe packet may be sent by a TCP host when the remote host advertizes a window size of zero. By specification, a zero window probe *may* contain one byte of the next segment of data. If the zero window condition has been resolved, the receiver sends an acknowledgment for the new byte received. If the zero window condition has not been resolved, the receiver sends an ACK, but does not acknowledge the new byte.

What Triggers "Zero Window Probe ACK"

Zero Window Probe ACKs are listed under the Notes tab in the Expert Info Composite window. This packet is a response to the Zero Window Probe packet. If the zero window condition has been resolved, the Zero Window Probe ACK will acknowledge the new byte received. If the zero window condition has not been resolved, the Zero Window Probe ACK will not acknowledge the new byte received.

What Triggers "Keep Alive ACK"

Keep Alive ACKs are listed under the Notes tab in the Expert Info Composite window. Keep Alive ACKs are sent in response to a Keep Alive. If the Keep Alive ACK contains a window size of zero, the zero window condition has not been resolved.

What Triggers "Out-of-Order"

Out of Order packets are listed under the Warnings tab in the Expert Info Composite window. If a packet contains data and does not advance the sequence number, it is either a retransmission or fast retransmission (using the same sequence number as the previous one) or an Out of Order packet. An out of order packet contains a lower sequence number than a previous packet.

What Triggers "Fast Retransmission"

Fast Retransmissions are listed under the Warnings tab in the Expert Info Composite window. The difference between a Retransmission and a Fast Retransmission is timing. A Fast Retransmission occurs within 20ms of a Duplicate ACK whereas a regular Retransmission has a greater delta time between the Duplicate ACK and the retransmission. Always check for Retransmissions under the Notes tab when you notice Fast Retransmissions under the Warnings tab.

Setting a filter for `tcp.analysis.flags` and the time column to Seconds since Previous Displayed Packets helps compare the time between Duplicate ACK packets and retransmissions in a trace file.

What Triggers "Window Update"

Window Update packets are listed under the Chats tab in the Expert Info Composite window. A Window Update packet contains no data, but indicates that the sender's TCP window size field value has increased[63].

What Triggers "Window is Full"

Window is Full packets are listed under the Notes tab in the Warnings Info Composite window. Wireshark tracks a receiver's window size and notes when a data packet is sent that will fill up the remaining buffer space. This packet itself will not have the Window size value of 0—this packet is an indication that a window size value of 0 may come from the other side if their receive window size is not updated.

Disable Wireshark's Expert Feature... with Caution

To disable the Expert feature, disable Analyze TCP sequence numbers in the TCP preferences section. Note that your filter for `tcp.analysis.flags` *will yield no results as no packets will match the filter if this setting is disabled.*

---

[63] Note that Wireshark does not have an Expert notification for decreasing window sizes. This Window Update only pertains to increases in the sender's window size value.

Case Study: Expert Info Catches Remote Access Headaches

Submitted by: Guy Talbot, CISSP
  Conseiller Principal en Sécurité de l'Information et Réseautique

I am a network architect for a large organization.

Our network consists of close to 2,000 sites and includes more than 100,000 workstations. I am usually not involved in network incidents unless: (1) things really get out of hand; (2) nobody else can figure out what is happening; or (3) my boss decides that I need to get involved.

It must have been a Friday afternoon. (These things always happen on a Friday afternoon to ruin your weekend or on a Monday morning to convince you that Monday morning is a bad idea and should simply be cancelled.)

Anyway, a technician came into my office indicating that the call center is receiving multiple complaints from users stating that Internet access is very slow or is not available at all.

Level 1 and 2 technicians and even the network analysts couldn't understand the causes. Multiples sites are affected and we already know that all the affected sites are on low speed (ADSL) access. The other common factor is that all the affected sites are using the Internet through a web proxy service. Don't ask why, but users on our network can access the Internet either through a web proxy service or they can request to bypass this service. Level 1 technicians are already using the bypass option as a workaround for the incident, so this is a number (2) situation where I need to get involved.

The local networks of the affected sites can almost certainly be eliminated as the cause of those incidents because everything is fine when bypassing the web proxy service. The conclusion is then: the web proxy service is the cause of the problem.

But wait, we have approximately 1,000 sites still using that web proxy service and they are not reporting any incidents.

So here we are: we have a network problem!

Wireshark to the rescue. Trying to capture traffic at the web proxy service is futile. Yes, we have network taps available very close to the equipment, but trying to isolate problematic sessions in the volumes of traffic going through this service is literally the proverbial "needle in the haystack."

Network taps and port mirroring are not available on affected sites' networks.

In an earlier situation, we needed to be able to capture traffic on workstations for long periods of time (days actually). We could not rely on the users to make sure that Wireshark was running at all times on their systems every time their systems were rebooted or a shift change occurred.

So we bought a few 250GB USB external drives, installed the Tshark executable as well as WinPcap. We added a few scripts to install and remove WinPcap and Tshark as a service on a Windows workstation—we called it "Deepthroat"—no, that wasn't a good name—we called it "USBTSHARK". That's better.

This setup captured all the traffic from the workstations and stored it on the USB drive in 200MB chunks. (If you are into stupid stunts, capture to your "C" drive, let it run for a while and you'll have a problem that is definitely not network related.)

We sent a few of these USB drives to the local administrators and asked them to set them up on workstations. We also asked the local administrators to switch the configuration of Internet Explorer between the web proxy service and the bypass on those workstation, and finally to log web browsing with both configurations and note any problems accessing the Internet.

When the traces came back, we began the analyses. I will spare you all the filtering and the latency calculations that were done on theses traces because it is long, boring and the problem was not there. But still, they needed to be done.

Looking at the different tabs of the Expert Info Composite in Wireshark, I eventually came across an oddity, the number of Duplicated ACKs was, let say, a little on the high side as shown in the following image.

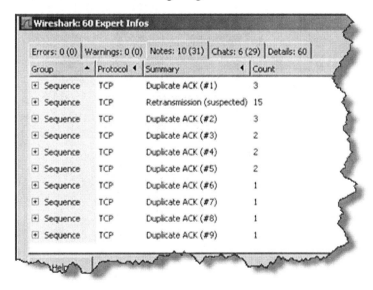

When I isolated the sessions that were impacted, I noticed that, yes, the Duplicate "ACK" indicated lost frames and sometimes the lost frames were eventually resent and acknowledged.

In certain situations however, the web proxy server retransmitted the last acknowledged frame instead of retransmitting the lost frame. This retransmission was acknowledged by a Duplicated ACK again. After a few rounds of that, the workstation eventually got fed up and reset the session.

What can make an average web filtering server suddenly become dumb and not be able to figure out the proper frame to retransmit?

Looking a few frames back in the trace, I noticed that before the web filtering server began retransmitting the wrong frame, a few frames were also acknowledged with a Duplicate ACK. This is normal—those frames were simply transmitted after the lost frame, arriving as they should.

An analysis of the TCP header showed that the session was using the SACK option. That's good news—this should help prevent unneeded retransmissions if we start losing multiple frames.

But wait something is *not* right. The values of the TCP sequence numbers in the TCP header and those in the SACK option field are not in the same range—I mean really, completely, definitely those numbers are very far from each other as you can see in the following figure.

```
⊞ Frame 290 (66 bytes on wire, 66 bytes captured)
⊞ Ethernet II, Src:                                          DS
⊞ Internet Protocol, Src:
⊟ Transmission Control Protocol, Src Port: chmd (3099),
     Source port: chmd (3099)
     Destination port: http-alt (8080)
     [Stream index: 6]
     Sequence number: 483     (relative sequence number)
     Acknowledgement number: 4141    (relative ack number)
     Header length: 32 bytes
  ⊞ Flags: 0x10 (ACK)
     Window size: 64860
  ⊞ Checksum: 0xac03 [correct]
  ⊟ Options: (12 bytes)
        NOP
        NOP
     ⊟ SACK: 975687856-975690616
          left edge = 975687856 (relative)
          right edge = 975690616 (relative)
  ⊞ [SEQ/ACK analysis]
  ⊞ [Timestamps]
```

Something happened to that TCP header. The Acknowledgement number is 4141, but the left and right edges in the SACK option field are 975687856 and 975690616.

This time I have no options—no more Mr. Nice Guy. I will need a multi-point trace to find out who the heck is modifying my TCP headers. Not on my network, not on my watch!

I had a site and a workstation where I could replicate the incident. I could install probes along the path between the workstation and the web filtering service. I could create capture filters that would control the size of the traces because I had the IP addresses of the clients and the web filtering device. I installed 4 probes; one next to the web proxy server, one next to the WAN router of our data center, one next to the WAN router of the site where my workstation is located and finally "USBTSHARK" on the workstation itself.

Long setup, very short analysis—the TCP headers are modified between the 2 WAN routers.

Our WAN is built around multiple Multiprotocol Label Switching VPNs with firewalls isolating the VPNs. This infrastructure is managed by an external operator. I sent a request to the operator asking if they were aware of any device in this infrastructure that could modify TCP headers. After the normal exchanges with an operator convinced that their network was not the problem, the answer finally came back. They informed us that that Cisco's Firewall blade module used in our infrastructure had a "feature" called "TCP randomization". Its purpose was to mitigate a vulnerability in the Initial Sequence Number (ISN) generation as defined in RFC 793. This feature replaced the ISNs generated by the client and the server by "more secure ISNs" and maintained the new sequences numbers in the TCP headers. The bad news about this feature is that it's not able to maintain the new sequence numbers in the "SACK" option field.

Now an average web proxy server exposed to contradicting information on which parts of a session are received and which parts need to be transmitted again might decide that this client "lost it," and try to bring it back to reality with something they should both agree on. On the client side, it's receiving the same frame over and over again, this conversation is going nowhere—"I give up and we'll start over when you are ready to have a normal conversation!"

To this date, this "feature" is not an option. I mean, it cannot be completely turned off. In certain situations, the TCP randomization feature can be bypassed, but—you guessed it—our configuration was not one of them.

To randomize or not to randomize? For now the answer is "you have no options" and you have to give up using "SACK".

Note from Laura: For more information on Selective ACK (SACK), refer to *Chapter 20: Analyze Transmission Control Protocol (TCP) Traffic*. For details on the TCP randomization feature that Guy mentioned in this case study, visit *www.cisco.com/warp/public/707/cisco-sa-20010301-ios-tcp-isn-random.shtml*.

Summary

Wireshark's Expert System offers a quick look at traffic that hints of network problems or unusual activity. There are five sections in the Expert System: Errors, Warnings, Notes, Chats and Details. The Expert Info Composite button on the Status Bar indicates the highest level of Expert notification triggered in the trace file. Clicking on this button is the fastest way to launch the Expert Info Composite window.

Expert Info details for a protocol are maintained in the protocol's dissector. TCP has the largest number of Expert notifications defined at this time. To view all the TCP Expert notifications, apply a display filter for `tcp.analysis.flags`. By default, Wireshark has a coloring rule for this traffic.

You should always verify problems identified by the Expert System.

Practice What You've Learned

 Download the trace files available in the Download section of the book website, *www.wiresharkbook.com*. Open the following trace files and examine the Expert Info Composite details identified for each. Answer the questions listed.

ftp-ioupload-partial.pcap   No one will live long enough to upload files to this FTP server. Is the server at fault? The client? The network? Examine the Warnings and Notes in the Expert Info Composite to get the whole picture.

What is the IP address of the host that is sending data?

What type of file is being transferred?

What is the most common error noted in the trace file?

How many retransmissions are seen?

How many fast retransmissions are seen?

Can you reassemble the file that is transferred?

http-download-bad.pcap   The client complains that there is a problem with the Internet connection—they are trying to download the OpenOffice binary, but it is just taking too long. Use the Expert Info and Expert Info Composite to identify the problems in this trace file.

What are the three primary causes of poor performance?

Review Questions

Q13.1   **What is the fastest way to launch the Expert Info Composite window?**

Q13.2   **How can you make specific Expert Info elements stand out in the Packet List pane?**

Q13.3   **How can you filter on all packets that trigger TCP Expert notifications?**

Answers to Review Questions

Q13.1   **What is the fastest way to launch the Expert Info Composite window?**

A13.1   Click on the Expert Info Composite button on Wireshark's Status Bar.

Q13.2   **How can you make specific Expert Info elements stand out in the Packet List pane?**

A13.2   By default, Wireshark colors all Expert Info elements with a black background and red foreground. You can make Expert Info elements stand out by creating a coloring rule for the element (e.g., `tcp.analysis.retransmission`) and placing it above the "Bad TCP" coloring rule.

Q13.3   **How can you filter on all packets that trigger TCP Expert notifications?**

A13.3   Apply a display for `tcp.analysis.flags` to filter on all TCP Expert notifications.

Chapter 14: TCP/IP Analysis Overview

Wireshark Certified Network Analyst Exam Objectives covered:

- TCP/IP Functionality Overview
- The Multi-Step Resolution Process
- Step 1: Port Number Resolution
- Step 2: Network Name Resolution (optional)
- Step 3: Route Resolution when the Target is Local
- Step 4: Local MAC Address Resolution
- Step 5: Route Resolution—when the Target is Remote
- Step 6: Local MAC Address Resolution for a Gateway

- ❖ Case Study: Absolving the Network from Blame
- ❖ Summary
- ❖ Practice What You've Learned
- ❖ Review Questions and Answers

TCP/IP Functionality Overview

In order to troubleshoot or secure a network using Wireshark (or any network analyzer), you must possess a solid understanding of TCP/IP communications. In the next twelve chapters we examine the most common traffic patterns seen on a TCP/IP network.

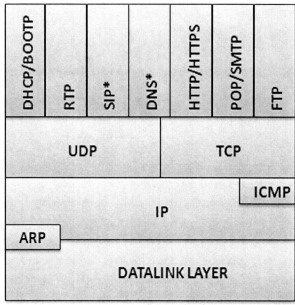

can also be run over TCP

Figure 162. The TCP/IP stack elements

Many network faults or breaches can be attributed to TCP/IP protocol or application issues. When we troubleshoot from the bottom up, we first look for errors at the physical and data link layers—can a host send bits onto the wire? Are those packets properly formed with a correct checksum?[64] Next we move up the TCP/IP stack to determine if problems are visible. To recognize these problems, we need to know what normal behavior is.

- Internet Protocol (IP) acts as the routable network layer protocol used to get packets from end-to-end on a network. Routers use the information contained in the IP header to make forwarding decisions. "Layer 3" switches can route traffic as well.

- User Datagram Protocol (UDP) and Transmission Control Protocol (TCP) provide connectionless and connection-oriented transport layer services, respectively. The port fields in UDP and TCP headers define the application in use. TCP headers contain fields that offer sequencing and acknowledgment services as well.

---

[64] Checksum offloading can throw you off here. If all packets sent from your Wireshark system are listed with invalid checksums, likely that network interface card and driver uses checksum offloading and Wireshark has captured packets before the checksums (IP, TCP or MAC) have been applied.

- Routing Information Protocol (RIP) and Open Shortest Path First (OSPF) are two examples of protocols that provide network and path information exchange between routing devices.

- Internet Control Message Protocol (ICMP) is used to provide network information and is typically recognized as the protocol used for ping.

- Domain Name System (DNS) provides host name-to-IP address resolution services. When you type "`telnet station3`," DNS resolves the name *station3* to its IP address. Other name elements can be resolved with DNS as well.

- Dynamic Host Configuration Protocol (DHCP) provides dynamic client configuration and service discovery services—not just IP address information. DHCP can also provide default gateway settings, DNS server settings and more.

- Address Resolution Protocol (ARP) provides hardware address lookup services for a local destination device. ARP also enables us to check and see if an IP address is already in use (duplicate address test).

There are many more elements to the entire complex TCP/IP protocol stack. First we examine how TCP/IP communications work when everything goes right.

When Everything Goes Right

If all goes well in TCP/IP communications, clients locate services quickly. Those services respond rapidly to requests and the client systems never need to request a service more than once. An analyzer can reveal large delays between communications, name resolution faults, duplicate requests and retransmissions, insecure applications and much more.

Before analyzing traffic to identify faults, you need to know what is considered *normal* network communication. This is where a baseline can be quite useful. For more detail on what traces should be taken to create a baseline of normal network communications, refer to *Chapter 28: Baseline "Normal" Traffic Patterns.*

The Multi-Step Resolution Process

TCP/IP uses a multi-step resolution process when a client communicates with a server, as shown in Figure 163. In our example, both the client and the server are on the same network. This process includes the following steps:

- Define the source and destination port (port number resolution) used by the application.

- Resolve the target name to an IP address (network name resolution), if necessary.

- If the target is on the local network, obtain the hardware address of the target (local MAC address resolution).

- If the target is remote, identify the best router to use to get to the target (route resolution).

- If the target is remote, identify the MAC address of the router (local MAC address resolution again).

We will use the example scenario in Figure 163 and the TCP/IP flow diagram in Figure 164 to examine the TCP/IP resolution processes.

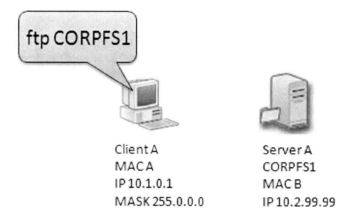

Figure 163. The client wants to make an FTP connection to CORPFS1

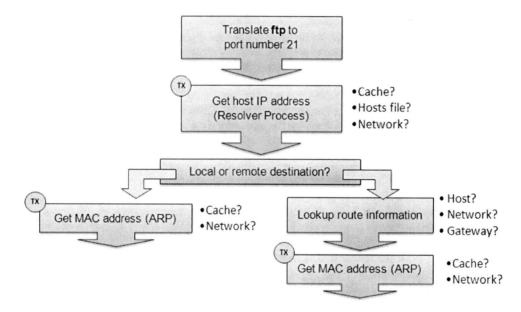

Figure 164. TCP/IP resolution processes

Step 1: Port Number Resolution

In our example, the user has typed "`ftp CORPFS1`." FTP typically uses port 20 or a dynamic port to transfer data and port 21 for commands such as login and password submission functions, USER and PASS.[65] In our example, the client is attempting to connect to the FTP server using port 21. This port number is contained in the *etc/services* file on the client. This number would be placed in the TCP header destination port field of the outbound packet. The client would use a dynamic (ephemeral) port for the source port field value.

This process does not generate traffic on the network.

Step 2: Network Name Resolution (optional)

If an explicit destination IP address has been defined by the client, the network name resolution process is not necessary. If the client has defined a destination host name (CORPFS1 in our example), the network name resolution process is required to obtain the IP address of the target host.

The name resolution specification dictates that you must follow a specific order when performing the resolver process:

1.   Look in DNS resolver cache for the name.

2.   If the entry is not in DNS resolver cache, examine the local *hosts* file (if one exists).

3.   If the local *hosts* file does not exist or the desired name/address is not in the *hosts* file, send requests to the DNS (Domain Name System) server (if one has been configured for the local system).

If there is no answer from the first DNS server on the configured DNS server list, the client can retry the query to the first DNS server or query the next DNS server known. Still no answer? No more DNS servers known? The client cannot build the packet if it cannot resolve the value to be placed in the destination IP address field.

In our example, we may see the client send a DNS query to the first DNS server listed in the client's local configuration. We should (if all goes well) see a reply that contains CORPFS1's IP address from a DNS server.

This process may generate traffic on the network as designated with "TX" in Figure 164. If the name resolution uses the local *hosts* file or obtains the desired information from cache, no packets will be sent. If a DNS query must be sent, it will be seen in the trace file.

Step 3: Route Resolution when the Target is Local

During this process, the client determines if the destination device is local (on the same network) or remote (on the other side of a router). The client compares its own network address to the target network address to determine if a target is on the same network. In the example shown in Figure 163,

---

[65] Applications can overwrite this default port value. For example, our client could use CORPFS1:89 to indicate that it will use port 89 to connect to the FTP server.

the client's IP address is 10.1.0.1/16 (network 10). The server's IP address is 10.2.99.99. The target is also on network 10.

Consider the possible results depending on the client's IP address and subnet mask:

Source Address	Subnet Mask	Is CORPFS1 Local or Remote?
10.1.22.4	255.0.0.0	Local (go to step 4)
10.1.22.4	255.255.0.0	Local (go to step 4)
10.2.22.4	255.255.0.0	Remote (go to step 5)

This process does not generate traffic on the network.

Step 4: Local MAC Address Resolution

If the destination device is local, the client must resolve the MAC address of the local target. First the client checks its ARP cache for the information.[66] If it does not exist, the client sends an ARP broadcast looking for the target's hardware address. Upon receipt of an ARP response, the client updates its ARP cache.

This process may generate traffic on the network as designated with "TX" in Figure 164. If the MAC address is in cache, no packets will be sent. If an ARP query must be sent, it will be seen in the trace file.

Step 5: Route Resolution—when the Target is Remote

If the destination device is remote, the client must perform route resolution to identify the appropriate next-hop router. The client looks in its local routing tables to determine if it has a host or network route entry for the target.[67] If neither entry is available, the client checks for a default gateway entry. This process does not generate traffic on the network.

The default gateway offers a path of 'blind faith'—since the client does not have a route to the destination, it sends the packet to the default gateway and just hopes the default gateway can figure out what to do with the packet.

Default gateways typically either forward the packet (if they have the best route to the destination), send an ICMP redirection response that points to another local router that has the best route to the destination, or reply indicating they have no idea where to send the packet (ICMP Destination Unreachable/Host or Network Unreachable).

Step 6: Local MAC Address Resolution for a Gateway

Finally, the client must resolve the MAC address of the next-hop router or default gateway. The client checks its ARP cache first. If the information does not exist in cache, the client sends an ARP broadcast to get the MAC address of the next-hop router, and updates its ARP cache.

---

[66] To view your ARP cache, type `arp -a` at the command-line.

[67] To view your route tables, at the command prompt type `route print`.

This process may generate traffic on the network as designated with "TX" in Figure 164. If the MAC address of a desired router is in cache, no packets will be sent. If an ARP query must be sent for the desired router, it will be seen in the trace file.

Building the Packet

If all goes well (and in this case the destination is local), we should have resolved the following information during this process as shown in Figure 165:

- Destination MAC address
- Destination IP address
- Source and destination port numbers

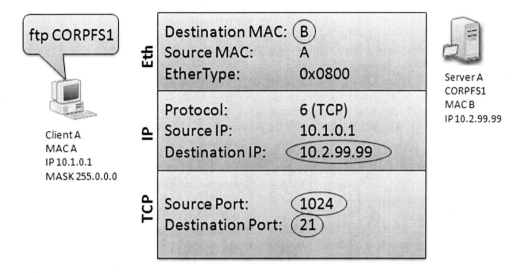

Figure 165. Discovered information for the TCP/IP over Ethernet packet

Let's examine this process in a trace file. Figure 166 shows the packets captured when a client browses to *www.cacetech.com*. By examining this trace file we can identify which information is currently in the client's ARP cache or DNS cache.

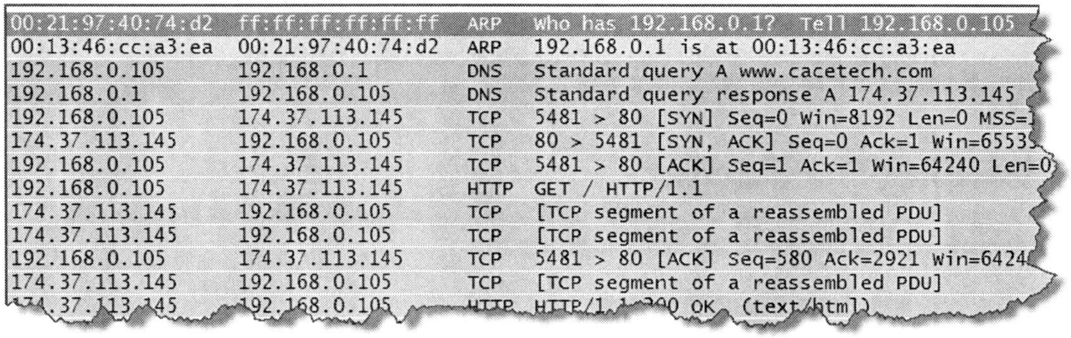

```
00:21:97:40:74:d2   ff:ff:ff:ff:ff:ff   ARP    Who has 192.168.0.1? Tell 192.168.0.105
00:13:46:cc:a3:ea   00:21:97:40:74:d2   ARP    192.168.0.1 is at 00:13:46:cc:a3:ea
192.168.0.105       192.168.0.1         DNS    Standard query A www.cacetech.com
192.168.0.1         192.168.0.105       DNS    Standard query response A 174.37.113.145
192.168.0.105       174.37.113.145      TCP    5481 > 80 [SYN] Seq=0 Win=8192 Len=0 MSS=
174.37.113.145      192.168.0.105       TCP    80 > 5481 [SYN, ACK] Seq=0 Ack=1 Win=6553
192.168.0.105       174.37.113.145      TCP    5481 > 80 [ACK] Seq=1 Ack=1 Win=64240 Len=0
192.168.0.105       174.37.113.145      HTTP   GET / HTTP/1.1
174.37.113.145      192.168.0.105       TCP    [TCP segment of a reassembled PDU]
174.37.113.145      192.168.0.105       TCP    [TCP segment of a reassembled PDU]
192.168.0.105       174.37.113.145      TCP    5481 > 80 [ACK] Seq=580 Ack=2921 Win=6424
174.37.113.145      192.168.0.105       TCP    [TCP segment of a reassembled PDU]
174.37.113.145      192.168.0.105       HTTP   HTTP/1.1 200 OK (text/html)
```

Figure 166. Following the process of browsing to a website

Our trace contains the following packets:

1. ARP query for the MAC address of the DNS server which happens to be the default gateway as well—the client did not have the DNS server's hardware address in ARP cache.

2. Response from the DNS server providing its hardware address. This information is placed in the client's ARP cache and is now visible when we run `arp -a`. When this client needs to connect to a target on another network it will examine ARP cache for the hardware address of the default gateway—which it now has in ARP cache.

3. DNS query for *www.cacetech.com* (this query indicates that the client does not have the IP address for *www.cacetech.com* in cache—in our example, the DNS server process is running on the default gateway; the client does not need to locate the hardware address of a separate local DNS server).

4. DNS response providing the address of the *www.cacetech.com* (this information is now placed in the client's DNS cache and can remain in the cache for the time defined in the Time to Live field in the DNS Answer section).

5. TCP SYN using the correct source/destination ports, sent to the hardware address of the default gateway, sent to the IP address of *www.cacetech.com*.

The rest of the trace file shows the TCP connection process and the request to get the main page at *www.cacetech.com*.

Launch Wireshark on your own host and capture trace files as you browse to websites, ping local targets or login to your server. Next, clear your ARP cache and your DNS cache. Start capturing again and browse to the same websites. Compare the traffic in both trace files noting any changes in the ARP and DNS queries.

Besides being an excellent troubleshooting and security tool, Wireshark is the perfect learning tool allowing you to see how TCP/IP protocols and applications work.

Case Study:
Absolving the Network from Blame

Watching the traffic enables us to point the finger at the problem and also point the finger at the areas that are not part of the problem.

When we noticed our email connections weren't working suddenly and Outlook just sat there in a state of confusion, we grabbed a trace file of the traffic.

No.	Source	Destination	Protocol	Info
1	00:d0:59:aa:	ff:ff:ff:ff:ff	ARP	who has 172.16.0.254? Tell 172.16.1.10
2	00:01:e1:01:	00:d0:59:aa:af	ARP	172.16.0.254 is at 00:01:e1:01:20:e8
3	172.16.1.10	172.16.0.254	DNS	Standard query A smtp.packet-level.com
4	172.16.0.254	172.16.1.10	DNS	Standard query response A 198.173.244.3
5	172.16.1.10	198.173.244.32	TCP	nicetec-nmsvc > smtp [SYN] Seq=0 Win=64
6	172.16.1.10	198.173.244.32	TCP	nicetec-nmsvc > smtp [SYN] Seq=0 Win=6
7	172.16.1.10	198.173.244.32	TCP	nicetec-nmsvc > smtp [SYN] Seq=0 Win=64

We could see the ARP process to locate the DNS server followed by the DNS request for *smtp.packet-level.com*. The response provided us with the correct IP address of the SMTP server.

Then the problem appeared.

We saw the client make a handshake attempt to the SMTP server. No answer. The client tried again and again. Still no answer.

The problem could be along the path or at the SMTP server itself. We saw successful TCP handshake processes when trying to connect to the SMTP server on another port that we knew was open. We tried to connect to the SMTP port from another location and experienced the same problem. We could connect successfully to the other port, however. It felt like the path was not the problem and that the SMTP server was the problem.

Restarting the SMTP server restored access to email services.

By examining the traffic we could rule out problems with the local network interface card, the ARP discovery process and the DNS server. Analyzing the traffic takes out so much of the guesswork.

Summary

TCP/IP communications must follow a standard set of rules that includes numerous resolution processes to determine the port numbers to use, the target IP address, the route to use and the target hardware address.

If one of the resolution processes is unsuccessful, a host cannot communicate with another host. Some of the resolution processes generate traffic on the network—others do not. In some instances, a host can obtain information from cache or local tables. If the information cannot be obtained locally, the host can query a target on the network.

These resolution processes include port number resolution, network name resolution, route resolution, and local MAC address resolution (for the target or a gateway). DNS and ARP queries are commonly seen during the resolution process.

Practice What You've Learned

 Download the trace files available in the Download section of the book website, *www.wiresharkbook.com*. Examine the following trace file to track a resolution process. Capture your own communications to watch your resolution processes.

net-resolutions.pcap   Follow the resolution steps listed in this chapter while you examine this trace file.

You can test `arp` and `dns` display filters on this trace file.

Notice the source/destination port numbers, destination hardware address and destination IP address in packet 5. This information was obtained using the port resolution, MAC address resolution and IP address resolution processes.

Review Questions

Q14.1 **What file is referenced to determine the port to use in a communication when the application does not explicitly specify a port?**

Q14.2 **What can you assume when a client does not generate a DNS query to resolve a target's IP address?**

Q14.3 **What configuration fault might cause a host to ARP for a remote target?**

Answers to Review Questions

Q14.1   **What file is referenced to determine the port to use in a communication when the application does not explicitly specify a port?**

A14.1   The client references the *etc/services* file to determine which port to use for a communication.

Q14.2   **What can you assume when a client does not generate a DNS query to resolve a target's IP address?**

A14.2   When a client does not generate a DNS query to resolve a target IP address you can assume the client either has the target's IP address in cache or the client has a *hosts* file.

Q14.3   **What configuration fault might cause a host to ARP for a remote target?**

A14.3   The client might have a subnet mask that is too short. For example, if a client with IP address 10.2.4.5 has a subnet mask of 255.0.0.0 instead of 255.255.0.0, the client will ARP for any target that has an IP address starting with 10.

Chapter 15: Analyze Domain Name System (DNS) Traffic

Wireshark Certified Network Analyst Exam Objectives covered:

- The Purpose of DNS
- Analyze Normal DNS Queries/Responses
- Analyze DNS Problems
- Dissect the DNS Packet Structure
- Filter on DNS/MDNS Traffic

The Purpose of DNS

DNS is used to convert symbolic host names, such as *www.wiresharkU.com*, to IP addresses. DNS can also be used to transfer name information between DNS servers, identify the host name associated with an IP address (an inverse or pointer query) and lookup other name elements such as the MX (mail exchange) record.

DNS is one of the most important applications on the network. A DNS failure will prevent hosts from locating each other.

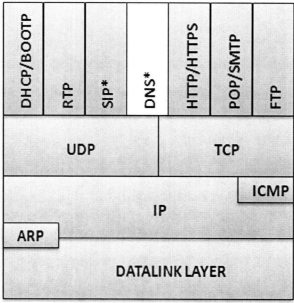

Figure 167. DNS queries/responses most often use UDP and zone transfers use TCP

The *resolver* process runs to perform DNS name resolution.

DNS can run over UDP or TCP. Most commonly you will see DNS queries and replies using UDP. Zone transfers or particularly large DNS queries will run over TCP, however. The default port for DNS is port 53.

RFC 1035, Domain Names – Implementation and Specification, limits DNS over UDP packet payload to 512 bytes. This is typically sufficient for a DNS query. When a response requires more than 512 bytes of space, however, a truncation flag bit is sent in the response. This triggers the resolver to send the DNS query again using TCP which allows for a larger packet size.

RFC 2671, Extension Mechanisms for DNS (EDNS0), allows for greater than 512 bytes over UDP. This added capability caused problems for many folks when Microsoft DNS server added support for

EDNS0, but the Cisco PIX Firewall versions prior to 6.3(2) did not. The PIX Firewall would drop DNS packets greater than the maximum configured length (the default was 512 bytes).

Multicast DNS (mDNS) offers a name resolution process for smaller networks that do not have a DNS server installed. The top level mDNS names end with ".local". Any mDNS query for a name ending with ".local." must be sent to the to the mDNS multicast address (224.0.0.251 or its IPv6 equivalent FF02::FB). For more information on Multicast DNS, refer to *www.multicastdns.org*.

Analyze Normal DNS Queries/Responses

Network name resolution DNS query and response processes are very simple. A client sends a DNS query to a DNS server typically asking for an IP address in exchange for a host name. The DNS server either responds directly with information it possesses or it asks other DNS servers on behalf of the clients (recursive queries).

Figure 168 shows a standard DNS request for the A record (host address) for *www.msnbc.com*. This DNS query was generated automatically when the user entered this host name in the browser URL window and pressed Enter.

```
⊞ Frame 1: 73 bytes on wire (584 bits), 73 bytes captured (584 bits)
⊞ Ethernet II, Src: 08:00:46:f4:3a:09 (08:00:46:f4:3a:09), Dst: 00:01
⊞ Internet Protocol, Src: 67.169.189.113 (67.169.189.113), Dst: 68.87
⊞ User Datagram Protocol, Src Port: 1042 (1042), Dst Port: 53 (53)
⊟ Domain Name System (query)
    [Response In: 2]
    Transaction ID: 0x4269
  ⊞ Flags: 0x0100 (Standard query)
    Questions: 1
    Answer RRs: 0
    Authority RRs: 0
    Additional RRs: 0
  ⊟ Queries
    ⊟ www.msnbc.com: type A, class IN
        Name: www.msnbc.com
        Type: A (Host address)
        Class: IN (0x0001)
```

Figure 168. A standard DNS query

Figure 169 shows the DNS response for the A record request for *www.msnbc.com*.

The name a client requests may not be the actual name of a target. In this case, a canonical name (CNAME), or true name, has been returned for *www.msnbc.com*. The CNAME is *lb.msnbc.com* and the address for that host is 207.46.150.21. Apply a DNS display filter (dns) and run Wireshark as you browse various websites.

```
Frame 2: 106 bytes on wire (848 bits), 106 bytes captured (848 bits)
Ethernet II, Src: 00:01:5c:22:a5:82 (00:01:5c:22:a5:82), Dst: 08:00
Internet Protocol, Src: 68.87.76.178 (68.87.76.178), Dst: 67.169.18
User Datagram Protocol, Src Port: 53 (53), Dst Port: 1042 (1042)
Domain Name System (response)
    [Request In: 1]
    [Time: 0.015912000 seconds]
    Transaction ID: 0x4269
    Flags: 0x8180 (Standard query response, No error)
    Questions: 1
    Answer RRs: 2
    Authority RRs: 0
    Additional RRs: 0
    Queries
        www.msnbc.com: type A, class IN
            Name: www.msnbc.com
            Type: A (Host address)
            Class: IN (0x0001)
    Answers
        www.msnbc.com: type CNAME, class IN, cname lb.msnbc.com
            Name: www.msnbc.com
            Type: CNAME (Canonical name for an alias)
            Class: IN (0x0001)
            Time to live: 3 minutes, 44 seconds
            Data length: 5
            Primary name: lb.msnbc.com
        lb.msnbc.com: type A, class IN, addr 207.46.150.21
            Name: lb.msnbc.com
            Type: A (Host address)
            Class: IN (0x0001)
            Time to live: 24 seconds
            Data length: 4
            Addr: 207.46.150.21
```

Figure 169. A standard DNS query response

Analyze DNS Problems

The most common DNS problem is an error generated because a name does not exist in the name server database. This could be caused by entering an incorrect name or entering a new name that has not yet propagated through the Internet name servers. In Figure 170 a user is trying to browse to *www.us.gov*. The name server responds indicating that there is no such name. The client appends the parent suffix (local domain information) to the query. This is an optional DNS configuration set at the client, but the new name is also not found. If the user cannot resolve the name, it cannot reach the target host.

No. .	Time	Source	Destination	Protocol	Info
1	0.000000	192.168.0.67	192.168.0.1	DNS	Standard query A www.us.gov
2	0.021377	192.168.0.1	192.168.0.67	DNS	Standard query response, No such name
3	0.001102	192.168.0.67	192.168.0.1	DNS	Standard query A www.us.gov.verio.com
4	0.049249	192.168.0.1	192.168.0.67	DNS	Standard query response, No such name

Figure 170. A DNS response indicates that no such name exists

Server failure responses indicate that the name server could not resolve the information for the client due to some error. It could be that the name server sent a query to another name server (through a recursive query) and timed out waiting for a response or the response was not understood or not linked to a query due to an internal failure of some sort. Figure 171 shows a server failure response when trying to get to *www.nmap.org*. We know this is a valid address, but DNS cannot resolve it. We cannot get to the site because of a DNS problem. Note the time column—we can tell how long this client waited before giving up.

No. .	Time	Source	Destination	Protocol	Info
1	0.000000	192.168.0.113	192.168.0.1	DNS	Standard query A www.nmap.org
2	0.999676	192.168.0.113	192.168.0.1	DNS	Standard query A www.nmap.org
3	1.000001	192.168.0.113	192.168.0.1	DNS	Standard query A www.nmap.org
4	2.000003	192.168.0.113	192.168.0.1	DNS	Standard query A www.nmap.org
5	1.095858	192.168.0.1	192.168.0.113	DNS	Standard query response, Server failure
6	0.000003	68.87.76.183	192.168.0.113	DNS	Standard query response, Server failure
7	0.952011	192.168.0.1	192.168.0.113	DNS	Standard query response, Server failure
8	0.000003	68.87.78.136	192.168.0.113	DNS	Standard query response, Server failure
9	15.777859	192.168.0.113	192.168.0.1	DNS	Standard query A d.getdropbox.com

Figure 171. DNS server failures prevent name resolution

Finding the cause of DNS problems may require that you move Wireshark upstream of the DNS server to watch the lookup process at that location. In Figure 172 our client is sending DNS queries to 10.0.0.1 which replies with ICMP Destination Unreachable/Port Unreachable responses indicating that port 53 is not open on that host.

Who is at fault in this case depends on whether the client has the correct IP address of the DNS server or the DNS server daemon is not running on 10.0.0.1. In this case, the client tries again—it only has one DNS server configured so it attempts the lookup again to 10.0.0.1. Again, the client's request is refused because the server indicates that it is not listening on that port.

For more information on ICMP, refer to *Chapter 18: Analyze Internet Control Message Protocol (ICMP) Traffic*.

No. .	Time	Source	Destination	Protocol	Info
1	0.000000	Lite-OnC_30:c8:db	Broadcast	ARP	Who has 10.33.2.1? Tell 10.0.0.99
2	5.000993	Lite-OnC_30:c8:db	Broadcast	ARP	Who has 10.44.5.32? Tell 10.0.0.99
3	5.011500	10.0.0.99	10.0.0.1	DNS	Standard query A ftpcorp1.NAI
4	0.000166	10.0.0.1	10.0.0.99	ICMP	Destination unreachable (Port unreac
5	5.012839	Lite-OnC_30:c8:db	Broadcast	ARP	Who has 10.33.2.1? Tell 10.0.0.99
6	3.008742	Lite-OnC_30:c8:db	Broadcast	ARP	Who has 10.44.5.32? Tell 10.0.0.99
7	3.006709	10.0.0.99	10.0.0.1	DNS	Standard query A ftpcorp1.NAI
8	0.000182	10.0.0.1	10.0.0.99	ICMP	Destination unreachable (Port unreac
9	3.008495	Lite-OnC_30:c8:db	Broadcast	ARP	Who has 10.33.2.1? Tell 10.0.0.99

Figure 172. ICMP responses indicate port 53 is not open on the target

Dissect the DNS Packet Structure

Unlike other applications that utilize a single transport mechanism (either UDP or TCP), DNS utilizes both UDP and TCP. DNS typically uses UDP port 53 for name requests and responses and TCP port 53 for zone transfers and larger name requests and responses. All DNS packets use a single basic structure—consisting of four primary sections as shown in Figure 173.

- Questions
- Answer Resource Records
- Authority Resource Records
- Additional Resource Records

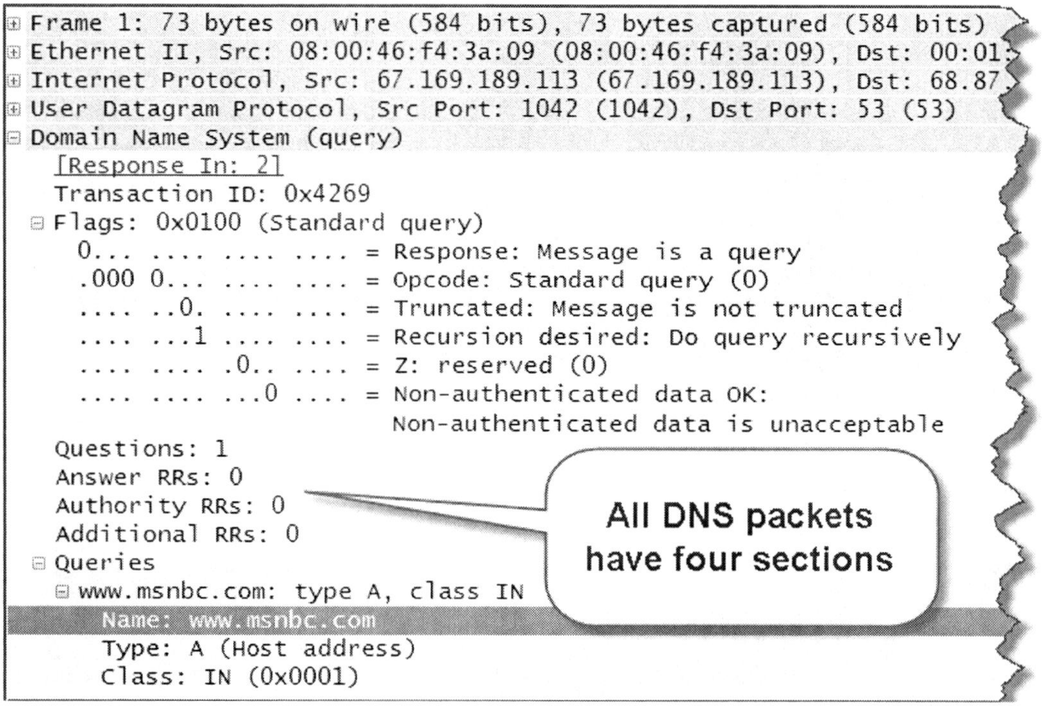

```
⊞ Frame 1: 73 bytes on wire (584 bits), 73 bytes captured (584 bits)
⊞ Ethernet II, Src: 08:00:46:f4:3a:09 (08:00:46:f4:3a:09), Dst: 00:01:
⊞ Internet Protocol, Src: 67.169.189.113 (67.169.189.113), Dst: 68.87
⊞ User Datagram Protocol, Src Port: 1042 (1042), Dst Port: 53 (53)
⊟ Domain Name System (query)
    [Response In: 2]
    Transaction ID: 0x4269
  ⊟ Flags: 0x0100 (Standard query)
    0... .... .... .... = Response: Message is a query
    .000 0... .... .... = Opcode: Standard query (0)
    .... ..0. .... .... = Truncated: Message is not truncated
    .... ...1 .... .... = Recursion desired: Do query recursively
    .... .... .0.. .... = Z: reserved (0)
    .... .... ...0 .... = Non-authenticated data OK:
                          Non-authenticated data is unacceptable
    Questions: 1
    Answer RRs: 0
    Authority RRs: 0
    Additional RRs: 0
  ⊟ Queries
    ⊟ www.msnbc.com: type A, class IN
         Name: www.msnbc.com
        Type: A (Host address)
        Class: IN (0x0001)
```

All DNS packets have four sections

Figure 173. A DNS name request for www.msnbc.com

This next section defines the purpose of each DNS packet field.

Transaction ID

The Transaction ID field associates DNS queries with responses. You can filter on this field and value (`dns.id==0x4269`) to view all associated DNS queries/responses.

Flags

The Flags byte consists of numerous fields that define the query characteristics.

Query/Response

The Query/Response bit indicates whether the packet is a query (0) or a response (1). You can build a Wireshark filter to display DNS queries (`dns.flags.response == 0`) or responses (`dns.flags.response == 1`).

Opcode

The Opcode field specifies the type of query. Most commonly, this field contains 0000 for standard queries and the field is left at 0000 in the responses.

Authoritative Answer

Used in responses, the Authoritative Answer field indicates that the response is from an authoritative server for the domain name.

Truncation

The Truncation field indicates the DNS response was truncated because of the length. If a client sees a truncated DNS response, it should retry the query over TCP. It is not very common to see TCP based queries/responses.

Recursion Desired

Recursion can be defined in DNS queries to indicate whether the server may use recursive query processes. Recursion allows a DNS server to ask another server for an answer on the client's behalf. If the local name server has the answer, it will reply directly. If it does not have the answer, it will begin the lookup process on behalf of the client.

If recursion is not desired, then the query is considered an iterative query. Using Iterative queries, the DNS server will return the information if it is locally available. Otherwise the DNS server may return the IP address of another DNS server to ask. Most DNS queries use recursion.

Recursion Available

Defined in responses, this setting indicates whether recursion is available at the DNS server.

Reserved

This field is set to 0.

Rcode (Response Code)

The Rcode field indicates whether an error condition exists in the response. The following table lists possible Rcode values.

Code	Value
0	No error condition.
1	Format error—query could not be interpreted.
2	Server failure—server could not process query due to a problem with the name server.
3	Name error—domain name does not exist.
4	Not implemented.
5	Refused—name server refuses to perform function due to policy.

Question Count

This field indicates the number of questions in the Question section. Typically you will see only one question per query packet.

Answer Resource Record (RR) Count

This field indicates the number of answers in the Answer RRs section. If a response contains CNAME information you will likely see a count of two in the Answer RR Count area—one for the CNAME and another for the IP address of the CNAME record. [68]

Authority RRs Count

This field indicates the number of answers in the Authority RRs section. These responses come from servers that are closer to the target name in the naming hierarchy.

Additional RRs Count

This field indicates the number of answers in the Additional RRs section. In this section you may find A records for servers in the Authority RR section.

Questions

This variable-length field defines the name that is being resolved.

Name

This field includes the name being resolved. The format is variable-length using a numerical delimiter to indicate the number of alphanumeric bytes in the name. The following are some examples:

```
3www9wireshark3org0
3www4iana3org0
```

---

[68] Bot-infected hosts may receive DNS responses with a high number of Answer RRs. For more information on this evidence, refer to *Name Resolution Process Vulnerabilities* on page 602.

Type

This field indicates the type of query. Refer to *www.iana.org/assignments/dns-parameters* for a complete list of registered type numbers.

Type	Description
A	Host address
NS	Authoritative name server
CNAME	Canonical name for an alias
SOA	Start of Zone Authority
PTR	Pointer record
HINFO	Host information
MX	Mail exchange
AAAA	IPv6 address

Class

This field is set a 1 to indicate an Internet class address for TCP/IP communications.

Answer RRs

This is the same format as this section in the Questions field.

RR Time to Live

This field is used in DNS responses and contains an RR Time to Live value that indicates how long the client can maintain the DNS response in cache.

Authority RRs

This field uses the same format as this section in the Questions field.

Additional RRs

This field uses the same format as this section in the Questions field.

Filter on DNS/MDNS Traffic

The capture filter syntax for DNS traffic is based on the port number because the tcpdump filter format does not understand the string dns. This may change as libpcap and WinPcap are updated.

The capture filter for standard DNS traffic over UDP or TCP is port 53 while mDNS uses port 5353 and the capture syntax is port 5353.

The display filter syntax is simply dns. This filter displays both DNS and mDNS traffic.

The following lists additional DNS display filters.

Display Filter	Description
`dns.flags.response == 0`	DNS queries
`dns.flags.response == 1`	DNs responses
`dns.flags.rcode != 0`	DNS response contains an error[69]
`dns.count.answers >= 5`	DNS response contains more than 5 responses
`dns.qry.name == "www.abc.com"`	DNS query is for *www.abc.com*
`dns contains "abc"`	DNS query or response contains the string "abc"
`dns.qry.type == 0x0001`	DNS query is for a host name
`dns.qry.type == 0x000c`	DNS query is a domain name pointer query (inverse query)
`dns.resp.type == 0x0005`	DNS response contains a CNAME value (canonical name)
`dns.resp.type == 0x0005`	DNS response contains SOA (Start of Authority) information
`dns.flags.recdesired == 1`	DNS query with recursion desired
`dns.flags.recavail == 1`	DNS response stating recursion available

More display filter options can be found in Wireshark's Display Filter Reference section at *www.wireshark.org/docs/dfref/d/dns.html*.

---

[69] Wireshark colorizes the display filter area yellow because of the "!=" operator that often does not provide the expected results. In this case, however, the operator works fine. Try it out on *dns-errors-partial.pcap*.

Case Study:
DNS Killed Web Browsing Performance

One customer complained about slow web browing. They said that sometimes it would take 10 or 15 seconds to load a website—other times sites just wouldn't load at all.

The problem seemed to have started overnight—one day browsing response time was acceptable; the next day it wasn't.

To troubleshoot this problem we placed a full-duplex tap on the network between one of the more "outspoken" users on the network[70] and the local switch.

We didn't need to create a capture filter for this analysis. The switch would only forward traffic destined to our complainer's network interface card. If there were broadcasts and multicasts flowing to this station we were definitely interested to see what they were.

We watched the traffic as our user hit a number of web sites. The web browsing sessions were fast—pages "popped" on the screen. The traffic indicated, however, that the user was visiting sites they'd been to before—there were no DNS queries to resolve the site URLs and the HTTP GET requests all contained "If-Modified-Since" request modifiers. For more details on cached web page analysis issues, refer to *Chapter 23: Analyze Hypertext Transfer Protocol (HTTP) Traffic*.

We asked the user to visit a number of *new* sites. Invariably, if you ask a user to do this they can't think of a single site to browse to. Aargh. We began listing a number of sites we were sure they hadn't surfed to recently—*www.mensa.org*, *www.apa.org* and *www.angermgmt.com* (we had to have *some* fun after all). We had the user browse to about 20 sites while we captured the traffic.

Sitting next to the complainer allowed us to experience their pain. Some web sites were excruciatingly slow to load. Other web sites loaded just fine. While we were there, however, all websites eventually did load—some were just really slow.

Watching the web browsing traffic for a few minutes revealed the problem. We saw three DNS queries go out to one of the DNS servers and then a DNS query go out to a second DNS server. For every page that needed to be loaded there were way too many DNS queries.

The IT staff recognized the issue right away—the primary DNS server was located at a branch office. The complainer's DNS queries were traveling across the Internet all the way to a remote office—and there were obviously some communication problems because they didn't get responses to many of these queries.

---

[70] You know the kind—the person who complains when the network is doing fine—the person who whines about their keyboard suddenly seeming "more sensitive" today. There are uses for these people—we use them as guinea pigs in our troubleshooting procedures. They are willing to stop work to focus on a problem—it is within their comfort zone.

After unsuccessfully trying to resolve the name to the remote DNS server, the complainer's system would then make a DNS query to the local DNS server. We built a simple IO Graph comparing the number of DNS requests and responses. The graph showed a higher number of requests than responses.

DNS Requests   `dns.flags.response==0`

DNS Responses `dns.flags.response==1`

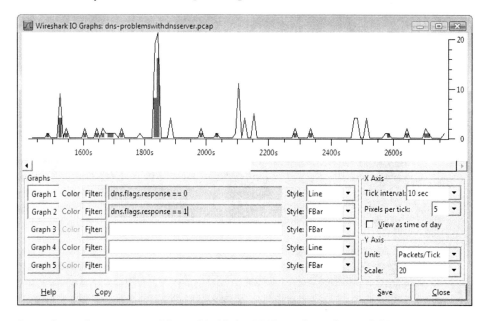

So we knew there was a problem with (a) the DNS configuration and (b) communications to the branch office.

Why was this station talking to the remote DNS server first? Well—the client received its DNS configuration information through DHCP. A review of the DHCP server showed that all local hosts were pointed to the remote DNS server first to resolve names.

The problem really wasn't a web browsing problem—it was a name resolution problem. We could prove it at the complainer's station by simply revisiting a website. We cleared the complainer's web cache (but not the DNS cache). The second and successive times that the complainer visited the sites they loaded fast because there were no DNS delays.

The figure below shows the crazy configuration that had been put in place.

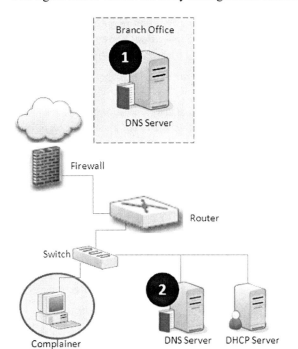

Now the finger pointing began between the IT team. That was my signal to close up the analyzer and start writing my report. Obviously someone configured the local DHCP server incorrectly. Just a couple of minutes and we'd found the problem and identified a solution.

Summary

DNS is used to resolve name information. Most commonly, DNS requests and replies provide hosts with the IP address associated with names used by an application. For example, when you browse to *www.wireshark.org*, your host must resolve the name *www.wireshark.org* to an IP address.

DNS can be used to resolve more than just host names.

When the name resolver process is launched, a host must first look in local cache to see if the information is already known. If no entry exists in cache, the client checks for an entry in a local *hosts* file. If no *hosts* file exists, or no entry for the desired name exists in the *hosts* file, the host can generate a DNS request to a pre-defined DNS server. DNS requests can be recursive or iterative, as defined in the DNS flags field.

DNS servers respond with a numerical code indicating if the lookup was successful. A reply code 0 indicates a successful request.

Practice What You've Learned

Download the trace files available in the Download section of the book website, *www.wiresharkbook.com*. Analyze the DNS communications in the trace files listed and answer the following questions.

http-espn2007.pcap	My favorite 'ugly' website (other than *www.ebay.com*) is *www.espn.com*. How many DNS queries were generated to load this website? Were any DNS queries unsuccessful? What was the typical round trip time between DNS requests and responses? Select **Statistics	HTTP	HTTP Packet Counter** to view the number of redirections (Code 301 and 302) and client errors (Code 404).
dns-misc.pcap	Compare the DNS lookups required to access *www.winpcap.org*, *www.msnbc.com* and *www.espn.com*. Were all of the DNS requests successful? Check the DNS traffic generated when you connect to your corporate servers. Consider baselining that traffic. Refer to *Chapter 28: Baseline "Normal" Traffic Patterns* for a complete list of baselines you should perform.
dns-ptr.pcap	If you see an excessive number of DNS PTR queries, look at the source. Make sure it's not your Wireshark system (turn off network name resolution to squelch the DNS PTR traffic from Wireshark).
	Were all the DNS PTR requests successful?
dns-serverfailure.pcap	DNS server failures indicate that the server couldn't offer a positive or negative response. Perhaps the upstream DNS server didn't respond in a timely manner (or at all). Were these recursive requests? Consider building a display filter for dns.flags.rcode==2 to view these DNS server failure responses.

Review Questions

Q15.1   **What is the purpose of DNS?**

Q15.2   **When does DNS traffic use TCP as the transport?**

Q15.3   **What is the difference between recursive and iterative DNS queries?**

Q15.4   **What are the four sections of DNS queries and answers?**

Answers to Review Questions

Q15.1   **What is the purpose of DNS?**

A15.1   DNS offers a name resolution service. Most commonly, DNS is used to obtain the IP address associated with a host name, but it can also be used to discover host name associated with an IP address (a PTR query), mail exchange server names and IP addresses and more.

Q15.2   **When does DNS traffic use TCP as the transport?**

A15.2   DNS uses TCP as the transport for zone transfers and large DNS packets. If a DNS response is too large to fit into the default 512 byte DNS payload size limitation, the DNS server sets the truncation flag bit in the response. The resolver process generates a new DNS query over TCP.

Q15.3   **What is the difference between recursive and iterative DNS queries?**

A15.3   A recursive query enables a DNS server to look up name information on behalf of the client. An iterative query provides the DNS client with the next DNS server to query if the answer is not available locally.

Q15.4   **What are the four sections of DNS queries and answers?**

A15.4   The four sections of DNS queries and answers are:

> Questions
> Answers
> Authority RR
> Additional RR

Chapter 16: Analyze Address Resolution Protocol (ARP) Traffic

Wireshark Certified Network Analyst Exam Objectives covered:

- The Purpose of ARP
- Analyze Normal ARP Requests/Responses
- Analyze Gratuitous ARP
- Analyze ARP Problems
- Dissect the ARP Packet Structure
- Filter on ARP Traffic

The Purpose of ARP

ARP is used to associate a hardware address with an IP address on a local network and to test for duplicate IP addresses (gratuitous ARP process). As simplistic as ARP is, it can be the protocol that signals problems with network addressing or configurations. ARP is defined in RFC 826, Ethernet Address Resolution Protocol.

ARP packets are unique compared to the majority of traffic on a TCP network because they do not contain an IP header. This characteristic means that ARP packets are non-routable packets.

ARP is Local Only

Keep this in mind while you are analyzing ARP traffic—you must be on the same network segment as a host sending ARP packets in order to capture its ARP packets.

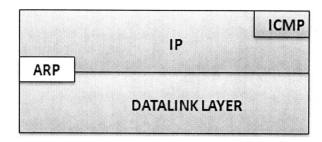

Figure 174. ARP offers address resolution between MAC and IP address layers

Analyze Normal ARP Requests/Responses

Normal ARP communications consist of a simple request and a simple response. A host sends an ARP broadcast that includes target IP address (but no target hardware address—that is what is being resolved).

```
⊟ Address Resolution Protocol (request)
   Hardware type: Ethernet (0x0001)
   Protocol type: IP (0x0800)
   Hardware size: 6
   Protocol size: 4
   Opcode: request (0x0001)
   [Is gratuitous: False]
   Sender MAC address: Elitegro_40:74:d2 (00:21:97:40:74:d2)
   Sender IP address: 192.168.0.113 (192.168.0.113)
   Target MAC address: 00:00:00_00:00:00 (00:00:00:00:00:00)
   Target IP address: 192.168.0.1 (192.168.0.1)
```

Figure 175. Standard ARP request

In Figure 175 a host with hardware address 00:21:97:40:74:d2 and IP address 192.168.0.113 is looking up the hardware address for 192.168.0.1.

The response packet, shown in Figure 176 now contains a sender IP address of 192.168.0.1 and contains the hardware address for that device. Note that the sender and target addresses are associated with the current packet sender in ARP requests and replies. In our request in Figure 175, the sender IP address is 192.168.0.113. The sender IP address in the response shown in Figure 176 is 192.168.0.1.

```
Address Resolution Protocol (reply)
    Hardware type: Ethernet (0x0001)
    Protocol type: IP (0x0800)
    Hardware size: 6
    Protocol size: 4
    Opcode: reply (0x0002)
    [Is gratuitous: False]
    Sender MAC address: D-Link_cc:a3:ea (00:13:46:cc:a3:ea)
    Sender IP address: 192.168.0.1 (192.168.0.1)
    Target MAC address: Elitegro_40:74:d2 (00:21:97:40:74:d2)
    Target IP address: 192.168.0.113 (192.168.0.113)
```

Figure 176. Standard ARP reply

Analyze Gratuitous ARPs

Gratuitous ARPs are sent to determine if another host on the network has the same IP address as the sender. All hosts send gratuitous ARPs regardless of whether their IP address was statically or dynamically assigned. Wireshark can identify gratuitous ARP packets.

In Figure 177 a host is checking to see if another device on the network is using the IP address 10.64.0.64. An ARP filter has been applied to the trace file and the Time column has been set to Seconds since Previous Displayed packet.

When a new host boots up on the network and receives an IP address from a DHCP server or a host boots with a static address, the host sends out at least one gratuitous ARP request. The host waits approximately one second for an answer.

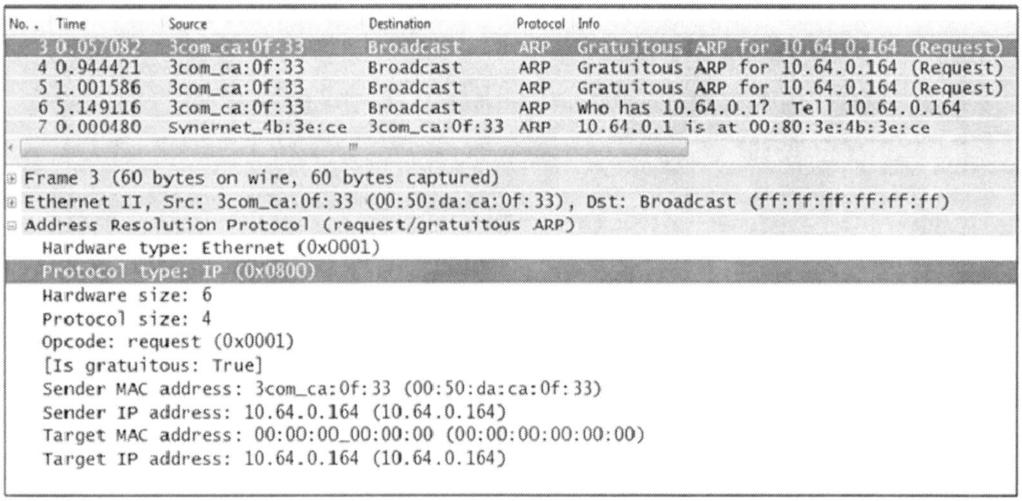

```
No. .  Time      Source           Destination       Protocol  Info
3 0.057082   3com_ca:0f:33    Broadcast        ARP     Gratuitous ARP for 10.64.0.164 (Request)
4 0.944421   3com_ca:0f:33    Broadcast        ARP     Gratuitous ARP for 10.64.0.164 (Request)
5 1.001586   3com_ca:0f:33    Broadcast        ARP     Gratuitous ARP for 10.64.0.164 (Request)
6 5.149116   3com_ca:0f:33    Broadcast        ARP     Who has 10.64.0.1?  Tell 10.64.0.164
7 0.000480   Synernet_4b:3e:ce 3com_ca:0f:33   ARP     10.64.0.1 is at 00:80:3e:4b:3e:ce

Frame 3 (60 bytes on wire, 60 bytes captured)
Ethernet II, Src: 3com_ca:0f:33 (00:50:da:ca:0f:33), Dst: Broadcast (ff:ff:ff:ff:ff:ff)
Address Resolution Protocol (request/gratuitous ARP)
    Hardware type: Ethernet (0x0001)
    Protocol type: IP (0x0800)
    Hardware size: 6
    Protocol size: 4
    Opcode: request (0x0001)
    [Is gratuitous: True]
    Sender MAC address: 3com_ca:0f:33 (00:50:da:ca:0f:33)
    Sender IP address: 10.64.0.164 (10.64.0.164)
    Target MAC address: 00:00:00_00:00:00 (00:00:00:00:00:00)
    Target IP address: 10.64.0.164 (10.64.0.164)
```

Figure 177. Gratuitous ARP packet

In our example in Figure 177, the host sends three gratuitous ARP packets—waiting one second between each attempt. After the third attempt and another one second delay with no response, the host can begin to initialize its IP stack. If a gratuitous ARP receives a response, another host is using the desired IP address. This typically generates a "duplicate IP address" alert which stops the IP address initiation process.

Analyze ARP Problems
Network addressing problems can cause ARP issues. For example, in Figure 178, Client A has been configured with the wrong subnet mask. When Client A goes through the resolution process to determine if the target, Server A at 10.2.99.99, is local or remote, Client A determines the server is local. Client A believes it is on network 10.0.0.0/8. Client A believes the server also sits on network 10.0.0.0/8. This is because Client A's subnet mask is set at 255.0.0.0.

Since ARP packets are non-routable, they will never make it to Server A.[71]

---

[71] Some texts state that ARP packets are not routed because they are broadcasts. This is incorrect. An ARP reply packet is not a broadcast, but it cannot be routed. ARP packets have no IP header and this prevents ARP packets from being routed.

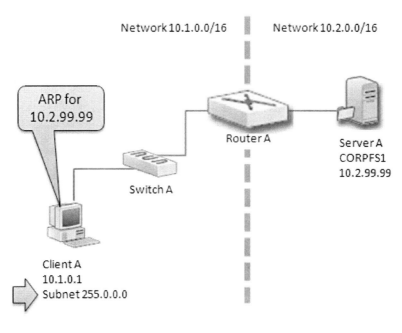

Figure 178. An ARP problem caused by a misconfigured host subnet value

---

Watch Out for Proxy ARP

Routers that support Proxy ARP (defined in RFC 1027, Using ARP to Implement Transparent Subnet Gateways) may answer on behalf of devices on other networks. There are numerous disadvantages to using proxy ARP including an increase in overall ARP traffic. For an example of filtering for proxy ARP traffic, see Filter on ARP Traffic on page 326.

If you examine ARP traffic, but do not see responses to ARP broadcasts, you (a) might not tapped in to a location where you can see unicast responses—you only saw the ARP broadcast because it was forwarded throughout the switched network—or (b) the ARP broadcast is a gratuitous ARP and the lack of response indicates that there is not an IP address conflict.

ARP poisoning traffic looks quite unique as well. In Figure 179 Wireshark has detected that duplicate address use has occurred. We can see a host at 00:d0:59:aa:af:80 advertising both 192.168.1.103 and 192.168.1.1. This is the classic signature of ARP-based man-in-the-middle traffic.

For more details on ARP poisoning, refer to *Chapter 32: Analyze Suspect Traffic*.

```
  Protocol Info
  ARP   192.168.1.103 is at 00:d0:59:aa:af:80
01 ARP   192.168.1.1 is at 00:d0:59:aa:af:80 (duplicate use of 192.168.1.103 detected!)
  ARP   who has 192.168.1.1? Tell 192.168.1.103
80 ARP   192.168.1.1 is at 00:20:78:d9:0d:db
01 ARP   who has 192.168.1.103? Tell 192.168.1.1 (duplicate use of 192.168.1.1 detected!)
80 ARP   192.168.1.103 is at 00:d0:59:12:9b:01 (duplicate use of 192.168.1.1 detected!)
  ARP   192.168.1.103 is at 00:d0:59:aa:af:80
01 ARP   192.168.1.1 is at 00:d0:59:aa:af:80 (duplicate use of 192.168.1.103 detected!)
  ARP   who has 192.168.1.1? Tell 192.168.1.103
80 ARP   192.168.1.1 is at 00:20:78:d9:0d:db
01 ARP   who has 192.168.1.103? Tell 192.168.1.1 (duplicate use of 192.168.1.1 detected!)
80 ARP   192.168.1.103 is at 00:d0:59:12:9b:01 (duplicate use of 192.168.1.1 detected!)
  ARP   192.168.1.103 is at 00:d0:59:aa:af:80
01 ARP   192.168.1.1 is at 00:d0:59:aa:af:80 (duplicate use of 192.168.1.103 detected!)
```

Figure 179. Wireshark can detect duplicate IP addresses

You can disable Wireshark's duplicate IP address detection mechanism in the ARP preferences configuration as shown in Figure 180.

You can also enable Wireshark's ARP storm detection. To enable this feature you must define the number of ARP packets to detect during a detection period. If you enable the ARP storm detection, Wireshark looks for 30 ARP packets occurring within 100ms before triggering an event.

Duplicate IP addresses are noted in the Packet List pane. ARP storm conditions are added to the Notes section of the Expert Info window.

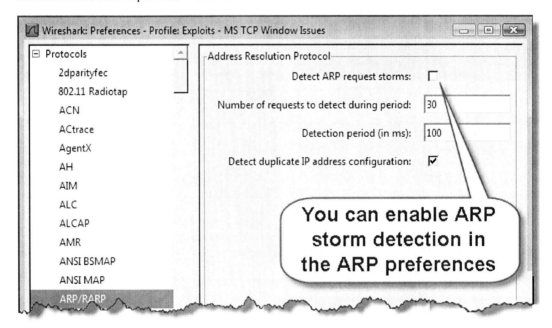

Figure 180. ARP duplicate IP address detection is on by default, but ARP storm detection is not

Dissect the ARP Packet Structure

There are two basic ARP packets—the ARP request packet and the ARP reply packet. Both packets use the same format. The most confusing part of ARP is the interpretation of the sender and target address information. When an ARP broadcast is being sent from a host (host A for example), the sending host puts their hardware and IP address in the sender address fields.

The target protocol address field includes the IP address of the device being sought. The target hardware address field is set to all 0's to indicate the information is not known. In an ARP reply, the target and sender information is reversed to show that the ARP responder is now the sender. The original station performing the lookup is now the destination.

Hardware Type

This defines the hardware or data link type in use. This field is also used to determine the hardware address length, which makes the 'Length of Hardware Address' field redundant. Hardware type "1" is assigned to Ethernet and defines a 6-byte hardware address length. The complete Hardware Type field value listing is available at *www.iana.org*.

Protocol Type

This field defines the protocol address type in use. This field uses the standard protocol ID values that are also used in the Ethernet II frame structures. These protocol types are defined at *www.iana.org/assignments/protocol-numbers*. This field also determines the length of the protocol address making the 'Length of Protocol Address' field redundant.

Length of Hardware Address

This field defines the length (in bytes) of the hardware addresses used in this packet. This field is redundant since this value is determined by the hardware type field.

Length of Protocol Address

This field defines the length (in bytes) of the protocol (network) addresses used in this packet. This field is redundant since this value is determined by the protocol type field.

Opcode

This defines whether this is a request or reply packet and the type of address resolution taking place. RARP is a process that enables a device to learn a network address from a MAC address. RARP is defined in RFC 903, A Reverse Address Resolution Protocol. The following lists the ARP and RARP (reverse ARP) operation codes:

Opcode	Purpose
1	ARP request
2	ARP reply
3	RARP request
4	RARP reply

Sender's Hardware Address

This field indicates the hardware address of the device that is sending this request or reply.

Sender's Protocol Address

This field indicates the protocol or network, address of the device that is sending this request or reply.

Target Hardware Address

This field indicates the desired target hardware address, if known. In ARP requests, this field is typically filled with all 0s. In ARP replies, this field should contain the hardware address of the device being sought (or the next-hop router to that device).

Target Protocol Address

This field indicates the desired target protocol or network, address.

Filter on ARP Traffic

The capture filter syntax for ARP traffic is simply `arp`.

The display filter syntax is simply `arp`. The following lists additional ARP display filters.

Display Filter	Description
`arp.opcode == 0x0001`	ARP request
`arp.opcode == 0x0002`	ARP reply
`arp.src.hw_mac == 00:13:46:cc:a3:ea`	ARP source hardware address is 00:13:46:cc:a3:ea (request or reply)
`(arp.src.hw_mac == 00:21:97:40:74:d2) && (arp.opcode == 0x0001)`	ARP request with source hardware address 00:13:46:cc:a3:ea
`(arp.src.hw_mac == 00:d0:59:aa:af:80) && !(arp.src.proto_ipv4 == 192.168.1.1)`	ARP packet where a host at 00:d0:59:aa:af:80 is not advertising its own IP address (192.168.1.1)—why not? Strange.
`(arp.opcode == 0x0002) && !(arp.src.proto_ipv4 == 192.168.0.1/16)`	ARP packet where IP address resolved is for remote device (ARP proxy response)— watch out for proxy ARP

Case Study:
Death by ARP

Submitted by: **Todd Dokey**

I did an Infosec gig last year, and that saw lots of "Wiresharkage." I worked for a large grocery chain in the central valley. Prior to that, and while there, I was involved in the Novell Beta test team for their new Teaming and Conferencing Software bundle.

So, in both cases, I used Wireshark, and always use it to see what the heck is going on. (SIP traffic is always fun!)

One of the things we had at the Infosec job was a packet storm coming from (mostly) HP printers.

They would start ARP requesting, and after a time, the whole network was ARPing up a storm. So much so, my Linux boxes had their tables flooded out.

Why? Oh, the *&$!#* that designed their network was a *&$!#*—the network was all one big bridged network between all sites! All that lovely Cisco gear, paid for by public money, and the *&$!#* had it all bridged!

Later they had issues with people using streaming clients—this was not a big deal for the internet gateway per se, although I am sure it influenced the hits to the domain web site somewhat. But the real effect was from all these secretaries listening to their music (or streaming music videos from YouTube) and log jamming the routes between the sites.

The end result there was that the client connections to useful things like back-end databases would time out. I don't have to tell you how much fun that is. So, they'd call support (vendor) and the vendor would not be able to figure it out. This was especially exciting during billing and payroll time.

Note from Laura: It's easy to learn how much bandwidth is required when someone watches a YouTube video. Just use your "My MAC" capture filter and watch a video. Apply a conversation filter for traffic to and from the YouTube server—the stream should be pretty easy to spot if you're not doing much else in the background. Note what the Stream Index value is in the TCP header and create a filter for this (`tcp.stream == x`) in your IO Graph.

Summary

Basic ARP is used to resolve the hardware address of local targets. Those local targets may be the final destination of the communication or they could be a local router.

The ARP process examines the local ARP cache first before generating an ARP request on the network. Both ARP requests and responses use the same packet format.

A typical ARP request is sent to the data link broadcast address while responses are sent directly to the hardware address of the requester. ARP can be used to discover all devices on the local network—even devices that try to hide behind firewalls.

Gratuitous ARP is used to detect duplicate IP addresses on the network and must be performed by IP hosts regardless of whether their IP address is statically or dynamically assigned.

ARP packets are non-routable because they do not have an IP header.

Practice What You've Learned

 Download the trace files available in the Download section of the book website, *www.wiresharkbook.com*. Open the trace files listed and answer the questions listed in this section.

arp-bootup.pcap   This is a classic client bootup sequence.

What is the purpose of the ARP packets in this trace file?

Were the ARP requests answered?

What is the delay between each of the ARP packets seen? Why is the delay necessary?

arp-ping.pcap   What is the purpose of each of the ARP packets in this trace file?

Was each process successful?

arp-badpadding.pcap   ARP packets are minimum-sized packets and must be padded to meet the minimum 64-byte length for this Ethernet network.

What is in the ARP padding in these packets?

Why can't we follow an ARP stream?

Could this padding be considered a security flaw?

Review Questions

Q16.1   **What is the purpose of ARP?**

Q16.2   **What configuration problem can cause a host to ARP for a remote host?**

Q16.3   **Why can't ARP packets cross routers?**

Q16.4   **What is the syntax of capture and display filters for ARP traffic?**

Answers to Review Questions

Q16.1   **What is the purpose of ARP?**

A16.1   ARP is used to obtain the hardware address of a target host or gateway/router.

Q16.2   **What configuration problem can cause a host to ARP for a remote host?**

A16.2   If a client's subnet mask is too short, it may think more targets are on the local network and broadcast ARP packets to resolve the hardware addresses of those targets.

Q16.3   **Why can't ARP packets cross routers?**

A16.3   ARP packets cannot be routed because they do not have a routing (IP) header.

Q16.4   **What is the syntax of capture and display filters for ARP traffic?**

A16.4   Capture filter: `arp`
Display filter: `arp`

Chapter 17: Analyze Internet Protocol (IPv4) Traffic

Wireshark Certified Network Analyst Exam Objectives covered:

- The Purpose of IPv4
- Analyze Normal IPv4 Traffic
- Analyze IPv4 Problems
- Dissect the IPv4 Packet Structure
- Set Your IP Protocol Preferences
- Filter on IPv4 Traffic

- ❖ Case Study: Everyone Blamed the Router
- ❖ Case Study: It's Not the Network's Problem
- ❖ Summary
- ❖ Practice What You've Learned
- ❖ Review Questions and Answers

Note: This Study Guide and the Wireshark Certified Network Analyst Exam focus on IPv4 only. For IPv6 information, refer to *wiki.wireshark.org/IPv6*.

The Purpose of IPv4

IPv4 is covered in RFC 791. IP provides the datagram delivery services for networked systems as well as fragmentation and reassembly for low MTU networks. IP also offers quality of service designation capability to enable certain traffic to be prioritized over other traffic.

IP is connectionless and unreliable, providing best effort delivery of datagrams between IP hosts. IP itself offers no way to determine if a packet arrived at a target location. An application that needs guaranteed delivery should use TCP over IP.

The IP header is typically 20 bytes long although it does contain an Options field that can extend the IP header length (in 4 byte increments).

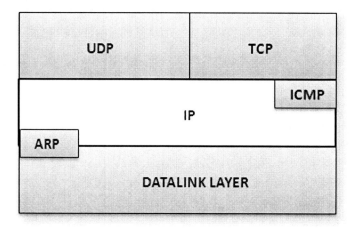

Figure 181. IP provides datagram delivery services

Analyze Normal IPv4 Traffic

Normal IPv4 communications simply gets packets from one location to another using the most efficient packet size.

As IP packets are forwarded by routers, the target IP address is examined to make routing decisions, the MTU size is checked against the next link (to determine if fragmentation is needed and allowed), the MAC header is stripped off and a new one is applied for the next network and the time to live value is decremented in the IP header. The IP header is also checked for forwarding prioritization (see *Differentiated Services Field and Explicit Congestion Notification* on page 335).

If all works well in an IPv4 communication, traffic should flow to and from IP addresses. The IP address in the header should not change unless a NAT/PAT device intercepts the traffic and alters the address. Refer back to *Proxy, Firewall and NAT/PAT Overview* on page 13 for details.

If a packet is too large to be forwarded to the next link in a path, the router examines the IP header's fragmentation setting. If the Don't Fragment bit is set, the packet cannot be forwarded. The router should send an ICMP Type 3, Code 4 message (Fragmentation Needed, but the Don't Fragment Bit was Set) defining the MTU limitation to the packet originator. The originator should retransmit the packet at a smaller MTU. If fragmentation is allowed, the router should split the single large packet into two (or more) smaller packets, define the fragment offset and indicate that the packets are fragments and forward them on.

In Figure 182, a 1500-byte MTU packet from Client A to Server A cannot flow through the path. The limitation is in the link between Router B and Router C. Router B should generate the ICMP Type 3, Code 4 message back to Client A. For more information on MTU limits, refer to *wiki.wireshark.org/MTU*.

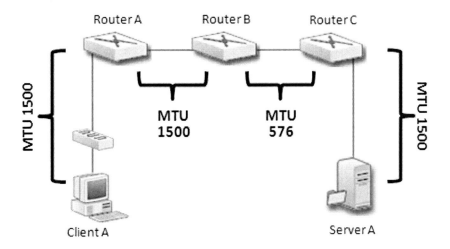

Figure 182. IP can fragment packets when a link's MTU doesn't support the datagram size

Fragmentation is not desirable on a network as it reduces the efficiency of data flow. It may, however, be unavoidable. Examine **Statistics | Packet Lengths** or apply a filter for ICMP Type 3/Code 4 packets to identify possible MTU problems.

For more information on ICMP filtering, refer to *Chapter 18: Analyze Internet Control Message Protocol (ICMP) Traffic*.

Analyze IPv4 Problems

IPv4 problems typically deal with fragmentation, unusual IP addresses and excessive broadcasts.

Fragmentation problems can arise when ICMP Type 3, Code 4 packets are blocked preventing a host from learning why its packets did not make it to a destination. The ICMP Type 3, Code 4 packet is used for "black hole detection."

Unusual IP addresses may be duplicate addresses or addresses that are not allowed on the network, such as the address shown in Figure 183. The IP source address cannot be the loopback address (127.0.0.0/8), a multicast address or a broadcast address.

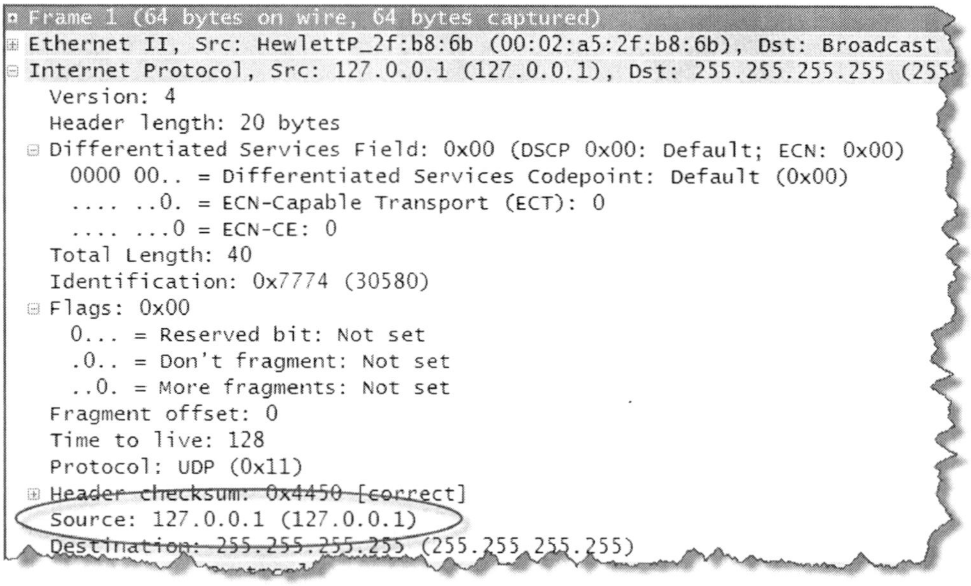

```
□ Frame 1 (64 bytes on wire, 64 bytes captured)
⊞ Ethernet II, Src: HewlettP_2f:b8:6b (00:02:a5:2f:b8:6b), Dst: Broadcast
□ Internet Protocol, Src: 127.0.0.1 (127.0.0.1), Dst: 255.255.255.255 (255
    Version: 4
    Header length: 20 bytes
  □ Differentiated Services Field: 0x00 (DSCP 0x00: Default; ECN: 0x00)
      0000 00.. = Differentiated Services Codepoint: Default (0x00)
      .... ..0. = ECN-Capable Transport (ECT): 0
      .... ...0 = ECN-CE: 0
    Total Length: 40
    Identification: 0x7774 (30580)
  □ Flags: 0x00
      0... = Reserved bit: Not set
      .0.. = Don't fragment: Not set
      ..0. = More fragments: Not set
    Fragment offset: 0
    Time to live: 128
    Protocol: UDP (0x11)
  ⊞ Header checksum: 0x4450 [correct]
    Source: 127.0.0.1 (127.0.0.1)
    Destination: 255.255.255.255 (255.255.255.255)
```

Figure 183. A source IP address of 127.0.0.1 is questionable

Excessive broadcasts flowing throughout a network can be easily detected by connecting Wireshark into a network switch. For more information on IP broadcasts and multicasts, refer to *Broadcast/Multicast Traffic* on page 339.

Dissect the IPv4 Packet Structure

This section details the header fields and their functions. For more details on each field, refer to RFC 791. Figure 184 shows a standard IPv4 header.

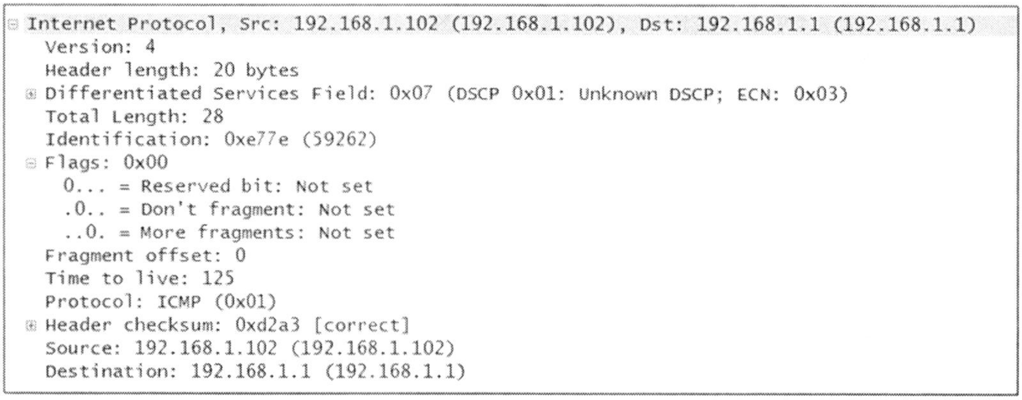

```
□ Internet Protocol, Src: 192.168.1.102 (192.168.1.102), Dst: 192.168.1.1 (192.168.1.1)
    Version: 4
    Header length: 20 bytes
  ⊞ Differentiated Services Field: 0x07 (DSCP 0x01: Unknown DSCP; ECN: 0x03)
    Total Length: 28
    Identification: 0xe77e (59262)
  □ Flags: 0x00
      0... = Reserved bit: Not set
      .0.. = Don't fragment: Not set
      ..0. = More fragments: Not set
    Fragment offset: 0
    Time to live: 125
    Protocol: ICMP (0x01)
  ⊞ Header checksum: 0xd2a3 [correct]
    Source: 192.168.1.102 (192.168.1.102)
    Destination: 192.168.1.1 (192.168.1.1)
```

Figure 184. IPv4 header

Version Field

The first field in the IP header is the version field. We are focusing on IPv4 in this book.

Header Length Field

This field is also referred to as the "Internet Header Length" field or IHL. This field denotes the length of the IP header only—just the IP header. This is necessary because the IP header can support options and therefore, may be varying lengths. This field value is provided in multiples of 4 bytes. For example, the actual decimal decode will be 5. Wireshark multiplies that value by 4 bytes to come up with the true IP header length value of 20 bytes. In Figure 184, the IP header is 20 bytes long. There are no options in this IP header.

Differentiated Services Field and Explicit Congestion Notification

The six-bit Differentiated Services Field (DiffServ) is used to prioritize traffic and provide a certain level of Quality of Service (QoS). The field contains a Differentiated Services Code Point (DSCP) value that is used to determine how to handle the packet (the per-hop behavior). Figure 185 shows the DSCP value for a SIP packet that is set with Assured Forwarding.

```
⊟ Differentiated Services Field: 0x68 (DSCP 0x1a: Assured Forwarding 31; ECN: 0x00)
   0110 10.. = Differentiated Services Codepoint: Assured Forwarding 31 (0x1a)
   .... ..0. = ECN-Capable Transport (ECT): 0
   .... ...0 = ECN-CE: 0
```

Figure 185. This Differentiated Services Codepoint field (DSCP) defines Assured Forwarding for a packet

For more information on Differentiated Services, view RFC 2474, Definition of the Differentiated Services Field (DS Field) in the IPv4 and IPv6 Headers. The RFCs related to DiffServ do not dictate the way to implement per-hop behavior; this is the responsibility of the vendor. In this section we will look at Cisco's implementation—we recommend that you refer to your router vendor's technical references as they may use different values.

Assured Forwarding and Expedited Forwarding Per-Hop Behavior

RFC 2597, Assured Forwarding PHB Group, defines Assured Forwarding as a means for a DiffServ provider to offer different levels of forwarding assurances for IP packets received from a DiffServ customer.

RFC 2598, an Expediting Forwarding PHB, defines that Expedited Forwarding "can be used to build a low loss, low latency, low jitter, assured bandwidth, end-to-end service through DS (DiffServ) domains. Such a service appears to the endpoints like a point-to-point connection or a "virtual leased line." This service has also been described as Premium service." Cisco routers that support DiffServ look for a DSCP value of 46 to support Expedited Forwarding.

The two-bit Explicit Congestion Notification (ECN) field is used by the sender and/or routers along the path to identify network congestion along route.[72]

---

[72] Refer to RFC 3168, The Addition of Explicit Congestion Notification (ECN).

The DiffServ and ECN sections of the IP header were formerly used as the Type of Service (TOS) field.

Total Length Field

This field defines the length of the IP header and any valid data (this does not include any data link padding). In the example shown in Figure 184, the total length field value is 48 bytes. The first 20 bytes of that is the IP header—this indicates that the remaining packet length (not including any data link padding) is 28 bytes.

Identification Field

Each individual IP packet is given a unique ID value when it is sent. If the packet must be fragmented to fit on a network that supports a smaller packet size, the same ID number will be placed in each fragment in order to indicate that these fragments are part of the same original packet.

Use the IP ID Field to Spot Looping Packets

When analyzing a network that is flooded with what appears to be the same packet looping the network, examine the IP header ID field and fragment settings. If the IP ID field is different in each packet, the packet cannot be looping—a host is flooding the network with separate packets—you need to find the host and shut it off. If, however, the IP ID field is the same and the packet is not a fragment (all fragments of a set contain the same IP ID value), then you can assume it is the same packet that is looping the network—look to an infrastructure loop as the cause of the problem.

Flags Field

The Flags field is actually three bits in length and has the following bit value assignments:

- Bit 0: Reserved—set to 0.
- Bit 1: The Don't Fragment Bit
  (0=may fragment; 1=don't fragment)
- Bit 2: The More Fragments Bit
  (0=last fragment; 1=more to come)

An application may be written to disallow fragmentation. If so, the application will set the Don't Fragment bit to 1. If fragmentation is allowed and a packet must be fragmented to cross a network that supports a smaller MTU, the Don't Fragment bit would be set to 0. When the packet is split into multiple fragments—three fragments, for example—the first and second fragments will have the More Fragments to Come bit set to 1. The last fragment will have the More Fragments bit set to 0 indicating that it is the final fragment in the set. All fragments would use the same IP ID value. Fragmentation reassembly occurs at the endpoint.

If you have mixed media types (Ethernet and PPP, for example), you may need fragmentation to get a 1500 MTU packet through a 1,476-byte Generic Routing Encapsulation (GRE) tunnel by splitting it up into multiple packets. Fragmentation takes time and extra overhead however.

Fragment Offset Field

If the packet is a fragment, this field indicates where to place this packet's data when the fragments are being reassembled into a single packet again (at the destination host). This field provides the offset in 8-byte values. For example, the first fragment may have an offset of 0 and contain 1400 bytes of data (not including any headers). The second fragment would have offset value 175 (175 x 8 = 1400). This field is only in use if the packet is a fragment—otherwise it is set to 0.

Time to Live Field

This field indicates the remaining lifetime (in seconds and hops through routers) of the packet. Typical starting TTL values are 32, 60, and 128.

Default TTL values are incorporated into the vendor's TCP/IP stack. Applications (such as traceroute) can override these defaults as desired. Each time a packet is forwarded by a router, the router must decrement the TTL field by 1. If the router must hold the packet in its queue for an extended period of time (longer than one second), it must decrement that TTL value by the number of seconds the packet was held in the queue as well as decrementing the TTL for the hop.

If a packet with TTL=1 arrives at a router, the router must discard the packet because it cannot decrement the TTL to 0 and forward the packet. A router may generate an ICMP Type 11, Code 0 response to the sender (Time Exceeded, Time to Live Exceeded in Transit) indicating the packet was not forwarded due to the Time to Live value.

If a packet with TTL=1 arrives at a host, what should the host do? Process the packet, of course. The hosts do not need to decrement the TTL value upon receipt.

Since low TTL values are considered unusual, Wireshark has a coloring rule called *TTL low or unexpected* that helps identify these packets in a trace file. The coloring rule filter is (! ip.dst == 224.0.0.0/4 && ip.ttl < 5) || (ip.dst == 224.0.0.0/24 && ip.ttl != 1).

When a packet gets fragmented, all fragments are given the same TTL value. If they take different paths through a network, they may end up at the destination with varying TTL values. When the first fragment arrives at the destination, however, the destination host will begin counting down from the TTL value of that packet in seconds. All fragments must arrive before that timer expires or the fragment set is considered 'incomplete' and unusable. The destination would send an ICMP Type 11, Code 1 reply (Time Exceeded, Fragment Reassembly Time Exceeded) to the source to indicate that the packet's lifetime had expired during the reassembly process. This prompts the client to retransmit the original unfragmented packet.

Protocol Field

All headers have a field that defines what is coming up next. For example, in a TCP/IP packet, an Ethernet II header has a Type field to indicate that IP is coming up next. The IP header has a Protocol field to indicate what is coming up next.

The more commonly seen values in the protocol field are listed below:

Num.	Description
1	ICMP
2	IGMP
6	TCP
8	EGP
9	Any private interior gateway, such as Cisco's IGRP
17	UDP
45	IDRP
88	Cisco EIGRP
89	OSPF

To obtain the most current list of Protocol field values, visit *www.iana.org/assignments/protocol-numbers*.

Header Checksum Field

The IP header Checksum field provides error detection on the contents of the IP header only—this field does not cover the contents of the packet other than the IP header. This checksum does not include the checksum field itself in the calculation.

Source Address Field

This is the IP address of the device that sent the packet. In some cases, such as during the DHCP bootup process, the client may not know its IP address, so it may use 0.0.0.0 in this field. This field cannot contain a multicast or broadcast address.

Destination Address Field

This field can include a unicast, multicast, broadcast (and in the case of IPv6, anycast) address. This address defines the final destination of the packet.

Options Field

The IP header can be extended by a number of options (although these options are not often used). If the header is extended with options, those options must end on a 4-byte boundary because the Internet Header Length (IHL) field defines the header length in 4-byte boundaries.

The following list only displays a partial set of options. For the complete list, refer to *www.iana.org*.

Number	Name
0	End of Options List (defines when IP options end)
3	Loose Source Route (provide some path information)
4	Time Stamp (timestamp along path)
7	Record Route (mark routers passed along a path)
9	Strict Source Route (provide specific path information)

Broadcast/Multicast Traffic

There are two basic types of broadcasts/multicasts on the network: lookups and announcements. An example of a lookup would be the discovery broadcast that a DHCP client sends when it boots up and needs a new IP address and needs to find a DHCP server. Another example of a lookup broadcast is the ARP MAC-to-IP address resolution broadcast.

General Broadcast	255.255.255.255
Subnet Broadcast	10.2.255.255
Multicast	224.x.x.x – 239.x.x.x

An example of an announcement would be an OSPF advertisement multicast. These packets are unsolicited announcements about known link state routing entries.

Concern over broadcasts and multicasts taking up valuable bandwidth may be overemphasized on today's high capacity network links. The other concern has been processing power required by these packets in the forwarding or receiving devices. If a switch or router is overloaded and appears to be dropping packets or holding them in the queue for an extended amount of time, consider examining the broadcast/multicast rate on the network.

Sanitize Your IP Addresses in Trace Files

At times you may want to share a trace file with someone else—a vendor or other analysts who are helping you troubleshoot problems perhaps. You may want to sanitize the trace file if you don't want to expose internal company IP addresses.

You can sanitize trace files by using a hex editor and performing a search and replace function for all IP addresses in the trace file. This will not recalculate the header checksum so your trace will trigger Wireshark's Checksum Error coloring rule. Of course you can let the person opening your edited trace file know they should disable this coloring filter.

Another option is to use a tool to automatically change the IP addresses and calculate the new checksum values.[73] Bit-Twiste is one of these tools—learn more about Bit-Twiste at *bittwist.sourceforge.net* and download Bit-Twiste from *sourceforge.net/projects/bittwist*.

There are two tools included in the Bit-Twist project—Bit-Twist and Bit-Twiste (with an "e" at the end of the name). Bit-Twist is a packet generator. Bit-Twiste is the trace file editor—this is the one we are using in Figure 186. Bit-Twist is available for FreeBSD, OpenBSD, NetBSD, Linux and Windows platforms. Both *bittwist.exe* and *bittwiste.exe* are contained in the *\src* directory.

Let's say you want to change your internal host's IP address (67.161.19.78) in *ftp-ioupload-partial.pcap*, available at *www.wiresharkbook.com*.

The command used for this process is:

```
bittwiste -I ftp-ioupload-partial.pcap -O ftpmod.pcap
-T ip -s 67.161.19.78,10.10.19.78 -d 67.161.19.78,10.10.19.78
```

As shown in Figure 186, the IP address 67.161.19.78 has been changed to 10.10.19.78 in both the source and destination IP address fields.

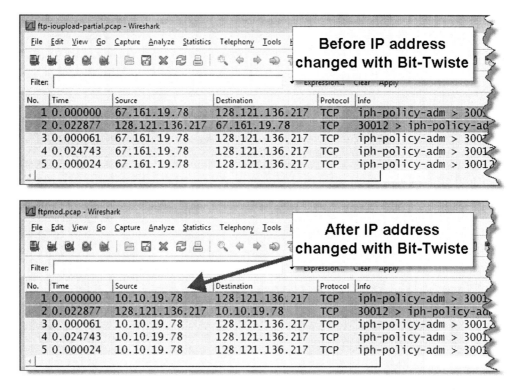

Figure 186. Bit-Twiste can easily alter IP addresses in a trace file and automatically recalculate checksums

---

[73] Not all automated tools can recalculate header checksums. Bit-Twiste, for example, can recalculate checksums for non-fragmented IP, ICMP, TCP, and UDP packets only.

Set Your IP Protocol Preferences

To quickly access the IP protocol preferences or enable/disable settings, right click on an IP field in the **Packet Bytes** pane. A few of the key settings that you'll want to understand are defined next.

Reassemble Fragmented IP Datagrams

Use this setting to have Wireshark reassemble sets of fragmented IP datagrams. When you enable this feature, the bottom of the IP header contains links to each fragment of the set. The last packet of the fragment set contains a tab under the Status Bar that enables you to view the reassembled fragment set in the Packet Bytes pane. Open *ip-fragments.pcap* and compare the view when this feature is enabled or disabled.

Enable GeoIP Lookups

When you enable this IP preferences setting and GeoIP is configured properly (see *Plot IP Addresses on a World Map* on page 140), Wireshark includes the source and destination GeoIP information at the end of the IP header in the Packet Details pane.

Interpret the Reserved Flag as a Security Flag (RFC 3514) ☺

In order to understand this amazing feature, you should read RFC 3514, A Security Flag in the IPv4 Header—we've included the introduction section below—and make sure you notice the date.[74]

> "Firewalls packet filters, intrusion detection systems, and the like often have difficulty distinguishing between packets that have malicious intent and those that are merely unusual. The problem is that making such determinations is hard. To solve this problem, we define a security flag, known as the "evil" bit, in the IPv4 [RFC791] header. Benign packets have this bit set to 0; those that are used for an attack will have the bit set to 1."

Troubleshoot Encrypted Communications

Troubleshooting can be very frustrating when you analyze traffic on a network that supports encrypted communications that you (a) do not have the encryption key for or (b) Wireshark cannot decrypt.

Figure 187 shows an IPsec communication between two peers. The security services of IPsec are provided by two security protocols—the Authentication Header (AH) and the Encapsulating Security Payload (ESP). The Protocol field in the IP header indicates that AH follows the IP header.

Together the two headers provide integrity, data origin authentication, anti-replay protection, and confidentiality. If you know the encryption keys, you can set them in the ESP preferences.

---

[74] Unfortunately, not enough malicious folks out there read and follow the recommendations of this April Fools' Day RFC. If they did, life would be so much easier—true?

If you are troubleshooting traffic that Wireshark cannot decrypt, however, the best process is bottom-up troubleshooting. Ensure everything is working properly based on what is visible. For example, in this communication, ensure there are no problems with the Ethernet communications or the IP header. Watch the packet sizes if the encrypted traffic is designed to support file transfers.

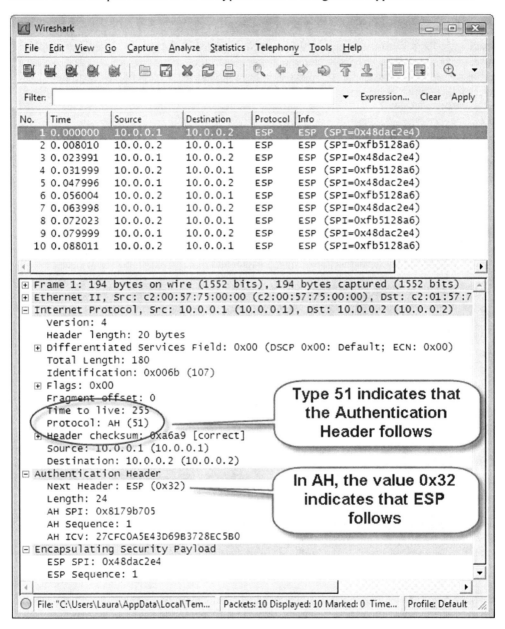

Figure 187. You can't troubleshoot an encrypted payload

For an example of decrypting traffic, read *Decrypt HTTPS Traffic* on page 466.

Filter on IPv4 Traffic

The capture filter syntax for IPv4 traffic is simply `ip`.

The display filter syntax is also simply `ip`. The following lists additional IP display filters.

Display Filter	Description
`ip.src == 192.168.1.1`	IP packets that contain 192.168.1.1 in the source IP address field
`ip.dst == 192.168.1.103`	IP packets that contain 192.168.1.103 in the destination IP address field
`ip.addr == 192.168.1.103`	IP packets that contain 192.168.1.103 in either the source or destination IP address fields
`!ip.addr == 192.168.1.103`	Packets that do not contain 192.168.1.103 in either the source or destination IP address fields
`ip.hdr_len > 20`	IP header with options (header length longer than 20 bytes)

`(ip.flags.mf == 1) ||`
`!(ip.frag_offset == 0) &&`
`ip`
	Fragmented packet—looks for "more fragments" bit and value in the IP fragment offset field. Added "`&& ip`" to deal with unusual results with ARP showing. Test on *ip-fragments.pcap*.

`ip.ttl < 10`	IP Time to Live values less than 10

Case Study: Everyone Blamed the Router

Submitted by: Russ F.

One day we received a report of a router problem. It would periodically not respond to pings.

A colleague suggested we start by replacing the router's Ethernet NIC. Before doing that, I suggested we connect Wireshark to the same VLAN and get a network trace using no mirroring—we expected to see a broadcast storm.

The trace showed an IP multicast storm occurring at the same time the router stopped responding. We could see the IP address of one of the servers in the multicast packets.

We located the server and disconnected it from the network, resolving the router issue. Further investigation revealed a misconfiguration on the server, which was easily corrected.

Without Wireshark, we would have caused a major network outage while we replaced the router NIC and then probably the router—neither of which would have resolved the problem.

Case Study:
It's Not the Network's Problem!

Submitted by: *Jennifer Keels*
                   Coastal Bend College

Our primary data information system was experiencing connection issues with external resources. The programming department spoke with their technical support, who pointed fingers at our DNS server.

I was still new to Wireshark but knew enough that I could perform some basic troubleshooting. I set a span on the switch port to the system (I didn't own a tap yet) and captured the packets.

I instantly saw the system was using an IP address from an old addressing scheme. For some reason, the system would periodically use that old IP address when sending packets.

I was able to inform technical support that they did not remove the old IP address configuration and that was why the system was having network related issues.

I really enjoyed the experience of being able to prove, once again, IT WAS NOT THE NETWORK!!

Summary

IPv4 offers connectionless routing services for packets traveling through an internetwork. In addition, IP offers the ability to fragment packets and include QoS information in the IP header's Differentiated Services Codepoint area. The Time to Live field in an IP header is decremented each time a router forwards a packet.

Each packet of a fragment set maintains the same IP ID field value. If non-fragmented packets contain the same IP ID value, the packets may be looping the network. When an IP packet does not permit fragmentation, but the packet is too large to be forwarded onto a link, the packet is dropped and an ICMP response should be returned to indicate the maximum MTU supported. This should trigger a new, smaller packet to be resent from the originating host. If the ICMP responses are blocked, however, the sending IP host cannot learn about the MTU limitation and will not be able to communicate with the target. This creates a "black hole"—this MTU detection process is referred to as "black hole detection."

The IP header's Protocol field indicates the next protocol included in the packet. The value 0x11 indicates that a UDP header follows the IP header while the value 0x06 indicates that a TCP header follows the IP header.

IPv4 multicast addresses begin with 224-239. Broadcasts are either "all nets" broadcasts (255.255.255.255) or subnet broadcasts (such as 10.2.255.255).

Practice What You've Learned

 Download the trace files available in the Download section of the book website, *www.wiresharkbook.com*. Examine the trace files listed below and answer the following questions.

ip-127guy.pcap	What is wrong with the IP addressing in this trace file?
	Can you look at the MAC header to identify the original sender of the packet?
ip-checksum-invalid.pcap	Wireshark's coloring rule indicates that there are checksum errors in this trace file.
	Which host's traffic has IP header checksum problems?
	Did the communication work properly regardless of the checksum problem?
	What could be causing these checksum errors? What can you do to make the trace file more readable?
ip-fragments.pcap	The client is sending fragment ICMP Echo packets to the target.
	What is the difference when you view this trace with and without IP fragment reassembly enabled? (**Edit | Preferences | Protocols | IP**)

Review Questions

Q17.1   **What is the purpose of IP?**

Q17.2   **Which three IP header fields are used with IP fragmentation?**

Q17.3   **What should a router do when a packet to be forwarded arrives with a TTL value of one?**

Q17.4   **What is the purpose of the Differentiated Services field?**

Q17.5   **What is the syntax for capture and display filters for IP traffic?**

Answers to Review Questions

Q17.1   **What is the purpose of IP?**

A17.4   IP provides the datagram delivery services for networked systems, fragmentation and reassembly for low MTU networks and quality of service designation to enable certain traffic to be prioritized over other traffic.

Q17.2   **Which three IP header fields are used with IP fragmentation?**

A17.4   The three fields are the Don't Fragment bit, the More Fragments bit and Fragment Offset field.

Q17.3   **What should a router do when a packet to be forwarded arrives with a TTL value of one?**

A17.3   The router should discard the packet. This process may occur silently or cause the router to generate an ICMP Type 11, Code 0 response to the sender (Time Exceeded, Time to Live Exceeded in Transit).

Q17.4   **What is the purpose of the Differentiated Services field?**

A17.4   The Differentiated Services field can be used to prioritize traffic along a path. This prioritization requires that routers along the path support Differentiated Services and recognize the prioritization value set.

Q17.5   **What is the syntax for capture and display filters for IP traffic?**

A17.5   Capture filter: `ip`
Display filter: `ip`

Chapter 18: Analyze Internet Control Message Protocol (ICMP) Traffic

Wireshark Certified Network Analyst Exam Objectives covered:

- The Purpose of ICMP
- Analyze Normal ICMP Traffic
- Analyze ICMP Problems
- Dissect the ICMP Packet Structure
- Filter on ICMP Traffic

  ❖ Case Study: The Dead-End Router
  ❖ Summary
  ❖ Practice What You've Learned
  ❖ Review Questions and Answers

The Purpose of ICMP

ICMP is used as a messaging system for errors, alerts, and general notifications on an IP network. There are many ICMP message types including the following:

- **Echo messages**: used by ping and traceroute to test end-to-end connectivity. Too many of these might signal a reconnaissance process or possibly a Denial of Service attack.

- **Redirect messages**: used by routers to let the source know there is a better path to a destination. If this packet is not sent by a router, it should be considered suspect.

- **Destination unreachable messages**: used to tell the source that their packet could not be delivered for some reason—the reason is stated in the Destination Unreachable message. A large number of these reply packets could indicate an unsuccessful UDP port scan is underway.

By examining the ICMP traffic on your network for a few hours or days, you can determine how efficiently the network is designed and spot numerous configuration errors, functional problems or security breaches. ICMP is defined in RFC 792.

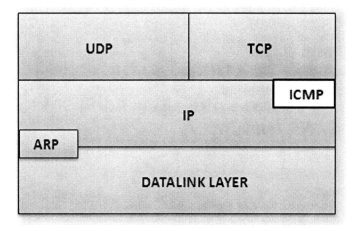

Figure 188. ICMP offers messaging services on IP networks

Analyze Normal ICMP Traffic

It is difficult to define "normal" ICMP traffic as this is subjective to each network. Some network IT staff use pings to perform connectivity tests while other companies restrict ICMP Echo Requests and Replies.

In this book, we define ICMP traffic from these ping tests and ICMP traffic from traceroute tests as "normal ICMP traffic." ICMP-based pings use ICMP Type 8 for Echo Requests and ICMP Type 0 as Echo Replies. Figure 189 shows a normal ICMP ping process.

Measure Round Trip Time Using an ICMP Filter

Setting the time column to Time Since Previous Displayed Packet and applying an ICMP filter provides you with round trip time values from the capture location when running echo tests. The Wireshark timing is typically more granular than the command line response time.

No.	Time	Source	Destination	Protocol	Info
1	0.000000	10.0.0.29	10.0.0.2	ICMP	Echo (ping) request
2	0.000161	10.0.0.2	10.0.0.29	ICMP	Echo (ping) reply
3	0.203309	10.0.0.29	10.0.0.2	ICMP	Echo (ping) request
4	0.000197	10.0.0.2	10.0.0.29	ICMP	Echo (ping) reply

⊞ Frame 1 (60 bytes on wire, 60 bytes captured)
⊞ Ethernet II, Src: Sony_15:4c:c0 (08:00:46:15:4c:c0), Dst: RPTInter_30:8
⊞ Internet Protocol, Src: 10.0.0.29 (10.0.0.29), Dst: 10.0.0.2 (10.0.0.2)
⊟ Internet Control Message Protocol
    Type: 8 (Echo (ping) request)
    Code: 0 ()
    Checksum: 0x014b [correct]
    Identifier: 0xac00
    Sequence number: 0 (0x0000)
  ⊟ Data (16 bytes)

Figure 189. A normal ICMP-based ping process

There are three variations of traceroute—ICMP-based, TCP-based and UDP-based. The ICMP-based traceroute uses ICMP Echo Requests and alters the Time to Live (TTL) value in the IP header. As packets arrive at routers along the path, the incoming TTL value is examined. If the incoming TTL value is 1, the router responds with an ICMP Time Exceeded/Time to Live Exceeded in Transit (Type 5, Code 0) (unless this response is disabled at the router). This allows you to discover that router's IP address.

Figure 190 shows the typical "striping" that Wireshark shows when colorization is enabled during a traceroute operation. Inside the ICMP Echo Request packet's IP header, the TTL value is set to 1 for the first packet.

Analyze ICMP Problems

One common ICMP problem is an echo test that does not receive a reply, implying there is no connectivity to a target. Identifying the point where the ICMP traffic is dropped requires moving the Wireshark system along the path until you reach the point where packet loss occurs.

ICMP itself, however, can help locate many other network problems and security issues. For example, if a DNS query elicits a Destination Unreachable/Port Unreachable (Type 3/Code 3)— either the client is sending DNS queries to the wrong target or the name service daemon is not running on the DNS server.

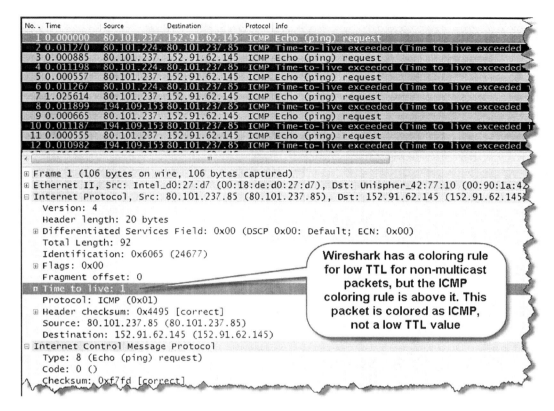

Figure 190. ICMP-based traceroute traffic

Another example would be excessive redirects. Figure 191 shows an ICMP Redirect packet pointing to another gateway at 10.2.99.98. This packet is sent when a receiving router identifies a better router for the sender. The receiving router generates an ICMP Redirect (Type 5/Code 1) packet with a recommended router to use. Upon receipt, a host should update its routing table. Redirects should only be sent by routers.

Some ICMP packets, such as ICMP Redirect packets, include a portion of the original packet that triggered the ICMP response. In Figure 191, the ICMP header is followed by the original IP header and the ICMP Echo packet contents that triggered the ICMP response. The packet that triggered this ICMP Redirect was sent from 10.2.10.2 to 10.3.71.7 (circled in Figure 191).

The next time 10.2.10.2 wants to reach 10.3.71.7, it should send it's packets through 10.2.the 10.2.99.98 router.

For more information on the interpretation of ICMP communications for network security, refer to *Chapter 31: Detect Scanning and Discovery Processes* and *Chapter 32: Analyze Suspect Traffic*.

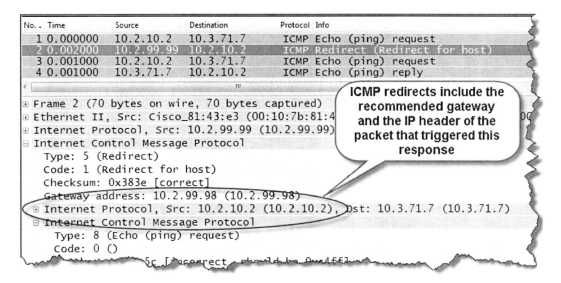

Figure 191. An ICMP Redirect packet

ICMP Destination Unreachable responses to TCP handshake connection requests are unusual as TCP connection requests should elicit either a TCP SYN/ACK or a TCP Reset. An ICMP response to these TCP handshake connection requests is a likely indication that a firewall is blocking a port—a verbose firewall. You may not want your firewall explicitly stating that a port is not accessible. For more information on ICMP responses to TCP packets, refer to *Chapter 31: Detect Scanning and Discovery Processes*.

Dissect the ICMP Packet Structure

ICMP packets do not contain a UDP or TCP header—port filtering settings cannot affect ICMP traffic. ICMP packets only contain three required fields after the IP header: type, code and checksum. Some ICMP packets contain additional fields to provide information or details on the message. For example, an ICMP redirect packet needs to include the address of the gateway that a host is being redirected to use. Upon receipt of this packet, a host should add a dynamic route entry to their routing tables and begin using the new routing information immediately.

Type

The following list defines the types of ICMP messages that can be sent on the network. This list is based on IANA documentation last update on July 17, 2009. To obtain the most current version of this list, visit *www.iana.org/assignments/icmp-parameters*.

Type	Name
0	Echo Reply [RFC 792]
1	Unassigned
2	Unassigned
3	Destination Unreachable [RFC 792]

Type	Name
4	Source Quench [RFC 792]
5	Redirect [RFC 792]
6	Alternate Host Address
7	Unassigned
8	Echo [RFC 792]
9	Router Advertisement [RFC 1256]
10	Router Solicitation [RFC 1256]
11	Time Exceeded [RFC 792]
12	Parameter Problem [RFC 792]
13	Timestamp [RFC 792]
14	Timestamp Reply [RFC 792]
15	Information Request [RFC 792]
16	Information Reply [RFC 792]
17	Address Mask Request [RFC 950]
18	Address Mask Reply [RFC 950]
19	Reserved (for Security)
20-29	Reserved (for Robustness Experiment)
30	Traceroute [RFC 1393]
31	Datagram Conversion Error [RFC 1475]
32	Mobile Host Redirect
33	IPv6 Where-Are-You
34	IPv6 I-Am-Here
35	Mobile Registration Request
36	Mobile Registration Reply
37	Domain Name Request
38	Domain Name Reply
39	SKIP
40	Photuris

You Should Know About Jon Postel

The initials of Jon B. Postel (JBP) are listed throughout many of the key protocols in the TCP/IP suite. Jon Postel was one of the founders of the Internet protocol suite. With a long beard and an intensely brilliant mind, he helped shape the communications system of the Internet and millions of private networks until his untimely and unexpected death in October 1998. You can learn more about this luminary at www.postel.org/postel.html.

Code

Many ICMP packet types have several possible "code" field values.

The following list provides the descriptions of the more common code fields.

Type Number and Code Descriptions

Type 3 Destination Unreachable Codes

0	Net Unreachable—the ICMP sender knows about network, but believes it is not "up" at this time—perhaps it is too far away or only available through an unknown route
1	Host Unreachable—the ICMP sender knows about the host, but doesn't get an ARP reply indicating the host is not "up" at this time
2	Protocol Unreachable—the protocol defined in the IP header cannot be processed for some reason—this response is seen in an IP scan as shown in *Chapter 31: Detect Scanning and Discovery Processes*
3	Port Unreachable—ICMP sender does not support the port number you are trying to reach—a large number of these packets indicates a configuration problem or possibly a UDP port scan; if these packets are sent in response to a TCP handshake attempt, they indicate the target port is likely firewalled
4	Fragmentation Needed and Don't Fragment was Set—a Router needed to fragment to forward the packet across a link that supports a smaller MTU size, but the application set the Don't Fragment bit
5	Source Route Failed—the ICMP sender cannot use the strict or loose source routing path specified in the original packet
6	Destination Network Unknown—the ICMP sender does not have a route entry for the destination network indicating it may never have been an available network
7	Destination Host Unknown—the ICMP sender does not have a host entry indicating it may never have been available on the connected network
8	Source Host Isolated—the ICMP sender (router) has been configured to not forward packets from source. Most routers will not generate this response code—they will generate a code 0 (network unreachable) and code 1 (host unreachable)—whichever one is appropriate
9	Communication with Destination Network is Administratively Prohibited—the ICMP sender (router) has been configured to block access to the desired destination network
10	Communication with Destination Host is Administratively Prohibited—the ICMP sender (router) has been configured to block access to the desired destination host
11	Destination Network Unreachable for Type of Service—the Type of Service (TOS) indication used by the original sender is not available through this router for that specific network—note that more current networks may not use TOS or Precedence—they may use DiffServ instead

Type Number and Code Descriptions	
12	Destination Host Unreachable for Type of Service—the TOS indication used by the original sender is not available through this router for that specific host—note that more current networks may not use TOS or Precedence—they may use DiffServ instead
13	Communication Administratively Prohibited—the ICMP sender is not available for communications at this time; this might be sent by a verbose firewall
14	Host Precedence Violation—the Precedence value defined in sender's original IP header is not allowed (for example, using Flash Override precedence)—note that more current networks may not use TOS or Precedence—they may use DiffServ instead
15	Precedence Cutoff in Effect—the Network administrator has imposed a minimum level of precedence to be serviced by a router, but a lower precedence packet was received

Type 5 Redirect Codes

0	Redirect Datagram for the Network (or subnet)—the ICMP sender (router) is not the best way to get to the desired network. Reply contains IP address of best router to destination. Dynamically adds a network entry in original sender's route tables
1	Redirect Datagram for the Host—the ICMP sender (router) is not the best way to get to the desired host. Reply contains IP address of best router to destination. Dynamically adds a host entry in original sender's route tables
2	Redirect Datagram for the Type of Service and Network—the ICMP sender (router) does not offer a path to the destination network using the TOS requested. Dynamically adds a network entry in original sender's route tables—note that more current networks may not use TOS or Precedence—they may use DiffServ instead
3	Redirect Datagram for the Type of Service and Host—the ICMP sender (router) does not offer a path to the destination host using the TOS requested. Dynamically adds a host entry in original sender's route tables—note that more current networks may not use TOS or Precedence—they may use DiffServ instead

Type 11 Time Exceeded Codes

0	Time to Live Exceeded in Transit—the ICMP sender (router) indicates that originator's packet came in with a TTL of 1. Routers cannot decrement the TTL value to 0 and forward a packet on
1	Fragment Reassembly Time Exceeded—the ICMP sender (destination host) did not receive all fragment parts before the expiration (in seconds of holding time) of the TTL value of the first fragment received

Type 12 Parameter Problem Codes

0	Pointer indicates the Error—this error is defined in greater detail within the ICMP packet.
1	Missing a Required Option—the ICMP sender expected some additional information in the Option field of the original packet.
2	Bad Length—the original packet structure had an invalid length.

Checksum

The checksum field covers the ICMP header only.

Filter on ICMP Traffic

The capture filter syntax for ICMP traffic is simply `icmp`.

The display filter syntax is simply `icmp`. The following lists additional ICMP display filters.

Display Filter	Description
`icmp.type == 8`	ICMP ping—echo request
`icmp.type == 8 || icmp.type == 0`	ICMP ping request or response
`(icmp.type == 8) && !(icmp.code == 0x00)`	Unusual ICMP ping packets (code field is not set at 0)
`icmp.type == 13 || icmp.type == 15 || icmp.type == 17`	ICMP Timestamp Request, Information Request or Address Mask Request (possible OS fingerprinting)—refer to *Chapter 31: Detect Scanning and Discovery Processes*
`tcp && icmp.type==3 && (icmp.code==1 || icmp.code==2 || icmp.code==3 || icmp.code==9 || icmp.code==10 || icmp.code==13)`	ICMP Destination Unreachable response to a TCP handshake (possible firewalled TCP target)—this is a unique filter as it looks for a TCP header embedded after the ICMP header
`icmp.type==11`	ICMP Time to Live Exceeded (traceroute underway?)
`icmp.type == 3 and icmp.code == 4`	Fragmentation Needed, but Don't Fragment Bit Set (path MTU discovery packet—don't block this packet!)

Case Study:
The Dead-End Router

My customer complained that some of their hosts could not reach the internet on certain days—they would reboot their workstations and everything would work fine.

The traffic showed the clients transmitting Router Solicitations because the default gateway provided by the DHCP server did not reside on the local network.

The accounting server, a Sun host, was configured to respond with Router Advertisements. That Sun host was not a router, however. If the Sun host's Router Advertisement arrived before the Cisco router's Router Advertisement arrived. The client used the Sun host's IP address in its routing tables as the default gateway. The figure below shows the situation that caused this problem.

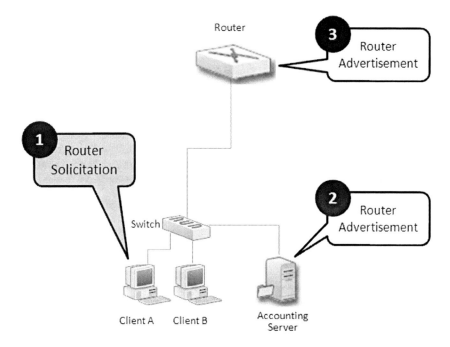

When the clients received the Router Advertisements from the accounting server, they would update their routing tables with the IP address of the accounting server as their default gateway. When the clients wanted to communicate with hosts that were on other networks, they would consult their routing tables and send the packets to the default gateway.

Packets sent to the Sun box for routing were discarded by that box because it didn't really offer routing services—this caused the isolated host problem.

It was easy to spot the problem in just a few minutes in this case.

Summary

ICMP offers a messaging service to indicate network configuration problems, unavailable services, hosts that are too far away from each other, fragmentation problems and more.

ICMP packets do not contain TCP or UDP headers—port filtering cannot block ICMP traffic.

Many ICMP packets contain the original header that triggered the ICMP packet.

ICMP Echo Requests are commonly used for standard ping tests and traceroute operations.

Practice What You've Learned

 Download the trace files available in the Download section of the book website, *www.wiresharkbook.com*. Analyze the trace files listed below and answer the questions to practice what you've learned in this chapter.

icmp-payload.pcap	What is in the payload of these ICMP packets?
	Why would this type of traffic be a security concern?
	Why can't you follow the stream to reassemble the communications?
icmp-ping-2signatures.pcap	What is in the payload of these ICMP packets?
icmp-dest-unreachable.pcap	What could be the reason why this ICMP ping is unsuccessful?
icmp-traceroute-normal.pcap	This is a classic ICMP-based traceroute operation shows the dependency on the ICMP Time to Live Exceeded/Time to Live Exceeded in Transit response that is used to locate routers along a path.
	Were all the routers along the path discovered?

Review Questions

Q18.1   **What is the purpose of ICMP?**

Q18.2   **What type of device might generate an ICMP Type 3, Code 13 (Destination Unreachable, Communication Administratively Prohibited) packet?**

Q18.3   **You have captured only ICMP packets on your network. How can you determine what triggered the ICMP Type 3 (Destination Unreachable) packets on your network?**

Q18.4   **Which ICMP packets are used for the standard ICMP-based ping process?**

Q18.5   **What should a host do when it receives an ICMP Type 5, Code 0 (Redirection, Redirect Datagram for the Network/Subnet) packet?**

Q18.6   **What is the syntax for capture and display filters for ICMP traffic?**

Answers to Review Questions

Q18.1   **What is the purpose of ICMP?**

A18.1   ICMP is used as a messaging system for errors, alerts, and general notifications on an IP network.

Q18.2   **What type of device might generate an ICMP Type 3, Code 13 (Destination Unreachable, Communication Administratively Prohibited) packet?**

A18.2   This packet might be generated by a verbose firewall. Many firewalls will silently discard blocked packets rather than send this packet.

Q18.3   **You have captured only ICMP packets on your network. How can you determine what triggered the ICMP Type 3 (Destination Unreachable) packets you see in your trace file?**

A18.3   ICMP Type 3 packets contain the IP header and at least the next 8 bytes of the packet that triggered this response. Examine the IP header and bytes that following ICMP portion to determine why this packet was sent. In the example shown below, this ICMP Type 3, Code 1 packet was triggered by an ICMP Echo Request from 10.4.88.88 to 10.2.10.2.

```
⊞ Frame 2: 74 bytes on wire (592 bits), 74 bytes captured (592 bits)
⊞ Ethernet II, Src: 00:10:7b:81:43:e3 (00:10:7b:81:43:e3), Dst: 00:20:78:e1:5a:80
⊞ Internet Protocol, Src: 10.2.99.99 (10.2.99.99), Dst: 10.2.10.2 (10.2.10.2)
⊟ Internet Control Message Protocol
     Type: 3 (Destination unreachable)
     Code: 1 (Host unreachable)
     Checksum: 0xa7a2 [correct]
   ⊞ Internet Protocol, Src: 10.2.10.2 (10.2.10.2), Dst: 10.4.88.88 (10.4.88.88)
   ⊟ Internet Control Message Protocol
        Type: 8 (Echo (ping) request)
        Code: 0
        Checksum: 0x265c [incorrect, should be 0xd0ff]
        Identifier: 0x0200
        Sequence number: 9472 (0x2500)
```

Q18.4   **Which ICMP packets are used for the standard ICMP-based traceroute process?**

A18.4   Standard ICMP-based traceroute processes use ICMP Type 8 (Echo Request) and ICMP Type 0 (Echo Reply) packets.

Q18.5   **What should a host do when it receives an ICMP Type 5, Code 0 (Redirection, Redirect Datagram for the Network/Subnet) packet?**

A18.5   When a host receives an ICMP Type 5, Code 0 (Redirection, Redirect Datagram for the Network/Subnet) packet, it should update its routing tables with the gateway address included in the ICMP packet. When it wants to communicate with that network again at a later time, it will use the new gateway entry in its routing tables.

Q18.6   What is the syntax for capture and display filters for IP traffic?

A18.6   Capture filter: `icmp`
          Display filter: `icmp`

Chapter 19:
Analyze User Datagram Protocol (UDP) Traffic

Wireshark Certified Network Analyst Exam Objectives covered:

- The Purpose of UDP
- Analyze Normal UDP Traffic
- Analyze UDP Problems
- Dissect the UDP Packet Structure
- Filter on UDP Traffic

  ❖ Case Study: Troubleshooting Time Synchronization
  ❖ Summary
  ❖ Practice What You've Learned
  ❖ Review Questions and Answers

The Purpose of UDP

If you capture a trace of broadcast/multicast traffic you already have a lot of UDP-based communications. UDP provides for connectionless transport services. Broadcast and multicast traffic flows over UDP.

The UDP header port fields identify the application using the transport. Because UDP uses a simple 8-byte header that consists of four fields, UDP itself rarely experiences much trouble. UDP is defined in RFC 768, User Datagram Protocol.

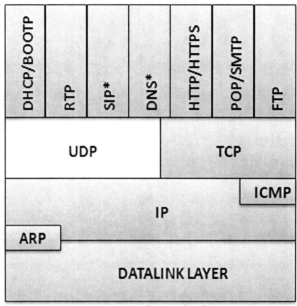

Figure 192. UDP offers connectionless transport service

Common applications that use UDP are DHCP/BOOTP, SIP, RTP, DNS, TFTP and various streaming video applications.

Analyze Normal UDP Traffic

Normal UDP communications, such as DHCP Discover packets, are sent with the destination port number of the desired service. Figure 193 shows a DHCP bootup sequence. DHCP uses UDP as transport and begins with a DHCP Discover packet addressed to the broadcast address. DHCP communications use port 68 for the client port number and port 67 as the server port number.

The majority of applications use an ephemeral or temporary port number for the client side of the communications. For example, a DNS query is sent to port 53. The source port is a temporary port number.

```
No. .  Time       Source     Destination      Protocol  Info
   1 0.000000   0.0.0.0    255.255.255.255  DHCP  DHCP Discover - Transaction ID 0xde03de03
   2 0.001512  10.0.0.1   10.0.99.2          DHCP  DHCP Offer    - Transaction ID 0xde03de03
   3 0.000790   0.0.0.0   255.255.255.255   DHCP  DHCP Request  - Transaction ID 0xde03de03
   4 0.007509  10.0.0.1   10.0.99.2          DHCP  DHCP ACK      - Transaction ID 0xde03de03
◄                                    III
⊞ Frame 1 (346 bytes on wire, 346 bytes captured)
⊞ Ethernet II, Src: Lite-OnC_30:c8:db (00:a0:cc:30:c8:db), Dst: Broadcast (ff:ff:ff:ff:ff:ff)
⊞ Internet Protocol, Src: 0.0.0.0 (0.0.0.0), Dst: 255.255.255.255 (255.255.255.255)
⊟ User Datagram Protocol, Src Port: bootpc (68), Dst Port: bootps (67)
     Source port: bootpc (68)
     Destination port: bootps (67)
     Length: 308
   ⊞ Checksum: 0xba92 [correct]
⊞ Bootstrap Protocol
```

Figure 193. A UDP-based DHCP startup sequence

For more information on DHCP communications, refer to *Chapter 22: Analyze Dynamic Host Configuration Protocol (DHCP) Traffic*.

Analyze UDP Problems

There are very few problems that occur directly with UDP. One potential problem is blocked traffic based on the UDP port number value. Figure 194 shows the results of capturing UDP traffic on a network that consists of a firewall configured to block traffic to certain port numbers. In this case, the firewall is blocking traffic to ports 161 (SNMP) and 5060 (SIP). Rather than responding with ICMP Destination Unreachable/Port Unreachable (Type 3/Code 3) packets, the firewall silently discards the packets. Your trace file only shows the UDP traffic—no responses are seen.

```
No. .  Time      Source         Destination     Protocol  Info
 575 0.007200  192.168.1.141  192.168.1.123   SNMP  get-next-request RFC1213-MIB::mib-2
 576 0.017056  192.168.1.141  192.168.1.123   SNMP  get-next-request RFC1213-MIB::mib-2
 579 0.016899  192.168.1.141  192.168.1.123   SNMP  get-next-request RFC1213-MIB::mib-2
 580 0.012030  192.168.1.141  192.168.1.123   SNMP  get-next-request RFC1213-MIB::mib-2
 581 0.002890  192.168.1.141  192.168.1.123   SIP   Request: OPTIONS sip:192.168.1.123
 582 0.009090  192.168.1.141  192.168.1.123   SNMP  get-next-request RFC1213-MIB::mib-2
 585 0.011976  192.168.1.141  192.168.1.123   SNMP  get-next-request RFC1213-MIB::mib-2
 586 0.012065  192.168.1.141  192.168.1.123   SNMP  get-next-request RFC1213-MIB::mib-2
 589 0.011995  192.168.1.141  192.168.1.123   SNMP  get-next-request RFC1213-MIB::mib-2
 590 0.011942  192.168.1.141  192.168.1.123   SNMP  get-next-request RFC1213-MIB::mib-2
 591 0.011984  192.168.1.141  192.168.1.123   SNMP  get-next-request RFC1213-MIB::mib-2
 592 0.012162  192.168.1.141  192.168.1.123   SNMP  get-next-request RFC1213-MIB::mib-2
 593 0.011853  192.168.1.141  192.168.1.123   SNMP  get-next-request RFC1213-MIB::mib-2
 594 0.012383  192.168.1.141  192.168.1.123   SNMP  get-next-request RFC1213-MIB::mib-2
 595 0.011612  192.168.1.141  192.168.1.123   SNMP  get-next-request RFC1213-MIB::mib-2
                                III
```

Figure 194. The lack of responses is caused by a port filtering firewall

UDP scans are evident when you see the "striping" of UDP packets and ICMP responses using Wireshark's default coloring rules. Again, if a port filtering firewall blocks the traffic you may not see the ICMP responses.

Figure 195 shows a UDP scan targeted at 192.168.1.123. The UDP scan has not located an open UDP port yet as each UDP packet has triggered an ICMP Destination Unreachable/Port Unreachable response. For more information on UDP scans, refer to *Chapter 31: Detect Scanning and Discovery Processes*.

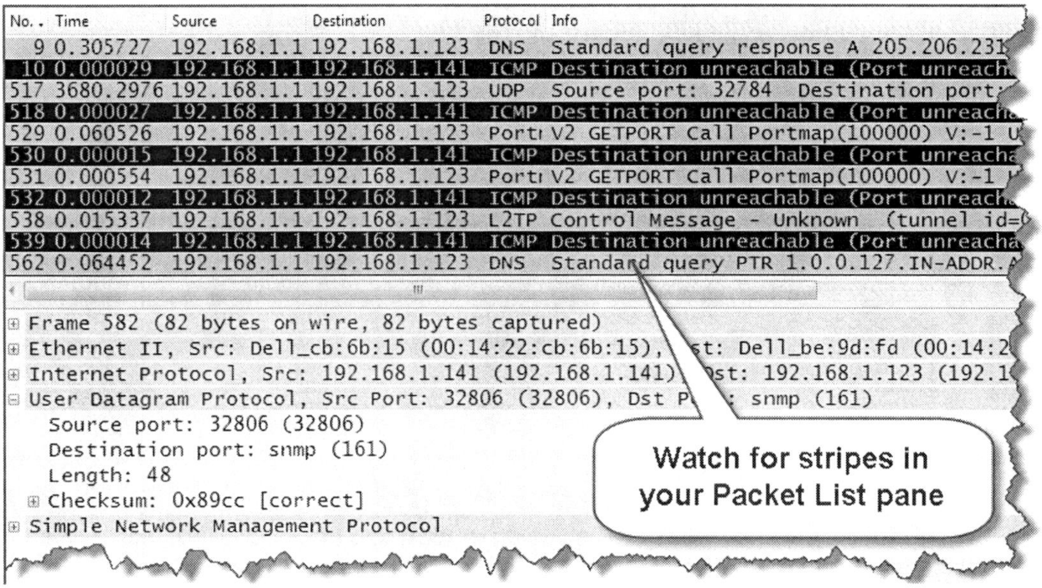

Figure 195. A UDP scan triggers a series of ICMP Destination Unreachable/Port Unreachable respones

Dissect the UDP Packet Structure

The UDP header is defined with the value 17 (0x11) in the IP header Protocol field. The UDP header only contains four fields and is always 8 bytes long, as shown in Figure 196.

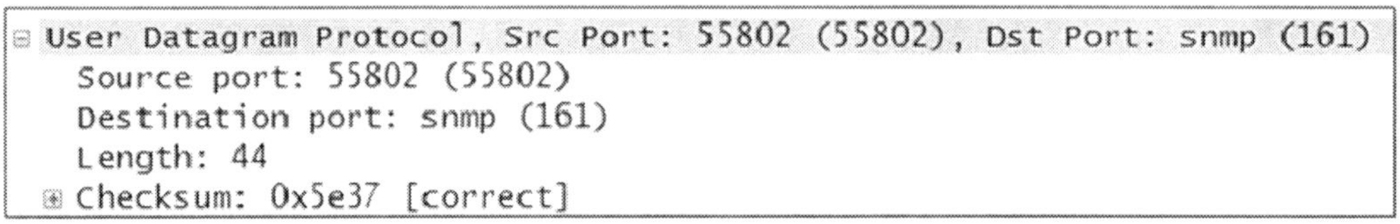

```
⊟ User Datagram Protocol, Src Port: 55802 (55802), Dst Port: snmp (161)
    Source port: 55802 (55802)
    Destination port: snmp (161)
    Length: 44
  ⊞ Checksum: 0x5e37 [correct]
```

Figure 196. The UDP header is only 8 bytes long

Source Port Field

The source port field has the same purpose in TCP and UDP—to open a listening port for response packets, and in some cases, define the application or protocol that is sending the packet.

Destination Port Field

This field value defines the destination application or process for the packet. In some instances the source and destination port numbers are the same for client and server processes. In other instances, you may find a separate and unique number for the client and server process (as in the case of DHCP). Still another variation is to allow the client to use temporary port numbers for their side of the communications and a well known port number for the server side of the communications.

Length Field

The length field defines the length of the packet from the UDP header to the end of valid data (not including any data link padding, if required). This is a redundant field and really quite unnecessary in the whole communication process. Consider the following three length fields and their interpretations:

IP Header Length = 5 (denoted in 4 byte increments)

- The IP header is 20 bytes long.
- IP Total Length Field = 329 bytes
- The data after the IP header is 309 bytes—remember that 20 bytes is the IP header.
- UDP Length Field = 309

The data after the IP header (including the UDP header) is 309 bytes. We figured this out from the Total Length Field in the IP header. Subtract the 8-byte UDP header and you know there are 301 bytes of data.

Checksum Field

The checksum is performed on the contents of the UDP header (except the checksum field itself), the data and a pseudo-header that is derived from the IP header. The pseudo-header is made up from the IP header source address field, destination address field, protocol field and UDP length field. UDP-based communications do not always require a checksum—sometimes you will see this field set to all zeros (0x0000).

Filter on UDP Traffic

The capture filter syntax for UDP traffic is simply udp.

The display filter syntax is simply udp. The following lists additional UDP display filters.

Display Filter	Description
udp.srcport == 161	SNMP response (based on port 161)
udp.dstport == 137	NetBIOS Name Service (based on port 137)
udp.length > 248	UDP packets containing more than 240 data bytes (8 bytes is reserved for the UDP header)

UDP is relatively boring compared to the exciting, complex world of TCP.

Case Study:
Troubleshooting Time Synchronization

Submitted by: Delfino L. Tiongco
ESU Seattle Networks Branch

I was asked to troubleshoot a switch that was not getting updates from our NTP (Network Time Protocol) server. Further investigation revealed that a few routers and switches were also not synchronizing with the NTP server.

I opened a Technical Assistance Center (TAC) case with Cisco and we went to troubleshoot the issue.

We found out that all NTP traffic (`udp.port==123`) was being forwarded by the router to the NTP server before the last switch. So it was *not* a Cisco routing issue.

I started using Wireshark to determine where the traffic from the NTP server was going.

To my surprise, the next hop for the Layer 2 traffic from the NTP server was going to the firewall instead of the nearest switch and router. The NTP server was not configured with our default gateway. Reconfiguring the NTP server fixed the problem.

So, again—Wireshark to the rescue!

Summary

UDP offers connectionless transport services. The UDP header itself is a simple 8-byte header primarily used to define the port number of the services supported. The checksum field in the UDP header may not even be used.

When a target does not support services on the desired port, the target responds with an ICMP Destination Unreachable/Port Unreachable response.

Practice What You've Learned

Download the trace files available in the Download section of the book website, *www.wiresharkbook.com*. Open the following trace files and answer the questions listed to practice what you've learned in this chapter.

udp-general.pcap   DHCP, DNS, NetBIOS Name Service and Microsoft Messenger make up the UDP-based communications in this trace.

How would you apply a display filter to see just the NetBIOS traffic on a network?

Did any of the communications trigger ICMP Destination Unreachable/Port Unreachable responses?

udp-echo.pcap   Although most people think of ICMP Echo Requests and ICMP Echo Replies when you mention the term "echo," there are also TCP and UDP echo communications. Anything sent to the TCP or UDP echo port must be echoed back.

What port numbers are used for this UDP communication?

What would happen if the source and destination port was set to the echo port?

Review Questions

Q19.1   **What is the purpose of UDP?**

Q19.2   **How does a UDP-based application recover from packet loss?**

Q19.3   **Why would a UDP packet contain a checksum value of 0x0000?**

Answers to Review Questions

Q19.1   **What is the purpose of UDP?**

A19.1   UDP provides for connectionless transport services. The UDP header identifies the application using the transport in the port fields.

Q19.2   **How does a UDP-based application recover from packet loss?**

A19.2   UDP itself is connectionless so it cannot help recover from packet loss. Applications must use their own retransmission process including timeout value and retry count value.

Q19.3   **Why would a UDP packet contain a checksum value of 0x0000?**

A19.3   Since the UDP checksum is optional; this field may contain 0x0000 when UDP checksums are not used.

Chapter 20: Analyze Transmission Control Protocol (TCP) Traffic

Wireshark Certified Network Analyst Exam Objectives covered:

- The Purpose of TCP
- Analyze Normal TCP Communications
- The Establishment of TCP Connections
- When TCP-based Services are Refused
- How TCP Tracks Packets Sequentially
- Understand TCP Flow Control
- How TCP Recovers from Packet Loss
- Improve Packet Loss Recovery with Selective Acknowledgments
- Analyze TCP Problems
- Dissect the TCP Packet Structure
- Filter on TCP Traffic
- Set TCP Protocol Preferences

  ❖ Case Study: Connections Require Four Attempts
  ❖ Summary
  ❖ Practice What You've Learned
  ❖ Review Questions and Answers

The Purpose of TCP

TCP offers a connection-oriented transport over a connection that begins with a handshake between two devices. Data is sequenced and acknowledged to ensure proper delivery and automatic recovery for lost packets. Where UDP may be considered similar to the standard mail delivery system for a letter or postcard, TCP would be likened to an express carrier who tracks the delivery of your letter or postcard and sends you notice of receipt.

TCP supports windowing—the process of sending numerous data packets in sequence without waiting for an intervening acknowledgment. The size of the window is based on the amount of traffic the network can handle (the network congestion rate) and the receiver's available buffer space. Most file transfer protocols use TCP to ensure data is delivered reliably. TCP is covered in RFC 793.

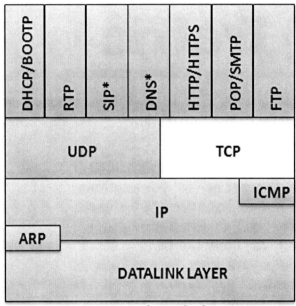

Figure 197. TCP offers transport for applications such as HTTP, HTTPS, email, FTP and more

Analyze Normal TCP Communications

Normal TCP communications includes connection establishment, sequence tracking, data loss recovery and connection teardown processes.

The Establishment of TCP Connections

TCP connections are established through a three-way handshake. The basic handshake process requires three packets—SYN, SYN/ACK and ACK.

The SYN packets synchronize the sequence numbers to ensure both sides know each other's starting sequence numbers. This is how they will keep track of the sequence of data exchanged between them.

In Figure 198, 192.168.0.105 establishes a TCP connection to 128.241.194.25. Packet 1 contains the designation [SYN] in the Info column, packet 2 lists [SYN, ACK] and packet 3 lists [ACK]. This recognizable pattern is the TCP three-way handshake used to establish a connection.

No.	Source	Destination	Protocol	Info
95	192.168.0.105	128.241.194.25	TCP	19377 > ftp [SYN] Seq=0 Win=8192 Len=0 MSS=14
96	128.241.194.25	192.168.0.105	TCP	ftp > 19377 [SYN, ACK] Seq=0 Ack=1 Win=16384
97	192.168.0.105	128.241...	TCP	19377 > ftp [ACK] Seq=1 Ack=1 Win=8192 Len=0
98			P	Response: 220 Microsoft FTP Service
9				19377 > ftp [ACK] Seq=1 Ack=28 Win=8165 Len=
10				Request: USER lchappell
10				Response: 331 Password required for lchappel
10				19377 > ftp [ACK] Seq=17 Ack=66 Win=8127 Len=
110			P	Request: PASS fakepwd
111	128.241.194.25	192.168.0.105	FTP	Response: 530 User lchappell cannot log in.
112	192.168.0.105	128.241.194.25	TCP	19377 > ftp [ACK] Seq=31 Ack=101 Win=8092 Len
113	192.168.0.105	128.241.194.25	FTP	Request: QUIT
114	128.241.194.25	192.168.0.105	FTP	Response: 221
115	128.241.194.25	192.168.0.105	TCP	ftp > 19377 [FIN, ACK] Seq=108 Ack=37 Win=65
116	192.168.0.105	128.241.194.25	TCP	19377 > ftp [ACK] Seq=37 Ack=109 Win=8085 Len
117	192.168.0.105	128.241.194.25	TCP	19377 > ftp [FIN, ACK] Seq=37 Ack=109 Win=808
118	128.241.194.25	192.168.0.105	TCP	ftp > 19377 [ACK] Seq=109 Ack=38 Win=65499 L

The TCP handshake process is SYN, SYN/ACK, ACK

Figure 198. The three-way TCP handshake establishes an FTP connection

When TCP-based Services are Refused

If the target server did not support FTP, it would respond to the SYN packet with a TCP Reset. If the target responds with ICMP Destination Unreachable packets, most likely the target port is firewalled either through firewall software on the target system or a firewall along the path. The ICMP Destination Unreachable response is being generated by the firewall.

In this case, the ICMP Destination Unreachable packet would be Type 3 and have one of the following codes:

Code	Definition
Code 1	Host Unreachable
Code 2	Protocol Unreachable
Code 3	Port Unreachable
Code 9	Communication with Network is Administratively Prohibited
Code 10	Communication with Host is Administratively Prohibited
Code 11	Destination Unreachable for Type of Service

If a TCP SYN does not receive any response, we must assume that (a) our SYN packet did not arrive at the target, or (b) the SYN/ACK did not make it back to our host for some reason, or (c) a firewall silently discarded the SYN packet. The TCP stack will automatically retransmit the SYN to attempt to establish the connection. TCP stacks vary in the number of times they reattempt a connection.

The Termination of TCP Connections

TCP connections can be terminated in several ways. In Figure 198 the client did not provide the correct password and the user closed the FTP window. The client FTP application sends the QUIT command to the server which triggers the server to respond with a FIN/ACK. The client replies with an ACK and then generates a FIN/ACK to the server. The server finished up the four-way process with an ACK. In this case, both peers are closing the connection simultaneously.

If the connection close process is started by one side of a connection (not a simultaneous connection close process), this process includes three packets—a FIN, FIN/ACK, ACK. For example, a client will send a FIN and enter a FIN-WAIT state until its FIN is acknowledged and the peer sends its own FIN back. You may also see a Reset used to terminate a TCP connection. Figure 199 shows an HTTP connection that is established by 192.168.1.215. The client generates a HEAD command and the server responds that authorization is required. The client acknowledges the response and sends a TCP Reset to terminate the connection. No FIN is required—the connection is terminated immediately when a reset (RST) is sent or received.

No.	Source	Destination	Protocol	Info
529	192.168.1.215	192.168.1.1	TCP	igi-lm > http [SYN] Seq=0 Win=64512 Len=0
530	192.168.1.1	192.168.1.215	TCP	http > igi-lm [SYN, ACK] Seq=0 Ack=1 Win=5
531	192.168.1.215	192.168.1.1	TCP	igi-lm > http [ACK] Seq=1 Ack=1 Win=64512 Le
532	192.168.1.215	192.168.1.1	HTTP	HEAD / HTTP/1.1
533	192.168.1.1	192.168.1.215	TCP	[TCP segment of a reassembled PDU]
534	192.168.1.1	192.168.1.215	HTTP	HTTP/1.1 401 Authorization Required (text
535	192.168.1.215	192.168.1.1	TCP	igi-lm > http [ACK] Seq=236 Ack=518 Win=63
541	192.168.1.215	192.168.1.1	TCP	igi-lm > http [RST] Seq=236 Win=0 Len=0

Figure 199. A TCP Reset is used to close a TCP connection

How TCP Tracks Packets Sequentially

The sequencing/acknowledgment process tracks the order of packets and detects and recovers from missing segments.

During the handshake process, each side of the connection selects its own starting sequence number (the Initial Sequence Number)[75]. Each side increments this sequence number by the amount of data included in each packet. When you analyze the sequencing/acknowledgment process, keep in mind this simple equation:

$$\begin{array}{r} \text{Sequence Number In} \\ +\ \underline{\text{Bytes of Data Received}} \\ =\ \text{Acknowledgment Number Out} \end{array}$$

---

[75] The Initial Sequence Number should be randomized to prevent Sequence Number Prediction Attacks as defined in RFC 1948, Defending against Sequence Number Attacks. As an example, Microsoft Server 2003 uses an RC4-based random number generator initialized with a 2048-bit random key upon system startup.

Here's a quick example of how a sequenced communication may occur in simple terms/numbers (remember, the acknowledgment number field contains the value of the next sequence number expected from the other side).

The Acknowledgment number field only increments when data is received. By default, Wireshark uses Relative Sequence Numbering—starting the sequence number values at 0 for easier readability. Instead of displaying a sequence number such as 4026919899[76], Wireshark begins with a sequence number of zero because it is easier to work with smaller numbers. If you want to see the actual sequence numbers, disable TCP Relative Sequence Numbers and Window Scaling in the TCP preferences.

The example shown in Figure 200 demonstrates the exception to the sequence numbering rule shown above. During the handshake and the teardown process, the sequence number increments by 1 even though a byte of data was not sent.

After the handshake is established, the sequence numbers only increment by the number of actual data bytes sent. In this example, the client is the first peer to send data (a request to get the main page on a web server).

---

[76] The Sequence Number field is a 4-byte field—without Relative Sequence Numbering enabled, the Sequence Number can be long and difficult to deal with.

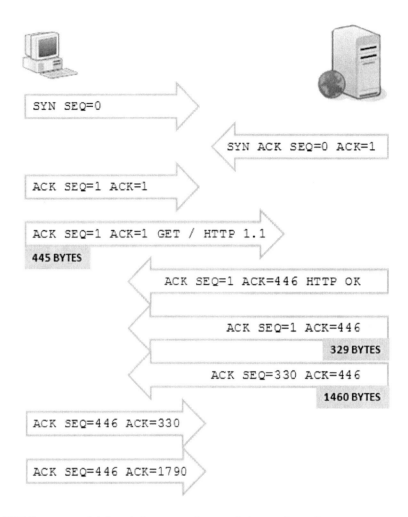

Figure 200. TCP Sequence and Acknowledgment numbers track data exchanged

Figure 200 shows how the Sequence and Acknowledgment Number field (ACK=) are incremented as data is exchanged. Note that not every data packet needs an explicit acknowledgment. As shown in Figure 201, multiple data packets can be acknowledged with a single ACK.

Source	Destination	Protocol	SEQ#	ACK#	Window size	Info
128.121.136.217	67.180.72.76	FTP-DATA	17085	1	33580	FTP Data: 1460 bytes
128.121.136.217	67.180.72.76	FTP-DATA	18545	1	33580	FTP Data: 1460 bytes
67.180.72.76	128.121.136.217	TCP	1	20005	17520	seraph > 30012 [ACK]
128.121.136.217	67.180.72.76	FTP-DATA	20005	1	33580	FTP Data: 1460 bytes
128.121.136.217	67.180.72.76	FTP-DATA	21465	1	33580	FTP Data: 1460 bytes
67.180.72.76	128.121.136.217	TCP	1	22925	17520	seraph > 30012 [ACK]
128.121.136.217	67.180.72.76	FTP-DATA	22925	1	33580	FTP Data: 1460 bytes
128.121.136.217	67.180.72.76	FTP-DATA	24385	1	33580	FTP Data: 1460 bytes
67.180.72.76	128.121.136.217	TCP	1	25845	17520	seraph > 30012 [ACK]

Figure 201. Not every TCP data segment needs a separate acknowlededgment

How TCP Recovers from Packet Loss

TCP has the capability to identify packet loss (based on missing sequence numbers) and recover by either requesting missing segments of data (the receiver side) or timing out and resending unacknowledged segments (the sender side).

Packet Loss Detected by the Receiver

When a receiver notes the expected sequence number is not in a packet, it assumes the packet has been lost. At this point, the receiver adjusts its Acknowledgment Number field to include the missing sequence number from the peer. It then sends ACK packets as an indication that a packet was lost. The receipt of three identical ACKs will trigger a retransmission.[77] For example, if sequence 275 is missing, the receiver sends three ACKs with 275 in the Acknowledgment Number field.

In the case of a high latency path, you may witness more than three identical ACKs in the trace file. For example, in Figure 202, the web browsing client sent 12 identical ACKs (the original ACK and 11 duplicate ACKs)—each ACK is requesting sequence 275 from the TCP peer.

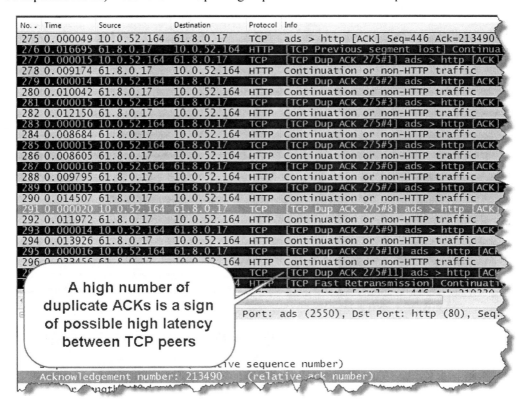

Figure 202. High latency paths may be the cause of more than three identical ACKs

---

[77] This included the original ACK and two duplicate ACKs (as noted by Wireshark's Expert system).

Packet Loss Detected by the Sender

TCP senders maintain a TCP Retransmission Timeout (RTO) value to determine when it should retransmit a packet that has not been acknowledged by a TCP peer.

If a data packet is sent and not acknowledged, a TCP sender can retransmit the packet using the sequence number of the original packet.

Figure 203 shows an HTTP client resending a GET request after waiting for an ACK for almost three seconds. Another retransmission is resent after approximately six seconds. TCP's backoff algorithm defines that the intervening time doubles for each retransmission attempt until the packet is acknowledged or the sending TCP host gives up.

```
No. . Time       Source         Destination      Protocol  Info
127  70.98928  172.17.8.66  161.58.73.17  TCP   wfremotertm > http [SYN] Seq=0 Win=645
134  0.775859  161.58.73.17 172.17.8.66   TCP   http > wfremotertm [SYN, ACK] Seq=0 Ack
135  0.000159  172.17.8.66  161.58.73.17  TCP   wfremotertm > http [ACK] Seq=1 Ack=1 Wi
140  0.000691  172.17.8.66  161.58.73.17  HTTP  GET /images/courses.qif HTTP/1.1
167  2.972601  172.17.8.66  161.58.73.17  HTTP  [TCP Retransmission] GET /images/course
222  6.019205  172.17.8.66  161.58.73.17  HTTP  [TCP Retransmission] GET /images/cours

⊞ Frame 140 (403 bytes on wire, 403 bytes captured)
⊞ Ethernet II, Src: AmbitMic_aa:af:80 (00:d0:59:aa:a    0), Dst: Intel_bc:c0:b9 (00:
⊞ Internet Protocol, Src: 172.17.8.66 (172.17                          61.58.73.
⊟ Transmission Control Protocol, Src Port: w         The sender retransmits    tp (80),
      Source port: wfremotertm (1046)               the segment when its
      Destination port: http (80)                   retransmission timeout
      [Stream index: 16]                                 (RTO) expires
      Sequence number: 1      (relative sequence
      [Next sequence number: 350     (relative se
      Acknowledgement number: 1    (relative ack number)
      Header length: 20 bytes
      Flags: 0x18 (PSH, ACK)
```

Figure 203. The HTTP server retransmits a packet when the retransmission timeout value is reached

Move Wireshark Around when Packet Loss is Identified

When taking a trace of the traffic close to the sender, you cannot be certain whether GET requests are not reaching the target or the ACKs are lost upon the return. Consider moving Wireshark further along the path to determine which case is true.

Improve Packet Loss Recovery with Selective Acknowledgments

Selective Acknowledgments (Selective ACKs) are defined in RFC 2018, TCP Selective Acknowledgment Options. TCP Selective Acknowledgment is used to acknowledge segments of TCP data that have arrived while still defining missing segments. Selective ACK capability must be set up during the TCP handshake process using the TCP options shown in Figure 204.

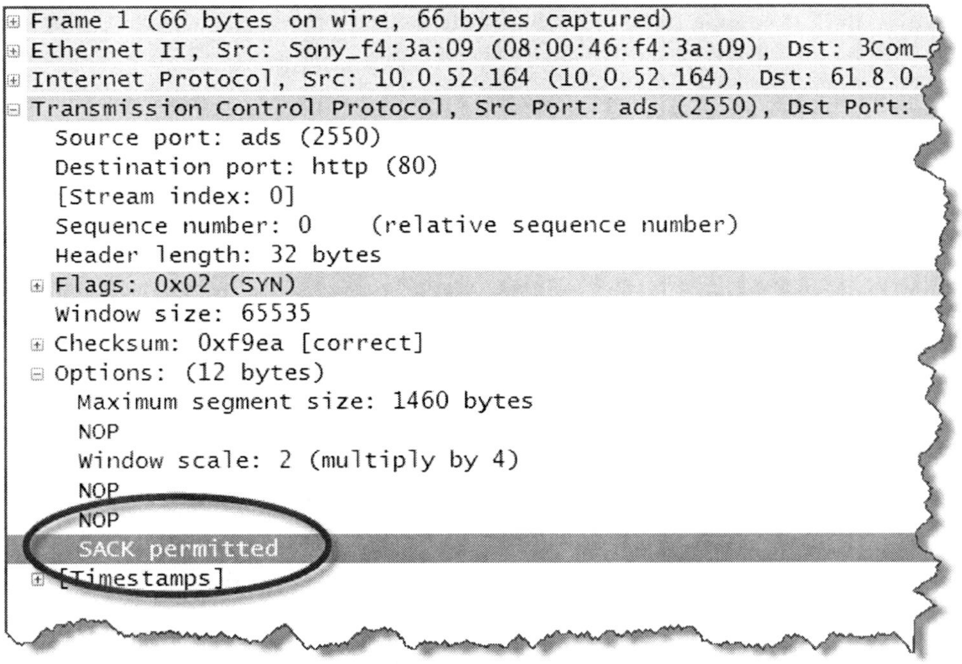

```
⊞ Frame 1 (66 bytes on wire, 66 bytes captured)
⊞ Ethernet II, Src: Sony_f4:3a:09 (08:00:46:f4:3a:09), Dst: 3Com_
⊞ Internet Protocol, Src: 10.0.52.164 (10.0.52.164), Dst: 61.8.0.
⊟ Transmission Control Protocol, Src Port: ads (2550), Dst Port:
    Source port: ads (2550)
    Destination port: http (80)
    [Stream index: 0]
    Sequence number: 0      (relative sequence number)
    Header length: 32 bytes
  ⊞ Flags: 0x02 (SYN)
    Window size: 65535
  ⊞ Checksum: 0xf9ea [correct]
  ⊟ Options: (12 bytes)
      Maximum segment size: 1460 bytes
      NOP
      Window scale: 2 (multiply by 4)
      NOP
      NOP
      SACK permitted
    ⊞ [Timestamps]
```

Figure 204. This TCP host supports Selective ACKs

In order to use Selective ACKs, both TCP hosts must indicate they support Selective ACKs in the TCP options area during the handshake process.

When packet loss occurs and Selective ACK is in use, duplicate ACKs indicate the missing segment in the Acknowledgment Number field and contain a left edge and right edge value in the TCP options area. These values acknowledge data that has been received since the lost packet. The sender does not need to resend any data other than the missing packet.

Understand TCP Flow Control

TCP offers a method of flow control to ensure that excessive traffic is not sent across a link that is known to be congested or to a host that is already overloaded.

The throughput rate of TCP communications is based on the congestion window. The congestion window defines the number of bytes that can be outstanding (unacknowledged) at a time. It is, in essence a flow control mechanism imposed by the sender. The congestion window is not a setting—it is dynamically determined based on two primary factors:

- The receiver's TCP buffer space advertised
- The amount of traffic allowed on the network (based on network congestion/packet loss)

The window will always be the lower of the two values. Network congestion is defined as a condition that causes packets to be lost in transmission because the network itself cannot support the data transfer rate. For example, on an Ethernet network suppose a receiver advertises a window of 65,535 bytes, but the connection experiences packet loss on a regular basis—before ever taking advantage of the 65,535 receive buffer of the peer.

The actual congestion window is not 65,535 bytes, but a lower value based on what the network will support. The process of determining the congestion window after packet loss is eloquently defined in RFC 2001: Slow Start, Congestion Avoidance and Fast Retransmit.

The congestion window is often referred to as *cwnd*. The receive window is often referred to as *rwin*.

The TCP sliding window offers a reliable data transfer method utilizing flow control. Figure 205 shows a set of eight TCP segments that are part of a data transfer. Segments A+B have already been sent and acknowledged. The current window has segments C+D+E and the sender is waiting for an acknowledgment. As acknowledgements arrive, the window slides to the left and expands to be larger.

The window will move to the left to send the next segments F+G+H. The window continues to slide to the left as acknowledgments are received.

Figure 205. TCP sliding windows

The TCP receive window is the TCP buffer space on the receiving end of a TCP connection. The maximum size of the receive buffer is dependent upon the settings and capabilities at the receiver. The current receive buffer size is based on the amount of available space to accept more data from a peer before handing the data up to an application.

Each side of a TCP connection maintains its own receive window size values and the values may be entirely different numbers. For example, a server may have 65,535 bytes available in its receive buffer while a client only has 14,600 bytes available.

If the receive window size drops down to zero, the window is "frozen" and the sender must stop transmitting data until the window opens again.

The TCP Window Size > Zero Can Still Stop Data Transfer

If the receiver advertizes a window smaller than one Maximum Segment Size (MSS), the sender may consider the window too small and wait for the window size to increase to the value of the MSS or one-half the size of the receive buffer, whichever is smaller. In effect, the data transfer stops—just as it does in the case of a Window Zero condition.

Understand Nagling and Delayed ACKs

The Nagle algorithm was defined to reduce the 'small packet problem' where a host sends a series of small TCP segments. For example, consider an application that sends 10 bytes of data at a time.

Using the Nagle algorithm, outgoing TCP data is buffered if there is a previous unacknowledged segment outstanding from that host. The Nagle algorithm is defined in RFC 896. The Nagle algorithm can slow down network communications for small data transfers and is disabled by many TCP implementations.

TCP's delayed ACK offers a method to reduce the number of packets in a TCP communication. Rather than sending a single ACK for every TCP segment received, TCP implementations using delayed ACKs won't send ACKs when either of the following conditions is met:

> (a)   no ACK was sent for the previous segment received or

> (b)   a segment is received, but no other segment arrived within 200 ms for that connection.

Typically you will see an acknowledgment sent for every other TCP segment that is received on a TCP connection. If the delayed ACK timer expires (200 ms), the ACK should be sent. TCP Delayed ACKs are covered in Section 4.2.3.2 of RFC 1122, Requirements for Internet Hosts - Communication Layer.

If you have problems with delayed ACKs, your TCP Time-Sequence graph will show the 200ms delays as shown in Figure 206. For more information on using Wireshark's TCP Time-Sequence graph, refer to *Chapter 21: Graph IO Rates and TCP Trends*.

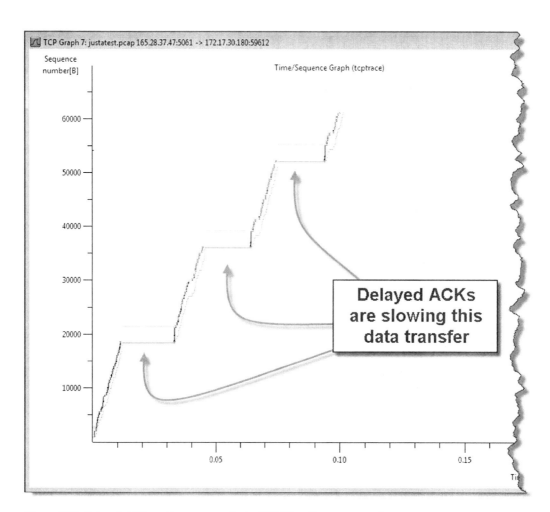

Figure 206. Delayed ACK problems appear in the TCP Time-Sequence graph

Analyze TCP Problems

There are numerous problems that can occur at the TCP layer, from problems with the handshake process, to packet loss, to TCP disconnects, to frozen windows. Refer to *Chapter 29: Find the Top Causes of Performance Problems* for more details on TCP-based communication problems.

We begin with TCP handshake problems. A TCP connection refusal is shown in Figure 207. In Figure 207, the initial packet of the handshake (SYN) receives a Reset (RST/ACK) response. The connection cannot be established. If the handshake process does not complete successfully, no data can be exchanged between the hosts.

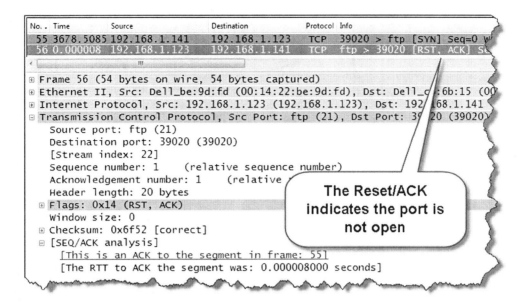

Figure 207. The TCP connection is refused with RST ACK

An excessive number of failed TCP connection attempts may indicate a TCP scan is underway. For more information on analyzing network scans, refer to *Chapter 31: Detect Scanning and Discovery Processes*.

Figure 208 shows another problem with the handshake process. The trace file was taken close to the client (67.171.32.69).

- The handshake appears normal—SYN, SYN/ACK, ACK in packets 3-5. Notice that in the first packet of the handshake (SYN) the sequence number of the client, 67.161.32.69, is shown as 0, a relative sequence number defined by Wireshark. The next packet sent from this client—packet number 5—indicates the client's sequence number is now 1 even though the client did not send any data in the SYN packet. The TCP specification (RFC 793, Transmission Control Protocol) defines that the first data packet after SYN packets must increment the Initial Sequence Number (ISN) by 1.[78]

- After the handshake process, the client sends a packet with 14 bytes of data to the server and sets the Push (PSH) and ACK bits on packet 6.

- Packet 7 is the first indication that something is wrong. The client's RTO value has expired waiting for an ACK to packet 6. Packet 7 is a retransmission of packet 6.

- Packet 8 is a retransmission as well. The server has resent the SYN/ACK packet from the TCP handshake. It appears the server has not received the third packet of the handshake process. The server sets the Acknowledgment Number field value to 1 to request the handshake ACK packet from the client.

---

[78] It is easy to think of this as the "phantom byte"—a byte that does not actually reside in a packet, but causes the sequence number value to increment by 1.

- The server continuously asks for the third packet of the handshake. The client, however, has sent two packets with Sequence Number 1. The client retransmits the first data packet instead of the final packet of the handshake.

- This problem cannot resolve itself. The server will not acknowledge the 14 bytes of data until it sees the handshake process resolve properly. The application that launched a TCP connection to the RWhois (Referral Whois) service on port 4321 must be restarted to create a new connection attempt.

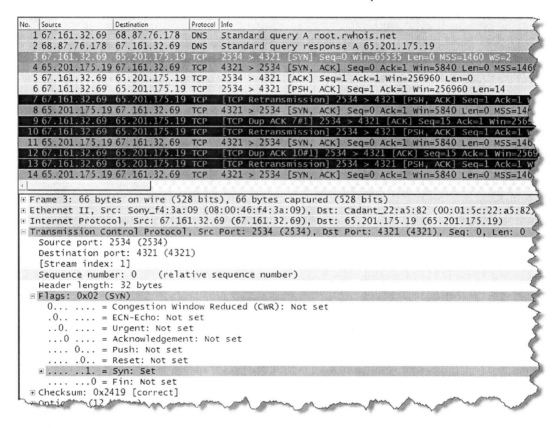

Figure 208. A failed TCP connection due to packet loss

Figure 209 depicts a problem with TCP data flow due to a Window Zero condition. In packet 364 the client advertises a window size of 0, effectively telling the peer that it can no longer accept data. This problem may be caused by an application that is not emptying the buffer in a timely manner or a host that is lacking processing power so applications cannot function efficiently.

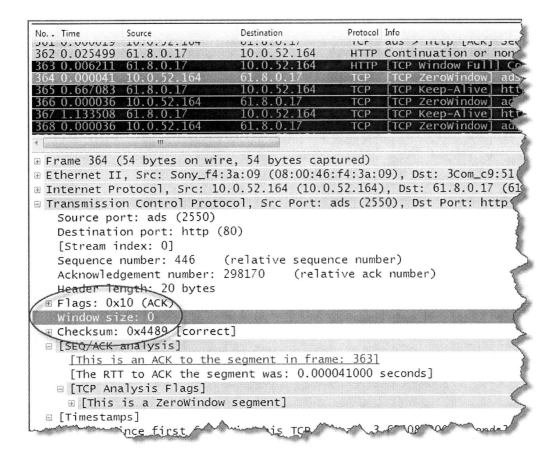

Figure 209. The TCP transfer is halted because the receiver's window is at zero

For more information on troubleshooting TCP communications, refer to *Chapter 29: Find the Top Causes of Performance Problems.*

Dissect the TCP Packet Structure

The TCP header is typically 20 bytes long, but the TCP header supports an Options field that can extend the header length.

Source Port Field

The TCP source port is the listening port open at the sender. The assigned port list is available online at *www.iana.org/assignments/port-numbers.*

Destination Port Field

The TCP destination port is the target port open at the receiver. The assigned port list is available online at *www.iana.org/assignments/port-numbers.*

Sequence Number Field

This field contains a number that uniquely identifies the TCP segment (the data that follows the TCP header is referred to as a TCP 'segment'). This sequence number provides an identifier for the TCP segment and enables receivers to determine when parts of a communication stream are missing. The sequence number increments by the number of data bytes contained in each packet.

Each TCP device assigns its own Initial Sequence Number (ISN). The process of incrementing this sequence number is was covered in *How TCP Tracks Packets Sequentially* on page 376.

Acknowledgment Number Field

The Acknowledgment Number field indicates the next expected sequence number from the other side of the communications. An Acknowledgment Number field that is never incremented by a host simply indicates that no data is being received by that host.

Data Offset Field

This defines the length of the TCP header. It is defined in 4 byte increments, so a value of 5 in this field indicates that the TCP header is 20 bytes long. We need this field because the TCP header length can vary depending on the TCP header options used. The TCP option field is often used during the TCP connection setup to establish the Maximum Segment Size (MSS).

Flags Field

The following list describes the flags used in the TCP header:

Flag Field Name	Description
URG (Urgent)	Indicates Urgent Pointer field should be examined; the Urgent Pointer field is only added to TCP header if this bit is set
ACK (Acknowledgment)	Acknowledgment packet
PSH (Push)	Bypass buffering and pass data directly onto the network—do not buffer incoming data—pass it directly to the application
RST (Reset)	Close the connection explicitly
SYN (Synchronize)	Synchronize sequence numbers—used in the handshake process
FIN (Finish)	Transaction finished, but don't close connection explicitly

The following list gives a brief interpretation of how you can use these field values in your analysis.

Urgent Bit (URG)

This bit setting is rarely seen and indicates that the sender wants the receiver to read the data in a packet beginning with a specific location as defined in the Urgent Pointer field that will be included in the packet if this bit is set to 1. The display filter for all packets using the URG bit is `tcp.flags.urg == 1`.

Acknowledgment Bit (ACK)

Setting this bit indicates that this is an acknowledgment packet. If this is missing from the process, then the data stream cannot continue to be sent. Back-to-back ACKs indicate a packet is missing from a set (see RFC 2001, TCP Slow Start, Congestion Avoidance, Slow Start). The display filter for all packets using the ACK bit is `tcp.flags.ack == 1`.

Push Bit (PSH)

The TCP buffer holds outgoing data to send a decent size packet rather than send individual bytes as they arrive in the buffer. This buffer also holds incoming data. The PSH flag indicates that a TCP segment should not be held in the buffer at the sending side or receiving side. An application that is very time sensitive and user driven (such as character-at-a-time telnet) may set the PSH flag on every packet making TCP act in a ping-pong (packet out, ACK in, packet out, ACK in, etc.) manner. The display filter for all packets using the PSH bit is `tcp.flags.push == 1`.

Reset Bit (RST)

A TCP packet with the RST bit set terminates a TCP connection. If an application does not send a RST when it is shut down, the connection is still open. The application may rely on a TCP connection timeout to shut down the connection. If an application encounters a fault, it may send a RST in the middle of the communication. The display filter for all packets using the RST bit is `tcp.flags.reset == 1`.

Synchronize Bit (SYN)

The SYN bit is set in first two packets of the TCP handshake process to provide the ISN to the TCP peer. One form of a Denial of Service attack floods a target with SYNs while incrementing the sequence number in each packet. The purpose of the attack may be to overload the connection table of the target. Firewalls can be configured to block SYN packets coming in from an untrusted source to stop connections from being established between hosts. The display filter for all packets using the SYN bit is `tcp.flags.syn == 1`.

Finish Bit (FIN)

This indicates that a process has completed and the data stream has been sent. This packet does not explicitly shut down the connection, however. Many times the PSH flag will be set with the FIN flag. The display filter for all packets using the FIN bit is `tcp.flags.fin == 1`.

Filter on the TCP Flags Summary Line

Rather than make a filter using individual bit settings such as `tcp.flags.urg == 0 &&` `tcp.flags.ack == 1 && tcp.flags.push == 0 && tcp.flags.reset == 0` `&& tcp.flags.syn == 1 && tcp.flags.fin == 0, consider creating a filter based on the TCP flags summary line. For example, the previous filter can be replaced with* `tcp.flags == 0x12`.

Window Field

This field indicates the size of the TCP receiver buffer in bytes. A window size of 0 indicates that the receiver has no buffer space available. The maximum value that can be denoted in this two-byte field is 65,535. Window scaling (established during the TCP handshake process) enables hosts to use larger window sizes. The display filter for all packets using a Window Size field value of less than 65,535 is `tcp.window_size < == 65535`.

Checksum Field

The TCP checksum is performed on the contents of the TCP header and data (not including data link padding) as well as a pseudo header derived from the IP header. Refer to RFC 793 for more information.

Urgent Pointer Field (optional)

This field is only relevant if the URG bit is set. If the URG bit is set, the receiver must examine this field to see where to look/read first in the packet. This is not a common function. The display filter for all packets that contain an Urgent Pointer field is `tcp.urgent_pointer`.

TCP Options Area (optional)

One option you will see often is Maximum Segment Size (MSS)—it is used in the first two packets of the three-way handshake process. The purpose of this option is to define what segment size the hosts support. The hosts will use the lowest common denominator between the two MSS values. The display filter for all packets that contain TCP options is `tcp.options`. The following table lists a few of the more commonly seen TCP options.

Other TCP options can be found at *www.iana.org/assignments/tcp-parameters*.

Option Number	Definition
0	End of Option List
1	No-Operation (padding to ensure header ends on 4-byte boundary)
2	Maximum Segment Size (defines the MSS value of each peer)
3	WSOPT - Window Scale (required on both sides to use)
4	SACK Permitted (required on both sides to use)
5	SACK (used to recover from packet loss)

Filter on TCP Traffic

The capture filter syntax for TCP traffic is simply `tcp`.

The display filter syntax is simply `tcp`. The following lists additional TCP display filters.

Display Filter	Description
`tcp.srcport == 21`	FTP response (assuming FTP is running on port 21)
`tcp.dstport == 80`	Traffic destined to port 80 (HTTP is most often running on port 80)
`tcp.hdr_len > 20`	TCP headers that contain one or more options.
`(tcp.window_size < 1460) && (tcp.flags.reset == 0)`	TCP window size smaller than one MSS on a packet that does not have the RST bit set—this would slow down the data transfer process; window updates are required to recover
`!(tcp.flags.cwr == 0) || !(tcp.flags.ecn == 0)`	Packets that have the Congestion Window Reduced flag or ECN-Echo flag set
`tcp.options.mss_val < 1460`	TCP MSS setting less than 1,460 bytes (this would be seen in the handshake process)
`tcp.options.wscale_val`	The TCP window scale option exists in the TCP header
`tcp.analysis.flags`	Packets have been flagged with TCP issues or notifications (will not work if Analyze TCP Sequence Numbers is disabled in the TCP preferences)
`tcp.analysis.lost_segment`	A lost segment was detected before this packet—one of many individual TCP analysis flags available. Use the auto-complete feature (`tcp.analysis.`)—include the period—or Expressions to view other TCP analysis flags

Set TCP Protocol Preferences

The TCP protocol settings offer numerous options that affect the reassembly, analysis and display of TCP-based traffic.

Validate the TCP Checksum if Possible

This feature examines the TCP header checksum. If you are capturing trace files on your own system and each TCP packet sent from your host indicates that the TCP checksum is invalid, your network interface card and driver may support checksum offloading. You may consider disabling the Checksum Errors colorization filter or disable specific checksum validation processes. Disabling the TCP checksum validation process will slightly increase Wireshark performance.

Allow Subdissector to Reassemble TCP Streams

When working with a TCP data stream, you can choose to have Wireshark reassemble the stream and provide links to each packet containing data from the stream. The setting also alters the display in the Packet List pane as shown in Figure 210.

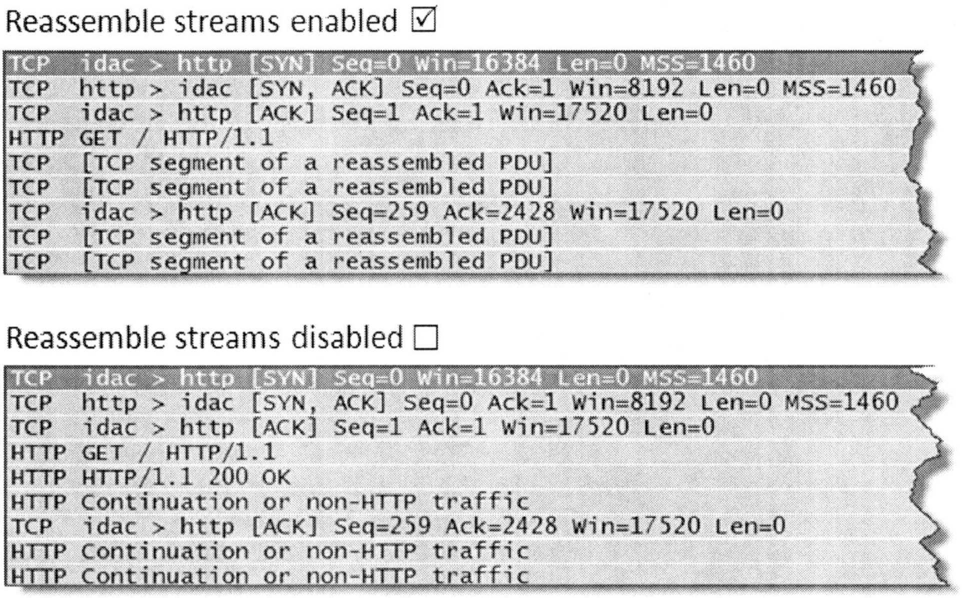

Reassemble streams enabled ☑

```
TCP   idac > http [SYN] Seq=0 Win=16384 Len=0 MSS=1460
TCP   http > idac [SYN, ACK] Seq=0 Ack=1 Win=8192 Len=0 MSS=1460
TCP   idac > http [ACK] Seq=1 Ack=1 Win=17520 Len=0
HTTP  GET / HTTP/1.1
TCP   [TCP segment of a reassembled PDU]
TCP   [TCP segment of a reassembled PDU]
TCP   idac > http [ACK] Seq=259 Ack=2428 Win=17520 Len=0
TCP   [TCP segment of a reassembled PDU]
TCP   [TCP segment of a reassembled PDU]
```

Reassemble streams disabled ☐

```
TCP   idac > http [SYN] Seq=0 Win=16384 Len=0 MSS=1460
TCP   http > idac [SYN, ACK] Seq=0 Ack=1 Win=8192 Len=0 MSS=1460
TCP   idac > http [ACK] Seq=1 Ack=1 Win=17520 Len=0
HTTP  GET / HTTP/1.1
HTTP  HTTP/1.1 200 OK
HTTP  Continuation or non-HTTP traffic
TCP   idac > http [ACK] Seq=259 Ack=2428 Win=17520 Len=0
HTTP  Continuation or non-HTTP traffic
HTTP  Continuation or non-HTTP traffic
```

Figure 210. Comparing TCP stream reassembly settings

Figure 211 shows the reassembled segment information inside a packet. Each frame line is linked to another packet in the stream. Using stream reassembly you can move quickly between packets involved in a data transfer.

```
  TCP segment data (293 bytes)
⊟ [Reassembled TCP Segments (30460 bytes): #20(967), #21
    [Frame: 20, payload: 0-966 (967 bytes)]
    [Frame: 21, payload: 967-2426 (1460 bytes)]
    [Frame: 23, payload: 2427-3886 (1460 bytes)]
    [Frame: 24, payload: 3887-5346 (1460 bytes)]
    [Frame: 26, payload: 5347-6806 (1460 bytes)]
    [Frame: 27, payload: 6807-8266 (1460 bytes)]
    [Frame: 29, payload: 8267-9726 (1460 bytes)]
    [Frame: 30, payload: 9727-11186 (1460 bytes)]
    [Frame: 32, payload: 11187-12646 (1460 bytes)]
    [Frame: 33, payload: 12647-14106 (1460 bytes)]
    [Frame: 35, payload: 14107-15566 (1460 bytes)]
    [Frame: 36, payload: 15567-17026 (1460 bytes)]
    [Frame: 38, payload: 17027-18486 (1460 bytes)]
    [Frame: 39, payload: 18487-19946 (1460 bytes)]
    [Frame: 41, payload: 19947-21406 (1460 bytes)]
    [Frame: 42, payload: 21407-22866 (1460 bytes)]
    [Frame: 44, payload: 22867-24326 (1460 bytes)]
    [Frame: 45, payload: 24327-25786 (1460 bytes)]
    [Frame: 47, payload: 25787-27246 (1460 bytes)]
    [Frame: 48, payload: 27247-28706 (1460 bytes)]
    [Frame: 50, payload: 28707-30166 (1460 bytes)]
    [Frame: 51, payload: 30167-30459 (293 bytes)]
```

Figure 211. Reassembled TCP data streams include a linked packets list

If you are interested in reassembled TCP traffic, consider creating a custom column for
`tcp.reassembled_length`. In Figure 212 we have enabled TCP preferences for "Allow
subdissector to reassemble TCP streams" and added a column to show us how much data is in the
reassembled packets. Sorting this column lists the size of the files downloaded during an HTTP
browsing session.

No.	Time	Source	Destination	ReLen ▼	Protocol	Info
1441	7.296080	67.131.237.17	24.6.150.44	87930	HTTP	HTTP/1.1 200 OK (JPEG JFI
253	1.266525	67.131.237.17	24.6.150.44	56019	HTTP	HTTP/1.1 200 OK (applicat
1870	8.665833	67.131.237.17	24.6.150.44	52619	HTTP	HTTP/1.1 200 OK (JPEG JFI
616	2.662568	67.131.237.17	24.6.150.44	51166	HTTP	[TCP Out-Of-Order] HTTP/1.
149	0.837842	67.131.237.17	24.6.150.44	49890	HTTP	HTTP/1.1 200 OK (applicat
1540	7.527406	67.131.237.17	24.6.150.44	45089	HTTP	[TCP Out-Of-Order] HTTP/1.
1080	4.080921	199.181.132.244	24.6.150.44	43946	HTTP	HTTP/1.1 200 OK (applicat
1642	7.784193	67.131.237.17	24.6.150.44	32948	HTTP	HTTP/1.1 200 OK (JPEG JFI
141	0.810801	67.131.237.17	24.6.150.44	31032	HTTP	[TCP Out-Of-Order] HTTP/1.
51	0.347522	199.181.132.244	24.6.150.44	30460	HTTP	HTTP/1.1 200 OK (text/htm
1097	4.116791	12.120.1.155	24.6.150.44	30346	HTTP	HTTP/1.1 200 OK (JPEG JFI
1151	4.385897	12.120.69.15	24.6.150.44	29349	HTTP	HTTP/1.1 200 OK (applicat
858	3.522698	199.181.132.244	24.6.150.44	27830	HTTP	HTTP/1.1 200 OK (applicat
708	3.103371	12.120.1.155	24.6.150.44	26967	HTTP	HTTP/1.1 200 OK (JPEG JFI

Figure 212. Create a column to display the reassembled length of linked packets

Analyze TCP Sequence Numbers

This setting is enabled by default and provides more efficient analysis by tracking the sequence number and acknowledgement number values. This feature is used by Wireshark to identify TCP conditions such as:

- Lost segments
- Out-of-order segments
- Duplicate ACKs
- Retransmissions and Fast Retransmissions
- Window is Full
- Frozen Window
- Window Updates

Disabling this feature also disables the Expert Info Composite information related to these TCP conditions.

Relative Sequence Numbers and Window Scaling

This setting is enabled by default and provides more efficient analysis by setting the starting TCP sequence number value to 0 for both sides of a TCP connection. In addition, this setting evaluates the TCP window scale option value and performs the calculation to display the actual window size being advertised.

In Figure 213 the Window Size field value is actually 64,240. During the TCP handshake, however, this sender defines that its window size should be multiplied by 4. With this setting enabled, Wireshark shows the scaled value and indicates that the field value has been scaled.

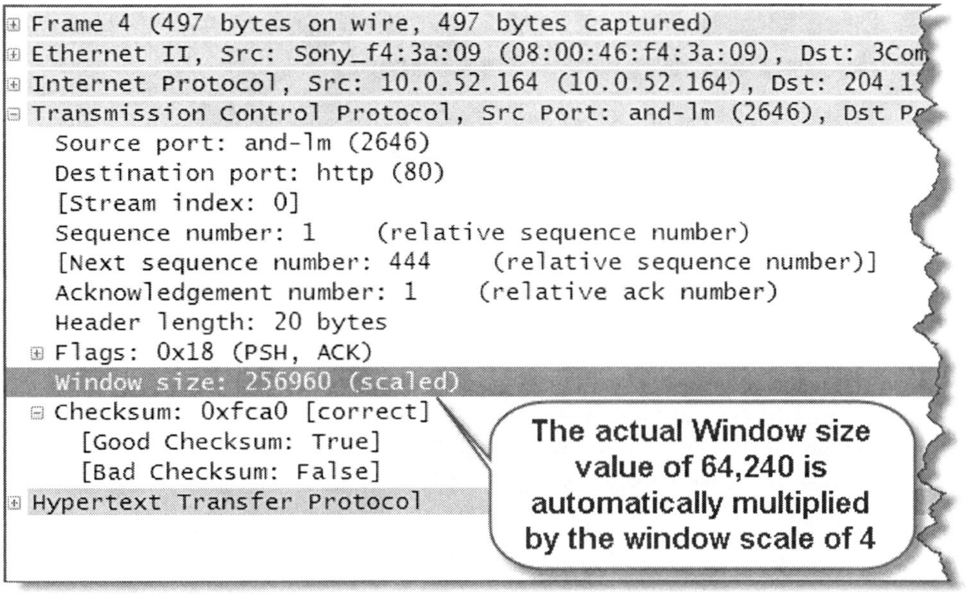

```
⊞ Frame 4 (497 bytes on wire, 497 bytes captured)
⊞ Ethernet II, Src: Sony_f4:3a:09 (08:00:46:f4:3a:09), Dst: 3Com
⊞ Internet Protocol, Src: 10.0.52.164 (10.0.52.164), Dst: 204.1
⊟ Transmission Control Protocol, Src Port: and-lm (2646), Dst Po
     Source port: and-lm (2646)
     Destination port: http (80)
     [Stream index: 0]
     Sequence number: 1      (relative sequence number)
     [Next sequence number: 444     (relative sequence number)]
     Acknowledgement number: 1     (relative ack number)
     Header length: 20 bytes
  ⊞ Flags: 0x18 (PSH, ACK)
     Window size: 256960 (scaled)
  ⊟ Checksum: 0xfca0 [correct]
        [Good Checksum: True]
        [Bad Checksum: False]
⊞ Hypertext Transfer Protocol
```

The actual Window size value of 64,240 is automatically multiplied by the window scale of 4

Figure 213. Wireshark can calculate the true window value based on the scale factor established in the TCP handshake

Track Number of Bytes in Flight

This setting enables Wireshark to track the number of unacknowledged bytes flowing on the network as shown in Figure 214. When this setting is enabled, you can create an IO Graph depicting the total number of bytes in the trace file and the number of bytes in flight using the display filter value `tcp.analysis.bytes_in_flight`. Graph this feature if you suspect congestion window issues are slowing file transfer processes. For more information on graphing TCP communications, refer to *Chapter 21: Graph IO Rates and TCP Trends*. The Analyze TCP Sequence Numbers setting must be enabled to use this setting.

Calculate Conversation Timestamps

This setting tracks the time values for a conversation, including the time since the first packet in the conversation and the time since the previous packet in conversation as shown in Figure 214. This setting is disabled by default.

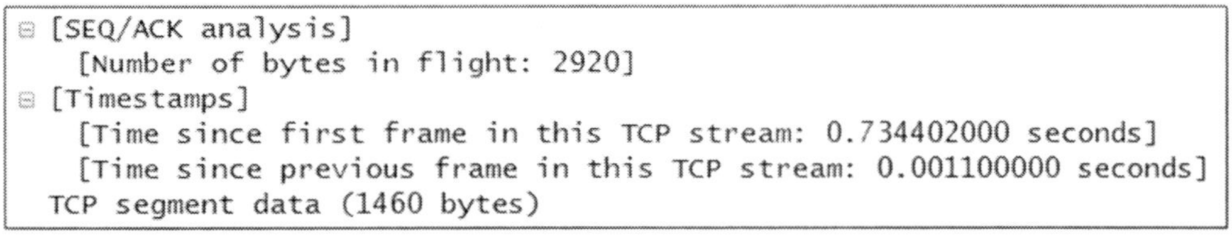

```
⊟ [SEQ/ACK analysis]
     [Number of bytes in flight: 2920]
⊟ [Timestamps]
     [Time since first frame in this TCP stream: 0.734402000 seconds]
     [Time since previous frame in this TCP stream: 0.001100000 seconds]
  TCP segment data (1460 bytes)
```

Figure 214. Calculate Conversation Timestamps are based on the stream timestamps

Case Study:
Connections Require Four Attempts

Submitted by: Todd DeBoard and Team
Tyco Electronics Corporation

We had a chronic trouble report from one of our remote users who reported that he would have to make four connection attempts with our remote access client before he was able to make a successful connection. The remote access client would then work every additional time he connected with it until his system was power cycled, at which time it failed again during the initial attempts.

This behavior presented itself at home, at the local library, and at the local coffee shop, but not when he was traveling on the road away from his home town. Our technical support team informed him that it sounded like a problem with his local Internet Service Provider (ISP), but when he contacted them they assured him that they were not blocking any traffic from their customers.

After a couple of months of repeated calls, we decided that it merited some focused attention. We installed Wireshark and some remote access software on his home PC and ran some targeted tests.

Wireshark showed us plain as day that when the client was first run after the computer was power cycled, it would always try initiating the first connection to our corporate network using the same TCP port and would increment it by one for subsequent attempts.

No response was received for the first three connection attempts, but responses were received for the fourth. Armed with the Wireshark packet capture, we had the user contact his ISP again.

This time, with the Wireshark evidence in hand, they confirmed that they were in fact blocking the ports in question and that they would open them, but only for the list of IP addresses of our remote access gateways.

We now have a happy user, but I can't help but wonder how many other customers of this ISP are encountering similar issues and wondering why it takes them so many attempts to get connected to their corporate network.

Summary

TCP offers connection-oriented transport services. TCP data is sequenced and acknowledged to ensure data arrives at the destination. TCP offers automatic retransmission for lost segments and flow control mechanisms to avoid saturating a network or TCP host.

TCP communications begin with a three-way handshake process (SYN, SYN/ACK and ACK). During data transfer, the Sequence Number field counts up by the number of data bytes contained in each packet. Each side of a TCP connection tracks their own sequence number as well as their peer's sequence number.

If a packet is lost, retransmissions are either triggered by duplicate ACKs or a retransmit timeout (RTO) condition. Three identical ACKs trigger a retransmission.

Selective Acknowledgments are used to reduce the number of TCP packets on the network in case of packet lost. Window scaling is used to increase the advertised receive buffer space above the 65,535 byte limit. When a host advertises a window size of zero, it cannot receive more data from the sending TCP host—the data transfer is stopped.

Wireshark contains many TCP Expert notifications to detect packet loss, window zero conditions, retransmissions and out-of-order packets.

Practice What You've Learned

Download the trace files available in the Download section of the book website, *www.wiresharkbook.com*. Analyze the trace files listed below and answer the questions to practice what you've learned in this chapter.

tcp-con-up.pcap	This is a simple TCP handshake process. What is the actual TCP starting sequence number used by the client that requests the TCP connection? Why did the TCP sequence number increment between packets 1 and 3?
	Does this connection support SACK? Does this connection support window scaling?
tcp-fin-3way.pcap	This trace shows the 3-way TCP FIN process. Do you see a "phantom byte" in this process?
http-download-bad.pcap	Does this connection support SACK? Does this connection support window scaling?
	The TCP Selective ACK option is used in packet 136. What do the left and right edge values indicate?
	In packet 679, what sequence number is 10.0.52.164 waiting for from 61.8.0.17? Is Wireshark downstream (closer to the client receiving the data) or upstream (closer to the TCP host that is sending data) from packet loss?

tcp-137port.pcap   It looks like NetBIOS... It feels like NetBIOS... but it doesn't smell like NetBIOS. Something just feels wrong. Follow the TCP stream.

What service is running over this port? How can you configure Wireshark to dissect this traffic properly?

Review Questions

Q20.1   **What is the purpose of TCP?**

Q20.2   **What three packets establish a TCP connection?**

Q20.3   **What is the purpose of the Sequence Number field? What is the purpose of the Acknowledgment Number field?**

Q20.4   **How does a TCP host refuse a connection request?**

Q20.5   **How does a TCP-based application recover from packet loss?**

Q20.6   **What is the maximum value that can be used in the TCP Window field?**

Answers to Review Questions

Q20.1   **What is the purpose of TCP?**

A20.1   TCP offers connection-oriented transport, data sequencing and acknowledgment, automatic recovery for lost packets.

Q20.2   **What three packets establish a TCP connection?**

A20.2   The three packets of the TCP handshake are SYN, SYN/ACK and ACK.

Q20.3   **What is the purpose of the Sequence Number field? What is the purpose of the Acknowledgment Number field?**

A20.3   The Sequence Number field is used to uniquely track each TCP segment. The Sequence Number field value increments based on the number of data bytes sent. The Acknowledgment Number field indicates the next expected sequence number from the other TCP host on the connection.

Q20.4   **How does a TCP host refuse a connection request?**

A20.4   TCP hosts set the Reset (RST) bit in a response to a TCP SYN packet to refuse a TCP connection.

Q20.5   **How does a TCP-based application recover from packet loss?**

A20.5   If the sender times out waiting for an acknowledgment, it generates a retransmission. If a receiver notices a missing segment, it sends duplicate acknowledgments to the TCP host it is connected to. Upon receipt of three identical acknowledgments the TCP sender generates a retransmission.

Q20.6   **What is the maximum value that can be used in the TCP Window field?**

A20.6   The TCP Window field is a two-byte field. The maximum value is 0xFFFF or 65,535. To use larger window size values, TCP peers must support window scaling.

Chapter 21: Graph IO Rates and TCP Trends

Wireshark Certified Network Analyst Exam Objectives covered:

- Use Graphs to View Trends
- Generate Basic IO Graphs
- Filter IO Graphs
- Generate Advanced IO Graphs
- Compare Traffic Trends in IO Graphs
- Graph Round Trip Time
- Graph Throughput Rates
- Graph TCP Sequence Numbers over Time
- Interpret TCP Window Size Issues
- Interpret Packet Loss, Duplicate ACKs and Retransmissions

- ❖ Case Study: Watching Performance Levels "Drop"
- ❖ Case Study: Graphing RTT to the Corporate Office
- ❖ Case Study: Testing QoS Policies
- ❖ Summary
- ❖ Practice What You've Learned
- ❖ Review Questions and Answers

Use Graphs to View Trends

Wireshark offers numerous graphs to depict traffic flow trends. Some graphs are directional, focusing on traffic flowing in a specific direction. Other graphs, such as the Input/Output (IO) graph, depict traffic flowing in both directions.

In the case of IO Graphs, you can manipulate the X and Y axis values—most other graphs automatically define the X and Y axis values based on the traffic being graphed.

IO Graphs support display filters and expressions and in the case of Advanced IO Graphs, they also support calculations. Some graphs can be exported and saved.

In this chapter, we examine the following graphs:

- Basic IO Graphs
- Advanced IO Graphs
- TCP round trip time graphs
- TCP throughput graphs
- TCP time-sequence graphs

Empty Graphs May Indicate You Selected the Wrong Packet

If your graph appears empty or shows too few plot points, it might be a unidirectional graph. Examine the title bar to see what traffic is being graphed. If it is a unidirectional graph and you have selected a packet flowing in the wrong direction, close the graph and select a packet flowing in the opposite direction before rebuilding the graph.

Generate Basic IO Graphs

IO Graphs are very useful in showing the overall traffic seen in unsaved or saved trace files. IO Graphs depict the total amount of bytes seen including data and headers.

Select **Statistics | IO Graphs** to plot the packets per second rate of all the traffic in the trace file.[79] By default the X axis is set to a tick interval of one second and the Y axis is set to packets/tick.

You can graph five traffic channels in standard and advanced IO Graph modes. You can alter the X axis to change the tick interval and the pixels per tick. You can adjust the Y axis to adjust the units and scale. Figure 215 shows a standard IO Graph. No display filters have been applied so all traffic seen in the trace file has been graphed.

Click on a point in the IO graph to jump to the first packet used in the range to calculate that graph point.

---

[79] IO graphs look at all the traffic in the trace file regardless of direction whereas some other graphs (such as Round Trip Time graphs and Throughput graphs look at traffic flowing in one way only.

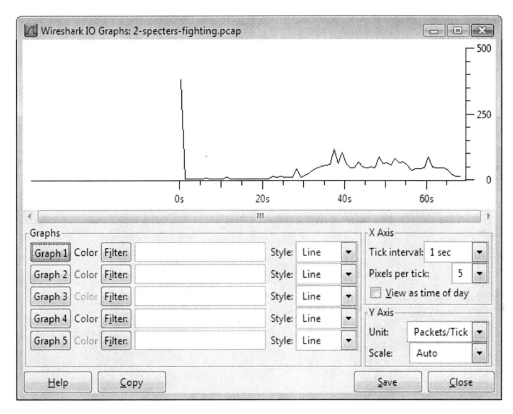

Figure 215. Wireshark automatically defines the X and Y axis scales based on the traffic

Filter IO Graphs

To graph specific traffic and compare it to the overall traffic, apply a filter to any of the five graph channels. For example, in Figure 216, we have applied a filter for `tcp.analysis.retransmission` on the Graph 2 channel. We have also selected the FBar style for this channel.

To apply pre-defined display filters to your IO Graph, click the **Filter** button. In addition, you can right click on a field in the Packet Details pane of a trace file, select **Copy | Field** or **Copy | As a Filter**. This buffers the field value in the format of a display filter. Now you can paste the filter into an IO Graph channel.

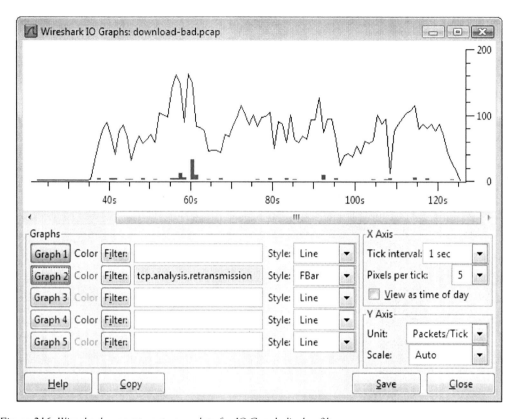

Figure 216. Wireshark supports auto-complete for IO Graph display filters

Coloring

Wireshark's IO Graphs support five channels that are set to use specific colors:[80]

- Graph 1 Black
- Graph 2 Red
- Graph 3 Green
- Graph 4 Blue
- Graph 5 Pink

_____

[80] At this time you cannot define other colors on the Wireshark IO Graphs, but that would be a great addition someday. Visit *wiki.wireshark.org/WishList* to see ideas that have been submitted for future Wireshark enhancements.

Red is Bad, Green is Good—Using "Color Assumptions"

If possible, consider "color assumptions" when selecting colors for good and bad traffic. For example, if you are graphing lost segment flags, color those packets in red. When graphing normal traffic flows, consider using green. People have an inert interpretation of certain colors—red is bad, green is good. Your color assumptions are not as important as clarity of the graph—see the Styles selection below regarding the layering of graph channels.

Styles and Layers

There are four styles available for IO Graphing:

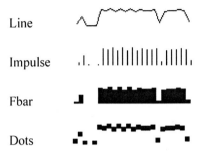

Line

Impulse

Fbar

Dots

Experiment with these styles to determine which one creates the most comprehensive graph.

When using multiple graph channels you might end up losing view of one of the channels because they are layered. Graph 1 is the foreground layer—if you create Graph 1 using an Fbar format and that channel uses the highest plotting points, it will block out all other channels you have graphed. Define your graph channels and styles accordingly.

X and Y Axis

Wireshark automatically defines the X axis and the Y axis based on the traffic being plotted. The Tick interval indicates how often traffic should be plotted on the graph. If the interval is set to 1 second (the default), data will be examined for one full second and then plotted. You can adjust the time interval to one of the following settings:

- 0.001 seconds
- 0.01 seconds
- 0.1 seconds
- 1 second
- 10 seconds
- 1 minute
- 10 minutes

To alter the spacing of the ticks on the view of the graph, redefine the number of pixels per tick from 1, 2, 5 or 10 pixels per tick. Select **View as Time of Day** to alter the X axis labels from seconds to time of day.

The Y axis supports three settings:

- Packets/Tick
- Bytes/Tick
- Bits/Tick
- Advanced (launches Advanced IO Graph view)

The Scale is set to Auto by default—using the minimum and maximum values of the traffic being graphed to create the Y axis values.

The scale can be set to a definite value from 10 to 2 billion or as a logarithmic value. Logarithmic scales are useful when you need to use a logarithm of a quantity instead of the quantity itself. For example, an IO Graph using logarithmic Y axis values may contain 1, 10, 100 and 1000 instead of 1, 2, 3, and 4.

Generate Advanced IO Graphs

Access Advanced IO Graphs under the Y Axis Unit drop down menu as shown in Figure 217. Advanced IO Graphs offer the following Calc options:

SUM(*)	Adds up and plots the value of a field for all instances seen during the tick interval
MIN(*)	Plots the minimum value seen in the field during the tick interval
AVG(*)	Plots the average value seen in the field during the tick interval
MAX(*)	Plots the maximum value seen in the field during the tick interval
COUNT(*)	Counts the number of occurrences of a field or characteristic seen during the tick interval
LOAD(*)	Measures response time fields only

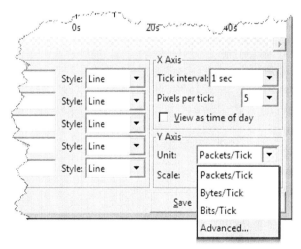

Figure 217. Access Advanced IO Graphs from the Y Axis Unit menu on a basic IO Graph

SUM(*) Calc

This calculation adds up the value of a field. For example, if you want to plot the amount of TCP data in your trace file use the value *tcp.len*. If you are interested in the amount of data crossing in a single direction of a bi-directional flow of traffic, add a filter for the IP source and destination addresses as shown in Figure 218.

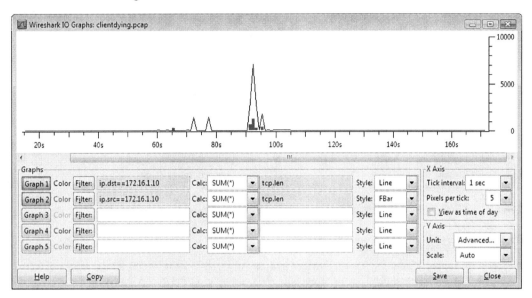

Figure 218. Use SUM(*) with `tcp.len` *to measure the IO of the TCP payload*

Another good example of using SUM(*) is to define `tcp.seq` to graph out the TCP sequence number as it increments as shown in Figure 219. In this example we see the gradual increase in the TCP sequence number value until approximately 18 seconds into the trace. The sudden drop indicates a problem in the data transfer process. We can click on that point in the IO Graph to jump to that packet in the Packet List pane. Note that this is adding up the TCP sequence number of bi-directional traffic.

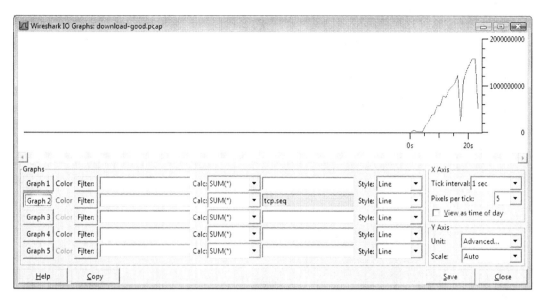

Figure 219. Use SUM(*) with `tcp.seq` *to spot data transfer problems*

MIN(*), AVG(*) and MAX(*) Calcs

These calculations plot the minimum, average and maximum of a field value. This is very useful when graphing the latency time between packets. For example, in the graph shown in Figure 220 we have graphed the minimum, average and maximum time from the end of one packet to the end of the next packet in a trace file using `frame.time_delta`.

Increases in round trip latency times become visible with this graph. In this case, a window zero condition caused the TCP backoff algorithm to be used with window probes. You can see the exponential growth in the delta time between packets.

Using filters for a single conversation you can measure the points in the conversation where communications slowed. The Y axis indicates the delta time values plotted while the X axis shows you how far into the trace file each delay occurred.

Find a Packet Plotted in Your IO Graph
You can click on any plotted point in the IO Graph to have Wireshark jump to that area in the trace file. This makes it very easy to examine the traffic around a problem spot in the IO flow.

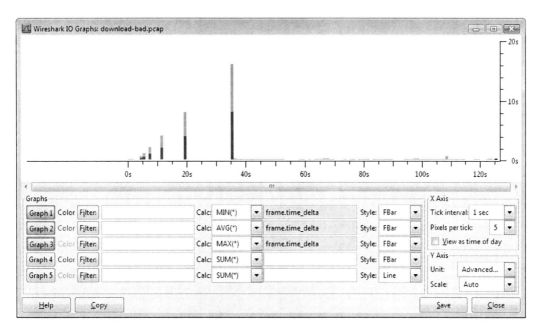

Figure 220. The TCP backoff process is visible with `frame.time_delta`

COUNT(*) Calc

This calculation counts the occurrence of a characteristic. This is most useful when graphing Wireshark's TCP analysis flags such as `tcp.analysis.retransmission` or `tcp.analysis.duplicate_ack`.

If you apply this calculation to field such as `ip.ttl`, it will only count and display the number of times the `ip.ttl` fields are seen, not the value in the fields.

In Figure 221 we have graphed the following TCP analysis flags occurring in a trace file:

```
tcp.analysis.duplicate_ack
tcp.analysis.retransmission
tcp.analysis.fast_retransmission
tcp.analysis.lost_segment
```

This advanced IO Graph illustrates the relationship between lost packets, duplicate ACKs and retransmissions.[81]

---

[81] As this book is printed in black and white, we cannot accurately show the colorization of this advanced IO graph. We have, however, included an image of this advanced IO graph on the back cover of this book. In the example on the back cover we altered the tick interval, the Y axis scale and the style for Graph 3 and Graph 4.

Understand and Plot TCP Packet Loss Recovery Processes
The graph depicted in Figure 221 is one you should master.

When a receiver notices packet loss (skipped TCP sequence numbers), these lost segments lead to duplicate ACKs which lead to retransmissions.

Check out the back cover of the book to see an IO graph comparing `tcp.analysis.lost_segment, tcp.analysis.duplicate_ack` *and* `tcp.analysis.retransmission` *packets.*

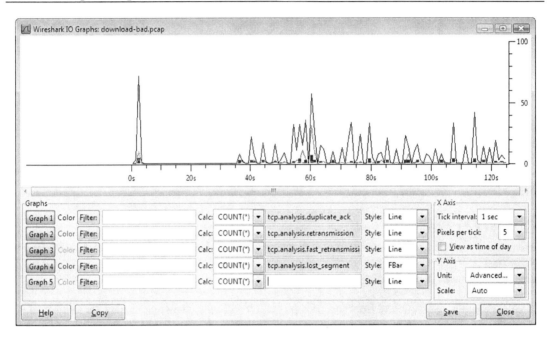

Figure 221. Graphing packet loss and recovery

LOAD(*) Calc

These graphs are used with response time fields only such as `smb.time` and `rpc.time`. In essence, LOAD graphs can be used to plot the client load on the server. For example, using the value `smb.time`, you can determine how many commands are traveling to the server at any time. The scale is number of commands times 1,000.

A value of 1,000 on the Y axis means one command at that time.

In Figure 222 we see large gaps between SMB requests. During these gaps, the server is idle waiting for requests. This is a classic example of a slow client. We must consider the Y axis in units of 1000 per SMB request. This trace shows a maximum of one SMB request in flight at a time.

If the server were slow, we would see the requests in flight increase. If our gaps on the graph were small or non-existent, then the client is keeping constant SMB requests in flight.

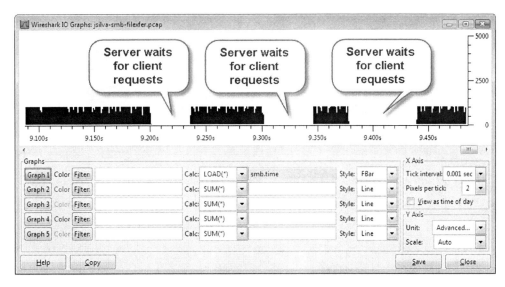

Figure 222. Gaps in the graph indicate times when the server site idle waiting for the client to make another SMB request

Compare Traffic Trends in IO Graphs

There may be times when you want to compare the IO Graph of a baseline to another trace file. For example, we have two trace files—one contains traffic from a good file transfer process and another contains traffic from a slow file transfer process.

We want to compare the two traffic flows side-by-side. This is a 4 step process:

1. Examine the time difference between the trace files
2. If necessary, alter one of the trace file timestamps so it will plot directly in front of or behind the other trace file
3. Merge the two trace files
4. Open the merged trace file and generate an IO Graph

For more information on altering trace file timestamps and merging trace files, refer to *Chapter 33: Effective Use of Command Line Tools.*

Figure 223 shows the IO Graph from the merged trace files. We can clearly see that the slow file transfer process at the beginning of the graph has a low IO rate over a longer period of time. In addition, we can see a large gap during the download when no data is transferred.

On the right side of the graph we see a high bits per tick rate—the data transfer took less time and was more efficient. We still see a short time when no data was transferred, but it is much shorter than the problem seen in the first trace file.

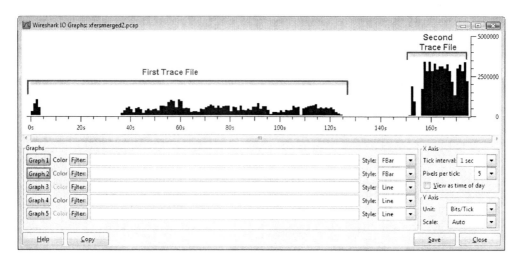

Figure 223. Comparing two file downloads in a single IO Graph

A picture is worth a thousand words—this is especially true in network analysis. It's one thing to capture thousands or millions of packets—it's another thing to make sense of it.

Use New –S Capinfos Setting to Time-Shift Trace Files

In the example shown above, the two trace files I merged were taken days apart. If I had just merged the two trace files and then created an IO graph, the time separating the data graphing sections would have destroyed the usefulness of this graph. After reading this example in the book, Gerald added a new –S parameter to the Capinfos utility in Wireshark v1.3 (development release) which is available on later revisions of Wireshark as well. The new –S parameter displays the start and end capture times in raw seconds. This information makes it much easier to use Editcap to time shift a trace file (with the Editcap –t <seconds> parameter) so the traces can fit in one IO graph. Refer to the List Trace File Details with Capinfos on page 687 for more details on Capinfos parameters. (Thanks, Gerald!)

Graph Round Trip Time

Select **Statistics | TCP Stream Graph | Round Trip Time Graph** to depict the round trip time from a data packet to the corresponding ACK packet. The Y axis is created based on the highest round trip latency time. Latency times are calculated as the time between a TCP data packet and the related acknowledgment.

Round Trip Time graphs are unidirectional—if you do not see anything plotted when you open a round trip time graph, you might be looking at a packet traveling in the opposite direction than data is flowing. Select a data packet and load the graph again.

Figure 224 illustrates the round trip time seen in a trace containing a slow file transfer process. The Y axis defines the round trip time in seconds. The X axis defines the TCP sequence number. We can see the latency times are very high at many points in the trace file and there are specific moments when the traffic is bursty in nature.

In order to determine what happens during the points when you notice vertical stripes, **Ctrl+click** on one of the plot points.

Consistent vertical stripes can be seen when packet loss occurs and a high number of duplicate ACKs are sent. Vertical stripes can also be seen when data is queued along a path and then suddenly forwarded through the queuing device. **Left click** to zoom in on an area of the graph. **Shift+click** to zoom out.

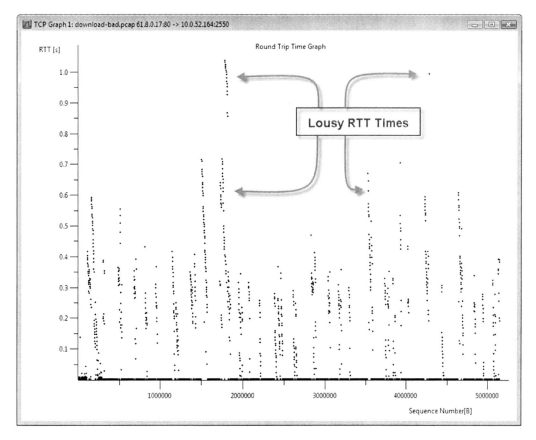

Figure 224. The Round Trip Time graph indicates very high latency times

In Figure 225 we see a lower Y axis value because the trace file does not have latency times as high as those graphed in Figure 224. We still see a vertical stripe in the trace file. In this situation, the sudden vertical stripe is plotted at the same time packets are lost, multiple duplicate ACKs are sent and finally a retransmission occurs.

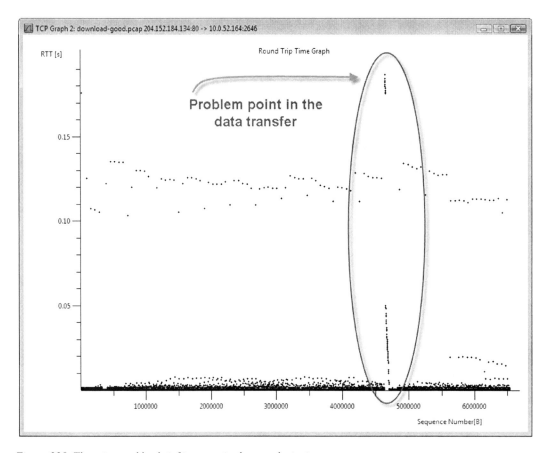

Figure 225. There is a sudden brief increase in the round trip time

Remember that you can also use Advanced IO Graphs to plot the average round trip time using `tcp.analysis.ack_rtt`.

Graph Throughput Rates

Select **Statistics | TCP Stream Graph | Throughput Graph** to view trends related to traffic flow. The TCP Throughput graph is closely related to the IO Graph, but plots are done with dots only.

TCP Throughput graphs are unidirectional—if you do not see anything plotted when you open a Throughput graph, you might be looking at the wrong side of the communication. Highlight a packet going in the reverse direction and load the graph again. Figure 226 shows the TCP Throughput graph for a trace file taken during a slow download process. Note that this is the same trace file we created a Round Trip Time graph of in Figure 224. You can see how similar the two graphs are in general flow information.

Since TCP Throughput graphs are created based on the packet you select in the Packet List pane, you can easily create these graphs for any conversation in the trace file.

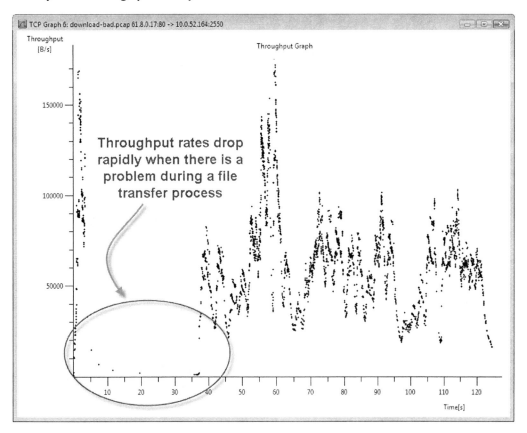

Figure 226. A TCP Throughput graph plots the throughput rate in bytes per second

Graph TCP Sequence Numbers over Time

Select **Statistics | TCP Stream Graph** and either **Time-Sequence Graph (Stevens)** or **Time-Sequence Graph (tcptrace).**[82] Wireshark's Time-Sequence Graphs visualize TCP-based traffic.

TCP headers contain a sequence number field that increments by the number of bytes sent during data transfer. If a TCP header sequence number is 1,000 and there are 200 bytes of data in the packet, the TCP header from this source should contain the sequence number 1,200. If the next packet contains sequence number 1,000 again, this is a retransmission packet. If the next TCP packet contains sequence number 1,400, a segment must have been lost.

---

[82] The tcptrace graph provides more information than the Stevens graph, so we recommend it over the Stevens graph. In this book we focus on the tcptrace graph.

Wireshark's Time-Sequence graphs visualize TCP-based traffic. In an ideal situation, the graph plots should run from the lower left corner to the upper right corner in a smooth diagonal line. TCP segments are plotted in an "I bar" format. Taller I bars contain more data.

The TCP Time-Sequence Graph graphs data moving in one direction. Ensure you have selected a packet in the Packet List pane that contains data or is traveling in the direction of data flow. If your graph appears empty, look at the title bar—which direction are you examining? Click on a packet traveling in the opposite direction and try plotting the traffic again.

Interpret TCP Window Size Issues

The TCP window size advertises the amount of buffer space available. When the TCP window size grey line moves closer to the plotted I bars, the receive window size is decreasing. When they touch, the receiver has indicated their TCP window size is zero and no more data may be received. In Figure 227 we have noted where the window size line meets the I bar.

In Figure 227 we zoomed in on a TCP Time-Sequence Graph to examine the receive window line (light grey line) and the plotted I bars that represent TCP segments in the trace file.

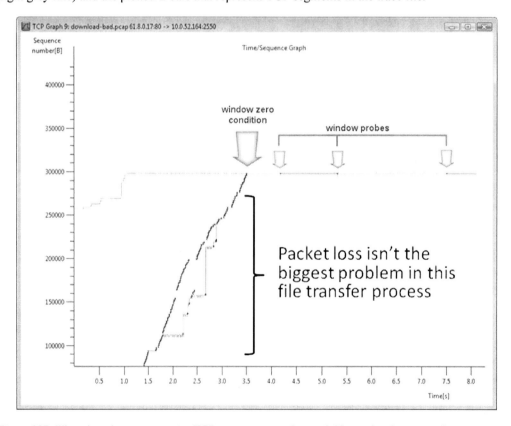

Figure 227. When the I bars representing TCP segments meet the available window line, a window zero condition has occurred

As data is taken out of the receive buffer, the receive window should increase. In Figure 227, we can see that the receive window does not increase—eventually the segment data transferred fills up the receive window as noted by the arrow. The data transfer stops until the receive window opens up again.

The smaller arrows point out the window probe packets that are sent to determine if the window has opened up.

Interpret Packet Loss, Duplicate ACKs and Retransmissions

If you are upstream from packet loss (at a location that sees packets before packet loss occurs), you will see duplicate I bars (same sequence number, but located at two different times in the graph).

If you are downstream from packet loss (at a location that shows skipped TCP sequence numbers), you will see gaps in the I bars.

Duplicate ACKs are noted as numerous ticks along the receive line as shown in the Figure 228. A high number of duplicate ACKs may indicate high path latency between the sender and the receiver. A retransmission triggered by duplicate ACKs will occur along the horizontal line across from the duplicate ACKs.

When retransmissions are triggered by the RTO (a timeout from the sender), they are not preceded by duplicate ACKs, again shown in Figure 228.

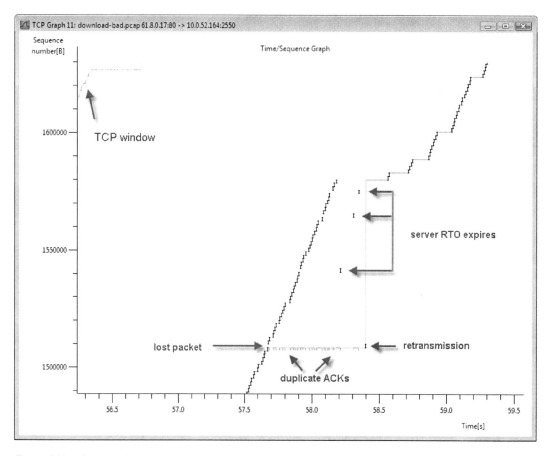

Figure 228. TCP Time-Sequence graphs display the packet loss, duplicate ACK and retransmission processes

Screen Capture those TCP Time-Sequence Graphs
At the present time, Wireshark does not allow you to save or print the Time-Sequence graph. Consider using a screen capture utility such as SnagIt (www.techsmith.com) to capture and print the graph.

Case Study:
Watching Performance Levels "Drop"

Submitted by: Mark R.
                Sr. Network Technician

We were plagued with intermittent complaints from end users who said their machines locked up occasionally when going to the Internet.

All our traffic went through a proxy server on port 8080.

We started capturing trace files of traffic to and from port 8080 as our users hit different servers on the Internet. We told the users to contact us by beeper when they had a lock up. It didn't take long before we were getting buzzed left and right.

When we looked at the trace files we kept seeing the client reporting "TCP Zero Window" and then 10 seconds or so go by before the client system sent a TCP reset.

We had taken some of Laura's courses on the top performance issues and recognized this was a problem with the client's resources—data wasn't being pulled out of the TCP buffer in a timely manner. It seemed they sent the reset when they tried to connect to another web host (after they got fed up waiting—we could gauge the patience level of our users by looking at the time difference between the Zero Window packets and the resets—an added bonus).

We examined the client machines to see what was running on them when they complained. We found a bunch of clients were using a program called Dropbox to keep copies of their pictures and videos shared between them. Those were the users that complained and it always happened when they synchronized their Dropbox folders.

Once we disabled Dropbox on their systems, they could browse just fine. We gave them the option of staying with Dropbox or having a better browsing experience.

It was really nice to point at the users and say "it's your fault"!
;-)

Case Study: Graphing RTT to the Corporate Office

Submitted by: ***Christy Z.***
 Network Administrator

To compare round trip times between different sites and the corporate office of a customer, we used AVG(*) with `tcp.analysis.ack_rtt`. Working closely with the internal IT team, we focused on three branch offices to start. We captured the traffic at the corporate headquarters building.

We used three filters—one for each of the branch offices as you can see below. Each filter looked for traffic to/from a different branch network address. In order to see the graphed traffic more clearly we set Graph 3 and Graph 4 to use FBar format.

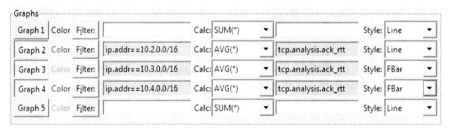

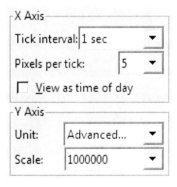

For even more clarity, we played around with the X axis and Y axis values—we usually have to manually choose a Y axis scale around 1,000,000 which is equal to 1 second as the time value is listed in milliseconds.

When we finished graphing the traffic we could see that the round trip time to our 10.2 and 10.4 networks were much higher than our RTT to the 10.3 network.

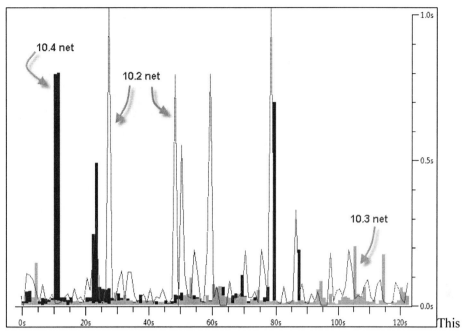

This matched what we were hearing from the users from those two branch offices—they complained that file transfers were slow.

Next we wanted to see if all traffic was experiencing the same delay. We focused on network 10.2 to begin with. We created additional IO Graphs to separate the traffic type to one of the branches. Our Advanced IO Graph setting is shown below.

We used the same network address, but defined a different port number to look at in Graphs 2, 3 and 4.

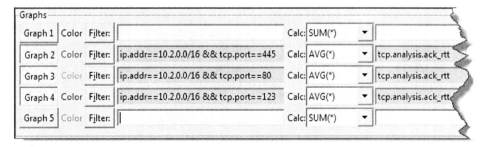

We kept the `tcp.analysis.rtt` setting and AVG(*) Calc with this new graph.

The results pointed out that SMB traffic was experiencing higher RTT times than the HTTP or even NTP traffic to/from the branch office.

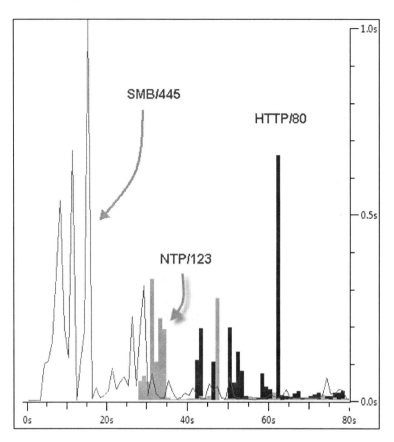

Our graph prompted us to investigate QoS configurations between the branches. We discovered the QoS configurations had been altered in preparation for the VoIP rollout. Traffic to and from port 445 was placed at a lower priority than other traffic types.

The IT team adjusted the QoS settings and the users noticed the performance difference.

Case Study:
Testing QoS Policies

Submitted by: Todd Lerdal

I was given a pretty fun task of setting up what I consider a fancier quality of service policy so that an external partner is only allowed X amount of bandwidth off of a 100mbps link.

I knew all the theory on what needed to be done and how to do it, but wanted to verify that the bandwidth restrictions would hold strong even if the external partner had something misconfigured (like anti-virus software) and would try and flood the connection.

I set up my test lab and simulated a few hosts on each end of the link, one pretending to be our equipment, the other to simulate the external partners. With Wireshark set up in the middle of the traffic path, I would fire off my packet generator to send more than the allowed amount of bandwidth to the external partner.

I was able to run through a few different scenarios, then take the packets and generate a few graphs for the "manager's interface" (pretty pictures with colors).

Summary

Wireshark's IO Graph, TCP Round Trip Time Graph, Time-Sequence Graph and Throughput Graph build pictures of TCP data flow and can help identify the cause of network performance problems.

Advanced IO Graphs enable you to use CALC values such as SUM(*), COUNT(*), MIN(*), MAX(*) and LOAD(*) on the traffic. Display filters can also be placed on the traffic in the Advanced IO Graphs.

The Round Trip Time is a unidirectional traffic that tracks the time between data being transmitted and the associated TCP ACK.

Throughput Graphs are unidirectional and plot the total amount of bytes seen in the trace at specific points in time. If throughput values are low, data transfer time increases.

TCP Time-Sequence Graphs (also unidirectional) plot the individual TCP packets based on the TCP Sequence number changes over time. In additional, this graph type depicts the ACKs seen and the window size. In a smooth data transfer process, the "I bar line" goes from the lower left corner to the upper right corner along a smooth path.

Practice What You've Learned

Download the trace files available in the Download section of the book website, *www.wiresharkbook.com*. To practice analyzing TCP communications, open the following trace files and answer the questions listed.

udp-mcastream-queued2.pcap	Can you see the queuing issue when you select Statistics | IO Graphs?
	What setting will help you examine the erratic IO rate when packets are held temporarily in a queue along this path?
net-latency-au.pcap	This trace consists of just DNS queries/responses and the first two packets of TCP handshakes to each target.
	How can you use an advanced IO Graph to depict the delays between packets in the trace file?
tcp-bad-download-again.pcap	Why is a TCP Time-Sequence graph based on packet 2 almost empty?
	How can you properly graph the TCP Time-Sequence values?
	Build a Round Trip Time graph. What is the highest RTT(s) value seen in this trace file? Is the RTT value contributing to the slow download?

Review Questions

Q21.1   **How much of a packet is counted when plotting an IO Graph?**

Q21.2   **What is the likely cause of an empty graph?**

Q21.3   **How can you use an IO Graph to plot overall traffic compared to a single conversation?**

Q21.4   **What is the purpose of the SUM(*) calculation in an advanced IO Graph?**

Q21.5   **On what data is the Round Trip Time graph based?**

Q21.6   **What is an ideal pattern to see in a TCP Time-Sequence graph?**

Answers to Review Questions

Q21.1 **How much of a packet is counted when plotting an IO Graph?**

A21.1 The entire packet including payload and headers is counted in IO Graphs.

Q21.2 **What is the likely cause of an empty graph?**

A21.2 Most likely the graph is unidirectional and you have selected a packet traveling in the wrong traffic direction before building the graph.

Q21.3 **How can you use an IO Graph to plot overall traffic compared to a single conversation?**

A21.3 Apply a conversation filter on a second graph line.

Q21.4 **What is the purpose of the SUM(*) calculation in an advanced IO Graph?**

A21.4 This calculation counts up the value of a field or characteristic (such as `tcp.len`) for the tick interval defined and plots the value on the graph.

Q21.5 **On what data is the Round Trip Time graph based?**

A21.5 Wireshark calculates and plots the time between a data packet and the corresponding ACK packet.

Q21.6 **What is an ideal pattern to see in a TCP Time-Sequence graph?**

A21.6 The ideal TCP Time-Sequence graph pattern is a steep slope from the lower left corner to the upper right corner.

Chapter 22: Analyze Dynamic Host Configuration Protocol (DHCP) Traffic

Wireshark Certified Network Analyst Exam Objectives covered:

- The Purpose of DHCP
- Analyze Normal DHCP Traffic
- Analyze DHCP Problems
- Dissect the DHCP Packet Structure
- Filter on DHCP Traffic
- Display BOOTP-DHCP Statistics

The Purpose of DHCP

DHCP enables clients to obtain their IP addresses and configuration information in a dynamic manner. Based on BOOTP, DHCP is the standard for address/configuration assignments.

DHCP uses UDP for transport offering connectionless services for numerous configuration options. The current definition for DHCP on IPv4 networks is RFC 2131.

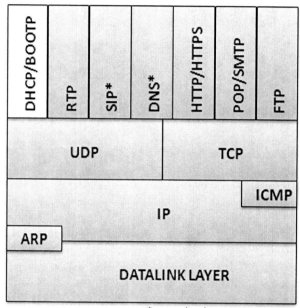

Figure 229. DHCP/BOOTP runs over UDP

Analyze Normal DHCP Traffic

The default ports for DHCP communications are port 68 (client process) and port 67 (server daemon).

Normal DHCP traffic differs depending on the client's current configuration state and what the client wants to know from the server. In Figure 230 a client is booting up. The client is outside its lease time, prompting the Discover broadcast.

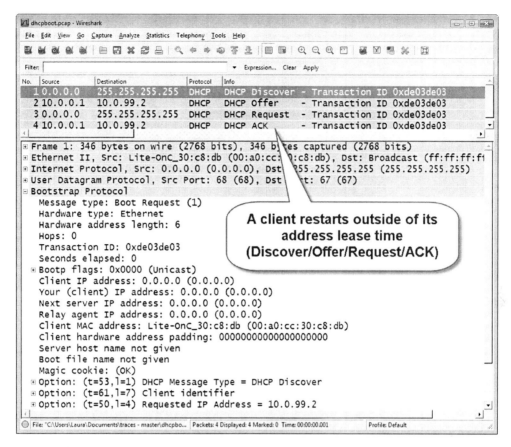

Figure 230. A four-packet DHCP startup sequence

Discover-Offer-Request-Acknowledgment is the sequence used in the default startup of a DHCP client that is outside its address lease time. If a client is inside its address lease time, the sequence Request-Acknowledgment is used.

There are eight DHCP message types. The table below lists the message types and their description from RFC 2131.

Number	Message Type	Description
1	DHCP Discover	Client broadcast to locate available DHCP servers
2	DHCP Offer	Server to client in response to DHCP Discover with offer of configuration parameters
3	DHCP Request	Client message to servers either (a) requesting offered parameters from one server and implicitly declining offers from all others, (b) confirming correctness of previously allocated address after a system reboot, for example, or (c) extending the lease on a particular network address

Number	Message Type	Description
4	DHCP Decline	Client to server indicating the offered network address is not acceptable (perhaps the client discovered the address already in use through a gratuitous ARP test process)
5	DHCP Acknowledgment	Server to client with configuration parameters, including committed network address
6	DHCP Negative Acknowledgment	Server to client indicating client's network address is incorrect (e.g., client has moved to new subnet) or client's lease as expired
7	DHCP Release	Client to server relinquishing network address and cancelling remaining lease
8	DHCP Informational	Client to server, asking only for local configuration parameters; client already has externally configured network address

One of the most common uses of DHCP is dynamic address assignment. Figure 230 shows the four-packet process of acquiring an address lease and parameters when a host is starting up. Once the DHCP client successfully receives and acknowledges an IP address from a DHCP server, the client enters the "bound" state.

During the address request and assignment process, the client obtains three time values:[83]

- Lease Time (LT)
- Renewal Time (T1)
- Rebind Time (T2)

The Lease Time (LT) defines how long the client is allowed to use the IP address assigned. The renewal time (T1) is .50 * LT. The rebind time (T2) is .875 * LT.

At T1, the client moves to the renewal state and sends a unicast DHCP request to extend the lease time to the DHCP server. If the DHCP server responds with an acknowledgment, the client may return to the bound state.

The client retries the DHCP request at intervals equal to one-half of the remaining time until T2 down to the minimum of 60 seconds. If the client does not receive an acknowledgment before T2 arrives, the client enters the rebinding state. In the rebinding state, the client sends a broadcast DHCP Request to extend its lease. If the client receives an acknowledgment, the client returns to the bound state.

The client retries the DHCP request at intervals equal to one-half of the remaining time until expiration of the LT.

If the client does not receive an acknowledgment before the expiration of LT, the client must return to an uninitialized state, release its IP address and send a DHCP broadcast to locate a DHCP server, if possible. Most DHCP client software uses a "sticky IP address"—the client system remembers the

---

[83] The DHCP server does not necessarily provide all three timers. The DHCP client can calculate the Renewal Time and Rebind Time based on the Lease Time.

last assigned IP address and requests to explicitly use that address again. *Dynamic* IP addressing is not as dynamic as the name implies.

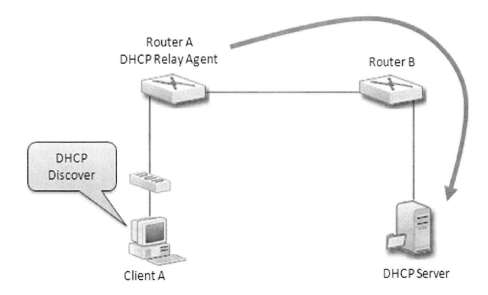

Figure 231. A DHCP Relay Agent forwards messages between DHCP clients and the DHCP server

Since DHCP relies on broadcasts for the initial DHCP Discover process, either the DHCP server or a DHCP Relay Agent must be on the same network segment as the DHCP client.

DHCP Relay Agents forward messages between DHCP clients and DHCP servers. Figure 233 shows a packet that has been forwarded through a DHCP Relay Agent. The DHCP Relay Agent's IP address, 10.2.99.99, is listed in the DHCP Request. The MAC address of the DHCP client is listed in the Client MAC address field. If you examine the Ethernet header, you will notice this packet is coming from a Cisco router that has the DHCP Relay Agent functionality enabled.

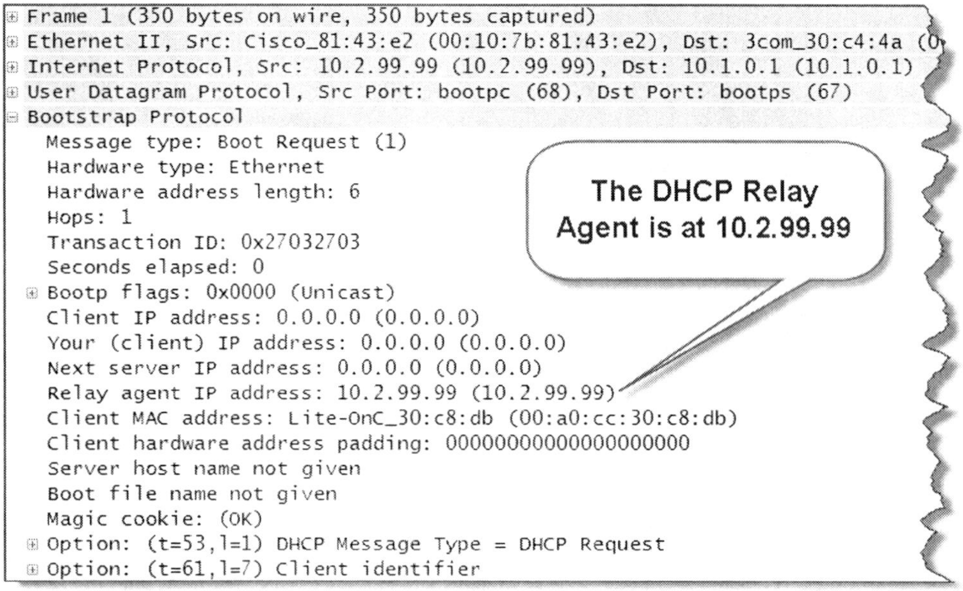

```
⊞ Frame 1 (350 bytes on wire, 350 bytes captured)
⊞ Ethernet II, Src: Cisco_81:43:e2 (00:10:7b:81:43:e2), Dst: 3com_30:c4:4a (0
⊞ Internet Protocol, Src: 10.2.99.99 (10.2.99.99), Dst: 10.1.0.1 (10.1.0.1)
⊞ User Datagram Protocol, Src Port: bootpc (68), Dst Port: bootps (67)
⊟ Bootstrap Protocol
    Message type: Boot Request (1)
    Hardware type: Ethernet
    Hardware address length: 6
    Hops: 1
    Transaction ID: 0x27032703
    Seconds elapsed: 0
  ⊞ Bootp flags: 0x0000 (Unicast)
    Client IP address: 0.0.0.0 (0.0.0.0)
    Your (client) IP address: 0.0.0.0 (0.0.0.0)
    Next server IP address: 0.0.0.0 (0.0.0.0)
    Relay agent IP address: 10.2.99.99 (10.2.99.99)
    Client MAC address: Lite-OnC_30:c8:db (00:a0:cc:30:c8:db)
    Client hardware address padding: 00000000000000000000
    Server host name not given
    Boot file name not given
    Magic cookie: (OK)
  ⊞ Option: (t=53,l=1) DHCP Message Type = DHCP Request
  ⊞ Option: (t=61,l=7) Client identifier
```

> **The DHCP Relay Agent is at 10.2.99.99**

Figure 232. This packet is being forwarded by a DHCP Relay Agent

Analyze DHCP Problems

If DHCP doesn't work properly, clients may not be able to obtain or maintain IP addresses or other client configurations. If hosts on the network have statically assigned addresses and the DHCP server is unaware of this, it may inadvertently offer an address that is already in use unless it performs a duplicate address test (typically using ICMP Echo Requests).

Alternately, the client can perform the duplicate address test. If the client locates another host with the same address, the DHCP client must decline the IP address provided in the DHCP Offer.

Figure 233 depicts a problem with a DHCP client IP address configuration. This trace file was captured using a capture filter for traffic to or from the DHCP server (port 67).

In the DHCP Discover packet, the client requested the address 192.168.0.102 (the last address the client used). In the DHCP Offer, the server offers the client 192.168.0.104. The client continues the DHCP process, but then sends a DHCP Decline packet to the server.

Typically this decline is sent when the client performs a duplicate address test and receives a response indicating the address is in use. In this network configuration, a printer had already been assigned a static IP address 192.168.0.104. The problem shown in Figure 233 is covered in the case study "Declining Clients" at the end of this chapter.

This demonstrates the problem with applying a capture filter instead of working with display filters only. Because we used a capture filter for all traffic to or from port 67, we cannot go back and see the client performing the duplicate address test. Use capture filters sparingly.

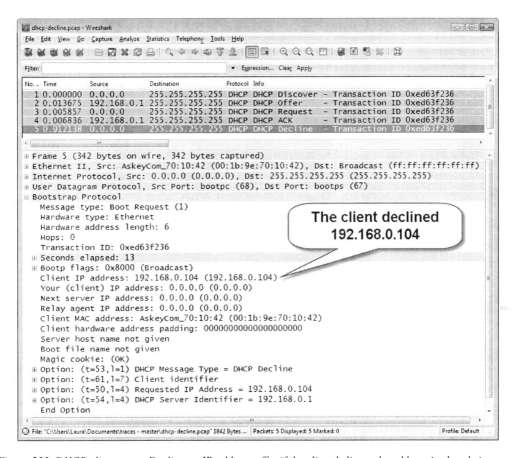

Figure 233. DHCP clients must Decline an IP address offer if the client believes the address is already in use

Dissect the DHCP Packet Structure

DHCP packets are variable length.

Message Type

Also referred to as the Opcode field, a 1 indicates a DHCP request and a 2 indicates a DHCP reply.

Hardware Type

This field defines the type of hardware address in use and matches the ARP hardware address type definitions. The value 0x0001 indicates the hardware address is an Ethernet address.

Hardware Length

This field indicates the length of the hardware address which is 6 for Ethernet addresses.

Hops

This field is used by DHCP relay agents to define the number of networks that must be crossed to get to the DHCP server.

Transaction ID

This field is used to match DHCP request and response packets.

Seconds Elapsed

This field indicates the number of seconds that have elapsed since the client began requesting a new address or renewal of an address.

BOOTP Flags

These flags indicate whether clients accept unicast or broadcast MAC packets before the IP stack is completely configured.

Client IP Address

The client fills in their client IP address after it is assigned by the DHCP server.

Your (Client) IP Address

This field indicates the address offered by the DHCP server. Only the DHCP server fills in this field.

Next Server IP Address

This field contains the address of DHCP server when a relay agent is used.

Relay Agent IP Address

This field shows the address of the DHCP relay agent if one is in use.

Client MAC Address

This field contains the client MAC address. This is a useful field to filter on if a user complains about the bootup process and you expect it might be a DHCP problem.

Server Host Name

This field can contain the name of the DHCP server (optional).

Boot File Name

This field indicates a boot file name (optional).

Magic Cookie

This field indicates the type of the data that follows. The value 0x63825363 indicates data is DHCP.

Option

The options are used to provide the IP address and configuration requests to the DHCP server and replies to the client. The following table lists some of the more common option types. A more complete list is available at *www.iana.org*.

Option	Name
1	Subnet Mask
3	Router
4	Time Server
5	Name Server
6	Domain Server
12	Host Name
15	Domain Name
31	Router Discovery

Filter on DHCP Traffic

The capture filter syntax for DHCP traffic is `port 67 or port 68` (alternately you can use just one of the port filters as all DHCP traffic should flow to or from port 67 or port 68).

DHCP is derived from BOOTP and uses the `bootp` display filter string. The following table lists additional DHCP display filters.

Display Filter	Description
`bootp.option.value == 0`	DHCP Discover message
`bootp.option.value == 04`	DHCP Decline message
`bootp.hw.mac_addr == 00:1b:9e:70:10:42`	DHCP message contains the MAC address 00:1b:9e:70:10:42
`bootp.option.type == 12`	The message contains a host name value (option type 12)
`!bootp.ip.relay == 0.0.0.0`	The message contains a DHCP Relay Agent value
`(bootp.ip.your == 192.168.0.104) && (bootp.option.value == 05)`	DHCP ACK message from a client using IP address 192.168.0.104
`bootp.option.type == 55 && bootp.option.value contains 1F`	DHCP parameter request list contains Perform Router Discover (0x1F)

Display BOOTP-DHCP Statistics

The BOOTP-DHCP statistics window summarizes the DHCP message types in the trace file. The following lists commonly seen DHCP message Types 53 values (listed in *Analyze Normal DHCP Traffic* on page 428.

Figure 234 shows the DHCP statistics for a trace file.

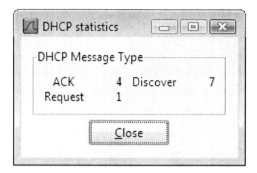

Figure 234. DHCP/BOOTP Statistics

The entire list of DHCP message types are listed at *www.iana.org/assignments/bootp-dhcp-parameters*.

Case Study: Declining Clients

A customer hit a problem where suddenly a number of hosts could not communicate on the Internet. A quick look at the local configurations confirmed that they did not have an IP address assigned.

So obviously something went wrong with the DHCP process, but the DHCP server seemed to be running fine. We launched Wireshark with a capture filter for all DHCP traffic (port 67 or port 68).

No.	Time	Source	Destination	Protocol	Info
1	0.000000	0.0.0.0	255.255.255.255	DHCP	DHCP Discover
2	0.013675	192.168.0.1	255.255.255.255	DHCP	DHCP Offer
3	0.005857	0.0.0.0	255.255.255.255	DHCP	DHCP Request
4	0.006836	192.168.0.1	255.255.255.255	DHCP	DHCP ACK
5	0.912138	0.0.0.0	255.255.255.255	DHCP	DHCP Decline

```
⊞ User Datagram Protocol, Src Port: bootpc (68), Dst Port: boo
⊟ Bootstrap Protocol
    Message type: Boot Request (1)
    Hardware type: Ethernet
    Hardware address length: 6
    Hops: 0
    Transaction ID: 0xed63f236
  ⊞ Seconds elapsed: 13
  ⊞ Bootp flags: 0x8000 (Broadcast)
    Client IP address: 0.0.0.0 (0.0.0.0)
    Your (client) IP address: 0.0.0.0 (0.0.0.0)
    Next server IP address: 0.0.0.0 (0.0.0.0)
    Relay agent IP address: 0.0.0.0 (0.0.0.0)
    Client MAC address: 00:1b:9e:70:10:42 (00:1b:9e:70:10:42)
    Client hardware address padding: 00000000000000000000
    Server host name not given
    Boot file name not given
    Magic cookie: (OK)
  ⊞ Option: (t=53,l=1) DHCP Message Type = DHCP Discover
  ⊞ Option: (t=116,l=1) DHCP Auto-Configuration = AutoConfigure
  ⊞ Option: (t=61,l=7) Client identifier
  ⊞ Option: (t=50,l=4) Requested IP Address = 192.168.0.102
```

The trace file showed that the clients booted up and sent the DHCP Discover packet and received an offer. We noticed that the server wasn't offering the same IP address requested by the client, but we assumed that the requested address was already assigned.

The client requested 192.168.0.102, but the server offered 192.168.0.104. The client sent the request for that address and an ACK finished the DHCP startup process—so far, so good.

Then… approximately one second later, the client sent a Decline to the DHCP server. Why?

This taught us a valuable lesson—DON'T use capture filters when troubleshooting the bootup process. We totally missed the problem.

When we took the trace again without the capture filter we saw the client perform a ping to the offered address immediately after being offered 192.168.0.104 (yes, the server offered the same address each time we tried it).

To our surprise the ping to 192.168.0.104 was answered by a printer. We learned that the printer's IP address had been assigned statically. The DHCP server never checked to see if an address was in use by performing its own ping process (the vendor assumed too many hosts won't respond to a ping process so it "isn't a reliable method to find an address in use").

The IT staff reconfigured the DHCP server with static entries for the printers. Never again has the DHCP server offered those addresses to the clients on the network.

Summary

DHCP can be used to provide more configuration settings than just the client IP address, although that is the most common use of DHCP.

When a client boots up outside of its lease time, we see a four packet DHCP process—Discover, Offer, Request and Acknowledge. When a client boots up inside its lease time, we see a two packet DHCP process—Request and Acknowledge. Clients can request their last used IP address in their DHCP Discover or Request packets.

Packets sent from IP address 0.0.0.0 are typically DHCP Discover packets. The sender does not have an IP address at that time. These packets are sent to the broadcast address (255.255.255.255).

If a DHCP server is not on the local network, a DHCP relay agent is required to forward DHCP requests to the remote DHCP server.

Practice What You've Learned

Download the trace files available in the Download section of the book website, *www.wiresharkbook.com*. Practice analyzing DHCP traffic by opening the trace files below and answering the questions listed.

dhcp-boot.pcap	This trace shows a basic DHCP boot sequence.
	Is this client inside or outside of its lease time?
	Did this client receive the IP address it requested?
dhcp-relay-serverside.pcap	Compare the source MAC address in the Ethernet header with the Client MAC Address inside the DHCP packet to note that this communication is coming from the DHCP Relay Agent to the DHCP Server.
	What IP address does the client request?
	What is the IP address of the DNS server?
	How long can the client keep the address?
	Did the client receive the address it requested?
dhcp-renewtorebind.pcap	The DHCP client is unsuccessful in renewing its IP address from 10.1.0.1 so the client broadcasts the DHCP Request in hopes of finding a new DHCP server.
	What does the client do when it doesn't get an answer from the DHCP server?
	What is this process called?
dhcp-decline.pcap	The DHCP client wants 192.168.0.102, but the server offers 192.168.0.104. The client seems OK with that until we see it

generates a DHCP Decline. Typically this indicates that the client thinks someone else has that IP address—sure enough, when we ARP scan the network we see a statically assigned 192.168.0.104. We filtered on just the DHCP traffic though so we can't see that other station talking.

dhcp-jerktakesaddress.pcap   The DHCP server is down, but the client remembers its last address and decided just to take it back. Of course it does a gratuitous ARP (packet 3). The client uses router solicitation (ugh) to try to find a default gateway as well. Finally, 12 seconds in to the trace the DHCP server resurfaces (packet 8).

Review Questions

Q22.1   **What is the purpose of DHCP?**

Q22.2   **What is the DHCP traffic sequence when a DHCP client boots up outside of its lease time?**

Q22.3   **What is the purpose of a DHCP Decline packet?**

Q22.4   **Why would a DHCP client enter the rebinding phase?**

Q22.5   **What is the syntax for capture and display filters for IP traffic?**

Answers to Review Questions

Q22.1 **What is the purpose of DHCP?**

A22.1 DHCP enables clients to obtain their IP addresses and configuration information in a dynamic manner. Based on BOOTP, DHCP is the standard for address/configuration assignments.

Q22.2 **What is the DHCP traffic sequence when a DHCP client boots up outside of its lease time?**

A22.2 When a DHCP client is outside of its lease time, the startup traffic sequence is Discover—Offer—Request—Acknowledge.

Q22.3 **What is the purpose of a DHCP Decline packet?**

A22.3 This DHCP packet is sent from a DHCP client to DHCP server to indicate that the offered network address is already in use.

Q22.4 **Why would a DHCP client enter the rebinding phase?**

A22.4 A DHCP client enters the rebinding phase when the renewal process is unsuccessful. In the rebinding state the DHCP client must release its IP address and broadcast a DHCP Discover packet.

Q22.5 **What is the syntax for capture and display filters for DHCP traffic?**

A22.5 Capture filter: `port 67 or port 68`
Display filter: `bootp`

Chapter 23: Analyze Hypertext Transfer Protocol (HTTP) Traffic

Wireshark Certified Network Analyst Exam Objectives covered:

- The Purpose of HTTP
- Analyze Normal HTTP Communications
- Analyze HTTP Problems
- Dissect HTTP Packet Structures
- Filter on HTTP or HTTPS Traffic
- Export HTTP Objects
- Display HTTP Statistics
- Graph HTTP Traffic Flows
- Set HTTP Preferences
- Analyze HTTPS Communications
- Decrypt HTTPS Traffic

- ❖ Case Study: HTTP Proxy Problems
- ❖ Summary
- ❖ Practice What You've Learned
- ❖ Review Questions and Answers

The Purpose of HTTP

Hypertext Transfer Protocol (HTTP) is referred to as a "distributed hypermedia information distribution application." HTTP is the application used when someone browses (unsecurely) on the Internet. HTTP uses a request/response model.

HTTP v1.0 is not used as often as HTTP v1.1, the current version in use. HTTP v1.1 is covered in RFC 2616, Hypertext Transfer Protocol – HTTP/1.1.

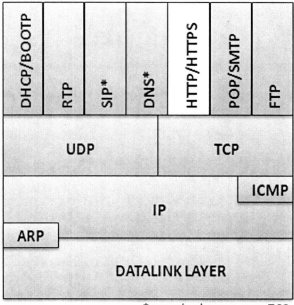

Figure 235. HTTP and HTTPS use the TCP transport

Analyze Normal HTTP Communications

Normal HTTP communications use a request/response communication style. Clients make requests of HTTP servers and servers respond with Status Codes.

Figure 236 shows an HTTP communication following an ARP process for the local gateway and a DNS query for *www.wireshark.org*. The HTTP communication begins with the TCP three-way handshake to establish the connection on port 80 (listed as HTTP because transport name resolution is enabled). By default, Wireshark is configured to dissect HTTP on 8 ports: 80, 3128, 3132, 8080, 8088, 11371, 3689 and 1900. HTTP communications can use other ports as well.

After the TCP connection is established successfully, the client makes an HTTP GET request for "/". The server responds with the Status Code 200 OK and begins sending the client the contents of the

www.wireshark.org main page. It takes six HTTP connections to view the main page at
www.wireshark.org.

Disable Stream Reassembly to See HTTP More Clearly

*For the clearest view of HTTP traffic in the Packet List pane, disable the TCP preference
"Allow subdissector to reassemble TCP streams." This enables you to see the HTTP GET
requests and the HTTP response codes in the Packet List pane.*

No. .	Time	Source	Destination	Protocol	Info
1	0.000000	Elitegro_40:74:d2	Broadcast	ARP	Who has 192.168.0.1? Tell
2	0.000559	D-Link_cc:a3:ea	Elitegro_40:74:d2	ARP	192.168.0.1 is at 00:13:46:
3	0.000023	192.168.0.113	192.168.0.1	DNS	Standard query A www.wiresh
4	0.089751	192.168.0.1	192.168.0.113	DNS	Standard query response A 6
5	0.003296	192.168.0.113	67.228.110.120	TCP	serverview-rm > http [SYN] S
6	0.031410	67.228.110.120	192.168.0.113	TCP	http > serverview-rm [SYN, A
7	0.000190	192.168.0.113	67.228.110.120	TCP	serverview-rm > http [ACK] Se
8	0.000645	192.168.0.113	67.228.110.120	HTTP	GET / HTTP/1.1
9	0.030699	67.228.110.120	192.168.0.113	TCP	http > serverview-rm [ACK] S
13	1.781965	67.228.110.120	192.168.0.113	HTTP	HTTP/1.1 200 OK (text/html
14	0.000879	67.228.110.120	192.168.0.113	HTTP	Continuation or non-HTTP tra
15	0.000652	192.168.0.113	67.228.110.120	TCP	serverview-rm > http [ACK] Se
16	0.031077	67.228.110.120	192.168.0.113	HTTP	Continuation or non-HTTP t
17	0.020732	192.168.0.113	67.228.110.120	HTTP	GET /css/ws-2.css HTTP/1.1
18	0.001979	192.168.0.113	67.228.110.120	TCP	serverview-icc > http [SYN]
19	0.003384	192.168.0.113	67.228.110.120	TCP	armi-server > http [SYN] Seq
20	0.005237	192.168.0.113	67.228.110.120	TCP	t1-e1-over-ip > http [SYN] S
21	0.021239	67.228.110.120	192.168.0.113	TCP	http > serverview-rm [ACK] S
22	0.002755	67.228.110.120	192.168.0.113	HTTP	HTTP/1.1 200 OK (text/css)
23	0.000607	67.228.110.120	192.168.0.113	HTTP	Continuation or non-HTTP tra
24	0.000513	192.168.0.113	67.228.110.120	TCP	serverview-rm > http [ACK] Se
25	0.000015	67.228.110.120	192.168.0.113	HTTP	Continuation or non-HTTP tra
26	0.000792	67.228.110.120	192.168.0.113	TCP	http > serverview-icc [SYN,
27	0.000118	192.168.0.113	67.228.110.120	TCP	serverview-icc > http [ACK]
28	0.000012	67.228.110.120	192.168.0.113	TCP	http > armi-server [SYN, ACK
29	0.000062	192.168.0.113	67.228.110.120	TCP	armi-server > http [ACK] Se

Figure 236. HTTP uses a request/response pattern

The HTTP Status Code Registry is maintained at *www.iana.org/assignments/http-status-codes*. The
Status Codes registered as of October 17, 2007 are listed below.

Value	Description	Reference
1xx Informational		
100	Continue	[RFC2616]
101	Switching Protocols	[RFC2616]
102	Processing	[RFC2518]
2xx Success		
200	OK	[RFC2616]
201	Created	[RFC2616]
202	Accepted	[RFC2616]
203	Non-Authoritative Information	[RFC2616]

Value	Description	Reference
204	No Content	[RFC2616]
205	Reset Content	[RFC2616]
206	Partial Content	[RFC2616]
207	Multi-Status	[RFC4918]
226	IM Used	[RFC3229]
3xx Redirection		
300	Multiple Choices	[RFC2616]
301	Moved Permanently	[RFC2616]
302	Found	[RFC2616]
303	See Other	[RFC2616]
304	Not Modified	[RFC2616]
305	Use Proxy	[RFC2616]
306	Reserved	[RFC2616]
307	Temporary Redirect	[RFC2616]
4xx Client Error		
400	Bad Request	[RFC2616]
401	Unauthorized	[RFC2616]
402	Payment Required	[RFC2616]
403	Forbidden	[RFC2616]
404	Not Found	[RFC2616]
405	Method Not Allowed	[RFC2616]
406	Not Acceptable	[RFC2616]
407	Proxy Authentication Required	[RFC2616]
408	Request Timeout	[RFC2616]
409	Conflict	[RFC2616]
410	Gone	[RFC2616]
411	Length Required	[RFC2616]
412	Precondition Failed	[RFC2616]
413	Request Entity Too Large	[RFC2616]
414	Request-URI Too Long	[RFC2616]
415	Unsupported Media Type	[RFC2616]
416	Requested Range Cannot be Satisfied	[RFC2616]
417	Expectation Failed	[RFC2616]
422	Unprocessable Entity	[RFC4918]
423	Locked	[RFC4918]

Value	Description	Reference
424	Failed Dependency	[RFC4918]
426	Upgrade Required	[RFC2817]
5xx Server Error		
500	Internal Server Error	[RFC2616]
501	Not Implemented	[RFC2616]
502	Bad Gateway	[RFC2616]
503	Service Unavailable	[RFC2616]
504	Gateway Timeout	[RFC2616]
505	HTTP Version Not Supported	[RFC2616]
506	Variant Also Negotiates (Experimental)	[RFC2295]
507	Insufficient Storage	[RFC4918]
510	Not Extended	[RFC2774]

One of the interesting response codes is the infamous 404 Not Found. Note that this is listed as a client error under the assumption that the client made a mistake in selecting the URL to visit. In truth, however, most 404 Not Found errors are sent in response to client's following broken links on web sites.

Watch Out For Cache-Loaded Web Pages

If an HTTP client has visited a page recently and that page is cached locally, the client may send the If Modified Since parameter and provide a date and time of the previous page download. The server may respond with a 304 Not Modified—the server will not resend the page that is already cached.

This is an important part of HTTP to understand when analyzing HTTP performance. If a user complains of poor performance when accessing a website the first time only, they may be loading pages from cache—you may not be seeing a true full page download.

Analyze HTTP Problems

HTTP communication problems can occur because of problems in site name resolution, issues with the TCP connection process, HTTP requests for non-existent pages or items, packet loss as well as congestion at the HTTP server or client.

Everyone at some time has typed in the wrong website address. If the site name cannot be resolved, you cannot access the site. This would generate a DNS Name Error. It is important to pay attention to DNS traffic when analyzing web browsing problems.

In addition, TCP errors may occur when the HTTP daemon is not running on the web server. After the client issues a TCP SYN, the server responds with a TCP RST or RST/ACK. The connection cannot be established as shown in Figure 237.

For more information on TCP connection problems, refer to *Chapter 20: Analyze Transmission Control Protocol (TCP) Traffic* and *Chapter 29: Find the Top Causes of Performance Problems.*

No.	Source	Destination	Protocol	Info
3	192.168.0.113	128.30.52.168	TCP	aicc-cmi > http [SYN] Seq=
6	192.168.0.113	128.30.52.168	TCP	vsaiport > http [SYN] Seq<
8	192.168.0.113	128.30.52.168	TCP	vsaiport > http [SYN] Seq=
9	128.30.52.168	192.168.0.113	TCP	http > cdid [RST] Seq=1 V
12	192.168.0.113	128.30.52.168	TCP	ssrip > http [SYN] Seq=0
14	192.168.0.113	128.30.52.168	TCP	vsaiport > http [SYN] Se<
28	128.30.52.168	192.168.0.113	TCP	http > aicc-cmi [RST] Se<
33	192.168.0.113	128.30.52.168	TCP	ssrip > http [SYN] Seq=0
46	192.168.0.113	128.30.52.168	TCP	vnsstr > http [SYN] Seq=0
59	192.168.0.113	128.30.52.168	TCP	vnsstr > http [SYN] Seq=(
102	192.168.0.113	128.30.52.168	TCP	ssrip > http [SYN] Seq=0
195	128.30.52.168	192.168.0.113	TCP	http > vsaiport [RST] Se<
196	192.168.0.113	128.30.52.168	TCP	vnsstr > http [SYN] Seq=C

Figure 237. Three unsuccessful HTTP connection attempts and the start of a fourth attempt

If the HTTP client connects successfully to the HTTP server, but then requests a page that is non-existent, HTTP 404 Not Found errors are generated by the web server. Interestingly, 404 Not Found errors are listed as 4xx Client Errors even though they may be caused by a missing page or file on a website.

Some redirection services will replace the standard 404 Not Found message with "suggested links" or redirect the HTTP client to another site completely. Consider building a color filter for HTTP 404 responses (`http.response.code == 404`).

Don't Use the `http` Filter to Analyze Web Browsing

This may seem quite counter-intuitive. When you apply the http display filter to a trace file that contains a web browsing session, Wireshark only displays packets that contain HTTP commands and response codes as well as data packets carrying web page elements. You won't see the TCP handshake used to set up the HTTP connection or the ACKs sent for downloaded pages or uploaded information. Use `tcp.port==80` (or designate the port used for the web browsing session if not 80) for your display filter. You'll be able to see the entire web browsing session with this filter.

Figure 238 shows a problem when opening up a list of laptops for sale at the *frys.com* website. We were able to resolve the IP address for the site and the page exists. By following the TCP stream we can see the server respond with the page heading. The laptop items are not displayed on the page, however—the page is blank.

Looking at the trace file we can see the *frys.com* web server reported an internal server error. This is not a problem on the client's system or the network. This problem is likely caused by a database problem within Fry's web services infrastructure.

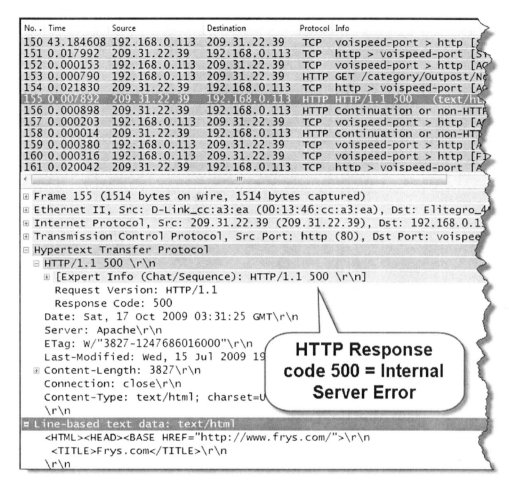

Figure 238. The frys.com server responds with an internal server error

In Figure 239 we are trying to fill out a form online—again we are browsing on the *www.frys.com* website. Upon clicking the Submit button, however, the client system appears to hang. In this case we can look at the HTTP traffic and observe a 403 Forbidden status code from the server.

Following the TCP stream reveals clear text and HTML tags with more information about the situation (we have removed the HTML tags):

```
The page cannot be displayed - you have attempted to
execute a CGI, ISAPI, or other executable program
from a directory that does not allow programs to be
executed.
```

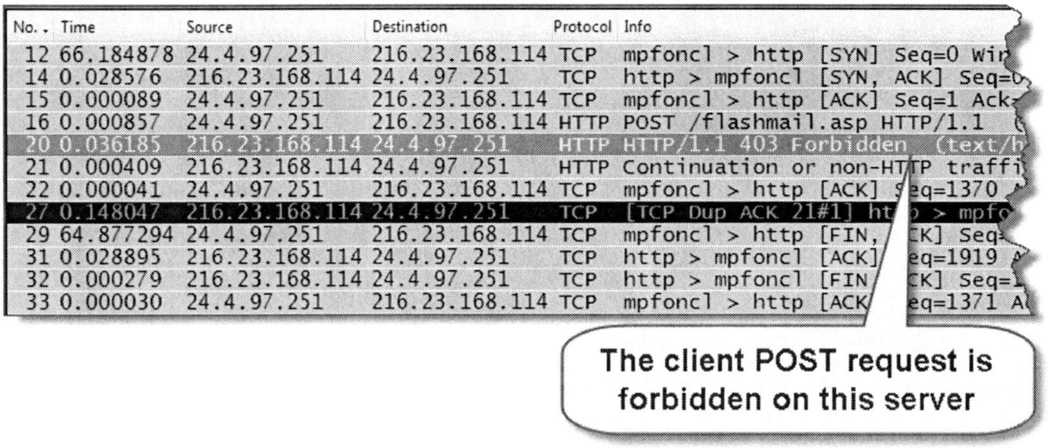

```
No. . Time        Source          Destination     Protocol Info
  12 66.184878 24.4.97.251     216.23.168.114 TCP   mpfoncl > http [SYN] Seq=0 Wir
  14 0.028576  216.23.168.114 24.4.97.251     TCP   http > mpfoncl [SYN, ACK] Seq=0
  15 0.000089  24.4.97.251     216.23.168.114 TCP   mpfoncl > http [ACK] Seq=1 Ack
  16 0.000857  24.4.97.251     216.23.168.114 HTTP  POST /flashmail.asp HTTP/1.1
  20 0.036185  216.23.168.114 24.4.97.251     HTTP  HTTP/1.1 403 Forbidden  (text/h
  21 0.000409  216.23.168.114 24.4.97.251     HTTP  Continuation or non-HTTP traffi
  22 0.000041  24.4.97.251     216.23.168.114 TCP   mpfoncl > http [ACK] Seq=1370
  27 0.148047  216.23.168.114 24.4.97.251     TCP   [TCP Dup ACK 21#1] http > mpfc
  29 64.877294 24.4.97.251     216.23.168.114 TCP   mpfoncl > http [FIN, CK] Seq=
  31 0.028895  216.23.168.114 24.4.97.251     TCP   http > mpfoncl [ACK] eq=1919
  32 0.000279  216.23.168.114 24.4.97.251     TCP   http > mpfoncl [FIN CK] Seq=
  33 0.000030  24.4.97.251     216.23.168.114 TCP   mpfoncl > http [ACK eq=1371 A
```

The client POST request is forbidden on this server

Figure 239. The client's post is unsuccessful and indicates a web server problem

Again, the problem does not appear to be a client issue and we do not see TCP transport errors as an issue. The problem is at the server.

When troubleshooting web browsing, look for TCP errors first before focusing on the HTTP traffic.

Dissect HTTP Packet Structures

HTTP packets are variable length. In this section we list some of the key areas in the HTTP packet structure. HTTP requests consist of a Method which defines the purpose of the HTTP request. HTTP responses contain a numerical response code referred to as a Status Code.

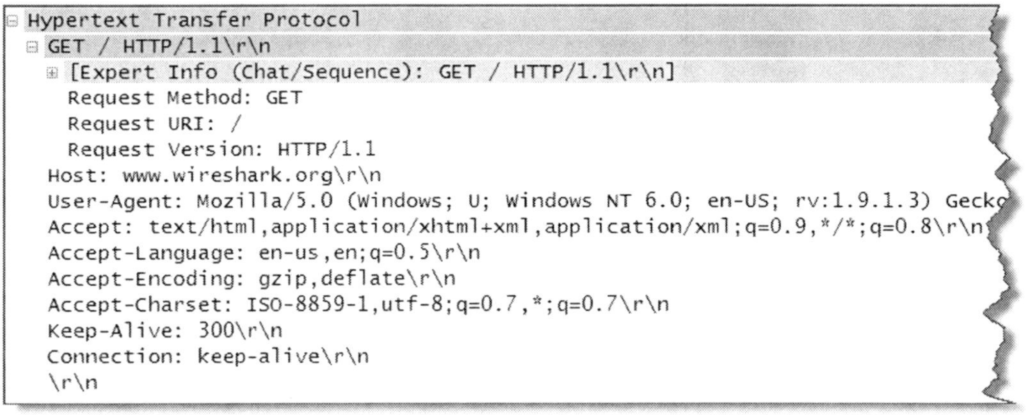

```
⊟ Hypertext Transfer Protocol
  ⊟ GET / HTTP/1.1\r\n
    ⊞ [Expert Info (Chat/Sequence): GET / HTTP/1.1\r\n]
      Request Method: GET
      Request URI: /
      Request Version: HTTP/1.1
    Host: www.wireshark.org\r\n
    User-Agent: Mozilla/5.0 (Windows; U; Windows NT 6.0; en-US; rv:1.9.1.3) Gecko
    Accept: text/html,application/xhtml+xml,application/xml;q=0.9,*/*;q=0.8\r\n
    Accept-Language: en-us,en;q=0.5\r\n
    Accept-Encoding: gzip,deflate\r\n
    Accept-Charset: ISO-8859-1,utf-8;q=0.7,*;q=0.7\r\n
    Keep-Alive: 300\r\n
    Connection: keep-alive\r\n
    \r\n
```

Figure 240. An HTTP GET request packet

HTTP Methods

Also referred to as the HTTP commands, the Methods define the purpose of the HTTP packet.

Method	Description
GET	Retrieves information defined by the URI (Uniform Resource Indicator) field
HEAD	Retrieves the meta data related to the desired URI
POST	Sends data to the HTTP server
OPTIONS	Determines the options associated with a resource
PUT	Sends data to the HTTP server
DELETE	Deletes the resource defined by the URI
TRACE	Invokes a remote loopback so the client can see what the server received from the client; this is rarely seen as many companies disable this to protect against a Cross-Site Tracing vulnerability
CONNECT	Connects to a proxy device

Host

The Host header field is required in all HTTP/1.1 request messages. The host field identifies the internet host and port number of the resource being requested. In our previous example, the host is *www.wireshark.org*. If no port number is specified, the default port for the service (for example, port 80 for HTTP).

Request Modifiers

HTTP requests and responses use request modifiers to provide details for the request. The following table lists the more commonly used request modifiers.

Request Modifiers	
Accept	Acceptable content types
Accept-Charset	Acceptable character sets
Accept-Encoding	Acceptable encodings
Accept-Language	Acceptable languages
Accept-Ranges	Server can accept range requests
Authorization	Authentication credentials for HTTP authentication
Cache-Control	Caching directives
Connection	Type of connection preferred by user agent
Cookie	HTTP cookie
Content-Length	Length of the request body (bytes)
Content-Type	Mime type of body (used with POST and PUT requests)
Date	Date and time message sent

Request Modifiers	
Expect	Defines server behavior expected by client
If-Match	Perform action if client-supplied information matches
If-Modified-Since	Provide date/time of cached data; 304 Not Modified if current
If-Range	Request for range of missing information
If-Unmodified-Since	Only send if unmodified since certain date/time
Max-Forwards	Limit number of forwards through proxies or gateways
Proxy-Authorization	Authorization credentials for proxy connection
Range	Request only part of an entity
Referrer	Address of previous website linking to current one
TE	Transfer encodings accepted
User-Agent	User agent—typically browser and operating system
Via	Proxies traversed

Filter on HTTP or HTTPS Traffic

The capture filter syntax for HTTP or HTTPS traffic is `tcp port http` or `tcp port https`.

If HTTP or HTTPS are running on non-standard ports, use the capture filter `tcp port x` where x denotes the port HTTP or HTTPS are using.

The display filter for HTTP is simply `http`. Note that this filter will only display HTTP packets that contain commands or responses. It will not display data packets or TCP ACKs. To view an entire HTTP session including data transferred during the HTTP session, use the display filter `tcp.port == 80` (or designate the port HTTP is using).

The filter for HTTP or HTTPS must be based on the port in use, such as port 443 for HTTPS (`tcp.port==443`). Alternately, you could use `ssl` as the display filter as HTTPS traffic uses Transport Layer Security (TLS) which is based on SSL.

The following table lists additional HTTP/HTTPS display filters.

Display Filter	Description
`http.request.method == "GET"`	HTTP GET request
`http.request.method == "POST"`	HTTP POST request
`http.response.code > 399`	HTTP 4xx or 5xx (client or server errors)
`http contains "If-Modified-Since"`	Determine if a client has cached a page already

Display Filter	Description
`http.host == "www.wireshark.org"`	Target host is *www.wireshark.org*
`http.user_agent contains "Firefox"`	HTTP client is using Firefox browser
`http.referer contains "wireshark.org"`	HTTP client has reached the current location from *wireshark.org*
`tcp.port == 443`	HTTPS
`ssl`	Secure Socket Layer (secure browsing session)
`ssl.record.content_type == 22`	TLSv1 handshake
`ssl.handshake.type == 1`	TLSv1 client hello in handshake
`ssl.handshake.type == 16`	TLSv1 client key exchange
`ssl.record.content_type == 20`	TLSv1 Change cipher spec
`http.content_type contains "ocsp"`	Online Certificate Status Protocol (OCSP) is used

Export HTTP Objects

Select **File** | **Export** | **Objects** | **HTTP** to save objects downloaded while using HTTP. When you export HTTP objects, the original object name is retained.

For examples of reassembling data downloaded during an HTTP session, refer to *Follow and Reassemble TCP Conversations* on page 238.

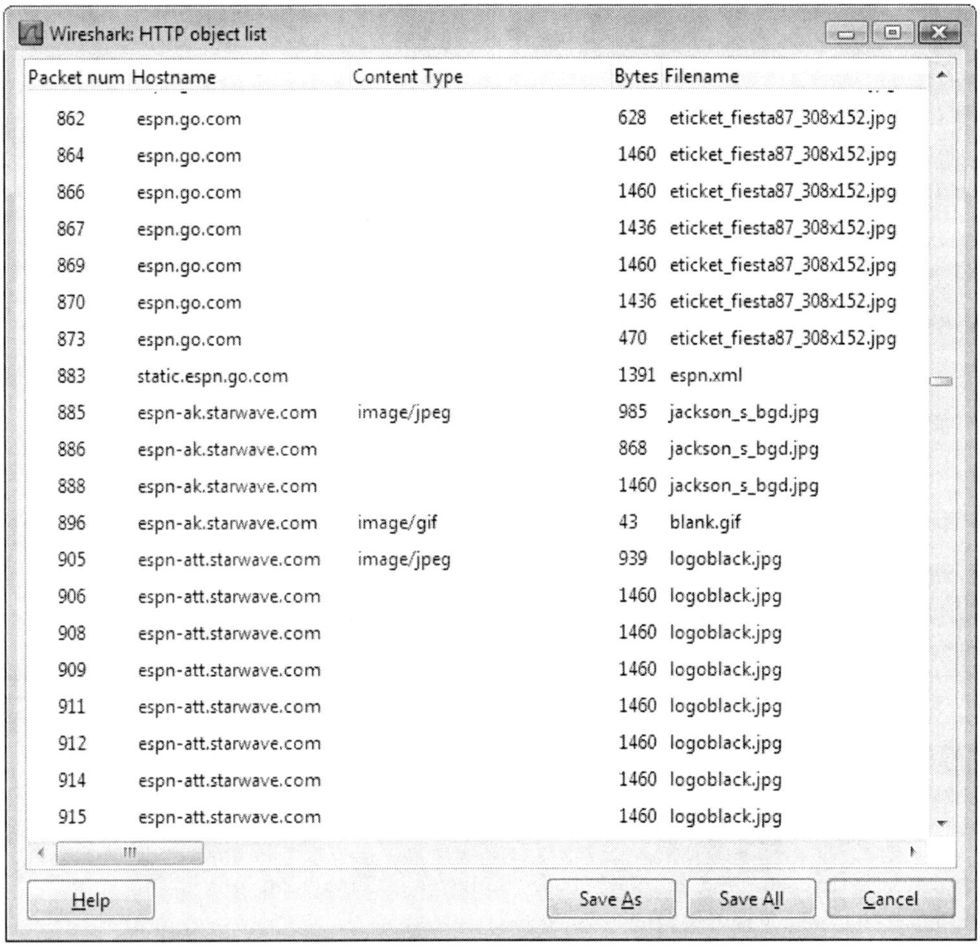

Figure 241. We can export the objects downloaded from a site we were referred to from ESPN's page.

Rebuild a Web Page Using Copy

When a client accesses a web site, typically it generates a GET request for the page. If the page is found, the server provides it to the client following an HTTP OK. To rebuild the page, disable the **"Allow subdissector to reassemble TCP streams"** setting, select the **"HTTP/1.0 200 OK"** packet in the Packet List pane. Expand the HTTP portion in the Packet Details pane and right click on **Line-based text data: text/html** and select **Copy | Bytes (Printable text only)**. Paste the buffered data into a text editor to rebuild the page. Save the file with an .html extension and open it in a browser. You will see the original page form.

Display HTTP Statistics

Wireshark tracks HTTP statistics for load distribution, packet counters, and HTTP requests. Select **Statistics | HTTP** and select the type of statistic you are interested in.

You are provided an option to apply a display filter to the statistics. For example, if you have a trace file that contains web browsing session to numerous hosts, you might apply an `http.host == www.wireshark.org` display filter to examine statistics for web browsing sessions to *www.wireshark.org* only.

HTTP Load Distribution

HTTP Load Distribution lists the HTTP requests and responses by server. Expanding the HTTP Requests by HTTP Host section lists the hosts contacted and the number of request packets sent to each one.

The HTTP Load Distribution statistic is an excellent resource for determining web site redirections and dependencies. In Figure 242 we are viewing the HTTP referrals and dependencies when we browse to *www.espn.com*.

Examining this statistic, we learned that a simple browsing session to *www.espn.com* creates HTTP sessions with 18 different servers that include content providing partners and advertisers. It is easy to understand why the *www.espn.com* site is slow to load.

Figure 242. The HTTP load distribution defines the number of servers we contacted when browsing to www.espn.com

HTTP Packet Counter

When analyzing HTTP communications, the HTTP Packet Counter is invaluable because it lists the Status Code responses. Spotting 4xx Client Error or 5xx Server Error responses is simple.

Figure 243 shows the HTTP Packet Counter for our browsing session to *www.espn.com*. We can see some HTTP 301 and 304 redirections and a 404 Not Found response.

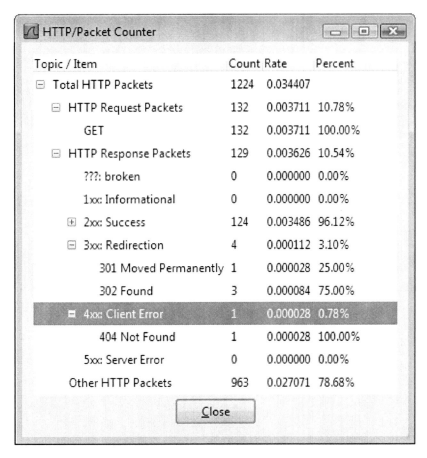

Figure 243. The HTTP Packet Counter displays the HTTP request method and the Status Code responses

HTTP Requests

HTTP Requests lists each item requested of each HTTP server. In Figure 244, we are examining the HTTP Requests sent during our web browsing session to *www.espn.com*. As you can see, we downloaded content from *doubleclick.net* during our browsing session.

Figure 244. The HTTP Request statistic details each HTTP request made to each HTTP server

Graph HTTP Traffic Flows

Flow Graphs provide a visual representation of the communications that occur during an HTTP session. This is an ideal statistic window to open when troubleshooting slow web browsing sessions. Each target host is listed in a column and every packet is listed in a row.

Create a Flow Graph to Spot Web Site Dependencies

Consider creating a Flow Graph based on your web browsing traffic. Capture your own browsing traffic to a popular website and notice the number of columns created because of other linked servers.

Select **Statistics | Flow Graph** to choose the three options for viewing the Flow Graph window, as shown in Figure 245.

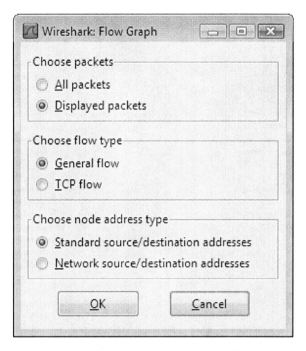

Figure 245. Create Flow Graphs based on the general flow or just the TCP headers

Choose Packets

You can graph the flow of all packets in the trace file or just the displayed packets. If your trace file contains more than one conversation, you may want to filter on the conversation you want to graph and then open the Flow Graph window.

Choose Flow Type

The general flow view includes application-layer information, such as requests and replies. The TCP Flow Graph shows just the TCP header values such as the sequence number and acknowledgment number value and the TCP flag settings.

Choose Node Address Type

The Standard source/destination addresses option shows IP addresses of devices listed in the graph and is the recommended setting due to space constraints when many hosts are communicating with each other. Choose the network source/destination addresses if you are using network name resolution with Wireshark.

Figure 246 shows the Flow Graph for our web browsing session to *www.espn.com*. The Flow Graph contains 20 IP address columns (the HTTP client, the DNS server and the 18 HTTP servers that we contacted when browsing to *www.espn.com*).

Wireshark will highlight the corresponding packet when you click on a packet description in the IP address column.

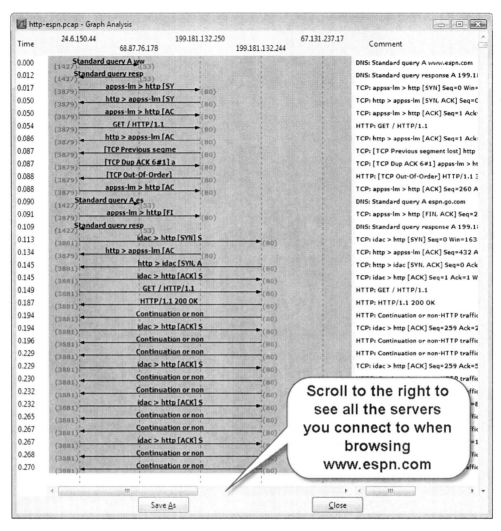

Figure 246. The Flow Graph adds a column for each host in the trace file

After creating a Flow Graph, click **Save As** to save the contents of the Flow Graph in a text file. Depending on the number of IP address columns depicted in the Flow Graph, the text file width could be extremely wide and may print best in landscape mode.

Set HTTP Preferences

There are seven preference settings for HTTP communications as shown in the HTTP Preferences window as shown in Figure 247.

One of the important settings that may need to be changed is the TCP Ports list. These are the ports associated with the HTTP dissector and the SSL/TLS port number to associate with the SSL/TLS dissector. Ensure the port used by your HTTP communications is listed in TCP Ports.

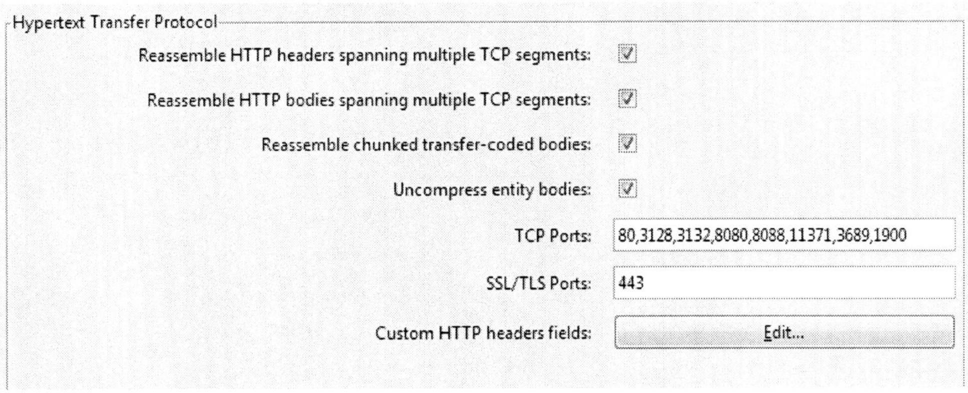

```
┌─Hypertext Transfer Protocol─────────────────────────────────────────────────┐
│        Reassemble HTTP headers spanning multiple TCP segments:   ☑           │
│         Reassemble HTTP bodies spanning multiple TCP segments:   ☑           │
│              Reassemble chunked transfer-coded bodies:   ☑                   │
│                        Uncompress entity bodies:   ☑                        │
│                                                                              │
│                              TCP Ports:  80,3128,3132,8080,8088,11371,3689,1900│
│                                                                              │
│                          SSL/TLS Ports:  443                                 │
│                                                                              │
│               Custom HTTP headers fields:  [         Edit...         ]       │
└──────────────────────────────────────────────────────────────────────────────┘
```

Figure 247. The HTTP Preferences settings

Analyze HTTPS Communications

Your web browsing analysis will likely include analysis of HTTPS communications. At the start of a secure HTTP conversation, a standard TCP handshake is executed followed by a secure handshake process.

RFC 2818 defines the use of HTTP over TLS[84] for secure communications. RFC 2246 details Transport Layer Security version 1.0 which is based on SSL version 3.0. Although there are minimal differences between TLS 1.0 and SSL 3.0, the two are not interoperable.

When working with HTTPS traffic, enable your TCP preferences to "Allow subdissector to reassemble TCP streams" as shown in Figure 248. This enables you to see and filter all four SSL/TLS handshake packets[85].

---

[84] TLS is the successor to Secure Socket Layer (SSL). In this chapter we will refer to the two protocols collectively as TLS/SSL.

[85] When analyzing standard HTTP communications, we recommend you disable the "Allow subdissector to reassemble TCP streams" to see the HTTP requests and responses in the Packet List Info column.

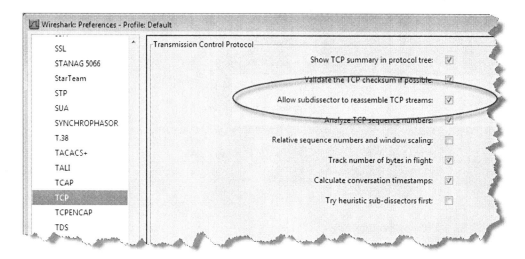

Figure 248. Allow the subdissector to reassemble TCP streams when working with HTTPS traffic

The HTTPS Handshake

The HTTPS communication begins with the TCP handshake on the port that will be used for the secure communications. In our example, we are using the standard HTTPS port number 443. If you are using another port for SSL/TLS traffic, add those ports in the HTTP preferences setting for SSL/TLS ports. Port 443 is already defined by default.

In this chapter we examine the encrypted traffic first and then we will copy the decryption key to the local drive and add the path to the key in the SSL preferences setting in Wireshark.

The SSL/TLS handshake consists of a series of packets with a content type value of 22. Use the display filter `ssl.record.content_type == 22` to view just the SSL/TLS handshake packets as shown in Figure 249.

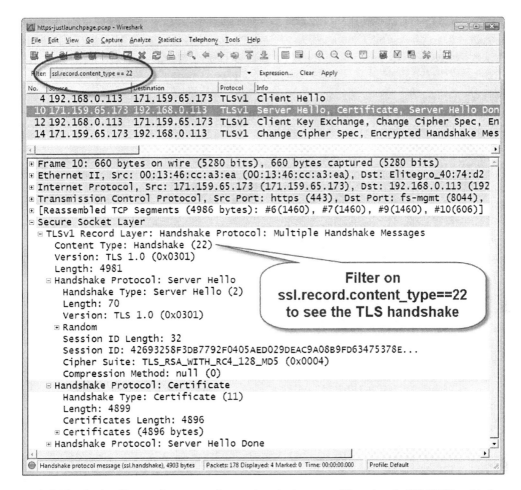

Figure 249. The display filter `ssl.record.content_type==22` *to view the SSL/TLS handshake*

The first packet of the SSL/TLS handshake is a Client Hello as noted in the handshake protocol field. The client also denotes that it is using TLS version 1.0.

This packet also contains the Universal Coordinated Time (UTC) at the client provided in UNIX format. The Session ID field is set at 0 which indicates this is a new session. If the Session ID field contains a non-zero value, this is a resumed session.

This packet also contains 28 random bytes which will be used later in this handshake.

The client provides the list of cipher suites supported by the browser. In this case, the client supports 34 cipher suites and lists them all in the Client Hello packet as shown in Figure 250. Ultimately, the server will make the decision of which cipher suite to use, but the top cipher listed is the client's preference.

Extensions add functionality to SSL/TLS. The presence of extensions is detected because there are bytes following the Compression Methods field at the end of the Client Hello packet.

One extension provides the server name, which in this case is *www.bankofamerica.com* as is shown in the packet bytes pane at the bottom of Figure 249. The server name extension enables the client to create a secure connection to a virtual server that may be hosted on a machine that supports numerous servers at a single IP address.

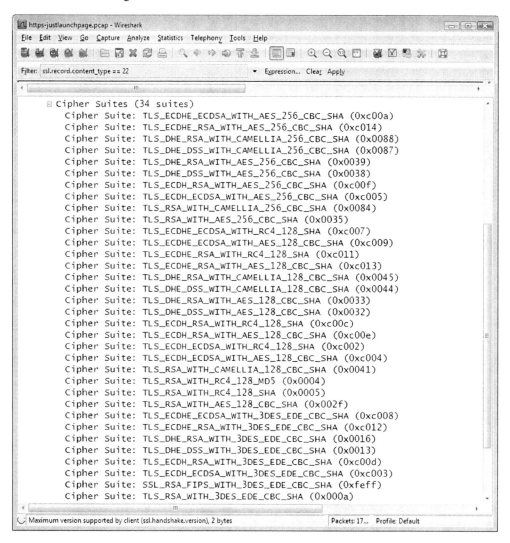

Figure 250. The client lists 34 supported cipher suites; the server will choose which will be used

The Server responds with a packet that consists of three functions. It is a Server Hello packet, a Certificate packet and a Server Hello Done packet as shown in Figure 249. The server indicates that it will use TLS 1.0 for the connection.

In the Random section, the server provides 28 random bytes (that will be used later in this connection) and a 32-byte Session ID value to allow the client to reconnect later.

Out of the 34 cipher suites offered, the server has selected TLS_RSA_with_RC4_128_MD5 (0x0004) which means:

- The RSA public key algorithm will be used to verify certificate signatures and exchange keys.
- The RC4 encryption algorithm will be used to encrypt data exchanged.
- The 128-bit MD5 hash function will be used to verify the contents of the messages exchanged.

This second packet of the handshake process also includes the certificate from the server. Inside this same packet, the server includes Server Hello Done to indicate that the server is done with the Hello process.

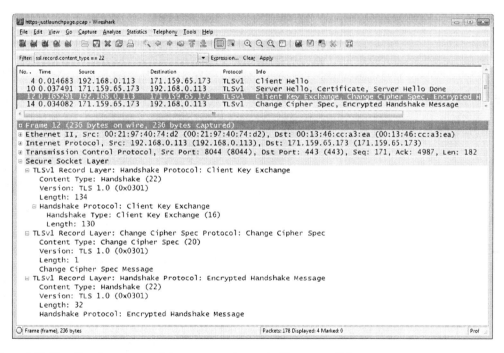

Figure 251. The client has computed the premaster key and will encrypt all future messages

The next packet from the client indicates that the client has computed a premaster secret from both the client and server random values. The Change Cipher Spec designation indicates that all future messages from the client will be encrypted using the keys and algorithms defined.

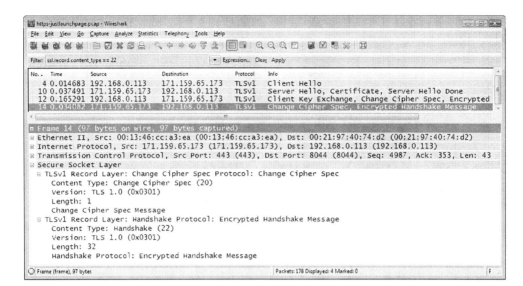

Figure 252. The server indicates it will encrypt all future messages

The handshake process finishes with the server indicating that all future messages it sends will be encrypted as well.

Decrypt HTTPS Traffic

We must have the RSA key and configure Wireshark to use it in order for Wireshark to decrypt the HTTPS traffic.

To decrypt this data, we need the private key of the server certificate. To get the private key, you need access to the server—you cannot get the private key from client side of the communication. Since our example used a browsing session to Bank of America's website and we do not have the ability to obtain the key, we will focus on another HTTPS trace file that was provided with the key.

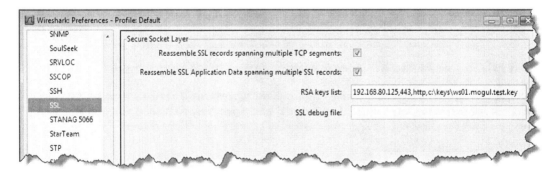

Figure 253. Enter the path to the RSA key file to decrypt the traffic.

In November 2009, Steve Dispensa and Marsh Ray of PhoneFactor wrote an 8-page overview of the security issues surrounding the TLS renegotiation process. The security issues were demonstrated against recent Microsoft IIS and Apache HTTPD versions. In essence, the renegotiate attack method defined is used to inject malicious code into the "secure" connection.

You can read the Case Study from Steve Dispensa in *Chapter 30: Network Forensics Overview*.

In the following example, we are working with the *client_init_renego.pcap* file provided as a supplement with the PhoneFactor document. In addition, PhoneFactor provided an RSA key named *ws01.mogul.test.key*.

To decrypt the HTTPS traffic, we copied the RSA key into a *keys* directory on the local Wireshark host. In order for Wireshark to recognize the key we must configure the SSL preferences to recognize the conversation we want to decrypt and point to the *keys* directory. Wireshark's RSA keys list setting includes the IP address of the server, the port used for the encrypted communications, the name of the application that is encrypted and the path to the key as well as the key name.

Figure 253 shows the settings used.

```
192.168.80.125,443,http,c:\keys\ws01.mogul.test.key
```

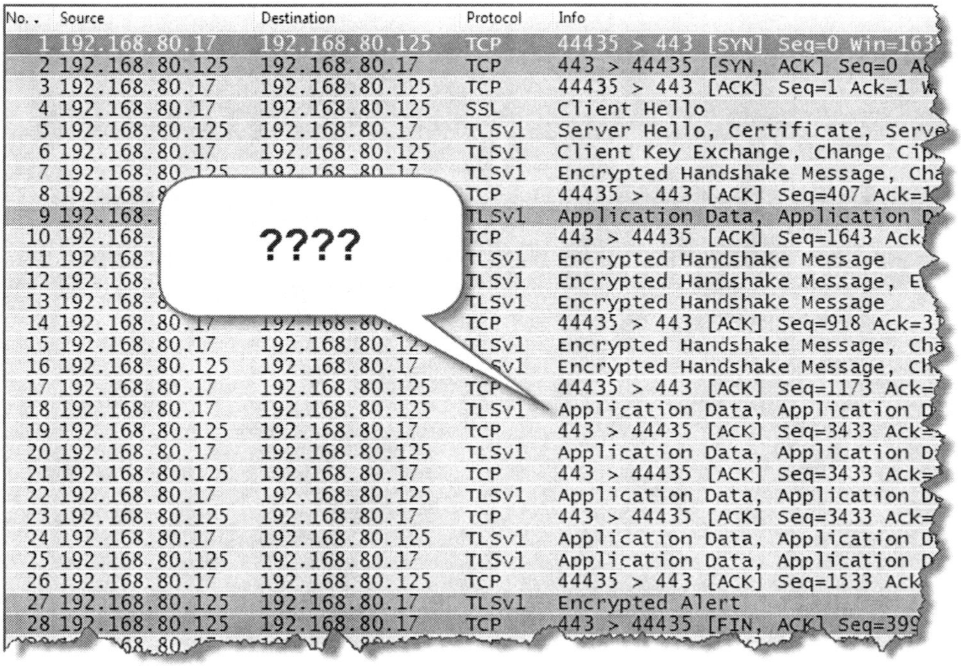

Figure 254. The HTTPS traffic cannot be decrypted without the RSA key configuration

Figure 254 shows the trace file before we provided the key. Notice the Protocol column indicates TCP, SSL or TLSv1. We cannot see decrypted traffic yet.

Figure 255 shows the results of applying the key. We still see TCP and TLSv1 in the Protocol column but we also see HTTP listed for the decrypted traffic. In addition, we can now right click on an HTTP packet listed in the Packet List pane and select **Follow SSL Stream** to clearly see the communications.

No. .	Source	Destination	Protocol	Info
1	192.168.80.17	192.168.80.125	TCP	44435 > 443 [SYN] Seq=0 Win=1638
2	192.168.80.125	192.168.80.17	TCP	443 > 44435 [SYN, ACK] Seq=0 Ack
3	192.168.80.17	192.168.80.125	TCP	44435 > 443 [ACK] Seq=1 Ack=1 Wi
4	192.168.80.17	192.168.80.125	TLSv1	Client Hello
5	192.168.80.125	192.168.80.17	TLSv1	Server Hello, Certificate, Serv
6	192.168.80.17	192.168.80.125	TLSv1	Client Key Exchange, Change Ciph
7	192.168.80.125	192.168.80.17	TLSv1	Encrypted Handshake Message, Cha
8	192.168.80.17	192.168.80.125	TCP	44435 > 443 [ACK] Seq=407 Ack=1
9	192.168.80.17	192.168.80.125	SSL	[SSL segment of a reassembled PD
10	192.168.80.125	192.168.80.17	TCP	443 > 44435 [ACK] Seq=1643 Ack=
11	19...		TLSv1	Client Hello
12	19...		TLSv1	Server Hello, Certificate,
13	19...		TLSv1	Server Hello Done
14	19...		...P	44435 > 443 [ACK] Seq=918 Ack=3
15	19...		...v1	Client Key Exchange, Change Ciph
16	192...		TLS...1	Encrypted Handshake Message, Ch
17	192.168.80.17	192.168.80.125	TCP	44435 > 443 [ACK] Seq=1173 Ack=
18	192.168.80.17	192.168.80.125	HTTP	Continuation or non-HTTP traffi
19	192.168.80.125	192.168.80.17	TCP	443 > 44435 [ACK] Seq=3433 Ack=
20	192.168.80.17	192.168.80.125	HTTP	Continuation or non-HTTP traffi
21	192.168.80.125	192.168.80.17	TCP	443 > 44435 [ACK] Seq=3433 Ack=
22	192.168.80.17	192.168.80.125	HTTP	Continuation or non-HTTP traffi
23	192.168.80.125	192.168.80.17	TCP	443 > 44435 [ACK] Seq=3433 Ack=
24	192.168.80.17	192.168.80.125	HTTP	Continuation or non-HTTP traffi
25	192.168.80.125	192.168.80.17	HTTP	HTTP/1.1 404 Not Found (text/ht
26	192.168.80.17	192.168.80.125	TCP	44435 > 443 [ACK] Seq=1533 Ack=3
27	192.168.80.125	192.168.80.17	TLSv1	Alert (Level: Warning, Descript
28	192.168.80.125	192.168.80.17	TCP	443 > 44435 [FIN, ACK] Seq=3997

Callout: Decrypted as HTTP communications

Figure 255. Once the key is configured and applied, we can see the HTTP communications clearly

 The Phone Factor report, trace files, keys and protocol diagrams are located in the Download section on the book website, *www.wiresharkbook.com*. To stay up to date on the SSL/TLS vulnerability, visit *www.phonefactor.com/sslgap*.

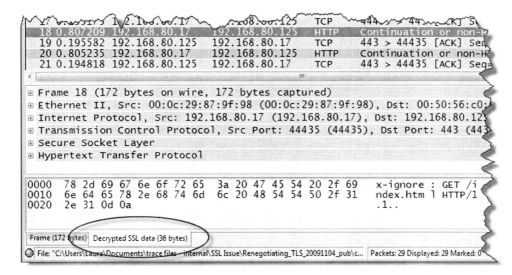

Figure 256. A decryption tag appears below the packet bytes pane when you have applied decryption to the traffic

When you decrypt SSL/TLS traffic (just as when you decrypt WLAN traffic), a tab appears just below the Packet Bytes pane. Click the **Decrypted SSL data** tab to view the decrypted traffic in the packet bytes pane. This tab will only appear when you have (a) decrypted traffic and (b) make the packet bytes pane visible.

Case Study:
HTTP Proxy Problems

Submitted by: **Richard Hicks**
                    Senior Sales Engineer, Product Specialist
                    Edge Security Solutions, Celestix Networks, Inc.

When troubleshooting connectivity issues through proxy servers that perform application layer traffic inspection, having a tool like Wireshark is invaluable.

A common scenario is one in which requests made through a router or simple packet filtering firewall work without issue, yet the same request made through a proxy fails.

An example of this was brought to my attention recently when a customer called our support team with just this complaint. Attempts to access a third-party web-based application were failing when accessed through the proxy, in this case a Microsoft ISA Server 2006.

The error message received was an ambiguous HTTP 502 error, an indication that the proxy objected to the request for a reason that was not readily apparent. Since the client could access the application when communicating directly through a router, naturally the customer assumed that the ISA firewall must be broken.

Knowing that the ISA firewall performs application layer traffic inspection, of course I knew that wasn't the case.

Immediately I was able to reproduce the error and used Wireshark to capture traffic on both sides of the proxy. What I found was most interesting.

Looking at the response from the application server, the trace showed that the request version was HTTP 2.0 (as shown on the next page).

```
⊟ Hypertext Transfer Protocol
  ⊟ HTTP/2.0 302 Found\r\n
        Request Version: HTTP/2.0
        Response Code: 302
     Server: SmarterTools/2.0.2692.18364\r\n
     Date: Fri, 16 Jan 2009 19:06:41 GMT\r\n
     X-AspNet-Version: 2.0.50727\r\n
     Location: /Login.aspx\r\n
     Set-Cookie: ASP.NET_SessionId=fd211145nf5wum45td
     Cache-Control: private\r\n
     Content-Type: text/html; charset=utf-8\r\n
  ⊞ Content-Length: 128\r\n
     Connection: Close\r\n
```

Fascinating, because there is no RFC specification for HTTP 2.0! The ISA firewall, with its deep application layer inspection capabilities, limits communication over TCP port 80 to only valid, RFC-compliant HTTP. Since this was technically a violation of the RFC, the ISA firewall denied the traffic.

Uncovering these details would not have been possible without Wireshark.

Summary

HTTP uses a request/response model to transfer data between hosts. HTTP communications use TCP as the transport mechanism—the most commonly used HTTP port number is 80.

Clients send commands such as GET and POST to the HTTP server. HTTP servers respond with a numerical response code. Codes greater than 399 identify client and server errors. Many people are familiar with the dreaded "404 Not Found" response seen when a page does not exist.

When analyzing HTTP communications, watch for the "If-Modified-Since" request modifier. This indicates that the client has a page in cache. If the server responds with code 304 Not Modified, the client will load the page from cache instead of across the network. This will affect your web loading time analysis.

Slow web browsing sessions can be caused by TCP problems as well as interdependencies on other web sites (such as advertisers), and non optimized web sites. Wisher enables you to rebuild web pages and export HTTP objects.

HTTPS traffic uses TLS to create a secure connection for HTTP traffic. These connections begin with a TCP connection which is followed by a secure handshake connection. During this connection process, the client and server negotiate security parameters such as the cipher suite that will be used for the secure communications.

Wireshark can decrypt HTTPS sessions as long as you have the decryption key and configure Wireshark to apply that key to the HTTPS conversation. The Phone Factor report, trace files, decryption keys and protocol diagrams are located in Download section on the book website, *www.wiresharkbook.com*. To stay up to date on the SSL/TLS vulnerability information released by Phone Factor, visit *www.phonefactor.com/sslgap*.

Practice What You've Learned

 The following table lists several trace files available from the Download section on the book website, *www.wiresharkbook.com*. Download and use these trace files to practice analyzing HTTP communications.

http-winpcap.pcap   This trace contains a web browsing session to *www.winpcap.org*.

How long did the DNS server take to respond to the DNS request?

Will this connection support window scaling?

What browser do you think the user is running? What operating system do you think the user is running?

Does the client want to load any of the website from cache?

What is the size of the new.gif file? What image does the new.gif file contain?

Does this site contain references to other web sites? How long did it take to load this site? (Do not count the FIN process.)

https-justlaunchpage.pcap	In this trace file we have simply opened a website. You'll see the HTTPS handshake after the TCP handshake.
	What site did we connect to?
	How many cipher suites were offered to the HTTPS server?
	Which cipher suite was chosen for this HTTPS connection?
	How long did it take the load the website? (Do not include the FIN process.)
https-ssl3session.pcap	There appear to be some problems during the establishment of this SSL connection (HTTPS).
	Hint: Disable **Preferences	Protocols	TCP	Allow subdissector to reassemble TCP streams** when examining the SSL/TLS handshake process.
	What problems occur during the HTTPS connection?
	How many cipher suites were offered to the HTTPS server?
	Which cipher suite was chosen for this HTTPS connection?

Review Questions

Q23.1   You are analyzing an HTTP session as a user browses a new website. What HTTP response code should be sent by an HTTP server after the client sends an *HTTP GET / HTTP/1.1* request?

Q23.2   How is an HTTP 404 Not Found categorized?

Q23.3   How can you determine that a client is loading web pages out of cache?

Q23.4   What display filter should you *avoid* if you want to view the TCP handshake and TCP ACKs during a web browsing session?

Q23.5   What is the HTTP request method used to send data up to an HTTP server?

Q23.6   What is the syntax for capture and display filters for HTTP traffic running over port 80?

Q23.7   How can you configure Wireshark to always recognize port 444 as an SSL/TLS port?

Q23.8   What steps are required to decrypt HTTPS traffic with Wireshark?

Q23.9   Which side of an HTTPS communication offers a list of acceptable cipher suites and which side of the HTTPS communication selects the desired cipher suite to use?

Answers to Review Questions

Q23.1   **You are analyzing an HTTP session as a user browses a new website. What HTTP response code should be sent by an HTTP server after the client sends an *HTTP GET / HTTP/1.1* request?**

A23.1   The HTTP response code 200 indicates that the desired page was located successfully.

Q23.2   **How is an HTTP 404 Not Found categorized?**

A23.2   This response is categorized as a client error (even though it may be caused by an invalid link on a website).

Q23.3   **How can you determine that a client is loading web pages out of cache?**

A23.3   To determine that a client is loading web pages from cache, look for the If-Modified-Since request modifier from the client or a response code 304 Not Modified.

Q23.4   **What display filter should you *avoid* if you want to view the TCP handshake and TCP ACKs during a web browsing session?**

A23.4   The `http` display filter will not display the TCP handshake or the TCP ACKs during the session. Consider using `tcp.port==80` to view the entire HTTP conversation.

Q23.5   **What is the HTTP request method used to send data up to an HTTP server?**

A23.5   HTTP clients use *POST* to send data up to an HTTP server.

Q23.6   **What is the syntax for capture and display filters for HTTP traffic running over port 80?**

A23.6   Capture filter: `tcp port http`
Display filter: `http`

Q23.7   **How can you configure Wireshark to always recognize port 444 as an SSL/TLS port?**

A23.7 To add port 444 as an SSL/TLS port, select **Edit | Preferences | Protocols | HTTP** and add port 444 in the SSL/TLS ports section.

Q23.8 **What steps are required to decrypt HTTPS traffic with Wireshark?**

A23.8 You must obtain the decryption key and copy it to your Wireshark system. Next you must configure Wireshark's SSL preferences RSA Key List setting with the proper syntax. The HTTPS session should be decrypted when you load the HTTPS traffic trace file.

Q23.9 **Which side of an HTTPS communication offers a list of acceptable cipher suites and which side of the HTTPS communication selects the desired cipher suite to use?**

A23.9 The HTTPS client offers a list of acceptable cipher suites and the HTTPS server selects the cipher suite to use for the communication.

Chapter 24: Analyze File Transfer Protocol (FTP) Traffic

Wireshark Certified Network Analyst Exam Objectives covered:

- The Purpose of FTP
- Analyze Normal FTP Communications
- Analyze FTP Problems
- Dissect the FTP Packet Structure
- Filter on FTP Traffic
- Reassemble FTP Traffic

   ❖ Case Study: Secret FTP Communications
   ❖ Summary
   ❖ Practice What You've Learned
   ❖ Review Questions and Answers

The Purpose of FTP

FTP is used to transfer files over TCP as shown in Figure 257 and is covered in RFC 959. TFTP (Trivial File Transfer Protocol) uses connectionless transport (UDP). In this chapter we focus on FTP only.

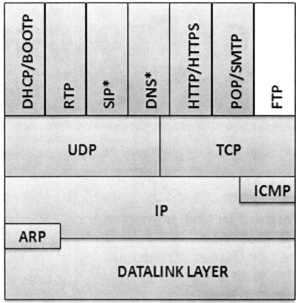

Figure 257. FTP uses TCP for transport

In a typical FTP communication, a command channel is established to port 21 on the FTP server. To transfer data (such as directory contents or files), a secondary data channel is established using dynamic port numbers. The specification defines that port 20 is to be used for the data channel, but in reality, you will notice dynamic port numbers in use for this channel.

Analyze Normal FTP Communications

FTP connections begin with a TCP handshake followed by the client waiting for the banner.

Clients issue commands and servers respond with numerical codes. You can create a filter looking for all hosts attempting to login to an FTP server using the display filter `ftp.request.command == "USER"`.

Although you may type "PUT" at the command line, FTP translates this command into STOR in the packets. Likewise, when you type "GET", FTP translates this to RETR in the packet. The following table lists the standard FTP client commands.

Client Command	Description
USER	Identifies the user accessing the FTP server
PASS	Indicates the user's password
CWD	Change working directory
QUIT	Terminates the connection
PORT	Sets up a data connection IP address and port number at the client (active mode FTP)
PASV	Requests the server to listen on a non-default data port for the client to establish a data connection (passive mode FTP)
TYPE	Indicates the type of data to be transferred
RETR	Retrieve a file from the FTP server
STOR	Send a file to the FTP server
DELE	Delete a file
RMD	Remove a directory
MKD	Make a directory
PWD	Print (display) working directory contents
NSLT	Name list—displays directory on server
HELP	Shows commands supported by the server

You can create a filter for individual or groups of FTP response codes. For example, the filter `ftp.response.code == 227` displays all responses indicating that an FTP server has entered passive mode. The following table lists the standard server response codes for FTP communications.

Response Code	Description
110	Restart marker reply. In this case, the text is exact and not left to the particular implementation; it must read: MARK yyyy = mmmm where yyyy is User-process data stream marker, and mmmm server's equivalent marker (note the spaces between markers and "=").
120	Service ready in nnn minutes.
125	Data connection already open; transfer starting.
150	File status okay; about to open data connection.
200	Command okay.
202	Command not implemented, superfluous at this site.

Response Code	Description
211	System status, or system help reply.
212	Directory status.
213	File status.
214	Help message. On how to use the server or the meaning of a particular non-standard command. This reply is useful only to the human user.
215	NAME system type. Where NAME is an official system name from the list in the Assigned Numbers document.
220	Service ready for new user.
221	Service closing control connection. Logged out if appropriate.
225	Data connection open; no transfer in progress.
226	Closing data connection. Requested file action successful (for example, file transfer or file abort).
227	Entering Passive Mode (h1,h2,h3,h4,p1,p2) where h1,h2,h3,h4 indicates the IP address and p1,p2 indicates the port number
230	User logged in, proceed.
250	Requested file action okay, completed.
257	"PATHNAME" created.
331	User name okay, need password.
332	Need account for login.
350	Requested file action pending further information.
421	Service not available, closing control connection. This may be a reply to any command if the service knows it must shut down.
425	Can't open data connection.
426	Connection closed; transfer aborted.
450	Requested file action not taken. File unavailable (e.g., file busy).
451	Requested action aborted: local error in processing.
452	Requested action not taken. Insufficient storage space in system.
500	Syntax error, command unrecognized. This may include errors such as command line too long.
501	Syntax error in parameters or arguments.

Response Code	Description
502	Command not implemented.
503	Bad sequence of commands.
504	Command not implemented for that parameter.
530	Not logged in.
532	Need account for storing files.
550	Requested action not taken. File unavailable (e.g., file not found, no access).
551	Requested action aborted: page type unknown.
552	Requested file action aborted. Exceeded storage allocation (for current directory or dataset).
553	Requested action not taken. File name not allowed.

The FTP client sends the USER command (all FTP commands are in upper case) followed by a username then the PASS command followed by the password. If the FTP username is incorrect, the server still responds with 331 Password Required for *username*. If the password is incorrect, the server responds with 530 Password Not Accepted. Once the user is logged in, they can use commands to examine the directory contents, change directories and launch a second channel for data transfer.

Data transfer takes place over a separate connection from the command connection. Data transferred may be a file or the contents of a directory.

There are two modes for data transfer—passive mode and active mode.

Analyze Passive Mode Connections
The PASV command is issued by the client to request that the server listen for a separate connection to be established by the FTP client. When the server responds to the PASV command, it includes its IP address and the port number that it will be listening on for the PASV connection.

Figure 258 shows a portion of an FTP connection (this trace does not contain the TCP handshake or TCP ACK packets). The client changes the working directory (CWD) and then sets the representation type to I for image or binary.

In packet 7, the client sends the PASV command.

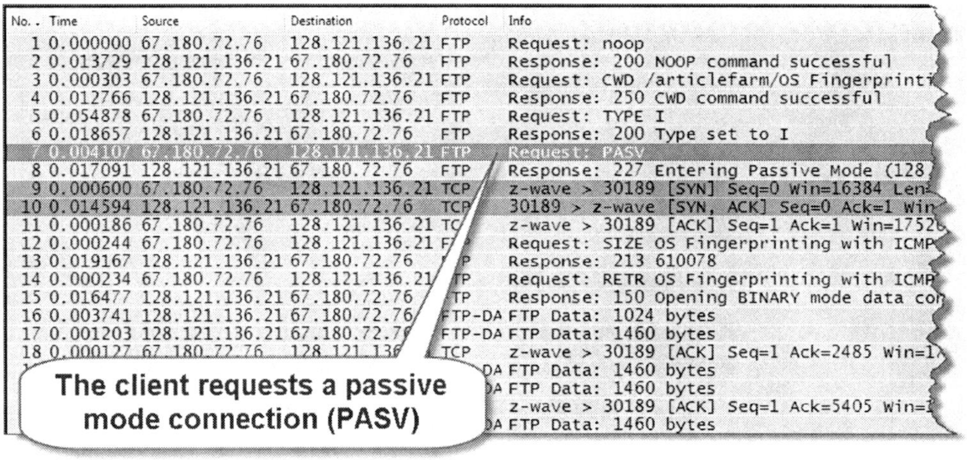

Figure 258. An FTP passive mode connection for data transfer

Wireshark can interpret the 227 response that indicates the server is entering passive mode as shown in Figure 259. FTP commands flow over the command channel while data travels across the second channel established using the PASV command. In our example, the client issues the retrieve command (RETR) and the server responds with code 150 to indicate it is opening a binary mode data connection for the file transfer.

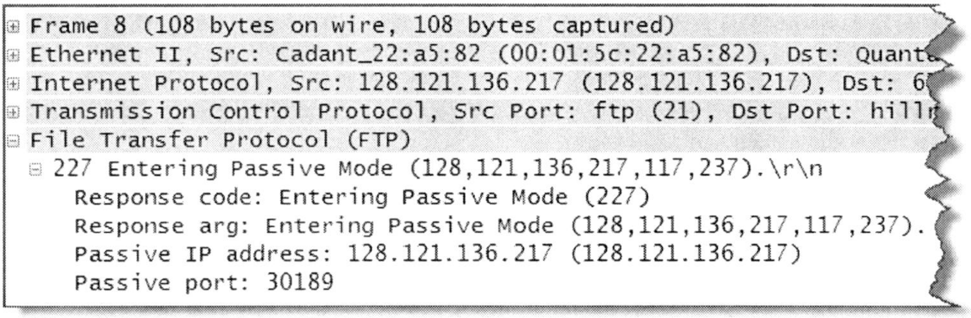

Figure 259. The response to PASV includes IP address and port number the server will listen on

You can use the display filter `ftp || ftp-data` to view both the FTP command channel and the FTP data channel. Wireshark is smart! Since FTP data channel traffic can be run over a dynamically defined port number, Wireshark parses the address and port information contained in packets that contain the PORT command or in response packets to the PASV command to identify traffic that should match the `ftp-data` filter.

Some FTP servers may not support passive mode data transfers. For an example of such a case, refer to *Analyze FTP Problems* on page 484.

Analyze Active Mode Connections

In an active mode data transfer, the client issues the PORT command and indicates the IP address and port number that it will listen on for a data channel connection that will be established by the server.

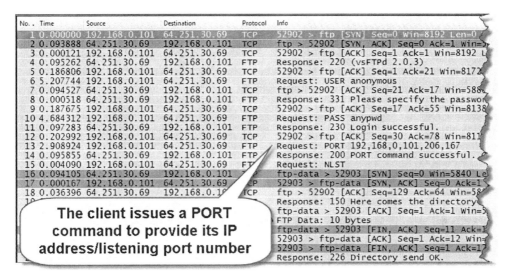

Figure 260. The FTP client issues a PORT command to establish an active mode channel for data transfer

In Figure 260 the FTP client has logged in and issued the PORT command to transfer a directory list (NLST). The PORT command packet includes the client's IP address and port on which it will listen to the server's connection request.

```
⊞ Frame 13 (82 bytes on wire, 82 bytes captured)
⊞ Ethernet II, Src: Intel_d0:27:d7 (00:18:de:d0:27:d7), D
⊞ Internet Protocol, Src: 192.168.0.101 (192.168.0.101),
⊞ Transmission Control Protocol, Src Port: 52902 (52902),
⊟ File Transfer Protocol (FTP)
   ⊟ PORT 192,168,0,101,206,167\r\n
      Request command: PORT
      Request arg: 192,168,0,101,206,167
      Active IP address: 192.168.0.101 (192.168.0.101)
      Active port: 52903
```

Figure 261. The FTP PORT command includes the client IP address and port for the data connection

Analyze FTP Problems

FTP communication problems begin with the TCP handshake. If a server does not have the FTP daemon running, it responds to TCP SYN packets on the FTP port with a TCP RST response. If the FTP server is configured to use a different port than the client uses, the FTP connection cannot be established properly.

In addition, if a firewall blocks passive mode support, the passive mode connection attempt will fail as shown in Figure 262. In this example, the client sends the PASV command and the server responds with its IP address and a port number for the passive mode connection. This indicates that the server itself supports passive mode connections.

The client attempts to make a connection on the port provided, but the server does not respond to the connection attempts. If the port is open, the server should respond with a SYN/ACK. If the port is closed, the server should respond with a TCP RST response. If no response is received, a firewall along the path or on the server may be blocking connection attempts to this port. After five attempts to make a connection, the client gives up. In addition, the client does a graceful shutdown of the command channel.

The server responds with the message "You could at least say goodbye." What attitude!

```
26 0.003413 207.33.247.67   192.233.80.108 FTP   Request: PWD
27 0.059446 192.233.80.108 207.33.247.67  FTP   Response: 257 "/" is current directory.
28 0.001022 207.33.247.67   192.233.80.108 FTP   Request: PASV
29 0.098251 192.233.80.108 207.33.247.67  TCP   ftp > 3ds-lm [ACK] Seq=4267 Ack=57 Win=876
30 0.021251 192.233.80.108 207.33.247.67  FTP   Response: 227 Entering Passive Mode (192,2
31 0.006504 207.33.247.67   192.233.80.108 TCP   intellistor-lm > 22807 [SYN] Seq=0 Win=819
32 0.177388 207.33.247.67   192.233.80.108 TCP   3ds-lm > ftp [ACK] Seq=57 Ack=4317 Win=75
33 2.805024 207.33.247.67   192.233.80.108 TCP   intellistor-lm > 22807 [SYN] Seq=0 Win=81
34 6.035010 207.33.247.67   192.233.80.108 TCP   intellistor-lm > 22807 [SYN] Seq=0 Win=819
35 12.04998 207.33.247.67   192.233.80.108 TCP   intellistor-lm > 22807 [SYN] Seq=0 Win=81
36 24.04856 207.33.247.67   192.233.80.108 TCP   [TCP Port numbers reused] intellistor-lm
37 0.031289 207.33.247.67   192.233.80.108 TCP   3ds-lm > ftp [FIN, ACK] Seq=57 Ack=4317 W
38 0.054821 192.233.80.108 207.33.247.67  TCP   ftp > 3ds-lm [ACK] Seq=4317 Ack=58 Win=87
39 0.004732 192.233.80.108 207.33.247.67  FTP   Response: 221 You could at least say goodb
40 0.000169 207.33.247.67   192.233.80.108 TCP   3ds-lm > ftp [RST] Seq=58 Win=0 Len=0
41 0.002592 192.233.80.108 207.33.247.67  TCP   ftp > 3ds-lm [FIN, ACK] Seq=4354 Ack=58 W
42 0.000118 207.33.247.67   192.233.80.108 TCP   3ds-lm > ftp [RST] Seq=58 Win=0 Len=0
43 2.897724 207.33.247.67   192.233.80.108 TCP   intellistor-lm > 22807 [SYN] Seq=0 Win=81
44 6.025047 207.33.247.67   192.233.80.108 TCP   intellistor-lm > 22807 [SYN] Seq=0 Win=819
```

Figure 262. The client is unable to establish a passive mode connection

In Figure 263, another client attempts a passive mode connection. In this case, the server responds with a 425 Error: Possible bounce attack/FXP transfer. The passive mode connection cannot be established. In this case, the passive mode connection cannot be established, but the server explains why.

For more information on FTP bounce attacks, refer to *Chapter 32: Analyze Suspect Traffic.*

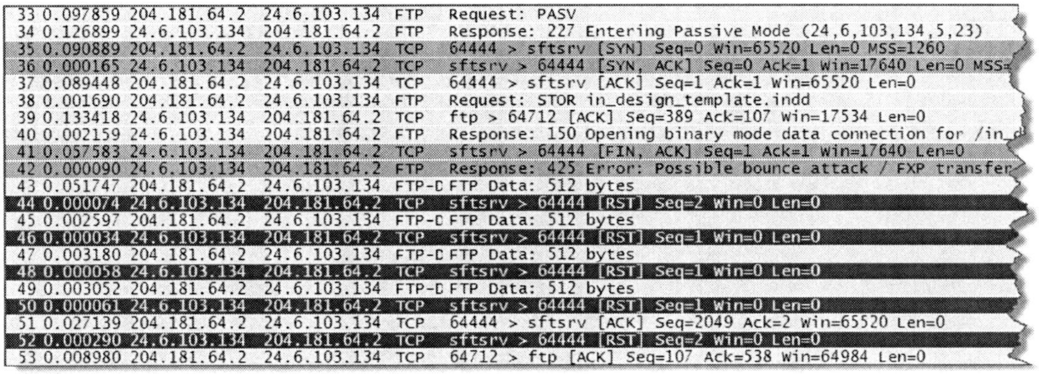

```
33 0.097859 204.181.64.2    24.6.103.134    FTP   Request: PASV
34 0.126899 24.6.103.134    204.181.64.2    FTP   Response: 227 Entering Passive Mode (24,6,103,134,5,23)
35 0.090889 204.181.64.2    24.6.103.134    TCP   64444 > sftsrv [SYN] Seq=0 Win=65520 Len=0 MSS=1260
36 0.000165 24.6.103.134    204.181.64.2    TCP   sftsrv > 64444 [SYN, ACK] Seq=0 Ack=1 Win=17640 Len=0 MSS=
37 0.089448 204.181.64.2    24.6.103.134    TCP   64444 > sftsrv [ACK] Seq=1 Win=65520 Len=0
38 0.001690 204.181.64.2    24.6.103.134    FTP   Request: STOR in_design_template.indd
39 0.133418 24.6.103.134    204.181.64.2    TCP   ftp > 64712 [ACK] Seq=389 Ack=107 Win=17534 Len=0
40 0.002159 24.6.103.134    204.181.64.2    FTP   Response: 150 Opening binary mode data connection for /in_d
41 0.057583 204.181.64.2    24.6.103.134    TCP   sftsrv > 64444 [FIN, ACK] Seq=1 Ack=1 Win=17640 Len=0
42 0.000090 24.6.103.134    204.181.64.2    FTP   Response: 425 Error: Possible bounce attack / FXP transfer
43 0.051747 204.181.64.2    24.6.103.134    FTP-C FTP Data: 512 bytes
44 0.000074 24.6.103.134    204.181.64.2    TCP   sftsrv > 64444 [RST] Seq=2 Win=0 Len=0
45 0.002597 204.181.64.2    24.6.103.134    FTP-C FTP Data: 512 bytes
46 0.000034 24.6.103.134    204.181.64.2    TCP   sftsrv > 64444 [RST] Seq=1 Win=0 Len=0
47 0.003180 204.181.64.2    24.6.103.134    FTP-C FTP Data: 512 bytes
48 0.000058 24.6.103.134    204.181.64.2    TCP   sftsrv > 64444 [RST] Seq=1 Win=0 Len=0
49 0.003052 204.181.64.2    24.6.103.134    FTP-C FTP Data: 512 bytes
50 0.000061 24.6.103.134    204.181.64.2    TCP   sftsrv > 64444 [RST] Seq=1 Win=0 Len=0
51 0.027139 204.181.64.2    24.6.103.134    TCP   64444 > sftsrv [ACK] Seq=2049 Ack=2 Win=65520 Len=0
52 0.000290 24.6.103.134    204.181.64.2    TCP   sftsrv > 64444 [RST] Seq=2 Win=0 Len=0
53 0.008980 204.181.64.2    24.6.103.134    TCP   64712 > ftp [ACK] Seq=107 Ack=538 Win=64984 Len=0
```

Figure 263. The FTP server sends a 425 response indicating security concerns

Dissect the FTP Packet Structure

The FTP packet structure is very simple.

Commands from the FTP client follow immediately after the TCP header, as shown in Figure 264. Some commands include an argument as in the case of the RETR command. A list of commands that use arguments is shown below.

Command	Argument
USER	username
PASS	password
RETR	directory/file name
TYPE	representation type
PORT	IP address, port number

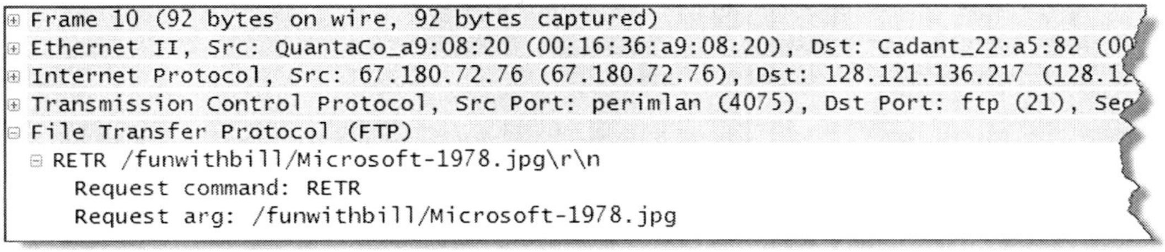

```
⊞ Frame 10 (92 bytes on wire, 92 bytes captured)
⊞ Ethernet II, Src: QuantaCo_a9:08:20 (00:16:36:a9:08:20), Dst: Cadant_22:a5:82 (00
⊞ Internet Protocol, Src: 67.180.72.76 (67.180.72.76), Dst: 128.121.136.217 (128.12
⊞ Transmission Control Protocol, Src Port: perimlan (4075), Dst Port: ftp (21), Seq
⊟ File Transfer Protocol (FTP)
   ⊟ RETR /funwithbill/Microsoft-1978.jpg\r\n
       Request command: RETR
       Request arg: /funwithbill/Microsoft-1978.jpg
```

Figure 264. FTP commands follow the TCP header

Responses contain a numerical code and text as shown in Figure 265. The response code and the response argument are in plain text in the response packet.

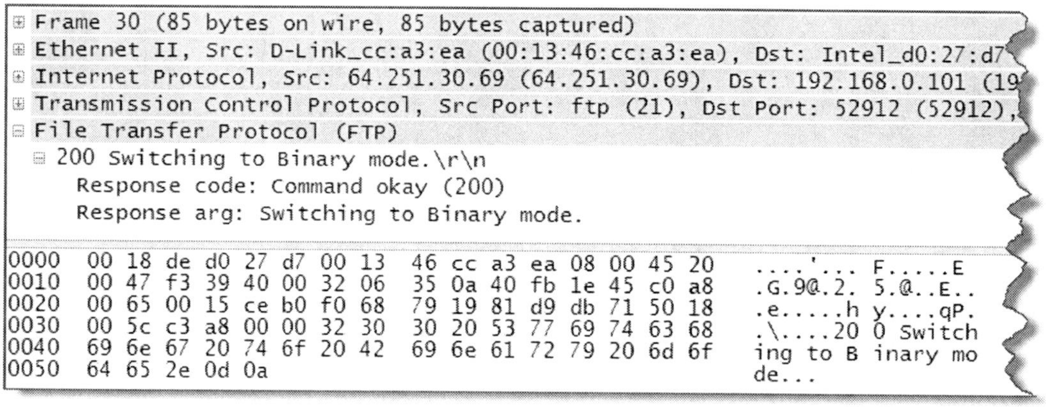

```
⊞ Frame 30 (85 bytes on wire, 85 bytes captured)
⊞ Ethernet II, Src: D-Link_cc:a3:ea (00:13:46:cc:a3:ea), Dst: Intel_d0:27:d7
⊞ Internet Protocol, Src: 64.251.30.69 (64.251.30.69), Dst: 192.168.0.101 (19
⊞ Transmission Control Protocol, Src Port: ftp (21), Dst Port: 52912 (52912),
⊟ File Transfer Protocol (FTP)
  ⊟ 200 Switching to Binary mode.\r\n
      Response code: Command okay (200)
      Response arg: Switching to Binary mode.

0000   00 18 de d0 27 d7 00 13   46 cc a3 ea 08 00 45 20    ....'...  F.....E
0010   00 47 f3 39 40 00 32 06   35 0a 40 fb 1e 45 c0 a8    .G.9@.2.  5.@..E..
0020   00 65 00 15 ce b0 f0 68   79 19 81 d9 db 71 50 18    .e.....h  y....qP.
0030   00 5c c3 a8 00 00 32 30   30 20 53 77 69 74 63 68    .\....20  0 Switch
0040   69 6e 67 20 74 6f 20 42   69 6e 61 72 79 20 6d 6f    ing to B  inary mo
0050   64 65 2e 0d 0a                                       de...
```

Figure 265. Response codes are followed by text

Data packets have an even simpler format—the data follows the TCP header as shown in Figure 266. No extra commands are required or allowed on this channel.

```
⊞ Frame 110 (1514 bytes on wire, 1514 bytes captured)
⊞ Ethernet II, Src: D-Link_cc:a3:ea (00:13:46:cc:a3:ea), Dst: Intel_d0:27:d7
⊞ Internet Protocol, Src: 64.251.30.69 (64.251.30.69), Dst: 192.168.0.101 (1
⊞ Transmission Control Protocol, Src Port: ftp-data (20), Dst Port: 52914 (5
⊟ FTP Data
    [truncated] FTP Data: 7\372\271\343V\004V6$\0359aITu1\256J\242\376\336h\
```

Figure 266. In an FTP data transfer, data follows the TCP header

Filter on FTP Traffic

The capture filter syntax for FTP command channel traffic is tcp port 21. The filter for the FTP data channel is dependent upon the port used for this traffic. If the data traffic crosses on port 20, the capture filter would be tcp port 20.

The display filter for FTP is simply ftp. Note that this filter will only display traffic on the FTP command channel if it uses the default port 21. The data channel traffic will not be displayed. To display the FTP data channel traffic, use the ftp-data display filter. If Wireshark cannot discern which connection is used for the FTP data channel, you will need to apply a filter based on the TCP port used for the FTP data transfer (tcp.port==30189).

The following table lists additional FTP display filters.

Display Filter	Description
`ftp.request.command == "USER"`	FTP USER packets
`ftp.request.command == "USER" || ftp.request.command == "PASS"`	FTP USER or PASS packets
`ftp.request.command == "USER" && ftp.request.arg == "Fred"`	FTP USER command with the user name Fred (the user name argument is case sensitive)
`ftp.request.command == "PASS" && ftp.request.arg == "Krueger"`	FTP PASS command with the password Krueger (the password argument is case sensitive)
`ftp.response.code == 230`	Successful FTP logins
`ftp.request.command == "PASV"`	FTP passive mode requests
`ftp.request.command == "MKD" && ftp.request.arg == "dir01"`	FTP MKD (make directory) command for a directory named "dir01" (the directory name argument is case sensitive)
`ftp.response.code == 257`	Successful directory creation response

Reassemble FTP Traffic

Reassembling FTP traffic is very easy because the data channel contains just the data being transferred. No extra commands are embedded in the data stream.

To reassemble FTP traffic, **Follow TCP Stream** on the data channel, define the format as **raw** and choose **Save As**. If you captured the command sequence preceding the data transfer in your trace file, you should have the name of the original file being transferred. This is useful in case you are unsure of the format of the file and do not recognize the file identifier.

For more information on reassembling FTP traffic, refer to *Chapter 10: Follow Streams and Reassemble Data*.

Case Study:
Secret FTP Communications

When a new computer comes into the office we typically perform an idle analysis of the system.

One day a new Windows XP Home Edition laptop arrived. It would eventually be updated to Windows Vista for testing. We started it up, installed the operating system and then just let it sit alone, untouched while we captured traffic to and from the idle system.

No.	Time	Source	Destination	Protocol	Info
1	0.000000	24.4.97.251	68.87.76.178	DNS	Standard query A rockford.discoverconsole.com
2	0.011752	68.87.76.178	24.4.97.251	DNS	Standard query response A 207.154.29.20
3	0.005382	24.4.97.251	207.154.29.20	TCP	alpha-sms > ftp [SYN] Seq=0 Win=65535 Len=0 MS
4	0.128676	207.154.29.20	24.4.97.251	TCP	ftp > alpha-sms [SYN, ACK] Seq=0 Ack=1 Win=163
5	0.000127	24.4.97.251	207.154.29.20	TCP	alpha-sms > ftp [ACK] Seq=1 Ack=1 Win=65535 Le
6	0.129952	207.154.29.20	24.4.97.251	FTP	Response: 220 Microsoft FTP Service
7	0.001125	24.4.97.251	207.154.29.20	FTP	Request: USER discover
8	0.125348	207.154.29.20	24.4.97.251	FTP	Response: 331 Password required for discover.
9	0.000260	24.4.97.251	207.154.29.20	FTP	Request: PASS qu1ckp41ncry
10	0.121442	207.154.29.20	24.4.97.251	FTP	Response: 230 User discover logged in.
11	0.056784	24.4.97.251	207.154.29.20	FTP	Request: CWD DISCoverFTP/SystemUpdates/HP_DEC
12	0.117536	207.154.29.20	24.4.97.251	FTP	Response: 550 DISCoverFTP/SystemUpdates/HP_DEC
13	0.029994	24.4.97.251	68.87.76.178	DNS	Standard query PTR 20.29.154.207.in-addr.arpa
14	0.002781	24.4.97.251	207.154.29.20	FTP	Request: QUIT
15	0.118283	207.154.29.20	24.4.97.251	FTP	Response: 221
16	0.000255	207.154.29.20	24.4.97.251	TCP	ftp > alpha-sms [FIN, ACK] Seq=185 Ack=79 Win=
17	0.000097	24.4.97.251	207.154.29.20	TCP	alpha-sms > ftp [ACK] Seq=79 Ack=186 Win=65351
18	0.023106	24.4.97.251	207.154.29.20	TCP	alpha-sms > ftp [FIN, ACK] Seq=79 Ack=186 Win=
19	0.123097	207.154.29.20	24.4.97.251	TCP	ftp > alpha-sms [ACK] Seq=186 Ack=80 Win=65457

```
0000  00 17 31 e0 d3 f7 00 01  5c 22 a5 82 08 00 45 00   ..1..... \"....E.
0010  00 7b 8c 43 40 00 6e 06  19 8c cf 9a 1d 14 18 04   .{.C@.n. ........
0020  61 fb 00 15 07 39 d0 a4  fa 4e 60 b8 95 38 50 18   a....9.. .N`..8P.
0030  ff 67 33 1e 00 00 35 35  30 20 44 49 53 43 6f 76   .g3...55 0 DISCov
0040  65 72 46 54 50 2f 53 79  73 74 65 6d 55 70 64 61   erFTP/Sy stemUpda
0050  74 65 73 2f 48 50 5f 44  45 43 3a 20 54 68 65 20   tes/HP_D EC: The
0060  73 79 73 74 65 6d 20 63  61 6e 6e 6f 74 20 66 69   system c annot fi
0070  6e 64 20 74 68 65 20 66  69 6c 65 20 73 70 65 63   nd the f ile spec
0080  69 66 69 65 64 2e 20 0d  0a                        ified. . .
```

After returning to the machine later in the day and reviewing the traffic to and from the unattended system, we spotted an interesting traffic pattern—an FTP connection.

Considering that we had not done anything other than install the operating system, we did not expect to see any interesting traffic.

Instead, we saw a successful FTP connection to a server called *rockford.discoverconsole.com*. We could see the username "discover" and the password "qu1ckp41cry" in clear text.

We also saw a CWD request for DISCoverFTP/SystemUpdates/HP_DEC. Why would a new system try to make an FTP connection to a remote FTP server? What was it trying to do? Surely a vendor wouldn't release a system that performed such a lame operation transparent to the user?

A bit of research uncovered information about *discoverconsole.com* (which is now CompuExpert). It turned out that HP shipped their Windows XP Media Center edition with this 'value added' set of games pre-installed and automatically updated on the system. During our research we found many people complaining about slow startup times on their HP laptops. Many IT-savvy folks correlated the slow start up with the DISCover game console item. The following is a tech forum question relating to the problem.

> *"Does anyone know how to remove the DISCover game console from startup? It significantly delays my startup. I cannot find it in my configuration, yet it starts and appear with the following processes C:\Program Files\DISC\DiscStreamHub.exe, C:\Program Files\DISC\DISCover.exe, and C:\Program Files\DISC\GameGuide\browser\DiscoverSA.exe. These programs do not appear in Add/Remove Programs."*

Our startup wasn't effected much (as you can see in the time column of the image on the previous page) simply because it couldn't find the directory. If we had not looked at the startup traffic, we would never have seen this kind of ugly behavior in the background.

Now it is mandatory that all new laptops are analyzed the moment they start up.

Summary

FTP is a TCP-based file transfer application. FTP communications use a separate connection for commands and data transfer. The most common port number used for the FTP command channel is port 21, but FTP can be configured to run over any other port number if desired. The data channel may use port 20 or use a port number established through the PORT or PASV command channel process.

There are two types of FTP transfer processes—active mode and passive mode. Active mode FTP data transfers use the PORT command; the data transfer connection is established by the FTP server to the FTP client. Passive mode data transfers use the PASV command; the data transfer connection is established by the FTP client to the FTP server.

Interestingly, the commands that many FTP users are familiar with—*get* and *put*—are not the actual commands that FTP communications use on the network. When the user types a *get* command, FTP sends a RETR request. When the user types *put*, FTP issues an STOR command.

FTP servers respond with a numerical code indicating the status of the request. Response codes in the 400 and 500 range indicate that a problem has occurred.

FTP data transfers can be reassembled using Follow TCP Streams and the Save As option. If you don't know what type of file is being transferred, look for a file identifier to determine what type of file it is.

Practice What You've Learned

 Download the trace files available in the Download section of the book website, *www.wiresharkbook.com*. Open the following files to analyze the FTP communications and answer the questions below.

ftp-download-good.pcap   There's a bit of humor hidden in this FTP file transfer.

Is this an active mode FTP transfer or a passive mode transfer?

What type of file is being sent on the data channel?

Can you reassemble the file?

ftp-ioupload-partial.pcap   This FTP upload process is taking too long.

 Is the server at fault? The client? The network? Examine the Warnings and Notes in the Expert Info Composite to get the whole picture.

ftp-filesizeproblem.pcap   Why didn't this file transfer process work?

Was this a passive mode or active mode transfer?

What is the name of the file that the client FTP requested?

Review Questions

Q24.1 **What is the purpose of FTP?**

Q24.2 **What are the two connections used for in FTP communications?**

Q24.3 **What is the purpose of the FTP PORT command?**

Q24.4 **What is the purpose of the FTP PASV command?**

Q24.5 **How secure is FTP traffic?**

Q24.6 **What is the syntax for capture and display filters for FTP command traffic running over port 21?**

Answers to Review Questions

Q24.1   **What is the purpose of FTP?**

A24.1   FTP is a basic file transfer protocol. Any type of file can be transferred using FTP.

Q24.2   **What are the two connections used for in FTP communications?**

A24.2   FTP communications use one connection as a command channel and a second connection as a data channel.

Q24.3   **What is the purpose of the FTP PORT command?**

A24.3   The PORT command is used by the client to establish an active mode FTP connection. PORT is used by the client to tell the server the IP address and port number the client will listen on for a data channel connection to be established by the FTP server.

Q24.4   **What is the purpose of the FTP PASV command?**

A24.4   The PASV command is used by the client to establish a passive mode FTP connection. If the FTP server supports passive mode connections, the server responds to PASV packets with the IP address and port number that the server will listen on for a data channel connection that will be established by the FTP client.

Q24.5   **How secure is FTP traffic?**

A24.5   FTP is not secure. The FTP user name and password are sent in clear text.

Q24.6   **What is the syntax for capture and display filters for FTP command traffic running over port 21?**

A24.6   Capture filter: `tcp port 21`
Display filter: `ftp`

Chapter 25: Analyze Email Traffic

Wireshark Certified Network Analyst Exam Objectives covered:

- The Purpose of POP
- Analyze Normal POP Communications
- Analyze POP Problems
- Dissect the POP Packet Structure
- Filter on POP Traffic
- The Purpose of SMTP
- Analyze Normal SMTP Communications
- Analyze SMTP Problems
- Dissect the SMTP Packet Structure
- Filter on SMTP Traffic

The Purpose of POP

POP (Post Office Protocol) is still a very popular method of retrieving email and is covered in RFC 1939. IMAP (Internet Message Access Protocol) is another popular email retrieval application. IMAP is covered in RFC 1730.

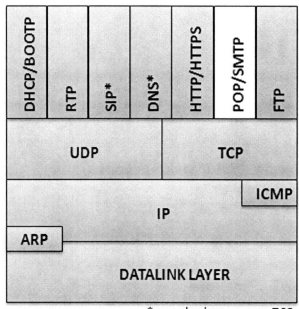

*can also be run over TCP

Figure 267. Email programs always run over TCP

This chapter covers POP and SMTP (Simple Mail Transfer Protocol).

POP itself does not provide security in email data transfer. Third-party applications and tools provide this added functionality.

Analyze Normal POP Communications

In Figure 268 we have applied a `pop` display filter to shows a user retrieving an email message. As you can see in the trace file, Wireshark's Info column provides enough detail on POP communications to interpret the entire process quite easily.

The POP user provides their username and password. The POP server opens the mailbox and tells the user that one message is waiting (the message is 11,110 bytes long). The client asks for the Unique Identification Listing (UIDL) before issuing the RETR command and the POP server begins sending the data to the client over multiple TCP packets if necessary.

No.	Time	Source	Destination	Protocol	Info
1	0.000000	67.161.34.229	128.241.194.25	TCP	isis-ambc > pop3 [SYN] Seq=0 Win=65535 Len=
2	0.086899	128.241.194.25	67.161.34.229	TCP	pop3 > isis-ambc [SYN, ACK] Seq=0 Ack=1 wi
3	0.086943	67.161.34.229	128.241.194.25	TCP	isis-ambc > pop3 [ACK] Seq=1 Ack=1 Win=256
4	4.680620	128.241.194.25	67.161.34.229	POP	S: +OK POP3 [128.241.194.25] v2000.70 serv
5	4.681007	67.161.34.229	128.241.194.25	POP	C: USER rgantrey1
6	4.770897	128.241.194.25	67.161.34.229	POP	S: +OK User name accepted, password please
7	4.771077	67.161.34.229	128.241.194.25	POP	C: PASS abcdefgh
8	4.886065	128.241.194.25	67.161.34.229	POP	S: +OK Mailbox open, 1 messages
9	4.886357	67.161.34.229	128.241.194.25	POP	C: STAT
10	4.978243	128.241.194.25	67.161.34.229	POP	S: +OK 1 11110
11	4.978520	67.161.34.229	128.241.194.25	POP	C: UIDL
12	5.071986	128.241.194.25	67.161.34.229	POP	S: +OK Unique-ID listing follows
13	5.072202	67.161.34.229	128.241.194.25	POP	C: LIST
14	5.166592	128.241.194.25	67.161.34.229	POP	S: +OK Mailbox scan listing follows
15	5.168841	67.161.34.229	128.241.194.25	POP	C: RETR 1
16	5.256687	128.241.194.25	67.161.34.229	POP	S: +OK 11110 octets
17	5.256983	128.241.194.25	67.161.34.229	POP	S: DATA fragment, 1460 bytes
18	5.257008	67.161.34.229	128.241.194.25	TCP	isis-ambc > pop3 [ACK] Seq=58 Ack=3154 Win=
19	5.257248	128.241.194.25	67.161.34.229	POP	S: DATA fragment, 1176 bytes
20	5.258325	128.241.194.25	67.161.34.229	POP	S: DATA fragment, 1460 bytes
21	5.258342	67.161.34.229	128.241.194.25	TCP	isis-ambc > pop3 [ACK] Seq=58 Ack=5790 win=
22	5.258644	128.241.194.25	67.161.34.229	POP	S: DATA fragment, 1460 bytes

Figure 268. A user retrieves one email message

Upon successful download of the email message, the client sends the delete command (DELE). The server responds indicating it has deleted the message. The POP communications are then terminated by the client.

POP does not maintain a persistent connection—the connection is established to retrieve the email and then terminated upon successful completion.

Analyze POP Problems
POP communication problems can begin with the TCP connection process and can also be affected by high latency and packet loss.

Problems at the POP server can also affect the client's ability to get their email. As shown in Figure 269, a client cannot even login to the POP server. The server indicates that it is too busy. Before the - ERR response, there is another indication of a possible problem in this trace file. The client had to issue two TCP handshake requests (SYN) to make the connection to the server.

This trace file indicates a capacity issue at the POP server. At peak points of the day, email retrieval is unavailable to the clients.

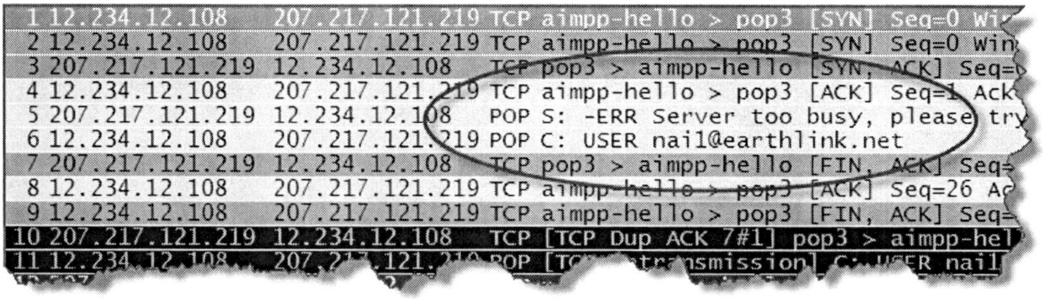

```
 1 12.234.12.108      207.217.121.219 TCP aimpp-hello > pop3 [SYN] Seq=0 Wi
 2 12.234.12.108      207.217.121.219 TCP aimpp-hello > pop3 [SYN] Seq=0 Win
 3 207.217.121.219 12.234.12.108      TCP pop3 > aimpp-hello [SYN, ACK] Seq=
 4 12.234.12.108      207.217.121.219 TCP aimpp-hello > pop3 [ACK] Seq=1 Ack
 5 207.217.121.219 12.234.12.108       POP S: -ERR Server too busy, please try
 6 12.234.12.108      207.217.121.219 POP C: USER nail@earthlink.net
 7 207.217.121.219 12.234.12.108      TCP pop3 > aimpp-hello [FIN, ACK] Seq=
 8 12.234.12.108      207.217.121.219 TCP aimpp-hello > pop3 [ACK] Seq=26 Ac
 9 12.234.12.108      207.217.121.219 TCP aimpp-hello > pop3 [FIN, ACK] Seq=
10 207.217.121.219 12.234.12.108      TCP [TCP Dup ACK 7#1] pop3 > aimpp-hel
11 12.234.12.108      207.217.121.219 POP [TCP transmission] C: USER nail
```

Figure 269. A POP error message indicates the POP server is busy

Spam clogged mailboxes can also affect performance. In Figure 270 we are looking at the email download process for a client whose mailbox is filled with spam messages. Each spam message has a binary attachment (a .pif file in this case). The client complained because downloading email seemed to take an extremely long time (over 30 minutes). The user did not complain about spam, however.

Examining the user's email retrieval process shows the spam messages and the attachments. Hundreds of these emails were being transferred to the user when they retrieved their email. Most of the spam messages were automatically moved to the user's spam folder (hence their lack of awareness regarding the high quantity of spam being retrieved).

The spam retrieval process was slowing down the retrieval of good email traffic. More aggressive spam filtering should be applied at the POP server.

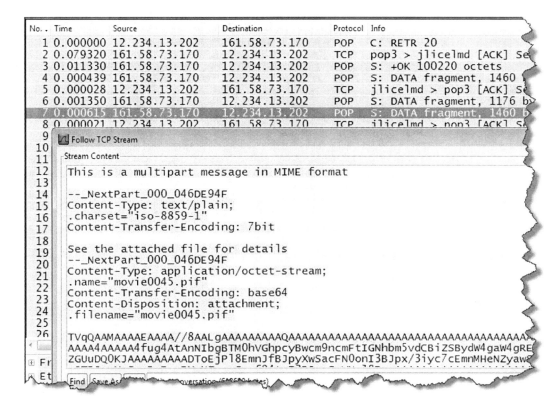

Figure 270. SPAM messages clog an inbox—email retrieval takes over 30 minutes

Dissect the POP Packet Structure

POP packet structures are very simple. POP requests consist of a Request Command and Request Parameter. Responses consist of a Response Indicator and Response Description. The request commands are listed in the following table.

Command	Description
USER	Used to indicate the user name
PASS	Used to indicate the password
QUIT	Terminate the connection
STAT	Obtain the server status
LIST	List message and message size
RETR	Retrieve a message
DELE	Delete a message
PIPELINING	Server can accept multiple commands at a time [RFC2449]
UIDL	Unique ID List—list all emails [RFC2449]

Figure 271 shows a POP request to retrieve a message. The request command is RETR and the request parameter is 1, indicating the client wants to retrieve message number 1.

```
⊞ Frame 15 (62 bytes on wire, 62 bytes captured)
⊞ Ethernet II, Src: Sony_f4:3a:09 (08:00:46:f4:3a:09), Dst: Cadant_22:a5:82 (00:0
⊞ Internet Protocol, Src: 67.161.34.229 (67.161.34.229), Dst: 128.241.194.25 (128.
⊞ Transmission Control Protocol, Src Port: isis-ambc (1643), Dst Port: pop3 (110)
⊟ Post Office Protocol
  ⊟ RETR 1\r\n
      Request command: RETR
      Request parameter: 1
```

Figure 271. A POP retrieve request for message number 1

Figure 272 shows an email response. The response begins with the response indicator and the response description.

There are only two response indicators used in POP communications:

> +OK

> -ERR

We can follow the POP mail message header to identify the path the packet took through mail exchange servers.

```
⊟ Post Office Protocol
  ⊟ +OK 11110 octets\r\n
      Response indicator: +OK
      Response description: 11110 octets
      Return-Path: bbelch@packet-level.com\r\n
      Received: from mx20.stngva01.us.mxservers.net (204.202.242.7)\r\n
      \tby mail11d.verio-web.com (RS ver 1.0.95vs) with SMTP id 3-0575327743\r\n
      \tfor <rgantrey1@packet-level.com>; Mon, 15 Jan 2007 16:49:06 -0500 (EST)\r\n
      Received: from mxw1100.verio-web.com [161.88.148.09] (EHLO GIGA)\r\n
      \tby mx20.stngva01.us.mxservers.net (mxl_mta-1.3.8-10p4) with ESMTP id d05fba54.25
      \tMon, 15 Jan 2007 16:41:33 -0500 (EST)\r\n
      From: "Barnel Belch" <bbelch@packet-level.com>\r\n
      To: "'Rolly Gantry12'" <rgantry11@packet-level.com>\r\n
      Subject: FW: Self-Paced Courseware: Performing Network and Security Analysis with
      Date: Mon, 15 Jan 2007 13:48:56 -0800\r\n
      MIME-Version: 1.0\r\n
      Content-Type: multipart/alternative;\r\n
      \tboundary="----=_NextPart_000_004E_01C738AB.EB5D93D0"\r\n
```

Figure 272. The response to the RETR command includes the email header information and the email itself

Filter on POP Traffic

The capture filter syntax for POP traffic is `tcp port 110`. If your POP traffic runs over another port number, the syntax would be `tcp port x` where x is the port you are using for your POP traffic.

The display filter for POP is simply `pop`. Note that this filter will only display POP command and email traffic—it will not display the TCP handshake or TCP ACK packets. To view all packets related to a POP communication, use the filter `tcp.port==110` or a conversation filter.

The following table lists additional POP display filters.

Display Filter	Description
`pop.response.indicator == "+OK"`	POP +OK responses
`pop.response.indicator == "-ERR"`	POP –ERR responses
`pop.request.command == "USER"`	POP USER commands
`(pop.request.command == "USER") && (pop.request.parameter == "Fred")`	POP USER commands with the username Fred (the username is case sensitive)
`(pop.response.indicator == "+OK") && (pop.response.description contains "octets")`	POP responses that contain email UIDL values and the length of each email message (good for spotting groups of spam messages with attachments)

The Purpose of SMTP

SMTP is the de facto standard application used for sending email and is defined in RFC 821, Simple Mail Transfer Protocol. SMTP uses Sender-SMTP and Receiver-SMTP processes. By default, SMTP communications are not secure. SMTP emails that are created in text format are delivered in Internet Message Format (IMF) which is covered in RFC 2822.

The default port used for SMTP communications is port 25, however SMTP can (like many applications) be configured to run over another port number. An increasing number of ISP's and firewall configurations block SMTP connections on port 25—this has been done primarily to try and stop spam going out through the ISP's networks.

```
⊞ Frame 19 (59 bytes on wire, 59 bytes captured)
⊞ Ethernet II, Src: Sony_f4:3a:09 (08:00:46:f4:3a:09), Dst: Cadant_22:a5:82 (0
⊞ Internet Protocol, Src: 67.161.34.229 (67.161.34.229), Dst: 128.241.194.25 (
⊞ Transmission Control Protocol, Src Port: nkd (1650), Dst Port: smtp (25), Se
⊟ Simple Mail Transfer Protocol
    C: .
  ⊞ [DATA fragments (4342 bytes): #15(1460), #16(1460), #17(1422)]
⊟ Internet Message Format
  ⊞ From: "Brian Readdy16" <breaddy16@packet-level.com>, 1 item
  ⊞ To: "'Barnel Belch'" <bbelch@packet-level.com>, 1 item
    Subject: Test email
    Date: Mon, 15 Jan 2007 13:55:23 -0800
    Message-ID: <006d01c738ef$e544a990$e522a143@hq.wnbnet>
    MIME-Version: 1.0
  ⊞ Content-Type: multipart/alternative;\r\n\tboundary="----=_NextPart_000_006
    X-Mailer: Microsoft Office Outlook 11
    Thread-Index: Acc479ph2gILPVD6QgiKnNrF3RpHpQ==
    X-MimeOLE: Produced By Microsoft MimeOLE V6.00.2900.3028\r\n
  ⊞ MIME Multipart Media Encapsulation, Type: multipart/alternative, Boundary:
```

Figure 273. SMTP messages are delivered in Internet Message Format

Analyze Normal SMTP Communications

After a successful TCP handshake, the SMTP server responds with a numerical code 220 indicating the service is ready. This response also identifies the SMTP server and indicates that the server supports mail extensions through the inclusion of "ESMTP" in this greeting.

The client sends a HELO or an EHLO with its host name. A HELO initiates a standard SMTP session, whereas EHLO initiates an SMTP session that supports mail service extensions. This client uses EHLO because the server indicated it supports mail service extensions in its greeting.

At this point the server can send capability information to the client. In our example, the server sends a packet indicating it supports pipelining. Pipelining allows the client to send another request without waiting for the response to the previous one(s).

The SMTP client sends the MAIL FROM and provides its source email address to the SMTP server. This address must be approved by the SMTP server. Next the client sends a RCPT TO indicating who the email will be destined to.

The DATA command indicates the client is ready to send the email, and if the server is ready it responds with 354 Start Mail Input. Now the client can send the email to the SMTP server.

No. .	Time	Source	Destination	Protocol	Info
1	0.000000	67.161.34.229	128.241.194.25	TCP	nkd > smtp [SYN] Seq=0 Win=65535 Len=0
2	0.088301	128.241.194.25	67.161.34.229	TCP	smtp > nkd [SYN, ACK] Seq=0 Ack=1 Win
3	0.000055	67.161.34.229	128.241.194.25	TCP	nkd > smtp [ACK] Seq=1 Ack=1 Win=25696
4	4.594681	128.241.194.25	67.161.34.229	SMTP	S: 220 mx100.stngva01.us.mxservers.ne
5	0.000270	67.161.34.229	128.241.194.25	SMTP	C: EHLO Vaio
6	0.098716	128.241.194.25	67.161.34.229	SMTP	S: 250-mx100.stngva01.us.mxservers.net
7	0.124529	67.161.34.229	128.241.194.25	TCP	nkd > smtp [ACK] Seq=12 Ack=147 Win=2
8	0.088823	128.241.194.25	67.161.34.229	SMTP	S: 250-SIZE 0	250 PIPELINING
9	0.000142	67.161.34.229	128.241.194.25	SMTP	C: MAIL FROM: <breaddy16@packet-leve
10	0.100986	128.241.194.25	67.161.34.229	SMTP	S: 250 Sender Ok
11	0.000363	67.161.34.229	128.241.194.25	SMTP	C: RCPT TO: <bbelch@packet-level.com>
12	0.201889	128.241.194.25	67.161.34.229	SMTP	S: 250 bbelch@packet-level.com ok (no
13	0.000243	67.161.34.229	128.241.194.25	SMTP	C: DATA
14	0.086553	128.241.194.25	67.161.34.229	SMTP	S: 354 Start mail input; end with <CR
15	0.011263	67.161.34.229	128.241.194.25	SMTP	C: DATA fragment, 1460 bytes
16	0.000025	67.161.34.229	128.241.194.25	SMTP	C: DATA fragment, 1460 bytes
17	0.000013	67.161.34.229	128.241.194.25	SMTP	C: DATA fragment, 1422 bytes
18	0.099800	128.241.194.25	67.161.34.229	TCP	smtp > nkd [ACK] Seq=277 Ack=3015 Win
19	0.000022	67.161.34.229	128.241.194.25	IMF	from: "Brian Readdy16" <breaddy16@pac
20	0.004146	128.241.194.25	67.161.34.229	TCP	smtp > nkd [ACK] Seq=277 Ack=4437 Win
21	0.217512	128.241.194.25	67.161.34.229	TCP	smtp > nkd [ACK] Seq=277 Ack=4442 Win=
22	0.642102	128.241.194.25	67.161.34.229	SMTP	S: 250 0-0484658135 Message accepted f
23	0.151263	67.161.34.229	128.241.194.25	TCP	nkd > smtp [ACK] Seq=4442 Ack=325 Wir
24	2.358602	67.161.34.229	128.241.194.25	SMTP	C: QUIT
25	0.000120	67.161.34.229	128.241.194.25	TCP	nkd > smtp [FIN, ACK] Seq=4448 Ack=32
26	0.087663	128.241.194.25	67.161.34.229	SMTP	S: 221 mx100.stngva01.us.mxservers.ne
27	0.000044	67.161.34.229	128.241.194.25	TCP	nkd > smtp [RST, ACK] Seq=4449 Ack=39
28	0.000951	128.241.194.25	67.161.34.229	TCP	nkd > smtp [FIN, ACK] Seq=399 Ack=444
29	0.000020	67.161.34.229	128.241.194.25	TCP	nkd > smtp [RST] Seq=4448 Win=0 Len=0
30	0.004519	128.241.194.25	67.161.34.229	TCP	smtp > nkd [ACK] Seq=400 Ack=4449 Win
31	0.000012	67.161.34.229	128.241.194.25	TCP	nkd > smtp [RST] Seq=4449 Win=0 Len=0

Figure 274. An SMTP client sends an email message

Once the email is sent, the client issues the QUIT command to begin the connection termination process.

Analyze SMTP Problems

SMTP communication problems can begin with the TCP connection process and can also be affected by high latency and packet loss.

If the SMTP server responds with numerical codes above 399, the server is indicating there is a problem with the email transmission process.

Figure 275 shows an unusual SMTP traffic pattern. A host's email program is performing an SMTP relay test by generating a series of MAIL FROM addresses to test whether the server will accept them.

This could be caused by a virus or other malware that attempts to email traffic from the infected host. In this case, however, we have used NetScanTools Pro to perform a test on an SMTP server.

One of the SMTP server responses (packet 42) is quite interesting. Although the interpretation of response code 554 is "Transaction Failed," this server responded with "Validating Sender". The text is included in the response with the code number. Others have reported seeing messages such as "554 Transaction Failed Listed in connection control deny list." In general, 554 is a general transaction failure message. Some SMTP servers will provide more details on why the transaction failed while other SMTP servers may respond with ambiguous messages that do not help one understand why the email sending process failed.

We can see in Figure 275 that the MAIL FROM addresses are accepted with 250 Sender OK. Many of the RCPT TO lines generate a 553 Invalid Recipient (Mailbox name not allowed), DN (domain name).

After each attempt, the sending email program generates a RST.

```
39 0.001406 67.161.34.229   128.241.194.25  SMTP  C: MAIL FROM:<spamtest@[128.241.194.25]>
40 0.105674 128.241.194.25  67.161.34.229   SMTP  S: 250 Sender Ok
41 0.001255 67.161.34.229   128.241.194.25  SMTP  C: RCPT TO:<securitytest@packet-level.com>
42 0.128310 128.241.194.25  67.161.34.229   SMTP  S: 554 Validating Sender
43 0.007522 67.161.34.229   128.241.194.25  SMTP  C: RSET
44 0.237237 128.241.194.25  67.161.34.229   TCP   smtp > skip-mc-gikreq [ACK] Seq=505 Ack=420
45 1.763451 128.241.194.25  67.161.34.229   SMTP  S: 250 Reset Ok
46 0.010043 67.161.34.229   128.241.194.25  SMTP  C: MAIL FROM:<spamtest@mx20.stngva01.us.mxse
47 0.141977 128.241.194.25  67.161.34.229   SMTP  S: 250 Sender Ok
48 0.001561 67.161.34.229   128.241.194.25  SMTP  C: RCPT TO:<securitytest%packet-level.com@mx2
49 0.269478 128.241.194.25  67.161.34.229   TCP   smtp > skip-mc-gikreq [ACK] Seq=534 Ack=545
50 0.082707 128.241.194.25  67.161.34.229   SMTP  S: 250 securitytest%packet-level.com@mx20.stn
51 0.002292 67.161.34.229   128.241.194.25  SMTP  C: RSET
52 0.089465 128.241.194.25  67.161.34.229   SMTP  S: 250 Reset Ok
53 0.001249 67.161.34.229   128.241.194.25  SMTP  C: MAIL FROM:<spamtest@mx20.stngva01.us.mxser
54 0.116160 128.241.194.25  67.161.34.229   SMTP  S: 250 Sender Ok
55 0.001702 67.161.34.229   128.241.194.25  SMTP  C: RCPT TO:<securitytest%packet-level.com@[12
56 0.089098 128.241.194.25  67.161.34.229   SMTP  S: 553 Invalid recipient, DN
57 0.002031 67.161.34.229   128.241.194.25  SMTP  C: RSET
58 0.271742 128.241.194.25  67.161.34.229   TCP   smtp > skip-mc-gikreq [ACK] Seq=668 Ack=668
59 1.731211 128.241.194.25  67.161.34.229   SMTP  S: 250 Reset Ok
60 0.002041 67.161.34.229   128.241.194.25  SMTP  C: MAIL FROM:<spamtest@mx20.stngva01.us.mxse
61 0.104278 128.241.194.25  67.161.34.229   SMTP  S: 250 Sender Ok
62 0.001496 67.161.34.229   128.241.194.25  SMTP  C: RCPT TO:<"securitytest@packet-level.com">
63 0.087792 128.241.194.25  67.161.34.229   SMTP  S: 553 Invalid recipient, DN
64 0.001840 67.161.34.229   128.241.194.25  SMTP  C: RSET
65 0.149467 128.241.194.25  67.161.34.229   TCP   smtp > skip-mc-gikreq [ACK] Seq=724 Ack=770
```

Figure 275. A host is running a relay test against the SMTP server

This certainly isn't normal behavior on the network. Email communications should be baselined to identify normal communications on your network. For more information on baselining network communications, refer to *Chapter 28: Baseline "Normal" Traffic Pattern.*

Dissect the SMTP Packet Structure

SMTP communications consist of commands and response codes. The SMTP commands and response codes follow immediately after the TCP header.

Figure 276 shows an EHLO command packet. In this packet, the command is followed by a request parameter, the name of the host sending the email.

```
⊞ Frame 5 (65 bytes on wire, 65 bytes captured)
⊞ Ethernet II, Src: Sony_f4:3a:09 (08:00:46:f4:3a:09), Dst: Cadant_22:a5:82
⊞ Internet Protocol, Src: 67.161.34.229 (67.161.34.229), Dst: 128.241.194.2
⊞ Transmission Control Protocol, Src Port: nkd (1650), Dst Port: smtp (25),
⊟ Simple Mail Transfer Protocol
   ⊟ Command: EHLO Vaio\r\n
      Command: EHLO
      Request parameter: Vaio
```

Figure 276. Inside an SMTP EHLO command packet

The following table lists the most commonly seen SMTP client commands.

Command	Description
HELO	Initiates an SMTP session
EHLO	Initiates an SMTP session from a sender that supports SMTP mail service extensions
MAIL	Initiates mail transfer
RCPT	Identifies mail recipient
DATA	Initiates mail data transfer
VRFY	Verifies recipient exists
RSET	Aborts mail transaction
NOOP	Tests connection to server
QUIT	Closes SMTP connection
EXPN	Expands mailing list
HELP	Lists help information

The following table lists the most commonly seen SMTP reply codes which are sent from the SMTP server.

Code	Description
211	System status
214	Help message
220	<domain> service ready
221	<domain> service closing channel
250	Requested action okay and completed
251	User not local; will forward to <path>
354	Start mail input
421	<domain> service not available
450	Mailbox unavailable
451	Local error
452	Insufficient storage
500	Syntax error, command unrecognized
501	Syntax error in parameters or arguments
502	Command not implemented
503	Bad sequence of commands
504	Command parameter not implemented
521	<domain> does not accept mail (see rfc1846)

Code	Description
550	Mailbox unavailable
551	User not local, please try <path>
552	Exceeded storage allocation
553	Mailbox name not allowed
554	Transaction failed

Filter on SMTP Traffic

The capture filter syntax for SMTP traffic is `tcp port 25`. If your SMTP server is using a different port number for the mail daemon, you must adjust this capture filter accordingly.

The display filter for SMTP is simply `smtp`. Note that this filter will only display SMTP commands and data. The TCP handshake and TCP ACKs are not displayed. If you want to view the TCP handshake and TCP ACKs, use `tcp.port==25`. (As always, substitute the port you are using for SMTP if not using port 25.) The following table lists additional SMTP display filters.

Display Filter	Description
`smtp.req.command == "EHLO"`	User and server support mail extensions and are setting up an SMTP communication
`(smtp.req.command == "MAIL") && (smtp.req.parameter == "FROM: <laura@chappellu.com>")`	An email is being sent from *laura@chappellu.com*
`(smtp.req.command == "RCPT") && (smtp.req.parameter == "TO: <brenda@chappellu.com>")`	An email is being sent to *brenda@chappellu.com*
`smtp.response.code > 399`	The email server indicates there is a problem with the email

Case Study:
SMTP Problem—Scan2Email Job

Submitted by: Christian Kreide

Facts

1) Scan device was a multifunctional device (MFD).

2) The device was connected to the SMTP server via an IPsec VPN over the Internet.

3) The Scan device supported passive MTU discovery and did not allow IP fragmentation.

Symptoms

Without Wireshark, we only knew that the Scan2Email job was aborted by an unknown cause.

With Wireshark, we could see the SMTP "handshake" worked fine, but data transmission failed as a router claimed a packet size issue by sending an ICMP Type 3 Code 4 packet. The MFD didn't resend the rejected packet using a smaller MTU even though Path MTU discovery is supported on the MFD.

Cause

The customer uses a Cisco PIX firewall, which did a TCP sequence number randomizing. This means the TCP sequence number of the original packet, from the MFD, differs from the TCP sequence number received in the TCP header part carried by the ICMP Type 3 Code 4 packet.

The MFD rejected the ICMP packet, as it never sent out the TCP (SMTP) packet with the altered sequence number. (This is a security function!)

This meant that the email could not be transferred over the VPN connection.

Our Solution

a) On the customer network, we reduced the MTU size of VPN gateway router, at least to the max MTU size of next hop as defined in the received ICMP Type 3 Code 4 packet.

b) Allow IP fragmentation on the MFD

Summary

POP and SMTP communications are used to receive and send email, respectively. POP communications rely on a username and password whereas basic SMTP communications do not. Both POP and SMTP run over TCP. Oftentimes, an authorized POP communication must be established before an SMTP communication can be established.

POP and SMTP communications rely on clear text request commands. There are only two response indicators in POP communications: +OK or -ERR. SMTP responses, however, use numerical codes. Response codes greater than 400 indicate there is a problem with the SMTP communications.

Practice What You've Learned

Download the trace files available in the Download section of the book website, *www.wiresharkbook.com.* Open the trace files below to analyze the email communications and answer the questions.

pop-normal.pcap   This trace depicts a normal POP communication—you might want to disable the Checksum Errors coloring rule to review it.

How many email messages did the user retrieve?

Did the user delete the message after picking it up from the POP server?

Did you see any slow behavior in this trace? If so, is there a slow network, client or server issue?

pop-problem.pcap   The POP email application gives no indication as to why it is taking so long to pick up mail.

What is the reason for the slow behavior?

smtp-sendone.pcap   This trace shows a standard single email being sent through SMTP.

What email application is the client using?

smtp-prob.pcap   A user (10.1.0.1) complains that they cannot send email to the SMTP server (10.2.23.11).

Does the fault lie with the client, the server or the network?

Review Questions

Q25.1   **What is the purpose of POP? What is the purpose of SMTP?**

Q25.2   **What command is used by a POP client to request that the POP server download emails to the client?**

Q25.3   **What are the two POP response codes?**

Q25.4   **What is the difference between an SMTP EHLO and HELO message?**

Q25.5   **What is the syntax for capture and display filters for POP communications?**

Q25.6   **What is the syntax for capture and display filters for SMTP communications?**

Answers to Review Questions

Q25.1   **What is the purpose of POP? What is the purpose of SMTP?**

A25.1   POP is an application used to retrieve email. SMTP is used to send email.

Q25.2   **What command is used by a POP client to request that the POP server download emails to the client?**

A25.2   The POP client issues an RETR command to the POP server to request emails.

Q25.3   **What are the two POP response codes?**

A25.3   The two POP response codes are +OK and –ERR.

Q25.4   **What is the difference between an SMTP EHLO and HELO message?**

A25.4   A HELO initiates a standard SMTP session, whereas EHLO initiates the client supports SMTP with mail service extensions.

Q25.5   **What is the syntax for capture and display filters for POP communications?**

A25.5   Capture filter: `tcp port 110`
Display filter: `pop`

Q25.6   **What is the syntax for capture and display filters for SMTP communications?**

A25.6   Capture filter: `tcp port 25`
Display filter: `smtp`

Chapter 26:
Introduction to
802.11 (WLAN)
Analysis

Wireshark Certified Network Analyst Exam Objectives covered:

- Analyze Signal Strength and Interference
- Capture WLAN Traffic
- Compare Monitor Mode vs. Promiscuous Mode
- Set Up WLAN Decryption
- Select to Prepend Radiotap or PPI Headers
- Compare Signal Strength and Signal-to-Noise Ratios
- Understand 802.11 Traffic Basics
- Analyze Normal 802.11 Communications
- Filter on All WLAN Traffic
- Analyze Frame Control Types and Subtypes

  ❖ Case Study: Cruddy Barcode Communications
  ❖ Summary
  ❖ Practice What You've Learned
  ❖ Review Questions and Answers

Analyzing WLAN Traffic

Wireless LANs (WLANs) are based on the IEEE 802.11 standard.

One key trait of 802.11 WLANs is that they use Carrier Sense (every WLAN host is listening), Multiple Access (shared medium) and Collision Avoidance (focus on avoiding collisions rather than just recovering from them) or CSMA/CA protocol.

The ultimate reference on 802.11 behaviors is the IEEE specification which can be downloaded for free from the IEEE at *standards.ieee.org/getieee802/*. There is an interesting purpose defined in the standard—to appear to higher layers as a wired network.

It is the movable station (STA) and open, shared medium requirements that add an extra level of complexity to WLAN analysis.

As you analyze network traffic, it is important to know what "normal" looks like. Normal signal strength values, normal radio frequency signals in the area (without interference), normal association processes, normal data exchange over 802.11, normal disassociation, etc. Performing a site survey and including trace files in the process can provide you with a valuable baseline of WLAN traffic.

Rule Out the Wired Network to Point to the WLAN

You can identify some WLAN problems when you've only tapped into the wired network. If you don't see the WLAN station's SYN packet (in attempt to establish a connection to the server), then there's something happening over on the WLAN side.

When analyzing WLAN traffic, think of a Basic Service Set (BSS) as a subnet controlled by the access point (AP). Figure 277 shows a very simple WLAN network connected to a wired network. We will use this simple network diagram when examining WLAN traffic in this chapter.

Each BSS has an identification (ID) value which is based on the Media Access Control (MAC) address.

When you communicate from the wireless network to an Ethernet wired network, the associated access point strips off the 802.11 header and encapsulates your packet into an Ethernet frame before forwarding the packet onto the wired network.

We begin with analysis of the signal strength and interference on a WLAN.

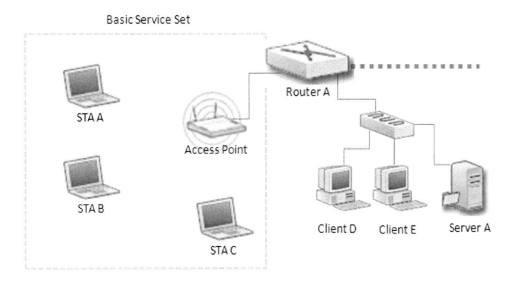

Figure 277. Simple WLAN network

Analyze Signal Strength and Interference

WLAN networks are dependent upon the strength of radio frequency (RF) signals to get management and data traffic through the wireless medium. As a wireless signal travels, its signal strength diminishes as it travels through and around the medium and obstacles. In addition, other RF energy can interfere with the signals.

When analyzing a WLAN, we need to examine the strength of the signal at the location of the WLAN stations and the location of the access points to look for interference from other RF activity (such as interference from a cordless phone, microwave or Bluetooth mouse). Even an overpowered Access Point can cause interference.

One of the most valuable tools used to examine WLAN signals is a spectrum analyzer. These devices can be very expensive, but they are *must-have* tools for anyone installing, troubleshooting and analyzing WLANs. Without a spectrum analyzer, you are blind to RF interference.

Wireshark cannot identify, capture or display RF energy unless it is modulated as in the case of 802.11 frames. Likewise, spectrum analyzers cannot capture and display packets. The two technologies working together offer the best option for troubleshooting wireless networks.

In this chapter we use the spectrum analyzer tools from Metageek—the Wi-Spy adapter and Chanalyzer software. [86]

Figure 278. The Metageek Wi-Spy adapter listens to RF signals

When a user complains about WLAN performance set up your Wi-Spy/Chanalyzer system as close as possible to that complaining user. RF signals are measured from the receipt point of your Wi-Spy adapter. You want to examine the RF signals from that station's or access point's perspective.

You can use the Wi-Spy/Chanalyzer system to perform numerous tasks:

- Examine RF energy (both Wi-Fi and non-Wi-Fi)
- Locate interfering devices
- Discover WLAN networks and their channel usage
- Determine the best channel for WLAN configurations
- Add notes to examine RF activity later

Figure 279 shows the Chanalyzer software's interpretation of RF signals received by the Wi-Spy adapter. In this example, there is strong RF interference seen near channel 1 on the WLAN (circled in Figure 279). Weaker RF activity is seen near channels 3, 5, 8 and 11 (side lobes).

This signal burst is generated when a Uniden 2.4 GHz phone is turned on. Throughout the time that the phone is in use, the WLAN network devices operating within 20 feet on channel 1 lose connectivity to the access point. The phone causes weaker RF activity near channels 3, 5, 8 and 11 as well (side lobes).

Once you have determined that RF energy and interference is not an issue, move up to the packet level to examine the WLAN traffic such as the connection process and authentication.

Examine WLAN control and management processes to make sure everything is functioning properly before inspecting the data packets.

---

[86] You can get information about Metageek spectrum analysis products at *metageek.net*.

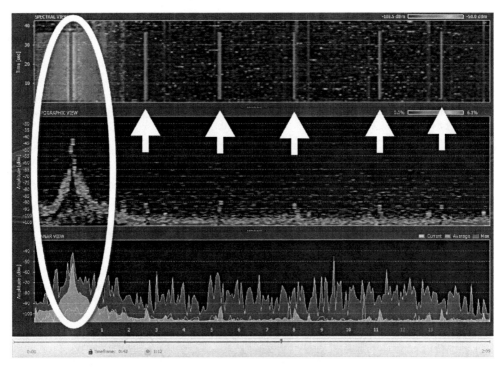

Figure 279. Chanalyzer illustrates the RF activity strength—sudden RF activity is seen when the Uniden phone is turned on

Capture WLAN Traffic

When you analyze WLAN traffic using Wireshark, get as close as you can to the complaining user. You want to see the communication issues from their perspective. This is the same capture technique used on wired networks.

If all users connecting through a particular access point are complaining, consider capturing traffic close to the access point. Look for low signal strength as reported from the receipt point, retransmissions, problems locating the access point, access point "disappearance," problems with the authentication process, etc. For information on capturing WLAN traffic with Wireshark, refer to *Analyze Wireless Networks* on page 90.

Compare Monitor Mode vs. Promiscuous Mode

In promiscuous mode, an 802.11 adapter only captures packets of the SSID the adapter has joined.

In order to capture all traffic that the adapter can receive, the adapter must be put into "monitor mode," sometimes called "rfmon mode." When using monitor mode, the driver does not make the adapter a member of any service set on the network. In monitor mode *all* packets of *all* SSID's from the currently selected channel are captured.

In monitor mode, the adapter won't support general network communications (web browsing, email, etc.) because the adapter is not part of any service set. The driver only supplies received packets to a packet capture mechanism, not to the network stack.

Monitor mode is not supported by WinPcap—this limits the WLAN analysis capabilities of Wireshark and TShark on Windows. It is supported, for at least some network interface cards, on some versions of Linux, FreeBSD, NetBSD, OpenBSD, and Mac OS X. No additional cards or drivers may be needed for WLAN analysis when using these operating systems. Test your network interface cards/drivers on these platforms to see if they will work in monitor mode.

If you receive the error message shown in Figure 280, consider disabling promiscuous mode during your WLAN capture. You won't be able to listen in on traffic of other devices—you must run Wireshark directly on the host whose traffic you are interested in.

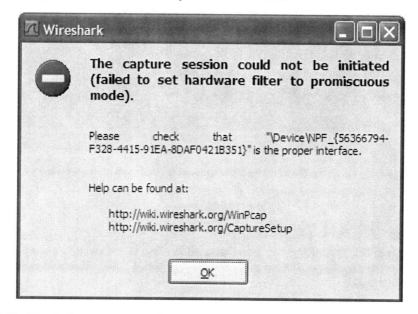

Figure 280. The Wireshark error message indicates a problem with promiscuous mode capture

Test your WLAN capture process before you need it—there's nothing more frustrating than having an "emergency analysis" request come in and finding out that you are unable to see all the data, management and control frames.

Get Help Setting Up WLAN Capture

Sometimes the WLAN capture process can be frustrating. You need to find an operating system/adapter/driver solution that works. For some great assistance and information on WLAN capture, refer to wiki.wireshark.org/CaptureSetup/WLAN.

The table below shows the four possible combinations of promiscuous mode and monitor mode configurations.

Promiscuous Mode`	Monitor Mode	Capture Capabilities	Issues to Consider
On	**Off**	Fake Ethernet header prepended to packet; no Management or Control packets captured	Problems? (Disable Promiscuous Mode)
Off	**Off**	Fake Ethernet header prepended to packet; no Management or Control packets captured	Need to capture traffic on the host you're interested in
Off	**On**	802.11 header; Management and Control packets captured	Need to capture traffic on the host you're interested in
On	**On**	802.11 header; Management and Control packets captured	Great. Can capture traffic on various channels and from all SSIDs

Select the Wireless Interface

Figure 281 shows the Capture Interfaces window on a system that has three AirPcap adapters connected via USB hub.

- AirPcap USB wireless capture adapter nr. 00 configured to listen on Channel 1
- AirPcap USB wireless capture adapter nr. 01 configured to listen on Channel 6
- AirPcap USB wireless capture adapter nr. 02 configured to listen on Channel 11
- The Microsoft driver is used as the native WLAN interface
- The MS Tunnel Interface Driver configured with IPv6 support
- The NVIDIA nForce MCP Networking Adapter Driver used for wired network access.

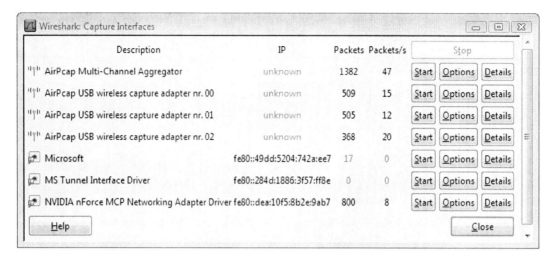

Figure 281. The Capture Interfaces list shows three AirPcap adapters and the Multi-Channel Aggregator driver

The AirPcap Control Panel was used to configure each AirPcap adapter to listen to a different channel. The AirPcap Multi-Channel Aggregator driver allows simultaneous capture on the three configured adapters.

Set Up WLAN Decryption

You must have the decryption key in order to decrypt WLAN traffic. Decryption keys can be input using the Decryption Mode and Decryption Key Management on the Wireless Toolbar or in the IEEE 802.11 preferences setting as shown in Figure 282.

Using the Wireless Toolbar, you can choose between three decryption modes—none (no decryption), Wireshark (decryption done by Wireshark) and Driver (decryption done by the AirPcap driver). The decryption keys can also be set in Wireshark using the Wireless Toolbar as shown in Figure 283.

Let Wireshark Resolve WLAN Decryption Key Conflicts

If you already have decryption keys defined using the AirPcap Control Panel, Wireshark will prompt you to determine which keys to keep or whether the keys from AirPcap and Wireshark should be merged. If you specify "none", then no decryption keys will be applied to the traffic, even if they are listed.

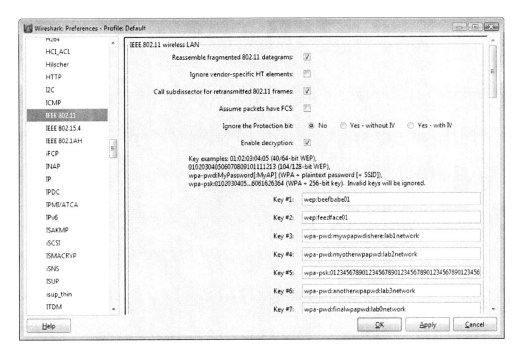

Figure 282. Enter decryption keys in the IEEE 802.11 preferences setting

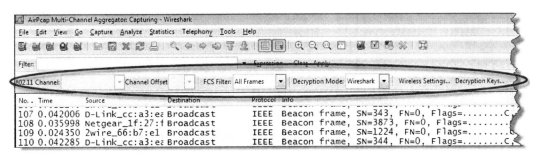

Figure 283. Wireshark's Wireless Toolbar

If you specify Driver mode, you can only use WEP keys to decrypt the traffic. This uses the AirPcap driver to perform the decryption. The AirPcap driver is limited to WEP decryption.

Wireshark can decrypt WEP, WPA and WPA2 traffic.

Put Most Often Used Decryption Keys on Top of the Key List
The keys will be applied in the order in which they are listed. For most efficient operation, move the decryption key you want to use currently to the top of the list.

Consider creating a WLAN profile that will store all your WLAN-specific columns, WLAN-specific display filters and WLAN-specific color filters. When you are opening up WLAN trace files or capturing on a WLAN, select **Edit | Profiles** and use your new profile. For more information on creating and using profiles, refer to *Chapter 11: Customize Wireshark Profiles.*

```
⊞ Frame 362 (189 bytes on wire, 189 bytes captured)
⊞ Radiotap Header v0, Length 20
⊞ IEEE 802.11 Data, Flags: .p.....TC
⊞ Logical-Link Control
⊞ Internet Protocol, Src: 192.168.1.64 (192.168.1.64), Dst: 192.168.1.254 (192.
⊞ User Datagram Protocol, Src Port: 35951 (35951), Dst Port: 53 (53)
⊞ Domain Name System (query)

0000  aa aa 03 00 00 00 08 00   45 00 00 7d 4c 68 00 00   ........ E..}Lh..
0010  80 11 69 79 c0 a8 01 40   c0 a8 01 fe 8c 6f 00 35   ..iy...@ .....o.5
0020  00 69 d8 13 61 d7 01 00   00 01 00 00 00 00 00 00   .i..a... ........
0030  01 30 08 32 32 30 39 31   30 38 31 05 37 30 30 33   .0.22091 081.7003
0040  33 04 31 34 62 35 04 31   36 61 64 04 33 65 39 62   3.14b5.1 6ad.3e9b
0050  02 31 30 01 30 1a 31 61   68 32 72 62 72 39 61 6c   .10.0.1a h2rbr9al
0060  39 31 61 68 71 6d 71 75   32 39 7a 75 32 6a 6e 76   91ahqmqu 29zu2jnv
0070  04 61 76 71 73 06 6d 63   61 66 65 65 03 63 6f 6d   .avqs.mc afee.com
0080  00 00 01 00 01                                      .....

Frame (189 bytes) ⟨ Decrypted WEP data (133 bytes) ⟩
AirPcap USB wireless capture adapter pr_00: <live capture in progress> File: C:\Users\Laura\AppDat...  Packets: 8534 Displayed: 373 Marked: 0
```

Figure 284. A decryption tag appears below the packet bytes pane when you have applied decryption to the traffic

When you decrypt WLAN traffic (just as when you decrypt SSL/TLS traffic), a tab appears just below the packet bytes pane. Click the **Decrypted WEP data** tab to view the decrypted traffic in the packet bytes pane. This tab will only appear when you have (a) decrypted traffic and (b) make the packet bytes pane visible.

Select to Prepend Radiotap or PPI Headers
You have three choices in WLAN settings for headers.

- 802.11 header only[87]
- Prepend a Radiotap pseudoheader
- Prepend a PPI (Per-Packet Information) pseudoheader

Use Wireless Settings (on the Wireless Toolbar) to define the header to be applied. The Radiotap and PPI pseudoheaders provide more information about the frames than exists in the 802.11 header only.

---

[87] This will provide you with the actual 802.11 header, but no information obtained by the local capturing interface. It is the least desirable option to use.

Figure 285 shows a standard 802.11 header that does not use a pseudo header.

```
⊞ Frame 9 (106 bytes on wire, 106 bytes captured)
⊟ IEEE 802.11 Beacon frame, Flags: ........
    Type/Subtype: Beacon frame (0x08)
  ⊟ Frame Control: 0x0080 (Normal)
      Version: 0
      Type: Management frame (0)
      Subtype: 8
    ⊟ Flags: 0x0
        .... ..00 = DS status: Not leaving DS or network is operating in AD-HOC mode
        .... .0.. = More Fragments: This is the last fragment
        .... 0... = Retry: Frame is not being retransmitted
        ...0 .... = PWR MGT: STA will stay up
        ..0. .... = More Data: No data buffered
        .0.. .... = Protected flag: Data is not protected
        0... .... = Order flag: Not strictly ordered
    Duration: 0
    Destination address: Broadcast (ff:ff:ff:ff:ff:ff)
    Source address: D-Link_cc:a3:ea (00:13:46:cc:a3:ea)
    BSS Id: D-Link_cc:a3:ea (00:13:46:cc:a3:ea)
    Fragment number: 0
    Sequence number: 2699
```

Figure 285. Standard 802.11 frame

The Radiotap and PPI headers supply additional information about frames captured. The Radiotap header provides this information from the AirPcap or libpcap driver to Wireshark. Figure 286 shows an 802.11 packet with a Radiotap header prepended to it.

The PPI header was developed in 2007. "The Per-Packet Information (PPI) Header is a general and extensible meta-information header format originally developed to provide 802.11n radio information, but can handle other information as well." To learn more about the PPI header format, download *PPI_Header_format_1.0.1.pdf* from *www.cacetech.com/documents*. Figure 287 shows an 802.11 packet with a PPI header prepended to it.

Use a Radiotap or PPI Header to Filter on WLAN Channels

You must apply the Radiotap or PPI header in order to filter on the 802.11 channel/frequency information. This information is not sent with a packet as a field value. When the WLAN packet is received by the adapter, the frequency that the packet was captured on is used to define which channel the packet was on— this frequency/channel information is shown in the Radiotap and PPI headers.

```
⊟ Radiotap Header v0, Length 24
    Header revision: 0
    Header pad: 0
    Header length: 24
⊟ Present flags: 0x000058ee
        .... .... .... .... .... .... .... ...0 = TSFT: False
        .... .... .... .... .... .... .... ..1. = Flags: True
        .... .... .... .... .... .... .... .1.. = Rate: True
        .... .... .... .... .... .... .... 1... = Channel: True
        .... .... .... .... .... .... ...0 .... = FHSS: False
        .... .... .... .... .... .... ..1. .... = DBM Antenna Signal: True
        .... .... .... .... .... .... .1.. .... = DBM Antenna Noise: True
        .... .... .... .... .... .... 1... .... = Lock Quality: True
        .... .... .... .... .... ...0 .... .... = TX Attenuation: False
        .... .... .... .... .... ..0. .... .... = DB TX Attenuation: False
        .... .... .... .... .... .0.. .... .... = DBM TX Attenuation: False
        .... .... .... .... .... 1... .... .... = Antenna: True
        .... .... .... .... ...1 .... .... .... = DB Antenna Signal: True
        .... .... .... .... ..0. .... .... .... = DB Antenna Noise: False
        .... .... .... .... .1.. .... .... .... = RX flags: True
        .... .... .... .0.. .... .... .... .... = Channel+: False
        0... .... .... .... .... .... .... .... = Ext: False
⊟ Flags: 0x10
    .... ...0 = CFP: False
    .... ..0. = Preamble: Long
    .... .0.. = WEP: False
    .... 0... = Fragmentation: False
    ...1 .... = FCS at end: True
    ..0. .... = Data Pad: False
    .0.. .... = Bad FCS: False
    0... .... = Short GI: False
    Data Rate: 54.0 Mb/s
    Channel frequency: 2462 [BG 11]
⊟ Channel type: 802.11g (pure-g) (0x00c0)
        .... .... ...0 .... = Turbo: False
        .... .... ..0. .... = Complementary Code Keying (CCK): False
        .... .... .1.. .... = Orthogonal Frequency-Division Multiplexing (OFDM): True
        .... .... 1... .... = 2 GHz spectrum: True
        .... ...0 .... .... = 5 GHz spectrum: False
        .... ..0. .... .... = Passive: False
        .... .0.. .... .... = Dynamic CCK-OFDM: False
        .... 0... .... .... = Gaussian Frequency Shift Keying (GFSK): False
        ...0 .... .... .... = GSM (900MHz): False
        ..0. .... .... .... = Static Turbo: False
        .0.. .... .... .... = Half Rate Channel (10MHz Channel Width): False
        0... .... .... .... = Quarter Rate Channel (5MHz Channel Width): False
    SSI Signal: -68 dBm
    SSI Noise: -100 dBm
    Signal Quality: 86
    Antenna: 0
    SSI Signal: 32 dB
⊟ RX flags: 0x50d0
        .... .... .... .... .... ..0. = Bad PLCP: False
```

Figure 286. 802.11 Radiotap header

Note that both the Radiotap and PPI headers include information about signal strength. The signal strength value is based on the signal strength at the location and time that the packet was received. The Radiotap header and PPI headers contain a channel/frequency values as well.

```
⊟ PPI version 0, 32 bytes
    Version: 0
  ⊟ Flags: 0x00
      .... ...0 = Alignment: Not aligned
      0000 000. = Reserved: 0x00
    Header length: 32
    DLT: 105
  ⊟ 802.11-Common
      Field type: 802.11-Common (2)
      Field length: 20
      TSFT: 0 [invalid]
    ⊟ Flags: 0x0001
        .... .... .... ...1 = FCS present flag: Present
        .... .... .... ..0. = TSFT flag: microseconds
        .... .... .... .0.. = FCS validity: Valid
        .... .... .... 0... = PHY error flag: No errors
      Rate: 54.0 Mbps
      Channel frequency: 2462 [BG 11]
    ⊟ Channel type: 802.11g (pure-g) (0x00c0)
        .... .... ...0 .... = Turbo: False
        .... .... ..0. .... = Complementary Code Keying (CCK): False
        .... .... .1.. .... = Orthogonal Frequency-Division Multiplexing (OFDM): True
        .... .... 1... .... = 2 GHz spectrum: True
        .... ...0 .... .... = 5 GHz spectrum: False
        .... ..0. .... .... = Passive: False
        .... .0.. .... .... = Dynamic CCK-OFDM: False
        .... 0... .... .... = Gaussian Frequency Shift Keying (GFSK): False
      FHSS hopset: 0x00
      FHSS pattern: 0x00
      dBm antenna signal: -58
      dBm antenna noise: -100
```

Figure 287. 802.11 PPI header

Compare Signal Strength and Signal-to-Noise Ratios

The signal strength indicator value defines the power, but not the quality of the signal. The value is defined in dBm (power ratio in decibels referenced to one milliwatt).

From 0 to -65 dBm is considered excellent to acceptable signal strength whereas the signal strength becomes an issue as it moves lower (closer to -100 dBm). Problems will likely occur if the signal strength goes below -80 dBm. Signal strength issues between the WLAN hosts and access points may lead to retransmissions and eventually loss of connectivity.

The signal-to-noise ratio defines the difference between the signal and noise values. Higher ratio numbers indicate less noise obstruction. If this value reaches as low as < 15 dB, performance is degraded.

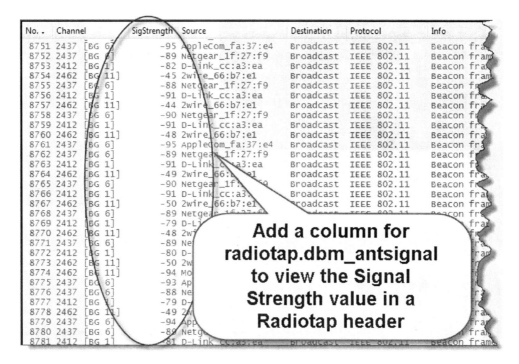

Figure 288. Consider adding a column for the signal strength value

You can create columns to show the values of the receive signal strength using either the IEEE 802.11 RSSI predefined column or the individual fields contained in the Radiotap or PPI headers. In Figure 288 we have added a column for the `radiotap.dbm_antsignal` field.

For more information on customizing Wireshark for WLAN analysis, refer to *Customize Wireshark for WLAN Analysis* on page 533.

Understand 802.11 Traffic Basics

There are three types of 802.11 frames seen on WLANs.

Data   Contains data of some sort

Management   Used to establish MAC-layer connectivity; Association Request/Responses, Probe Requests/Responses and Beacons are examples of management frames.

Control   Used to enable delivery of data and management frames; Request-to-Send (RTS) and Clear-to-Send (CTS) and ACKs are Control frames

The management and control frames are used to enable the basic 802.11 processes. Data frames are quite simply used to transfer data across the WLAN.

Data Frames

Data frames are the only WLAN frame types that can be forwarded to the wired network.[88]

Although the IEEE 802.11 specifications state that the MAC Service Data Unit (MSDU) can be up to 2304 bytes, you will probably see smaller data frames as these frames are bridged to an Ethernet network.

For example, if a STA makes a connection to an HTTP server on the wired network, the MSS will be negotiated during the TCP handshake process. This is the size of the TCP segment that will be prepended by the TCP and IP headers and encapsulated in an 802.11 header.

For more information on 802.11 frame sizes, refer to *Dissect the 802.11 Frame Structure* on page 526.

Management Frames

The following lists some of the most commonly seen 802.11 management frames. Refer to *Analyze Frame Control Types and Subtypes* on page 527 for a more complete list of 802.11 management frames.

Management Frames	
Authentication	STA sends to AP with identity. OpenSysAuth: AP sends Authentication frame back indicating success or failure; SharedKey: AP sends challenge text. NIC sends encrypted version of challenge text using key. AP sends Authentication frame indicating success or failure
Deauthentication	STA sends to terminate secure communications
Association	Used by AP to synchronize with STA radio and define capabilities
Reassociation	Sent by STA to new AP; triggers AP to get buffered data (if any) from previous AP
Disassociation	Sent by STA to terminate an association with the AP
Beacon	Sent every 100 ms (default) by AP to announce its presence and provide info; STAs continuously scan for other APs
Probe	Request/Response. STA uses to obtain info from another STA; e.g., find APs in range (request/response)

One of the most important management frames on the WLAN is the beacon frame. If users complain about intermittent loss of connectivity to the WLAN, consider creating an IO Graph using a filter for beacon frames. These frames should occur at an interval of approximately 100ms.

---

[88] The only exception to this is the Null Data frame which carries no data at all and do not cross onto the wired network as they are typically used to carry information to other WLAN stations.

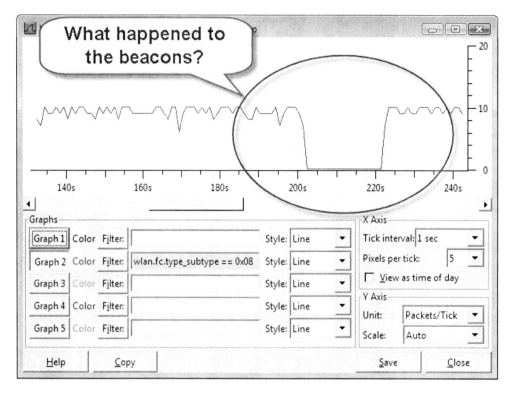

Figure 289. Filtering an IO Graph on beacons indicates that we cannot see beacons at the expected interval

The beacon issue illustrated in Figure 289 could be caused by two factors—either the access point stopped beaconing for a period[89] or we were unable to capture the beacons for some reason. We can determine which situation is true by capturing the beacons on a second analyzer. Refer to *Filter on All WLAN Traffic* on page 526 for a list of display filters you can use in your IO Graphs.

Control Frames

The following lists the most commonly seen 802.11 control frames seen. Refer to *Analyze Frame Control Types and Subtypes* on page 527 for a more complete list of 802.11 control frames.

Control Frames	
Request-to-Send	(optional) Used as part of 2-way handshake to request transmission privileges
Clear-to-Send	(optional) Second part of 2-way handshake.
ACK	Sent by receiver to indicate data frame received OK. No ACK would trigger an 802.11 retransmission by the sender.

---

[89] This is considered a very unusual condition, but the 802.11 specifications acknowledge that beacons "the transmission of any beacon may be delayed due to a medium busy condition." Such a long delay, however, would indicate a major problem that could indicate RF interference or a malfunctioning AP.

Analyze Normal 802.11 Communications

In this section we will look at some WLAN communications to view how stations connect to wireless networks. This process requires that a station locate a wireless network, authenticate and associate to the network. When a station wants to access a wireless network, it must connect with an access point that supports the desired SSID.

The station can either wait (passive mode) for a beacon frame from the access point or the station can send a probe request to find the access point (active mode). When an access point is configured not to broadcast an SSID, stations that are configured with an SSID value will need to broadcast probe requests onto the WLAN to find an access point with that SSID. By default, beacon frames are sent at approximately 100ms intervals.

```
No.    Time       Source            Destination   Protocol   Info
   1 0.000000  Cisco-Li_73:b5:56  Broadcast   IEEE 802.11  Beacon frame, SN=121, F
   2 0.102400  Cisco-Li_73:b5:56  Broadcast   IEEE 802.11  Beacon frame, SN=122, F

+ Frame 2: 78 bytes on wire (624 bits), 78 bytes captured (624 bits)
- IEEE 802.11 Beacon frame, Flags: ........
   Type/Subtype: Beacon frame (0x08)
 - Frame Control: 0x0080 (Normal)
    Version: 0
    Type: Management frame (0)
    Subtype: 8
 - Flags: 0x0
    .... ..00 = DS status: Not leaving DS or network is operating in AD-HOC mod
    .... .0.. = More Fragments: This is the last fragment
    .... 0... = Retry: Frame is not being retransmitted
    ...0 .... = PWR MGT: STA will stay up
    ..0. .... = More Data: No data buffered
    .0.. .... = Protected flag: Data is not protected
    0... .... = Order flag: Not strictly ordered
   Duration: 0
   Destination address: Broadcast (ff:ff:ff:ff:ff:ff)
   Source address: Cisco-Li_73:b5:56 (00:14:bf:73:b5:56)
   BSS Id: Cisco-Li_73:b5:56 (00:14:bf:73:b5:56)
   Fragment number: 0
   Sequence number: 122
- IEEE 802.11 wireless LAN management frame
 - Fixed parameters (12 bytes)
    Timestamp: 0x000000001960E145
    Beacon Interval: 0.102400 [Seconds]
  + Capability Information: 0x0471
 - Tagged parameters (42 bytes)
  - SSID parameter set
     Tag Number: 0 (SSID parameter set)
     Tag length: 11
     Tag interpretation: CorporateAP: "CorporateAP"
  + Supported Rates: 1.0(B) 2.0(B) 5.5(B) 11.0(B) 22.0
  + DS Parameter set: Current Channel: 11
  + Traffic Indication Map (TIM): DTIM 0 of 1 bitmap empty
  + ERP Information: no Non-ERP STAs, do not use protection, short or long preamb
  + Extended Supported Rates: 6.0 9.0 12.0 18.0 24.0 36.0 48.0 54.0
Interpretation of tag (wlan_mgt.tag.interpretation), 11 bytes    Packets: 104 Displayed: 104 Marked: 0 Time: 00:00:00
```

Figure 290. Beacon frames announce the SSID parameter set

Connection to a WLAN requires that the STA (a) decide which AP to join, (b) successfully complete the authentication process, and (c) successfully complete the association process.

Dissect the 802.11 Frame Structure

802.11 headers contain much more information than a simple Ethernet header that contains 3 fields (excluding the FCS at the end of the packet). For example, An 802.11 association frame contains 17 fields in the header. Many of the fields are only a single bit long. The retry flag, for example, is only 1 bit long.

The frame body is variable length—even the maximum size is variable length depending on the encryption type in use. As mentioned earlier in this chapter, the IEEE 802.11 specifications state that the MSDU (MAC Service Data Unit) is 2304 bytes[90].

Figure 291. The basic 802.11 frame structure

Note that you'll see the number 2312 listed often as the maximum frame body length of 802.11 frames. That length assumes a WEP-encrypted frame—encryption routines affect the length of the 802.11 packets:

- WEP: add 8 bytes to the MSDU length (2,312)
- WPA (TKIP): add 20 bytes to the MSDU length (2,324)
- CCMP (WPA2): add 16 bytes to the MSDU length (2,320)

Although the Frame Control field is only 2 bytes, it carries much information and we can build many filters on the fields contained therein. For more details on the Frame Control field, refer to *Analyze Frame Control Types and Subtypes* on page 527.

The gray fields are required in all 802.11 frames. For information on 802.11 addressing, refer to Figure 293 and the "To DS/From DS" table that follows. The 802.11 frames end with a Frame Check Sequence (FCS) which provides error checking on the contents of the frame.

Filter on All WLAN Traffic

The capture filter syntax for specific WLAN hosts is `wlan host wlan_mac` for example `wlan host 08:00:34:2a:f3:3b`. In addition, you can create capture filters for specific types of frames using the syntax `wlan[0] = 0x80` (this capture filter is used to capture beacons only).

The basic display filter for 802.11 traffic is `wlan`.

---

[90] This is the maximum frame size before encryption. In reality, however, you will likely see smaller packets due to the fact that your data traffic has to bridge to an Ethernet network and, in the case of TCP, an MSS value is defined during the handshake.

The following table lists numerous 802.11 display filters.

WLAN Display Filter	Description
`radiotap.channel.freq == 2412`	Channel 1 traffic (Radiotap header)
`radiotap.channel.freq == 2437`	Channel 6 traffic (Radiotap header)
`radiotap.channel.freq == 2462`	Channel 11 traffic (Radiotap header)
`wlan.fc.type_subtype == 8`	Beacon frames only
`!wlan.fc.type_subtype == 8`	All frames except Beacons
`wlan.fc.type_subtype == 4 ||` `wlan.fc.type_subtype == 5`	Probe requests and probe responses
`wlan.fc.retry == 1`	Frame is a retransmission

Analyze Frame Control Types and Subtypes

The Frame Control field in an 802.11 header is shown in Figure 292. As you can see, the Frame Control field contains numerous individual fields.

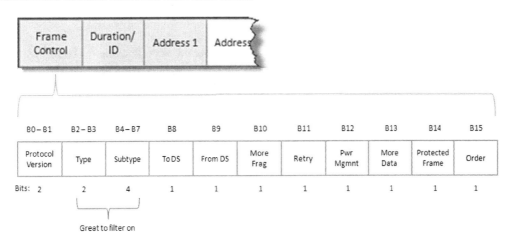

Figure 292. Inside the 802.11 Frame Control field

The following lists the basic 802.11 Frame Control field elements:

Field	Description
Protocol Version	Protocol Version Number—always set to 00 at this time
Type/Subtype	Management, Control, Data Frame
To DS/From DS	0,0 between stations in same BSS (DS distribution system) - 0,1 to DS - 1,0 From DS - 1,1 From DS to DS

Field	Description
More Fragments	Set to 1, fragmentation is set at the 802.11 MAC layer
Retry	Set to 1, this is an 802.11 retransmission[91]
Power Management	Set to 1, the STA is stating it is in power save mode
More Data	Typically used by AP to tell STA in power save mode that more data is buffered for it
Protected Frame	Set to 1 when data is encrypted
Order	Set to 1 when order is important; discard frame if out of order

As shown in Figure 291, 802.11 frames can use up to four address fields that are abbreviated as follows:

- BSSID—Basic Service Set identifier
- DA—Destination address
- SA—Source address
- RA—Receiver address
- TA—Transmitter address

The addressing in WLAN packets can be confusing. Keith Parsons from Institute for Network Professionals (*wirelesslanprofessionals.com*) created the following table and Figure 293 to demonstrate how the "To DS" and "From DS" bits are set on traffic moving through an extended WLAN.

To DS	From DS	Address 1	Address 2	Address 3	Address 4
0	0	RA/DA	TA/SA	BSSID	n/a
0	1	RA/DA	TA/BSSID	SA	n/a
1	0	RA/BSSID	TA/SA	DA	n/a
1	1	RA	TA	DA	SA

---

[91] When the Retry bit is set, it indicates that the frame is an 802.11 retransmission. This is a MAC-layer retransmission—additional retransmissions may occur at the transport layer (as in the case of TCP retransmissions, for example) or at the application layer. To spot retransmissions easier, consider setting a coloring rule to highlight 802.11 packets that have this bit set.

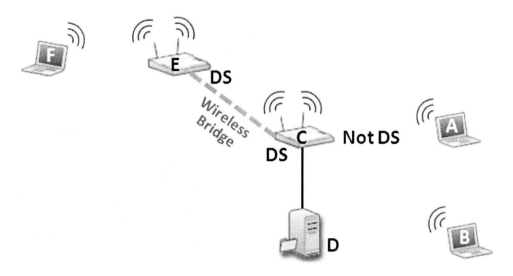

Figure 293. The WLAN header indicates if traffic is destined to or from or contained within a distribution system (DS)

Translate WLAN Type/Subtype Values to Hex for Easy Filtering

When you are creating display filters on these values and using these next pages as a reference, translate the type/subtype values to hex and use the `wlan.fc.type_subtype` *field value.*

For example, to filter on Probe Response packets:

> Convert 000101 to hex
> The first two bits = 00 = 0x0, the next four bits = 0101 = 0x5
> The display filter is `wlan.fc.type_subtype == 0x05`

In Figure 294 we have applied a display filter for probe requests and probe replies. In addition, we have created a color filter for retransmission packets. On this network we can see a high number of retransmissions.

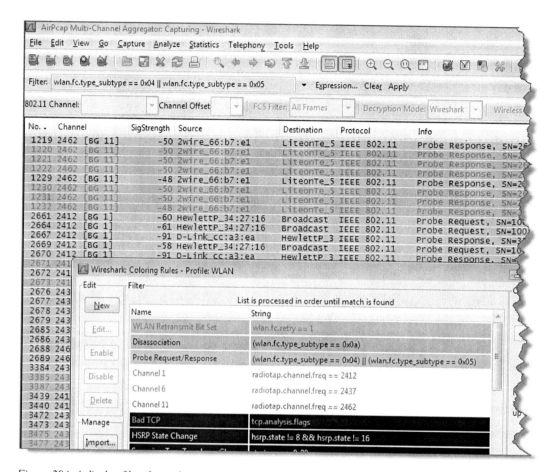

Figure 294. A display filter for probe requests and probe responses used in conjunction with a color filter for retransmissions

The following table lists the Wireshark filters for management, control and data frame type and subtype values in 802.11 packets.

Wireshark Type/Subtype Display Filter	Type	Subtype
`wlan.fc.type_subtype ==0`	Management	Association Request
`wlan.fc.type_subtype ==1`	Management	Association Response
`wlan.fc.type_subtype ==2`	Management	Reassociation Request
`wlan.fc.type_subtype ==3`	Management	Reassociation Response
`wlan.fc.type_subtype ==4`	Management	Probe Request

Wireshark Type/Subtype Display Filter	Type	Subtype
`wlan.fc.type_subtype ==5`	Management	Probe Response
`wlan.fc.type_subtype ==6 ‖` `wlan.fc.type_subtype ==7`	Management	Reserved
`wlan.fc.type_subtype ==8`	Management	Beacon
`wlan.fc.type_subtype ==9`	Management	ATIM
`wlan.fc.type_subtype ==10`	Management	Disassociation
`wlan.fc.type_subtype ==11`	Management	Authentication
`wlan.fc.type_subtype ==12`	Management	Deauthentication
`wlan.fc.type_subtype ==13`	Management	Action
`wlan.fc.type_subtype ==14 ‖` `wlan.fc.type_subtype ==15`	Management	Reserved
`wlan.fc.type_subtype > 15 &&` `wlan.fc.type_subtype <= 0x23`	Control	Reserved
`wlan.fc.type_subtype ==24`	Control	Block Ack Request
`wlan.fc.type_subtype ==25`	Control	Block Ack
`wlan.fc.type_subtype ==26`	Control	PS-Poll
`wlan.fc.type_subtype ==27`	Control	Request to Send
`wlan.fc.type_subtype ==28`	Control	Clear to Send
`wlan.fc.type_subtype ==29`	Control	ACK
`wlan.fc.type_subtype ==30`	Control	CF-End
`wlan.fc.type_subtype ==31`	Control	CF-End + CF-ACK
`wlan.fc.type_subtype ==32`	Data	Data
`wlan.fc.type_subtype ==33`	Data	Data + CF-ACK

Wireshark Type/Subtype Display Filter	Type	Subtype
`wlan.fc.type_subtype ==34`	Data	Data + CF-Poll
`wlan.fc.type_subtype ==35`	Data	Data+CF-ACK + CF-Poll
`wlan.fc.type_subtype ==36`	Data	Null (no data)
`wlan.fc.type_subtype ==37`	Data	CF-Ack (no data)
`wlan.fc.type_subtype ==38`	Data	CF-Poll (no data)
`wlan.fc.type_subtype ==39`	Data	CF-ACK + CF-Poll (no data)
`wlan.fc.type_subtype ==40`	Data	QoS Data
`wlan.fc.type_subtype ==41`	Data	QoS Data + CF-ACK
`wlan.fc.type_subtype ==42`	Data	QoS Data + CF-Poll
`wlan.fc.type_subtype ==43`	Data	QoS Data + CF-ACK + CF-Poll
`wlan.fc.type_subtype ==44`	Data	QoS Null (no data)
`wlan.fc.type_subtype ==45`	Data	Reserved
`wlan.fc.type_subtype ==46`	Data	QoS CF-Poll (no data)
`wlan.fc.type_subtype ==47`	Data	QoS CF-ACK + CF-Poll (no data)
`wlan.fc.type_subtype > 47 && wlan.fc.type_subtype <= 63`	Reserved	Reserved

Customize Wireshark for WLAN Analysis

The following checklist defines items that you may consider when creating a WLAN profile for Wireshark. These settings assume you have prepended the Radiotap header to the received packets as explained in *Select to Prepend Radiotap or PPI Headers* on page 518.

Customization	Description
`radiotap.channel.freq == 2412`	Coloring rule: Channel 1 (white background; green foreground)
`radiotap.channel.freq == 2437`	Coloring rule: Channel 6 (white background; red foreground)
`radiotap.channel.freq == 2462`	Coloring rule: Channel 11 (white background; blue foreground)
`wlan.fc.retry == 1`	Coloring rule: WLAN retries (orange background; black foreground)[92]
Frequency/Channel	Column: Available as a predefined column
`radiotap.dbm_antsignal`	Column: Displaying the antenna signal information in the Radiotap header
`radiotap.datarate`	Column: Displays the detected data rate of the WLAN frame
`wlan.fc.ds`	Column: Indicates the settings of the "To DS" and "From DS" bits

Consider creating a "WLAN" profile with the settings above. For more information on creating Wireshark profiles, refer to *Chapter 11: Customize Wireshark Profiles*.

---

[92] If this coloring rule is moved above the channel coloring rules you will not be able to detect which channel you are experiencing retries on without opening the packets. You can either combine the channel and retry coloring rules (for example you could create a coloring rule with an orange background and green foreground for `radiotap.channel.freq == 2412 && wlan.fc.retry == 1`) or you could add a frequency/channel column to the Packet List pane.

Case Study:
Cruddy Barcode Communications

Submitted by: Vik Evans

Recently I worked as a wireless engineer for a large shipping company. We had wireless deployments from a couple vendors in place at hundreds of sites for the purpose of scanning packages/freight. We also had large numbers of legacy 802.11b as well as newer 802.11b/g scanners in use.

I had performed a wireless switch software upgrade at a number of sites and shortly after that we started getting calls about application slowness on the legacy scanners. These scanners and the application they used had been in production for years, with no real maintenance performed on them.

Anyway, sites started calling in and complaining that the scanners were now slow. The actual symptom was that the screen refresh between scans was taking several seconds for every scan. "Normal" was 1-3 seconds between screens, but users were reporting 7-10 seconds now. The users could not continue scanning packages until the refresh between scans completed.

The wireless switches in question were running an OS version that included a basic version of Wireshark, or rather T-shark, as it was run from a command line with a "pktcap" command. I could execute a capture on the ETH ports of the switch or on the VLAN interfaces. The switch had dual ETH ports, eth1 and eth2, respectively.

Capturing on eth1 did not do much for me as it only captured the layer-2 frames from the access-ports, as they were called, encapsulated by some proprietary method. I had reason to believe that the "problem" lied within the communication of the application to the server; capturing on eth2 would give me decrypted IP packets from the wireless clients to the wired side server, which I could then decode with Wireshark.

Reviewing the capture, we could see the scan transaction take place—the barcode is scanned, the server acknowledges receipt and then sends screen refresh to client. However; the data returned by the server was coming back in 64-byte packets and further, there was no acknowledgment for the first data packet sent, but for the remaining packets client acknowledgments were seen.

Decoding the packets from the server, we noticed that the server was sending the refresh data as single character, one packet at a time. Because of the initial lost acknowledgment from the client, the server would then retransmit the data, yet this time the transaction was sent in a single "full" 1500-byte packet. Upon receiving that single packet, the client screen would refresh and scanning could continue. Adding up the time from the first packet sent by the server to the final "full" packet and subsequent client acknowledgment was always around 7 to 10 seconds, as reported by the users.

Why was the server sending such small packets? This isn't efficient at all!

Well, to get to the "meat," we spoke to the sys-admin responsible for that server, which was running UNIX and he was able to configure the server so that the server would buffer return data until it could send a single 1500-byte packet.

This resulted in a successful transmit—receive—acknowledge transaction between the scanner clients and server and "fixed" a problem that had been present for years, but was revealed as a result of my wireless switch OS upgrade. This upgrade included improvements in switching speed and over all better efficiency of data processing, bringing our problem to the surface.

That "lost" acknowledgment for the first 64-byte packet that the server sent was the result of the scanner going into sleep mode. The scanner was not returning to a ready state in time to receive that first packet, yet it received and acknowledged every other packet after that.

Yes—there were more problems, including scanner drivers that had never been kept up with the infrastructure upgrades (scanners were not within our responsibilities), but I digress.

Summary

Wireless networks (WLANs) are based on the IEEE 802.11 standard and rely on radio frequency (RF) signals to communicate. WLANs use CSMA/CA—Carrier Sense, Multiple Access with Collision Avoidance. The integrity and strength of RF signals should be evaluated with a spectrum analyzer when WLAN problems occur.

In a typical WLAN environment, traffic flows between stations (STAs) and access points (APs). If traffic from a STA is destined to a target on the wired network and that traffic never arrives on the wired network, we can assume a problem occurred on the WLAN side of the communications.

Ideally, your Wireshark WLAN interface should support both promiscuous and monitor mode operations to capture traffic to and from other devices, regardless of the SSID they are associated with.

WLAN traffic can be encrypted in a number of ways. Wireshark must be configured with the correct key or passphrase in order to decrypt this traffic.

Wireshark can prepend two different types of pseudoheaders onto the 802.11 header—a Radiotap header or a PPI header. These headers provide additional information about the frames received—information that is not available in the 802.11 header itself.

There are three WLAN traffic types: control, management and data. The WLAN frame type is defined in the Type/Subtype fields. Control frames are used to enable the delivery of data and management frames. Management frames are used to establish the MAC-layer connectivity between STAs and APs. Data frames contain data of some type.

Wireshark's WLAN statistics lists the SSID, channel numbers and packet types of all network traffic or just the selected channel. When analyzing WLAN traffic on different channels, consider using coloring rules to differentiate the channel traffic and adding columns for channel/frequency and signal strength information.

Practice What You've Learned

The book website, *www.wiresharkbook.com*, contains numerous Chanalyzer recordings (listed in Appendix A). Download the latest version of Chanalyzer from *www.metageek.net* and select **File | Open Recording** to review the RF signal recordings.

Refer to *Appendix A* for more information on the Chanalyzer recordings included on the book website.

The following table lists several trace files available from the Download section on the book website, *www.wiresharkbook.com*. Download and use these trace files to answer the questions about WLAN traffic.

wlan-ppi.pcap   This is a TCP handshake running over a WLAN and prepending with a PPI (Per-Packet-Information) header. Expand the PPI header completely.

What channel were these packets received on?

What was the data rate of these packets?

What was the dBm antenna signal strength value of these packets at the time of capture by the WLAN adapter?

wlan-radiotap.pcap

This is a TCP handshake running over a WLAN and prepending with a Radiotap header. Expand the Radiotap header completely.

What channel were these packets received on?

What was the data rate of these packets?

What was the dBm antenna signal strength value of these packets at the time of capture by the WLAN adapter?

wlan-signalissue.pcap

This traffic was captured by an AirPcap adapter and Wireshark on 192.168.0.106 as it pings the WLAN access point at 192.168.0.1. During this capture, 192.168.0.106 is moving around—at times almost touching the AirPcap adapter directly to the WLAN AP antenna.

Create and apply a display filter for the PPI antenna signal value. What is the range of the antenna signals seen in this trace file?

Add this PPI antenna signal value as a custom column and apply a display filter for traffic from 192.168.0.106. What is the range of the antenna signals in packets from this host?

Apply a filter for traffic from 192.168.0.1 now. What is the range of the antenna signals in packets from this host?

Can you find points in the trace where the signal strength was too weak to reach the target? Can you locate where the AirPcap adapter was closest to the AP antenna?

wlan-ap-problem.pcap

Create an IO Graph for this beacon traffic.

Why are users having problems connecting to the WLAN at times?

Review Questions

Q26.1   What does an Access Point do with the 802.11 header when it forwards a packet onto an Ethernet network?

Q26.2   What tool can be used to identify RF interference and RF energy?

Q26.3   What is monitor mode?

Q26.4   What are your capture limitations if the WLAN adapter does not support promiscuous mode?

Q26.5   What graph can you create to verify access point availability?

Q26.6   What is the advantage of prepending a Radiotap header to your 802.11 traffic?

Q26.7   What are the three WLAN traffic types used to transport data, establish MAC-layer connectivity and enable delivery of frames?

Q26.8   What is the purpose of Association frames on a WLAN?

Q26.9   What is the default interval of WLAN beacon frames?

Answers to Review Questions

Q26.1   **What does an Access Point do with the 802.11 header when it forwards a packet onto an Ethernet network?**

A26.1   The access point strips off the 802.11 header and applies an Ethernet header before forwarding the packet on.

Q26.2   **What tool can be used to identify RF interference and RF energy?**

A26.2   A spectrum analyzer, such as Wi-Spy and Chanalyzer, offer an insight into RF interference and RF energy.

Q26.3   **What is monitor mode?**

A26.3   In monitor mode, an adapter does not associate with any SSID—all packets from all SSIDs on the selected channel are captured.

Q26.4   **What are your capture limitations if the WLAN adapter does not support promiscuous mode?**

A26.4   If an adapter does not support promiscuous mode, you will not be able to listen to traffic destined to other hardware addresses. You must capture traffic directly on the host in which you are interested.

Q26.5   **What graph can you create to verify access point availability?**

A26.5   To verify access point availability you can create an IO Graph and add a filter for beacon frames (`wlan.fc.type_subtype == 0x08`).

Q26.6   **What is the advantage of prepending a Radiotap header to your 802.11 traffic?**

A26.6   The Radiotap header contains the `radiotap.channel.freq` field. Prepending this header on the packets enables you to filter on the WLAN channel.

Q26.7 **What are the three WLAN traffic types used to transport data, establish MAC-layer connectivity and enable delivery of frames?**

A26.7 The three WLAN traffic types are data, management and control.

Q26.8 **What is the purpose of Association frames on a WLAN?**

A26.8 Association request and response frames are sent by stations to synchronize with the access point and exchange capability information.

Q26.9 **What is the default interval of WLAN beacon frames?**

A26.9 By default, beacon frames are sent approximately every 100ms.

Chapter 27: Introduction to Voice over IP (VoIP) Analysis

Wireshark Certified Network Analyst Exam Objectives covered:

- Understand VoIP Traffic Flows
- Analyze VoIP Problems
- Examine SIP Traffic
- Examine RTP Traffic
- Play Back VoIP
- Create a VoIP Profile
- Filter on VoIP Traffic

Understand VoIP Traffic Flows

Wireshark can dissect many of the call setup protocols and the voice stream itself.

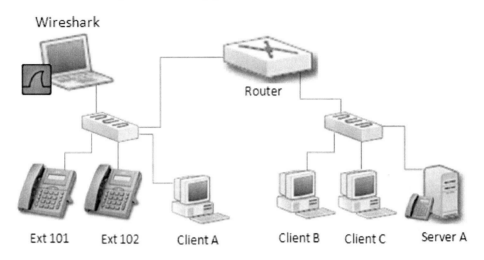

Figure 295. To troubleshoot VoIP, consider capturing traffic as close to the phone unit as possible

VoIP communications consist of two primary parts—the signaling protocol for call setup and teardown and the transport protocol for the voice communications.

Session Initiation Protocol (SIP) is an example of a VoIP signaling protocol. SIP can run over UDP or TCP port 5060 (it is more common to see SIP running over UDP).

Realtime Transport Protocol (RTP) carries the voice call itself. Wireshark includes an RTP player that enables you to playback VoIP conversations[93].

Another protocol, Realtime Transport Control Protocol (RTCP) provides out-of-band statistics and control information for an RTP flow.

RTP can run over any even port number whereas RTCP runs over the next higher odd port number. For example, if RTP runs over port 8000, RTCP runs over port 8001.

You may also see Dual-Tone Multi-Frequency (DTMF) telephony events during your VoIP analysis sessions. DTMF is the tones sent when you push a button on a phone, for example, when you push an extension number. Sometimes these signals are sent in the voice channel in which case it's referred to as in-band signaling. More often you'll see separate control packets for DTMF which is called out-of-band signaling. Wireshark recognizes and dissects out-of-band DTMF traffic.

Figure 295 shows a simple VoIP network configuration. Server A is the telephony server and our network has two VoIP phones in this area of the network. To analyze the VoIP traffic, consider

---

[93] Wireshark cannot decrypt and play back secure VoIP traffic.

placing the analyzer as close as possible to the VoIP phone to obtain round trip times and packet loss from that phone's perspective.

If Wireshark doesn't see the signaling protocol, it may not be able to identify the VoIP datastream and mark the conversation simply as UDP traffic in the protocol column of the Packet List pane. Select **"Try to decode RTP outside of conversations"** in the RTP preference setting. Alternately, if you are certain the traffic is RTP, right click a packet and select **Decode As...** Select the UDP port option for **"both"** and choose **RTP** in the protocols list.

In the following example, we examine the call setup process when one phone at extension 201 connects to another phone at extension 204.

When a VoIP call is initiated, the signaling protocol is used to set up the call. In this example, the signaling traffic flows through our telephony server when the phone sends an invite. The telephony server sends an Invite to the target phone while sending a 100 Trying message to the caller. The receiving phone indicates that it is ringing (180 Ringing)—this information is also forwarded to the call initiator.

When the user at extension 204 picks up the phone, it sends 200 OK indicating the call has been accepted.

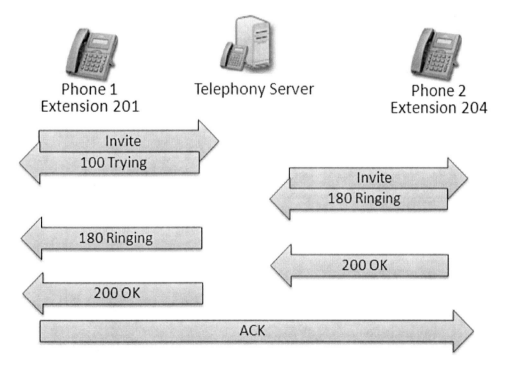

Figure 296. The VoIP call setup process

Figure 297 shows a VoIP call setup and call in Wireshark. In this case, the caller is contacting the telephony server (dialing 0). The telephony server responds with a tone indicating it is listening. In this example, both SIP and RTP are using UDP—no TCP handshake is used for the call setup or the call itself.

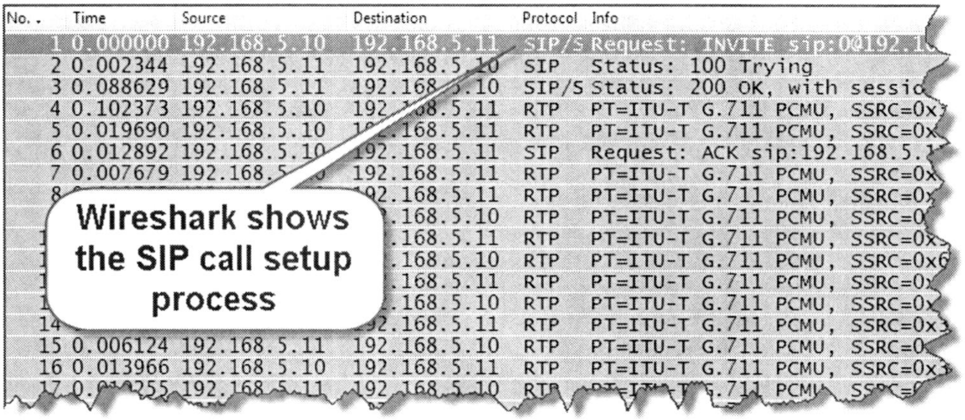

Figure 297. A VoIP call setup using SIP precedes the call that uses RTP

Wireshark offers dissectors for many protocols used in VoIP communications. These protocols are listed at *wiki.wireshark.org/VOIPProtocolFamily* and include:

- Call control: SIP, SDP, RTSP, H.323, H225, Q.931, H.248/MEGACO, MGCP, Cisco Skinny (SCCP)
- Transport: RTP, RTCP, SRTP
- Authentication, Authorization and Accounting: Radius, Diameter

To keep up-to-date on the latest VoIP analysis capabilities, visit *wiki.wireshark.org/VoIP_calls*.

Session Bandwidth and RTP Port Definition

Figure 298 shows the contents of the 200 OK response. This SIP packet contains Session Description Protocol (SDP). SDP is used to provide information about media streams in multimedia sessions. Refer to RFC 4566, Session Description Protocol (SDP) and RFC 3264, An Offer/Answer Model with the Session Description Protocol (SDP).

The SDP information includes:

- (*o*) owner/creator of the session
- (*s*) session name (if any)
- (*c*) connection information (IP address)
- (*b*) bandwidth estimate (see the bandwidth per call information later in this chapter)
- (*m*) media name (in this case RTP will be used for the call on port 25,426)
- (*a*) session attributes (the G.711 codec is offered)

Codecs are used to convert an analog voice signal into a digitally encoded signal. Codecs vary in quality, compression rate and bandwidth requirements. In Figure 297 the VoIP call is using G711 as the codec.

The codec that will be used for the voice call is defined in the SDP portion of the SIP communications. Figure 298 shows the bandwidth value estimate (for a bidirectional call) and RTP port that will be used for the call.

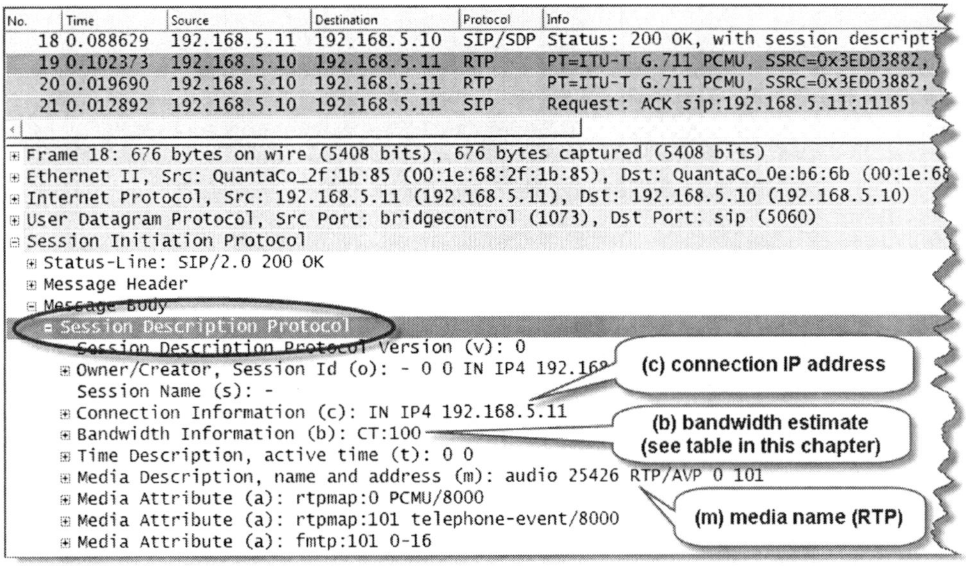

Figure 298. The VoIP codec and bandwidth information is included in the SDP portion of SIP conversation

Figure 298. The VoIP codec and bandwidth information is included in the SDP portion of SIP conversation

Creating IO Graphs to examine the packets per second rate based on the codec used can help you easily depict problems in either direction of a call. The following table shows the packets per second and bandwidth required for each side of a VoIP call.

Codec	Packets Per Second Rate	Bandwidth Per Call (kbps)[94]
G711	50	87.2
G729	50	31.2
G723.1	34	21.9
G726	50	47.2
G728	34	31.5

The case study in *Chapter 8: Interpret Basic Trace File Statistics* demonstrates how to build an IO Graph showing each side of a VoIP call.

---

[94] This calculation is based on a VoIP call traversing an Ethernet network and takes into account the Ethernet header overhead (18 bytes), the 20 byte IP header and 8 byte UDP header.

Analyze VoIP Problems

When VoIP communications experience problems, calls may not go through or the call quality may be degraded—the caller may hear echoing, or their voice may drop out sporadically.

VoIP communications are negatively affected by packet loss and jitter. In this section we will examine the characteristics and causes of both conditions.

Packet Loss

Realtime Transport Protocol typically carries call data over UDP, a connectionless protocol. UDP does not track packets to ensure they arrive at the destination. If a packet is lost, it is not resent by UDP. An application must retransmit the traffic. In the case of VoIP, retransmissions would not be a good thing because the retransmissions may create a conversation where words are out of order or further garbled. Imagine if the call came through as "Hello, Laura. How... you are?"

In Figure 299, we have selected Telephony | RTP | Show All Streams to identify over 12% packet loss in one call direction. From this window we can create a filter based on that stream's source and destination IP addresses and ports or we can mark all the packets in a stream[95].

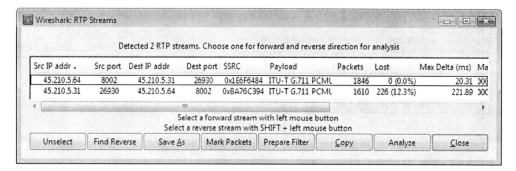

*Figure 299. Use **Telephony | RTP | Show All Streams** to identify packet loss in VoIP calls*

When you select Analyze, Wireshark lists the packets in the RTP stream and provides additional details on the VoIP call. The Status column indicates problems in the RTP streams. In Figure 300 packet loss is denoted by *Wrong sequence* indications in the Status column.

Packet loss can occur because of timing issues such as excessive jitter or clock skew between VoIP end points.

---

[95] This is a quick way to save an RTP stream while still working in the trace. Mark the stream from this window and later select **File | Save As** and choose Marked packets.

Packet ▲	Sequence ◀	Delta(ms) ◀	Filtered Jitter(ms) ◀	Skew(ms) ◀	IP BW(kbps ◀	Marker ◀	Status ◀
20	20180	0.00	0.00	0.00	1.60	SET	[Ok]
22	20181	20.00	0.00	-0.00	3.20		[Ok]
24	20182	19.99	0.00	0.01	4.80		[Ok]
26	20183	19.97	0.00	0.04	6.40		[Ok]
28	20184	20.00	0.00	0.04	8.00		[Ok]
30	20185	20.10	0.01	-0.06	9.60		[Ok]
32	20186	19.86	0.02	0.08	11.20		[Ok]
34	20187	19.97	0.02	0.11	12.80		[Ok]
36	20188	20.12	0.02	-0.01	14.40		[Ok]
38	20189	20.00	0.02	-0.01	16.00		[Ok]
41	20191	39.98	0.02	0.01	17.60		Wrong sequenc
43	20192	19.98	0.02	0.03	19.20		[Ok]
45	20193	19.99	0.02	0.04	20.80		[Ok]
46	20193	0.19	0.03	-0.15	22.40		Wrong sequenc
47	20193	0.19	0.04	-0.34	24.00		Wrong sequenc
50	20195	39.60	0.06	0.06	25.60		Wrong sequenc
52	20196	20.02	0.06	0.04	27.20		[Ok]
54	20197	19.95	0.06	0.09	28.80		[Ok]
56	20198	19.97	0.06	0.12	30.40		[Ok]
58	20199	20.08	0.06	0.05	32.00		[Ok]
61	20201	40.04	0.06	0.00	33.60		Wrong sequenc
62	20201	0.19	0.07	-0.18	35.20		Wrong sequenc
63	20201	0.19	0.07	-0.27	36.80		Wrong sequenc

Max delta = 221.89 ms at packet no. 2577
Max jitter = 567.30 ms. Mean jitter = 217.26 ms.
Max skew = -1290.68 ms.
Total RTP packets = 1836   (expected 1836)   Lost RTP packets = 226 (12.31%)   Sequence errors = 759
Duration 36.70 s (-37 ms clock drift, corresponding to 7992 Hz (-0.10%)

Figure 300. Wireshark's VoIP analysis denotes where packet loss occurred in the communication

The delta time column in Figure 300 shows the time since the last RTP packet was received, and should remain fairly consistent. In the figure, most of the deltas are around 20ms which corresponds to the packetization time (ptime) of the codec being used. The ptime refers to the length of the recorded voice in each packet. In other words, if the ptime is "20," each RTP packet contains 20ms of voice time (or silence if the caller is not speaking). The ptime value is shown in the (*a*) attribute in Figure 301.

Jitter

Jitter is a variance in the packet rate. Wireshark calculates jitter according to RFC 3550 (RTP).

Excessive jitter can be caused by congested networks, load balancing, quality of service configurations, or low bandwidth links. Jitter buffers act like "elastic bands" that help buffer packets to even out the variance in arrival times. A high jitter rate (above 20ms) will affect the call to the point that users will become annoyed. If the jitter level is excessively high, packets can be dropped by the jitter buffer in the receiving VoIP host. Figure 300 shows the maximum jitter at 567.30 milliseconds, enough to cause packet loss.

Examine SIP Traffic

SIP is defined in RFC 3261 and, although it is typically associated with VoIP call setup, SIP can be used to set up other application sessions as well. RFC 3665, Session Initiation Protocol (SIP) Basic Call Flow Examples, is a great place to start when analyzing VoIP communications as it provides packet-by-packet examples of typical and atypical call setup scenarios.

Figure 301 shows a SIP Invite packet. This invitation is being sent for extension 204 (204@192.168.5.20) and has been referred through the operator (0@192.168.5.11). The call has been initiated by John Haller (201@192.168.5.10).

The SDP media attribute section indicates that the RTP stream should run over UDP port 8002 (the *m* attribute) and the sender is offering the following (the *a* attributes):

- G.729 @ 8KHz (G729/8000)
- G.711 mu-law @ 8KHz (PCMU/8000)
- G.711 A-law @ 8Khz (PCMA/8000)
- DTMF payload type 101 (e.g. out of band DTMF tones)
- 20ms packetization (standard) (ptime)
- "fmtp" is passing "0-16" to item 101 (DTMF signaling) saying it supports encoding of all 16 DTMF digits (0-9, *, #, A-D)

```
⊟ Session Initiation Protocol
  ⊟ Request-Line: INVITE sip:204@192.168.5.20:5060 SIP/2.0
      Method: INVITE
    ⊞ Request-URI: sip:204@192.168.5.20:5060
      [Resent Packet: False]
  ⊟ Message Header
      Record-Route: <sip:192.168.5.11:7818;lr>
    ⊞ To: <sip:204@192.168.5.11>
      Referred-By: <sip:0@192.168.5.11>;cid="673b0437-dc3f99dd-699f99a7-92fd8066@192.168.5.10"
      Accept: application/sdp,text/plain,message/sipfrag,application/sip
      User-Agent: YV5/1.1.4
    ⊞ Via: SIP/2.0/UDP 192.168.5.11:7818;branch=z9hG4bKaee54e8f23
    ⊞ Via: SIP/2.0/UDP 192.168.5.10:5060;rport;branch=z9hG4bK4a367a1e
    ⊞ From: "John Haller"<sip:201@192.168.5.11>;tag=4b33797e
      Allow: INFO,REFER,NOTIFY,INVITE,ACK,OPTIONS,BYE,CANCEL
      Allow-Events: refer
      History-Info: <sip:204@192.168.5.11>;index=1
      Call-ID: f49fa0af-e84c7379-6649d13e-60bbc1c9@192.168.5.10
      Max-Forwards: 69
    ⊞ Contact: <sip:201@192.168.5.10:5060>
      Content-Type: application/sdp
      Supported: tdialog,replaces,norefersub,histinfo
    ⊞ CSeq: 28836 INVITE
      Content-Length: 257
  ⊟ Message Body
    ⊟ Session Description Protocol
        Session Description Protocol Version (v): 0
      ⊞ Owner/Creator, Session Id (o): ipr1E680EB66B 4684168 4684168 IN IP4 192.168.5.10
        Session Name (s): -
      ⊞ Connection Information (c): IN IP4 192.168.5.10         RTP will use port 8002
      ⊞ Time Description, active time (t): 0 0
      ⊞ Media Description, name and address (m): audio 8002 RTP/AVP 18 0 8 101
      ⊞ Media Attribute (a): rtpmap:18 G729/8000
      ⊞ Media Attribute (a): rtpmap:0 PCMU/8000        Three codecs are offered.
      ⊞ Media Attribute (a): rtpmap:8 PCMA/8000
      ⊞ Media Attribute (a): rtpmap:101 telephone-event/8000
      ⊞ Media Attribute (a): ptime:20
      ⊞ Media Attribute (a): fmtp:101 0-16
```

Figure 301. A SIP Invite packet definesthe RTP port to use and offers codecs

SIP Commands

Wireshark defines the SIP commands and response codes in the Info column of the Packet List pane. The following table defines the SIP commands.

SIP Command	Description
INVITE	Invites a user to a call
ACK	Acknowledgement is used to facilitate reliable message exchange for INVITEs.
BYE	Terminates a connection between users
CANCEL	Terminates a request, or search, for a user. It is used if a client sends an INVITE and then changes its decision to call the recipient.
OPTIONS	Solicits information about a server's capabilities.
SUBSCRIBE	Requests state change information regarding another host
REGISTER	Registers a user's current location
INFO	Used for mid-session signaling

SIP Response Codes

SIP response codes are broken down into six groups.

- 1xx: Provisional—request received, continuing to process the request
- 2xx: Success—the action was successfully received, understood, and accepted
- 3xx: Redirection—further action needs to be taken in order to complete the request
- 4xx: Client Error — the request contains bad syntax or cannot be fulfilled at this server
- 5xx: Server Error — the server failed to fulfill an apparently valid request
- 6xx: Global Failure — the request cannot be fulfilled at any server

Refer to *Filter on VoIP Traffic* on page 556 for details on how to filter on error response codes.

The following table lists many of the more commonly seen the SIP Response Codes. For a complete of SIP response codes, refer to *www.iana.org/assignments/sip-parameters*.

SIP Response Code	Description
100	Trying
180	Ringing
181	Call is Being Forwarded
182	Queued
183	Session Progress
200	OK
202	Accepted (used for referrals)
300	Multiple Choices
301	Moved Permanently
302	Moved Temporarily
305	Use Proxy
380	Alternative Service
400	Bad Request
401	Unauthorized: *Used only by registrars. Proxies should use proxy authorization 407*
402	Payment Required (Reserved for future use)
403	Forbidden
404	Not Found: *User not found*
405	Method Not Allowed
406	Not Acceptable
407	Proxy Authentication Required
408	Request Timeout: *Couldn't find the user in time*

SIP Response Code	Description
409	Conflict
410	Gone: *The user existed once, but is not available here anymore.*
413	Request Entity Too Large
414	Request-URI Too Long
415	Unsupported Media Type
416	Unsupported URI Scheme
420	Bad Extension: *Bad SIP Protocol Extension used, not understood by the server*
421	Extension Required
422	Session Interval Too Small
423	Interval Too Brief
480	Temporarily Unavailable
481	Call/Transaction Does Not Exist
482	Loop Detected
483	Too Many Hops
484	Address Incomplete
485	Ambiguous
486	Busy Here
487	Request Terminated
488	Not Acceptable Here
491	Request Pending
493	Undecipherable: *Could not decrypt S/MIME body part*
500	Server Internal Error
501	Not Implemented: *The SIP request method is not implemented here*
502	Bad Gateway
503	Service Unavailable
504	Server Time-out
505	Version Not Supported: *The server does not support this version of the SIP protocol*
513	Message Too Large
600	Busy Everywhere
603	Decline
604	Does Not Exist Anywhere
606	Not Acceptable

Select **Telephony | SIP** to view SIP statistics as shown in Figure 302. This statistics window offers a fast method for identifying SIP responses indicating client errors, server errors or global failure. In Figure 302, the SIP statistics indicate that our trace file contains two client errors—488 Not Acceptable Here. This may be an indication that a common codec cannot be defined.

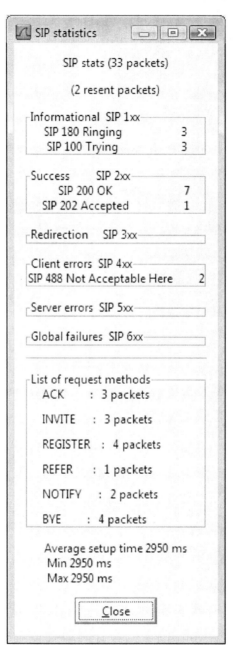

Figure 302. Wireshark's SIP Statistics window

Examine RTP Traffic

RTP provides end-to-end transport functions for real-time data such as audio, video or simulation data over multicast or unicast network services. Real-time Transport Protocol (RTP) is defined in RFC 3550. Figure 303 shows an RTP packet that contains VoIP call data.

```
Real-Time Transport Protocol
  [Stream setup by SDP (frame 3)]
    10.. .... = Version: RFC 1889 Version (2)
    ..0. .... = Padding: False
    ...0 .... = Extension: False
    .... 0000 = Contributing source identifiers count: 0
    0... .... = Marker: False
    Payload type: ITU-T G.711 PCMU (0)
    Sequence number: 416
    [Extended sequence number: 65952]
    Timestamp: 3460831035
    Synchronization Source identifier: 0x3edd3882 (1054685314)
    Payload: 7D7E7878FF7C7EFF7CFFFFFDF8FAFF78737877767775747B...
```

Figure 303. An RTP packet carrying a VoIP call

RTP is supplemented by a control protocol (RTCP) to allow monitoring of the RTP data delivery and to provide minimal control and identification functionality.

Figure 304 shows an RTCP packet. There are five RTCP packet types. Figure 304 is an RTCP goodbye packet.

Abbreviation	Name	Value
SR	sender report	200
RR	receiver report	201
SDES	source description	202
BYE	goodbye	203
APP	application-defined	204

```
⊟ Real-time Transport Control Protocol (Sender Report)
  ⊞ [Stream setup by SDP (frame 1)]
    10.. .... = Version: RFC 1889 Version (2)
    ..0. .... = Padding: False
    ...0 0001 = Reception report count: 1
    Packet type: Sender Report (200)
    Length: 12 (52 bytes)
    Sender SSRC: 0x6bd480aa (1809088682)
    Timestamp, MSW: 3460815870 (0xce47dbfe)
    Timestamp, LSW: 4072781824 (0xf2c1b800)
    [MSW and LSW as NTP timestamp: Sep 1, 2009 17:44:30.9483 UTC]
    RTP timestamp: 3488764456
    Sender's packet count: 289
    Sender's octet count: 46240
  ⊟ Source 1
      Identifier: 0x3edd3882 (1054685314)
    ⊞ SSRC contents
    ⊞ Extended highest sequence number received: 442
      Interarrival jitter: 15
      Last SR timestamp: 0 (0x00000000)
      Delay since last SR timestamp: 0 (0 milliseconds)
⊟ Real-time Transport Control Protocol (Goodbye)
  ⊞ [Stream setup by SDP (frame 1)]
    10.. .... = Version: RFC 1889 Version (2)
    ..0. .... = Padding: False
    ...0 0001 = Source count: 1
    Packet type: Goodbye (203)
    Length: 7 (32 bytes)
    Identifier: 0x6bd480aa (1809088682)
    Length: 19
    Text: Session terminated
```

Figure 304. A Real-Time Transport Control packet

Play Back VoIP Conversations

To play back a VoIP RTP stream, select **Telephony | VoIP Calls** as shown in Figure 305. Select a call (or multiple calls using the **Ctrl** key) and click **Player**.

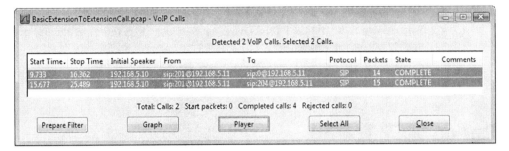

Figure 305. Wireshark identifies and lists the VoIP calls in the trace file

You can emulate a specific jitter buffer setting before replaying the VoIP calls as shown in Figure 306. Lowering the jitter buffer value will cause more packets to be dropped. Click the **Decode** button to view and play the VoIP call.

Figure 306. You can alter the jitter buffer value before playing back the VoIP call

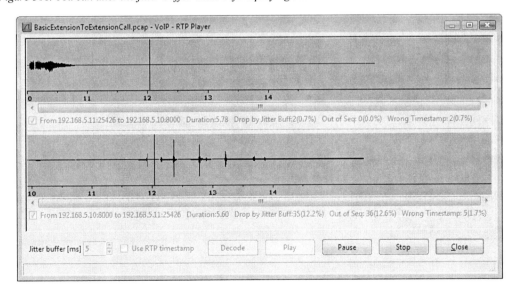

Figure 307. Wireshark can play back G711 A-Law and G711 u-Law RTP streams

Create a VoIP Profile

For efficient VoIP analysis and troubleshooting, consider creating a VoIP profile. The VoIP profile might contain the following elements:

- Set the time column to "Seconds Since Previous Displayed Packet"
- Add a column for IP DSCP (Differentiated Services Code Point) to identify traffic quality of service settings
- Colorize all SIP resends (see *Filter on VoIP Traffic* on page 556)
- Colorize all SIP response codes greater than 399

Filter on VoIP Traffic

To capture only VoIP traffic you can build capture filters based on the ports used for SIP (udp.port=5060 for example). The port number used for RTP may not be known however. It may be best to simply create a capture filter for all UDP traffic (udp) since SIP and RTP both can travel over UDP. For example, in Figure 301, port 8002 was selected for the RTP communications. In Figure 298, port 25,426 was selected for the RTP communications.

VoIP display filters can be based on the protocols or specific fields inside protocol traffic. The following table lists numerous possible VoIP display filters.

Display Filter	Description
`sip`	SIP traffic only
`rtp`	RTP traffic only
`rtcp`	Real-time Transport Control Protocol
`sip.Method == "INVITE"`	SIP Invites[96]
`sip.Method == "BYE"`	SIP Connection closings
`sip.Method == "NOTIFY"`	SIP Notify packets
`sip.Status-Code > 399`	SIP response codes indicating client, server or global faults
`sip.resend == 1`	Detect when SIP packet had to be resent[97]
`rtp.p_type == 0`	G.711 codec definition for payload type
`rtpevent.event_id == 4`	Dual-tone multifrequency—a 4 was pushed on the phone keypad
`(sip.r-uri.user == "0")`	The SIP packet is used to establish a session with the operator (0) or ACK to the operator (0)
`rtcp.pt == 200`	RTCP sender report

---

[96] Note that almost all Wireshark display filters use lower-case characters for the field names. A few of the SIP fields, however, use some upper-case characters.

[97] This great display filter tip was submitted by Martin Mathieson, one of the core Wireshark developers, that he uses as "the first sign of a crash or that I'd managed to overload a server :)." Nice tip, Martin!

Case Study:
Lost VoIP Tones

Submitted by: Sean Walberg
Network Engineer

Troubleshooting DTMF problems crosses the usual boundary between signaling and voice traffic. I had written an application for our Interactive Voice Response (IVR) system that would take a message from a caller and then try to reach a technician by dialing out from a preconfigured list of phone numbers. If someone answered, the message would be played and the technician would have to acknowledge the message by pressing the '1' key. The application underwent extensive testing, but the first night in production some technicians complained that even though they acknowledged the message the call went on to the next person in the list.

The digits were collected fine if the call went to the operations desk that used IP phones, so the first thought was that it had something to do with the cell phones being used. Land lines were no better, in fact, only IP phones seemed to work.

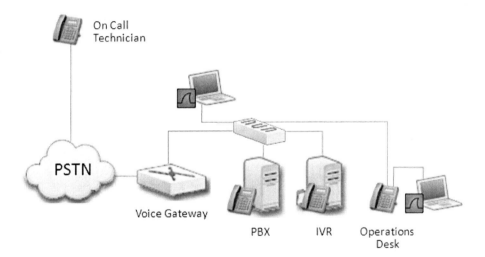

At this point I started collecting packet traces of people calling in, and the subsequent calls being made by the system. Wireshark collected the traces at the operations desk IP phone (by bridging the calls to the attached PC) and also at the voice gateway's Ethernet port (through a SPAN session). Because of all the signaling between the different components it's usually easiest to start at the edges of the network and work your way in if necessary.

Starting with the VoIP gateway's capture file of a call that didn't work, I went into Telephony | VoIP Calls, which shows all the calls made in the trace, and picked out the call from the IVR to the phone. From there, I clicked the Graph button which gives a visual indication of where the signaling and RTP traffic are flowing. At this point I wanted to make sure that the trace was good in that it showed signaling between the gateway, the PBX, and the IVR, and also had the voice traffic. It did, so I closed that window and replayed the conversation by pressing the Play button.

The call was clear and I could hear the DTMF digit being pressed. I then did the same for the IP phone trace that worked. Curiously, I only heard a click instead of a digit. Back to the graph of the call, I could see that there was an H.245 User Input packet sent out of band instead of the tones for the digit in the RTP stream. The call that didn't work had no such thing because the digit was being played in band. I then went back to look at a trace where someone called in, and they too had out of band signaling.

With this in mind, I started poring through the manuals for the IVR system and finally found that it required out of band signaling for DTMF digits. After that it was a matter of debugging on the voice gateway to find out that if the IVR initiated a call out the PSTN that DTMF relaying would not be used. If the call came from the gateway to the IVR, relaying was used. For IP phone to IVR calls, the devices would just negotiate relay by default.

Summary

VoIP traffic consists of two specific elements—the call setup traffic (signaling traffic) and the call traffic itself. SIP is an example of a protocol used for call setup whereas RTP is an example of a protocol used for the actual VoIP call.

SIP can run over UDP or TCP on port 5060. It is more common to see SIP running over UDP, but some vendors also support SIP over TCP. A typical SIP call setup would include Invite, 100 Trying, 180 Ringing, 200 OK and ACK sequence. SIP response codes greater than 399 indicate client errors, server errors or global failures. Wireshark's SIP statistics can be used to spot these errors easily.

RTP carries the voice call itself. Wireshark contains an RTP player that enables you to listen to unencrypted VoIP conversations. If Wireshark does not recognize the call traffic, enable Try to decode RTP outside of conversations or manually use Decode As to force the RTP dissector on the traffic that you know is RTP. RTP is supplemented by RTCP which offers monitoring of the RTP data delivery system.

Call bandwidth requirements vary depending on the codec used for the call. The call bandwidth requirements and codec are defined in the SIP communications.

Packet loss, jitter and asynchronous QoS settings can negatively affect VoIP communications. Jitter is a variance in the packet rate. Asynchronous QoS settings can be detected by adding a column for the DSCP field in the IP header.

Practice What You've Learned

 Download the trace files available in the Download section of the book website, *www.wiresharkbook.com*. Practice your VoIP analysis skills by opening the trace files listed below and answering the questions.

voip-extension.pcap

This VoIP communication begins with a SIP call setup process. The call is directed to the VoIP server (operator). Later in the trace file the user enters extension 204. This was just a test call.

Colorize the SIP conversation starting with packet 1 using Color 1. Colorize the RTP conversation starting with packet with Color 2. Are there other conversations later in the trace file? Does the call to extension 204 go through the VoIP server or go directly to that phone? Playback the call to the operator. What does the user hear when they connect to the operator? Add a column for the IP DSCP value. Does the traffic in both directions use the same DSCP value?

voip-extension2downata.pcap

Playback this VoIP call. What message does the user hear? In this case the analog telephone adapter on the target side of the call is down. Create a VoIP error coloring rule that identifies all SIP response codes greater than 399. Test this coloring rule on this trace file. Four packets should match your coloring rule.

Review Questions

Q27.1   **What is the purpose of SIP?**

Q27.2   **What is the purpose of RTP?**

Q27.3   **What configuration change can you make if Wireshark does not see the SIP traffic and can't identify a VoIP call?**

Q27.4   **What is jitter?**

Q27.5   **What causes a *wrong sequence number* indication in Wireshark's RTP Stream Analysis window?**

Q27.6   **What is the default port used by SIP traffic? Where is the RTP port number defined?**

Q27.7   **What types of packets are displayed using the filter `sip.Status-Code > 399`?**

Q27.8   **What is a useful column to add to the Packet List pane when looking for QoS issues in handling VoIP traffic?**

Q27.9   **What capture filter can be used to capture all SIP traffic?**

Answers to Review Questions

Q27.1   **What is the purpose of SIP?**

A27.1   SIP, the Session Initiation Protocol, is the signaling protocol used for call setup and teardown.

Q27.2   **What is the purpose of RTP?**

A27.2   RTP, Realtime Transport Protocol, carries the voice call itself.

Q27.3   **What configuration change can you make if Wireshark does not see the SIP traffic and can't identify a VoIP call?**

A27.3   If Wireshark cannot identify the RTP stream that carries the call, consider enabling **Try to Decode RTP Outside of Conversations** in **Edit | Preferences | RTP**.

Q27.4   **What is jitter?**

A27.4   Jitter is a variance in the packet rate.

Q27.5   **What causes a *wrong sequence number* indication in Wireshark's RTP Stream Analysis window?**

A27.5   Packet loss or packets that are out of order will trigger the wrong sequence number indication in the RTP Stream Analysis window.

Q27.6   **What is the default port used by SIP traffic? Where is the RTP port number defined?**

A27.6   By default, SIP uses port 5060 (over UDP or TCP). The SIP packet media attribute section indicates the port number that the RTP stream should run over.

Q27.7   **What types of packets are displayed using the filter `sip.Status-Code > 399`?**

A27.7   If you use this filter you would capture all SIP client errors, server errors and global failures.

Q27.8   **What is a useful column to add to the Packet List pane when looking for QoS issues in handling VoIP traffic?**

A27.8   To identify possible QoS issues, add a DSCP column to examine the priority settings of VoIP call setup and call data traffic.

Q27.9   **What capture filter can be used to capture all SIP traffic?**

A27.9   You can use the capture filter `udp port 5060` to capture all SIP traffic running over UDP. If your VoIP solution uses SIP over TCP, use the capture filter `tcp port 5060` to capture all SIP traffic running over UDP.

Chapter 28: Baseline "Normal" Traffic Patterns

Wireshark Certified Network Analyst Exam Objectives covered:

- Understanding the Importance of Baselining
- Baseline Broadcast and Multicast Types and Rates
- Baseline Bootup Sequences
- Baseline Login/Logout Sequences
- Baseline Traffic during Idle Time
- Baseline Application Launch Sequences and Key Tasks
- Baseline Web Browsing Sessions
- Baseline Name Resolution Sessions
- Baseline Throughput Tests
- Baseline Wireless Connectivity
- Baseline VoIP Communications

- ❖ Case Study: Login Log Jam
- ❖ Case Study: Solving SAN Disconnects
- ❖ Summary
- ❖ Practice What You've Learned
- ❖ Review Questions and Answers

Understanding the Importance of Baselining

Baselining is the process of creating a set of trace files that depict "normal" communications on the network. Having baselines that were created before network problems or security breaches occur can speed up the process of identifying unusual network activity. Ultimately, baselines enable you to resolve problems more effectively and efficiently.

One method of using baselines is to identify normal traffic patterns on a problem network. For example, if a user complains about performance one day, you can take the trace file of the current traffic. Referring back to your baseline trace file you can filter out "normal" traffic and focus on the unusual traffic. This can reduce your troubleshooting time significantly.

In a security breach situation, knowing the normal protocols, applications and traffic patterns helps you spot unusual communications. For example, if your hosts never use internet relay chat, but you suddenly begin seeing this type of traffic, your host may be infected with a bot. Further traffic analysis may reveal which bot you are facing and help you determine how to deal with it. Figure 308 shows an SMTP baseline trace. The TCP handshake indicates a round trip time of a little over 92 ms and a connection established to *mmp1102.verio-web.com*. Our server and client support Enhanced SMTP and authenticated logins. The Summary information for this baseline indicates that the average bytes per second rate is approximately 1,490.

Your baseline process may consist of more than trace files—the process could also include images of the client screens or server screens and summary data, IO Graph information.

No. .	Time	Source	Destination	Protocol	Info
1	0.000000	192.168.0.113	161.58.148.77	TCP	accelenet > submission [SYN] Seq=0 W
2	0.092538	161.58.148.77	192.168.0.113	TCP	submission > accelenet [SYN, ACK] Seq
3	0.000185	192.168.0.113	161.58.148.77	TCP	accelenet > submission [ACK] Seq=1 A
4	0.103386	161.58.148.77	192.168.0.113	SMTP	S: 220 mmp1102.verio-web.com ESMTP
5	0.000375	192.168.0.113	161.58.148.77	SMTP	C: EHLO vid01
6	0.095295	161.58.148.77	192.168.0.113	SMTP	S: 250-mmp1102.verio-web.com	250-F
7	0.000334	192.168.0.113	161.58.148.77	SMTP	C: AUTH LOGIN
8	0.093660	161.58.148.77	192.168.0.113	SMTP	S: 334 VXNlcm5hbwU6
9	0.000311	192.168.0.113	161.58.148.77	SMTP	C: bGF1cmEuY2hhcHA0
10	0.110312	161.58.148.77	192.168.0.113	SMTP	S: 334 UGFzc3dvcmQ6
11	0.000287	192.168.0.113	161.58.148.77	SMTP	C: YnViYmxlczI=
12	0.101629	161.58.148.77	192.168.0.113	SMTP	S: 235 ok, go ahead (#2.0.0)
13	0.000403	192.168.0.113	161.58.148.77	SMTP	C: MAIL FROM: <laura@chappellu.com>
14	0.093830	161.58.148.77	192.168.0.113	SMTP	S: 250 ok
15	0.000497	192.168.0.113	161.58.148.77	SMTP	C: RCPT TO: <brenda@chappellU.com>
16	0.093184	161.58.148.77	192.168.0.113	SMTP	S: 250 ok
17	0.000450	192.168.0.113	161.58.148.77	SMTP	C: DATA
18	0.093491	161.58.148.77	192.168.0.113	SMTP	S: 354 go ahead
19	0.008904	192.168.0.113	161.58.148.77	SMTP	C: DATA fragment, 1460 bytes
20	0.000011	192.168.0.113	161.58.148.77	SMTP	C: DATA fragment, 1460 bytes
21	0.095197	161.58.148.77	192.168.0.113	TCP	submission > accelenet [ACK] Seq=218
22	0.000089	192.168.0.113	161.58.148.77	IMF	from: "Laura Chappell" <laura@chappe
23	0.100033	161.58.148.77	192.168.0.113	SMTP	S: 250 ok 1256145014 qp 3531
24	0.199595	192.168.0.113	161.58.148.77	TCP	accelenet > submission [ACK] Seq=363
25	2.307074	192.168.0.113	161.58.148.77	SMTP	C: QUIT
26	0.000066	192.168.0.113	161.58.148.77	TCP	accelenet > submission [FIN, ACK] S
27	0.091858	161.58.148.77	192.168.0.113	TCP	submission > accelenet [ACK] Seq=245
28	0.063252	161.58.148.77	192.168.0.113	SMTP	S: 221 mmp1102.verio-web.com
29	0.000157	192.168.0.113	161.58.148.77	TCP	accelenet > submission [RST, ACK] Se
30	0.000029	161.58.148.77	192.168.0.113	TCP	submission > accelenet [FIN, ACK] Se

Figure 308. An SMTP baseline trace

In the following sections, we provide examples of baseline information you might consider gathering. This is not a comprehensive list as your baseline needs may differ.

Baseline Broadcast and Multicast Types and Rates

Baseline your broadcast and multicast traffic to identify a sudden increase in this traffic rate or to identify new hosts on the network in a passive manner.

- Who is broadcasting?
- What application is using broadcasts?
- What is the typical broadcast rate in packets per seconds?
- Who is multicasting?
- What application is using multicasts?
- What is the typical multicast rate in packets per seconds?

Baseline Protocols and Applications

Creating a baseline of normal protocols and applications on the network can help you spot breached hosts. For example, if you suspect a host has been breached, you can take a trace file of the current traffic and compare that to your baseline. If your network doesn't typically support IRC or TFTP traffic, you would likely be concerned when your Protocol Hierarchy window looks like Figure 309.

- Which applications are running on the network?
- What protocols are used for these applications?
- What UDP ports are in use?
- What TCP ports are in use?
- What routing protocol is in use?
- What does a routing update process look like?
- What ICMP traffic is seen on the network?

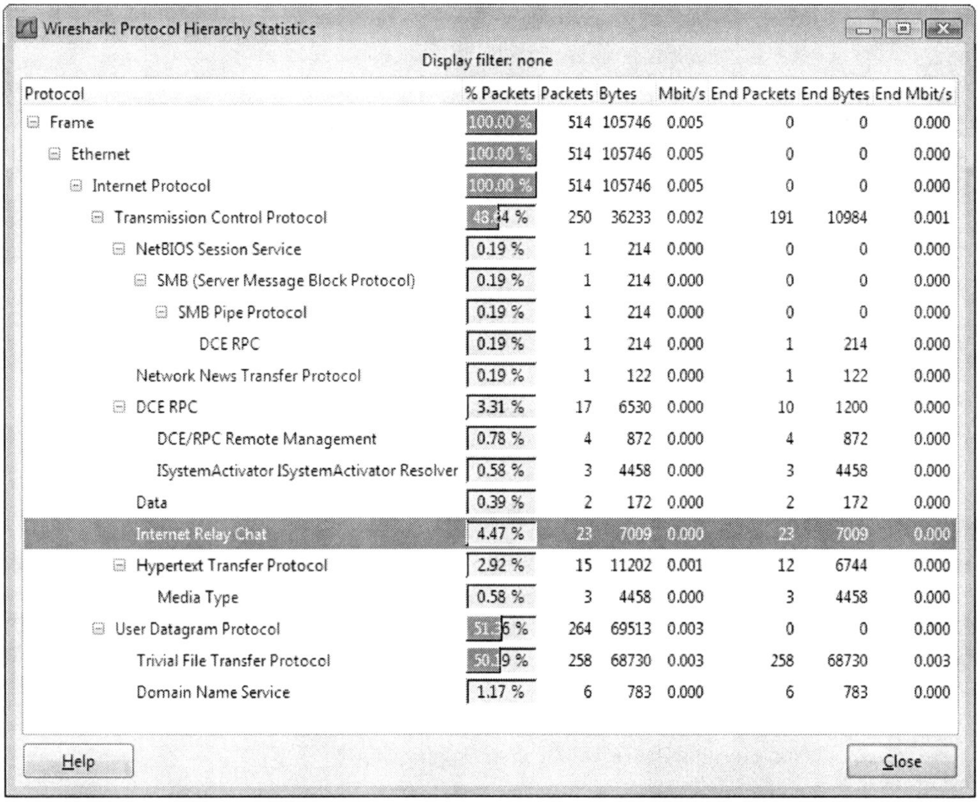

Figure 309. We know this network doesn't usually have IRC and TFTP traffic on it

Baseline Bootup Sequences

Analyzing the bootup sequence is important since this sequence sets up the client's general configuration and performance for the remaining up time. Bootup baselines can help you spot performance changes caused when a new bootup processes are implemented on a network. Periodic checks of the bootup sequence are also recommended.

- What is involved in the initial DHCP startup sequence (relay agent, parameter requests)?
- What applications generate traffic during the startup sequence?

Unlike most of the other baselines listed in this section, this baseline cannot be captured based on the traffic to and from the host that is running Wireshark. You must tap into an existing network connection (as close as possible to the client preferably), start capturing and then bootup the baseline host.

Baseline Login/Logout Sequences

The login sequence should be baselined each time a new configuration is deployed (and also in the lab environment before deployment). This helps understand what is considered "normal" and acceptable and the effects of small or large changes on this important process.

- What discovery process takes place during login?
- What server does the client connect to?
- What are the processes seen during login?
- How many packets does a typical login require?
- Are there any login dependencies?

This baseline may not be able to be captured based on traffic seen to and from the host that is running Wireshark. You must tap into an existing network connection (closely to the client if possible), start capturing with Wireshark and then login to the network from the baseline host.

Baseline Traffic during Idle Times

Watching the traffic flowing to and from a host during idle time (when no one is using the host) is important to identity background traffic that automatically occurs—traffic that is generated by the application(s) loaded on a host.

- What protocols or applications are seen during idle time?
- What hosts are contacted (IP address, host name)?
- How frequently does the idle traffic occur?
- What are the signatures of this traffic that you can filter out when removing this traffic from a trace file?

Baseline Application Launch Sequences and Key Tasks

Key applications on the network should be baselined as well. The first portion of application baselining focuses on the application launch to identify interdependencies and the general ports and startup procedure used. Key tasks should be baselined to learn how they work and what their typical response times are.

- What discovery process is the application dependent upon?
- Is the application TCP-based or UDP-based?
- If TCP-based, what are the TCP options set in the handshake packets?
- What port(s) does the application use?
- What hosts are contacted when the application starts (interdependencies)?
- How many packets/how much time until the launch is complete?
- What is the IO rate during the launch sequence?
- What happens during application idle time?
- Are any portions of the login visible in clear text?

- What is the round trip latency during the application launch?
- Are there any failures or retries during the application launch?
- Are there any server delays upon receipt of requests?
- Are there any client delays preceding requests?
- Are there lost packets, retransmissions or out-of-order packets during the launch?
- Analyze key tasks (application-dependent) individually.

Baseline Web Browsing Sessions

Create a baseline of web browsing sessions to the most popular web hosts to determine the typical behavior and latency times. This process relates closely to the name resolution baseline process defined next.

- What browser is used for the analysis?
- What is the target (if any) for the name resolution process?
- What is the name resolution response time?
- What is the round trip latency time between the client and the target server?
- What is the application response time to a page request?
- What other hosts do you communicate with during the web browsing session?
- Are there any HTTP errors in the trace file?

Baseline Name Resolution Sessions

Problems during the name resolution process can have a significant impact on performance. Creating a baseline of this process to compare against future trace files can help identify the cause of name resolution performance issues.

- What application is being used to test the name resolution process?
- What name and type is being resolved?
- What is the IP address of the target name server?
- What is the round trip response time for the name resolution process?

Baseline Throughput Tests

Consider using an application such as iPerf to perform throughput tests. Capture the trace file during the test to graph the IO rate and spot any performance problems already occurring.

- What application is being used to perform the throughput test?
- What are the configurations of host 1 and host 2?
- What is the packet size used for the throughput test?
- What transport was used for the test?
- What is the Kbytes per second rate from host 1 to host 2?
- What is the Kbytes per second rate from host 2 to host 1?

- What was the packet loss rate in each direction?
- What was the latency (if measurable) in each direction?
- Save the IO Graph from throughput tests.

Baseline Wireless Connectivity

Just as important as the site survey before WLAN deployment, the baseline of the WLAN traffic once the network is in place can help identify and solve problems at a later date.

- Where is the packet capture point?
- What packets are involved with the connection establishment to the access point?
- What encryption method is used?
- Were there WLAN retries? (filter on the retry bit)
- What is the beacon rate (IO Graph with beacon filter)?
- Copy and save the **Statistics | WLAN Traffic** baseline information.

Baseline VoIP Communications

Understanding the basic VoIP traffic patterns (including call setup and actual call processes) helps perform comparative analysis at a later date. Focus on the jitter rate, packet loss rate and call setup procedures.

- What protocol is used for the call setup procedure?
- What is the round trip latency time for the call setup procedure?
- What is the average call setup time (**Telephony | SIP**)?
- What codec is used for the compression (e.g., payload type G.711)
- Did Wireshark detect VoIP calls in the trace file (**Telephony | VoIP**)?
- Are there any SIP error responses (**Telephony | SIP**)?
- What is the jitter rate?
- Is there any packet loss in the communication (**Telephony | RTP | Stream Analysis**)?

Case Study:
Login Log Jam

One customer was shocked to learn their login sequence required over 70,000 packets. They felt their login process was slow, but they assumed the problem was due to the increased number of connections the server had to deal with in the morning hours.

The slow login process was due to the high packet rate exchanged before completion of the login process.

During an update process, the client's roaming profile had been set up improperly to download numerous fonts and data that had been in cache on the original host—data that should never have been in the original image to be copied down to the client upon login.

After a bit of research into the traffic, we created a list of elements that should be excluded from the profile to speed up the login process. The users actually noticed the difference and commented on it—a shock to the IT department!

Case Study:
Solving SAN Disconnects

Submitted by: Robert M.
        Network/Connectivity Team Lead
        Xerox Corporation

I recently had a field technician capture a network trace of a Multifunction Printer that was continuously failing to scan documents to a Storage Area Network (SAN) device using SMB protocol.

The field technician sent me two traces, one of the failure process and one of a successful scan to a Windows workstation.

After sorting the scans to show only traffic going between the printer and the destination, I noticed the printer was able to negotiate an SMB connection and ask for access to the destination folder. The printer would then immediately send a TCP FIN after a positive SMB response from the SAN.

I compared the SMB response from the SAN to the working one from the workstation and notice that the last line of the Tree Connect ANDX Response in the SMB header failed to announce the file system type (in this case NTFS).

Since the printer was unsure of the file system to use when communicating to the SAN, it dropped the connection.

Comparing these two files enabled us to resolve the issue with the customer. To fix the problem, they needed to make changes to their SAN configuration.

Summary

Baselines should be created when the network is running properly. These baselines can be used for comparative analysis sessions later when performance suffers or a security breach is suspected. You cannot identify *unusual* traffic unless you are aware of the *usual* traffic on your network.

Practice What You've Learned

This chapter listed numerous baselines that you should create *now*—right *now*. Take a break from your focus on troubleshooting to build the following baseline set. Check off the baselines as you create them.

- ☐ Broadcasts and multicasts
- ☐ General protocols and applications (capture from a number of hosts)
- ☐ Typical bootup sequence
- ☐ Login sequence
- ☐ Logout sequence
- ☐ Idle time traffic
- ☐ Application Launch Sequence (one trace file for each application)
- ☐ Application Key Tasks (one trace file for each task)
- ☐ Web browsing session (to the corporate site, if possible)
- ☐ Name resolution sessions
- ☐ Throughput tests—consider using iPerf if you don't have another tool
- ☐ Wireless connection process
- ☐ VoIP call setup and VoIP call

Download the trace files available in the Download section of the book website, *www.wiresharkbook.com*. The following files could be considered baselines of their respective processes. Review the trace files for practice.

app-zonealarm-update.pcap	This is a normal ZoneAlarm update—it's important to know how your personal firewall and virus detection tools perform their updates.
dns-misc.pcap	Compare the DNS lookups required to access *www.winpcap.org*, *www.msnbc.com* and *www.espn.com*. Check the DNS traffic generated when you connect to your corporate servers.
icmp-traceroute-normal.pcap	This is a classic ICMP-based traceroute operation shows the dependency on the ICMP Time to Live Exceeded/Time to Live Exceeded in Transit response that is used to locate routers along a path.

Review Questions

Q28.1   **What is the purpose of a baseline?**

Q28.2   **How can you obtain a baseline of a bootup sequence?**

Q28.3   **Why should you baseline traffic during idle times?**

Answers to Review Questions

Q28.1   **What is the purpose of a baseline?**

A28.1   Baselining is the process of creating a set of trace files that depict "normal" communications on the network. Compare unusual traffic patterns to your baseline to identify anomalies.

Q28.2   **How can you obtain a baseline of a bootup sequence?**

A28.2   You cannot obtain a bootup baseline on the actual host you are analyzing. You must tap into an existing network connection (as close as possible to the client preferably), start capturing and then bootup the baseline host.

Q28.3   **Why should you baseline traffic during idle times?**

A28.3   Watching the traffic flowing to and from a host during idle time (when no one is using the host) helps identity background traffic that automatically occurs.

Chapter 29: Find the Top Causes of Performance Problems

Wireshark Certified Network Analyst Exam Objectives covered:

- Troubleshoot Performance Problems
- Identify High Latency Times
- Point to Slow Processing Times
- Find the Location of Packet Loss
- Watching Signs of Misconfigurations
- Analyze Traffic Redirections
- Watch for Small Payload Sizes
- Look for Congestion
- Identify Application Faults
- Note Any Name Resolution Faults

Troubleshoot Performance Problems

One of the most popular troubleshooting methodologies begins at the physical layer and moves up through to the application layer in bottom-up order.

When a user complains of poor performance, the symptoms might be slow application loading time, slow file transfer time, inability to connect to specific services, etc.

Problems may arise in the resolution process (shown in Figure 310) as well. For example, DNS problems may prevent a host from obtaining the IP address for a target host. Incorrect subnet mask values may cause a host to perform discovery for a local host that is, in fact, remote. Incorrect route table values or unavailable gateways may isolate a host.

Baselines of normal network communications can be compared to faulty communications to locate differences and rapidly spot the source of problems.

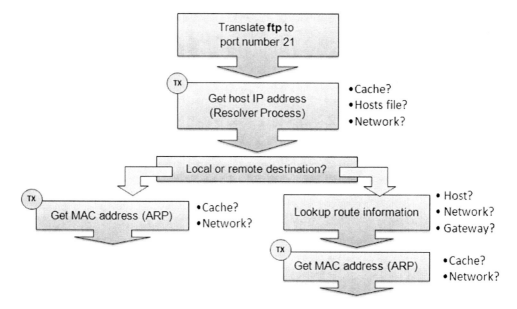

Figure 310. Errors can occur anywhere in the resolution process

When analyzing a TCP/IP trace, you should be able to determine which processes have completed successfully. You should also be able to determine where the communication faults reside.

The following pages review some of the most commonly seen problems that cause unacceptable performance.

Identify High Latency Times

High latency times can be caused by distance (as in the case of satellite communications), queuing delays along a path, processing delays, etc.

One of the easiest ways to identify delays in a trace file is to set the Time column to Seconds since Previous Displayed Packet then sort this column and note large gaps in time between packets in the trace file as shown in Figure 311.

Filter on a Conversation Before Sorting the Time Column

If your trace contains numerous conversations, ensure you filter on a conversation before sorting the time column to ensure you are comparing times within a single conversation. Alternately you could add a time column for "Delta Time (conversation)" to identify large gaps in time between packets in a conversation.

No.	Time	Source	Destination	Protocol	Info
375	16.07423	61.8.0.17	10.0.52.164	TCP	[TCP Keep-Alive]
373	8.064197	61.8.0.17	10.0.52.164	TCP	[TCP Keep-Alive]
371	4.128068	61.8.0.17	10.0.52.164	TCP	[TCP Keep-Alive] h
369	2.198012	61.8.0.17	10.0.52.164	TCP	[TCP Keep-Alive] h
367	1.133508	61.8.0.17	10.0.52.164	TCP	[TCP Keep-Alive] h
5966	0.681690	61.8.0.17	10.0.52.164	HTTP	[TCP Retransmissio
365	0.667083	61.8.0.17	10.0.52.164	TCP	[TCP Keep-Alive] h
379	0.279305	61.8.0.17	10.0.52.164	HTTP	Continuation or no
385	0.257458	61.8.0.17	10.0.52.164	HTTP	Continuation or nor
7153	0.247708	61.8.0.17	10.0.52.164	HTTP	Continuation or nc
7161	0.230970	61.8.0.17	10.0.52.164	HTTP	[TCP Previous segm
7171	0.225367	61.8.0.17	10.0.52.164	HTTP	Continuation or no
2861	0.224006	61.8.0.17	10.0.52.164	HTTP	Continuation or no
2877	0.208945	61.8.0.17	10.0.52.164	HTTP	[TCP Previous segm
7195	0.207764	10.0.52.164	61.8.0.17	TCP	ads > http [RST, A
5338	0.205759	61.8.0.17	10.0.52.164	HTTP	Continuation or

Figure 311. Sort on the Time column after filtering on a conversation

You can also filter on delta time values. Inside the frame information section there are several time values. Although these values are not actual fields in the packet, Wireshark can find packets based on their values. In Figure 312 we have expanded the Frame information preceding an Ethernet II header to view the four time fields listed therein.

```
Frame 4 (142 bytes on wire, 142 bytes captured)
  Arrival Time: Sep 28, 2009 12:21:31.121493000
  [Time delta from previous captured frame: 0.001536000 seconds]
  [Time delta from previous displayed frame: 0.001536000 seconds]
  [Time since reference or first frame: 0.002345000 seconds]
```

Figure 312. Expand the Frame section to view time details

Packet timestamps are provided by the WinPcap, libpcap, or AirPcap libraries at the time the packet is captured. It is saved with the trace file. These libraries support microsecond resolution. You might have greater resolution timestamps (down to the nanosecond), if you captured traffic with specialized hardware. Alternately, if you captured the traffic with a software solution that only offers timestamp resolution to the millisecond, you will not see microsecond-level time designations.

Filter on Arrival Times

The Arrival Time value is based on the system time at the time the packet was captured. The following list provides examples of filtering on the arrival time of packets.

```
frame.time == "Mar 1, 2010 12:21:31.121493000"

frame.time < "Jan 15, 2010 00:00:00.000000000"

frame.time > "Jan 27, 2010 23:59:59.000000000"
```

Filter on the Delta Times

The Time Delta from Previous Captured Frame depicts when a packet arrived compared to the previous captured packet—regardless of filters. For example, if you filtered on an HTTP communication, but your trace contains DNS queries before the TCP handshake to the HTTP server, the time value of the first TCP handshake packet would compare the time from the end of the DNS response packet to the end of the first TCP handshake packet. The following list provides some examples of filtering on this time value.

```
frame.time_delta == 0.001536000

frame.time_delta < 0.001

frame.time_delta > 1
```

The Time Delta from Previous Displayed Frame is based on the delta time from the end of one displayed packet to the end of the next displayed packet. Packets that are not displayed are not used in this time calculation. The following list provides examples of filtering on this time value.

```
frame.time_delta_displayed == 0.001536

frame.time_delta_displayed < 0.001

frame.time_delta_displayed > 1
```

Filter on the Time since Reference or First Packet

This time reference compares the current packet time to the first packet in the trace file or the most recent packet that has the time reference set. The following list provides examples of filtering on this time value.

```
frame.time_relative == 0

frame.time_relative < 0.001

frame.time_relative > 1
```

The `frame.time_relative == 0` display filter would show the first packet in the trace file and any packets marked with a time reference.

Point to Slow Processing Times

When a host doesn't have sufficient processing power or memory or an application does not respond in a timely manner, gaps in the response times may be seen between requests and replies.

These gaps may be accompanied by other evidence of the problem, such as a TCP window size of zero or a TCP window size smaller than the TCP MSS value. Alternately, application responses may indicate an overloaded condition. Consider reassembling streams to decipher any plain text messages if they exist. The messages may clearly define the application problem.

Find the Location of Packet Loss

Packet loss can affect performance when the receiver must request retransmissions and wait for those retransmissions before passing data to the application. For example, when packet loss occurs on a TCP connection that does not support Selective ACKs, numerous packets may be retransmitted as the receiver cannot acknowledge receipt of data after the lost packet.

In a UDP-based application, the retransmission timeout value is dictated by the application itself. An application that is slow to request retransmission will affect the overall performance of the application.

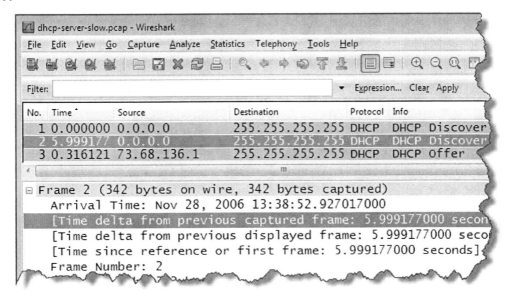

Figure 313. The DHCP client is slow to retransmit the DHCP Discover packet

Figure 313 shows the slow retransmission process of a DHCP client. The original DHCP Discover goes unanswered. The DHCP client waits almost 6 seconds before retransmitting the Discover packet. This causes nearly a 6 second delay in recovering from possible packet loss during the bootup process. Since the DHCP server or relay agent must be on the same network segment, this seems to be an excessive amount of time.

If you are capturing traffic in the infrastructure and you see the original packet *and* the retransmission, you are upstream from (at a point before) the point of packet loss. "Upstream" means you are closer to the sender of the data. To find out where packet loss is occurring, move along the path until you no longer see the original packet *and* retransmissions to find out exactly where the packets are being dropped.

Packet loss typically occurs at interconnecting devices such as switches and routers. This is a relatively simple process for TCP communications since Wireshark indicates which packets are retransmissions.

Watching Signs of Misconfigurations

Various misconfigurations can affect network performance. For example, video multicast traffic that is prioritized below file transfer, voice and email traffic may be held in queues along a path. This traffic that is held in a queue while higher priority traffic flows ahead of it may cause a 'striping' effect on a round trip time graph as shown in Figure 314.

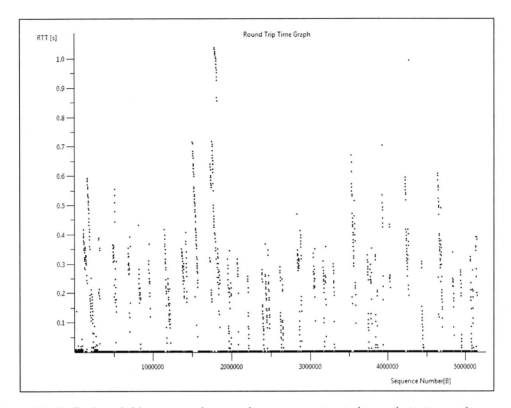

Figure 314. Traffic that is held in a queue along a path may cause stripes in the round trip time graphs

Analyze Traffic Redirections

The most common redirections seen on a network are based on default paths that may not be optimal or available. This could be a default gateway that does not offer the best route to the target network (responding with an ICMP redirection packet).

Another common redirection is seen in web browsing sessions when a browsing client connects to a website only to be redirected to other sites to build the pages. Figure 315 shows a redirection when a client connects to *www.espn.com*. The server indicates that the client must connect to *espn.go.com*. This prompts the client to generate a DNS query for the new site before generating a TCP handshake.

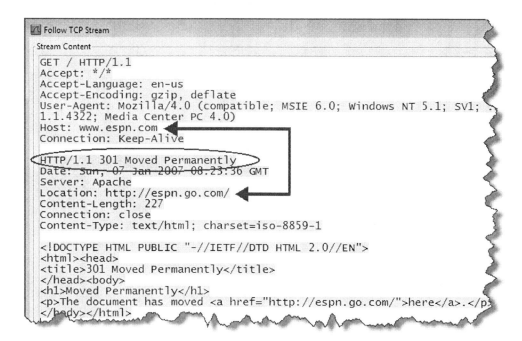

Figure 315. The web browsing client is redirected to another site

Watch for Small Payload Sizes

If a 500 MB file is exchanged in 512 byte segments instead of 1,460, increments, the data exchange will require almost 650 more data packets to complete the transfer.

Some applications may use smaller payload on purpose. For example, database applications may be transferring a record or set of records at a time. The records may be non-contiguous in the file so a steady stream of larger MTU data segments is not possible.

An example of this would be when two distant TCP hosts complete the handshake process indicating the MTU value of 1,460 bytes. If part of the network path only supports an MTU size of 512, packets must be fragmented by routers adjoining the limiting segment or the peers must use ICMP path discovery to identify the new MTU size to use when communicating.

Traditional path discovery using ICMP Type 3/Code 4 messages (Fragmentation Needed, but Don't Fragment Bit Set) is covered in RFC 1191, Path MTU Discovery.

Use a `tcp.len` Column to Easily See Payload Size

Create a column for `tcp.len` to display the payload size of the data packets. In addition, consider creating an IO Graph to depict the payload size of traffic as shown in Figure 316. Use the `AVG(*)tcp.len` value in an Advanced IO Graph.

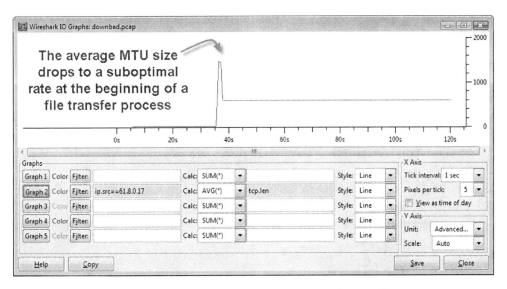

Figure 316. Graphing tcp.len shows a suboptimal MTU size used for the data transfer

Look for Congestion

Congestion along a network path may cause packet loss, queuing, or throttling back of possible throughput maximums.

A window zero condition is one example of possible congestion at a receiving host. Alternately this could be caused by a misbehaving application.

When a host hits a window size of zero, no data can be sent. In effect, the IO drops to zero bytes/second.

One possible solution to a Window Zero condition is to use Window Scaling, as referred to in RFC 1323. Window Scaling enables a host to exponentially increase the window size. Window Scaling is defined as a TCP option during the handshake process.

When the network experiences flooding—a condition of prolonged peak packets per second or bytes per second rates, communications may suffer. In some cases, the flood traffic may overwhelm Wireshark. Consider using Tshark to capture the traffic to file sets and examine the trace files separately.

Identify Application Faults

Application faults may manifest themselves through dissected response codes or by simply not allowing efficient data flow.

One of the more commonly experienced faults is when an HTTP 404 Not Found response is received by a web browsing client. No data is transferred from the target page after this condition and no redirection takes place.

Figure 317 displays an IO Graph depicting a sudden drop in throughput. This is caused when Internet Explorer stops pulling data out of the TCP receive buffer.

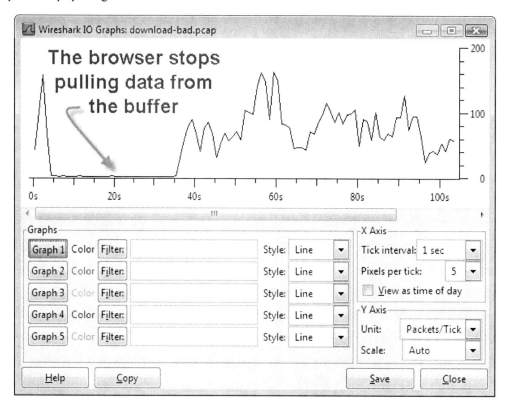

Figure 317. The IO rate drops as Internet Explorer stops pulling data out of the receive buffers

Note Any Name Resolution Faults

Name resolution faults, whether DNS, LDAP, NetBIOS Name Service or another name resolution process is used, can be significantly detrimental to network performance. These types of errors are typically quite evident in the trace file.

In Figure 318, DNS Server Failure responses indicate there are name resolution problems. The time column shows the delays between each successive DNS query.

No.	Source	Destination	Protocol	Info
1	192.168.1.1	192.168.0.2	DNS	Standard query PTR 109.1.168.192.in-a
2	192.168.0.2	192.168.1.1	DNS	Standard query response, No such name
3	192.168.1.1	192.168.0.2	DNS	Standard query PTR 44.133.17.66.in-ad
4	192.168.0.2	192.168.1.1	DNS	Standard query response, Server failu
5	192.168.200	192.168.200	DNS	Standard query PTR 1.0.0.127.in-addr.
6	192.168.200	192.168.200	DNS	Standard query response
7	192.168.200	192.168.200	DNS	Standard query PTR 1.0.0.127.in-addr.
8	192.168.200	192.168.200	DNS	Standard query response
9	192.168.200	192.168.200	DNS	Standard query A 198.162.100
10	192.168.1.1	192.168.0.2	DNS	Standard query PTR 14.1.168.192.in-ad
11	192.168.0.2	192.168.1.1	DNS	Standard query response, No such name
12	192.168.200	192.168.200	DNS	Standard query A 198.162.100
13	192.168.200	192.168.200	DNS	Standard query PTR 116.17.52.216.in-a
14	192.168.200	192.168.200	DNS	Standard query A 198.162.100
15	192.168.200	192.168.200	DNS	Standard query PTR 116.17.52.216.in-ac
16	192.168.1.1	192.168.0.2	DNS	Standard query PTR 44.133.17.66.in-add
17	192.168.0.2	192.168.1.1	DNS	Standard query response, Server fail

Figure 318. Evident name resolution problems cause poor performance

An Important Note about Analyzing Performance Problems

When you are analyzing network performance indicated by slow response, the first rule is "watch the time column." Although some processes may appear to cause problems, consider the amount of delay time incurred by each of the processes.

For example, if you find your Windows XP clients continuously query network drives for desktop.ini—measure the total amount of time consumed by the search process. You may find that the process only takes 100 milliseconds—hardly noticeable to the user. Do not get fixated on traffic that seems to indicate a fault, but does not affect performance issue.

Case Study:
One-Way Problems

Submitted by: *P.C.*
                         Sr. Network Technician

We had the most bizarre problems and used Wireshark to move along the path between devices to find out where the problem surfaced.

Our users were able to transfer files across our WAN link in one direction, but not in the reverse direction. For example, we could transfer files from our branch office #1 to branch office #2, but we could not transfer files from branch office #2 to branch office #1. When we tried transferring data in that direction, the transfer just "stalled" and the system generated various errors for each file transfer.

The trace file showed that we had packet loss only when we transferred in one direction. We moved Wireshark around closer to our WAN router when we found the switch that was dropping the packets.

We showed the switch vendor our trace files of the traffic before and after going through the switch—they ended up sending me a replacement card for the switch and that fixed the problem.

It was the first time I'd ever sent a Wireshark trace file to a vendor, but it really helped get them on board to fix the problem right away. The packets showed exactly where the problem was. They couldn't deny it.

Case Study:
The Perfect Storm of Network Problems

Submitted by: **P. Erskine**
          Network Analyst

After months of noticing slow file transfer speeds in one direction on the network, this customer finally decided to stop guessing and take the recommended trace files. Following gut-instinct that the problems were along the path, the customer handed the trace files off to several vendors responsible for the infrastructure devices. In addition, they reviewed the trace files internally.

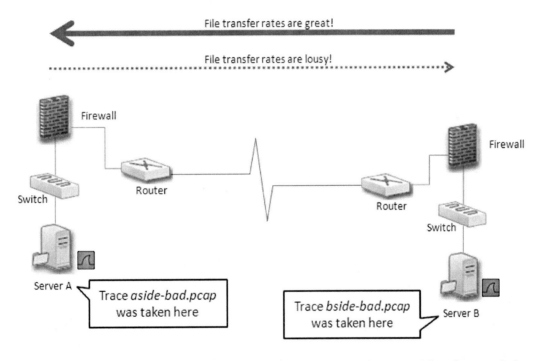

Performance is great when data travels from Server B to Server A. When data travels in the opposite direction, however, we notice some really lousy performance! To check out what could be causing the problem, the customer installed Wireshark directly on Server A and Server B. Then they performed a file transfer over FTP. They transferred the same file in both directions.

Source	Destination	Transfer Time
Server A	Server B	8 seconds
Server B	Server A	157 seconds

In each situation we captured the file transfer process on both ends of the connection. When we opened the trace files from the slow file transfer process, we saw some really interesting traffic.

aside-bad.pcap Results

In this trace file we noticed that packets flowed down to Server A nicely. Server A acknowledged the data and everything looked great… until all of a sudden, Server B began resending data packets from the middle of the download process. Weird. We also noticed that Wireshark said packet 173 was an Out-of-Order packet—which it is—but first and foremost, this packet is a retransmission. Sequence number 110401 occurred earlier in the trace file.

In addition, the duplicate ACKs that began in packet 176 are asking for the next packet expected if everything moved along smoothly (#157321). As we looked through the trace, we saw lots of retransmissions. It looked like Server B thought Server A didn't get sequence 110401 so it resent it. Then Server B resent all the other packets until it caught up to sequence 157321. This is a clear indication that Selective ACK is not being used.

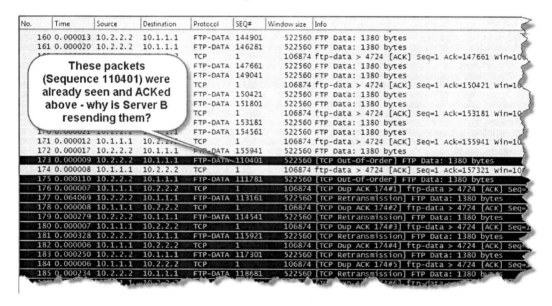

When we looked at the TCP Time-Sequence graph, we could retransmissions occurring throughout the trace file. When examining the trace file taken at Server A, we saw the original data packets and Server A's acknowledgments. Why did Server B suddenly start retransmitting packets? Were the ACKs from Server A getting dropped along the path? Time to look at the traffic from Server B's perspective.

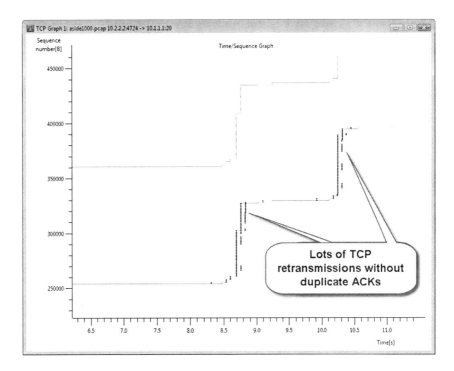

bside-bad.pcap Results

Ok… this was weird. At Server B we saw lots of duplicate ACKs coming in from Server A. Server B was just resending data as requested. Where were the duplicate ACKs coming from?

As we delved further into this issue, we found that an "intelligent security device" along the path was (a) stripping off the Selective ACK option from the TCP headers in the handshakes and (b) periodically generating duplicate ACKs on behalf of Server A.

```
⊞ Frame 1: 78 bytes on wire (624 bits), 78 bytes captured (624 bits)
⊞ Ethernet II, Src: Cisco_88:86:ff (00:12:43:88:86:ff), Dst: HewlettP_94:83:10 (00:12:79:94:83:10)
⊞ Internet Protocol, Src: 10.1.1.1 (10.1.1.1), Dst: 10.2.2.2 (10.2.2.2)
⊟ Transmission Control Protocol, Src Port: ftp-data (20), Dst Port: 4724 (4724), Seq: 0, Len: 0
    Source port: ftp-data (20)
    Destination port: 4724 (4724)
    [Stream index: 0]
    Sequence number: 0    (relative sequence number)
    Header length: 44 bytes
⊞ Flags: 0x02 (SYN)
⊞ Checksum: 0x9e91 [correct]
⊟ Options: (24 bytes)
    Maximum segment size: 1380 bytes
    NOP
    Window scale: 1 (multiply by 2)
    NOP
    NOP
    Timestamps: TSval 0, TSecr 0
    NOP
    NOP
    NOP
    NOP
```

> Where is the Selective ACK option that the packet was sent with originally? Why all the NOPs instead?

We knew some device in the center was messing up our traffic – we saw TCP handshake packets that had a bunch of NOP (No Option) placeholders instead of our Selective ACK option. That explained why our server was retransmitting more than just the packet it thought was lost. Ugly. After taking more traces on either side of one of the "intelligent security devices," we were able to watch that device strip off the Selective ACK option. We also saw that device start sending duplicate ACKs in the middle of a transmission.

The ultimate cause of slow performance was the server slowing down because the congestion window has been reduced because of "lost packets" (which weren't lost at all. The server resent more than it needed to because SACK was disabled so we watched the server slow down sending packets. The server had to wait for some ACKs before sending more data.

This really slowed everything down to a crawl!

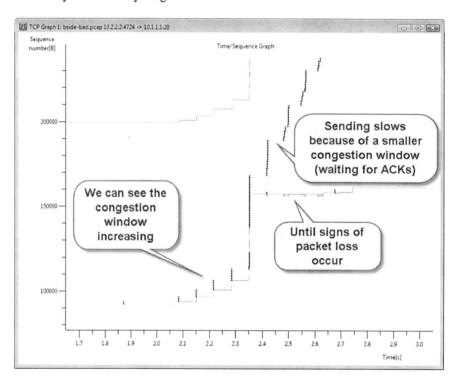

We had to sit with the vendor and go through the trace file packet-by-packet to explain that our servers were behaving properly, but their device was interfering with our communications in one direction.

Summary

Wireshark is the ideal tool for network troubleshooting. Poor network performance is typically due to delays, packet loss, misconfigurations, faulty applications, poorly-designed applications, non-optimized hosts or applications, redirections, network or host congestion or name resolution faults.

The first problem to watch for is delay. Consider setting Wireshark's Time column to Seconds Since Previous Displayed Packets. Sort the Time column to spot large gaps in time. Delays can occur due to high path latency, QoS settings, client congestion or server congestion.

Packet loss also affects network performance. When TCP-based traffic experiences packet loss, TCP automatically attempts to recover from the problem. UDP-based traffic relies on the applications to define the timeout values and retry counts.

Applications that are either misconfigured (and possibly deny services) or poorly designed (and perhaps transfer files using minimal packet sizes) can also affect performance to the point that users begin to complain.

Name resolution problems (or any other resolution problems) can completely disrupt network communications.

Practice What You've Learned

Download the trace files available in the Download section of the book website, *www.wiresharkbook.com*. Examine the trace files listed below to practice identifying the causes of poor performance.

dns-lousyhotelnetwork.pcap This trace begins with a really slow DNS response. How much delay was caused by this slow DNS response? Are there any other problems in this trace file that are affecting network performance?

How much time passed from the first packet of the TCP handshake to the last packet of the trace file? Where do you see delays in the trace file?

http-slow-filexfer.pcap Why is this file transfer process so slow? What Expert Info Composite notifications are listed for this trace file?

tcp-pktloss94040.pcap This trace depicts a browsing session to *www.cnn.com*—with massive packet loss.

Create an IO Graph of the packet loss situations. Is packet loss consistent through the trace file or just at one specific time?

tcp-window-frozen.pcap A window frozen condition can kill file transfer speed.

Right click on the first **ZeroWindow** packet (packet 30) to Set a Time Reference. How much time did this window frozen condition waste?

http-download-bad.pcap   The client complains that there is a problem with the Internet connection—they are trying to download the OpenOffice binary, but it is just taking too long. Use the Expert Info and Expert Info Composite to identify the problems in this trace file. What are the three primary causes for the poor performance? Refer to *Chapter 13: Use Wireshark's Expert System* for information on identifying problems quickly.

http-download-good.pcap   The users are relatively happy with the download time required to obtain the OpenOffice binary depicted in this trace file. How long did the file transfer take? What is the average bytes/second rate? Refer to *Chapter 7: Define Time Values and Interpret Summaries* for details on using Wireshark's Summary window.

Review Questions

Q29.1   **How can you quickly spot large gaps in time between packets of a conversation?**

Q29.2   **What are the steps involved in finding the source of packet loss during a TCP-based file transfer process?**

Q29.3   **Which graph can you create to display small packet sizes during a file transfer process?**

Q29.4   **What condition occurs when a TCP receiver has no buffer space available?**

Q29.5   **When analyzing a trace file of a file transfer process you notice over 100 error responses during the file location process. Can you assume this will always cause a delay that is noticeable by the client?**

Answers to Review Questions

Q29.1   **How can you quickly spot large gaps in time between packets of a conversation?**

A29.1   To spot large gaps in time between packets of a conversation set the Time column to Seconds since Previous Displayed Packet, filter on a single conversation and then sort the Time column so the largest values are at the top.

Q29.2   **What are the steps involved in finding the source of packet loss during a TCP-based file transfer process?**

A29.2   Move the analyze along the path to determine the point when you see the original packet and the retransmission—packet loss has not occurred yet—the device that is dropping packets is downstream (closer to the receiver) than you are located.

Q29.3   **Which graph can you create to display small packet sizes during a file transfer process?**

A29.3   Graph the `AVG(*)tcp.len` value in an Advanced IO Graph.

Q29.4   **What condition occurs when a TCP receiver has no buffer space available?**

A29.4   When a TCP receiver runs out of buffer space, it advertises a *window zero* condition.

Q29.5   **When analyzing a file transfer trace file you notice over 100 error responses during the file location process. Can you assume this will always cause a delay that is noticeable by the client?**

A29.5   No. You must analyze the total amount of delay incurred by the errors before stating that they are causing a noticeable effect.

Chapter 30: Network Forensics Overview

Wireshark Certified Network Analyst Exam Objectives covered:

- Compare Host vs. Network Forensics
- Gather Evidence
- Avoid Detection
- Handle Evidence
- Recognize Unusual Traffic Patterns
- Color Unusual Traffic Patterns
- Check Out Complementary Forensic Tools

Compare Host vs. Network Forensics

Host forensics is the process of investigating media storage elements such as internal and external hard drives. Evidence may include data files, locally-stored emails, registry settings, browsing history and more.

Network forensics is the process of examining network traffic for evidence of unusual or malicious traffic. This traffic may include reconnaissance (discovery) processes, phone-home behavior, denial of service attacks, man-in-the-middle poisoning, botnet commands, etc. These types of unusual traffic are covered in *Chapter 32: Analyze Suspect Traffic*.

Network forensics can also be used to study traffic patterns of malicious activity to properly configure network defense mechanisms.

Gather Evidence

Network forensic evidence may be gathered for proactive or reactive analysis. Proactive analysis techniques may require placing network capture devices at various key locations on the network and saving large volumes of traffic.

An Intrusion Detection System (IDS) offers complementary capability for examining network traffic and alerting IT staff to unusual traffic patterns.

The placement of Wireshark depends on the issue being investigated.

Using Wireshark to capture traffic to and from a suspect host is an example of reactive analysis. If you suspect numerous compromised hosts are communicating with command and control (C&C) servers, you may prefer to place Wireshark close to the network egress point and filter on the IP addresses of the suspect hosts or the protocol in use.

The purpose of network forensics analysis is to reduce traffic data to useful information. Capturing high quantities of traffic and distilling it into separate conversations, protocols, or time sets helps locate possible breaches.

Avoid Detection

By default, Wireshark does not transmit data on the network. Other applications running on the same host as Wireshark may be communicating, however.

Wireshark may be detectable if you enable network name resolution. For example, in Figure 319, the host running Wireshark (192.168.0.111) is capturing traffic on an Ethernet network and sending DNS PTR queries for each IP address captured. Besides making Wireshark visible, this traffic may overwhelm the DNS server if the capture contains a high number of IP addresses.

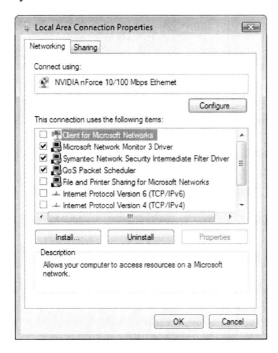

No.. T...			Protocol	Info
			LOC	Attribute Request, V1 Transaction ID
			LOC	Attribute Reply, V1 Transaction ID
				Who has 192.168.0.101? Tell 192.16
				Source port: 6646 Destination por
5			ARP	Who has 192.168.0.108? Tell 192.16
6 0.032385	IntelCor_46:9c:	Broadcast	ARP	Who has 192.168.0.102? Tell 192.168
7 0.249317	192.168.0.113	192.168.0.1	DNS	Standard query PTR 106.0.168.192.i
8 0.000045	192.168.0.113	192.168.0.1	DNS	Standard query PTR 100.0.168.192.i
9 0.000028	192.168.0.113	192.168.0.1	DNS	Standard query PTR 111.0.168.192.i
10 0.000024	192.168.0.113	192.168.0.1	DNS	Standard query PTR 255.0.168.192.i
11 0.013623	192.168.0.1	192.168.0.113	DNS	Standard query response, No such na
12 0.000123	68.87.76.182	192.168.0.113	DNS	Standard query response, No such na
13 0.035707	192.168.0.1	192.168.0.113	DNS	Standard query response, No such na
14 0.000111	68.87.78.134	192.168.0.113	DNS	Standard query response, No such na
15 0.503791	192.168.0.113	192.168.0.1	DNS	Standard query PTR 113.0.168.192.i
16 0.000273	192.168.0.113	192.168.0.1	DNS	Standard query PTR 1.0.168.192.in-a
17 0.012139	192.168.0.1	192.168.0.113	DNS	Standard query response, No such na
18 0.035816	192.168.0.1	192.168.0.113	DNS	Standard query response, No such na
19 0.118815	IntelCor_46:9c:	Broadcast	ARP	Who has 192.168.0.117? Tell 192.1
20 0.582947	192.168.0.113	192.168.0.1	DNS	Standard query PTR 182.76.87.68.in
21 0.000274	192.168.0.113	192.168.0.1	DNS	Standard query PTR 134.78.87.68.in-
22 0.013053	192.168.0.1	192.168.0.113	DNS	Standard query response PTR cns.san
23 0.036540	192.168.0.1	192.168.0.113	DNS	Standard query response PTR cns.sa
24 1.455165	192.168.0.108	192.168.0.100	SRVLOC	Attribute Request, V1 Transaction
25 0.000976	192.168.0.100	192.168.0.108	SRVLOC	Attribute Reply, V1 Transaction ID

Wireshark is sending DNS PTR queries because network name resolution is enabled

Figure 319. Wireshark may generate PTR queries when network name resolution is enabled

Interestingly, Wireshark can still capture traffic even if the TCP/IP stack is disabled, as shown in Figure 320. This is one way to avoid detection.

Figure 320. Wireshark can still capture traffic when the IP stacks are disabled

Some products, such as NetScanTools Pro (*www.netscantools.com*) can perform discovery processes to identify hosts in promiscuous mode, a requirement for capturing traffic addressed to other hosts' hardware addresses.[98]

Figure 321 shows the results of the NetScanTools' Promiscuous Mode Scanner tool run against a network in search of a host running Wireshark or another packet capture tool.

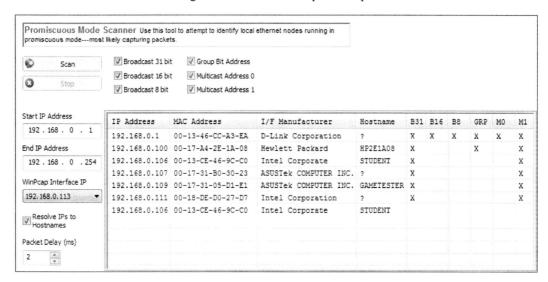

Figure 321. NetScanTools Pro contains a promiscuous mode scanner

This promiscuous mode scan first sends an ARP scan to discover all devices on the local network. The result columns indicate responses to the following tests:

Column	Description
B31	31-bit Broadcast MAC Address (0xff:ff:ff:ff:ff:fe)
B16	16-bit Broadcast MAC Address (0xff:ff:00:00:00:00)
B8	8-bit Broadcast MAC Address (0xff:00:00:00:00:00)
M0	Multicast MAC Address ending in 0 (0x01:00:5e:00:00:00)
M1	Multicast MAC Address ending in 1 (0x01:00:5e:00:00:01)

In Figure 321, NetScanTools Pro lists the results of the test. If more than two X's follow an adapter listed, there is a chance the adapter is in promiscuous mode and could be capturing packets. Note that only one device is actually running Wireshark in our test—the number of false positives negates the effectiveness of most promiscuous mode tests.

The traffic pattern of this promiscuous mode scan is easy to identify. Figure 322 shows the variations in the destination MAC address field during this ARP scan.[99]

---

[98] Since many network interface cards and adapters are in promiscuous mode by default, this scan may have a high rate of false positives making it unreliable as an analyzer detection method.

No..	Time	Source	Destination	Protocol	Info
59	5.736470	Elitegro_40:74:d2	Broadcast	ARP	who has 192.168.0.22
364	1.805207	Elitegro_40:74:d2	ff:ff:ff:ff:ff:fe	ARP	who has 192.168.0.22
526	1.695822	Elitegro_40:74:d2	ff:ff:00:00:00:00	ARP	who has 192.168.0.22
395	1.601962	Elitegro_40:74:d2	ff:00:00:00:00:00	ARP	who has 192.168.0.22
153	1.600968	Elitegro_40:74:d2	00:00:00_00:00:00	ARP	who has 192.168.0.22
112	1.597061	Elitegro_40:74:d2	IPv4mcast_00:00:00	ARP	who has 192.168.0.22
579	1.619130	Elitegro_40:74:d2	IPv4mcast_00:00:01	ARP	who has 192.168.0.22

Figure 322. This promiscuous mode scan uses ARP variations

Handle Evidence Properly

Handling of evidence should not alter or cause concern regarding its integrity. Trace files should always be stored in a secure location and chain of custody documentation should define the capture process and location, trace file control, transfer and analysis process details. IT staff should own a fireproof safe for securing magnetic media that contains evidence and follow all recommended evidence handling procedures.

Digital evidence handling procedure recommendations vary. Local laws and regulations should be considered to preserve the integrity and admissibility of digital evidence.[100] Review *Be Aware of Legal Issues of Listening to Network Traffic* on page 8.

Recognize Unusual Traffic Patterns

In order to recognize unusual traffic patterns, you must first recognize normal traffic patterns. Baselines are essential in differentiating traffic types.

Using penetration testing, reconnaissance and mapping tools to generate unusual traffic enables you to correlate this type of traffic with these tools. For example, in Figure 323 we have captured an OS fingerprinting operation performed with NetScanTools Pro. In some of the ICMP Echo Request packets, the code field is set at 1. This is unique as the specification indicates the code field of an ICMP Echo Request packet should be 0.

---

[99] Capture your own traffic when you run discovery or testing tools. Save the trace files as baselines of how these applications look on the network so you recognize their patterns when a third-party uses these tools against you.

[100] The High Technology Investigation Association (HTCIA) is a global membership group open to security professionals and law enforcement agents. Visit *www.htcia.org* for numerous forensic resources.

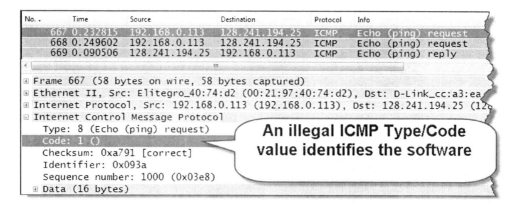

Figure 323. Unusual traffic patterns may identify the tool used on the network

Color Unusual Traffic Patterns

In order to spot unusual traffic more efficiently, consider creating coloring rules to highlight this traffic. For example, a coloring rule using the string (icmp.type == 8) && !(icmp.code == 0x00) would highlight the unusual ICMP Echo Request used by NetScanTools. The following table illustrates additional coloring rules that highlight unusual traffic.

Coloring Rule String	Coloring Rule Name/Description

`(tcp.flags == 0x00) ||`
`(tcp.options.wscale_val == 10) ||`
`(tcp.options.mss_val < 1460) ||`
`(tcp.flags == 0x29) &&`
`tcp.urgent_pointer == 0 ||`
`(tcp.flags==0x02 && frame[42:4] !=`
`00:00:00:00) || (tcp.flags==0x02 &&`
`tcp.window_size < 65535 &&`
`tcp.options.wscale_val > 0)`
	Nmap general traffic (a long filter looking for unusual traffic patterns)

`tcp.window_size < 65535 &&` `tcp.flags.syn==1`	Small WinSize SYN (Suboptimal setting or discovery packet?)

`tcp.port == 6666 || tcp.port == 6667`
`|| tcp.port == 6668 || tcp.port ==`
`6669`
	Default IRC TCP Ports 6666-6669 (IRC traffic—bot issue? Could also be created with > and < operators)

`dns.count.answers > 5`	DNS Answers > 5 (Bot C&C servers listed in this packet? Not always a problem, but suspect.)

Coloring Rule String	Coloring Rule Name/Description
`icmp.type==3 && icmp.code==2`	ICMP Protocol Unreachable (IP scan underway?)
`(icmp) && (tcp)`	ICMP Response to TCP Packet (Sender firewalled?)
`icmp.type==3 && icmp.code==4`	ICMP Type 3/Code 4 (Black hole detection?)
`icmp.type==13 || icmp.type==15 ||` `icmp.type==17`	ICMP Types 13, 15 or 17 (OS fingerprinting?)
`icmp.type==8 && !icmp.code==0`	Non-Standard ICMP Echo Request (Can we detect the application used?)
`tcp.window_size < 1460 &&` `tcp.flags.reset == 0`	TCP Window Size < 1460 (Receiver stopping data transfer?)
`(tcp.window_size == 0) &&` `(tcp.flags.reset == 0)`	TCP Zero Window (Receiver stopping data transfer.)

Check Out Complementary Forensic Tools

Numerous other security tools complement the packet capture abilities of Wireshark. A list of the Top 100 Network Security Tools is maintained by Gordon "Fyodor" Lyon (creator of Nmap) at *sectools.org*.[101] This is a partial list of tools that made the Top 100 list.

- Nessus (*www.nessus.org*)
- Snort (*www.snort.org*)
- Netcat (*netcat.sourceforge.net*)
- NetScanTools (*www.netscantools.com*)
- Metasploit Framework (*www.metasploit.com*)
- Hping2 (*www.hping.org*)
- Kismet (*www.kismetwireless.net*)
- Tcpdump (*www.tcpdump.org*)
- Cain and Abel (*www.oxid.it*)
- John the Ripper (*www.openwall.com/john*)
- Ettercap (*ettercap.sourceforge.net*)
- Nikto (*www.cirt.net/nikto2*)

For a list of other tools that complement Wireshark's capabilities, visit *wiki.wireshark.org/Tools*.

---

[101] In the most recent survey conducted by Fyodor, Wireshark ranked #2 in security tools.

Case Study:
SSL/TLS Vulnerability Studied

Submitted by: **Steve Dispensa**
                  Chief Technology Officer
                  PhoneFactor

Note from the author: On November 5, 2009, word spread through the IT community that the globally-deployed SSL/TLS was susceptible to man-in-the-middle attack. The vulnerability was actually discovered in August of 2009 by Marsh Ray and Steve Dispensa from PhoneFactor (*www.phonefactor.com*). Their publicly-released document describing the issue, trace files and decryption keys for the malicious SSL/TLS traffic is available on the book website, *www.wiresharkbook.com*. For more information on the status of this vulnerability, visit *www.phonefactor.com/sslgap/*.

At PhoneFactor, we've been heavy users of Wireshark (and Ethereal before it) for years. It'd be hard to imagine doing any serious protocol development without it. We used Wireshark at several points in the process during our research into the TLS vulnerability for the report that we published in November, 2009.

We identified the problem in TLS after a developer got suspicious about the way Apache handled certificate authentication. We did a number of packet captures that, coupled with source code analysis and a careful reading of the relevant standards documents, led us to the problem.

Because the protocol in question is TLS, Wireshark has to do an extra bit of magic to display meaningful information from the packet captures. When capturing packets in the middle of a TLS session (e.g., from a switch in the middle of the network), all you can see after the initial handshake are encrypted records—after all, that's the point of TLS. In order to decode these encrypted packets, Wireshark generally has to be supplied with a copy of the certificate in use on the connection, including its private key. This can be a little tricky to set up, but once it's configured, you'll have full access to decrypted data.

After the problem was identified, we wanted to get a working reproduction of the issue to prove to vendors that it was a real problem. That involved developing a working implementation of a lot of the TLS protocol, so once again, we relied heavily on Wireshark to make sure our packet structures were correct.

To prove the problem was real, we took a packet capture of the exploit code in action, just to make sure that there wasn't any kind of external interaction that could account for what we were seeing. Sure enough, we were able to show that the effects we were seeing couldn't possibly have been caused by anything other than the flaw we identified.

When it came to showing the problem to others, we started out by presenting protocol diagrams and packet captures to prove our point. Standards notwithstanding, the very best way to learn the mechanics of a protocol is by studying packet captures, and the packet captures we presented to the vendor community accurately communicated the details of the problem.

There are often differences between the way the writers of standards documents think things should be implemented and the way programmers actually write the code. Wireshark is a great reference tool, since it generally is well adapted to the actual implementations in the field. As we continue our research into TLS, this kind of information will continue to be invaluable.

Summary

Host forensics is the process of investigating the contents of electronic media such as hard drives, USB drives and even memory. Network forensics is the process of investigating data communications evidence.

Knowing where to capture the network traffic and how to capture the network traffic is the most important element of network forensics. If you miss capturing the traffic evidence, then you have nothing to analyze. Avoid using capture filters if possible. Once traffic is filtered out using capture filters you cannot get access to that traffic again. Use display filters during your network forensics investigation. If you are capturing a large amount of data, consider capturing to file sets.

Ensure you have not enabled Wireshark's network name resolution process to avoid detection.

Handle your evidence with the assumption that it may be used in a legal process someday. Use proper chain of custody procedures and ensure the network traffic evidence is kept in a secure location (such as a safe).

If you have performed your baselines processes, you are more likely to be able to spot unusual traffic patterns. When you spot these unusual patterns, consider creating coloring rules to make them even more highly visible.

There are numerous forensics tools that complement Wireshark. Fyodor, creator of Nmap, maintains a list of Top Security Tools at *sectools.org*.

Practice What You've Learned

 Download the trace files available in the Download section of the book website, *www.wiresharkbook.com*. Open the traces listed below to examine some unusual traffic patterns.

sec-dictionary2.pcap   This dictionary password crack is focused on breaking into the admin account on an FTP server. Apply the following filter to display all the passwords attempted: `ftp.request.command==PASS`. Did the cracker try using a blank password?

sec-evilprogram.pcap   This is a truly classic trace file of a system infected with the Stopguard browser hijack spyware/malware/scumware program.

     Create a DNS filter to see the client look up Virtumonde's website. That's when the troubles begin. Check out *www.spywarewarrior.com*—a great reference for spyware/adware/malware/scumware, etc.

sec-macof.pcap   Dug Song created Macof to flood network switch MAC address tables and cause them to go into 'hub mode.' This tool still wreaks havoc on the network. Can you identify the signature in this flood traffic?

Review Questions

Q30.1   **What is the purpose of network forensics?**

Q30.2   **What is one of the traffic patterns that can make a Wireshark system visible to others?**

Q30.3   **Why should you capture your own traffic when doing research with reconnaissance and attack tools?**

Q30.4   **How can you make unusual traffic easier to locate in Wireshark?**

Answers to Review Questions

Q30.1   **What is the purpose of network forensics?**

A30.1   Network forensics is the process of examining network traffic for evidence of unusual or unacceptable traffic. This traffic may include reconnaissance (discovery) processes, phone-home behavior, denial of service attacks, man-in-the-middle poisoning, bot commands, etc.

Q30.2   **What is one of the traffic patterns that can make a Wireshark system visible to others?**

A30.2   If network name resolution is enabled, Wireshark may generate a large number of DNS PTR queries to resolve IP addresses to host names.

Q30.3   **Why should you capture your own traffic when doing research with reconnaissance and attack tools?**

A30.3   Capture your own traffic when doing research with these tools to identify the signatures in their traffic and create defense mechanisms to block these tools from being used successfully on your network.

Q30.4   **How can you make unusual traffic easier to locate in Wireshark?**

A30.4   Consider creating coloring rules for unusual packets so you can identify them faster in the Packet List pane.

Chapter 31: Detect Scanning and Discovery Processes

Wireshark Certified Network Analyst Exam Objectives covered:

- The Purpose of Discovery and Reconnaissance
- Detect ARP Scans (aka ARP Sweeps)
- Detect ICMP Ping Sweeps
- Detect Various Types of TCP Port Scans
- Detect UDP Port Scans
- Detect IP Protocol Scans
- Understanding Idle Scans
- Know Your ICMP Types and Codes
- Analyze Traceroute Path Discovery
- Detect Dynamic Router Discovery
- Understand Application Mapping Processes
- Use Wireshark for Passive OS Fingerprinting
- Detect Active OS Fingerprinting
- Identify Spoofed Addresses in Scans

- ❖ Case Study: Learning the Conficker Lesson
- ❖ Summary
- ❖ Practice What You've Learned
- ❖ Review Questions and Answers

The Purpose of Discovery and Reconnaissance Processes

Just as a criminal may investigate the workings of a bank before robbing it, malicious programs and processes may investigate open ports and working hosts before attempting an exploit. Identifying these discovery and reconnaissance processes in a timely manner may thwart the effects of the eventual attack.

Understanding the purpose of these discovery methods will help you realize what the attacker is looking for and what options are available to block the traffic.

Nmap is one of the most popular tools used to discover network devices and services.[102] In this chapter we provide some details on how to run and identify various Nmap discovery processes.

Use Nmap on Your Network (with Permission)

Nmap is a free, multi-platform (Windows, Linux/UNIX, Mac OS X) security scanner available from nmap.org. This is a tool you should know as well as you know Wireshark. When you run Nmap, be certain to analyze the traffic Nmap generates as we show in this chapter.

Detect ARP Scans (aka ARP Sweeps)

ARP scans are used to find local hosts only because ARP packets are not routable—ARP packets do not have an IP header. One of the advantages of using ARP scanning on a local network is that you can discover hosts that might be firewalled and not answering typical pings.

Nmap—ARP Scanning Process

The Nmap parameter to run an ARP scan is −PR (referred to as an ARP ping), but this parameter is rarely used since Nmap automatically uses ARP scan whenever it can (e.g. when the target is on the same Ethernet segment as the source). Consider analyzing an Nmap Ping sweep operation as that process uses an ARP scan whenever it can so you can analyze both processes in a single analysis session.

The disadvantage of using an ARP scan is that the ARP traffic can't get through a router or any layer 3 device. The advantage of running an ARP scan is that you can discover local devices that may be hidden from other discovery methods by a firewall. If the firewall blocks ICMP-based pings, you can use an ARP scan to discover the device. You cannot disable ARP responses—that would "break" the TCP/IP communications system.

Keep in mind that ARP scans will not cross a router. If you detect an ARP scan taking place, the source and targets will be on the same network you are capturing traffic on.

---

[102] "Nmap: Network Scanning", written by Gordon "Fyodor" Lyon (the creator of Nmap), is the most comprehensive guide to using Nmap—a "must read" for any IT professional (ISBN: 978-0-9799587-1-7). Find out more about this great book at *nmap.org/book*.

No. .	Time	Source	Destination	Protocol	Info
1	0.000000	3com_de:42:c2	Broadcast	ARP	who has 10.64.44.3? Tell 10.64.44.20
2	0.019991	3com_de:42:c2	Broadcast	ARP	who has 10.64.44.4? Tell 10.64.44.20
3	0.020057	3com_de:42:c2	Broadcast	ARP	who has 10.64.44.5? Tell 10.64.44.20
4	0.060254	3com_de:42:c2	Broadcast	ARP	who has 10.64.44.8? Tell 10.64.44.20
5	0.020067	3com_de:42:c2	Broadcast	ARP	who has 10.64.44.9? Tell 10.64.44.20
6	0.039864	3com_de:42:c2	Broadcast	ARP	who has 10.64.44.11? Tell 10.64.44.2
7	0.020184	3com_de:42:c2	Broadcast	ARP	who has 10.64.44.12? Tell 10.64.44.20
8	0.039983	3com_de:42:c2	Broadcast	ARP	who has 10.64.44.14? Tell 10.64.44.20
9	0.040166	3com_de:42:c2	Broadcast	ARP	who has 10.64.44.16? Tell 10.64.44.2

⊞ Frame 1 (64 bytes on wire, 64 bytes captured)
⊞ Ethernet II, Src: 3com_de:42:c2 (00:10:4b:de:42:c2), Dst: Broadcast (ff:ff:ff:ff:
⊟ Address Resolution Protocol (request)
    Hardware type: Ethernet (0x0001)
    Protocol type: IP (0x0800)
    Hardware size: 6
    Protocol size: 4
    Opcode: request (0x0001)
    [Is gratuitous: False]
    Sender MAC address: 3com_de:42:c2 (00:10:4b:de:42:c2)
    Sender IP address: 10.64.44.20 (10.64.44.20)
    Target MAC address: 00:00:00_00:00:00 (00:00:00:00:00:00)
    Target IP address: 10.64.44.3 (10.64.44.3)

Figure 324. ARP scans can discover all local TCP/IP devices

Common ARP scan processes send ARP requests to the broadcast MAC address (0xff:ff:ff:ff:ff:ff).
Discovering ARP scan traffic can be difficult if the ARP traffic is not using a high packet per second
rate which would make it clearly visible in the trace file, as shown in Figure 324.

Detect ICMP Ping Sweeps

There are three possible variations of ping sweeps although most people refer to a ping sweep as a
scan using an ICMP Type 8 Echo Requests followed by an ICMP Type 0 Echo Reply. The other
variations are TCP ping scans and UDP ping scans. Both TCP and UDP variations use destination
port 8, the echo port. Most hosts should not support echo services on TCP or UDP port 8, so using
TCP and UDP ping scan methods are not very useful.

The standard ICMP-based ping sweep worked great for many years until firewalls (host and
network) were often configured to block these types of ICMP packets. Figure 325 shows a standard
ICMP-based ping process used to discover a target at 130.57.4.27.

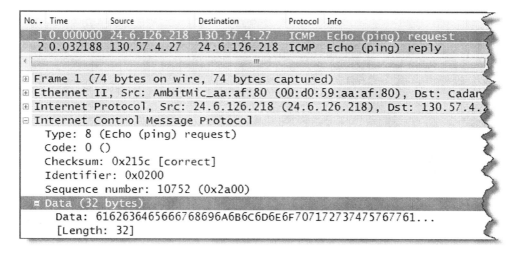

Figure 325. The most common variation of a ping sweep uses ICMP Echo Requests/Replies

ICMP-based ping sweeps are easy to detect with a simple filter for `icmp.type==8 ||`
`icmp.type==0`. The echo requests use ICMP type 8 while the ICMP echo replies use ICMP type
0. If a target blocks ICMP pings, consider using a TCP or UDP port scan to identify hosts on the
network.

Nmap Syntax—Ping Sweep Parameter

The Nmap syntax for an ICMP-based ping sweep is `-sP`.

Detect Various Types of TCP Port Scans

Port scans are used to discover targets and/or services offered on a target.[103]

The majority of popular services such as web browsing and email services run over TCP. The
following table lists a few popular services that run over TCP and may be interesting to someone
scanning the network.

Service	TCP Port Number
FTP	21
Secure Shell (SSH)	22
Telnet	23
SMTP	25
HTTP	80
POP	110

---

[103] Most people assume TCP scans are only used to discover active services. In fact, however, TCP scans may
be used to simply discover active targets as well.

Service	TCP Port Number
NTP	123
Endpoint Mapper Resolution	135
NetBIOS Session Service	139
HTTP over SSL/TLS	443
Microsoft Directory Services	445
Microsoft SQL Server	1433
VNC Server	5900
HTTP Alternate	8080

For a complete list of assigned port numbers, *visit www.iana.org/assignments/port-numbers*. For a recent list of the most popular scan target ports and their source IP addresses, visit the SANS Internet Storm Center (ISC) at *isc.sans.org/top10.html*.

There are several variations of TCP scans. In basic TCP connection establishment, one TCP host sends a TCP SYN to a port on a target. The target must respond with either a RST (port is not open) or SYN/ACK (port is open). This provides a quick connectivity test.

TCP Half-Open Scan (aka "Stealth Scan")

Nmap uses a TCP half-open (a.k.a. stealth scan) by default. It does not finish up the three-way handshake to make a complete connection if a port is open. Upon receipt of the SYN/ACK from the target, the host running Nmap will generate a TCP Reset to terminate the connection attempt.

Watch for Microsoft-Limited Connection Attempts

When Microsoft released Service Pack 2 for XP, they intentionally limited the number of half-open outgoing connections allowed to a maximum of 10. This caused some problems for legitimate applications that launched greater than 10 connection attempts—most notably peer-to-peer applications. Nmap (running on Windows hosts) generally avoids this restriction by sending packets at the Ethernet frame level—though it can dramatically slow down TCP connect scans (-sT).

A TCP Reset response indicates that the target port is closed. If no response is received, we cannot assume the port is open or closed. The TCP SYN or the response may have been dropped along the way. Advanced port scanners such as Nmap retransmit probe packets to distinguish intentional packet filtering from the occasional packet loss which can be expected on busy networks.

An ICMP Destination Unreachable (Type 3) response with a Code 1, 2, 3, 9, 10 or 13 indicates that the port is probably firewalled. Refer to *Dissect the ICMP Packet Structure* on page 353.

In a TCP half-open scan, since the scanner does not complete the three-way handshake, a target can look at their list of open connections and the scanning host will not show up (hence the name "stealth scan."). The half-open TCP scan is the desired type of TCP scan for the sake of stealthiness and resource preservation on the target.

Detecting TCP scans can be difficult to detect with Wireshark[104] unless the scans are in close proximity and evident in the trace file as shown in Figure 326. An unusually high number of RSTs or a high number of SYN/ACKs with a low volume of data transfer are strong indications that a TCP scan is underway.

No. .	Time	Source	Destination	Protocol	Info
27	0.000050	192.168.1.141	192.168.1.123	TCP	55784 > echo [SYN] Seq=0 Win=5840 Len
28	0.000010	192.168.1.123	192.168.1.141	TCP	echo > 55784 [RST, ACK] Seq=1 Ack=1 W
29	0.000130	192.168.1.141	192.168.1.123	TCP	55521 > 8 [SYN] Seq=0 Win=5840 Len=0
30	0.000010	192.168.1.123	192.168.1.141	TCP	8 > 55521 [RST, ACK] Seq=1 Ack=1 Wi
31	0.000052	192.168.1.141	192.168.1.123	TCP	50915 > discard [SYN] Seq=0 Win=5840
32	0.000010	192.168.1.123	192.168.1.141	TCP	discard > 50915 [RST, ACK] Seq=1 Ack=
33	0.000139	192.168.1.141	192.168.1.123	TCP	33342 > 10 [SYN] Seq=0 Win=5840 Len=0
34	0.000010	192.168.1.123	192.168.1.141	TCP	10 > 33342 [RST, ACK] Seq=1 Ack=1 Win
35	0.000048	192.168.1.141	192.168.1.123	TCP	59149 > systat [SYN] Seq=0 Win=5840
36	0.000009	192.168.1.123	192.168.1.141	TCP	systat > 59149 [RST, ACK] Seq=1 Ack=
37	0.000160	192.168.1.141	192.168.1.123	TCP	57308 > 12 [SYN] Seq=0 Win=5840 Len=
38	0.000010	192.168.1.123	192.168.1.141	TCP	12 > 57308 [RST, ACK] Seq=1 Ack=1 Wi

Figure 326. TCP scans in close proximity are easy to identify

TCP Full Connect Scan

TCP full scans complete the three-way handshake after receiving a SYN/ACK packet from an open port. A TCP Reset response indicates that the target port is closed. If no response is received, we cannot assume the port is open or closed. The TCP SYN or the response may have been dropped along the way. An ICMP Destination Unreachable (Type 3) response with a Code 1, 2, 3, 9, 10 or 13 indicates that the port is probably firewalled. Refer to *Dissect the ICMP Packet Structure* on page 353.

Just as with TCP half-open scans, detecting TCP full connect scans can be difficult to detect with Wireshark unless the scans are in close proximity and evident in the trace file. An unusually high number of RSTs or a high number of SYN/ACKs with a low volume of data transfer are strong indications that a TCP scan is underway as well.

Figure 327 shows the pattern of a TCP full connect scan. Note that in packet 106, the scanner completes the three-way handshake.

---

[104] This really differentiates Wireshark from specialized port scanning detectors or intrusion detection tools, such as Snort, which are designed to detect such scans.

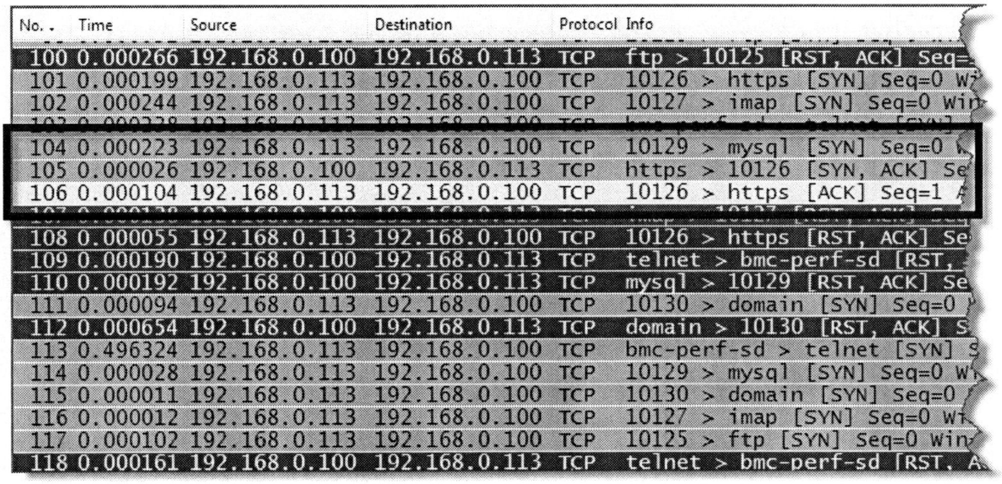

No. .	Time	Source	Destination	Protocol	Info
100	0.000266	192.168.0.100	192.168.0.113	TCP	ftp > 10125 [RST, ACK] Seq=
101	0.000199	192.168.0.113	192.168.0.100	TCP	10126 > https [SYN] Seq=0 Wi
102	0.000244	192.168.0.113	192.168.0.100	TCP	10127 > imap [SYN] Seq=0 Win
104	0.000223	192.168.0.113	192.168.0.100	TCP	10129 > mysql [SYN] Seq=0
105	0.000026	192.168.0.100	192.168.0.113	TCP	https > 10126 [SYN, ACK] Se
106	0.000104	192.168.0.113	192.168.0.100	TCP	10126 > https [ACK] Seq=1
108	0.000055	192.168.0.113	192.168.0.100	TCP	10126 > https [RST, ACK] Se
109	0.000190	192.168.0.100	192.168.0.113	TCP	telnet > bmc-perf-sd [RST,
110	0.000192	192.168.0.100	192.168.0.113	TCP	mysql > 10129 [RST, ACK] Se
111	0.000094	192.168.0.113	192.168.0.100	TCP	10130 > domain [SYN] Seq=0
112	0.000654	192.168.0.100	192.168.0.113	TCP	domain > 10130 [RST, ACK] S
113	0.496324	192.168.0.113	192.168.0.100	TCP	bmc-perf-sd > telnet [SYN]
114	0.000028	192.168.0.113	192.168.0.100	TCP	10129 > mysql [SYN] Seq=0 Wi
115	0.000011	192.168.0.113	192.168.0.100	TCP	10130 > domain [SYN] Seq=0
116	0.000012	192.168.0.113	192.168.0.100	TCP	10127 > imap [SYN] Seq=0 Wi
117	0.000102	192.168.0.113	192.168.0.100	TCP	10125 > ftp [SYN] Seq=0 Win
118	0.000161	192.168.0.100	192.168.0.113	TCP	telnet > bmc-perf-sd [RST, A

Figure 327. A full connect scan has found the HTTPS port open on the target

Null Scans

Null scans use an unusual TCP packet format—none of the TCP flags are set as shown in Figure 328. No response to a null scan indicates that the port is either open or filtered. A TCP Reset response indicates the port is closed. An ICMP Destination Unreachable (Type 3) response with a Code 1, 2, 3, 9, 10 or 13 indicates that the port is probably firewalled.[105]

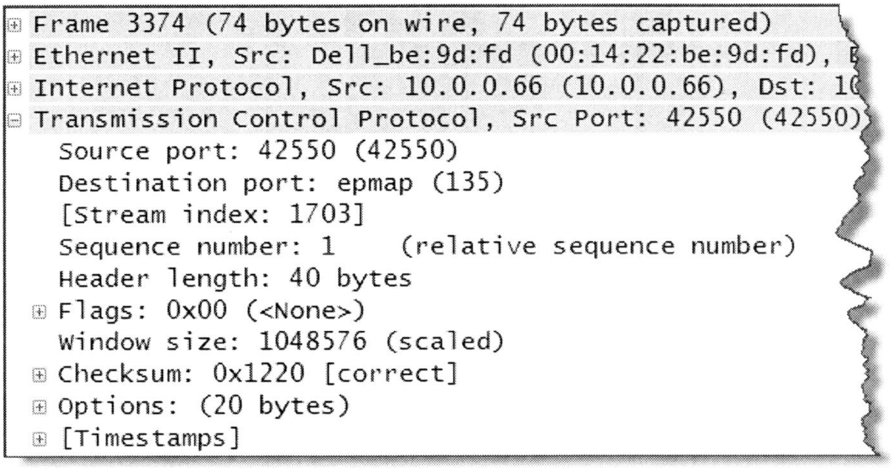

```
⊞ Frame 3374 (74 bytes on wire, 74 bytes captured)
⊞ Ethernet II, Src: Dell_be:9d:fd (00:14:22:be:9d:fd),
⊞ Internet Protocol, Src: 10.0.0.66 (10.0.0.66), Dst: 10
⊟ Transmission Control Protocol, Src Port: 42550 (42550)
     Source port: 42550 (42550)
     Destination port: epmap (135)
     [Stream index: 1703]
     Sequence number: 1     (relative sequence number)
     Header length: 40 bytes
   ⊞ Flags: 0x00 (<None>)
     Window size: 1048576 (scaled)
   ⊞ Checksum: 0x1220 [correct]
   ⊞ Options: (20 bytes)
   ⊞ [Timestamps]
```

Figure 328. Null scans do not have any TCP flags set

---

[105] Null scans, FIN scans and Xmas scans do not work against Microsoft hosts because they do not precisely follow RFC 793, Transmission Control Protocol. This RFC specifies how hosts should respond to "half-open connections and other anomalies."

To detect null scans, consider creating a coloring rule or display for TCP packets that have no TCP flags set - `tcp.flags == 0x00`.

Xmas Scan

Xmas scans have the URG, FIN and PUSH flags set.

No response to a Xmas scan indicates that the port is either open or filtered. A TCP Reset response indicates the port is closed. An ICMP Destination Unreachable (Type 3) response with a Code 1, 2, 3, 9, 10 or 13 indicates that the port is probably firewalled.

 Nmap Syntax—Xmas Scan Parameter

The Nmap syntax for an Xmas scan is −sX.

To detect Xmas scans, consider creating a coloring rule or display filter for TCP packets that have only these three flags set. You can do this two ways—by filtering on just those three flags or by filtering on the entire flags summary line. There is an advantage to filtering on the flags individually. A packet that contains the URG, FIN, PUSH and RST flags set to 1 would match the display filter or coloring rule.

The following is the syntax for a filter based on individual TCP flag settings:

```
(tcp.flags.urg == 1) && (tcp.flags.push == 1) &&
(tcp.flags.fin == 1)
```

The following is the syntax for a filter based on the TCP flags summary line. Figure 329 shows the Xmas scan packet format and the TCP flags summary line.

```
tcp.flags == 0x29
```

```
⊞ Frame 3380 (74 bytes on wire, 74 bytes captured)
⊞ Ethernet II, Src: Dell_be:9d:fd (00:14:22:be:9d:fd)
⊞ Internet Protocol, Src: 10.0.0.66 (10.0.0.66), Dst:
⊟ Transmission Control Protocol, Src Port: 42555 (4255
    Source port: 42555 (42555)
    Destination port: tcpmux (1)
    [Stream index: 1708]
    Sequence number: 1    (relative sequence number)
    Header length: 40 bytes
  ⊞ Flags: 0x29 (FIN, PSH, URG)
    Window size: 1048576 (scaled)
  ⊞ Checksum: 0x1278 [correct]
    Urgent pointer: 0
  ⊞ Options: (20 bytes)
  ⊞ [Timestamps]
```

Figure 329. Xmas scans have the Urgent, Push and Finish flags set

FIN Scan

FIN Scans only have the TCP FIN bit set.

No response to a FIN scan indicates that the port is either open or filtered. A TCP Reset response indicates the port is closed. An ICMP Destination Unreachable (Type 3) response with a Code 1, 2, 3, 9, 10 or 13 indicates that the port is probably firewalled.

Detecting FIN scans can be difficult unless the scans are in close proximity and evident in the trace file.

Nmap Syntax—FIN Scan Parameter

The Nmap syntax for a FIN scan is `-sF`.

ACK Scan

ACK scans are typically used to check firewall rules to see if ports are explicitly blocked. ACK scans are not used to identify open ports unless the window scan technique (`-sW` with Nmap) is used as well.[106]

An ACK scan uses a TCP packet with the ACK (Acknowledge) flag bit set to 1 as shown in Figure 330. No other TCP flag bits are set.

A TCP RST response indicates the port is unfiltered, which does not indicate the port is open—a TCP scan can be used to determine whether or not the port is open.

An ICMP Destination Unreachable response (Type 3, codes 1, 2, 3, 9, 10 or 13) indicates the port is likely filtered. No response is an indication that the port is likely filtered as well.

Wireshark's default color filtering rules contain a coloring rule for the ICMP Destination Unreachable packets (black background, vivid green foreground). The rule syntax is `icmp.type eq 3 || icmp.type eq 4 || icmp.type eq 5 || icmp.type eq 11`.

Nmap Syntax—ACK Scan Parameter

The Nmap syntax for an ACK scan is `-sA`.

---

[106] Window scanning examines the TCP window size field in a RST response from a target. Some hosts respond with a window size field value of zero if the port is closed and a non-zero window size field value if the port is open. The windows scan technique does not work on all devices as TCP/IP stacks get update to provide a more consistent response whether the port is open or closed.

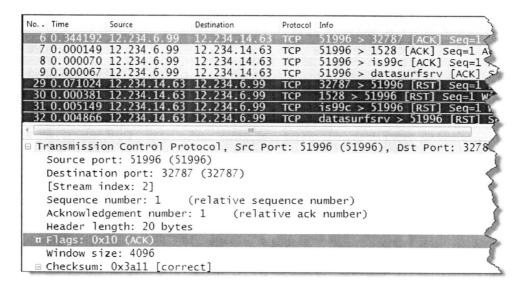

Figure 330. ACK scans are used to check firewall rules and identify blocked ports

Detect UDP Port Scans

Although the majority of popular services such as web browsing and email services run over TCP, certain very interesting services run over UDP.

The following table lists a few of the more interesting UDP-based services.

Service	UDP Port Number
DNS	53
SNMP	161/162
DHCP	67/68
SIP	5060
Microsoft Endpoint Mapper	135
NetBIOS Name Service	137/139

For a complete list of assigned port numbers, visit *www.iana.org/assignments/port-numbers*.

UDP port scans can be used to find services running on UDP ports or as a simple connectivity test.

An ICMP Destination Unreachable/Port Unreachable response indicates that the service is not available on the target as shown in Figure 331. No response indicates that the service might be available or the service might just be filtered. Any other ICMP response is an indication that the service is filtered.

No. .	Time	Source	Destination	Protocol	Info
1608	0.000014	192.168.1.123	192.168.1.141	ICMP	Destination unreachable (P
1609	0.067887	192.168.1.141	192.168.1.123	SNMP	get-next-request IF-MIB::å
1610	0.000016	192.168.1.123	192.168.1.141	ICMP	Destination unreachable (P
1611	0.020663	192.168.1.141	192.168.1.123	DNS	Standard query A www.googl
1612	0.017157	192.168.1.141	192.168.1.123	SNMP	get-request SNMPv2-MIB::sy
1617	2.418882	192.168.1.141	192.168.1.123	SNMP	get-next-request SNMPv2-SM
1618	0.000029	192.168.1.123	192.168.1.141	ICMP	Destination unreachable (P
1619	0.020867	192.168.1.141	192.168.1.123	XDMCP	Query
1620	0.000025	192.168.1.123	192.168.1.141	ICMP	Destination unreachable (P
1633	0.076650	192.168.1.141	192.168.1.123	UDP	Source port: 32929 Destin
1634	0.466263	192.168.1.141	192.168.1.123	DNS	Standard query A www.googl
1635	0.000017	192.168.1.123	192.168.1.141	ICMP	Destination unreachable (P
1638	0.016837	192.168.1.141	192.168.1.123	SNMP	get-request SNMPv2-MIB::sys
1663	1.105895	192.168.1.141	192.168.1.123	UDP	Source port: 32930 Desti
1664	0.000015	192.168.1.123	192.168.1.141	ICMP	Destination unreachable (P
1693	0.264598	192.168.1.141	192.168.1.123	UDP	Source port: 32930 Destin
1700	0.587418	192.168.1.141	192.168.1.123	UDP	Source port: 1024 Destina

Figure 331. UDP scans to closed ports trigger ICMP Destination Unreachable/Port Unreachable responses

An unusually high number of ICMP Destination Unreachable/Port Unreachable packets or a high number of unanswered UDP packets are strong indications that a UDP scan is underway.

Nmap Syntax—UDP Scan Parameter

The Nmap syntax for a UDP scan is `-sU`.

Wireshark's default color filtering rules contain a coloring rule for the ICMP Destination Unreachable packets (black background, vivid green foreground). The rule syntax is `icmp.type eq 3 || icmp.type eq 4 || icmp.type eq 5 || icmp.type eq 11`.

Detect IP Protocol Scans

IP protocol scans are designed to locate services running directly over IP. For example, an IP scan can locate a device that supports Enhanced Interior Gateway Routing Protocol (EIGRP).

Figure 332 shows the pattern of an IP protocol scan.

The following table lists several services that run directly over IP.

Service	IP Protocol Number
ICMP	1
IGMP	2
TCP	6
EGP	8
IGP (used for IGRP)	9
UDP	17

For a complete list of assigned IP protocol numbers, visit *www.iana.org/assignments/protocol-numbers.*

No. .	Time	Source	Destination	Protocol	Info
38	0.000091	192.168.1.118	192.168.1.117	IP	Unknown (0x93)
39	0.000002	192.168.1.118	192.168.1.117	IP	TLSP Kryptonet (0x38)
40	0.000086	192.168.1.118	192.168.1.117	IP	Stream (0x05)
41	1.000318	192.168.1.118	192.168.1.117	IP	SATNET Monitoring (0x
42	0.000006	192.168.1.118	192.168.1.117	IP	Wideband Expak (0x4f)
43	0.000083	192.168.1.118	192.168.1.117	IP	Unknown (0x63)
44	0.000002	192.168.1.118	192.168.1.117	IP	IPv6 hop-by-hop optio

```
⊞ Frame 1 (60 bytes on wire, 60 bytes captured)
⊞ Ethernet II, Src: Dell_be:9d:fd (00:14:22:be:9d:fd), Dst: Sony_f4:3a:09 (0
⊟ Internet Protocol, Src: 192.168.1.118 (192.168.1.118), Dst: 192.168.1.117
    Version: 4
    Header length: 20 bytes
  ⊞ Differentiated Services Field: 0x00 (DSCP 0x00: Default; ECN: 0x00)
    Total Length: 20
    Identification: 0xf593 (62867)
  ⊞ Flags: 0x00
    Fragment offset: 0
    Time to live: 46
    Protocol: Multiplex (0x12)
  ⊞ Header checksum: 0x1309 [correct]
    Source: 192.168.1.118 (192.168.1.118)
    Destination: 192.168.1.117 (192.168.1.117)
```

Figure 332. IP scans are used to locate services that run directly over IP

When a protocol is not supported on a target, the target may respond with an ICMP Destination Unreachable, Protocol Unreachable response (Type 3/Code 2). If no response is received, we assume the service is available or the response is filtered (open|filtered).

IP Protocol Scan Parameter

The Nmap syntax for an IP protocol scan is -sO.

To detect IP protocol scans, consider creating a coloring rule or display filter for ICMP Type 3/Code 2 packets – icmp.type==3 && icmp.code==2.

Understanding Idle Scans

Idle scans are used when a scanner is prohibited from talking directly to a target (perhaps a firewall is blocking the traffic based on the scanner's IP address).

Idle scans use another host that can reach the target. This host is referred to as the *zombie.*

Step 1:   First the scanner sends a TCP scan to the zombie on a TCP port that is expected to be closed. When the TCP Reset response is received, the scanner notes the IP header ID field value (ID=n). This value typically counts up sequentially for each IP packet transmitted through the TCP/IP stack.

Step 2: The scanner next sends a TCP scan to the target using the zombie's IP address as the source IP address.

If the target port is closed, the target will respond to the zombie with a TCP Reset packet. The zombie would discard this TCP Reset packet. The next IP packet from the zombie would be incremented by 1 (ID=n+1).

If the target port is open, the target sends a SYN/ACK to the zombie. The zombie did not initiate the handshake and it sends a TCP Reset packet to the target. This causes the zombie's IP ID value to increment by 1 (ID=n+1). The next IP packet from the zombie would be incremented by 2 (ID=n+2).

Step 3: Step 1 is repeated.

If the zombie's IP ID field is incremented by 1 then we assume it received a TCP RST from the target and the target port is not open. If the zombie's IP ID value has incremented by 2 we assume the port must have been open at the target.

Nmap Syntax—Idle Scan Parameter

The Nmap syntax for an idle scan is `-sI <zombie host>[:probeport]`.

Figure 333 shows the communication pattern of an IP idle scan when the target port is closed.

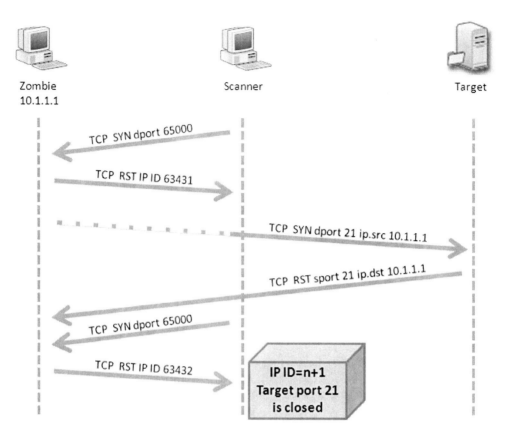

Figure 333. If the IP ID value of the zombie increments by 1, the target port is closed

Figure 334 shows the IP idle scan communications process when the target port is open. These types of scans can be difficult to detect in a trace file—look for TCP Resets that follow TCP SYN packets.

TCP Resets are color coded with a red background and yellow foreground by default. The coloring rule string is `tcp.flags.reset eq 1`.

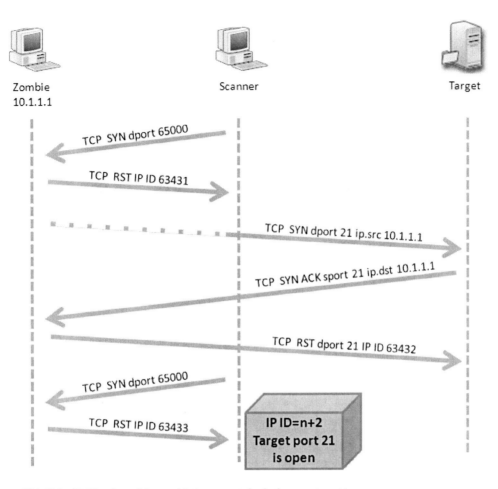

Figure 334. If the IP ID value of the zombie increments by 2, the target port is open

Know Your ICMP Types and Codes

In this book we have already discussed ICMP Type 3—Destination Unreachable—responses seen during UDP and TCP scans. There are numerous reasons that these responses may be sent.

You should know ICMP thoroughly to effectively troubleshoot and secure a network. Many reconnaissance processes use ICMP to detect active services or perform connectivity tests. In addition, ICMP can be used for route redirection (ICMP Type 5). More information on route redirection is contained in *Locating Route Redirection* on page 656.

The table below shows the codes that can be defined in ICMP Type 3 packets.

Codes	Description
0	Net Unreachable
1	Host Unreachable
2	Protocol Unreachable
3	Port Unreachable
4	Fragmentation Needed and Don't Fragment was Set
5	Source Route Failed
6	Destination Network Unknown
7	Destination Host Unknown
8	Source Host Isolated
9	Communication with Destination Network is Administratively Prohibited
10	Communication with Destination Host is Administratively Prohibited
11	Destination Network Unreachable for Type of Service
12	Destination Host Unreachable for Type of Service
13	Communication Administratively Prohibited
14	Host Precedence Violation
15	Precedence cutoff in effect

Don't Create a Black Hole

Although many of these ICMP packets may be blocked or hosts may be configured not to generate them, ICMP Type 3/Code 4 should never be blocked. This ICMP packet alerts a host that their packet was too large to traverse a link and the "Don't Fragment" bit in the IP header was set to 1. Upon receipt of this ICMP Type 3/Code 4 packet, a transmitting host should automatically split the original TCP segment data into smaller packets and resend the data.

Try These Nmap Scan Commands

Capture the traffic when you run these scans to test your color filters and display filters and practice identifying the signatures of these scans in your trace files. These examples are the default scan profiles of Zenmap, the default Nmap GUI. In each case, the target is 192.168.0.1.

Zenmap Profile Title	Command-Line Syntax
Intense Scan	`nmap -T4 -A -v -PE -PA21,23,80,3389 192.168.0.1`
Intense Scan Plus UDP	`nmap -sS -sU -T4 -A -v -PE -PA21,23,80,3389 192.168.0.1`

Zenmap Profile Title	Command-Line Syntax
Intense Scan, All TCP Ports	`nmap -p 1-65535 -T4 -A -v -PE -PA21,23,80,3389 192.168.0.1`
Intense Scan, no Ping	`nmap -T4 -A -v -PN 192.168.0.1`
Ping Scan	`nmap -sP -PE -PA21,23,80,3389 192.168.0.1`
Quick Scan	`nmap -T4 -F 192.168.0.1`
Quick Scan Plus	`nmap -sV -T4 -O -F --version-light 192.168.0.1`
Quick Traceroute	`nmap -sP -PE -PS22,25,80 -PA21,23,80,3389 -PU -PO --traceroute 192.168.0.1`
Regular Scan	`nmap 192.168.0.1`
Slow Comprehensive Scan	`nmap -sS -sU -T4 -A -v -PE -PP -PS21,22,23,25,80,113,31339 -PA80,113,443,10042 -PO --script all 192.168.0.1`

Analyze Traceroute Path Discovery

One common use of ICMP is as a path discovery mechanism using ICMP Echo Request (Type 8) and Echo Reply (Type 0) packets (aka "ping" packets). This is the default traceroute method used on Windows hosts. UNIX hosts, however, default to using UDP for traceroute path discovery.

In Figure 335, a system increments the IP header TTL field value in consecutive ping packets to discover the route to a target. When the TTL value decrements to a value of 1 as packets traverse the network, routers discard them when they reach TTL of 1. The routers generate an ICMP Time Exceeded in Transit (Type 11) packet.

Packets with a TTL value lower than 5 are considered suspicious. Wireshark includes a default coloring rule for packets that contain a low TTL value. The syntax of the coloring rule is `(! ip.dst == 224.0.0.0/4 && ip.ttl < 5) || (ip.dst == 224.0.0.0/24 && ip.ttl != 1)`. Notice that this coloring rule examines the destination IP address field to look for multicasts. Traffic will be colored with a red background and a white foreground if it is not a multicast, but has an IP TTL value lower than 5 or if it is a multicast and the IP TTL value is not equal to 1.

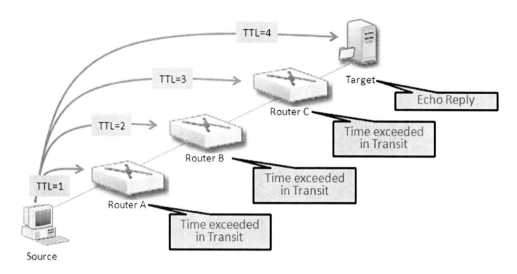

Figure 335. An ICMP-based traceroute also depends on ICMP Time Exceeded in Transit responses

Figure 336 shows the ICMP Time to Live Exceeded responses to ICMP Echo packets with a TTL=1.

No.	Time	Source	Destination	Protocol	Info
1	0.000000	80.101.237.85	152.91.62.145	ICMP	Echo (ping) request
2	0.011270	80.101.224.1	80.101.237.85	ICMP	Time-to-live exceeded
3	0.012155	80.101.237.85	152.91.62.145	ICMP	Echo (ping) request
4	0.023353	80.101.224.1	80.101.237.85	ICMP	Time-to-live exceeded
5	0.023910	80.101.237.85	152.91.62.145	ICMP	Echo (ping) request
6	0.035177	80.101.224.1	80.101.237.85	ICMP	Time-to-live exceeded
7	1.060791	80.101.237.85	152.91.62.145	ICMP	Echo (ping) request
8	1.072690	194.109.153.105	80.101.237.85	ICMP	Time-to-live exceeded
9	1.073355	80.101.237.85	152.91.62.145	ICMP	Echo (ping) request
10	1.084542	194.109.153.105	80.101.237.85	ICMP	Time-to-live exceeded
11	1.085097	80.101.237.85	152.91.62.145	ICMP	Echo (ping) request
12	1.096079	194.109.153.105	80.101.237.85	ICMP	Time-to-live exceeded
13	2.106735	80.101.237.85	152.91.62.145	ICMP	Echo (ping) request
14	2.118337	194.109.12.33	80.101.237.85	ICMP	Time-to-live exceeded
15	2.118958	80.101.237.85	152.91.62.145	ICMP	Echo (ping) request
16	2.130424	194.109.12.33	80.101.237.85	ICMP	Time-to-live exceeded
17	2.130978	80.101.237.85	152.91.62.145	ICMP	Echo (ping) request
18	2.142292	194.109.12.33	80.101.237.85	ICMP	Time-to-live exceeded
19	3.154587	80.101.237.85	152.91.62.145	ICMP	Echo (ping) request
20	3.165962	194.109.5.2	80.101.237.85	ICMP	Time-to-live exceeded
21	3.166616	80.101.237.85	152.91.62.145	ICMP	Echo (ping) request
22	3.177756	194.109.5.2	80.101.237.85	ICMP	Time-to-live exceeded
23	3.178237	80.101.237.85	152.91.62.145	ICMP	Echo (ping) request
24	3.189342	194.109.5.2	80.101.237.85	ICMP	Time-to-live exceeded
25	4.197611	80.101.237.85	152.91.62.145	ICMP	Echo (ping) request

Figure 336. Traceroute relies on ICMP Time to Live responses to locate routers on a path

Two other variations of traceroute include UDP traceroute and TCP traceroute.

- UDP traceroute sends UDP packets to a closed UDP port. The Time Exceeded in Transit responses from routers along the path are used to discover the path to the target. The expected response is an ICMP Type 3/Code 3—Destination Unreachable/Port Unreachable.
- TCP traceroute sends TCP packets to any TCP port. The Time Exceeded in Transit responses from routers along the path are used to discover the path to the target. The expected response is a TCP Reset or TCP SYN/ACK.

Detecting ICMP-based, UDP-based or TCP-based traceroute can be simple if the routers along the path respond with Time Exceeded in Transit ICMP packets. Consider creating a coloring rule or display filter for (icmp.type == 11) && (icmp.code == 0).

Detect Dynamic Router Discovery

When dynamic router discovery is enabled, routers periodically send ICMP Router Advertisements—ICMP Type 9, Code 0 packets.

Hosts can send ICMP Router Solicitations (ICMP Type 10) to the multicast address 224.0.0.2 (the all-routers multicast address), the local IP broadcast address or the IP broadcast address. Routers respond to these solicitations with ICMP Router Advertisement (Type 9) packets.

Besides being used to discover local routers, these ICMP Router Advertisements can affect network performance and security. Consider what would happen if an attacker crafts a Router Advertisement packet listing a host that is not a router?

```
⊞ Frame 21 (64 bytes on wire, 64 bytes captured)
⊞ Ethernet II, Src: NetworkG_10:22:1b (00:00:65:10:22:1b), Dst: IPv4mcast_00:00:02
⊞ Internet Protocol, Src: 10.1.22.2 (10.1.22.2), Dst: 224.0.0.2 (224.0.0.2)
⊟ Internet Control Message Protocol
    Type: 10 (Router solicitation)
    Code: 0 ()
    Checksum: 0xf5ff [correct]
```

Figure 337. ICMP Router Solicitation packets are easy to detect

Figure 337 shows an ICMP Router Solicitation packet.

To detect ICMP Router Solicitations and ICMP Router Advertisements, consider using coloring rule/display filter based on the ICMP type numbers used in these packets - icmp.type==9 || icmp.type==10.

Understand Application Mapping Processes

Application mapping identifies services on a target even when those services are not using standard ports. For example, if someone runs an FTP server process on port 80, an application mapping tool identifies that FTP is running on the port, not HTTP.

Nmap offers excellent application mapping capabilities and will be used as our example tool in this section. Another interesting tool is Amap (*www.thc.org/thc-amap*).

By default when scanning ports, Nmap references the *nmap-services* file to correlate a port number with a service.

Application mapping relies on two distinct functions –probing and matching. Probes are proactively sent to a target to generate responses. Responses are matched to predefined response patterns to identify the service discovered. In some cases, probes are not required in order to identify a service.

For example, once a TCP connection is established to a port, Nmap listens for five seconds. Many applications such as FTP, POP3 and SMTP offer a banner immediately following connection. Nmap compares the response received, if any, to the contents of the *nmap-services-probes* file.

This process of listening is called a NULL probe, but it is not related to a TCP Null Scan that generates a packet without any TCP flags set.

The following shows a portion of the FTP match section of the *nmap-services-probes* file.

```
match ftp m|^220[- ]FileZilla Server version (\d[-.\w ]+)\r\n|
p/FileZilla ftpd/ v/$1/ o/Windows/
match ftp m|^220 ([-\w_.]+) running FileZilla Server version (\d[-
.\w ]+)\r\n| p/FileZilla ftpd/ v/$2/ h/$1/ o/Windows/
match ftp m|^220 FTP Server - FileZilla\r\n| p/FileZilla ftpd/
o/Windows/
match ftp m|^220-Welcome to ([A-Z]+) FTP Service\.\r\n220 All
unauthorized access is logged\.\r\n| p/FileZilla ftpd/ h/$1/
o/Windows/
match ftp m|^220.*\r\n220[- ]FileZilla Server version (\d[-.\w
]+)\r\n|s p/FileZilla ftpd/ v/$1/ o/Windows/
match ftp m|^220-.*\r\n220-\r\n220 using FileZilla FileZilla Server
version ([^\r\n]+)\r\n|s p/FileZilla ftpd/ v/$1/ o/Windows/
match ftp m|^431 Could not initialize SSL connection\r\n|
p/FileZilla ftpd/ i/Mandatory SSL/ o/Windows/
match ftp m|^550 No connections allowed from your IP\r\n|
p/FileZilla ftpd/ i/IP blocked/ o/Windows/
```

You Need to Order the Nmap Book...Now!
The nmap-services-probes *file format is defined in detail in the Nmap Network Scanning book by Gordon "Fyodor" Lyon. A section of the book is online at nmap.org/book/vscan-fileformat.html. [ISBN: 978-0-9799587-1-7]*

The probing process sends packets out with a protocol definition and a string that should trigger a response. The response is compared to the match lines.

The following probe example is included in the Nmap Network Scanning book and provides a great example of putting probes together with matches.

```
Probe UDP Help q|help\r\n\r\n|
rarity 3
ports 7,13,37
match chargen m|@ABCDEFGHIJKLMNOPQRSTUVWXYZ|
match echo m|^help\r\n\r\n$|
```

In the example above, a "UDP Help" probe sends the ASCII string "help" followed by two sets of carriage return, line feeds to UDP ports 7, 13 and 37. If the response contains the string @ABCDEFGHIJKLMNOPQRSTUVWXYZ, the port is considered in use by the Character Generator (chargen) service. If the response contains the same text sent, `help` and the carriage return, line feed sets, the port is identified as a UDP Echo port.

```
⊞ Frame 321 (72 bytes on wire, 72 bytes captured)
⊞ Ethernet II, Src: Elitegro_40:74:d2 (00:21:97:40:74:d2), Dst: D-Link_cc:a3:ea (
⊞ Internet Protocol, Src: 192.168.0.113 (192.168.0.113), Dst: 128.241.194.25 (12
⊞ Transmission Control Protocol, Src Port: 5513 (5513), Dst Port: 80 (80), Seq: 1
⊟ Hypertext Transfer Protocol
  ⊟ GET / HTTP/1.0\r\n
    ⊞ [Expert Info (Chat/Sequence): GET / HTTP/1.0\r\n]
      Request Method: GET
      Request URI: /
      Request Version: HTTP/1.0
    \r\n
```

Figure 338. Nmap's probe is testing port 80 to verify HTTP services—it looks like any other GET request for the root document ("/")

Although in most instances you will find standard ports used for services, Nmap is a great tool for scanning targets to identify services running on non-standard port numbers.

Use Wireshark for Passive OS Fingerprinting

OS fingerprinting is the process of determining the operating system of a target through either active scanning or passive listening. Wireshark can be used as a passive listening device and Wireshark can identify active OS fingerprinting processes.

Trace files taken by Wireshark can be used to make some assumptions regarding the operating system running on hosts.

For example, if traffic travels to and from ports 135, 137, 139 and 445 on a host you can make some basic assumptions that the host is a Windows host. You might also make the assumption that the host is *not* a Windows version before Windows 2000 as those Windows versions did not support services on port 445 (SMB over TCP/IP).

Numerous packets contain evidence of a host's operating system as well.

HTTP GET requests contain a User-Agent definition as shown in Figure 339. In this case, the browsing client is a Windows host that is using Firefox v 3.5.5.

The following lists some possible User-Agent definitions.

- `Mozilla/5.0 (Windows; U; Windows NT 6.0; en-US; rv:1.9.1.5) Gecko/20091102 Firefox/3.5.5 (.NET CLR 3.5.30729)` *[likely a Vista host with .NET framework running Firefox v3.5.5]*
- `Mozilla/5.0 (Windows; U; Windows NT 5.1; de; rv:1.9.1.4) Gecko/20091016 Firefox/3.5.4 (.NET CLR 3.5.30729)` *[likely a Windows XP host running Firefox v3.5.4]*
- `Mozilla/4.0 (compatible; MSIE 6.0; Windows NT 5.1; SV1; GTB6.3; .NET CLR 2.0.50727; InfoPath.2)` *[likely a Windows XP host running Internet Explorer v6.0 and Service Pack 2]*
- `Mozilla/4.0 (compatible; MSIE 7.0; Windows NT 5.1; .NET CLR 1.1.4322; .NET CLR 2.0.50727; .NET CLR 3.0.04506.30; InfoPat` *[likely a Windows XP host with the .NET framework running Internet Explorer v7.0]*
- `Mozilla/4.0 (compatible; MSIE 7.0; Windows NT 6.1; WOW64; Trident/4.0; SLCC2; .NET CLR 2.0.50727; .NET CLR 3.5.30729; .N` *[likely a Windows 7 host with .NET framework running 32-bit version of Internet Explorer v8.0 compatibility view on a 64-bit Windows OS]*
- `Mozilla/5.0 (Windows; U; Windows NT 6.0; en-US) AppleWebKit/532.0 (KHTML, like Gecko) Chrome/3.0.195.33 Safari/532.0` *[likely a Vista host running Chrome v3.0.195.33]*
- `Mozilla/4.0 (compatible; MSIE 7.0; Windows NT 6.0; SLCC1; .NET CLR 2.0.50727; Media Center PC 5.0; OfficeLiveConnector.1` *[likely a Vista Media Center Edition host with .NET framework running Internet Explorer v7.0 with Office Live Workspace installed]*
- `vodafone/1.0/SFR_v3650/1.25.163.3 (compatible; MSIE 6.0; Windows CE; IEMobile 7.6)` *[likely Windows CE running Internet Explorer v7.6 on a mobile device (Vodafone)]*
- `Mozilla/5.0 (X11; U; Linux i686; en-US) AppleWebKit/532.5 (KHTML, like Gecko) Chrome/4.0.251.0 Safari/532.5` *[likely a Linux host running Chrome v4.0.251.0]*
- `Mozilla/5.0 (webOS/1.3.1; U; en-US) AppleWebKit/525.27.1 (KHTML, like Gecko) Version/1.0 Safari/525.27.1 Pre/1.0` *[likely a Palm Pre 1.0 running Safari v1.0]*
- `Mozilla/4.0 (compatible; MSIE 7.0; Windows NT 6.0; Trident/4.0; SLCC1; .NET CLR 2.0.50727; InfoPath.2; .NET CLR 3.5.3072` *[likely a Windows Vista host with .NET framework running Internet Explorer v8.0 compatibility view]*
- `Mozilla/5.0 (compatible; Nmap Scripting Engine; http://nmap.org/book/nse.html)` (Check this out! Nice, eh? Thanks to Fyodor, creator of Nmap, for sending this over!)

The User-Agent information includes the browser application name and version number, the version token (which defines the browser) and the platform token (which defines the operating system in use).

Application Name   Version Token
        ▼   ▼
User-Agent: Mozilla/5.0 (Windows; U; Windows NT 6.0; en-US; rv:1.9.1.5)

Gecko/20091102 Firefox/3.5.5 (.NET CLR 3.5.30729)\r\n
                        ▲
                 Platform Token

This line can be spoofed, so additional OS fingerprinting techniques should be used in conjunction with this passive fingerprinting method.

Generate Your HTTP User-Agent Value

To view the User-Agent string generated by your browser, type
`javascript:alert(navigator.userAgent)` *in the browser address bar.*

Most version tokens are relatively self-explanatory—MSIE 8.0 is Internet Explorer version 8.0. MSIE 8.0 followed by WOW64 indicates that the 32-bit version of Internet Explorer is running on a 64-bit platform. Firefox is followed by the version number.

Optional components installed may alter the User-Agent string. The following table lists some possible additions to the User-Agent string.

Element	Description
Trident/4.0	Used by Internet Explorer 8.0 in compatibility mode
.NET CLR	.NET Framework common language run time, followed by the version number
SV1	Internet Explorer 6 with enhanced security features (Windows XP SP2 and Windows Server 2003 only)
Tablet PC	Tablet services are installed; number indicates the version number
Win64; IA64	System has a 64-bit processor (Intel)
Win64; x64	System has a 64-bit processor (AMD)
WOW64	A 32-bit version of Internet Explorer is running on a 64-bit processor

For a humorous look at the numerous transitions of the User-Agent string, visit *webaim.org/blog/user-agent-string-history/*.

```
⊞ Frame 91 (546 bytes on wire, 546 bytes captured)
⊞ Ethernet II, Src: Elitegro_40:74:d2 (00:21:97:40:74:d2), Dst: D-Link_cc:a3:
⊞ Internet Protocol, Src: 192.168.0.113 (192.168.0.113), Dst: 65.198.49.78 (6
⊞ Transmission Control Protocol, Src Port: 5981 (5981), Dst Port: 80 (80), Se
⊟ Hypertext Transfer Protocol
  ⊟ GET /customer/pst_ihr/images/banner.gif HTTP/1.1\r\n
    ⊞ [Expert Info (Chat/Sequence): GET /customer/pst_ihr/images/banner.gif HT
       Request Method: GET
       Request URI: /customer/pst_ihr/images/banner.gif
       Request Version: HTTP/1.1
    Host: www.internetpulse.net\r\n
    User-Agent: Mozilla/5.0 (windows: U: windows NT 6.0: en-US: rv:1.9.1.5)
            Gecko/20091102 Firefox/3.5.5 (.NET CLR 3.5.30729)\r\n
    Accept: image/png,image/*;q=0.8,*/*;q=0.5\r\n
    Accept-Language: en-us,en;q=0.5\r\n
    Accept-Encoding: gzip,deflate\r\n
    Accept-Charset: ISO-8859-1,utf-8;q=0.7,*;q=0.7\r\n
    Keep-Alive: 300\r\n
    Connection: keep-alive\r\n
    Referer: http://www.internetpulse.net/\r\n
    Cookie: ASP.NET_SessionId=qxbspgmsqriqgi23sf22sh45\r\n
    \r\n
```

Figure 339. HTTP GET requests' User-Agent includes host information

Detect Active OS Fingerprinting

Active OS fingerprinting can be much more efficient than passive OS fingerprinting, but it can also be detected by listening applications such as Wireshark. Nmap is an excellent example of an OS fingerprinting tool.

Nmap can detect operating system version information based on a series of port scans, ICMP pings, sequence number detection packets, TCP Explicit Congestion Notification tests, closed port tests and numerous follow-up tests based on the responses received. These follow-up tests are defined in the `nmap-os-db` file.

Nmap Syntax—OS Fingerprinting Parameter

The Nmap parameter to run OS fingerprinting with verbosity and version detection is `-sV -O -v`.

Examining Nmap's process of OS fingerprinting provides numerous signatures of its traffic:

- ICMP Echo Request (Type 8) with no payload
- ICMP Echo Request (Type 8) with 120 or 150 byte payload of 0x00s
- ICMP Timestamp Request with Originate Timestamp value set to 0
- TCP SYN with 40 byte options area
- TCP SYN with Window Scale Value set to 10
- TCP SYN with Maximum Segment Size set to 256

- TCP SYN with Timestamp Value set to 0xFFFFFFFF
- TCP packet with options and SYN, FIN, PSH and URG bits set
- TCP packet with options and no flags set
- TCP Acknowledgment Number field non-zero without the ACK bit set
- TCP packets with unusual TCP Window Size field values

Figure 340 depicts some of the unique packets in an Nmap OS detection process. In this case we have added two columns—a TCP Header Length field column and a TCP Window Size field column.

Creating coloring rules for some of these unique packets makes detecting Nmap's OS detection process much easier. Consider setting up the following coloring rules with distinctive colorization.

Display Filter	Description
`(tcp.flags == 0x02) && (tcp.window_size < 1025)`	TCP SYN/ACK with a TCP Window Size field value less than 1025
`tcp.flags == 0x2b`	TCP SYN, FIN, PSH and URG bits set
`tcp.flags == 0x00`	No TCP flags set
`(icmp.type == 13) && (frame[42:4] == 00:00:00:00)`	ICMP Timestamp Request with Originate Timestamp Value set to 0 (Ethernet II header structure)
`tcp.options.wscale_val == 10`	TCP Window Scale Option set to 10
`tcp.options.mss_val < 1460`	TCP Maximum Segment Size value set to less than 1460

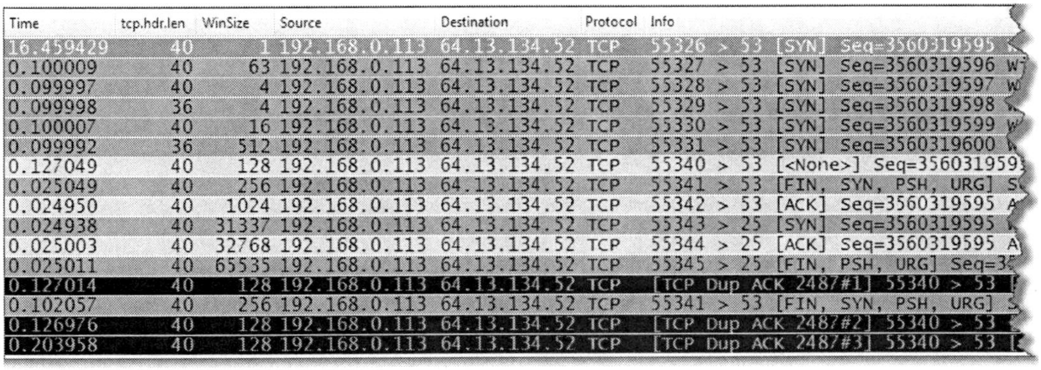

Figure 340. Nmap's OS detection process has numerous signatures

Another popular OS fingerprinting technique used by tools such as NetScanTools Pro and Xprobe is based on a series of ICMP packets:

Type 13 ICMP Timestamp Requests

Type 15 ICMP Information Requests

Type 17 ICMP Address Mask Requests

NetScanTools Pro consists of over 44 tools used for network testing, reconnaissance, discovery and more. For more information on NetScanTools Pro, visit *www.netscantools.com*.

Ofir Arkin (*www.sys-security.com*) created Xprobe, an OS fingerprinting tool that uses a combination of procedures to identify the target OS type and version.

Figure 341 shows NetScanTools Pro's OS fingerprinting process and the proximity of these ICMP packets.

```
No. .   Time       Source          Destination      Protocol  Info
     23 0.000509   192.168.0.113   64.13.134.52     ICMP      Echo (ping) request
     24 0.023183   64.13.134.52    192.168.0.113    ICMP      Echo (ping) reply
     25 0.875261   192.168.0.113   64.13.134.52     ICMP      Timestamp request
     26 0.249801   192.168.0.113   64.13.134.52     ICMP      Timestamp request
     27 4.177062   192.168.0.113   64.13.134.52     ICMP      Address mask request
     28 0.249900   192.168.0.113   64.13.134.52     ICMP      Address mask request
     29 4.171007   192.168.0.113   64.13.134.52     ICMP      Information request
     30 0.250188   192.168.0.113   64.13.134.52     ICMP      Information request
     31 4.170775   192.168.0.113   64.13.134.52     ICMP      Echo (ping) request
     32 0.013870   64.13.134.52    192.168.0.113    ICMP      Echo (ping) reply

⊞ Frame 25 (54 bytes on wire, 54 bytes captured)
⊞ Ethernet II, Src: Elitegro_40:74:d2 (00:21:97:40:74:d2), Dst: D-Link_cc:a3:ea (
⊞ Internet Protocol, Src: 192.168.0.113 (192.168.0.113), Dst: 64.13.134.52 (64.1
⊟ Internet Control Message Protocol
    Type: 13 (Timestamp request)
    Code: 0 ()
    Checksum: 0x4367 [correct]
    Identifier: 0x0792
    Sequence number: 1000 (0x03e8)
    Originate timestamp: 5 hours, 29 minutes, 28.049 seconds after midnight UTC
    Receive timestamp: 0 time after midnight UTC
    Transmit timestamp: 0 time after midnight UTC
```

Figure 341. ICMP Timestamp Requests, Address Mask Requests and Information Requests can be used for OS fingerprinting

You can set up Wireshark to detect these three ICMP packets using a coloring rule with the following filter string:

```
icmp.type==13 || icmp.type==15 || icmp.type==17
```

NetScanTools Pro, Xprobe and many other OS fingerprinting tools have another possible signature—unusual ICMP Echo Request packets. Figure 342 shows an ICMP Echo Request packet that contains the undefined Code value of 1.

NetScanTools Pro uses ICMP Type 8 with Code 1 whereas Xprobe uses ICMP Type 8 with Code 123. You can set up Wireshark to detect unusual ICMP Echo packets using a coloring rule with the following filter string:

```
(icmp.type == 8) && !(icmp.code == 0x00)
```

In addition, Xprobe generates an unsolicited DNS response packet to the target in order to elicit an ICMP Destination Unreachable/Port Unreachable response. The formation of this response is used to identify the target OS.

You can set up Wireshark to detect these DNS response packets using a coloring rule with the following filter string:

```
(dns.qry.name == "www.securityfocus.com") &&
(dns.flags.response == 1)
```

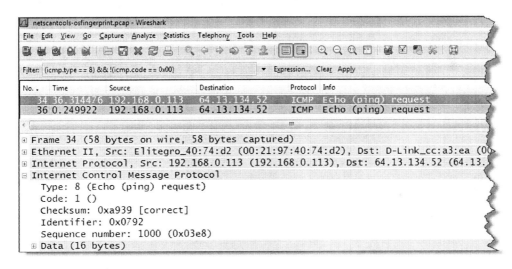

Figure 342. Unusual ICMP Echo packet formats are also used by some OS fingerprinting tools

Identify Spoofed Addresses in Scans

Attackers and scanners may use MAC or IP address spoofing to hide their actual hardware or network addresses or appear to be another system to get through filtering devices on the network.

In a Denial of Service flood style attack, where the attacker is not relying on two-way communications, they may spoof their MAC or IP address since they are not reliant upon receiving responses to their packets. To test IP address spoofing, try the Nmap −S parameter.

Anyone Can Spoof a MAC Address!

Don't believe everything you see. Nmap supports MAC address spoofing with the ––spoof-mac option! You can choose to send packets using a completely random MAC address or a MAC address starting with a specific value in the first bytes and then random bytes to finish off the address. You can also send packets using a specific OUI value assigned to a vendor such as Apple or Cisco. If you don't know the OUI value, Nmap can look it up for you in the –mac-prefixes file.

No.	Time	Source	Destination	Protocol	Info
186	0.001171	192.168.1.101	192.168.1.103	TCP	1416 > 111 [SYN] Seq=3914709952
187	0.000153	192.168.1.103	192.168.1.101	TCP	111 > 1416 [RST, ACK] Seq=0 Ack
188	0.000486	192.168.1.101	192.168.1.103	TCP	1417 > 113 [SYN] Seq=3914747064
189	0.000141	192.168.1.103	192.168.1.101	TCP	113 > 1417 [RST, ACK] Seq=0 Ack=
190	0.001459	192.168.1.101	192.168.1.103	TCP	1418 > 118 [SYN] Seq=3914800644
191	0.000161	192.168.1.103	192.168.1.101	TCP	118 > 1418 [RST, ACK] Seq=0 Ack
192	0.001194	192.168.1.101	192.168.1.103	TCP	1419 > 135 [SYN] Seq=3914861042
193	0.000179	192.168.1.103	192.168.1.101	TCP	135 > 1419 [SYN, ACK] Seq=29952
194	0.000024	192.168.1.101	192.168.1.103	TCP	1419 > 135 [ACK] Seq=3914861043
195	0.000608	192.168.1.101	192.168.1.103	TCP	1420 > 139 [SYN] Seq=3914905537
196	0.000170	192.168.1.103	192.168.1.101	TCP	139 > 1420 [SYN, ACK] Seq=29958
197	0.000020	192.168.1.101	192.168.1.103	TCP	1420 > 139 [ACK] Seq=3914905538
198	0.000955	192.168.1.101	192.168.1.103	TCP	1421 > 156 [SYN] Seq=3914953302
199	0.000195	192.168.1.103	192.168.1.101	TCP	156 > 1421 [RST, ACK] Seq=0 Ack
200	0.001017	192.168.1.101	192.168.1.103	TCP	1422 > 179 [SYN] Seq=3915006700
201	0.000147	192.168.1.103	192.168.1.101	TCP	179 > 1422 [RST, ACK] Seq=0 Ack
202	0.000446	192.168.1.101	192.168.1.103	TCP	1423 > 371 [SYN] Seq=3915055485
203	0.000139	192.168.1.103	192.168.1.101	TCP	371 > 1423 [RST, ACK] Seq=0 Ack

Figure 343. If the scanner does not complete the three-way handshake, it might be using a spoofed IP address

Figure 343 shows a TCP scan process. Packets 194 and 197 complete three-way handshake processes. This is a good indication that the scanner is actually using the IP address 192.168.1.101 during the time this trace file was taken.

Case Study:
Learning the Conficker Lesson

Submitted by: Bill Bach
Goldstar Software

I have one client, a school, who was receiving Internet access from a library next door via a simple fiber optic bridge. The library handled all the aspects of the link, including managing the fiber connection, the T1, the DHCP server, and so on, and the school and library comprised one big happy network on the same subnet.

Last week, we received a phone call that the Internet link for the school was down. Upon further investigation, we found that the IT folks at the library had pulled the plug when they sensed "virus-like" activity on the network. They said that they wouldn't reconnect the school back until all systems were cleaned.

Finally, we convinced them that all of the school PC's had been pulled from the wire, and we commenced scanning all of the PC's in the school lab. None were found to have any malware on them. Further discussions with the library IT staff yielded two machine names that were being blamed. A quick review showed that one of these two systems had been shut down for over two months—the other hadn't been used for over 6 months.

So, knowing that the two machines were shut down and all the other machines were checking out clean, we started letting users in the lab back onto the network. We also wanted to see if we could see anything "unusual" going on, so we enabled Wireshark on the bridged link. No sooner did we reboot the computer lab boxes, than we saw a series of tell-tale network packets.

Hmm... Some machine at the library was trying to connect to one of the newly-booted lab computers. That can't be right. Scrolling down through the trace (shown on the next page), it didn't take long (OK -- it was really 1/4 second later) to see the same system scanning the next IP address.

After that, we saw .96, .97, and subsequent network addresses showing up. Needless to say, we immediately terminated the bridge link (on our end, this time) and asked the IT staff at the library to remove the infected machine from their side of the link.

Before we reconnected the link, we set up a new subnet that provided complete NAT protection for all the devices in the school -- partitioning the network off from the devices in the library. As with many schools, there were no funds for this hardware, so we were stuck with a simple low-cost "home" router with DHCP capabilities, but this solution gave us a way to protect the school computers from further infection.

```
HewlettP_1c:fd:a6  Broadcast         ARP     60 who has 192.168.22.95?  Tell 192.168.22.124
Dell_b5:25:7a      HewlettP_1c:fd:a6 ARP     60 192.168.22.95 is at 00:13:72:b5:25:7a
192.168.22.124     192.168.22.95     TCP     62 payrouter > microsoft-ds [SYN] Seq=0 win=65535 Len=0 MSS=1460
192.168.22.95      192.168.22.124    TCP     62 microsoft-ds > payrouter [SYN, ACK] Seq=0 Ack=1 win=65535 Len=0
192.168.22.124     192.168.22.95     TCP     60 payrouter > microsoft-ds [ACK] Seq=1 Ack=1 win=65535 Len=0
192.168.22.124     192.168.22.95     SMB    105 Negotiate Protocol Request
192.168.22.95      192.168.22.124    SMB    163 Negotiate Protocol Response
192.168.22.124     192.168.22.95     SMB    131 Session Setup AndX Request, User: anonymous
192.168.22.95      192.168.22.124    SMB    143 Session Setup AndX Response
192.168.22.124     192.168.22.95     TCP     60 payrouter > microsoft-ds [FIN, ACK] Seq=129 Ack=199 win=65337 L
192.168.22.95      192.168.22.124    TCP     60 microsoft-ds > payrouter [FIN, ACK] Seq=199 Ack=130 win=65407
192.168.22.124     192.168.22.95     TCP     60 payrouter > microsoft-ds [ACK] Seq=130 Ack=200 win=65337 Len=0
192.168.22.124     192.168.22.95     TCP     62 visionpyramid > microsoft-ds [SYN] Seq=0 win=65535 Len=0 MSS=1
192.168.22.124     192.168.22.95     TCP     62 hermes > netbios-ssn [SYN] Seq=0 win=65535 Len=0 MSS=1460
192.168.22.95      192.168.22.124    TCP     62 microsoft-ds > visionpyramid [SYN, ACK] Seq=0 Ack=1 win=65535 Le
192.168.22.95      192.168.22.124    TCP     62 netbios-ssn > hermes [SYN, ACK] Seq=0 Ack=1 win=65535 Len=0 MSS
192.168.22.124     192.168.22.95     TCP     60 visionpyramid > microsoft-ds [ACK] Seq=1 Ack=1 win=65535 Len=0
192.168.22.124     192.168.22.95     TCP     60 hermes > netbios-ssn [RST] Seq=1 win=0 Len=0
192.168.22.124     192.168.22.95     SMB    191 Negotiate Protocol Request
192.168.22.95      192.168.22.124    SMB    235 Negotiate Protocol Response
192.168.22.124     192.168.22.95     SMB    294 Session Setup AndX Request, NTLMSSP_NEGOTIATE
192.168.22.95      192.168.22.124    SMB    408 Session Setup AndX Response, NTLMSSP_CHALLENGE, Error: STATUS_MO
192.168.22.124     192.168.22.95     SMB    316 Session Setup AndX Request, NTLMSSP_AUTH, User: \
192.168.22.95      192.168.22.124    SMB    184 Session Setup AndX Response
192.168.22.124     192.168.22.95     SMB    150 Tree Connect AndX Request, Path: \\192.168.22.95\IPC$
192.168.22.95      192.168.22.124    SMB    114 Tree Connect AndX Response
192.168.22.124     192.168.22.95     SMB    158 NT Create AndX Request, Path: \srvsvc
192.168.22.95      192.168.22.124    SMB     93 NT Create AndX Response, FID: 0x0000, Error: STATUS_ACCESS_DENI
192.168.22.124     192.168.22.95     SMB    160 NT Create AndX Request, Path: \browser
192.168.22.95      192.168.22.124    SMB    193 NT Create AndX Response, FID: 0x4000
192.168.22.124     192.168.22.95     DCERPC 194 Bind: call_id: 1 SRVSVC V3.0
192.168.22.95      192.168.22.124    SMB    105 write AndX Response, FID: 0x4000, 72 bytes
192.168.22.124     192.168.22.95     SMB    117 Read AndX Request, FID: 0x4000, 1024 bytes at offset 0
192.168.22.95      192.168.22.124    DCERPC 186 Bind_ack: call_id: 1 accept max_xmit: 4280 max_recv: 4280
192.168.22.124     192.168.22.95     SRVSVC 846 NetPathCanonicalize request
192.168.22.95      192.168.22.124    SRVSVC 950 NetPathCanonicalize response[Long frame (804 bytes)]
192.168.22.124     192.168.22.95     SMB     99 Close Request, FID: 0x4000
192.168.22.95      192.168.22.124    SMB     93 Close Response, FID: 0x4000
192.168.22.124     192.168.22.95     SMB     97 Logoff AndX Request
192.168.22.95      192.168.22.124    SMB     97 Logoff AndX Response
192.168.22.124     192.168.22.95     SMB     93 Tree Disconnect Request
192.168.22.95      192.168.22.124    SMB     93 Tree Disconnect Response
192.168.22.124     192.168.22.95     TCP     60 visionpyramid > microsoft-ds [FIN, ACK] Seq=2068 Ack=2104 win=
192.168.22.95      192.168.22.124    TCP     60 microsoft-ds > visionpyramid [FIN, ACK] Seq=2104 Ack=2069 win=6
192.168.22.124     192.168.22.95     TCP     60 visionpyramid > microsoft-ds [ACK] Seq=2069 Ack=2105 win=65414
```

Of course, we can never be sure where the problem originally came from, whether it came from the library or an errant download by a user in the school, but after spending the better part of three days cleaning Conficker from the network, we were able to allow everyone back in again.

What did we learn? Several things:

1) No matter how much you trust your network partners, you should always segregate your network from your neighbors, even if it is simple NAT device.

2) It is always a good idea to monitor your network boundary periodically with Wireshark to watch for trouble.

3) With a span port on a core switch, you can easily catch the source of new virus infections, almost on the fly!

Summary

Discovery and reconnaissance processes are used to locate hosts and services on a network. The ultimate purpose may be to map out network devices or locate vulnerable systems for an impending attack on the network or network devices. Recognizing these processes can help prevent network breaches.

Various scan techniques can be used to discover network devices, such as ARP scans, ping scans, UDP scans and TCP scans. Each of these scans generates recognizable traffic patterns on the network. A thorough understanding of how each of these protocols works for normal network communications will help you identify when these protocols may be used for malicious purposes.

Practice What You've Learned

Now is a great time to load Nmap on a system (maybe load it directly on your Wireshark system) and set up another host as a test target. This chapter provided details on the signatures of various discovery and reconnaissance processes.

 Download the trace files available in the Download section of the book website, *www.wiresharkbook.com*. Examine the trace files listed below to spot their unique signatures.

sec-nmap-ipscan.pcap

This is the kind of traffic you never want to see on your network—someone is doing an IP scan... not a UDP scan... not a TCP scan. This person wants to know what services are supported directly on top of the IP header. Examples include EGP, IDRP, ICMP and encapsulated IPv6.

Sort the Info column heading to see all the protocols queried.

sec-nst-osfingerprint.pcap

This trace shows an OS fingerprinting operation from NetScanTools Pro.

Create a coloring rule for ICMP Echo packets that have a non-zero code value.

This filter will help you discover what NetScanTools Pro's signature is in this trace.

sec-strangescan.pcap

What on Earth is the scanner doing?

Look at the TCP Flag settings in the scan packets. What is triggering the "TCP ACKed lost segment" expert notification in Wireshark?

arp-recon.pcap

This trace depicts an ARP reconnaissance process.

What would explain the non-sequential target IP addresses? Can you determine the subnet mask of the transmitter by the ARP target addresses?

Review Questions

Q31.1   What is the purpose of discovery and reconnaissance processes?

Q31.2   What is the limitation of ARP scanning?

Q31.3   What are the two reasons someone may run a TCP port scan?

Q31.4   How can you differentiate between a TCP full connect scan and a TCP half-open scan?

Q31.5   What type of device may send an ICMP Destination Unreachable response to a TCP connection attempt?

Q31.6   What process can be detected by an unusual number of IP packets that contain a low TTL value?

Q31.7   What are the two distinct functions of application mapping?

Q31.8   What is the advantage of performing passive OS fingerprinting with Wireshark?

Answers to Review Questions

Q31.1 **What is the purpose of discovery and reconnaissance processes?**

A31.1 Discovery and reconnaissance processes are used to identify hosts on the network, locate network services, learn operating system versions running on hosts and any other information on network devices.

Q31.2 **What is the limitation of ARP scanning?**

A31.2 Because ARP is a non-routable protocol, ARP scanning can only find local devices. The advantage of ARP scanning is that the process can locate devices that block ICMP pings through firewall use.

Q31.3 **What are the two reasons someone may run a TCP port scan?**

A31.3 TCP port scans can be used to identify TCP-based services running on a target or they can be used simply to determine which hosts are running on a network.

Q31.4 **How can you differentiate between a TCP full connect scan and a TCP half-open scan?**

A31.4 A TCP full connect scan completes the three-way TCP handshake when an open port is found. The packet sequence is SYN, SYN/ACK, ACK. A TCP half-open scan does not complete the three-way TCP handshake. The packet sequence is SYN, SYN/ACK.

Q31.5 **What type of device may send an ICMP Destination Unreachable response to a TCP connection attempt?**

A31.5 If a TCP connection attempt receives an ICMP Destination Unreachable response you can assume the target is behind a local or network firewall that is generating the ICMP response.

Q31.6 **What process can be detected by an unusual number of IP packets that contain a low TTL value?**

A31.6 A traceroute process generates a high number of packets that have a low TTL value. For example, in the first packet of a traceroute operation the TTL value is 1. The next packet contains a TTL value of 2. The next packet contains a TTL value 3 and so on.

Q31.7 **What are the two distinct functions of application mapping?**

A31.7 Application mapping relies on two distinct functions –probing and matching. Probes are proactively sent to a target to generate responses. Responses are matched to predefined responses to identify the service discovered.

Q31.8 **What is the advantage of performing passive OS fingerprinting with Wireshark?**

A31.8 Passive OS fingerprinting relies on silently listening to network traffic and does not generate any traffic and cannot be detected by IDS devices. Active OS fingerprinting generates packets to trigger responses that allows identification of the target.

Chapter 32: Analyze Suspect Traffic

Wireshark Certified Network Analyst Exam Objectives covered:

- What is "Suspect" Traffic?
- Identify Vulnerabilities in the TCP/IP Resolution Processes
- Identify Unacceptable Traffic
- Find Maliciously Malformed Packets
- Identify Invalid or 'Dark' Destination Addresses
- Differentiating Between Flooding or Standard Denial of Service Traffic
- Finding Clear Text Passwords and Data
- Identifying Phone Home Traffic
- Catching Unusual Protocols and Applications
- Locating Route Redirection that Uses ICMP
- Catching ARP Poisoning
- Catching IP Fragmentation and Overwriting
- Spotting TCP Splicing
- Watching Other Unusual TCP Traffic
- Identifying Password Cracking Attempts
- Know Where to Look: Signature Locations

What is "Suspect" Traffic?

Suspect traffic does not match network baselines—it is either out of place because of protocol type, port usage, packet frequency, requests, responses, etc. Suspect traffic may be normal network communications that we are not familiar with or traffic that has unusual patterns.

Alternately, suspect traffic may simply be caused by poorly behaving applications, misconfigurations, innocent mistakes or faulty devices.

In order to rule out the innocent causes of suspect traffic, you need to know what is normal. This is where your baseline becomes a precious resource.

In this chapter we focus on malicious traffic patterns that may occur after or without the discovery process. We begin with a review of the resolution process with an assumption that a breach has occurred.

Identify Vulnerabilities in the TCP/IP Resolution Processes

Understanding normal TCP/IP communications is important when you are trying to identify abnormal communications. Consider reviewing *Chapter 14: TCP/IP Analysis Overview* as you go through this chapter.

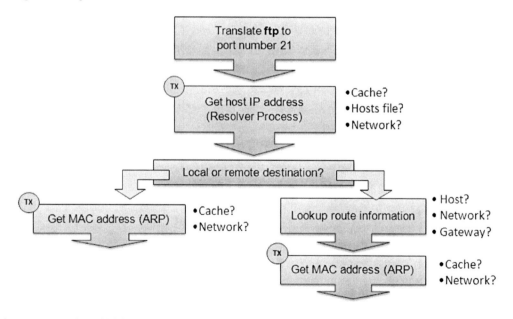

Figure 344. Vulnerabilities can be found throughout the resolution processes

Port Resolution Vulnerabilities

Port resolution relies on the integrity of the `services` file and the application requesting to use a particular port number.

If a malicious user or program has altered the content of the *services* file, the port resolution process may be affected. Applications can also define which ports they will use. A malicious FTP program might use port 80 knowing that many companies do not block traffic from this port.

Figure 345 shows an IRC communication that is not decoded as an IRC conversation because it uses a non-standard port number 18067.

Bot-infected hosts often use Internet Relay Chat (IRC) to communicate with Command and Control (C&C) servers. In this case, the bot-infected host connects to the IRC server on port 18067 and Wireshark defines the IRC communications as simply "Data". In the bytes pane we can see the packet contains the JOIN command used to connect to an IRC channel.

```
⊞ Frame 20 (72 bytes on wire, 72 bytes captured)
⊞ Ethernet II, Src: DellEsgP_58:93:fa (00:0b:db:58:93:fa), Dst: Watchgua_04:f8:
⊞ Internet Protocol, Src: 10.129.211.13 (10.129.211.13), Dst: 61.189.243.240 (61
⊞ Transmission Control Protocol, Src Port: 1048 (1048), Dst Port: 18067 (18067),
⊟ Data (18 bytes)
    Data: 4A4F694E202370382069686F64633968690A
    [Length: 18]

0000  00 90 7f 04 f8 35 00 0b  db 58 93 fa 08 00 45 00   .....5.. .X....E.
0010  00 3a 01 2c 40 00 80 06  00 00 0a 81 d3 0d 3d bd   .:.,@... ......=.
0020  f3 f0 04 18 46 93 ce d8  35 1f ed 88 e5 9b 50 18   ....F... 5.....P.
0030  fa a1 97 69 00 00 4a 4f  69 4e 20 23 70 38 20 69   ...i..JO iN #p8 i
0040  68 6f 64 63 39 68 69 0a                            hodc9hi.
```

Figure 345. Traffic using non-standard ports may use the wrong dissector or not be decoded at all

Using the right click | Decode As function, we can force Wireshark to temporarily dissect traffic to and from port 18067 as IRC traffic as shown in Figure 346.

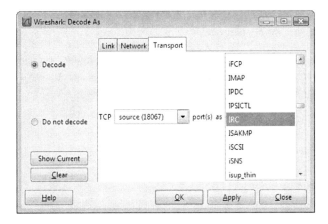

Figure 346. Use "Decode As" to force the IRC dissector on the traffic

Using the Decode As function temporarily applies the dissector to all traffic using the selected port. When you restart Wireshark, the dissector will not be in place. You can edit the *services* file in the Wireshark Program Files directory if you Wireshark want to permanently list the port number as IRC. This does not force the IRC dissector onto this traffic as shown in Figure 347.

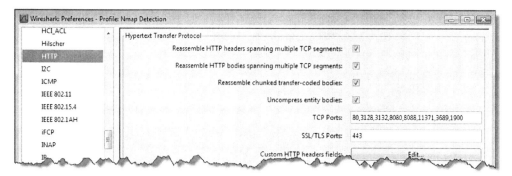

```
⊞ Frame 20 (72 bytes on wire, 72 bytes captured)
⊞ Ethernet II, Src: DellEsgP_58:93:fa (00:0b:db:58:93:fa), Dst: Watchgua_04:f8:3
⊞ Internet Protocol, Src: 10.129.211.13 (10.129.211.13), Dst: 61.189.243.240 (61
⊞ Transmission Control Protocol, Src Port: neod2 (1048), Dst Port: irc (18067), S
⊟ Data (18 bytes)
    Data: 4A4F694E2023703820696686F64633968690A
    [Length: 18]

0000  00 90 7f 04 f8 35 00 0b  db 58 93 fa 08 00 45 00   .....5.. .X....E.
0010  00 3a 01 2c 40 00 80 06  00 00 0a 81 d3 0d 3d bd   .:.,@... ......=.
0020  f3 f0 04 18 46 93 ce d8  35 1f ed 88 e5 9b 50 18   ....F... 5.....P.
0030  fa a1 97 69 00 00 4a 4f  69 4e 20 23 70 38 20 69   ...i..JO iN #p8 i
0040  68 6f 64 63 39 68 69 0a                            hodc9hi.
```

Figure 347. Adding or editing an entry in the services file does not apply the dissector

You can use define Preferences for some applications, such as HTTP, to set Wireshark to recognize additional or alternate port numbers for applications. Figure 348 shows the HTTP preferences setting listing TCP ports that will be decoded as HTTP traffic.

Figure 348. Some Preferences settings can add dissector associations

Rather than apply a temporary decode or alter the Preferences settings, you can create color filters to identify packets that contain specific strings.[107] To color code packets that contain the JOIN command in undecoded traffic, use the syntax `data contains "JOIN"`.

---

[107] These filters can be quite cumbersome to create if the strings may be in upper or lower case or alternating cases. For example, if you wanted to color code all traffic that contains the term "USER" in upper, lower or mixed case, your color filter would be `data contains "USER" || data contains "user" || data contains "USer" || data contains "USEr"` and so on.

Name Resolution Process Vulnerabilities

If a malicious application has altered the client's *hosts* file, the client system will use the information in that file before generating a DNS query.

Unless a secure form of DNS is used to validate responses and responding DNS server, clients accept the name information supplied any DNS responses as long as the transaction ID number and the restated query matches the original request.

If the DNS information supplied is not correct or leads to an alternate host, the client continues the resolution processes to connect to the incorrect host. If this information is kept in DNS cache, the client uses it again (until the information has expired).

Unless you know the IP address that corresponds to a host name, it is difficult to spot traffic with malicious intent.

In the case of bot-infected hosts, however, it is not uncommon to see a DNS query generate CNAME (canonical name) responses with many IP addresses. Figure 349 shows the details of a DNS response to a query for *bbjj.househot.com*. There are 12 responses for this DNS query.

Creating a color filter to identify DNS responses that contain more than 5 IP addresses may help you spot these packets. The syntax for the color filter is (dns.flags.response == 1) && (dns.count.answers > 5).

```
⊞ Frame 2 (399 bytes on wire, 399 bytes captured)
⊞ Ethernet II, Src: Watchgua_04:f8:35 (00:90:7f:04:f8:35), Dst: DellEsg
⊞ Internet Protocol, Src: 10.129.56.6 (10.129.56.6), Dst: 10.129.211.13
⊞ User Datagram Protocol, Src Port: domain (53), Dst Port: blackjack (1
⊟ Domain Name System (response)
    [Request In: 1]
    [Time: 0.237997000 seconds]
    Transaction ID: 0x0006
  ⊞ Flags: 0x8580 (Standard query response, No error)
    Questions: 1
    Answer RRs: 12
    Authority RRs: 2
    Additional RRs: 3
  ⊞ Queries
  ⊟ Answers
    ⊞ bbjj.househot.com: type CNAME, class IN, cname ypgw.wallloan.com
    ⊞ ypgw.wallloan.com: type A, class IN, addr 216.234.235.165
    ⊞ ypgw.wallloan.com: type A, class IN, addr 151.198.6.55
    ⊞ ypgw.wallloan.com: type A, class IN, addr 216.234.247.191
    ⊞ ypgw.wallloan.com: type A, class IN, addr 68.112.229.228
    ⊞ ypgw.wallloan.com: type A, class IN, addr 61.189.243.240
    ⊞ ypgw.wallloan.com: type A, class IN, addr 218.12.94.58
    ⊞ ypgw.wallloan.com: type A, class IN, addr 61.145.119.63
```

Figure 349. A high number of answers and a CNAME response may be worth investigating

MAC Address Resolution Vulnerabilities

When resolving the hardware address of a local target or a router, the client depends on the validity of the ARP response or entries that exist in the local ARP cache in order to use the proper MAC address in the subsequent packets.

This is MAC address redirection which can be used by some attackers to perpetrate a man-in-the-middle attack.

For an example of unusual ARP traffic, refer to *Catching ARP Poisoning* on page 657.

Route Resolution Vulnerabilities

When a client needs to send data to a target on a remote local network, the client consults its routing tables to identify the best gateway or a default gateway. If the local route table has been poisoned, the client sends the packets in the wrong direction.

This is a route redirection and can be used for man-in-the-middle attacks.

Identify Unacceptable Traffic

Wireshark may reveal unusual patterns of network scans (reconnaissance), attempted logins, insecure communications or strange protocols or unusual application behavior.

You can make the unusual traffic easier to identify by colorizing the traffic that is of concern. In this next section we examine unusual traffic patterns and define the syntax used by display filters and coloring rules to make this traffic more visible in Wireshark.

Scanning traffic is typically considered unacceptable on the network. In some cases, however, you may find the scans are generated by network monitoring devices that build and maintain a database of network devices.

The following traffic *may* be considered unacceptable—keep in mind your baseline information and the often illogical operation of network communications.

- Maliciously malformed packets—intentionally malicious packets
- Traffic to invalid or 'dark' addresses—packets addressed to unassigned IP or MAC addresses
- Flooding or denial of service traffic—traffic sent at a high packet per second rate to a single, group or all hosts
- Clear text passwords—passwords that are visible and therefore unsecure
- Clear text data—data that is visible or able to be reconstructed
- Phone home traffic—traffic patterns indicating an application is checking in periodically with a remote host
- Unusual protocols and applications—protocols and applications that are not commonly seen or allowed on the network

- Route redirections—ICMP-based route redirections in preparation of man-in-the-middle attacks
- ARP poisoning—altering target ARP tables for redirection of local traffic through another host—used for man-in-the-middle attacks
- IP fragmentation and overwriting—using the IP fragment offset field setting to overwrite previous data sent to a target
- TCP splicing—obscuring the actual TCP data to be processed at the peer
- Password cracking attempts—repeated attempts to guess an account password over a single connection or multiple connections

This is only a sampling of traffic patterns that should be investigated.

Find Maliciously Malformed Packets

Malicious packets take advantage of vulnerabilities in protocols and/or applications. In September 2009, we were presented with an example of a security breach caused by maliciously malformed packets—CVE-2009-3103 (detailed below).

> **CVE-2009-3103**
> *Array index error in the SMBv2 protocol implementation in srv2.sys in Microsoft Windows Vista Gold, SP1, and SP2, Windows Server 2008 Gold and SP2, and Windows 7 RC allows remote attackers to execute arbitrary code or cause a denial of service (system crash) via an & (ampersand) character in a Process ID High header field in a NEGOTIATE PROTOCOL REQUEST packet, which triggers an attempted dereference of an out-of-bounds memory location, aka "SMBv2 Negotiation Vulnerability." NOTE: some of these details are obtained from third party information.*

The details of this vulnerability pointed to packets that contained the value "&" in the Process ID High field in the SMB header. Figure 350 shows the packet detail pane of an SMB Negotiate Protocol Request packet.

```
⊞ Frame 28 (191 bytes on wire, 191 bytes captured)
⊞ Ethernet II, Src: Dell_be:9d:fd (00:14:22:be:9d:fd), Dst: AsustekC_8
⊞ Internet Protocol, Src: 192.168.0.88 (192.168.0.88), Dst: 192.168.0.
⊞ Transmission Control Protocol, Src Port: sgi-storman (1178), Dst Por
⊞ NetBIOS Session Service
⊟ SMB (Server Message Block Protocol)
  ⊟ SMB Header
      Server Component: SMB
      [Response in: 29]
      SMB Command: Negotiate Protocol (0x72)
      NT Status: STATUS_SUCCESS (0x00000000)
    ⊟ Flags: 0x18
        0... .... = Request/Response: Message is a request to the serve
        .0.. .... = Notify: Notify client only on open
        ..0. .... = Oplocks: OpLock not requested/granted
        ...1 .... = Canonicalized Pathnames: Pathnames are canonicalized
        .... 1... = Case Sensitivity: Path names are caseless
        .... ..0. = Receive Buffer Posted: Receive buffer has not been
        .... ...0 = Lock and Read: Lock&Read, Write&Unlock are not supp
    ⊟ Flags2: 0xc853
      Process ID High: 0
      Signature: 0000000000000000
      Reserved: 0000
      Tree ID: 0
      Process ID: 65279
      User ID: 0
      Multiplex ID: 0
  ⊟ Negotiate Protocol Request (0x72)
      Word Count (WCT): 0
      Byte Count (BCC): 98
```

Figure 350. The SMB header's Process ID High field should be set to 0

Microsoft responded on October 13th with "Microsoft Security Bulletin MS09-050 – Critical - Vulnerabilities in SMBv2 Could Allow Remote Code Execution (975517)".

Packet details released with vulnerabilities can be used to configure firewalls and IDS solutions to block such traffic. Wireshark can be configured to identify this traffic through display filters or coloring rules.

The following filter can be used alone or as a coloring rule to detect these malformed packets.

```
(smb.cmd == 0x72) && (smb.flags.response == 0)
&& !(smb.pid.high == 0)
```

This filter consists of three sections to identify these malicious packets:

`(smb.cmd == 0x72)`	SMB command 0x72 is a Negotiate Protocol Request
`(smb.flags.response == 0)`	SMB Flags Response is set to 0 in a request and 1 in a reply; we are interested in the requests
`!(smb.pid.high == 0)`	The SMB Protocol ID High should be set to 0; we are interested in packets that have a non-zero value in this field

When vulnerabilities are announced—and they provide packet details—consider creating coloring rules to highlight these packets in any trace file you open. In addition, you can use Tshark with the – R parameter to view traffic that meets your filter syntax. See *Tshark Syntax* on page 680 for more information on using display filters in command-line capture.

Identify Invalid or 'Dark' Destination Addresses

Given the numerous resolution processes for host and hardware addresses, it is considered unusual to see traffic destined to addresses that are not assigned. For example, if your network is configured as 10.2.0.0/16 and you have assigned 10.2.0.1 through 10.2.0.20, you would not expect to see traffic destined to 10.2.0.99.

Unassigned MAC addresses are referred to as "dark MAC addresses." Unassigned IP addresses are referred to as "dark IP addresses." Traffic sent to or referencing unassigned addresses may be indications of blind discovery processes—someone is trying to find hosts on the network by doing a scan of those host addresses and listening for responses.

Figure 351 shows ARP scan traffic referencing a number of dark IP addresses. If this traffic is not normally seen on the network by some monitoring device, it should be flagged for investigation.

Traffic sent to unusual target addresses is also an indication of a possible configuration or application problem. For example, traffic sent to 127.0.0.1 (the loopback address) would be considered quite unusual.

No. .	Time	Source	Destination	Protocol	Info
22	0.002020	LiteonTe_58:2b:0d	Broadcast	ARP	who has 192.168.0.1? Tell 192.168.0.108
23	0.001368	Elitegro_40:74:d2	Broadcast	ARP	who has 192.168.0.4? Tell 192.168.0.113
24	0.003884	Elitegro_40:74:d2	Broadcast	ARP	who has 192.168.0.5? Tell 192.168.0.113
25	0.005445	Elitegro_40:74:d2	Broadcast	ARP	who has 192.168.0.6? Tell 192.168.0.113
26	0.004018	Elitegro_40:74:d2	Broadcast	ARP	who has 192.168.0.7? Tell 192.168.0.113
27	0.003496	Elitegro_40:74:d2	Broadcast	ARP	who has 192.168.0.8? Tell 192.168.0.113
28	0.004066	Elitegro_40:74:d2	Broadcast	ARP	who has 192.168.0.9? Tell 192.168.0.113
29	0.005198	Elitegro_40:74:d2	Broadcast	ARP	who has 192.168.0.10? Tell 192.168.0.113
30	0.004226	Elitegro_40:74:d2	Broadcast	ARP	who has 192.168.0.11? Tell 192.168.0.113
31	0.003473	Elitegro_40:74:d2	Broadcast	ARP	who has 192.168.0.12? Tell 192.168.0.113
32	0.003401	Elitegro_40:74:d2	Broadcast	ARP	who has 192.168.0.13? Tell 192.168.0.113
33	0.004344	Elitegro_40:74:d2	Broadcast	ARP	who has 192.168.0.14? Tell 192.168.0.113
34	0.004984	Elitegro_40:74:d2	Broadcast	ARP	who has 192.168.0.15? Tell 192.168.0.113
35	0.003750	Elitegro_40:74:d2	Broadcast	ARP	who has 192.168.0.16? Tell 192.168.0.113
36	0.003750	Elitegro_40:74:d2	Broadcast	ARP	who has 192.168.0.17? Tell 192.168.0.113
37	0.003276	Elitegro_40:74:d2	Broadcast	ARP	who has 192.168.0.18? Tell 192.168.0.113
38	0.004142	Elitegro_40:74:d2	Broadcast	ARP	who has 192.168.0.19? Tell 192.168.0.113
39	0.003391	Elitegro_40:74:d2	Broadcast	ARP	who has 192.168.0.20? Tell 192.168.0.113
40	0.003598	Elitegro_40:74:d2	Broadcast	ARP	who has 192.168.0.21? Tell 192.168.0.113
41	0.003275	Elitegro_40:74:d2	Broadcast	ARP	who has 192.168.0.22? Tell 192.168.0.113
42	0.003025	Elitegro_40:74:d2	Broadcast	ARP	who has 192.168.0.23? Tell 192.168.0.113
43	0.00?425	Elitegro_40:74:d2	Broadcast	ARP	who has 192.168.0.24? Tell 192.168.0.113

Figure 351. This ARP scan hits numerous dark IP addresses

You can locate traffic to or from addresses that are not in use, but the display filter may be quite long if you use non-contiguous addressing.

As an example, consider if your network is configured to use the following IP address ranges:

192.168.0.1-4	assigned to routers
192.168.0.100-112	assigned to servers
192.168.0.140-211	assigned to clients

Your display filter for traffic to or from unassigned IP addresses within the 192.168 network range would be:

```
(ip.dst > 192.168.0.4 && ip.dst < 192.168.0.100) || (ip.dst >
192.168.0.112 && ip.dst < 192.168.0.140) || (ip.dst > 192.168.0.211
&& ip.dst < 192.168.0.254)
```

Notice the use of parentheses to group together the filters sections. The parentheses group together addresses we are interested in displaying. The filter would be interpreted as follows.

- A destination IP address between 192.168.0.4 and 192.168.0.100, or
- A destination IP address between 192.168.0.112 and 192.168.0.140, or
- A destination IP address of 192.168.0.211 and 192.168.0.254

To make these packets stand out more in a trace file, you might consider creating a coloring rule for this traffic.

Differentiating Between Flooding or Standard Denial of Service Traffic

Floods are a form of a denial of service attack. Consistent connection requests are another form of denial of service. Denial of service attacks are designed to make a resource unavailable to others. The attack may be focused on a target host, group of hosts or even the network infrastructure itself.

Flooding can be used to saturate a network link, a TCP connection table, the buffer on a network interface card, switch tables, routing tables or other elements of a network.

When analyzing network floods, consider that a configuration mistake could be the cause of the flood. Is the flood due to a loop in the network? If so, the IP ID field of all the flooding packets would likely be the same as it is the same packet circulating on the network. This type of flood is typically caused by a layer 2 loop—for example, when someone connects a hub into two switches. Spanning Tree is a protocol designed to resolve layer 2 loops.

If the IP ID field value (or other packet value) is different in each packet, then it is not a loop situation. Each packet is generated separately through the IP stack element.

Macof is a tool that purposefully floods a network. The purpose of Macof is to overload a switch's MAC address table hoping to cause the switch to stop making forwarding decisions and forward all packets out all ports (thereby becoming, in essence, a hub) or stop forward packets altogether (thereby becoming a brick).

Figure 352 and Figure 353 show a Macof flood in the Packet List pane[108]. The Time column is set to display the Seconds since Previously Displayed Packets. The majority of the flood is sent at 42 microseconds (millionths of a second) apart. By default, Macof sends SYN packets to the random target addresses.

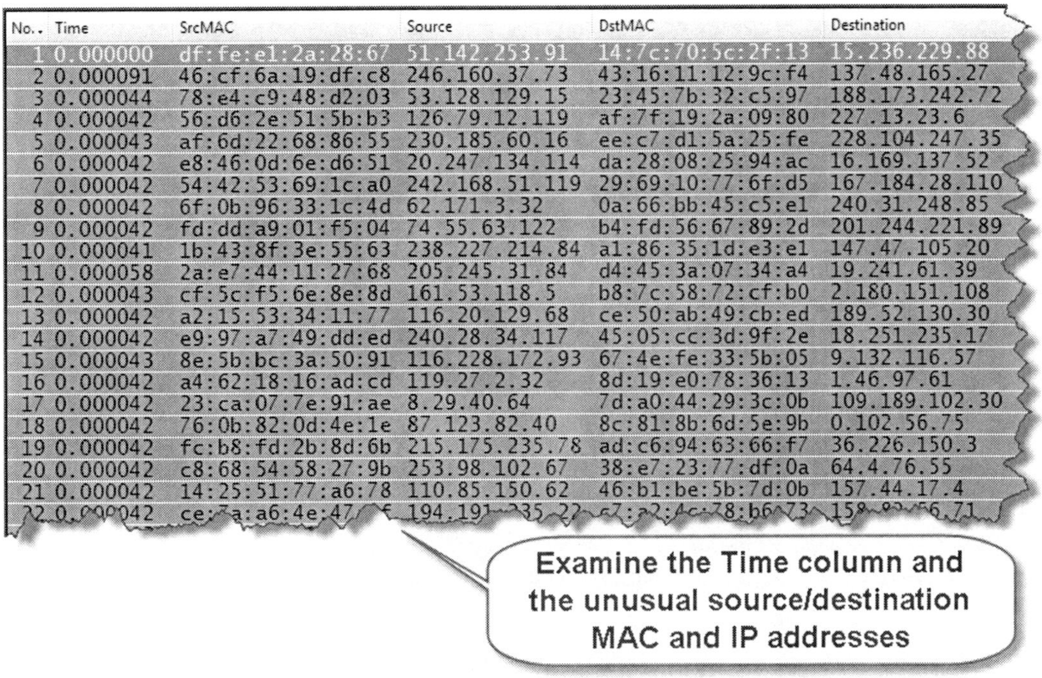

No..	Time	SrcMAC	Source	DstMAC	Destination
1	0.000000	df:fe:e1:2a:28:67	51.142.253.91	14:7c:70:5c:2f:13	15.236.229.88
2	0.000091	46:cf:6a:19:df:c8	246.160.37.73	43:16:11:12:9c:f4	137.48.165.27
3	0.000044	78:e4:c9:48:d2:03	53.128.129.15	23:45:7b:32:c5:97	188.173.242.72
4	0.000042	56:d6:2e:51:5b:b3	126.79.12.119	af:7f:19:2a:09:80	227.13.23.6
5	0.000043	af:6d:22:68:86:55	230.185.60.16	ee:c7:d1:5a:25:fe	228.104.247.35
6	0.000042	e8:46:0d:6e:d6:51	20.247.134.114	da:28:08:25:94:ac	16.169.137.52
7	0.000042	54:42:53:69:1c:a0	242.168.51.119	29:69:10:77:6f:d5	167.184.28.110
8	0.000042	6f:0b:96:33:1c:4d	62.171.3.32	0a:66:bb:45:c5:e1	240.31.248.85
9	0.000042	fd:dd:a9:01:f5:04	74.55.63.122	b4:fd:56:67:89:2d	201.244.221.89
10	0.000041	1b:43:8f:3e:55:63	238.227.214.84	a1:86:35:1d:e3:e1	147.47.105.20
11	0.000058	2a:e7:44:11:27:68	205.245.31.84	d4:45:3a:07:34:a4	19.241.61.39
12	0.000043	cf:5c:f5:6e:8e:8d	161.53.118.5	b8:7c:58:72:cf:b0	2.180.151.108
13	0.000042	a2:15:53:34:11:77	116.20.129.68	ce:50:ab:49:cb:ed	189.52.130.30
14	0.000042	e9:97:a7:49:dd:ed	240.28.34.117	45:05:cc:3d:9f:2e	18.251.235.17
15	0.000043	8e:5b:bc:3a:50:91	116.228.172.93	67:4e:fe:33:5b:05	9.132.116.57
16	0.000042	a4:62:18:16:ad:cd	119.27.2.32	8d:19:e0:78:36:13	1.46.97.61
17	0.000042	23:ca:07:7e:91:ae	8.29.40.64	7d:a0:44:29:3c:0b	109.189.102.30
18	0.000042	76:0b:82:0d:4e:1e	87.123.82.40	8c:81:8b:6d:5e:9b	0.102.56.75
19	0.000042	fc:b8:fd:2b:8d:6b	215.175.235.78	ad:c6:94:63:66:f7	36.226.150.3
20	0.000042	c8:68:54:58:27:9b	253.98.102.67	38:e7:23:77:df:0a	64.4.76.55
21	0.000042	14:25:51:77:a6:78	110.85.150.62	46:b1:be:5b:7d:0b	157.44.17.4
22	0.000042	ce:5a:a6:4e:47:e	194.191.35.22	c7:a2:4c:78:b6	159.89.56.71

> **Examine the Time column and the unusual source/destination MAC and IP addresses**

Figure 352. Macof sends packets to random MAC and IP addresses

Wireshark may not be able to keep up with traffic on a flooded network. If the packet per second rate is high enough, you may find that Wireshark drops packets. Dropped packets may be indicated on the Status Bar depending on whether the operating system enables the driver to determine if packets are lost.

There are several optimization techniques that can be used when capturing on a flooded network. The first, and most efficient method, is to use Tshark or dumpcap instead of Wireshark to capture the traffic. On a flooded network you may not need to capture very many packets to identify the characteristics of the flood.

If you choose to use Wireshark to capture the traffic, consider turning off unnecessary features such as updating the list of packets in real time, colorization and disable network name resolution.

---

[108] The Packet List pane view is split into two pieces for clarity. Two additional columns were set up in Preferences—the SrcMAC column lists the unresolved source MAC address and the DstMAC column lists the unresolved destination MAC address.

No..	Protocol	Info
1	TCP	2555 > 22746 [SYN] Seq=794289546 Win=512 Len=0
2	TCP	36850 > 38839 [SYN] Seq=905234887 Win=512 Len=0
3	TCP	65386 > 6909 [SYN] Seq=1901697088 Win=512 Len=0
4	TCP	17662 > 20614 [SYN] Seq=157705070 Win=512 Len=0
5	TCP	51795 > 23062 [SYN] Seq=907472509 Win=512 Len=0
6	TCP	41795 > 26887 [SYN] Seq=2019917873 Win=512 Len=0
7	TCP	59753 > 25893 [SYN] Seq=1034795420 Win=512 Len=0
8	TCP	28321 > 38294 [SYN] Seq=1806263381 Win=512 Len=0
9	TCP	2851 > 54476 [SYN] Seq=1477894039 Win=512 Len=0
10	TCP	34984 > 8752 [SYN] Seq=304223999 Win=512 Len=0
11	TCP	39452 > 14478 [SYN] Seq=1562005709 Win=512 Len=0
12	TCP	32630 > 17979 [SYN] Seq=1347560724 Win=512 Len=0
13	TCP	12744 > 57757 [SYN] Seq=215804050 Win=512 Len=0
14	TCP	18160 > 44078 [SYN] Seq=409677089 Win=512 Len=0
15	TCP	42484 > 16791 [SYN] Seq=438725010 Win=512 Len=0
16	TCP	26229 > 60736 [SYN] Seq=631154530 Win=512 Len=0
17	TCP	6202 > 9249 [SYN] Seq=1082214274 Win=512 Len=0
18	TCP	22748 > 18846 [SYN] Seq=1494194625 Win=512 Len=0
19	TCP	25290 > 58680 [SYN] Seq=160090481 Win=512 Len=0
20	TCP	59058 > 16030 [SYN] Seq=1871966233 Win=512 Len=0
21	TCP	15542 > 27872 [SYN] Seq=1175467068 Win=512 Len=0
22		22897 > 14712 [SYN] Seq=342485669 Win=512 Len=0

Figure 353. Macof can randomize the source and destination port numbers as well as the starting sequence number

Finding Clear Text Passwords and Data

Some applications are known to use clear text passwords and Wireshark can easily capture and display those passwords. These visible passwords are a security concern.

Wireshark can be used to display any clear text communications transmitted on the network. From the network security standpoint, these applications should be examined to determine if they are releasing sensitive data on the network. From an intruder standpoint, this information may be used to exploit network vulnerabilities.

Figure 354 depicts the traffic from an HTTP POST operation that is setting a user password. Certainly this password should not be sent in clear text—the password prompting page should have been accessed via secure encrypted connection.

Validating that applications are using encryption for password setting and password input is an important step in analyzing network security.

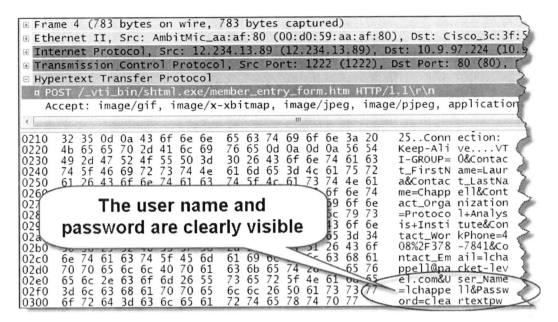

Figure 354. Wireshark displays a password setting process that is visible in clear text.

One method to identify if clear text passwords are crossing the network is to begin packet capture then access the host using a password. Use the Find feature to look for the string anywhere in the trace file or simple Follow the TCP Stream (or UDP Stream) to look for the password in readable format.

Clear text data is a concern as well. For example, if financial information is crossing the network you would want to know this and possibly alter the data transfer process to a more secure method.

Again, to detect clear text data you might capture the traffic and reassemble the stream to identify clear text data.

Identifying Phone Home Traffic

"Phone home" traffic is seen when an application periodically connects to a remote host for the purpose of updating the application, obtaining commands, etc. Phone home behavior typically occurs without user interaction.

The most commonly seen phone home behavior is generated by virus detection programs that periodically obtain new threat signatures. Figure 355 shows a host updating its Norton virus detection signatures without the user's interaction.

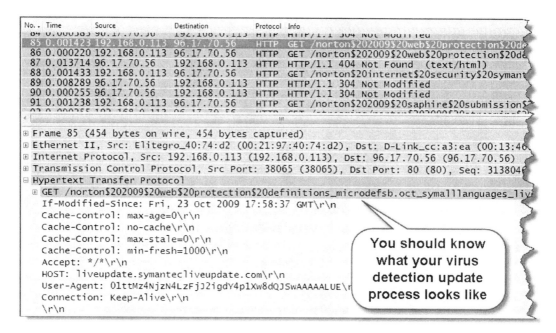

Figure 355. Virus detection services "phone home" to obtain signature updates

It is important to be able to differentiate between acceptable phone home behavior (as in the case of virus detection update processes) and malicious behavior (as in the case of bot-infected host processes).

Bot-infected hosts typically obtain their commands from Command and Control (C&C) servers. Without user interaction, the bot programs connect to these servers.

One method of detecting phone home traffic is to capture the traffic to and from a host that is idle. This is an important baseline and mentioned in *Baseline Traffic during Idle Time* on page 567.

Consider filtering out (removing from view) acceptable phone home traffic, such as virus and operating system update traffic. This filter may be quite long if the host has a large number of applications that phone home.

Catching Unusual Protocols and Applications

A solid baseline of normal communications assists in locating unusual protocols and applications on the network.

The Protocol Hierarchy Statistics window helps identify unusual protocols and applications in the traffic. Figure 356 shows the Protocol Hierarchy Statistics window opened for a trace file containing traffic to and from a breached host.

The breached host is a Windows machine. The DCE RPC traffic used for SMB is normal for this host. The IRC and Trivial File Transfer Protocol (TFTP) traffic is not normal.

Right clicking on the IRC or FTP line provides the option to filter on this traffic for further investigation.

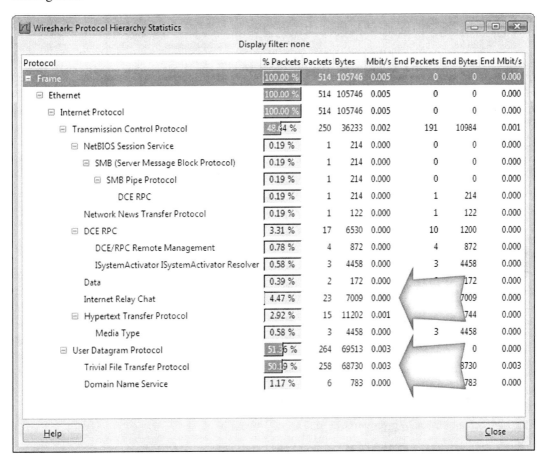

Figure 356. The Protocol Hierarchy Statistics window helps detect unusual protocols or applications

You will not see the statistics for all the traffic if you applied a display filter to the traffic before opening the Protocol Hierarchy Statistics window. The display filter applied is listed just below the title bar of the window.

If the unusual traffic is using a port that Wireshark does not recognize, the Protocol Hierarchy Statistics window may have a high percentage of packets listed as "Data" as shown in Figure 357. In this case you can right click to filter on this unrecognized traffic and reassemble the stream to look for something that identifies the purpose of the traffic.

Consider creating coloring rules for unusual traffic on standard ports (such as IRC and TFTP traffic, for example) to identify the traffic easily when you scroll through the trace file.

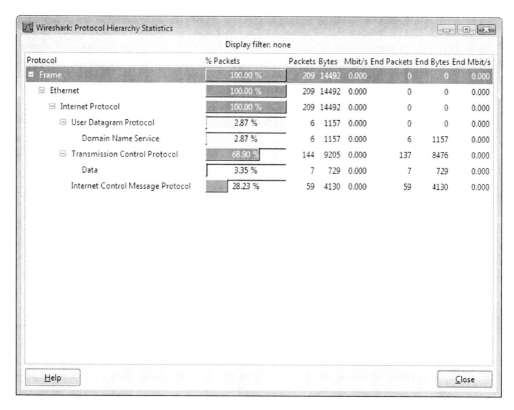

Figure 357. If Wireshark does not recognize the application, it is listed as "Data"

Locating Route Redirection that Uses ICMP

One method used for man-in-the-middle attacks is route redirection.

ICMP offers a method to dynamically discover the best router when more than one router is available on the network. When a host sends the packets to a gateway that knows of a better router to use (closer to the target network or host), it sends an ICMP Redirect (Type 5) that contains the IP address of the gateway offering a better path.

Figure 358 shows an ICMP Redirect from a gateway at 10.2.99.99 indicating that the best gateway to use is 10.2.99.98. Upon receipt of this packet, a host should update its routing tables to add an entry for 10.2.99.98.

When 10.2.0.2 wants to communicate with 10.3.71.1 (seen in the copy of the original IP header shown after the ICMP portion of the packet) it should send the packet through 10.2.99.98.

An attacker can use this redirection to intercept and forward traffic that normally would not be directed to the attacker's IP address.

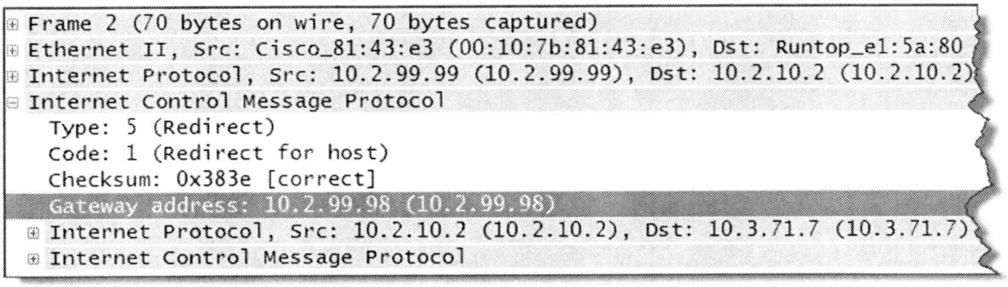

```
⊞ Frame 2 (70 bytes on wire, 70 bytes captured)
⊞ Ethernet II, Src: Cisco_81:43:e3 (00:10:7b:81:43:e3), Dst: Runtop_e1:5a:80
⊞ Internet Protocol, Src: 10.2.99.99 (10.2.99.99), Dst: 10.2.10.2 (10.2.10.2)
⊟ Internet Control Message Protocol
     Type: 5 (Redirect)
     Code: 1 (Redirect for host)
     Checksum: 0x383e [correct]
     Gateway address: 10.2.99.98 (10.2.99.98)
  ⊞ Internet Protocol, Src: 10.2.10.2 (10.2.10.2), Dst: 10.3.71.7 (10.3.71.7)
  ⊞ Internet Control Message Protocol
```

Figure 358. ICMP Redirect packets indicate a better router to use to reach a host

ICMP Redirect packets are easy to spot with a display filter or color filter for `icmp.type==5`.

Catching ARP Poisoning

ARP poisoning is typically used for man-in-the-middle attacks. The attacker generates a series of ARP packets with false information that alters the ARP tables of victim hosts.

Ettercap and Cain and Abel are two tools that can be used to perform ARP poisoning.

Figure 359 depicts the Protocol and Info columns of a trace file containing an ARP poisoning process. The poisoning host is using MAC address 00:d0:59:aa:af:80. The host at that address states that both 192.168.1.103 and 192.168.1.1 are at that address in packets 6 and 7.

In packet 7, Wireshark indicates "duplicate use of 192.168.1.103 detected" because that IP address is contained in the Target IP Address field in this packet is associated with MAC address 00:d0:59:12:9b:01. In packet 6, however, that IP address is associated with 00:d0:59:aa:af:80.

Figure 360 shows the Expert Info Composite Warnings tab indicating that a duplicate address has been detected. The Info column and Expert Info Composite columns simplify the process of detecting ARP poisoning.

```
No. . Protocol  Info
  6 ARP      192.168.1.103 is at 00:d0:59:aa:af:80
  7 ARP      192.168.1.1 is at 00:d0:59:aa:af:80 (duplicate use of 192.168.1.103 detected!)
  9 ARP      who has 192.168.1.1?  Tell 192.168.1.103
 10 ARP      192.168.1.1 is at 00:20:78:d9:0d:db
 11 ARP      who has 192.168.1.103?  Tell 192.168.1.1 (duplicate use of 192.168.1.1 detected!)
 12 ARP      192.168.1.103 is at 00:d0:59:12:9b:01 (duplicate use of 192.168.1.1 detected!)
 13 ARP      192.168.1.103 is at 00:d0:59:aa:af:80
 14 ARP      192.168.1.1 is at 00:d0:59:aa:af:80 (duplicate use of 192.168.1.103 detected!)
 15 ARP      who has 192.168.1.1?  Tell 192.168.1.103
 16 ARP      192.168.1.1 is at 00:20:78:d9:0d:db
 17 ARP      who has 192.168.1.103?  Tell 192.168.1.1 (duplicate use of 192.168.1.1 detected!)
 18 ARP      192.168.1.103 is at 00:d0:59:12:9b:01 (duplicate use of 192.168.1.1 detected!)
 19 ARP      192.168.1.103 is at 00:d0:59:aa:af:80
 20 ARP      192.168.1.1 is at 00:d0:59:aa:af:80 (duplicate use of 192.168.1.103 detected!)

⊞ Frame 7 (64 bytes on wire, 64 bytes captured)
⊞ Ethernet II, Src: 00:d0:59:aa:af:80 (00:d0:59:aa:af:80), Dst: 00:d0:59:12:9b:01 (00:d0:59
⊟ Address Resolution Protocol (reply)
     Hardware type: Ethernet (0x0001)
     Protocol type: IP (0x0800)
     Hardware size: 6
     Protocol size: 4
     Opcode: reply (0x0002)
     [Is gratuitous: False]
     Sender MAC address: 00:d0:59:aa:af:80 (00:d0:59:aa:af:80)
     Sender IP address: 192.168.1.1 (192.168.1.1)
     Target MAC address: 00:d0:59:12:9b:01 (00:d0:59:12:9b:01)
     Target IP address: 192.168.1.103 (192.168.1.103)
```

Figure 359. Wireshark detects duplicate use of an IP address during ARP poisoning

In this case, a host updates its ARP tables based on information learned during the ARP poisoning process. When it wants to send data to another IP address it consults its ARP table and forwards the packets to MAC address associated with the target IP address.

In the ARP poisoning shown in Figure 359, both 192.168.1.103 and 192.168.1.1 believe the other's MAC address is 00:d0:59:aa:af:80—the MAC address of the poisoning host. This ARP poisoning was performed using Ettercap.

Catch the Traffic When You Run Malicious Tools

As you evaluate attack tools in your lab, ensure you capture the traffic generated by these tools. Examine this traffic to understand how the attack tools work and the signatures of this traffic. These signatures can be used to block or identify the traffic on your production network.

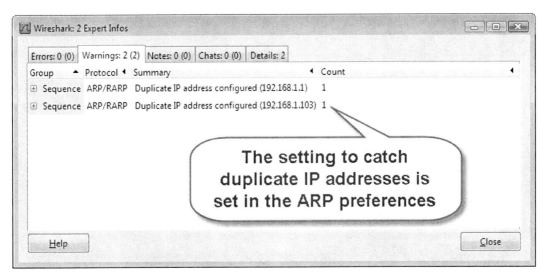

Figure 360. Wireshark indicates there are duplicate IP addresses in the Expert Info window

Catching IP Fragmentation and Overwriting

IP fragmentation is a process used to split a packet into smaller sizes in order to traverse network segments that support smaller MTU sizes.

The IP header contains three fields that define if an IP packet *may* be fragmented and if an IP packet *has* been fragmented. These fields are

Field	Details
May Fragment field (one bit long)	0 = may fragment; 1 = don't fragment
More Fragments field (one bit long)	0 = not set; 1 = more fragments to come
Fragment Offset field (13 bits long).	This field is used to reassemble the fragmented data in the correct order.

Fragmentation override occurs when data occurring later in a fragmented set overrides previous data based on its Fragmentation Offset field value when the data is reassembled.

Figure 361 shows the contents of the IP header in a fragmented communication. To spot fragmentation override, add an `ip.frag_offset` column to the Packet List pane. If the fragmentation offset value does not increment with each new fragment, then the entire communication is suspect. For example, if the `ip.frag_offset` column indicates that the fragment offset values are 0, 1480, 2960, 4400, 1480, 5920, 7400 and 8880, you must wonder about the fifth packet in the set. Is it a retransmission? If not, then it may be an IP fragment override situation.

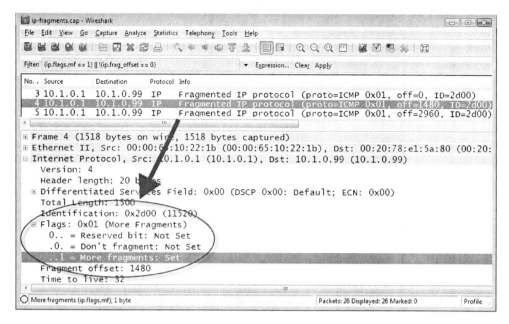

Figure 361. Wireshark lists the offset of IP fragments in the Info column

Spotting TCP Splicing

There are numerous TCP evasion techniques used to bypass firewalls, intrusion detection systems and intrusion prevention systems.

One method of TCP evasion is TCP splicing—splitting TCP segments over multiple packets. Each packet may contain only one byte of data (although some products detect when a single byte of data is transferred—a random number of smaller bytes may be more effective).

In order to run protection checking on TCP payload values, the firewall, IDS or IPS must reassemble the TCP segments and examine that payload before forwarding or triggering events.

One indication that splicing may be underway would be a continuous stream of small packets traveling in both directions on a TCP connection. Extremely small packets would be expected coming from the receiving host that is sending ACK packets. Extremely small packets would not be expected from the host that is sending data. Consider adding a `tcp.len` column in Wireshark to help spot these unusual packets. Right click to reassemble these spliced packets into a single stream.

Figure 362 shows an FTP communications that is sending TCP data across one byte at a time. This is easy to detect in Wireshark.

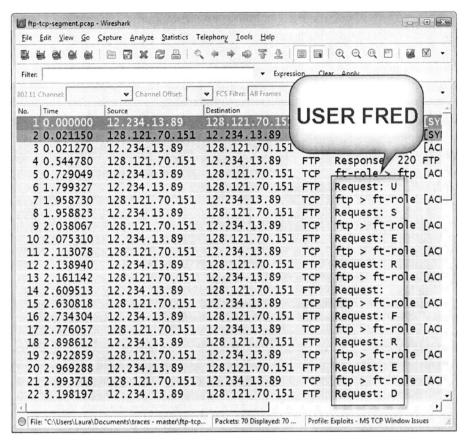

Figure 362. An FTP login sequence is sent one byte at a time

Watching Other Unusual TCP Traffic

There are numerous methods used to manipulate TCP communications to bypass IDS or firewall elements on the network.

The following lists some of the TCP packets that are considered unusual and possibly malicious on the network.

Vulnerability Name	Description
TCP Segment Overwrite	One or more TCP segments in a stream overwrite one or more segments occurring earlier in the stream[109]
TCP Options Occurring after an End of Options Indicator	Additional TCP options are seen in the TCP header options area after the End of Options (0) indicator

---

[109] Note that Wireshark's `tcp.segment.overlap.conflict` display filter can detect TCP segments that have overlapping offsets, but contain different data. Consider creating a "butt ugly" coloring rule to call your attention to this and other malicious packets.

Vulnerability Name	Description
TCP SYN Packet Contains Data	The initial TCP SYN handshake packets contain data[110]
TCP Bad Flags Combination	An illogical combination of TCP flags is seen
TCP URG Bit Set with Illogical Urgent Pointer Value	The Urgent Pointer bit is set and the Urgent Pointer field points to non-existent data
TCP Timestamp Not Allowed	A packet contains a TCP Timestamp value when that option is not allowed in the connection
TCP SYN/ACK but Not SYN Window Scale Option	The second handshake packet (SYN/ACK) contains the Window Scale Option setting when the SYN packet did not contain this option

Identifying Password Cracking Attempts

Password cracking attempts can be obvious on the wire—even if the connection is encrypted. Unsuccessful attempts generate error responses which may, in turn, cause another TCP connection to be established.

Unencrypted cracking attempts may generate clear text error responses as in the case of an incorrect FTP password. Consider creating a coloring filter to highlight password error responses.

An unencrypted password crack consists of multiple login attempts in clear text, as shown in Figure 363. In an encrypted login attempt, there typically are a high number of small packets and possibly an equally high number of new connections to the target server if the cracking attempt uses a separate connection for each attempt.

Brute Force Password Crack Attempts

Brute force password cracks use a sequence of characters, numbers and key values to identify the password.

Dictionary Password Crack Attempts

Dictionary attacks use common words, names and numbers maintained in a cracking dictionary. Figure 363 depicts a dictionary password cracking attempt on the Administrator account of an FTP server. The cracker has tried no *password*, *abc123*, *password*, *passwd*, and *123456* so far in this attempt.

Regardless of the type of cracking attempt, a higher-than-normal number of error responses would be seen on the network. The display filter or coloring rule to highlight FTP password errors is `ftp.response.code == 530`.

---

[110] Some TCP implementations have been observed sending data with the second packet of the TCP handshake—the SYN/ACK packet. This behavior is not explicitly prohibited by TCP specifications, but it is unusual.

No. . Time	Source	Destination	Protocol	Info
1 0.000000	200.90.26	67.161.39.	TCP	33928 > 21 [SYN] Seq=2518798394 win=5840 Le
2 0.000084	67.161.39	200.90.26.	TCP	21 > 33928 [SYN, ACK] Seq=3329031107 Ack=251
3 0.405761	200.90.26	67.161.39.	TCP	33928 > 21 [ACK] Seq=2518798395 Ack=332903110
4 0.037924	67.161.39	200.90.26.	FTP	Response: 220-creditus.com
5 0.618882	200.90.26	67.161.39.	TCP	33928 > 21 [ACK] Seq=2518798395 Ack=3329031
6 2.885715	200.90.26	67.161.39.	FTP	Request: USER Administrator
7 0.001391	67.161.39	200.90.26.	FTP	Response: 331 User name okay, Need password.
8 0.426148	200.90.26	67.161.39.	FTP	Request: PASS
9 0.000835	67.161.39	200.90.26.	FTP	Response: 530 Password not accepted.
10 0.642147	200.90.26	67.161.39.	FTP	Request: USER Administrator
11 0.000950	67.161.39	200.90.26.	FTP	Response: 331 User name okay, Need password
12 0.456493	200.90.26	67.161.39.	FTP	Request: PASS abc123
13 0.000843	67.161.39	200.90.26.	FTP	Response: 530 Password not accepted.
14 0.379510	200.90.26	67.161.39.	FTP	Request: USER Administrator
15 0.000836	67.161.39	200.90.26.	FTP	Response: 331 User name okay, Need password
16 1.781915	200.90.26	67.161.39.	FTP	Request: PASS password
17 0.001267	67.161.39	200.90.26.	FTP	Response: 530 Password not accepted.
18 0.534723	200.90.26	67.161.39.	FTP	Request: USER Administrator
19 0.000844	67.161.39	200.90.26.	FTP	Response: 331 User name okay, Need password
20 0.669539	200.90.26	67.161.39.	FTP	Request: PASS passwd
21 0.000882	67.161.39	200.90.26.	FTP	Response: 530 Password not accepted.
22 1.361404	200.90.26	67.161.39.	FTP	Request: USER Administrator
23 0.000845	67.161.39	200.90.26.	FTP	Response: 331 User name okay, Need password
24 3.040089	200.90.26	67.161.39.	FTP	Request: PASS 123456
25 0.000860	67.161.39	200.90.26.	FTP	Response: 530 Password not accepted.

Figure 363. This dictionary password cracking attempt runs over a single TCP connection

Know Where to Look: Signature Locations

If you write firewall rules, you are probably already familiar with the many locations where reconnaissance and attack signatures reside in traffic. Your firewall rules are based on these signatures. Explicit traffic signatures are often released when vulnerabilities are openly announced to the public.

In many cases you can correlate your firewall or IDS rules with Wireshark display filters or coloring rules. For example, if your IDS triggers on non-multicast packets with a Time to Live lower than 5, you can create a Wireshark display filter or coloring rule to match this rule.

The following is an example of a rule that may be used on a Snort IDS host:

```
alert tcp $EXTERNAL_NET any -> $HOME_NET 6004 (msg:"DOS iParty
DOS attempt"; flow:to_server,established; content:"|FF FF FF
FF FF FF|"; offset:0; reference:bugtraq,6844;
reference:cve,1999-1566; reference:nessus,10111;
classtype:misc-attack; sid:1605; rev:8;)
```

Based on the rule above, we could build a Wireshark display filter or coloring rule based on these elements:

- It is a TCP packet (`tcp`)
- Traffic is destined to the local network (`ip.dst==10.2.0.0/16` for example)
- Traffic is destined to the TCP port 6004 (`tcp.dstport==6004`)
- The content following the TCP header is 0xFF:FF:FF:FF:FF:FF (`data contains 0xFF:FF:FF:FF:FF:FF`)

Header Signatures

There are times when the signature resides in an IP, UDP or TCP header.

Header	Potential Signature
IP Header	TTL (too low?)
	ID field (unusual or recognized value?)
	Total length (small data packets—fragmented?)
	Fragmentation (fragmented attack?)
	Source IP address (known attacker?)
	Destination IP address (critical system?)
UDP Header	Destination port number (known target application?)
TCP Header	Destination port number (known target application?)
	Flags (unusual setting?)

Sequence Signatures

Sometimes it is not the individual packets that are of concern, but the proximity of specific packet types to each other and the order of those packets.

For example, ICMP Types 13, 15 and 17 in close proximity is the signature of ICMP-based OS fingerprinting.

Another example is a series of packets that have sequentially incremented TTL values starting at 1. This is the signature of a traceroute operation.

Payload Signatures

Numerous attacks are visible when looking at the payload. The payload may contain command strings, file ID values indicating an executable is being downloaded, or other traffic of concern.

Case Study:
The Flooding Host

Submitted by: *Martin B.*
                  Network Administrator

Whenever users complain about performance or I don't think the network is performing well myself, I generally get Wireshark running and start checking out the traffic.

Recently I fired up Wireshark and was really amazed to see a ton of broadcasts being sent from one network host to my machine and almost every other machine on our network. The source machine was hitting everyone on port 135 which I knew had been used for some exploits before, so I was really worried about what was going on.

I moved to the switch upstream from the flooding host and saw that no one was even sitting at that machine. That's when I really knew there was something wrong.

It only took me a few minutes to find a server it was communicating with on the Internet and reassemble the TCP streams to find out it was using port 18067 to set up an IRC channel. Using the basic information I found in the trace file I did some research and found out that the host was bot-infected. I could identify the exact bot it was infected with and we immediately shut down that host and began to check out every system on the network to see if others were infected.

Wireshark took out all the guesswork for us.

Case Study:
Catching Keylogging Traffic

Submitted by: *Jim McMahon*
            Founder
            "Our Security Guy" Strategic Consultants

One day we were scanning the network for administrative traffic flows using a piece of software we were demonstrating for ten days with the vendor's permission. We were looking at using the product to see what the loads and flows were for various types of traffic. We were scanning ports that had regular predictable traffic and ones where traffic was more uneven and or driven by particular activities to see how we might do some load balancing.

During this process we noticed a periodic packet departing the network (at exactly 10 minute intervals) AND a second larger packet once an hour going to an unrelated private domain.

Intrigued, we traced the internal IP address and noted that it was originating from a financial analyst account (very very bad for a company) and that it was going to an IP address at a non-business related domain.

We quickly looked at the stored data (it was poorly set up by the miscreant as it did not clean up after itself after sending), and determined what was happening was a series of screen shots were going out and then the larger packet was keystroke monitoring collection being dispatched hourly.

Quickly taking the machine off line we did an EnCase® exam and determined that there was evidence of a commercially available keylogger that had been installed on the machine and not very well hidden.

Interviewing the employee we learned that there was a very jealous fiancé in the background who had sent her a "pretty picture" to download. It of course carried a Trojan horse which installed when she opened the pretty picture and self installed. It then began sending the periodic contents of screen and keystroke monitoring.

We obtained a confession from the boyfriend, (he lost the girl and met new friends in small contained places).

Case Study:
Passively Finding Malware

Submitted by: *Labnuke99*

I used Wireshark as a malware infected host detector.

Given that Wireshark is multi-platform, I used it on a Linux computer on a Windows network listening on ports 139 and 445. This particular Linux host was not in Active Directory or in DNS, so the only way any connections should be made to it would be by either scanning the network or by directly connecting to the IP address.

On this particular network, there were a large number of machines where the antivirus application was showing buffer overflow detections. Because the network is on the other side of the world from me (11 hours time difference), it was very difficult to capture the information during these buffer overflow events.

I suspected that there was a malware infected machine on the network attempting to attack and exploit other computers.

Since there were a lot of Windows-to-Windows communications on this network, I decided that the best way to detect the infected host would be to start Wireshark on a Linux host and listen only on ports 139 and 445.

Lo and behold the next morning I found that the culprit had tried to gain access to this Linux host on both ports 139 and 445. Gotcha!

I notified the site administrator about the infected computer and it was rebuilt from clean media.

Wireshark is a great tool for detecting malware infected hosts!

Summary

"Suspect" traffic may include unusual protocols or applications, unusually formed packets, traffic to unused addresses or suspicious targets, high traffic rates or other traffic that just doesn't seem right or match your baselines[111].

A strong knowledge of TCP/IP communications can help you spot protocol and application traffic that is used for breaches. For example, a high number of ICMP Destination Unreachable packets may indicate a UDP discovery process underway—it may also indicate there is a problem with a host that is denying services for some reason.

Perhaps the unusual traffic simply consists of unusual conversation pairs. What if you see a high amount between a sensitive host and targets in country that you believe might be interested in your intellectual property?

Practice What You've Learned

Download the trace files available in the Download section of the book website, *www.wiresharkbook.com*. Open and examine the trace files listed below to become familiar with some obviously unusual traffic patterns.

arp-poison.pcap　　　Consider taking out a pen and paper to sketch the communications (pay close attention to the MAC header as well as the advertised MAC address in the ARP packets). Using a combination of ARP and ICMP Echo requests, a system is poisoning and testing the poison process.

Can you map out the contents of the ARP tables of each poisoned host?

What are the limitations of ARP poisoning?

sec-sql-attack.pcap　　After performing an SQL connection test to port 1433 (ms-sql-s), the attacker makes a login attempt with the client name SYD-S-21-ESXI and username *sa*. The response indicates an error because the login for user *sa* failed.

Apply a display filter on the SQL Error Number 18456. How many packets matched your filter?

sec-sickclient.pcap　　*Note*: Turn off the Checksum Error colorization on this trace or your head may explode. We ran this trace through an IP address cleaner program but it didn't recalculate header checksums.

This client hits an IRC channel as user l l l l (four lowercase "L"s separated by spaces) (packet 14) and later begins to do a scan on the network for anyone with port 139 open.

This feels like a bot looking for other systems to infect. Look at the rapid

---

[111] How will you know what is "suspect" if you don't know what is "normal?" I hate to beat a dead server, but... you really do need to create those baselines mentioned in Chapter 28.

rate of the scan—the responses are bunched up at the end of the trace.

Use the evidence shows in this trace and perform some research on the Internet. What might this host be infected with?

sec-macof.pcap   Dug Song created Macof to flood network switch MAC address tables and cause them to go into 'hub mode.' This tool still wreaks havoc on the network.

What is the IO rate of the traffic?

What is the packet per second rate of the traffic?

Can you identify the signature in this flood traffic?

sec-bruteforce.pcap   Someone is attempting a brute force password crack on an FTP server (*creditus.com*).

Apply a display filter for packets with the USER or PASS commands.

What usernames and passwords were attempted?

How many connections did this password crack establish?

Review Questions

Q32.1   **What is "suspect traffic?"**

Q32.2   **How can name resolution vulnerabilities affect network security?**

Q32.3   **What is a maliciously malformed packet?**

Q32.4   **What is a 'Dark' destination address?**

Q32.5   **What is a key signature of a packet that is looping a switched network?**

Q32.6   **Which Wireshark feature can help you spot unusual protocols and applications on the network?**

Q32.7   **What are two redirection processes that can facilitate man-in-the-middle attacks?**

Q32.8   **How can you determine the complete payload of TCP splicing traffic?**

Answers to Review Questions

Q32.1   **What is "suspect traffic?"**

A32.1   Suspect traffic is traffic that is considered unusual on the network. For example, if a network does not typically support large numbers of connections to sites in China or TFTP communications you might consider this suspect traffic.

Q32.2   **How can name resolution vulnerabilities affect network security?**

A32.2   If the name resolution process is breached, an attacker can redirect hosts to communicate with systems other than the intended ones. For example, if an attacker has added malicious entries to a DNS server's cache, that server will provide this information to querying hosts. From the host's perspective, the redirection is transparent.

Q32.3   **What is a maliciously malformed packet?**

A32.3   A maliciously malformed packet is a packet that is intentionally created to take advantage of protocol or application vulnerabilities. The 2009 SMB2 Negotiate Protocol Request packet containing an ampersand character in the Process ID High field is an example of a maliciously malformed packet.

Q32.4   **What is a 'Dark' destination address?**

A32.4   A 'dark' destination address is an address that falls within the network address range in use but is not currently assigned to a host.

Q32.5   **What is a key signature of a packet that is looping a switched network?**

A32.5   A packet that is looping on a switched network will contain the same IP ID value. If you capture a flood of packets and all of the packets have the same IP ID value, but the packet is part of a fragment set, it may not be a looping packet.

Q32.6   **Which Wireshark feature can help you spot unusual protocols and applications on the network?**

A32.6   Wireshark's Protocol Hierarchy window helps identify unusual protocols and applications. It is imperative that you have a baseline and know what is considered "normal" network communications so you can spot these unusual protocols and applications.

Q32.7 **What are two redirection processes that can facilitate man-in-the-middle attacks?**

A32.7 ARP poisoning and ICMP redirection are two redirection processes that can facilitate man-in-the-middle attacks.

Q32.8 **How can you determine the complete payload of TCP splicing traffic?**

A32.8 Use TCP reassembly to view the reconstructed TCP payload when the traffic has been spliced.

Chapter 33: Effective Use of Command-Line Tools

Wireshark Certified Network Analyst Exam Objectives covered:

- Understand the Power of Command-Line Tools
- Using Wireshark.exe (Command-Line Launch)
- List Trace File Details with Capinfos
- Edit Trace Files with Editcap
- Merge Trace Files with Mergecap
- Convert Text with Text2pcap
- Capture Traffic with Dumpcap
- Understand Rawshark

- ❖ Case Study: Getting GETS and a Suspect
- ❖ Summary
- ❖ Practice What You've Learned
- ❖ Review Questions and Answers

Understand the Power of Command-Line Tools

Wireshark includes a range of command-line tools including:

- Capinfos
- Dumpcap
- Editcap
- Mergecap
- Rawshark
- Text2pcap
- Tshark

In addition, the installation includes wireshark.exe which launches the GUI and offers numerous launch parameters. All these executables are installed by default, as shown in Figure 364.

Add Wireshark to Your Path

Consider adding the Wireshark program file directory to your path so you can run these tools from any directory.

This chapter provides several examples of how these applications can be used for network analysis.

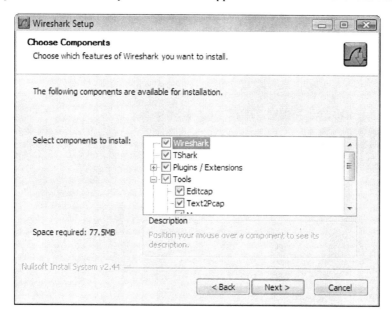

Figure 364. Tshark and the other command-line tools are installed by default

Using Wireshark.exe (Command-Line Launch)

Wireshark.exe launches the graphical view of Wireshark. There are numerous parameters that can be used to automatically begin capturing traffic from a specific interface, apply a capture filter, and set various capture parameters.

Wireshark Syntax

Usage: `wireshark [options] ...`

Function/Parameter	Description
Capture interface	
`-i <interface>`	name or id of interface (default: first non-loopback)
`-f <capture filter>`	packet filter in libpcap filter syntax
`-s <snaplen>`	packet snapshot length (default: 65535)
`-p`	don't capture in promiscuous mode
`-k`	start capturing immediately (default: do nothing)
`-Q`	quit Wireshark after capturing
`-S`	update packet display when new packets are captured
`-l`	turn on automatic scrolling while `-S` is in use
`-B <buffer size>`	size of kernel buffer (default: 1MB)
`-y <link type>`	link layer type (default: first appropriate)
`-D`	print list of interfaces and exit
`-L`	print list of link-layer types of interfaces and exit
Capture stop conditions	
`-c <packet count>`	stop after n packets (default: infinite)
`-a <autostop cond.> ...`	`duration:NUM` - stop after NUM seconds
	`filesize:NUM` - stop this file after NUM KB
	`files:NUM` - stop after NUM files
Capture output	
`-b <ringbuffer opt.> ...`	`duration:NUM` - switch to next file after NUM seconds
	`filesize:NUM` - switch to next file after NUM KB
	`files:NUM` - ringbuffer: replace after NUM files
Input file	
`-r <infile>`	set the filename to read from (read from an existing trace file)
Processing	
`-R <read filter>`	packet filter in Wireshark display filter syntax

Function/Parameter	Description
-n	disable all name resolutions (default: all enabled)
-N \<name resolve flags\>	\<name resolve flags\> enable specific name resolution(s): "mntC"
	m to enable MAC address resolution
	n to enable network address resolution
	t to enable transport-layer port number resolution
	C to enable concurrent (asynchronous) DNS lookups
User interface	
-C \<config profile\>	start with specified configuration profile
-g \<packet number\>	go to specified packet number after "-r"
-m \<font\>	set the font name used for most text
-t ad|a|r|d|dd|e	output format of timestamps. The default format is relative.
	ad absolute with date: The absolute date and time is the actual time and date the packet was captured
	a absolute: The absolute time is the actual time the packet was captured, with no date displayed
	r relative: The relative time is the time elapsed between the first packet and the current packet
	d delta: The delta time is the time since the previous packet was captured
	e epoch: The time in seconds since epoch (Jan 1, 1970 00:00:00)
-X \<key\>:\<value\>	extension options, see man page for details
-z \<statistics\>	show various statistics, see man page for details
Output	
-w \<outfile|-\>	set the output filename (or '-' for standard output, such as the screen)
Miscellaneous	
-h	Display help information and exits
-v	display version info and exit
-P \<key\>:\<path\>	personal configuration path—personal configuration files

Function/Parameter	Description
`-P <key>:<path>`	personal configuration data:path—personal data files
`-o <name>:<value> ...`	override preference or recent setting
`-K <keytab>`	keytab file to use for Kerberos decryption

Customize Wireshark's Launch

Figure 365 shows a series of Wireshark icons that launch separate instances of Wireshark with specific properties defined for each. The target syntax for each icon is listed below Figure 365.

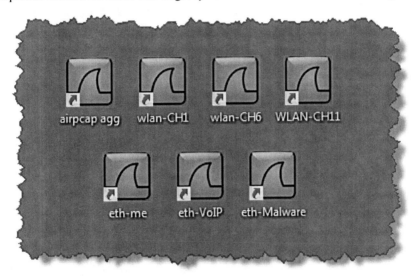

Figure 365. You can create shortcuts to launch customized Wireshark configurations

Shortcut Name and Target Syntax

airpcap agg (WLAN Profile)
`"C:\Program Files (x86)\Wireshark\wireshark.exe" -k -C "WLAN" -i`
`"\\.\airpcap_any"`

wlan-CH1 (uses first AirPcap adapter connected)
`"C:\Program Files (x86)\Wireshark\wireshark.exe" -k -C "WLAN" -i`
`"\\.\airpcap00"`

wlan-CH6 (uses second AirPcap adapter connected)
`"C:\Program Files (x86)\Wireshark\wireshark.exe" -k -C "WLAN" -i`
`"\\.\airpcap01"`

wlan-CH11 (uses third AirPcap adapter connected)
`"C:\Program Files (x86)\Wireshark\wireshark.exe" -k -C "WLAN" -i`
`"\\.\airpcap02"`

Shortcut Name and Target Syntax

eth-me (traffic to and from local Ethernet NIC)
```
"C:\Program Files (x86)\Wireshark\wireshark.exe" -k -R
eth.addr==00:21:97:40:74:d2 -i " \Device\NPF_{C4226BEC-969C-4E62-
A4A3-A0427B7AE12D}"
```

eth-VoIP (VoIP Profile)
```
"C:\Program Files (x86)\Wireshark\wireshark.exe" -k -C "VoIP" -i "
\Device\NPF_{C4226BEC-969C-4E62-A4A3-A0427B7AE12D}"
```

eth-Malware (Malware Profile)
```
"C:\Program Files (x86)\Wireshark\wireshark.exe" -k -C "Malicious"
-i " \Device\NPF_{C4226BEC-969C-4E62-A4A3-A0427B7AE12D}"
```

You can obtain the interface information from the Capture Options window as shown in Figure 366. Use the text and characters that follow the colon.

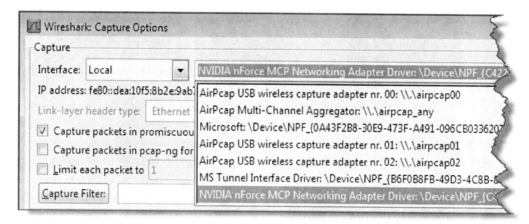

Figure 366. The Capture Options window provides device information

The following table includes numerous examples of command strings to launch Wireshark with specific settings.

Command Strings and Descriptions

`wireshark -k -S -l`

Launch Wireshark and start capturing immediately. Update the list of packets in real time and use automatic scrolling.

`wireshark -k -i 7`

Launch Wireshark and start capturing immediately on the seventh interface.

`wireshark -r noarp.pcap`

Launch Wireshark and open the trace file called *noarp.pcap*.

`wireshark -k -i 7 -c 1000`

Command Strings and Descriptions

Launch Wireshark and start capturing immediately on the seventh interface. Capture 1,000 packets and then stop capturing.

```
wireshark -k -i 7 -a duration:200
```

Launch Wireshark and start capturing immediately on the seventh interface. Capture for 200 seconds then automatically stop capturing.

```
wireshark -k -i 7 -b duration:7 -b files:2 -a files:4
-w capset.pcap
```

Launch Wireshark and start capturing immediately on the seventh interface. Capture using a ring buffer to save only the last two 7-second files of four files. Name each file *capset_[num]_[date/timestamp].pcap.*

```
wireshark -k -i 7 -n -f "ether host 00:21:97:40:74:d2"
```

Launch Wireshark and immediately start capturing traffic to and from MAC address 00:21:97:40:74:d2 on the seventh interface.

Capture Traffic with Tshark

Tshark can be used to capture live traffic or display a saved trace file. Packets can be displayed to the standard output (screen) or saved to a trace file.

Tshark Syntax

Usage: `tshark [options] ...`

Function/Parameter	Description
Capture interface	
`-i <interface>`	name or ID of interface (default: first non-loopback)
`-f <capture filter>`	packet filter in libpcap filter syntax
`-s <snaplen>`	packet snapshot length (default: 65535)
`-p`	don't capture in promiscuous mode
`-B <buffer size>`	size of kernel buffer (default: 1MB)
`-y <link type>`	link layer type (default: first appropriate)
`-D`	print list of interfaces and exit
`-L`	print list of link-layer types of interfaces and exit
Capture stop conditions	
`-c <packet count>`	stop after n packets (default: infinite)
`-a <autostop cond.> ...`	`duration:NUM` - stop after NUM seconds
	`filesize:NUM` - stop this file after NUM KB
	`files:NUM` - stop after NUM files
Capture output	
`-b <ringbuffer opt.> ...`	`duration:NUM` - switch to next file after NUM seconds
	`filesize:NUM` - switch to next file after NUM KB
	`files:NUM` - ringbuffer: replace after NUM files
Input file	
`-r <infile>`	set the filename to read from (read an existing trace file)
Processing	
`-R <read filter>`	packet filter in Wireshark display filter syntax
`-n`	disable all name resolutions (default: all enabled)

Function/Parameter	Description
`-N <name resolve flags>`	\<name resolve flags\> enable specific name resolution(s): "mntC"
	m to enable MAC address resolution
	n to enable network address resolution
	t to enable transport-layer port number resolution
	C to enable concurrent (asynchronous) DNS lookups
`-d <layer_type>== <selector>, <decode_as_ protocol> ...`	"Decode As"; example: tcp.port==8888,http
Output	
`-w <outfile|->`	set the output filename (or '-' for standard output, such as the screen)
`-C <config profile>`	start with specified configuration profile
`-F <output file type>`	set the output file type, default is libpcap an empty "−F" option will list the file types
`-v`	add output of packet tree (Packet Details)
`-S`	display packets even when writing to a file
`-x`	add output of hex and ASCII dump (Packet Bytes)

Function/Parameter	Description
`-T pdml|ps|psml|` ` text|fields`	format of text output (default: text)
	`pdml` Packet Details Markup Language, an XML-based format for the details of a decoded packet. This information is equivalent to the packet details printed with the **-V** flag.
	`psml` Packet Summary Markup Language, an XML-based format for the summary information of a decoded packet. This information is equivalent to the information shown in the one-line summary printed by default.
	`ps` PostScript for a human-readable one-line summary of each of the packets, or a multi-line view of the details of each of the packets, depending on whether the **-V** flag was specified.
	`text` Text of a human-readable one-line summary of each of the packets, or a multi-line view of the details of each of the packets, depending on whether the **-V** flag was specified. This is the default.
	`fields` The values of fields specified with the **-e** option, in a form specified by the **-E** option.
`-e <field>`	field to print if -Tfields selected (e.g. tcp.port); this option can be repeated to print multiple fields
`-E <fieldsoption>=` ` <value>`	set options for output when -Tfields selected as listed below
	`header=y|n` switch headers on and off
	`separator=/t|/s|<char>` select tab, space, printable character as separator
	`quote=d|s|n` select double, single, no quotes for values

Function/Parameter	Description
`-t ad|a|r|d|dd|e`	output format of time stamps. The default format is relative.
	ad absolute with date: The absolute date and time is the actual time and date the packet was captured
	a absolute: The absolute time is the actual time the packet was captured, with no date displayed
	r relative: The relative time is the time elapsed between the first packet and the current packet
	d delta: The delta time is the time since the previous packet was captured
	dd delta_displayed: The delta_displayed time is the time since the previous displayed packet was captured
	e epoch: The time in seconds since epoch (Jan 1, 1970 00:00:00)
`-l`	flush standard output after each packet
`-q`	be more quiet on output (e.g. when using statistics)
`-X <key>:<value>`	extension options, see the man page for details
`-z <statistics>`	various statistics, See View Tshark Statistics next.
Miscellaneous	
`-h`	Display help information and exits
`-v`	display version info and exit
`-o <name>:<value> ...`	override preference setting
`-K <keytab>`	keytab to use with Kerberos decryption

View Tshark Statistics

Tshark can be used to quickly gather statistics on live traffic or trace files. Filters can be applied to the packets to limit the statistics to specific packet types—these filters do not filter packets for capture.

Use the −q option if you only want the statistics and do not want to see the packets while running Tshark. For example, in Figure 367 we have run Tshark using the options −qz io,phs to display the protocol hierarchy statistics of traffic seen by Tshark, but not displayed on the screen. We have not captured any traffic during the process. Use **Ctrl+C** to stop Tshark.

```
C:\Users\Laura>tshark -qz io,phs
Capturing on NVIDIA nForce MCP Networking Adapter Driver
638 packets captured

=================================================================
Protocol Hierarchy Statistics
Filter: frame

frame                                          frames:638 bytes:98839
  eth                                          frames:638 bytes:98839
    ip                                         frames:307 bytes:77689
      tcp                                      frames:125 bytes:9756
        http                                   frames:10 bytes:2912
          data-text-lines                      frames:6 bytes:1512
        data                                   frames:4 bytes:256
      udp                                      frames:182 bytes:67933
        data                                   frames:14 bytes:19803
        srvloc                                 frames:82 bytes:22099
        http                                   frames:76 bytes:25174
        nbdgm                                  frames:1 bytes:253
          smb                                  frames:1 bytes:253
            mailslot                           frames:1 bytes:253
              browser                          frames:1 bytes:253
        dns                                    frames:9 bytes:604
    arp                                        frames:323 bytes:20478
    ipv6                                       frames:8 bytes:672
      udp                                      frames:8 bytes:672
        dns                                    frames:8 bytes:672
=================================================================

C:\Users\Laura>_
```

Figure 367. Use `tshark -qz io,phs` *to display the protocol hierarchy statistics only*

The −z option is used with Tshark to view protocol statistics, conversation statistics, IO statistics and more.

View Numerous Statistics with One Tshark Command Line

Most of the −z options can be used multiple times in one command-line string. For example, you can combine your request for Ethernet conversation statistics with IP conversation statistics and TCP conversation statistics in one command as shown in Figure 368.

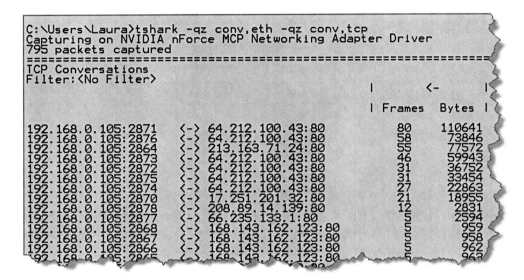

Figure 368. Many -q options can be used multiple times in one command-line string

The following table lists various Tshark command strings for examining statistics. Additional details on Tshark statistics can be found at *www.wireshark.org/docs/man-pages/tshark.html*.

-z \<statistics\> Examples	
tshark -qz io,phs	Display protocol hierarchy statistics as seen in Figure 367
tshark -qz conv,eth -qz conv,ip -qz conv,tcp	Display Ethernet, IP and TCP conversation statistics
tshark -qz conv,eth -qz conv,ip -qz conv,tcp	Display Ethernet, IP and TCP conversation statistics
tshark -qz io,stat,10,ip,udp,tcp	Display IO statistics for IP, UDP and TCP traffic at 10 second intervals
tshark -z io,stat,5,icmp - w allpkts.pcap	Displays IO statistics for ICMP traffic at 5 second intervals—all traffic is saved to a trace file called *allpkts.pcap* (Note the filter used for ICMP is not applied to the traffic captured—to apply this filter to the traffic captured, use the −f parameter)

Tshark Examples

The following table provides numerous examples of command strings to launch Tshark with specific settings.

Command Strings and Descriptions

`tshark -h`

List the Tshark parameters.

`tshark -D`

Display the interface list.

`tshark -b filesize:1000 -b files:2 -w traces-test.pcap`

Capture to a ring buffer with 2 files of 1000 KB each and write packets to trace files beginning with *traces-test.pcap*. Use **Ctrl+C** to stop capture.

`tshark -i 3 -a duration:20 -w shorttrace.pcap`

Capture for 20 seconds on the third interface and save to a trace file called *shorttrace.pcap*.

`tshark -c 100 -w 100pts.pcap -S`

Capture 100 packets and save them to a trace file called *100pkts.pcap*. Display the packets while creating the trace file.

`tshark -R "!arp && !bootp" -n -t dd`

Capture packets without using name resolution. Show the time in delta display format. Do not display ARP or BOOTP/DHCP packets.

`tshark -qz io,stat,5,ip.addr==255.255.255.255 -w bcasts.pcap`

Capture and display IO statistics in five second intervals for packets containing IP address 255.255.255.255 while writing the packets to a file called *bcasts.pcap*.

`tshark -r general.pcap -q -z conv,tcp`

Open a trace file and display TCP conversation statistics.

`tshark -r sip.pcap -R "sip.Call-ID contains "12013223"" -w sipcalls.pcap`

Open a trace file and apply a display filter for SIP packets that contain the Call ID value 12013223 and display just these packets.

`tshark -r test.pcap -R "ip.addr==192.168.0.1 && tcp.port==2058 && ip.addr==192.168.0.2 && tcp.port==80"`

Open *test.pcap*, apply a filter for a single conversation as listed in the command string and display the results.

`tshark -r gen1.pcap http.request -T fields -e http.host -e http.request.uri -c 100`

Open *gen1.pcap* and display the `http.host` and `http.request.uri` fields of `http.requests` for a maximum of 100 packets.

List Trace File Details with Capinfos
Capinfos.exe prints information about trace files.

Capinfos Syntax
Usage: `capinfos [options] <infile> ...`

Function/Parameter	Description
General	
`-t`	display the capture file type
`-E`	display the capture file encapsulation
`-H`	display the SHA1, RMD160, and MD5 hashes of the file
Size	
`-c`	display the number of packets
`-s`	display the size of the file (in bytes)
`-d`	display the total length of all packets (in bytes)
Time	
`-u`	display the capture duration (in seconds)
`-a`	display the capture start time
`-e`	display the capture end time
`-S`	display the capture start and end time as raw seconds[112]
Statistic	
`-y`	display average data rate (in bytes/sec)
`-i`	display average data rate (in bits/sec)
`-z`	display average packet size (in bytes)
`-x`	display average packet rate (in packets/sec)
Output	
`-L`	generate long report (default)
`-T`	generate table report
`-T`	generate table report
Table Report Options	
`-R`	generate header record (default)
`-r`	do not generate header record
`-B`	separate information with TAB character (default)

---

[112] This is a new feature added in the Wireshark v1.3 Development Release and Wireshark v1.4 Stable Release. For an example of when you might want to use the −S parameter to time-shift trace files, refer to *Compare Traffic Trends in IO Graphs* on page 433.

Function/Parameter	Description
-m	separate information with comma (,) character
-b	separate information with SPACE character
-N	do not quote information (default)
-q	quote information with single quotes (')
-Q	quote information with double quotes (")
Miscellaneous	
-h	Display help information and exits
-C	cancel processing if file open fails (default is to continue)
-A	generate all information (default)

As shown in Figure 369, you can string along multiple options on a single command-line.

```
C:\Users\Laura>capinfos gen1.pcap -t -E -c -s -d -u -a -e
File name:              gen1.pcap
File type:             Wireshark/tcpdump/... - libpcap
File encapsulation:    Ethernet
Number of packets:     18
File size:             5160 bytes
Data size:             4848 bytes
Capture duration:      2 seconds
Start time:            Tue Nov 24 17:09:05 2009
End time:              Tue Nov 24 17:09:07 2009

C:\Users\Laura>
```

Figure 369. Capinfos displays basic information about trace files

Capinfos Examples
The following table provides numerous examples of command strings to examine the contents of trace files.

Command Strings and Descriptions
`capinfos -h`
Display the Capinfos parameter information.
`capinfos -c -s -d 100pkts.pcap`
Display the number of packets, size of the file (in bytes) and total length of all packets in *100pkts.pcap*.
`capinfos -u -a -e 100pkts.pcap`
Launch Capinfos and display the capture duration as well as the start and end time of *100pkts.pcap*.
`capinfos -y -i -z -x 100pkts.pcap`
Launch Capinfos and display the average data rate in bytes and bits as well as the average packet size in bytes and average packet rate in packets/second for *100pkts.pcap*.

Command Strings and Descriptions

`capinfos -aeS before.pcap after.pcap`

Print the start and end times of two trace files, *before.pcap* and *after.pcap*, in raw seconds. This information can be used to time-shift *after.pcap* so its start time is closer to *before.pcap*'s end time and can be depicted closer together for comparison on an IO graph. After you run this command on the files, you must use `editcap -t <seconds>` on *after.pcap* before merging the trace files.

Edit Trace Files with Editcap

Use Editcap to split a trace file, alter the trace file timestamp, remove duplicates and perform other trace file editing tasks.

Editcap Syntax

Usage: `editcap [options] ... <infile> <outfile>`
`[ <packet#>[-<packet#>] ... ]`

You must specify both <infile> and <outfile>. A single packet or a range of packets can be defined.

Figure 370 depicts the process of splitting a single file into a file set consisting of a maximum of 2000 packets each. The file names include a file number and a date/timestamp so they can be linked as a file set. File sets can be accessed using **File | File Set** in Wireshark.

```
C:\Users\Laura>editcap -c 2000 gen2.pcap gen2split.pcap

C:\Users\Laura>dir gen2split*.*
 Volume in drive C is HP
 Volume Serial Number is 9264-B632

 Directory of C:\Users\Laura

11/24/2009  05:47 PM         1,047,453 gen2split_00000_20091124173252.pcap
11/24/2009  05:47 PM         1,122,811 gen2split_00001_20091124173351.pcap
11/24/2009  05:47 PM           918,333 gen2split_00002_20091124173540.pcap
11/24/2009  05:47 PM           877,626 gen2split_00003_20091124173740.pcap
11/24/2009  05:47 PM         1,170,726 gen2split_00004_20091124174001.pcap
11/24/2009  05:47 PM           980,938 gen2split_00005_20091124174148.pcap
11/24/2009  05:47 PM           985,072 gen2split_00006_20091124174335.pcap
11/24/2009  05:47 PM         1,001,676 gen2split_00007_20091124174524.pcap
11/24/2009  05:47 PM            61,838 gen2split_00008_20091124174725.pcap
               9 File(s)      8,166,473 bytes
               0 Dir(s)  304,448,176,128 bytes free

C:\Users\Laura>
```

Figure 370. Use Editcap to split a larger trace file into a file set

Use Editcap to Split a Large Trace into File Sets

*Use Editcap to split trace files that are too large to load in Wireshark. Editcap splits the file into a file set. After opening one of the files, use **File | File Sets** to list and move between files in a file set.*

Function/Parameter	Description
Packet selection	
`-r`	Keep the selected packets; default is to delete them
`-A <start time>`	Don't output packets whose timestamp is before the given time (format as YYYY-MM-DD hh:mm:ss).
`-B <stop time>`	Don't output packets whose timestamp is after the given time (format as YYYY-MM-DD hh:mm:ss).
Duplicate packet removal	

Function/Parameter	Description
`-d`	Remove packet if duplicate (the default window is 5 packets).
`-D <dupe window>`	Remove packet if duplicate; configurable <dup window> Valid <dup window> values are 0 to 1000000. NOTE: A <dup window> of 0 with -v (verbose option) is useful to print MD5 hashes.
`-w <dup time window>`	Remove packet if duplicate packet is found EQUAL TO OR LESS THAN <dup time window> prior to current packet. A <dup time window> is specified in relative seconds (e.g. 0.000001). NOTE: The use of the 'Duplicate packet removal' options with other editcap options except -v may not always work as expected. Specifically the -r and -t options will very likely NOT have the desired effect if combined with the -d, -D or -w.
Packet manipulation	
`-s <snaplen>`	Truncate each packet to max. <snaplen> bytes of data.
`-C <choplen>`	Chop each packet at the end by <choplen> bytes.
`-t <time adjustment>`	Adjust the timestamp of each packet; <time adjustment> is in relative seconds (e.g. -0.5).
`-E <error probability>`	Set the probability (between 0.0 and 1.0 incl.) that a particular packet byte will be randomly changed.
Output File(s)	
`-c <packets per file>`	Split the packet output to different files based on uniform packet counts with a maximum of <packets per file> each.
`-i <seconds per file>`	Split the packet output to different files based on uniform time intervals with a maximum of <seconds per file> each.
`-F <capture type>`	Set the output file type; default is libpcap. An empty "-F" option will list the file types.
`-T <encap type>`	Set the output file encapsulation type; default is the same as the input file. An empty "-T" option will list the encapsulation types.
Miscellaneous	
`-h`	Display help information and exits
`-v`	Verbose output. If -v is used with any of the 'Duplicate Packet Removal' options (-d, -D or -w) then Packet lengths and MD5 hashes are printed to standard-out.

Editcap Examples

The following table provides examples of command strings to edit trace files with Editcap.

Command Strings and Descriptions
`editcap -h`
Launch Editcap and view available options.
`editcap -d dupes.pcap nodupes.pcap`
Examine the *dupes.pcap* trace for duplicate packets within a 5-packet proximity. Remove duplicates and create a new trace file called *nodupes.pcap*.
`editcap -c 2000 dbad.pcap dbadsplit.pcap`
Split *dbad.pcap* into separate trace files starting with "dbadsplit"—each new file should have a maximum of 2,000 packets in it. The file number and date/timestamp will be added to the new file name automatically.
`editcap -t -0.2 oldtime.pcap newtime.pcap`
Make a new version of *oldtime.pcap* called *newtime.pcap* and subtract 0.2 seconds from all timestamps in the *newtime.pcap* trace file.

Merge Trace Files with Mergecap

Use Mergecap to merge two or more capture files into one.

Merge Traces to Compare Them Side by Side in an IO Graph

Merging two or more trace files together is a useful task for comparing their contents in IO Graphs. Consider using Editcap to alter the timestamps in one trace file to graph them in closer proximity in your IO Graphs.

There are three methods available for merging trace files:

- Click and drag two or more trace files onto the Wireshark desktop (trace files will be merged in chronological order based on packet timestamps).

- Select **File | Merge** (trace files are ordered based on most recent trace file merged—in other words, packets from a trace file timestamped 2008 may show up before packets from a trace file timestamped 2007).

- Use Mergcap.

Figure 371 shows the process of combining two trace files, *gen1.pcap* and *gen2.pcap* into a new trace file called *genall.pcap*.

```
C:\Users\Laura>dir gen*.*
 Volume in drive C is HP
 Volume Serial Number is 9264-B632

 Directory of C:\Users\Laura

11/24/2009  05:09 PM                 5,160 gen1.pcap
11/24/2009  05:47 PM             8,166,281 gen2.pcap
               2 File(s)          8,171,441 bytes
               0 Dir(s)     304,449,617,920 bytes free

C:\Users\Laura>mergecap -w genall.pcap gen1.pcap gen2.pcap

C:\Users\Laura>dir gen*.*
 Volume in drive C is HP
 Volume Serial Number is 9264-B632

 Directory of C:\Users\Laura

11/24/2009  05:09 PM                 5,160 gen1.pcap
11/24/2009  05:47 PM             8,166,281 gen2.pcap
11/24/2009  06:10 PM             8,171,417 genall.pcap
               3 File(s)         16,342,858 bytes
               0 Dir(s)     304,441,384,960 bytes free

C:\Users\Laura>_
```

Figure 371. Use Mergecap to combine trace files

Mergecap Syntax

Usage: `mergecap [options] -w <outfile>|- <infile> ...`

Function/Parameter	Description
Output	
`-a`	Concatenate rather than merge files. The default is to merge based on packet timestamps.
`-s <snaplen>`	Truncate packets to <snaplen> bytes of data
`-w <outfile>|-`	Set the output filename to <outfile> or '-' for standard output, such as the screen.
`-F <capture type>`	Set the output file type; default is libpcap. An empty "-F" option will list the file types.
`-T <encap type>`	Set the output file encapsulation type; default is the same as the first input file. An empty "-T" option will list the encapsulation types.
Miscellaneous	
`-h`	Display help information and exits
`-v`	Verbose output.

Mergecap Examples

The following table includes numerous examples of command strings to launch Wireshark with specific settings.

Command Strings and Descriptions
`mergecap -h`
View the Mergecap options.
`mergecap -w allinone.pcap file1.pcap file2.pcap`
Merge *file1.pcap* and *file2.pcap* into *allinone.pcap*—merge the files based on the file timestamps
`mergecap -a -w neworder.pcap download-good.pcap downloadbad.pcap`
Merge *download-good.pcap* and *download-bad.pcap* in the order listed—regardless of the file timestamps—into a new file called *neworder.pcap*.

Convert Text with Text2pcap

Text2pcap generates a trace file from an ASCII hex dump of packets. Figure 372 shows the plaintext version of traffic. Examination of the hex values indicates that these packets are both likely to be TCP packets (based on the values 0x0800 at offset 0x0c and 0x45 at offset 0x0e).

```
0000  ff ff ff ff ff ff 00 50 da ca 0f 33 08 00 45 00   .......P...3..E.
0010  01 48 00 00 00 00 80 11 39 a6 00 00 00 00 ff ff   .H......9.......
0020  ff ff 00 44 00 43 01 34 e6 fe 01 01 06 00 07 02   ...D.C.4........
0030  85 2a 00 00 00 00 00 00 00 00 00 00 00 00 00 00   .*..............
0040  00 00 00 00 00 00 00 50 da ca 0f 33 00 00 00 00   .......P...3....
0050  00 00 00 00 00 00 00 00 00 00 00 00 00 00 00 00   ................
0060  00 00 00 00 00 00 00 00 00 00 00 00 00 00 00 00   ................
0070  00 00 00 00 00 00 00 00 00 00 00 00 00 00 00 00   ................
0080  00 00 00 00 00 00 00 00 00 00 00 00 00 00 00 00   ................
0090  00 00 00 00 00 00 00 00 00 00 00 00 00 00 00 00   ................
00a0  00 00 00 00 00 00 00 00 00 00 00 00 00 00 00 00   ................
00b0  00 00 00 00 00 00 00 00 00 00 00 00 00 00 00 00   ................
00c0  00 00 00 00 00 00 00 00 00 00 00 00 00 00 00 00   ................
00d0  00 00 00 00 00 00 00 00 00 00 00 00 00 00 00 00   ................
00e0  00 00 00 00 00 00 00 00 00 00 00 00 00 00 00 00   ................
00f0  00 00 00 00 00 00 00 00 00 00 00 00 00 00 00 00   ................
0100  00 00 00 00 00 00 00 00 00 00 00 00 00 00 00 00   ................
0110  00 00 00 00 00 00 63 82 53 63 35 01 03 3d 07 01   ......c.Sc5..=..
0120  00 50 da ca 0f 33 32 04 0a 40 00 a4 0c 08 43 50   .P...32..@....CP
0130  51 31 32 30 38 00 37 07 01 0f 03 2c 2e 2f 06 ff   Q1208.7....,./..
0140  00 00 00 00 00 00 00 00 00 00 00 00 00 00 00 00   ................
0150  00 00 00 00 00 00                                 ......

0000  00 50 da ca 0f 33 00 80 3e 4b 3e ce 08 00 45 00   .P...3..>K>...E.
0010  01 5e c8 59 00 00 40 11 9c 11 0a 40 00 01 0a 40   .^.Y..@....@...@
0020  00 a4 00 43 00 44 01 4a 28 4c 02 01 06 01 07 02   ...C.D.J(L......
0030  85 2a 00 00 00 00 00 00 00 00 0a 40 00 a4 00 00   .*.........@....
0040  00 00 0a 40 00 01 00 50 da ca 0f 33 00 00 00 00   ...@...P...3....
0050  00 00 00 00 00 00 00 00 00 00 00 00 00 00 00 00   ................
0060  00 00 00 00 00 00 00 00 00 00 00 00 00 00 00 00   ................
0070  00 00 00 00 00 00 00 00 00 00 00 00 00 00 00 00   ................
0080  00 00 00 00 00 00 00 00 00 00 00 00 00 00 00 00   ................
0090  00 00 00 00 00 00 00 00 00 00 00 00 00 00 00 00   ................
00a0  00 00 00 00 00 00 00 00 00 00 00 00 00 00 00 00   ................
00b0  00 00 00 00 00 00 00 00 00 00 00 00 00 00 00 00   ................
00c0  00 00 00 00 00 00 00 00 00 00 00 00 00 00 00 00   ................
00d0  00 00 00 00 00 00 00 00 00 00 00 00 00 00 00 00   ................
00e0  00 00 00 00 00 00 00 00 00 00 00 00 00 00 00 00   ................
```

Figure 372. The plaintext version of captured traffic

Figure 373 shows the simple process to convert this text file to a pcap trace file. If the original text contains date/timestamps or does not include certain headers (Ethernet, IP, UDP or TCP for example), use the Text2pcap options to prepend dummy headers on the data to create properly formatted trace files.

```
C:\Users\Laura>text2pcap plain.txt plain.pcap
Input from: plain.txt
Output to: plain.pcap
Wrote packet of 342 bytes at 0
Wrote packet of 364 bytes at 342
Wrote packet of 60 bytes at 706
Wrote packet of 60 bytes at 766
Wrote packet of 60 bytes at 826
Wrote packet of 60 bytes at 886
Wrote packet of 60 bytes at 946
Read 7 potential packets, wrote 7 packets

C:\Users\Laura>_
```

Figure 373. Use Text2pcap to convert traffic from text format to pcap format

Text2pcap Syntax

Usage: `text2pcap [options] <infile> <outfile>`

Function/Parameter	Description
Input	
`-o hex|oct|dec`	Parse offsets as (h)ex, (o)ctal or (d)ecimal; default is hex.
`-t <timefmt>`	Treat the text before the packet as a date/time code; the specified argument is a format string of the sort supported by a string representation of time. Example: The time "10:15:14.5476" has the format code "%H:%M:%S." Note: Date/time fields from the current date/time are used as the default for unspecified fields.
Output	
`-l <typenum>`	Link layer type number; default is 1 (Ethernet). See the file *bpf.h* for list of numbers. Use this option if your dump is a complete hex dump of an encapsulated packet and you wish to specify the exact type of encapsulation. Rarely do people send me hex dumps of trace files, but if you need to work with one someday, this is the tool to use.
`-m <max-packet>`	Max packet length in output; default is 64000
Prepend dummy header	If someone gave you a file that contains packets without headers, you need to prepend dummy headers on the packets before you can open the resulting trace file in Wireshark.
`-e <l3pid>`	Prepend dummy Ethernet II header with specified L3PID (in HEX). Example: -e 0x806 to specify an ARP packet.
`-i <proto>`	Prepend dummy IP header with specified IP protocol (in DECIMAL). Automatically prepends Ethernet header as well.

Function/Parameter	Description
`-u <srcp>,<destp>`	Prepend dummy UDP header with specified destination and source ports (in decimal). Automatically prepends Ethernet & IP headers as well. Example: -u 1000 69 to make the packets look like TFTP/UDP packets.
`-T <srcp>,<destp>`	Prepend dummy TCP header with specified destination and source ports (in decimal). Automatically prepends Ethernet & IP headers as well. Example: -T 50,60
`-s <srcp>,<dstp>,` `<tag>`	Prepend dummy SCTP header with specified destination/source ports and verification tag (in decimal). Automatically prepends Ethernet & IP headers as well. Example: -s 30,40,34
`-S <srcp>,<dstp>,` `<ppi>`	Prepend dummy SCTP header with specified dest/source ports and verification tag 0. Automatically prepends a dummy SCTP data chunk header with payload protocol identifier ppi. Example: -S 30,40,34
Miscellaneous	
`-h`	Display help information and exits.
`-d`	Show detailed debug of parser states.
`-q`	Generate no output at all (automatically turns off -d).

Text2pcap Examples

The following table includes numerous examples of command strings to use Text2pcap to convert a text file to a pcap trace file.

Command Strings and Descriptions
`text2pcap -h`
Displays the Text2pcap options.
`text2pcap plainfile.txt newtrace.pcap`
Basic conversion from text to pcap format.
`text2pcap -e 0x0800 iptext.txt iptrace.txt`
Convert a text file to a pcap trace file by prepending a dummy Ethernet header—the `-e 0x0800` indicate the packets in iptext.txt are IP packets.

Capture Traffic with Dumpcap

Dumpcap is used to capture network packets and save them into a libpcap format file. Use Ctrl-C to stop capturing at any time. Dumpcap is used as the capture engine for Tshark. Dumpcap uses fewer resources than Tshark—an advantage in some situations.

Dumpcap Syntax

Usage: `dumpcap [options] ...`

Function/Parameter	Description
Capture interface	
`-i <interface>`	Name or index of interface (default: first non-loopback)
`-f <capture filter>`	Packet filter in libpcap filter syntax
`-s <snaplen>`	Packet snapshot length (default: 65535)
`-p`	Don't capture in promiscuous mode
`-B <buffer size>`	Size of kernel buffer (default: 1MB)
`-y <link type>`	Link layer type (default: first appropriate)
`-D`	Print list of interfaces and exit
`-L`	Print list of link layer types of interfaces and exit
`-S`	Print statistics for each interface once every second
`-M`	For -D, -L, and -S produce machine-readable output
rpcapd options	
`-r`	don't ignore own rpcap traffic in capture
`-u`	use UDP for rpcap data transfer
`-A <user>:<password>`	use rpcap password authentication
`-m`	use packet sampling
Stop conditions	
`-c <packet count>`	Stop after n packets (default: infinite)
`-a <autostop cond.> ...`	`duration:NUM` - stop after NUM seconds
	`filesize:NUM` - stop this file after NUM KB
	`files:NUM` - stop after NUM files
Output (files)	
`-w <filename>`	Name of file to save (default: tempfile)
`-b <ringbuffer opt.> ...`	`duration:NUM` - switch to next file after NUM seconds
	`filesize:NUM` - switch to next file after NUM KB
	`files:NUM` - ringbuffer: replace after NUM files
`-n`	Use pcapng format instead of pcap format

Function/Parameter	Description
Miscellaneous	
`-v`	Print version information and exit
`-h`	Display the help information and exit

Dumpcap Examples

The following table includes numerous examples of command strings to launch Wireshark with specific settings.

Command Strings and Descriptions
`dumpcap -h`
Display Dumpcap options.
`dumpcap -i 7 -b files:25 -b filesize:25000 -w capset.pcap`
Capture and save the most recent 25 files (ring buffer) with a maximum file size of 25,000 KB. Each file in the set should begin with "capset".
`dumpcap -a duration:3000 -w 5mins.pcap`
Captures traffic for 3000 seconds and saves it in a file called *5mins.pcap*.

Understand Rawshark

Rawshark expects raw libpcap packet headers, followed by packet data.

Unlike Tshark, Rawshark makes no assumptions about the encapsulation or input format. You must use the **-d <encap:dlt>|<proto:protoname>** and **-r <infile>** flags with Rawshark. It is recommended that you use the -F <field> option for useful output.

Most likely, you will use Tshark and dumpcap for command-line packet capture. For libpcap files, you must skip past the file header (the first 24 bytes), then start feeding the file data to Rawshark. For other kinds of data you must create a packet header for every packet that you send to Rawshark.

Rawshark Syntax

Usage: `rawshark [options] ...`

Function/Parameter	Description
Input file	
-r <infile>	Set the pipe or file name to read from
Processing	
-R <read filter>	Packet filter in Wireshark display filter syntax
-F <field>	Field to display
-s	Skip PCAP header on input
-n	Disable all name resolution (default: all enabled)
-N <name resolve flags>	<name resolve flags> enable specific name resolution(s): "mntC"
	m to enable MAC address resolution
	n to enable network address resolution
	t to enable transport-layer port number resolution
	C to enable concurrent (asynchronous) DNS lookups
-d <encap:dlt>|<proto:protoname>	Packet encapsulation or protocol
Output	
-S	Format string for fields (%D - name, %S - stringval, %N numval)
-t ad|a|r|d|dd|e	Output format of time stamps (default: r: rel. to first)
-l	Flush output after each packet

Function/Parameter	Description
Miscellaneous	
`-h`	Display help information and exits
`-v`	Display version info and exit
`-o <name>:<value> ...`	Override preference setting

Case Study:
Getting GETS and a Suspect

Submitted by: Anonymous (because "otherwise we'd look dumb")

We ran Wireshark for a week to watch all the traffic to and from an employee's PC. There were concerns that the employee was somehow connected to a competitor's site that had some of our corporate price sheets—we were sure they were illegally-obtained. We ended up with a series of trace files that were 100MB in size—way too big to open with Wireshark.

After researching Tshark a bit more, we found we could easily pull out any packets that referenced the file name in an HTTP GET request or even anywhere in the packet!

We used the following Tshark command:

```
tshark -r capcorp1.pcap -R "http.request.method==GET &&
frame contains "pricex""
```

The file name we were interested in contained the string `pricex`. That allowed us to look specifically at the HTTP GET requests. Alternately, we just ran the portion looking for `pricex`.

Soon we realized that we needed to save the results to a file so we added `-w project.pcap` to save those packets to a separate file. (We learned that the current version of Wireshark can't use the `-R` parameter as a capture filter on live traffic—so we captured the traffic to .pcap files and then ran Tshark against them. I think this is covered in Bug 2234—"filtering Tshark captures with display filters -R no longer works"). I hope this gets fixed.

After just three days—bingo! We thought we'd see our suspect looking at the site where the file was located, but we also saw them upload a newer copy that we released just days before.

We had clear evidence that the employee was sending all our pricing data to our competitor.

Summary

Wireshark includes a number of command-line tools that offer added functionality for capturing, manipulating and analyzing network traffic. In addition, even though wireshark.exe launches the GUI version of Wireshark, it can be set to launch with specific parameters in place for a specific interface, filter or other loading sequence.

Tshark provides a command-line tool for capturing traffic and even loading a trace file with specific parameters in place. The resource overhead is much lower than the GUI version of Wireshark, but higher than Dumpcap, which is another command-line capture tool. Rawshark is the third, but rarely used, command-line capture tool included with Wireshark. Capinfos can give you a quick view of trace file details such as the number of packets in a trace, the average data rate and average packet size. Mergecap can be used to merge multiple trace files. Merging is also available through **File | Merge**, but this tool can be used to merge trace files in an order other than one dictated by the timestamps in the files. Editcap is a great tool for altering trace file timestamps, splitting up a large trace file into file sets, remove duplicate packets or even changing the trace file type. Text2pcap can be used to convert a text file to a trace file. This allows you to manipulate the trace file using the other tools or load the trace in Wireshark.

Practice What You've Learned

Download the trace files available in the Download section of the book website, *www.wiresharkbook.com*. Practice your skills with the command-line tools using the following trace files.

ftp-clientside.pcap and *ftp-serverside.pcap*	These trace files depict an FTP file transfer—one trace file was taken at the client side of the transfer, another was taken at the server side. Examine the timestamp in these two trace files.
	If traces taken at two points in the network have been taken on hosts that are not time synchronized, you may need to alter the timestamp on one file.
	What is the timestamp of the first packet in each trace file? (Use editcap if you need to alter the timestamp of one trace file.)
	Use mergecap to combine the two trace files. Let Wireshark merge the files based on the timestamp information.
	When you examine the combined trace file, you will see what appear to be duplicates of the packets as they were captured at both the client location and the server location.
	They aren't duplicates, however. Examine the MAC header to see the differences. You could even add a hardware address column to the Packet List pane to make this situation more evident.

tcp-pktloss94040.pcap   This trace depicts a browsing session to *www.cnn.com*—with massive packet loss. Consider building an IO Graph to compare the various TCP problems. This is a healthy-sized file—over 94,000 packets to work with. If it takes too long to load, consider using Editcap to split the file into smaller pieces.

Review Questions

Q33.1   **What is the primary purpose of Tshark?**

Q33.2   **Which command line tool can be used to change the packet timestamps on a trace file?**

Q33.3   **Which command line tool can be used to display the capture file type, the number of packets and the capture duration of a trace file?**

Q33.4   **You are working on a system that is low on memory and a network that is saturated with packets. Would you rather use tcpdump or Tshark to capture traffic?**

Answers to Review Questions

Q33.1 **What is the primary purpose of Tshark?**

A33.1 Tshark's primary purpose is to offer command line packet capture. Tshark is preferred over the GUI capture because it requires fewer resources than the GUI Wireshark.exe.

Q33.2 **Which command line tool can be used to change the packet timestamps on a trace file?**

A33.2 Editcap can be used to change packet timestamps using the −t parameter.

Q33.3 **Which command line tool can be used to display the capture file type, the number of packets and the capture duration of a trace file?**

A33.3 Capinfos can be used to display numerous statistics about a trace file, but not information about protocols and applications contained in the trace file. For information about the protocols and applications in a trace file, use Tshark with the −z parameter.

Q33.4 **You are working on a system that is low on memory and a network that is saturated with packets. Would you rather use tcpdump or Tshark to capture traffic?**

A33.4 Between tcpdump and Tshark, tcpdump uses fewer system resources but does not offer as many capture configuration options.

Appendix A: Resources on the Book Website

 Visit *www.wiresharkbook.com* to download the items listed in this Appendix.

- Practice Trace Files (.pcap Files)
- Chanalyzer/Wi-Spy Recordings (.wsr Files)
- MaxMind GeoIP Database Files (.dat Files)
- PhoneFactor SSL/TLS Vulnerabilities Documents and Trace Files Created by Steve Dispensa and Ray Marsh
- Wireshark Customized Profiles Created for Use on WLAN, VoIP, Malicious Traffic, etc.

Chanalyzer/Wi-Spy Recordings (.wsr Files)

The Download section of the book website (*www.wiresharkbook.com*) contains a number of Wi-Spy Recordings that you can play back with Metageek's Chanalyzer software to examine interference in a WLAN environment.

Download the latest version of Chanalyzer from *www.metageek.net*.

.wsr Recording Name	Description
80211-microwave-xbox.wsr	In this 57-minute recording, check out the interference from a microwave across the entire 802.11b/g channel range. The most powerful signals (up to -7dBm) hit the worst around Channel 12. About 30 minutes into the recording, we turned on an Xbox—you can barely make out the relatively weak signals across the entire frequency range.
videoxmitter.wsr	Ouch! This is pure agony on the network. In this 5-minute trace, watch the signal skip from around 2430 to 2475 MHz. The video transmitter seemed to lock in on the higher frequency (farther away from the 802.11b/g network down on Channel 1. Chanalyzer has a signature for a Philips Video Transmitter— that's not the brand we used, but the signature is nearly identical.
uniden-hell.wsr	In this 2-minute recording a Uniden 2.4GHz phone (US $10 at Target stores) killed WLAN performance around Channel 1. The phone stripes across the frequencies, but 'lives' just below Channel 1. Whenever a call is made/received, our WLAN retransmission rates increase.
flight-lax-sjc-051509.wsr	This flight didn't offer WiFi services—it's one of those puddle-jumper plans that I hate. Notice the constant, low signal strength RF energy in the background? It's kinda interesting.
mo_moving-away_notes.wsr	In this short recording, we are watching the interference from a microwave oven as it moves away from the Wi-Spy adapter. We began popping popcorn at 1 minute into the trace—everything before that is our baseline. Select the **Notes** tab to read how far away the microwave was through this lab experiment.

.wsr Recording Name	Description
samsclub-appleton1109.wsr 	In this 25-minute recording you'll see some strange and constant signals—they may be from the RFID system set up throughout the store. I didn't ask. It's true—this is the RF signal information I recorded while walking around a Sam's Club in Appleton, Wisconsin. With my laptop perched on my cart and some 'distraction' items loaded in my cart—200 pairs of socks, a plastic plant and a 50-count toothbrush pack—I strolled from the front of the store around the outer aisles to the back (bakery section—time to pick up some cookies) and then back up to the front past the mattresses and electronics gear. How did I get outta the store without calling too much attention to myself? I said I was shopping for a party and my shopping list was on my laptop — hence the need to have the laptop open the whole time. They didn't seem to notice what a weird party it would be with socks and toothbrushes—oh well. On the way out the 'greeter' eyed my laptop (I didn't buy anything because I didn't have a Sam's Club card.)—I explained it was mine—they didn't have any laptops that looked better. [Head down… keep walking…]
alarm-microwave.wsr 	We were standing right below one of those Exit signs that are lit up—you know the ones—bright red sign that you probably won't be able to even see through the smoke when fire breaks out. About 4 minutes into the trace, life got even worse as someone started up the microwave in the kitchen around the corner from the conference room. No wonder these folks complain about the WLAN!

MaxMind GeoIP Database Files (.dat Files)

The Download section of the book website (*www.wiresharkbook.com/download*) contains the three MaxMind GeoIP database files that allow you to map IP addresses to their locations in an OpenStreetMap window. The three database files include ASN information, city information and country information. For the latest copy of these free database files, visit *www.maxmind.com*.

This directory also contains an MP4 training video (*geoip_wireshark.mp4*) showing how to get the latest MaxMind GeoIP database files and configure Wireshark to use GeoIP and locate IP addresses on an OpenStreetMap window.

PhoneFactor SSL/TLS Vulnerabilities Documents/Trace Files

The Download section of the book website (*www.wiresharkbook.com*) contains a zip file with the research document about the TLS renegotiation vulnerability written by Steve Dispensa and Ray Marsh of PhoneFactor, Inc. In addition, the zip file contains protocol diagrams, trace files and certificates and keys.

For more information on how Steve and Ray use Wireshark in their research, check out the Case Study entitled "SSL/TLS Vulnerability Studied" in *Chapter 30: Network Forensics Overview*.

Wireshark Customized Profiles

The Download section of the book website (*www.wiresharkbook.com/download*) contains four Profiles. For information on how to use these profiles, refer to *Chapter 11: Customize Wireshark Profiles*.

- Exploits—MS TCP Windows Issues
- lauras_config
- Nmap Detection
- VoIP
- WLAN

Practice Trace Files

The Download section of the book website (*www.wiresharkbook.com*) contains the trace files listed in this Appendix. Please note the license for use below and on the book website.

You agree to indemnify and hold Protocol Analysis Institute and its subsidiaries, affiliates, officers, agents, employees, partners and licensors harmless from any claim or demand, including reasonable attorneys' fees, made by any third party due to or arising out of your use of the included trace files, your violation of the TOS, or your violation of any rights of another.

NO COMMERCIAL REUSE

You may not reproduce, duplicate, copy, sell, trade, resell or exploit for any commercial purposes, any of the trace files available at *www.wiresharkbook.com*.

Trace File Name	Description
app-aptimize-off.pcap	This trace file is referenced in the case study in *Chapter 8: Interpret Basic Trace File Statistics*. This is the web browsing session without the Aptimize Web Accelerator disenabled.
app-aptimize-on.pcap	This second trace file is also referenced in the case study in *Chapter 8: Interpret Basic Trace File Statistics*. This is the web browsing session without the Aptimize Web Accelerator enabled.
app-aptimize-on-fromcache.pcap	This is what the *sharepoint.microsoft.com* site load time looks like with the Aptimize Web Accelerator enabled and the page served up out of cache. For information on the If-Modified-Since request method, refer to *Chapter 23: Analyze Hypertext Transfer Protocol (HTTP) Traffic.*
app-bit-torrent-background.pcap	Don't you just love that BitTorrent stuff? Well, your network doesn't! This is the background traffic from starting up BitTorrent on a clean system. Build an IO Graph to see the packets/second and bytes/second rate. Refer to *Chapter 8: Interpret Basic Trace File Statistics* for details on the basic IO Graph.
app-iperf-default.pcap	In this iPerf default test, traffic is sent from the client to the server only. Consider adding a `tcp.len` column in the Packet List pane and sort on the source column—you'll see all packets from 192.168.0.99 have a length of 0. Refer to *Chapter 21: Graph IO Rates and TCP Trends* and *Chapter 29: Find the Top Causes of Performance Problems* for details on tracking the tcp.len value.
app-iperf-parallel4-dualtest.pcap	This test runs 8 separate connections in parallel between the iPerf client and server. In the configuration we used the `-P` parameter to indicate that we wanted to run 4 tests in parallel—that created a total of 8 connections—four in each direction. This is a great way of testing the capabilities of multiple connections between two hosts. Refer to *Chapter 21: Graph IO Rates and TCP Trends* and *Chapter 29: Find the Top Causes of Performance Problems* for details on tracking the tcp.len value.

Trace File Name	Description
app-iperf-udp-b1_10_100.pcap	We ran an iPerf test over UDP using the −b parameter to define the bandwidth at 10Mbps and then at 100Mbps. In each instance we could only reach about 50% of the bandwidth level we set. Refer to *Chapter 8: Interpret Basic Trace File Statistics* for details on comparing UDP conversations and creating a basic IO Graph to show the iPerf setting change.
app-iradio.pcap	Radio is music to my ears! With minimal overhead, radio is preferred to video on the network. Refer to *Chapter 8: Interpret Basic Trace File Statistics* for details on creating an IO Graph on this traffic. Compare this IO Graph to the IO Graph for the *app-youtube1.pcap* or *app-youtube2.pcap* trace file.
app-is-pwdxfer.pcap	Invisible Secrets is primarily used for steganography, but it also can do secure password transfer. This trace shows the secure password transfer process. Note the clear text indication that this is an Invisible Secrets 4 communications. Refer to *Chapter 10: Follow Streams and Reassemble Data* for details on figuring out the purpose of traffic that is not dissected by Wireshark.
app-live-chat.pcap	This live chat to a support line creates a nice secure connection. Oh, wait... make that 122 nice secure connections. Whazzup with that? Isn't that overkill? Look at **Statistics	Packet Length** to see how much of the traffic uses little itty bitty stinkin' packets! Refer to *Chapter 8: Interpret Basic Trace File Statistics*.
app-mcafeeeupdateslow.pcap	Is this a problem with the client or the server or the network? The McAfee update took so long—over 60 seconds. Open **Statistics	Summary** to see the average Mbit/second rate. Refer to *Chapter 7: Define Time Values and Interpret Summaries* to examine the methods for troubleshooting time-based problems.
app-messenger-ugly.pcap	Anyone who buys products based on Messenger popups deserves what they get. This popup was refused using an ICMP Destination Unreachable/Port Unreachable response (packet 2). The "message" is in clear text format in both packets because the Windows target system includes the entire original request in the ICMP response (unnecessary since the spec says you only have to include the first 64 bits of the original datagram's data). Refer to *Chapter 18: Analyze Internet Control Message Protocol (ICMP) Traffic* for details on the various ICMP responses.
app-nodissector.pcap	Even though Wireshark doesn't have a dissector for this application, following the TCP stream reveals that this is AIDA32 traffic. If Wireshark doesn't have a dissector for your traffic, examine the payload to look for some evidence to help identify the application or look up the port on *www.iana.org*. Refer to *Chapter 10: Follow Streams and Reassemble Data* for details on figuring out the purpose of traffic that is not dissected by Wireshark.

Trace File Name	Description
app-norton-failed.pcap	Filter on `http` to see what's happening more clearly. This will remove the handshake packets and the ACK responses. Why did this Symantec LiveUpdate process fail? To learn why an `http` filter is different from a `tcp.port==80`, refer to *Chapter 23: Analyze Hypertext Transfer Protocol (HTTP) Traffic*.
app-norton-update.pcap	The client renews its subscription for the Symantec product with minimum HTTP 404 response codes. There appears to be a periodic GET request (in 15 second intervals) (packet 20) (packet 415) (packet 431). Filter on the `http.request.uri` field in one of these packets to find out how often this query goes out. Are all the replies the same? Refer to *Chapter 23: Analyze Hypertext Transfer Protocol (HTTP) Traffic*.
app-norton-update2.pcap	This Symantec update process doesn't seem to work very well. Consider building a filter for `http.response.code == 404` and note the number of "File Not Found" responses. Now compare the difference between applying: (1) `!http.response.code == 404` and (2) `http.response.code !=404`. Good lesson! Refer to *Chapter 9: Create and Apply Display Filters* for more details on using the negative operand.
app-twitter_post_tweet.pcap	This trace shows what a Tweet posting does on the network. You can find a full Twitter analysis report at *www.chappellseminars.com*. For more information on setting up filters for application testing, refer to *Chapter 4: Create and Apply Capture Filters*.
app-webcast-keepalive.pcap	This videocast ended 130 seconds into the trace file. Build an IO Graph to watch the keep alive process as the video concluded and the client kept the connection alive (packet 2562) (packet 2572) by sending a GET request for caption.aspx?filetype=1 every 6 seconds. This occurs all during the video download as well. Refer to *Chapter 23: Analyze Hypertext Transfer Protocol (HTTP) Traffic*.
app-wow-look4wireshark.pcap	This is a World of Warcraft session including a chat. Reassemble the TCP stream and use Find to locate "wireshark" in the stream. Funny… Refer to *Chapter 10: Follow Streams and Reassemble Data*.
app-youtube1.pcap	Time to do some application analysis—how much bandwidth does a YouTube video eat up? Create an IO Graph and set the Y axis to bits/tick. Refer to the application analysis process shown in *Chapter 8: Interpret Basic Trace File Statistics*.
app-youtube2.pcap	Another test of YouTube bandwidth—create an IO Graph and set the Y axis to bits/tick. Again, refer to the application analysis case study in *Chapter 8: Interpret Basic Trace File Statistics*.
app-zonealarm-update.pcap	This is a normal ZoneAlarm update—it's important to know how your personal firewall and virus detection tools perform their updates. Refer to the case study in *Chapter 8: Interpret Basic Trace File Statistics*.

Trace File Name	Description
arp-badpadding.pcap	ARP packets are minimum-sized packets and must be padded to meet the minimum 64-byte length for this Ethernet network. When we look at the padding on these packets, we see something frightening—there's data in the padding! This is a security flaw that surfaced back around 2003. Seems the NIC driver was padding the packets with information from cache. We still see this every once in a while—how long have your systems had the same NIC/driver? Refer to *Chapter 16: Analyze Address Resolution Protocol (ARP) Traffic.*
arp-bootup.pcap	This is a classic client bootup sequence beginning with the DHCP Request/ACK sequence (indicating the client is still within its lease time) and moving on to the gratuitous ARP process before sending out an ARP to the default gateway defined in the DHCP ACK (packet 2). This isn't a fast process however. Users typically accept sluggish boot processes, but not slow login sequences. Refer to *Chapter 22: Analyze Dynamic Host Configuration Protocol (DHCP) Traffic.*
arp-iphonestartup.pcap	Full of attitude and feelings of self-importance, an iPhone ARP storms the network and then uses some pretty unusual ARP packets—note the source of 0.0.0.0 before the gratuitous ARP? Notice the ARPs for 169.255.255.255? These phones perform special steps for the zero-configuration networking setup. Love 'em or hate 'em, ya gotta listen to them. *Chapter 16: Analyze Address Resolution Protocol (ARP) Traffic* covered the typical types of ARP traffic seen on the network.
arp-ping.pcap	This trace shows the startup sequence for using a newly-assigned IP address. What might be the cause for the delay between the Gratuitous ARP and the ARP for 10.1.0.1? Do you see recognizable padding in the ICMP Echo request? Refer to *Chapter 16: Analyze Address Resolution Protocol (ARP) Traffic* and *Chapter 18: Analyze Internet Control Message Protocol (ICMP) Traffic.*
arp-pmode-scan-nstpro.pcap	This trace shows NetScanTools Pro's promiscuous mode scanning process highlighted in *Chapter 30: Network Forensics Overview.* Notice the different source MAC addresses used in this scan process. No response means 192.168.0.22 cannot be identified as being in promiscuous mode. For more information on promiscuous mode scanning, refer to *Chapter 30: Network Forensics Overview.*
arp-poison.pcap	Consider taking out a pen and paper to sketch the communications (pay close attention to the MAC header as well as the advertised MAC address in the ARP packets). Using a combination of ARP and ICMP Echo requests, a system is poisoning and testing the poison process. Can you determine the IP address of the poisoner? Refer to *Chapter 32: Analyze Suspect Traffic* for more information about ARP poisoning.

Trace File Name	Description
arp-recon.pcap	This trace depicts an ARP reconnaissance process. What would explain the non-sequential target IP addresses? Can you determine the subnet mask of the transmitter by the ARP target addresses? Refer to *Chapter 31: Detect Scanning and Discovery Processes.*
arp-standard.pcap	This is a basic ARP request and reply as explained in *Chapter 16: Analyze Address Resolution Protocol (ARP) Traffic.* There should never be a large gap in time between requests and replies as all ARP responses should be from devices on the local network. What is the response time in this standard ARP lookup?
arp-sweep.pcap	This trace shows a class ARP sweep as mentioned in *Chapter 32: Analyze Suspect Traffic.* This ARP sweep isn't just one big nonstop sweep. Build an IO Graph and apply the filter `arp.src.proto_ipv4 == 192.168.0.102` to Graph 2 in *Fbar* format. That will display just the ARP sweep packets—not the responses.
cdp-general.pcap	This is the Cisco Discovery Protocol (CDP) chatting away on the network. Note the destination address and lack of an IP header—this is just local link stuff. Can you tell what VLAN is running on this network? Refer to *Chapter 3: Capture Traffic* for details on capturing traffic on a VLAN.
cldap-general.pcap	This a general Connectionless Lightweight Access Directory Access Protocol (CLDAP) lookup service in a Microsoft environment. Compare this lookup process to the DNS lookup processes shown in *Chapter 15: Analyze Domain Name System (DNS) Traffic.*
dhcp-addressproblem.pcap	Something went wrong with the DHCP server—who is trying to get an address and who has one that works just fine? Rebooting the DHCP server solved this problem. Refer to *Chapter 22: Analyze Dynamic Host Configuration Protocol (DHCP) Traffic.*
dhcp-boot.pcap	This trace shows a basic DHCP boot sequence for a client that is outside of its lease time. Examine the DHCP Discover packet to determine if this client received the IP address it requested. For more information on the four-packet DHCP boot sequence, refer to *Chapter 22: Analyze Dynamic Host Configuration (DHCP) Traffic.*
dhcp-decline.pcap	This trace is referred to in *Chapter 22: Analyze Dynamic Host Configuration Protocol (DHCP) Traffic.* The DHCP client wants 192.168.0.102, but the server offers 192.168.0.104. The client seems OK with that until we see it generates a DHCP Decline. Typically this indicates that the client thinks someone else has that IP address—sure enough, when we ARP scan the network we see a statically assigned 192.168.0.104. We filtered on just the DHCP traffic though so we can't see that other station talking.

Trace File Name	Description
dhcp-jerktakesaddress.pcap	The DHCP server is down, but the client remembers its last address and decided just to take it back. Of course it does a gratuitous ARP (packet 3). The client uses router solicitation (ugh) to try to find a default gateway as well. Finally, 12 seconds in to the trace the DHCP server resurfaces (packet 8). Refer to *Chapter 22: Analyze Dynamic Host Configuration Protocol (DHCP) Traffic.*
dhcp-offer-info.pcap	You can learn a lot about the other devices on the network—even if you are hanging off of a switch or you are on the other side of a router (as long as their DHCP traffic flows across your network). DHCP Offer packets sent to the broadcast address go everywhere on a switched network and contain some interesting information. Look at packet 3, for example. DHCP Discovery packets are also ripe with information. Refer to *Chapter 22: Analyze Dynamic Host Configuration Protocol (DHCP) Traffic.*
dhcp-relay-serverside.pcap	Compare the source MAC address in the Ethernet header with the Client MAC Address inside the DHCP packet to note that this communication is coming from the DHCP Relay Agent to the DHCP Server. The client sends a Requested IP Address and begins with a DHCP Request because it is still within its lease time. Refer to *Chapter 22: Analyze Dynamic Host Configuration Protocol (DHCP) Traffic.*
dhcp-renewtorebind.pcap	The DHCP client is unsuccessful in renewing its IP address from 10.1.0.1so the client broadcasts the DHCP Request in hopes of finding a new DHCP server. When the DHCP client doesn't get an answer, it gives up its IP address and begins the process of discovery from scratch (packet 7). Refer to *Chapter 22: Analyze Dynamic Host Configuration Protocol (DHCP) Traffic.*
dhcp-serverdiscovery.pcap	This trace shows the two different DHCP Discover packets used to locate rogue DHCP server on the network using NetScanTools Pro. Look in the client ID field in the DHCP packet for the difference. Refer to *Chapter 22: Analyze Dynamic Host Configuration Protocol (DHCP) Traffic.*
dns-errors-partial.pcap	In this situation we are trying to get to Nmap's site at either *www.nmap.org* or *www.insecure.org*. We don't seem to be able to connect—is the DNS server down? The trace file tells the answer. For more information on DNS analysis, refer to *Chapter 15: Analyze Domain Name System (DNS) Traffic.*
dns-icmp-fault.pcap	What's wrong with this DNS query? Why isn't it working? That's an easy one—if you know what the ICMP Type 3/Code 3 response means. Review *Chapter 18: Analyze Internet Control Message Protocol (ICMP).*

Trace File Name	Description
dns-lousyhotelnetwork.pcap	This trace begins with a really slow DNS response. In fact, the client sends out two DNS queries. When the first DNS response arrives, the client shuts down the listening port and responds to the second DNS response with an ICMP Destination Unreachable/Port Unreachable. How much delay was caused by packet loss? Refer to *Chapter 15: Analyze Domain Name System (DNS) Traffic.*
dns-misc.pcap	Compare the DNS lookups required to access *www.winpcap.org*, *www.msnbc.com* and *www.espn.com*. Check the DNS traffic generated when you connect to your corporate servers. Consider baselining that traffic. Refer to *Chapter 28: Baseline "Normal" Traffic Patterns* for a complete list of baselines you should perform.
dns-misc2.pcap	Browsing to *www.cnn.com*, *www.microsoft.com* and *www.espn.com* generates lots of DNS queries and responses (filtered out in this trace) as they direct you to their ad and data streaming affiliates. Many of the server names imply they are advertising sites. Refer to *Chapter 8: Interpret Basic Trace File Statistics* for information on Wireshark's HTTP statistics.
dns-mxlookup.pcap	Our client is only looking for the Mail Exchange (MX) server for *www.packet-level.net*. The response (packet 2) includes the name servers and their IP addresses. Refer to *Chapter 15: Analyze Domain Name System (DNS) Traffic.*
dns-ptr.pcap	If you see an excess number of DNS PTR queries, look at the source. Make sure it's not your Wireshark system (turn off network name resolution to squelch the DNS PTR traffic from Wireshark). Why are other devices on the network performing these DNS PTR queries— don't they know the network names of the targets? Refer to *Chapter 15: Analyze Domain Name System (DNS) Traffic.*
dns-root.pcap	This DNS query for <Root> generates a response with the MNAME (primary master server name) value of A.ROOT.SERVERS.NET. The reply indicates that the responsible authority's mailbox is at Verisign and the receiver can only cache this information for a measly 6 minutes and 19 seconds. Refer to *Chapter 15: Analyze Domain Name System (DNS) Traffic.*
dns-serverfailure.pcap	DNS server failures (packet 4) (packet 17) (packet 23-25) don't indicate that the name was not found—they indicate that the server couldn't get a positive or negative response. Perhaps the upstream DNS server didn't respond in a timely manner (or at all). Consider building a display filter for dns.flags.rcode==2 to view these DNS server failure responses. Refer to *Chapter 15: Analyze Domain Name System (DNS) Traffic* for details on creating DNS response filters.
dns-slow.pcap	Compare how quickly the first and second DNS response packets come to the delay before the first DNS response is sent. Is the DNS response time better later in the trace (packet 98)? Refer to *Chapter 15: Analyze Domain Name System (DNS) Traffic.*

Trace File Name	Description
dns-ttl-issue.pcap	This client can't get to a website because DNS isn't resolving properly. It's not the normal Name Error or Server Error response, however. Something strange is happening. Look at the source of the ICMP packets, the type of ICMP packets and the original DNS query packet contents spit back inside those ICMP packets. Which device would you examine first to find the source of this problem? Refer to *Chapter 18: Analyze Internet Control Message Protocol (ICMP) Traffic.*
dns-walk.pcap	This DNS 'walking' operation begins by looking up the SOA (Start of Zone Authority) for a domain and then the NS (name servers) for the same domain. After doing some research on the name servers, the client begins a TCP-based Zone Transfer (AXFR) (packet 7). Note the number and format of replies (packet 14). Refer to *Chapter 15: Analyze Domain Name System (DNS) Traffic.*
dtp-dynamictrunking-cisco.pcap	Proprietary to Cisco, the Dynamic Trunking Protocol (DTP) is used to negotiate trunking between two VLAN-enabled switches. Refer to *Chapter 3: Capture Traffic* for information on capturing VLAN traffic.
ftp-clientside.pcap	You'll want to disable the Checksum Errors coloring rule when viewing this trace file. This is an FTP file transfer—note that you can follow the TCP stream and see the type of camera used to take the picture. This trace is the client side of the *ftp-serverside.pcap* trace file. Refer to *Chapter 6: Colorize Traffic* for more information on the Checksum Errors coloring rule.
ftp-crack.pcap	Consider applying the following display filter on the traffic: `ftp.request.command == "USER" || ftp.request.command == "PASS"`. This reveals that the password cracking attempt is only focused on the admin account and the passwords are coming from a dictionary that includes names. Looks like they are cycling through the password list—we caught them on the letter M, but they start at the beginning later (packet 4739). Refer to *Chapter 24: Analyze File Transfer Protocol (FTP).*
ftp-dir.enc	This trace was saved in Sniffer DOS file format (.enc). Why on Earth would this be included in a Wireshark book? Well—when you open this trace file you are using the wiretap library to make the conversion to a format Wireshark can recognize. Refer to *Chapter 24: Analyze File Transfer Protocol (FTP).*
ftp-dir.pcap	This trace file shows someone using a variety of FTP commands including USER, PASS, PWD, SYST, HELP, PORT, LIST and QUIT. You can follow the TCP stream to rebuild the directory list sent across the data channel. What port was used for the data channel? Was this a passive or active transfer process? Refer to *Chapter 24: Analyze File Transfer Protocol (FTP).*

Trace File Name	Description
ftp-download-good.pcap	There's a bit of humor hidden in this FTP file transfer. First, however, check out the transfer type—is it an active FTP transfer or a passive mode transfer? What type of file is being sent on the data channel? Can you reassemble the file? Refer to *Chapter 24: Analyze File Transfer Protocol (FTP)*.
ftp-download-good2.pcap	An FTP user wants to download a file, but not until it knows the size of the file (packet 12). There are a few lost packets along the way, but nothing too significant. Consider setting **Time Display Format | Seconds Since Beginning of Capture** and then setting a Time Reference on the first data transfer packet (packet 16). Scroll to the end of the trace to find the download time. Refer to *Chapter 7: Define Time Values and Interpret Summaries* for details on using different Time column values.
ftp-failedupload.pcap	This is an interesting trace of an FTP file upload process that seemed to take forever and then generated an error. What happened here? Can you figure out which direction packet loss must have occurred on? Refer to *Chapter 24: Analyze File Transfer Protocol (FTP)*.
ftp-filesizeproblem.pcap	In this case, an FTP download is unsuccessful because of a limit imposed by the FTP server. The response message is quite clear (packet 38). Refer to *Chapter 24: Analyze File Transfer Protocol (FTP)*.
ftp-haha-at-client.pcap	Use this trace to test your skills rebuilding a file transferred over an FTP data channel. Pay attention to the command channel to determine the original name of the file transferred. Refer to *Chapter 10: Follow Streams and Reassemble Data* to see what file was transferred.
ftp-ioupload-partial.pcap	No one will live long enough to upload files to this FTP server. Is the server at fault? The client? The network? Examine the Warnings and Notes in the Expert Info Composite to get the whole picture. Refer to *Chapter 13: Use Wireshark's Expert System.*
ftp-pasv-fail.pcap	Although this FTP server seems to accept the PASV command (packet 30), when the user attempts to connect to the offered port, the server doesn't answer. Even though the FTP server shuts down the FTP data connection, it makes a snide remark to the client (packet 39). Refer to *Chapter 24: Analyze File Transfer Protocol (FTP)* for information on passive mode vs. active mode FTP connections.
ftp-putfile.pcap	The client uses the STOR command during an active FTP connection. Note the Wireshark decode of the PORT command packets (packet 16) (packet 37) (packet 55) (packet 71). What data is being transferred across the secondary connections established by the server? Refer to *Chapter 24: Analyze File Transfer Protocol (FTP)*.

Trace File Name	Description
ftp-secret.pcap	The traffic is already ugly on this new system that just had BitTorrent loaded on it. Look in the trace for the background FTP connection. The client didn't have any idea this connection was being established in the background. Some research indicated that all HP Media Center PCs included the game console program that made a secret FTP connection. Refer to *Chapter 32: Analyze Suspect Traffic*.
ftp-serverside.pcap	You'll want to disable the Checksum Errors coloring rule when viewing this trace file. This trace is the server side of the *ftp-clientside.pcap* trace file. Refer to *Chapter 33: Effective Use of Command-Line Tools* to learn how to merge the trace files and alter the timestamps if necessary.
ftp-tcp-segment.pcap	What is going on in this FTP communication? First of all, the traffic is not efficient. Secondly, it would raise the red flag of the security team. This is definitely a non-standard way of sending FTP traffic to a server. Refer to *Chapter 32: Analyze Suspect Traffic*.
ftp-transfer.pcap	This FTP transfer process consists of five TCP connections. Reviewing TCP Conversations information is the best way to see which connection supports the majority of the traffic. There are some problems as indicated in the Expert Info window as well. Refer to *Chapter 20: Analyze Transmission Control Protocol (TCP) Traffic*.
ftp-unusualport.pcap	Something about this communication just feels weird. Follow TCP Stream to find out what's really going on here. Now is the time to protocol force the correct decode on the traffic. Refer to *Chapter 2: Introduction to Wireshark* for information on forcing dissectors onto traffic.
ftp-up-disconnect.pcap	Trying to upload a file (you can see the PPT file name in the trace), the connection is lost. Note the retransmissions leading to a whole slew of FIN/ACK packets. Refer to *Chapter 20: Analyze Transmission Control Protocol (TCP) Traffic* for details on various ways that TCP connections can be terminated.
gen-googlemaps.pcap	This trace depicts the traffic generated when a host opens *maps.google.com*. The process begins with an ARP for the DNS server (which is also the router) hardware address. Then we see the DNS request and response. Finally, the page loads. Apply a filter for dns to see all the sites that you must connect to when you want to load a map. Refer to *Chapter 23: Analyze Hypertext Transfer Protocol (HTTP) Traffic*.
gen-googleopen.pcap	If you've ever hit Google's site (who hasn't?), then you know *google.com* is a seriously streamlined site. This site opening process only required 37 packets—nice, eh? Refer to *Chapter 23: Analyze Hypertext Transfer Protocol (HTTP) Traffic*.

Trace File Name	Description
http-1.pcap	This HTTP trace depicts someone using the HEAD command instead of the GET command. The HEAD command is similar to the GET command except it does not expect the file to be transferred—it just obtains the associated header lines. For example, if the HEAD command is followed by the If-Modified-Since line, the sender can determine if there is a newer version of a file on the HTTP server. Refer to *Chapter 23: Analyze Hypertext Transfer Protocol (HTTP) Traffic* for details on the If-Modified-Since request method.
http-500error.pcap	This trace shows an HTTP 500 error response from a web server that cannot handle the request. In this case we were trying to get a list of laptops on sale at Fry's Electronics' website (Outpost). The problem seemed to be with the backend database server. Refer to *Chapter 23: Analyze Hypertext Transfer Protocol (HTTP) Traffic* for details on analyzing web browsing problems.
http-a.pcap	This trace provides some interesting information about the target. In the response we can see that they employ Redline Networks Web I/O Processor. Refer to *Chapter 23: Analyze Hypertext Transfer Protocol (HTTP) Traffic* for details on HTTP response information.
http-aol.pcap	It takes 18 different TCP connections to load the *www.aol.com* website. Have you analyzed the connection to your corporate website lately? Refer to *Chapter 23: Analyze Hypertext Transfer Protocol (HTTP) Traffic* for information on using HTTP Flow Graphs to identify website relationships.
http-browse-ok.pcap	This user must have recently browsed to *www.packet-level.com* based on the high number of HTTP 304 Not Modified responses (39 in all) sent from the server. If the user complained of slow performance in the previous connection and we are troubleshooting the problem, we need to ensure they do not receive any HTTP 304 Not Modified responses—they should download all files and not pull them from cache. Refer to *Chapter 23: Analyze Hypertext Transfer Protocol (HTTP) Traffic.*
http-client-refuses.pcap	This client has more than one connection to a streaming video server, but nothing happens when they begin the stream viewing process. A quick review of the trace file indicates that the client rudely sends TCP RST packets (packet 28) (packet 29) to shut down the connections. The fault is at the client. Most likely a popup blocker process is getting in the way. Refer to *Chapter 20: Analyze Transmission Control Protocol (TCP) Traffic* for details on the various ways TCP connections can be terminated.

Trace File Name	Description
http-download-bad.pcap	The client complains that there is a problem with the Internet connection—they are trying to download the OpenOffice binary, but it is just taking too long. Use the Expert Info and Expert Info Composite to identify the problems in this trace file. What are the three primary causes for the poor performance? Refer to *Chapter 13: Use Wireshark's Expert System* for information on identifying problems quickly.
http-download-good.pcap	The users are relatively happy with the download time required to obtain the OpenOffice binary depicted in this trace file. How long did the file transfer take? What is the average bytes/second rate? Refer to *Chapter 7: Define Time Values and Interpret Summaries* for details on using Wireshark's Summary window.
http-espn2007.pcap	A favorite 'ugly' website (other than *www.ebay.com*) is *www.espn.com*. Consider selecting Statistics	HTTP	HTTP Packet Counter to view the number of redirections (Code 301 and 302) and client errors (Code 404). Now why is the client blamed for these 404 errors? It's ESPN's fault that we looked somewhere we weren't supposed to! Harrumph! Refer to *Chapter 23: Analyze Hypertext Transfer Protocol (HTTP) Traffic.*
http-espn2010.pcap	Compare this trace file to the one taken in 2007. Has ESPN improved their site since then? Refer to *Chapter 7: Define Time Values and Interpret Summaries* for details on comparing two Summaries.
http-fault-post.pcap	Although this company has a nice feedback form online, when you fill out the form and click submit they rudely send an HTTP error code 403 (packet 10) (packet 13). Someone needs to let the webmaster know the form is broken! Refer to *Chapter 23: Analyze Hypertext Transfer Protocol (HTTP) Traffic.*
http-google.pcap	Want to see a simple site that loads fast? You got it—that would be Google's main page. Measure the total amount of time required to load the page. Fast, eh? Refer to *Chapter 23: Analyze Hypertext Transfer Protocol (HTTP) Traffic.*
http-ifmodified.pcap	This short trace file shows the If-Modified-Since HTTP request modifier and the 304 Not Modified response. This page will be loaded from cache. Refer to *Chapter 23: Analyze Hypertext Transfer Protocol (HTTP) Traffic* for details on the If-Modified-Since request method.
http-microsoft.pcap	Here is a web browsing session to *www.microsoft.com*. Compare this to the *http-microsoft-fromcache.pcap* trace file. There are a lot fewer packets required when you load the packets from cache. Refer to *Chapter 23: Analyze Hypertext Transfer Protocol (HTTP) Traffic.*

Trace File Name	Description
http-microsoft-fromcache.pcap	Compare this trace file to *http-microsoft.pcap* to see the difference between loading the *www.microsoft.com* website from the server and from cache. Refer to *Chapter 23: Analyze Hypertext Transfer Protocol (HTTP) Traffic.*
http-proxy-problem.pcap	The client can't get off the network because of errors getting through the proxy server. You can read the proxy response in clear text— Follow TCP Stream. Also note the slow handshake response time. Not a good day for this user. Refer to *Chapter 10: Follow Streams and Reassemble Data.*
https-justlaunchpage.pcap	In this trace file we have simply opened the *www.bankofamerica.com* website. You'll see the HTTPS handshake after the TCP handshake. Refer to *Chapter 23: Analyze Hypertext Transfer Protocol (HTTP) Traffic* for more information on decrypting and troubleshooting HTTPS traffic.
http-slow-filexfer.pcap	Another problem file download caused by packet loss. Use the Expert Info Composite window to determine how many packets were lost in this file transfer. Refer to *Chapter 13: Use Wireshark's Expert System* to learn to spot packet loss.
https-ssl3session.pcap	During the establishment of this SSL connection (HTTPS) there appears to be communication problems causing retransmissions. Disable **Preferences	Protocols	TCP	Allow subdissector to reassemble TCP streams** when examining the SSL/TLS handshake process. Refer to *Chapter 23: Analyze Hypertext Transfer Protocol (HTTP) Traffic* for more information on decrypting and troubleshooting HTTPS traffic.
http-thesearchenginelist.pcap	This site is interesting—*www.thesearchenginelist.com*—it seeds the client with all the URLs of various search engines causing the client to make a series of DNS queries automatically when it loads the page. Refer to *Chapter 23: Analyze Hypertext Transfer Protocol (HTTP) Traffic.*
http-winpcap.pcap	This trace shows a simple web browsing session to *www.winpcap.org*. Consider adding a column for `tcp.reassembled.length` to see exactly how large each HTTP object is. Nice, eh? That's a new feature as of Wireshark 1.4. Refer to *Chapter 20: Analyze Transmission Control Protocol (TCP) Traffic* for examples on using this new filter value.
icmp-dest-unreachable.pcap	The client is trying to ping 10.4.88.88, but it appears that the local router can't locate the device on the next network. The local router sends an ICMP Destination Unreachable/Host Unreachable message indicating that it tried to ARP for the target, but didn't receive an answer. You MUST learn ICMP in depth to secure, optimize and troubleshoot your network effectively! Refer to *Chapter 18: Analyze Internet Control Message Protocol (ICMP) Traffic.*

Trace File Name	Description
icmp-lotsostuff.pcap	This trace contains some interesting ICMP traffic. If you look closely you can spot two systems that are behaving strangely on the network. What is triggering the ICMP Destination Unreachable/Protocol Unreachable responses? Refer to *Chapter 18: Analyze Internet Control Message Protocol (ICMP) Traffic.*
icmp-payload.pcap	ICMP Echo Requests are not supposed to have data in the payload, but that's what we see in these packets. You would want to ensure that the payload doesn't contain data coming off the local system. There is an old exploit called 'Loki' that tunneled traffic inside ICMP Echo packets. Refer to *Chapter 18: Analyze Internet Control Message Protocol (ICMP) Traffic.*
icmp-ping-2signatures.pcap	When you see ICMP echo request packets on the wire, check the payload to see if you can identify the application sending the data. Try using the following display filter: `data contains "from"`. Refer to *Chapter 9: Create and Apply Display Filters* for information on using `contains` with display filters.
icmp-ping-basic.pcap	This is a simple ICMP-based ping process preceded by a DNS request/response. This ping was performed by a Windows host using the ping.exe that is included with Windows—we can tell by the payload (Microsoft knows the alphabet… but not the whole alphabet—they can only go up to "w"—go figure). Refer to *Chapter 18: Analyze Internet Control Message Protocol (ICMP) Traffic.*
icmp-redirect.pcap	A clear case of ICMP redirection. As you examine this trace, pay close attention to the MAC address in the packets and the contents of the ICMP Redirect packet (packet 2). That packet contains the IP address of the recommended router to get to 10.3.71.7. The client must already have the MAC address of that router (or perhaps the analyst filtered out ARP traffic). Refer to *Chapter 32: Analyze Suspect Traffic.*
icmp-routersolicitation.pcap	Wow—my DHCP server (10.1.0.1) wasn't up when I needed to renew my IP address. When it did restart it offered me a different address and a bogus address for my default gateway. That triggered my system to perform ICMP Router Solicitation. This is typically not a good ICMP packet to see on the network. [Yes, you can see my name in the trace file. Why hide it—I'm the one that killed the DHCP server in the lab and I paid the price.]. Refer to *Chapter 18: Analyze Internet Control Message Protocol (ICMP) Traffic.*
icmp-standardping.pcap	This trace shows a standard ICMP-based ping process. By default, the ping.exe file sends a separate ICMP Echo Request packet out at approximately 1 second intervals. Refer to *Chapter 18: Analyze Internet Control Message Protocol (ICMP) Traffic.*

Trace File Name	Description
icmp-traceroute-normal.pcap	This is a classic ICMP-based traceroute operation shows the dependency on the ICMP Time to Live Exceeded/Time to Live Exceeded in Transit response that is used to locate routers along a path. One of the routers doesn't generate these responses though. Refer to *Chapter 18: Analyze Internet Control Message Protocol (ICMP) Traffic* for details on traceroute traffic.
icmp-tracert_au.pcap	This trace shows a traceroute operation from the Netherlands to a site in Australia. On the traceroute trace files, use GeoIP mapping to see the path taken in a visual format. Refer to *Chapter 8: Interpret Basic Trace File Statistics* for information on configuring GeoIP.
icmp-tracert-slow.pcap	This traceroute client is excruciatingly slow between some of the TTL increment sets. What triggers the ICMP Destination Unreachable/Port Unreachable message sent to the client (packet 64)? How many hops away is the target? Refer to *Chapter 18: Analyze Internet Control Message Protocol (ICMP) Traffic*.
igmp-joinleave.pcap	This trace shows IGMP traffic for a device that is joining a multicast group. Notice we have a device that is multicasting from an unassigned IP address—169.254.229.200—that needs to be fixed. Refer to *Chapter 8: Interpret Basic Trace File Statistics* for details on analyzing multicast traffic.
ip-127guy.pcap	This trace depicts an actual host that sends traffic to 127.0.0.1— something is terribly wrong with this host. Can you tell what application is triggering this traffic? Perhaps the application should be examined. Refer to *Chapter 17: Analyze Internet Protocol (IPv4) Traffic*.
ip-checksum-invalid.pcap	This is a classic case of checksum offloading (also referred to as task offloading). We are capturing traffic on 10.2.110.167 and all traffic from that source IP address appears to have invalid checksums. Open the Packet Details pane and look at which headers have invalid checksums. How do we know the checksums must be valid on the wire? Easy—the HTTP web browsing session was successful. Consider disabling the Checksum Errors coloring filter. Refer to *Chapter 6: Colorize Traffic*.
ip-fragments.pcap	The client is sending fragment ICMP Echo packets to the target. Try setting up Wireshark with and without IP fragment reassembly to note the difference. **Edit	Preferences	Protocols	IP**. Refer to *Chapter 5: Define Global and Personal Preferences*.
ip-icmp-frag-needed.pcap	Something is definitely wrong here. Look inside the Destination Unreachable/Fragmentation Needed packets to locate the IP header Total Length field. Was the triggering packet too long? What is the MTU of the next hop advertised? Refer to *Chapter 17: Analyze Internet Protocol (IPv4) Traffic* and *Chapter 18: Analyze Internet Control Message Protocol (ICMP) Traffic*.

Trace File Name	Description
ip-llmnr.pcap	Local Link Multicast Name Resolution (LLMNR) is just another name resolution process—notice how these packets use the same format as DNS queries. LLMNR is part of the "zero configuration networking". LLMNR is defined in RFC 4795. Compare these LLMNR packets to DNS packets in *Chapter 15: Analyze Domain Name System (DNS) Traffic.*
ip-pingfrag.pcap	This trace shows an ICMP Echo process (ping) fragmented using IP. Why can't you follow the stream to rebuild the communications? Adjust the **Preferences	Protocols	IP	Reassemble fragmented IP datagrams** setting to see how it affects the traffic display. Refer to *Chapter 5: Define Global and Personal Preferences.*
ipv6-mcasts.pcap	This trace depicts default IPv6 traffic on a host that sites on an IPv4 network. The traffic consists of LLMNR queries, ICMPv6 Router Solicitations and ICMPv6 Multicast Listener Reports. Refer to *Chapter 18: Analyze Internet Control Message Protocol (ICMP) Traffic* to compare these packets to ICMPv4 packets.
irc-channel.pcap	You're being hunted! This IRC channel was established by a system that was loaded with malware. Follow TCP Stream to see the entire IRC communication in plain text. Do you notice the file download commands? Not a good sign at all! Refer to *Chapter 32: Analyze Suspect Traffic.*
kerberos.pcap	This short trace shows a Kerberos communication that switches from UDP to TCP because of the ERR_RESPONSE_TOO_BIG reply in packet 2. Refer to the case study in *Chapter 19: Analyze User Datagram Protocol (UDP) Traffic* to see the issues with UDP vs. TCP for Kerberos.
net-latency-au.pcap	This trace consists of just DNS queries/responses and the first two packets of TCP handshakes to each target. Refer to *Chapter 21: Graph IO Rates and TCP Trends* to learn how to use `frame.time_delta` in an Advanced IO Graph.
net-loopflood.pcap	Examine the IP ID value in this trace file to validate that this is the same packet looping this network. You might want to disable the checksum coloring rule on this trace file. This traffic killed the network, but was easy to fix—the IP TTL value didn't decrement so this wasn't a layer 3 problem—this was a layer 2 loop. Refer to *Chapter 17: Analyze Internet Protocol (IPv4) Traffic.*
net-lost-route.pcap	Although the client can get to the Google toolbar page, it can't get to the Verio home page. It doesn't appear that there is a path to the target. Why aren't there any TCP RST packets or any ICMP Destination Unreachable packets? Refer to *Chapter 1: The World of Network Analysis.*

Trace File Name	Description
net-msloadbalance.pcap	This is the heartbeat message sent by Network Load Balancing cluster servers to other hosts in the cluster. These servers listen for the heartbeat of other hosts to identify when a cluster fails. If that occurs, the remaining hosts will adjust and redistribute the workload while continuing to provide service to their clients. Refer to *Chapter 1: The World of Network Analysis.*
net-noenet.pcap	This trace was taken on a host that was having problems connecting to the network. This is a classic sign of a speed/duplex mismatch. The host cannot get past problems at the data link layer. Refer to *Chapter 1: The World of Network Analysis.*
net-resolutions.pcap	This trace shows a nice clean connection to a web server. First we have the ARP resolution process to obtain the MAC address of the DNS server, then the DNS resolution process and finally the TCP handshake to port 80 for the web browsing session. All looks good in this trace. *Refer to Chapter 14: TCP/IP Analysis Overview.*
nicname.pcap	The NICNAME application traffic (using port 43) is generated by a WHOIS query. In this case, the query is based on an IP address. Is the query successful? Refer to *Chapter 32: Analyze Suspect Traffic.*
ntp-gettime.pcap	A client connects to *pool.ntp.org* on port 123 to time synchronize its time. You can see the static structure used in both the NTP client mode and the NTP server mode. Notice that there are 12 IP addresses provided in the DNS response (packet 2). Refer to *Chapter 15: Analyze Domain Name System (DNS) Traffic.*
ntp-timesync.pcap	This trace shows a system performing a DNS query for tock.usno.navy.mil and then running a Network Time Protocol request on port 123. Refer to *Chapter 15: Analyze Domain Name System (DNS) Traffic.*
pop-normal.pcap	This trace depicts a normal POP communication—you might want to disable the Checksum Errors coloring rule to review it. Consider using Follow TCP to view the POP communication more clearly. You will see the USER, PASS, STAT, UIDL, LIST, RETR, DATA, DELE and QUIT commands. Refer to *Chapter 25: Analyze Email Traffic.*
pop-problem.pcap	The POP email application gives no indication as to why it is taking so long to pick up mail. In this trace we can clearly see the problem lies with the email server that is sending back an '-ERR-' response (packet 5). Refer to *Chapter 25: Analyze Email Traffic.*
pop-spamclog.pcap	Users can't get their email. It appears that their email programs just hang when they try to send/receive. In truth, we can see that there are spam messages with large attachments (.pif) that take a long time to download. Users need to be patient and the company needs to consider filtering this spam before it gets to the client systems. Follow TCP Stream on any POP packet to view the spam messages. Refer to *Chapter 25: Analyze Email Traffic.*

Trace File Name	Description
ppp-general.pcap	This is a standard PPP (Point-to-Point Protocol) communication. The IP header Type field contains the value 47—GRE which stands for General Router Encapsulation. Refer to *Chapter 17: Analyze Internet Protocol (IPv4) Traffic.*
rpcap-findinterfaces.pcap	This is an rpcap connection that shows the list of remote interfaces being discovered. Consider reassembling the TCP connections to see the nice list of interfaces. For more information on remote capture with rpcap, refer to *Chapter 3: Capture Traffic.*
rpcap-refused.pcap	This didn't work right—the rpcap connection was refused. The packets show exactly why so it's easy to remedy this situation. Note that the rpcap connection is established on port 2002—that's the default port for rpcap. You can change Wireshark's *services* file to display this port as rpcap instead of "globe." For more information on remote capture with rpcap, refer to *Chapter 3: Capture Traffic.*
rwhois.pcap	This query uses RWHOIS (Referral WHOIS) on port 4321. RWHOIS extends the capabilities of WHOIS in a hierarchical structure. This trace shows a successful RWHOIS query handled by *root.rwhois.net*. Refer to *Chapter 20: Analyze Transmission Control Protocol (TCP) Traffic.*
sec-active-scan.pcap	This scan was performed by LANguard Network Security Scanner. Look for the unusual ICMP Echo request packet (Type 8; Code 19) which is the signature for LNSS. Refer to *Chapter 31: Detect Scanning and Discovery Processes.*
sec-bruteforce.pcap	Someone is attempting a brute force password crack on an FTP server (*creditus.com*). Apply the following filter to display all packets with the USER and PASS commands: `ftp.request.command==USER ||` `ftp.request.command==PASS`. Refer to *Chapter 32: Analyze Suspect Traffic.*
sec-clientdying.pcap	A client system (172.16.1.10) is in trouble. After it boots up the CPU utilization climbs to 100% and the system locks up within 3 minutes. You can see many problems in the trace—incoming DCERPC communications and the client establishing TFTP and IRC communications to remote systems. Follow TCP Stream on the IRC communication. This client is infected with a variant of the sdbot worm. Refer to *Chapter 32: Analyze Suspect Traffic.*
sec-dictionary2.pcap	This dictionary password crack is focused on breaking into the admin account on an FTP server. Apply the following filter to display all the passwords attempted: `ftp.request.command==PASS`. Did the cracker try using a blank password? Refer to *Chapter 32: Analyze Suspect Traffic.*

Trace File Name	Description
sec-ettercap-poisoner.pcap	This great trace file shows someone running ettercap's 'Check for Poisoner' function. The IP ID field of these ping packets contains the signature 0xe77e (eleet-speak for 'ette' which is short for ettercap). Systems that answer back with the same IP ID value are most likely running ettercap as well. Don't get distracted by the ICMP ID value of 0xe77e—responders all must echo back that value so the echo requests and replies can be associated properly. Refer to *Chapter 32: Analyze Suspect Traffic.*
sec-evilprogram.pcap	A truly classic trace file of a system infected with the Stopguard browser hijack spyware/malware/scumware program. It's imperative that the client not reboot, but luckily we got the trace. Create a DNS filter to see the client look up Virtumonde's website. That's when the troubles begin. Check out *www.spywarewarrior.com*—a great reference for spyware/adware/malware/scumware, etc. Refer to *Chapter 32: Analyze Suspect Traffic.*
sec-honeypots-fighting.pcap	It's a cat fight! Watch the change of direction in the scan process when one aggressive honeypot gets scanned by another aggressive honeypot. Consider making an IO Graph with two filters: Graph 1 line: `ip.src==24.6.137.85 && tcp.flags == 0x02`; Graph 2 line: `ip.src==24.6.138.50 && tcp.flags == 0x02`. You may need to adjust the X axis tick interval. Turn on the green graph line without any filter applied. Refer to *Chapter 9: Create and Apply Display Filters.*
sec-justascan.pcap	Is this really just a TCP scan? It appears so in the beginning. Examine the timing in this trace to see how the flow of the scan changes. Refer to *Chapter 31: Detect Scanning and Discovery Processes.*
sec-macof.pcap	Dug Song created Macof to flood network switch MAC address tables and cause them to go into 'hub mode.' This tool still wreaks havoc on the network. Can you identify the signature in this flood traffic? Refer to *Chapter 31: Detect Scanning and Discovery Processes.*
sec-nessus.pcap	Nessus (*www.nessus.org*), the penetration testing tool, doesn't try to be sneaky. Use the Find feature to search for the string 'nessus' in this trace file (do not search case sensitive). You'll find the 'nessus' signature all over in this trace file. In addition, you'll see the unusual ping packet (packet 3) used by Xprobe2 when the Nessus scan runs. Refer to *Chapter 32: Analyze Suspect Traffic.*
sec-nessus-recon.pcap	This trace shows a Nessus reconnaissance on a target. Consider creating a coloring rule for ICMP Echo packets that have an unusual code number—`(icmp.type == 8) && !(icmp.code == 0)`. Refer to *Chapter 31: Detect Scanning and Discovery Processes* for details on detecting scan signatures.

Trace File Name	Description
sec-nmap-fragscan.pcap	This trace file depicts a system sending an IP fragment scan. If you examine the IP header, the protocol field indicates that TCP follows. You can manually decode the TCP header to identify the purpose of the TCP packets. Do you see the follow up fragments? Refer to *Chapter 17: Analyze Internet Protocol (IPv4) Traffic* for information on reassembling IP fragments.
sec-nmap-ipscan.pcap	This is the kind of traffic you never want to see on your network—someone is doing an IP scan... not a UDP scan... not a TCP scan. This person wants to know what services are supported directly on top of the IP header. Examples include EGP, IDRP, ICMP and encapsulated IPv6. Sort the Info column heading to see all the protocols queried for. Refer to *Chapter 31: Detect Scanning and Discovery Processes.*
sec-nmap-osdetection.pcap	This trace shows an OS detection process using Nmap. Consider creating a coloring rule for ICMP Echo packets that have an unusual code number—`(icmp.type == 8) && !(icmp.code == 0)`. Once you apply that filter you can find the Nmap signature. Refer to *Chapter 31: Detect Scanning and Discovery Processes.*
sec-nmap-osdetect-sV-O-v.pcap	This Nmap scan is performing service/version detection and OS detection. At almost 3,000 TCP connection attempts, this isn't a very stealthy scan process. See *Chapter 8: Interpret Basic Trace File Statistics* and *Chapter 31: Detect Scanning and Discovery Processes.*
sec-nmapscan.pcap	This trace depicts an Nmap scan. Open the **Statistics	Conversation** window and examine the TCP conversations. Do you see any common port number used by Nmap to perform this scan? Did Nmap hit any ports more than once? Refer to *Chapter 8: Interpret Basic Trace File Statistics.*
sec-nmap-see-short-ping.pcap	There are some strange ICMP Echo requests in this Nmap scan (packet 1) (packet 8). What data is supposed to be echoed back? What is the payload in the other ICMP Echo requests? There are also some unusual scans on port 1 which trigger ICMP Destination Unreachable/Port Unreachable responses. Refer to *Chapter 31: Detect Scanning and Discovery Processes.*
sec-nst-axfr-refused.pcap	The AXFR command sticks out like a sore thumb. Someone is trying to do a DNS zone transfer and their request is being refused. Notice that this trace shows the two types of DNS queries—UPD-based and TCP-based. Refer to *Chapter 32: Analyze Suspect Traffic.*
sec-nst-nslookup-mx.pcap	Someone is looking up the name service entry for the mail exchange server (MX). This type of query isn't normal to have on the network and should send up a red flag! Refer to *Chapter 32: Analyze Suspect Traffic.*

Trace File Name	Description
sec-nst-osfingerprint.pcap	This trace shows an OS fingerprinting operation from NetScanTools Pro. Consider creating a coloring rule for ICMP Echo packets that have an unusual code number—`(icmp.type == 8) && !(icmp.code == 0)`. This filter will help you discover what NetScanTools Pro's signature is in this trace. Refer to *Chapter 31: Detect Scanning and Discovery Processes.*
sec-nstpro-automatic-recon.pcap	NetScanTools Pro (NSTPro) is a great multi-function tool. This trace shows the automated reconnaissance process on the wire. As part of the process, NSTPro performs a real-time blacklist check, a WHOIS query, name server lookup, traceroute [filter on `ip.ttl < 10`]. Also build a filter to look for successful FTP connections using the following filter: `(ip.dst==67.169.189.113) && (tcp.flags == 0x12)`. Refer to *Chapter 31: Detect Scanning and Discovery Processes.*
sec-nst-rblcheck-soforems.pcap	We wanted to know if *soforems* was blacklisted—we knew they were up to no good one day so we did an RBL check on them. It's interesting to see how a Realtime Blacklist (RBL) check works. Using DNS, the investigator sends numerous DNS queries out with the IP address and the domain name of the blacklist servers. Refer to *Chapter 32: Analyze Suspect Traffic.*
sec-password-setting.pcap	This website sign-up has a problem -the password setting process crosses the wire in clear text (packet 4). Whoops. Refer to *Chapter 30: Network Forensics Overview.*
sec-sickclient.pcap	This client hits an IRC channel as user l l l l (four lowercase "L"s separated by spaces) (packet 14) and later begins to do a scan on the network for anyone with port 139 open. Feels like a bot looking for other systems to infect. Look at the rapid rate of the scan—that's why the responses are bunched up at the end of the trace. [Note: Turn off the colorization on this trace or your head may explode. We ran this trace through an IP address cleaner program but it didn't recalculate the checksums.) Symantec: Wargbot; MS: Graweg; Trend: Worm_IRCbot; McAfee: Mocbot; F-Secure: IRCBot. Refer to *Chapter 30: Network Forensics Overview* and *Chapter 32: Analyze Suspect Traffic.*
sec-sql-attack.pcap	After performing an SQL connection test to port 1433 ms-sql-s), the attacker makes a login attempt with the client name SYD-S-21-ESXI and username sa. The response indicates an error because the login for user *sa* failed. Filter on the SQL Error Number 18456 by using the following syntax: `frame[65:4]==18:48:00:00`. Refer to *Chapter 32: Analyze Suspect Traffic.*
sec-strangescan.pcap	What on Earth is the scanner doing? Look at the TCP Flag settings in the scan packets. What is triggering the "TCP ACKed lost segment" expert notification in Wireshark? Refer to *Chapter 20: Analyze Transmission Control Protocol (TCP) Traffic* and *Chapter 13: Use Wireshark's Expert System.*

Trace File Name	Description
sec-weirdscan.pcap	This is an unusual scan—the TCP flag settings are illogical—FIN, RST, ACK. We would expect a target to send back a RST. Refer to *Chapter 31: Detect Scanning and Discovery Processes.*
sec-xprobe2.pcap	Xprobe2 is an OS fingerprinting tool developed by Ofir Arkin <*www.sys-security.com*>. This trace depicts the ICMP-based process using ICMP Echo, Timestamp, Address Mask and Information requests. Notice the unusual ICMP Echo request code field value (packet 3). This is a signature of Xprobe2. Refer to *Chapter 31: Detect Scanning and Discovery Processes.*
smb-filexfer.pcap	This trace shows the file transfer process between a Microsoft client and server using SMBv1. The file transferred is OOo_2.4.1_SolarisSparc_install_en-US.tar.gz. You can see the periodic SMB Read ANDX Request and Read ANDX Response interruptions during the file download process. Refer to *Chapter 20: Analyze Transmission Control Protocol (TCP) Traffic.*
smb-joindomain.pcap	This trace shows a computer joining a domain in a MS Windows environment. Notice the Kerberos errors that precede a successful join operation. In addition, you'll see the server indicate that the client should use TCP for the Kerberos communications (KRB5KRB_ERR_RESPONSE_TOO_BIG). Refer to the case study in *Chapter 19: Analyze User Datagram Protocol (UDP) Traffic.*
smb-protocol-request-reply.pcap	This is the much focused on SMB communication that was exploited at the end of 2009. The exploit used the Process ID High field. Refer to *Chapter 32: Analyze Suspect Traffic.*
smtp-fault.pcap	This trace shows what happens when the DNS lookup for an SMTP server works fine, but the actual connection attempt does not. Refer to *Chapter 14: TCP/IP Analysis Overview.*
smtp-normal.pcap	In a normal SMTP connection the user doesn't send a user name or password. Follow TCP Stream to clearly view the entire message. During the initial communication process, the server indicates that it supports pipelining and imposes no limitation on email size (packet 8). Refer to *Chapter 10: Follow Streams and Reassemble Data.*
smtp-prob.pcap	A user (10.1.0.1) complains that they cannot send email to the SMTP server (10.2.23.11). Examine the trace and determine if the fault lies with the client, the server or the network. Refer to *Chapter 10: Follow Streams and Reassemble Data.*
smtp-sendone.pcap	This trace shows a standard single email being sent through SMTP. Follow the stream and you can see the sending application (Outlook).

Trace File Name	Description
snmp.pcap	This trace includes a simple SNMP query-response pair of communications. Are they all looking for the same information? Perform some Internet research to locate .1.3.6.1.2.1.25.3.2.1.5.1 (or search for SNMP MIB-2.25.3.2.1.5.1). You'll notice the response code of INTEGER 5 indicates that the status of the device is "down." For information on adding SNMP MIBs, refer to *Chapter 5: Define Global and Personal Preferences.*
snmp-mibwalk.pcap	SNMP MIB walking is the process of exploring all the MIB (Management Information Base) objects defined at the target. For information on adding SNMP MIBs, refer to *Chapter 5: Define Global and Personal Preferences.*
srvloc-locateprinter.pcap	This is the Service Location Protocol (SLP) used to find the network printer. Compare SLP structure to DNS packet structures in *Chapter 15: Analyze Domain Name System (DNS) Traffic.*
stp-spanningtree-changes.pcap	This trace only consists of Spanning Tree traffic from the local switch. This traffic is coming down the client's port which is unnecessary since the client can't do anything with it. Refer to *Chapter 1: The World of Network Analysis.*
syslog.pcap	This trace shows SYSLOG traffic traveling over port 514 on the network. If SYSLOG is used to transfer firewall or IDS alerts, imagine what someone can learn about your security system. Eek. Refer to *Chapter 30: Network Forensics Overview.*
tcp-104-103problem.pcap	The client (192.168.0.104) is trying to connect to the printer at 192.168.0.103. Everything worked fine yesterday, but not today. Filter on `ip.src==192.168.0.103` to try to identify what this host really is—is it a printer? Refer to *Chapter 29: Find the Top Causes of Performance Problems.*
tcp-137port.pcap	It looks like NetBIOS... It feels like NetBIOS... but it doesn't smell like NetBIOS. Something just feels wrong. Follow TCP Stream on this communication to find out what it really is. Consider using protocol forcing (right-mouse click, Decode As) to make port 137 traffic get decoded as FTP. Refer to *Chapter 10: Follow Streams and Reassemble Data.*
tcp-ack-scan.pcap	An ACK scan isn't used to find an open port—it is used to determine whether there may be an unfiltered path to a target system. For example, the fact that we get a TCP RST response (packet 3) to the ACK scan to port 80 (HTTP) indicates that this outbound port value is not filtered at a firewall or router. Sort the Source column heading to view all the response from 12.234.14.63—if a response was received from an ACK scan on a port, then that port is not blocked by an intermediary device. Refer to *Chapter 31: Detect Scanning and Discovery Processes.*

Trace File Name	Description
tcp-bad-download-again.pcap	This file download process is excruciatingly slow. Open the Expert Info Composite window to see what Wireshark detected. Refer to *Chapter 13: Use Wireshark's Expert System* to learn what the causes are of the various alerts. Open **Statistics	Summary** to see how much time has elapsed in this download process already. Consider building an IO Graph on all the traffic and then use tcp.analysis.flags on Graph 2.
tcp-con-up.pcap	This is a plain and simple TCP handshake process. Consider setting your TCP Preferences so Wireshark does not use relative sequence numbers—you can see the actual sequence numbers of the communications. In this short trace you can witness the 'phantom' byte that increments the Sequence Number value during the handshake process. Refer to *Chapter 23: Analyze Hypertext Transfer Protocol (HTTP) Traffic.*
tcp-fin-3way.pcap	This trace shows the 3-way TCP FIN process. Refer to *Chapter 20: Analyze Transmission Control Protocol (TCP) Traffic.*
tcp-fin-4way.pcap	This trace shows the 4-way TCP FIN process. There are actually two common variations of this process (see *tcp-fin-3way.pcap*). This trace shows FIN, FIN ACK, ACK. Note that the TCP connection is still active and waiting for a timeout now. Refer to *Chapter 20: Analyze Transmission Control Protocol (TCP) Traffic.*
tcp-fin-orphaned.pcap	This is supposed to be a 4-way TCP FIN process, but one side isn't cooperating. Because this is reattempted over and over again, the connection stays open. Refer to *Chapter 32: Analyze Suspect Traffic* for more information on orphaned TCP connections.
tcp-handshake-problem.pcap	An amazingly simple communication that went all wrong because of the TCP handshake. Each packet of the handshake looks good (packet 3-5). When the client begins sending data to the RWHOIS server, however, it receives SYN ACK packets in response. All this trouble just because the third packet of the handshake never arrived. The duplicate ACKs are asking for Sequence number 1 again—unfortunately two of the client's packets have this same sequence number. This will never get resolved. Refer to *Chapter 20: Analyze Transmission Control Protocol (TCP) Traffic.*
tcp-keepalive.pcap	An application that wants to keep the TCP connection open during a long idle time can trigger the TCP keep alive function. This trace shows just such a process for traffic maintaining a connection between ports 1863 and 2042. Is there any data contained in these TCP keep alive packets? How do you think Wireshark determines that these are TCP keep alives? Refer to *Chapter 20: Analyze Transmission Control Protocol (TCP) Traffic.*

Trace File Name	Description
tcp-keepalive-applevel.pcap	This is an old trace file, but it illustrates an application-level keep alive process. The application appears to read from a file at offset 3584 for a maximum of 512 bytes (check out that data in the responses) (packet 1) (packet 5) (packet 9) (packet 13) (packet 17). Not a pretty site. What was that programmer thinking? Refer to *Chapter 20: Analyze Transmission Control Protocol (TCP) Traffic.*
tcp-low-mss.pcap	This HTTP file transfer is never going to achieve the maximum throughput potential because of a Maximum Segment Size (MSS) issue. Does the problem reside with the client or the HTTP server? The Flow Graph indicates that the client is communicating with more than one HTTP server. Is this problem evidence on the second server as well? Refer to *Chapter 17: Analyze Internet Protocol (IPv4) Traffic.*
tcp-pktloss94040.pcap	This trace depicts a browsing session to *www.cnn.com*—with massive packet loss. Consider building an IO Graph to compare the various TCP problems. This is a healthy-sized file—over 94,000 packets to work with. Refer to *Chapter 33: Effective Use of Command-Line Tools* to learn how to use Editcap to split trace files into trace file sets.
tcp-problem.pcap	When you set the Time Display Format to Seconds Since Previous Packet, you can easily see the TCP retry process with five retransmissions of the packet that did not receive an ACK (packet 2). Refer to *Chapter 20: Analyze Transmission Control Protocol (TCP) Traffic.*
tcp-traceroute.pcap	Not all traceroutes are created equal. You may be familiar with standard ICMP-based traceroute operations. This however is a TCP-based traceroute that can be used as a connectivity test to a host that doesn't respond to ICMP echo packets. Refer to *Chapter 31: Detect Scanning and Discovery Processes.*
tcp-tracert_au.pcap	This trace file shows a TCP-based traceroute. Using TCP for traceroute is a good option as many targets won't respond to an ICMP-based traceroute. The router discovery process is the same for both versions. In this case we are using TCP port 99. Refer to *Chapter 31: Detect Scanning and Discovery Processes.*
tcp-window-frozen.pcap	A window frozen condition can kill file transfer speed. Set the Time Display Format to Seconds Since Beginning of Capture and right click on the first Zero Window packet (packet 30) to Set Time Reference. How much time did this condition waste? Refer to *Chapter 13: Use Wireshark's Expert System.*
tcp-winscaling-bad.pcap	It would have been nice to set up TCP window scaling for this HTTP connection. The client advertises a window scale of 2 (multiply the 65,535 window by 4) (packet 1), but the server doesn't support TCP window scaling. Sigh. Refer to *Chapter 20: Analyze Transmission Control Protocol (TCP) Traffic.*

Trace File Name	Description
tcp-winscaling-good.pcap	Now this is the life! The client advertises a TCP window scale of 2 (multiply the window value by 4) and the server supports window scaling as well (although with a window scale of 0 which does it no good on the receive side of things). Check out Wireshark's ability to calculate the correct window size (packet 3) for the client. This is a feature you can turn on/off in the **Preferences	TCP** area. Refer to *Chapter 20: Analyze Transmission Control Protocol (TCP) Traffic.*
tcp-winscaling-wishful.pcap	The client and the server can do window scaling, but when we look at the scaled value for the client (packet 3), it's only set at 5840. Shouldn't it be higher (5,840 times 4)? Highlight the TCP window field and you'll find out why we are still at 5,840. Bummer. It's a weird HTTP communication anyway. Refer to *Chapter 20: Analyze Transmission Control Protocol (TCP) Traffic.*
tcp-wont-shutup.pcap	Which side of the communication is trying to terminate the TCP connection? What is the response from the other side of the connection? What size is the file being transferred? Do you think the entire graphic file was received by the client? Refer to *Chapter 20: Analyze Transmission Control Protocol (TCP) Traffic.*
telnet.pcap	Someone makes a telnet connection to a Cisco router to run the 'show version' command which is echoed back, as is the 'exit' command. The password, however, is not echoed back. Follow the DO, DON'T, WILL and WON'T command as the client and server negotiate the connection behavior. Refer to *Chapter 20: Analyze Transmission Control Protocol (TCP) Traffic* and *Chapter 30: Network Forensics Overview.*
telnet-questionable.pcap	Examine this trace to determine if the telnet client and telnet server agree on the communication settings. DO, DON'T are demands being made from the source to the target. WILL, WON'T are statements from the source indicate what it is willing or not willing to do. How long did it take to get to the Login prompt? Refer to *Chapter 20: Analyze Transmission Control Protocol (TCP) Traffic* and *Chapter 30: Network Forensics Overview.*
telnet-refuse via rst.pcap	This client's telnet connection request is refused by the target in the traditional TCP RST/ACK method. An excessive number of RST/ACKs on the cable may be indication of a TCP port scan. In this case it is just one wayward telnet client. Refer to *Chapter 20: Analyze Transmission Control Protocol (TCP) Traffic.*
udp-echo.pcap	Although most people think of ICMP Echo Requests and ICMP Echo Replies when you mention the term "echo," there are also TCP and UDP echo communications. Can you identify the port used for this UDP communication? What would happen if the source and destination port was set to the echo port? Refer to *Chapter 31: Detect Scanning and Discovery Processes.*

Trace File Name	Description
udp-general.pcap	DHCP, DNS, NetBIOS Name Service and Microsoft Messenger make up the UDP-based communications in this trace. You wouldn't wish this NetBIOS and Messenger traffic on your worst enemy—what a filthy network. Refer to *Chapter 19: Analyze User Datagram Protocol (UDP) Traffic.*
udp-mcastream-queued2.pcap	Build an IO Graph on this multicast video traffic—set the tick interval to 0.01 seconds to see when the queuing occurred. On steady rate traffic, make sure you alter the tick interval to look closely at variations in the traffic rate. For an example of using this technique, refer to *Chapter 27: Introduction to Voice over IP (VoIP) Analysis.*
udp-pentest.pcap	This trace contains just the UDP traffic from a Nessus scan and the numerous ICMP Destination Unreachable/Port Unreachable responses the scan has triggered. View **Statistics	Protocol Hierarchy** to see the range of target ports hit in this penetration test. Refer to *Chapter 19: Analyze User Datagram Protocol (UDP) Traffic.*
udp-tracert.pcap	When a ping connectivity test won't work because the target doesn't answer pings, consider a UDP connectivity test. This UDP-based traceroute is targeted at bogus port numbers starting with port 32767. The process relies on the target sending back a Destination Unreachable/Port Unreachable response (packet 59). It looks like this UDP traceroute utility does name resolution as well. Refer to *Chapter 31: Detect Scanning and Discovery Processes.*
vlan-general.pcap	This trace shows an X11 communication on a VLAN. You can see the VLAN tag directly after the Ethernet header and before the IP header. Refer to *Chapter 3: Capture Traffic.*
voip-extension.pcap	This VoIP communication begins with a SIP call setup process. The call is directed to the VoIP server (operator). Later in the trace file the user enters extension 204. This was just a test call. *Chapter 27: Introduction to Voice over IP (VoIP) Analysis.*
voip-extension2downata.pcap	Playback this VoIP call to hear the lovely "I'm sorry…" message indicating the call cannot be completed. In this case the analog telephone adapter on the target side of the call is down. *Chapter 27: Introduction to Voice over IP (VoIP) Analysis.*
voip-skype-conn-disconn.pcap	While watching a Skype call being established and terminated, we noted the numerous UDP connections that were required and what appeared to be a command channel using TCP during the beginning and end of the call. Strange that it didn't terminate the TCP connections. *Chapter 27: Introduction to Voice over IP (VoIP) Analysis.*
wlan-airplane-laptopson.pcap	This is the traffic broadcast on a flight that does not have a wireless network on board. So much for the old "please disable wireless on your laptops" speech, eh? Refer to *Chapter 26: Introduction to 802.11 (WLAN) Analysis.*

Trace File Name	Description
wlan-ap-problem.pcap	Graph out this traffic and see what happened to the access point on our wireless network. This happens every so often and we lose connectivity on the WLAN. Refer to *Chapter 26: Introduction to 802.11 (WLAN) Analysis.*
wlan-beacon-problem.pcap	Use an IO Graph to check out the recurring WLAN problem caused when the access point "goes missing". Refer to *Chapter 26: Introduction to 802.11 (WLAN) Analysis.*
wlan-dupes.pcap	This WLAN trace file looks like it has problems with duplicate packets. Expand the 802.11 header and you'll note that these packets are not duplicates. Expand the Frame Control/Flags section. The first packet is from a STA to DS via an AP. The second packet is from DS to STA via AP. If you want to filter out the second set of packets, use the display filter `wlan.fc.ds == 0x01`. Refer to *Chapter 26: Introduction to 802.11 (WLAN) Analysis* for more information on the "To DS" and "From DS" bit settings.
wlan-fragments.pcap	All these fragments are 802.11 fragments—use the display filter `wlan.frag > 0` to display all WLAN fragment packets. Refer to *Chapter 26: Introduction to 802.11 (WLAN) Analysis.*
wlan-ppi.pcap	This is a PPI (Per-Packet-Information) header on an 802.11 frame. Refer to *Chapter 26: Introduction to 802.11 (WLAN) Analysis.*
wlan-radiotap.pcap	This is a Radiotap header on an 802.11 frame. Refer to *Chapter 26: Introduction to 802.11 (WLAN) Analysis.*
wlan-signalissue.pcap	Watch the signal strength change (maybe graph the ppi.80211-common.dbm.antsignal field) as the pinging host is moved closer and further away from the access point. Refer to *Chapter 26: Introduction to 802.11 (WLAN) Analysis.*
wlan-videodownload.pcap	A WEP-encrypted WLAN trace of a client downloading a video—IO Graph the traffic to see the bursty nature of the video download. Refer to *Chapter 26: Introduction to 802.11 (WLAN) Analysis.*

Index

D

E

M

Macof tool, 650
macros. See display filters
mailing lists
  signing up for, 72
  Wireshark announcements, 72
  Wireshark bug tracker, 72
  Wireshark commits, 72
  Wireshark developers, 72
  Wireshark users, 72
Main Toolbar
  capture toolbar icons, 62
  color and scroll toolbar icons, 64
  filter, color and configuration toolbar
    icons, 64
  finding a packet, 63
  help toolbar icon, 64
  navigation toolbar icons, 63
  trace file and print toolbar icons, 62
  viewer toolbar icons, 64
malicious FTP program, 643
maliciously malformed packets, 647
man-in-the-middle attack, 323
manuf file
  contents, 128
  editing, 137
  update overrides, 130
maps.google.com, analyzing traffic to, 19
marked packets
  fast naviation with, 39
  saving, 155
  summary information, 175
  toggling on and off, 155
Mathieson, Martin, 556
Maximum Segment Size (MSS), 192, 382
Maximum Transmission Unit (MTU)
  Ethernet, 192
  low sizes, 332, 348
memory requirements
  Dumpcap vs. Tshark, 101
merge trace files. See Mergecap
Mergecap, 92
  examples of, 694
  overview, 693
  syntax, 693
  using with non-aggregating taps, 85
merging trace files. See Mergecap

merging trace files in the GUI interface, 37
Metageek Wi-Spy products, 90, 512
Metasploit Framework, 601
Microsoft
  opening a reassembled Word stream, 240
  Security Bulletin MS09-048, 133
  Security Bulletin MS09-050, 648
  Service Pack 2 for XP, 611
Mobile IP, filtering for, 216
monitor mode. See WLAN
  connectivity loss, 91
  overview of, 91
most active connections, detection of, 188
Mu Dynamics, 32
multicast DNS (mDNS), 305
multicasts
  address range, 339
  burst statistics, 196
  Ethernet, 196
  excessive, 339
  IGMP support, 196
  in endpoint window, 189
  setting burst thresholds, 196
  storms, 344
multifunctional device (MFD), case study of, 505
*Multiprotocol Label Switching (MPLS), effect on
  network traffic, 14*

N

name resolution
  in basic communications, 295
  MAC name resolution, 137
  network name resolution
    disable for optimization, 100
    DNS PTR queries, 138
    in basic FTP comunication, 293
    performance impact, 138
    warning, 44
  settings, 136
  vulnerabilities, 645
needle in the haystack issue, 9, 80
Neo hex editing program, 269
Nessus, 601
Netcat, 601

X

Xprobe, 632
Xprobe2, 272, 632

Z

Zero Window Probe ACK, cause of, 282
Zero Window Probe, cause of, 282
zombie, idle scans use, 618

LaVergne, TN USA
12 March 2010
175789LV00003B/2/P

9 781893 939998